WORD
BIBLICAL
COMMENTARY

WORD
BIBLICAL
COMMENTARY

VOLUME 3

Exodus

JOHN I DURHAM

WORD BOOKS, PUBLISHER • WACO, TEXAS

Word Biblical Commentary
EXODUS
Copyright © 1987 by Word, Incorporated

Library of Congress Cataloging in Publication Data
Main entry under title:

Word biblical commentary.

  Includes bibliographies.
  1. Bible—Commentaries—Collected works.
BS491.2.W67   220.7'7   81–71768
ISBN 0–8499–0202–9 (vol. 3) AACR2

Printed in the United States of America

Scripture quotations in the body of the commentary marked RSV are from the Revised Standard
Version of the Bible, copyright 1946 (renewed 1973), 1956, and © 1971 by the Division of
Christian Education of the National Council of the Churches of Christ in the USA and are
used by permission.

The author's own translation of the text appears in italic type under the heading "Translation."

12 — 03 02 01 00 99

For Jeremy and for Gwynne
בני ובתי
אהובי

Contents

Author's Preface

Any traversal of the Book of Exodus is a trip across holy ground. There is so much in the book that is both beginning and conclusion of faith for so many believers that simply taking the book in hand is a close thing to a religious act. I had studied the book of Exodus for nearly twenty years, and had already written a brief commentary on it, in 1971, when John Watts and the editorial board of the Word Biblical Commentary invited me to undertake the preparation of the present volume, in 1977. I accepted their invitation with enthusiasm after I learned that the commentary was to be based on each writer's own translation of the biblical text. Previous experience had convinced me that writing commentary on a translation made by other minds and hands is not the best way to go about the task.

My work on the present volume has had to be carried on during the midst of regular class terms, in summers, and in the first half of my 1983–84 sabbatical leave. I thank all who have helped shelter my time, my colleagues who took the summer classes, the trustees who granted me sabbatical leave, and above all my children, whose tolerance was generous and whose attention to one often preoccupied was exemplary. I must also thank my colleague Sam Balentine and my student Jeff Rogers who read the typescript and made helpful suggestions to me, John Watts and his readers who did the same, and Mrs. Carolyn Bailey, my secretary, who typed a long manuscript in addition to all her other duties. For the exacting and important work of proofreading and the preparation of the indices to this volume, I am grateful to my friend of many years, Betty Bethea, as also to the students who helped check author and Scripture references. There are then the librarians who helped with the location of needed books and articles, of course my students who so often have taught me when I was attempting to teach them, and my own teachers, who taught me what teaching is. I am grateful especially to Professor B. Elmo Scoggin, who taught me Hebrew, and to Dr. G. Henton Davies, who taught me the importance of the theology of Yahweh's Presence in the Book of Exodus.

To all of these and to the many more they symbolize, I express profound thanks. The fault lines in this studied translation are mine, not theirs.

Finally, I must acknowledge the role in the creation of this Book of Exodus of all those who are memorialized in the wider application of the book's Hebrew title, ואלה שמות: the twelve sons of Jacob/Israel, Moses and Aaron, and above all the one whose Name is so much a part of the revelation of the book itself, יהוה the God of our fathers and mothers, the God and father also of Jesus who is Christ.

March 11, 1984
Jerusalem

Editorial Preface

The launching of the *Word Biblical Commentary* brings to fulfillment an enterprise of several years' planning. The publishers and the members of the editorial board met in 1977 to explore the possibility of a new commentary on the books of the Bible that would incorporate several distinctive features. Prospective readers of these volumes are entitled to know what such features were intended to be; whether the aims of the commentary have been fully achieved time alone will tell.

First, we have tried to cast a wide net to include as contributors a number of scholars from around the world who not only share our aims, but are in the main engaged in the ministry of teaching in university, college and seminary. They represent a rich diversity of denominational allegiance. The broad stance of our contributors can rightly be called evangelical, and this term is to be understood in its positive, historic sense of a commitment to scripture as divine revelation, and to the truth and power of the Christian gospel.

Then, the commentaries in our series are all commissioned and written for the purpose of inclusion in the *Word Biblical Commentary.* Unlike several of our distinguished counterparts in the field of commentary writing, there are no translated works, originally written in a non-English language. Also, our commentators were asked to prepare their own rendering of the original biblical text and to use those languages as the basis of their own comments and exegesis. What may be claimed as distinctive with this series is that it is based on the biblical languages, yet it seeks to make the technical and scholarly approach to a theological understanding of scripture understandable by—and useful to—the fledgling student, the working minister as well as to colleagues in the guild of professional scholars and teachers.

Finally, a word must be said about the format of the series. The layout in clearly defined sections has been consciously devised to assist readers at different levels. Those wishing to learn about the textual witnesses on which the translation is offered are invited to consult the section headed "Notes." If the readers' concern is with the state of modern scholarship on any given portion of scripture, then they should turn to the sections on "Bibliography" and "Form/Structure/Setting." For a clear exposition of the passage's meaning and its relevance to the ongoing biblical revelation, the "Comment" and concluding "Explanation" are designed expressly to meet that need. There is therefore something for everyone who may pick up and use these volumes.

If these aims come anywhere near realization, the intention of the editors will have been met, and the labor of our team of contributors rewarded.

General Editors: *David A. Hubbard*
Glenn W. Barker †
Old Testament: *John D. W. Watts*
New Testament: *Ralph P. Martin*

Abbreviations

EKL	*Evangelisches Kirchenlexikon*
EncJud	*Encyclopaedia judaica* (1971)
EvQ	*Evangelical Quarterly*
EvT	*Evangelische Theologie (EvTh)*
ExpTim	*Expository Times*
FRLANT	Forschungen zur Religion und Literatur des Alten und Neuen Testaments
GKC	*Gesenius' Hebrew Grammar*, ed. E. Kautzsch, tr. and rev. A. E. Cowley. Oxford: Clarendon Press, 1982.
GTL	Göttinger Theologische Lehrbücher
HALAT	W. Baumgartner et al., *Hebräisches und Aramäisches Lexikon zum Alten Testament*. Lieferungen I–III. Leiden: E. J. Brill, 1967, 1974, 1983.
HAT	Handbuch zum Alten Testament
Herm	Hermeneia
HSM	Harvard Semitic Monographs
HTR	*Harvard Theological Review*
HUCA	*Hebrew Union College Annual*
IB	*Interpreter's Bible*
ICC	International Critical Commentary
IDB	*Interpreter's Dictionary of the Bible*
IDBSup	*Supplementary volume to IDB*
IEJ	*Israel Exploration Journal*
Int	*Interpretation*
JAOS	*Journal of the American Oriental Society*
JBL	*Journal of Biblical Literature*
JBLMS	*Journal of Biblical Literature Monograph Series*
JBR	*Journal of Bible and Religion*
JCS	*Journal of Cuneiform Studies*
JEA	*Journal of Egyptian Archaeology*
JNES	*Journal of Near Eastern Studies*
JQR	*Jewish Quarterly Review*
JSOT	*Journal for the Study of the Old Testament*
JSOTSup	Journal for the Study of the Old Testament Supplement Series
JSS	*Journal of Semitic Studies*
JTS	*Journal of Theological Studies*
Jub.	*Jubilees*
Judaica	*Judaica: Beiträge zum Verständnis . . .*
KB	L. Koehler and W. Baumgartner, *Lexicon in Veteris Testamenti Libros.* Leiden: E. J. Brill, 1958.
KVHS	Korte Verklaring der Heilige Schrift
LCL	Loeb Classical Library
Lisowsky	G. Lisowsky, *Konkordanz zum Hebräischen Alten Testament.* Stuttgart: Akademische Druck-U. Verlagsanstalt, 1955.
LSJ	Liddell-Scott-Jones, *A Greek-English Lexicon,* compiled by H. G. Liddell and R. Scott, revised by H. S. Jones, et al., with Supplement, 1968. Oxford: At the Clarendon Press, 1968.
Mandelkern	S. Mandelkern, *Veteris Testamenti Concordantiae Hebraicae atque*

	Chaldaicae. Graz: Akademische Druck-U. Verlagsanstalt, 1955.
MBA	Y. Aharoni and M. Avi-Yonah, *The Macmillan Bible Atlas.* New York: Macmillan, 1968.
NCB	*New Century Bible*
NedTTs	*Nederlands theologische tijdschrift* (NedThTs)
NICOT	New International Commentary on the Old Testament
NTS	*New Testament Studies*
Numen	*Numen: International Review for the History of Religions*
OBO	*Orbis biblicus et orientalis*
OLZ	*Orientalische Literaturzeitung*
OTL	Old Testament Library
OTS	*Oudtestamentische Studiën*
PEQ	*Palestine Exploration Quarterly*
POS	*Pretoria Oriental Series*
PTR	*Princeton Theological Review*
RB	*Revue Biblique*
RES	*Repertoire d'epigraphie semitique*
RÉtSém	*Revue des études sémitiques*
RHR	*Revue de l'histoire des religions*
SANT	Studien zum Alten und Neuen Testament
SBLDS	SBL Dissertation Series
SBS	Stuttgarter Bibelstudien
SBT	Studies in Biblical Theology
SC	Sources Chrétiennes
Sem	*Semitica*
SJT	*Scottish Journal of Theology*
Sperber	A. Sperber, ed., *The Bible in Aramaic,* Vol. I: The Pentateuch According to Targum Onkelos. Leiden: E. J. Brill, 1959.
ST	*Studia theologica (StTh)*
TBC	Torch Bible Commentary
TBl	*Theologische Blätter (ThBl)*
TBü	Theologische Bücherei
TDNT	G. Kittel and G. Friedrich (eds.), *Theological Dictionary of the New Testament.* 10 vols. Grand Rapids: Wm. B. Eerdmans Publishing Co., 1964–1976.
TDOT	G. Botterweck and H. Ringgren (eds.), *Theological Dictionary of the Old Testament.* In process of publication. 5 vols. to date. Grand Rapids: Wm. B. Eerdmans Publishing Co., 1974–1986.
TextsS	Texts and Studies
THAT	E. Jenni and C. Westermann (eds.), *Theologisches Handwörterbuch zum Alten Testament.* 2 vols. Munich: Chr. Kaiser Verlag, Vol. 1, 1971, vol. 2, 1976.
ThW	Theologische Wissenschaft
TLZ	*Theologische Literaturzeitung*
TRu	*Theologische Rundschau (ThR)*
TWAT	G. J. Botterweck and H. Ringgren (eds.), *Theologisches Wörterbuch zum Alten Testament (ThWAT).* In process of publication, Vols.

	I–IV, plus V: ½ to date. Stuttgart: Verlag W. Kohlhammer 1973, 1977, 1982, 1984.
TynB	*Tyndale Bulletin*
TZ	*Theologische Zeitschrift (ThZ)*
VT	*Vetus Testamentum*
VTSup	Vetus Testamentum Supplements
WC	Westminster Commentaries
Weil	*Massorah Gedolah iuxta Codicem Leningradensem B 19a*, ed. G. E. Weil. Vol. I. Rome: Pontifical Biblical Institute, 1971.
WMANT	Wissenschaftliche Monographien Zum Alten und Neuen Testament
WTJ	*Westminster Theological Journal*
WuD	*Wort und Dienst*
ZAW	*Zeitschrift für die alttestamentliche Wissenschaft*
ZDPV	*Zeitschrift des deutschen Palästina-Vereins*
ZKT	*Zeitschrift für katholische Theologie (ZKTh)*
ZTK	*Zeitschrift für Theologie und Kirche (ZThK)*

MODERN TRANSLATIONS

AB	Anchor Bible
JB	Jerusalem Bible
JPS	Jewish Publication Society of America, *The Holy Scriptures According to the Masoretic Text*, 1917
KJV	King James Version
NEB	New English Bible
NIV	New International Version
RSV	Revised Standard Version
RV	Revised Version

TEXTS, VERSIONS, AND ANCIENT WORKS

Dtr	Deuteronomistic History
LXX	Septuagint
A	Codex Alexandrinus
B	Codex Vaticanus
F	Codex Ambrosíanus
L	Codex Leningradensis, B 19a
MT	Masoretic text
NT	New Testament
OT	Old Testament
1QIsa^{a,b}	First or second copy of Isaiah from Qumran Cave I
4QPs^b	Pss 91–118: see P. W. Skehan, "A Psalm Manuscript from Qumran (4QPs^b)," *CBQ* 26 (1964) 313–22.
SamPent	*Samaritan Pentateuch, Der Hebräische Pentateuch der Samaritaner*, ed. A. F. von Gall. Giessen: Verlag von Alfred Topelmann, 1918.
Syr	Syriac text
Tg(s)	Targum(s)

Tg Onk	Targum Onkelos		
Tg Ps-J	Targum Pseudo-Jonathan		
Vg	*Vulgate, Biblia Sacra iuxta Vulgatam Versionem,* ed. R. Weber. 2 vols. Stuttgart: Wurttembergische Bibelanstalt, 1969.		

This commentary is based on the printed Hebrew text of the *Biblia Hebraica Stuttgartensia,* K. Elliger, W. Rudolph, et al., eds. (Stuttgart: Deutsche Bibelstiftung, 1977). Chapter and verse enumeration throughout are those of the Hebrew Bible. Where these differ from the standard English versions, references to the latter have been given in brackets following the Hebrew number. The LXX text cited is that of A. Rahlfs, *Septuaginta,* 6th ed., 2 vols. (Stuttgart: Priviligierte Württembergische Bibelanstalt, n.d.).

BIBLICAL AND APOCRYPHAL BOOKS

Gen	Genesis	Mic	Micah
Exod	Exodus	Nah	Nahum
Lev	Leviticus	Hab	Habakkuk
Num	Numbers	Zeph	Zephaniah
Deut	Deuteronomy	Hag	Haggai
Josh	Joshua	Zech	Zechariah
Judg	Judges	Mal	Malachi
Ruth	Ruth	1 Kgdms	1 Kingdoms
1 Sam	1 Samuel	2 Kgdms	2 Kingdoms
2 Sam	2 Samuel	3 Kgdms	3 Kingdoms
1 Kgs	1 Kings	4 Kgdms	4 Kingdoms
2 Kgs	2 Kings	Add Esth	Additions to Esther
1 Chr	1 Chronicles	Bar	Baruch
2 Chr	2 Chronicles	Bel	Bel and the Dragon
Ezra	Ezra	1 Esdr	1 Esdras
Neh	Nehemiah	2 Esdr	2 Esdras
Esth	Esther	4 Ezra	4 Ezra
Job	Job	Jdt	Judith
Ps	Psalms	Ep Jer	Epistle of Jeremiah
Prov	Proverbs	1 Macc	1 Maccabees
Eccl	Ecclesiastes	2 Macc	2 Maccabees
Cant	Song of Solomon	3 Macc	3 Maccabees
Isa	Isaiah	4 Macc	4 Maccabees
Jer	Jeremiah	Pr Azar	Prayer of Azariah
Lam	Lamentations	Pr Man	Prayer of Manasseh
Ezek	Ezekiel	Sir	Sirach
Dan	Daniel	Sus	Susanna
Hos	Hosea	Tob	Tobit
Joel	Joel	Wis	Wisdom of Solomon
Amos	Amos	Matt	Matthew
Obad	Obadiah	Mark	Mark
Jonah	Jonah	Luke	Luke
Jub	Jubilees		

John	John	2 Tim	2 Timothy
Acts	Acts	Titus	Titus
Rom	Romans	Phlm	Philemon
1 Cor	1 Corinthians	Heb	Hebrews
2 Cor	2 Corinthians	Jas	James
Gal	Galatians	1 Pet	1 Peter
Eph	Ephesians	2 Pet	2 Peter
Phil	Philippians	1 John	1 John
Col	Colossians	2 John	2 John
1 Thess	1 Thessalonians	3 John	3 John
2 Thess	2 Thessalonians	Jude	Jude
1 Tim	1 Timothy	Rev	Revelation

GRAMMATICAL AND OTHER ABBREVIATIONS

abs	absolute	JE	Yahwist plus the Elohist
act	active	K	Kethib, "written"
adj	adjective, adjectival	masc	masculine
ANE	Ancient Near East(ern)	MS(S)	manuscript(s)
art	article	niph	niphal
chap(s).	chapter(s)	nom	nominative
com	common	obj	object
conj	conjunction	P	Priestly writer, source
constr	construct	pass	passive
def	definite	pers	person, personal
dir	direct	pf	perfect
E	Elohist	pl	plural
ed(s).	editor(s), edited by	poss	possessive
ET	English translation	prep	preposition, prepositional
fem	feminine		
haplogr	haplography	pronom	pronominal
Heb.	consonantal Hebrew	ptcp	participle
hiph	hiphil	Q	Qere, to be "read"
hithp	hithpael	sg	singular
hoph	hophal	sq	followed by
impf	imperfect	subj	subject
impv	imperative	suff	suffix
inf	infinitive	=	equals
J	Yahwist	×	times

INTRODUCTION

1. THE BOOK OF EXODUS AS A WHOLE

Bibliography

Bentzen, A. *Introduction to the Old Testament.* Vols. 1 & 2. 6th ed. Copenhagen: G. E. C. Gad, 1961. **Beyerlin, W.** *Origins and History of the Oldest Sinaitic Tradition.* Oxford: Basil Blackwell, 1965. **Cazelles, H.** *Études sur le Code de L'Alliance.* Paris: Letouzey et Ané, 1946. **Daube, D.** *The Exodus Pattern in the Bible.* All Souls Studies II. London: Faber and Faber, 1963. **Eissfeldt, O.** *The Old Testament: An Introduction.* New York: Harper and Row, 1965. **Fohrer, G.** *Introduction to the Old Testament.* Nashville: Abingdon Press, 1968. ———. *Überlieferung und Geschichte des Exodus.* BZAW 91. Berlin: Walter de Gruyter, 1964. **Fuss, W.** *Die deuteronomistische Pentateuchredaktion in Exodus 3–17.* BZAW 126. Berlin: Walter de Gruyter, 1972. **Goldberg, M.** *Jews and Christians. Getting Our Stories Straight: The Exodus and The Passion-Resurrection.* Nashville: Abingdon, 1985. **Gressmann, H.** *Mose und seine Zeit: Ein Kommentar zu den Mose-Sagen.* FRLANT 18. Göttingen: Vandenhoeck & Ruprecht, 1913. **Knight, D. A.** *Rediscovering the Traditions of Israel.* SBLDS 9. Rev. ed. Missoula, MT: Scholars Press, 1975. **Koch, K.** *The Growth of the Biblical Tradition: The Form-Critical Method.* New York: Charles Scribner's Sons, 1969. **Loewenstamm, S. E.** *The Tradition of the Exodus in Its Development.* 2d ed. Jerusalem: At the Magnes Press, 1972. Heb., with summary in Eng. **Nicholson, E. W.** *Exodus and Sinai in History and Tradition.* Richmond: John Knox Press, 1973. **Noth, M.** *A History of Pentateuchal Traditions.* Englewood Cliffs, NJ: Prentice-Hall, 1972. **Pedersen, J.** "Passahfest und Passahlegende." *ZAW* 52 (1934) 161–75. **Pfeiffer, R. H.** *Introduction to the Old Testament.* New York: Harper and Brothers, 1948. **Rad, G. von.** "The Form-Critical Problem of the Hexateuch" in *The Problem of the Hexateuch and Other Essays.* Edinburgh: Oliver and Boyd, 1965. 1–78. **Rendtorff, R.** *Das Überlieferungsgeschichtliche Problem des Pentateuch.* BZAW 147. Berlin: Walter de Gruyter, 1977. **Rudolph, W.** *Der 'Elohist' von Exodus bis Josua.* BZAW 68. Berlin: Alfred Töpelmann, 1938. **Schmid, H. H.** *Der sogenannte Jahwist: Beobachtungen und Fragen zur Pentateuchforschung.* Zurich: Theologischer Verlag, 1976. **Seters, J. van.** *Abraham in History and Tradition.* New Haven: Yale University Press, 1975. ———. *In Search of History.* New Haven: Yale University Press, 1983. **Soggin, A.** *Introduction to the Old Testament.* Philadelphia: Westminster Press, 1976. **Walzer, M.** *Exodus and Revolution.* New York: Basic Books, 1985.

The Book of Exodus is the first book of the Bible. There in the ancient stories of Moses at Sinai, Israel in Egypt and Israel leaving Egypt, Israel in the Wilderness and Israel with Moses at Sinai are more beginnings for faith than are to be found in בראשית, the Book of Beginnings.

In the Book of Exodus God gives Israel his special name, his special deliverance, his special guidance, his special covenant, his special worship, his special mercy and his special description of himself. In the Book of Exodus, the people Israel is born; תּוֹרָה *Torah* is born, and with it the Bible; the theology of Presence and response to Presence is born, and with it the special iconography of that large part of the Hebrew-Christian tradition which symbolizes ideas rather than beings; and priesthood and cultus in ancient Israel are born, laying the ancient sub-foundations of Temple, Synagogue and Church.

In the Book of Exodus, Israel's celebration is followed by Israel's complaining, and Israel's promise of obedience to Yahweh first is followed by Israel's first disobedience of Yahweh. In the Book of Exodus, Yahweh's powerful proving of his Presence is disregarded because of the absence of Moses, his representative; the manna is provided to a hungry people who then criticize their unvaried menu; and a people eager and curious to know Yahweh become so frightened by his appearance that they ask to be spared any repetition of the experience. In the Book of Exodus, Passover is begun, and there is set in motion a continuity of testimony to a living faith that continues to this day.

The Book of Exodus contains history, of course, and tradition, and instruction, and sociology, and folk-wisdom, and story, and perpetual and occasional requirement, and aetiology, and geography, and genealogy, and anti-Egyptian sentiment, and folk-song and hymnody, and desert lore, and the foundations of Western jurisprudence and Judeo-Christian religious mystery, along with much else.

The primary burden of the Book of Exodus, however, is theological. The book is theological in concept, in arrangement, in content, and in implication. It is a book of faith, about faith, and directed primarily to those with faith. Those who read the Book of Exodus without faith, though they will inevitably profit from their reading, will not understand its message.

For this reason, among others, the Book of Exodus must be read as a whole. Despite the strands of narrative and legal and sacerdotal source-material that are clearly visible in the forty chapters that make up this book, and despite the fact that it is a compilation whose layers are still at least partly visible and to a degree recoverable, the Book of Exodus must be considered as a whole piece of theological literature, quite deliberately put into the form in which we have it, for very specific purposes.

The temptation has been great, since Wellhausen's revolutionary way of considering the beginning books of the OT, to concentrate on what the Book of Exodus is not, or is only in part. The source-documentary approach to Exodus correctly treats the book as one part of a larger literary whole, a whole made up of composites that extend from Genesis through Exodus to Leviticus and Numbers, and even on into Deuteronomy, Joshua, and beyond, according to some theorists. The history of the development and application of this approach has been frequently surveyed, sometimes in considerable detail, in the standard OT introductions (e.g., Bentzen, Eissfeldt, Fohrer, Soggin) and in such handy surveys as those of Noth and Knight, which reach beyond literary questions toward the influences that shaped the composites in tradition history. Despite a great many attempts at refinement, e.g., "fragmentary hypotheses" and the proposal of proto-sources such as "L" (Eissfeldt), "S" (Pfeiffer), "G" (Noth) and "N" (Fohrer), the source-documentary approach has remained a dominant theory in the interpretation of the first four books of the OT. At present, though the dating of the sources is under consideration (e.g., van Seters, Schmid), and though the question of the validity of a source-documentary approach as a key to theological understanding (so especially Pedersen and von Rad and Noth) is being raised (Rendtorff), the interweaving of the sources through the composites that make up Genesis,

Exodus, and Numbers in particular remains still a presupposition approaching dogma, as the reviews in the sections on *Form/Structure/Setting* in the Commentary that follows make plain. There too, and at other appropriate points in the pages that follow, reference is made to important form-critical and redaction-critical study on the Book of Exodus, from Gressmann to Rudolph to Cazelles to Koch to Beyerlin to Fohrer to Loewenstamm to Schmid to Nicholson to Fuss.

Despite the massive amount of information provided by these studies, much of it helpful, an understanding of the Book of Exodus as a whole, and as it stands in the received text of the OT, has been lacking. The undoubted and considerable advantages of source criticism, and then form criticism, and still later tradition criticism and rhetorical and structural analysis have helped us understand Exodus, then hindered us in understanding it by directing our attention somehow away from the "finished product," which we have, to the ingredients we can guess at, but do not have. The process by which the Book of Exodus came to its canonical form began as early as the time of Moses and continued at least into the third century B.C.; it is exceedingly complex and can only be surmised. The end result of that process is at last our one certainty, for we have it at hand.

Of course, Exodus is an assemblage of pieces of narrative and sequences of laws, strands of story, and a carefully ordered system of religious symbols. But it is not literary or theological goulash. It did not come together haphazardly or without a guiding purpose, or with no unified concept to hold it together. The discrepancies and shifts of style and emphasis that we so quickly detect were not invisible to the editors who put the Book of Exodus together, nor to those who heard and used these accounts even while the book was evolving. These differences and inconsistencies were simply not as important to them as they have been to us, for the very good reason that they were primarily interested in the whole Exodus, while we have been preoccupied overmuch with its pieces.

For its ancient compilers the whole of Exodus was theological. Their purpose in the composition of both intermediary forms and the final form of the book was a theological one. Thus all other considerations are shifted to the background, and the only unity that is of any real importance in the Book of Exodus is theological unity—and that the book displays on every hand.

The centerpiece of this unity is the theology of Yahweh present with and in the midst of his people Israel. Throughout the Book of Exodus in its canonical form, this theme is constantly in evidence, serving as a theological anchor and also as a kind of compass indicating the directions in which the book is to go. Indeed, the Book of Exodus may be seen as a series of interlocking concentric circles spreading outwards from the narratives of the coming of Yahweh: to Moses in chaps. 3 and 4, to all Israel in chaps. 19, 20 and 24, and to Moses representing Israel in chaps. 32, 33 and 34.

The revelation to Moses in chaps. 3 and 4 establishes Yahweh's Presence with Moses (3:6, 12; 4:5, 11–12, 15), points backward to his Presence with Israel in Egypt (3:7–10) and forward to the proof of his Presence to Israel and to the Egyptians and to Pharaoh (3:17, 19–22; 4:21–23), as does the parallel summary of this narrative in Exod 6:2–8. The revelation to Israel in chaps. 19–20 establishes Yahweh's Presence in Israel's midst (19:9–11, 16–18; 20:1–21), points backward to the proof of his Presence in Egypt and at the sea (19:4; 20:2) and forward to the proof of his Presence manifested in Israel's response to his nearness (19:5–6, 8; 20:3–17). The revelation to Moses interceding for Israel in chaps. 32, 33, and 34 establishes Yahweh's Presence as the essential and indispensable basis of Israel's very existence as Yahweh's people (32:7–10; 33:1–6, 12–17). That revelation also points backward to the fact of his Presence and its benefits (32:11–13) and forward to what Yahweh is yet to accomplish in Israel's midst, making Israel unique among all peoples (33:15; 34:9) both by Yahweh's deeds and by Yahweh's requirements (34:10–26).

Along with these principal passages and the themes that reach formatively out from them are numerous other references to the fact and the effect of Yahweh's Presence in and with Israel, so many of them that a theology of Yahweh's Presence as a kind of magnet for the gathering of the earliest and formative versions of what became the Book of Exodus may be suggested. For example, the multiplication of the sons of Jacob in the Egyptian delta, a fulfillment of the covenant promise to the fathers (Gen 17:1–8; 28:10–15, etc.), is effected by the Presence of God among them (Exod 1:7, 20); the dramatic series of the mighty acts in Egypt, by which first Israel, then the Egyptian people, then the Egyptian court, and finally, and nearly too soon at that, the Pharaoh of Egypt himself are convinced of the power of Yahweh, is represented repeatedly as the action of Yahweh on the scene (Exod 7:1–5, 14–17, 25; 7:26–29 [8:1–4]; 8:8–11 [8:12–15]; 8:17–20 [8:21–24]; 9:1–7, 12, 13–18, 23–26; 10:1–6, 12–15, 16–20, 27; 11:4–7; 12:12–13, 23, 27, 29–30, 36, etc.). The Presence of Yahweh/Elohim guides the people in the proper route of Exodus (Exod 13:3, 17–18, 21–22), interposes a protective screen between fleeing Israel and the pursuing Egyptians (14:19–20), cleaves the sea to make way for Israel to cross it dry-footed, then brings the waters rushing in upon the Egyptians following (14:21–31). The great hymn celebrating this event *and* the conquest and settlement of Canaan as well ends with a celebration of Yahweh's Presence in his mountain sanctuary that sounds very much like a hymn of Zion (15:11–18).

The Presence of Yahweh provides for Israel's need in the wilderness (15:22–27; 16:4, 9–16; 17:4–7). The Presence of Yahweh gives the principles by which Israel is to live in covenant (20:1–18) and the application of those principles to the needs and problems of daily living (20:22–23:33; note especially 20:22, 24; 21:6; 22:7–8 [22:8–9]; 22:25–26 [22:26–27]; 23:14–17). The Presence of Yahweh promises guidance, protection, and success in the settlement of the promised land (23:20–33). The Presence of Yahweh solemnizes the covenant, both with Israel (24:5–8, 18) and with Israel's leaders (24:9–17). And the Presence of Yahweh is at the center of the elaborate instructions for the media of worship in Exod 25–31 and of the account of their construction and consecration in Exod 35–40. Indeed, when that work was finished, Yahweh's Presence settled onto and into the Tabernacle (40:34–38), an indication both that the work had been done properly and that Yahweh had at last a permanent residence among his people, a theme elaborated still further by David and Solomon in the cult of Yahweh's Presence in Jerusalem.

These are only representative references; the full list is much longer still. I have attempted to indicate and to discuss them all in the commentary on the translation that follows. Two additional themes are natural extensions of the Presence theme in the Book of Exodus. The first of these themes is Deliverance, or Salvation, or Rescue. The second of them is Covenant, the provision of a means of Response to Deliverance. God's Presence in Israel's midst witnesses the need for Deliverance and brings it about. God's Presence in Israel's midst guides Israel, both in a reaction of gratitude and also in a continuing acknowledgement of the reality of God's nearness. The story of the first half of Exodus, in broad summary, is Rescue. The story of the second half, in equally broad summary, is Response, both immediate response and continuing response. And binding together and undergirding both Rescue and Response is Presence, the Presence of Yahweh from whom both Rescue and Response ultimately derive. If all this seems to make Exodus sound like a one-track book, that is so because that is exactly what the Book of Exodus is: the foundational biblical declaration that whatever else he may be, God is first of all a God at hand, a God with his people, a God who rescues, protects, guides, provides for, forgives, and disciplines the people who call him *their* God and who call themselves *his* people.

Now if the Book of Exodus is as theologically single-minded as I am here suggesting (and what I am here suggesting is only a brief survey of the emphasis of the commentary that follows), and if the Book of Exodus is in fact the kind of first book of the Bible I am proposing that it is, we might expect that it would have had a very great impact on the OT, and indeed on the Bible as a whole. That is exactly the case. No other biblical book surfaces elsewhere in the OT as frequently as the Book of Exodus does; in the NT only the Books of Psalms and Isaiah are cited more, and that for the fairly obvious reasons of liturgy and messianism.

Both within the Book of Exodus and beyond it, the exodus deliverance is depicted as the act by which Israel was brought into being as a people and thus as the beginning point in Israel's history. In the time of the fathers, God had revealed his Presence to individuals, had delivered and blessed, made promises to and sometimes judged them. But with the exodus, he revealed his Presence to a whole people and called them to nationhood and a special role by relating himself to them in covenant. This special role becomes a kind of lens through which Israel is viewed throughout the rest of the Bible, and the sequence of magnificent events that led up to the covenant and made it possible becomes a formative sequence, one that shapes much of the theology of the OT. It is this special role, indeed, that weaves the Book of Exodus so completely into the canonical fabric begun with Genesis and ended only with Revelation.

The exodus was given theological expression in Israel's life in a number of ways. Quite early, no doubt at the time of the event itself, the exodus was celebrated in hymnic poetry and memorialized in narrative summary. Though as time passed, both the poetry and the narrative underwent expansion until they reached the form in which they are preserved in our OT, there is little reason to doubt that the exodus traditions of the OT, for all their confessional and sometimes stylized language, yet contain ancient memories of historical event. This is particularly apparent in the oldest confessions and hymns, which speak of Yahweh's deliverance from Egypt in terms of a "bringing forth" of his mighty arm and his right hand, of his wondrous deeds, of his salvation, of his defeat of the Egyptians at the sea, of his guidance and provision, of his choice and purchase of the people, and of his majestic and permanent reign (Exod 15:1–18, 21; Josh 24:2–13; Deut 6:20–25; 26:5–11). These motifs and the language in which they are given expression appear throughout the OT in virtually every period of Israel's existence. This recurrent language is a reflection of the theological common denominator of the OT. I refer to it frequently in the commentary that follows as "theological rhetoric," the vocabulary of confession in its irreducible minimum, the repeated key words and phrases that are the unique and common forms of OT theology.

Within the extensive array of OT references to the exodus, further, a consistent pattern of meaning appears to have emerged. Whether reference was to the exodus from Egypt, as is the case in most of the OT, or to a new exodus yet to come in deliverance from Assyria or from Babylon, in general eschatological expectations, or in the more particularized expression of messianic hopes, the exodus/new exodus references always bear specific relation to the deliverance brought by the Presence of God. It is God on the scene and in the midst of the fray who can effect deliverance, and any deliverance is testimony to this real and effective Presence. As in the first exodus, any subsequent deliverance will establish both his authority and his power and will show him to be all-sufficient to meet any need of his people that arises (cf. the thematic study of D. Daube, and, for the continuing application of the Exodus themes, the works of Goldberg and Walzer).

2. THE EXODUS IN HISTORY AND THE EXODUS AS HISTORY

Bibliography

Bimson, J. J. *Redating the Exodus and Conquest.* JSOTSup 5. Sheffield: JSOT, 1978. **Coats, G.** "The Wilderness Itinerary." *CBQ* 34 (1972) 135–52. **Davies, G. I.** "The Wilderness Itineraries and The Composition of the Pentateuch." *VT* 33 (1983) 1–13. **Driver, S. R.** *The Book of Exodus.* CBSC. Cambridge: University Press, 1953. **Dyer, C. H.** "The Date of the Exodus Reexamined." *BSac* 140 (1983) 225–43. **Greenberg, M.** *The Ḫab/piru.* AOS 39. New Haven: American Oriental Society, 1955. **Herrmann, S.** *Israel in Egypt.* SBT 2d ser., 27. London: SCM Press, 1973. **McNeile, A. H.** *The Book of Exodus.* WC. London: Methuen and Company, 1908. **Nicholson, E. W.** *Exodus and Sinai in History and Tradition.* Richmond: John Knox Press, 1973. **Plaut, W. G.** "The Israelites in Pharaoh's Egypt—A Historical Reconstruction." *Judaism* 27 (1978) 40–46. **Rowley, H. H.** *From Joseph to Joshua: Biblical Traditions in the Light of Archaeology.* London: Published for the British Academy by the Oxford University Press, 1950. **Seters, J. van.** *The Hyksos: a New Investigation.* New Haven: Yale University Press, 1966. **Shanks, H.** "The Exodus and the Crossing of the Red Sea, According to Hans Goedicke." *BARev* 7 (1981) 42–50. **Thompson, T. L.** *The Historicity of the Patriarchal Narratives.* BZAW 133. Berlin: Walter de Gruyter, 1974. ————. "The Joseph and Moses Narratives: Historical Reconstructions of the Narratives." *Israelite and Judaean History.* Ed. J. H. Hayes and J. M. Miller. OTL. Philadelphia: Westminster Press, 1977. 149–66. **Vaux, R. de.** *The Early History of Israel.* Philadelphia: Westminster Press, 1978. **Vergote, J.** *Joseph en Égypte, Genèse chap. 37–50 à la lumière des études égyptologiques récentes.* Louvain: Publications Universitaires, 1959. **Walsh, J. T.** "From Egypt to Moab: A Source-Critical Analysis of the Wilderness Itinerary." *CBQ* 39 (1977) 20–33. **Waltke, K.** "Palestinian Artifactual Evidence Supporting the Early Date of the Exodus." *BSac* 129 (1972) 33–47. **Zenger, E.** *Israel am Sinai: Analysen und Interpretationen zu Exodus 17–34.* Altenberge: CIS-Verlag, 1982.

The problematical question of the historicity of the narratives of the Book of Exodus has been much discussed, particularly by commentators of the last fourth of the nineteenth century and the first fourth of the twentieth century. A number of careful studies (e.g., van Seters, Greenberg, Rowley, Herrmann, Nicholson, Vergote, Plaut) have established beyond cavil what may be called the contextual plausibility of the Exodus narrative without confirming the historicity of even one of its events or personages. We can prove of course that Egypt was there, and even that there were in Egypt displaced persons subjected to oppressive forced labor in a sequence of dynasties. We can prove that many of the laws and law-forms of both the Decalogue and the Book of the Covenant are anticipated by earlier and companion law-codes, whatever possible date is suggested for the earliest form of the Exodus laws. We can prove the presence of people very like the early Israelites appear to have been, in the Sinai peninsula, in the wilderness area of Kadesh-Barnea, and in general in all the other places where the Books of Exodus and Numbers and Joshua place the people of Israel. We can present archeological data to support more than one set of dates for the wilderness wandering and the conquest/settlement, as shown by such studies as those of de Vaux (291–472), Herrmann (1–91), Nicholson (xiii–xv, 1–90) and Bimson (7–324). We can make a case for three or four excellent Egyptian *Sitze im Leben* that would fit the sojourn-exodus narratives of Genesis and Exodus (Thompson).

What we cannot do, without more specific data than we have, however, is provide historical confirmation for anything or anybody mentioned in the Book of Exodus. No one yet has given any convincing extrabiblical hint, much less proof, of any single part of the Exodus narrative. Apart from the Pharaoh's store-cities, Pithom and Raᶜamses, which can be generally located, and the oasis of Kadesh-Barnea, which can be certainly located, we cannot fix with any degree of certainty one single place of the many mentioned in the Book of Exodus, not even Mount Sinai itself (Coats, Walsh, Davies, Zenger). This is not of course to say that the events and persons referred to by Exodus are not historical, only that we have no historical proof of them. Thus it is far better to speak of the narrative of Exodus *in* history rather than *as* history and to be content with the general historical context we *can* have rather than longing for specific historical proof we *cannot* have, at least until some dramatic new evidence is presented.

This subject in any case is the province of the historian, the geographer, the archeologist, the ethnographer, and the expert in ancient demographics. The translator and commentator is of course interested in the work of these scholars, as in anything else that can help the recovery of ancient meaning in the task of determining contemporary meaning. But the subject of historicity must not be a primary interest. The commentator has enough other subjects with which to stay busy and needs to leave such matters to those who know what they are (or in the case of the Book of Exodus, alas, are not) talking about. We should have learned this lesson from the long and straw-grasping excursuses on historicity in the works of the commentators who wrote in the sixty years following 1875 (e.g., Driver, McNeile, etc.).

The determination of any exact historical context for events mentioned in the Book of Exodus thus remains impossible. Given the purpose of the book, and the manner in which that purpose is attempted, such a determination is also relatively unimportant. Despite a variety of attempts to fix an earlier date for the oppression and the exodus (e.g., Waltke, Goedicke; see Shanks, Bimson, Dyer), no case is any more convincing than the case for the later date most frequently proposed, at the beginning of the nineteenth dynasty of Egypt (with Seti I as the Pharaoh of the oppression, Raamses II as the Pharaoh of the exodus, and Merneptah as the Pharaoh of Israel's early forays into Canaan). That is the dating assumed in the Commentary below, but the chronology of the events described in Exodus is of little importance to the theological message of the book in its present form, a form vastly removed from the connection of any of these events with an historical time-frame. To such an extent is this true, indeed, that a shift of dating to an earlier context would have no effect on the message of Exodus as I understand that message.

3. THE TEXT OF EXODUS AND ITS TRANSLATION

Bibliography

Déaut, R. le. *Targum du Pentateuque.* SC. Paris: Les Éditions du Cerf, 1979. **Elliger, K.,** and **W. Rudolf,** eds. *Biblia Hebraica Stuttgartensia.* Stuttgart: Deutsche Bibelstiftung, 1977. **Fitzmyer, Joseph A.** *The Dead Sea Scrolls: Major Publications and Tools for Study.* Missoula, MT: Scholars Press, 1977. **Gall, A. F. von.** *Der Hebräische Pentateuch der Samaritaner.* Giessen: Verlag Alfred Töpelmann, 1918. **Hatch, E.,** and **H. A. Redpath,** eds. *A Concordance to the Septuagint and the Other Greek Versions of the Old Testament.* Graz: Akademische Druck-U. Verlagsanstalt, 1954. **Mandelkern, S.** *Veteris Testamenti Concordantiae Hebraicae atque Chaldaicae.* Graz: Akademische Druck-U. Verlaganstalt, 1955. **Postma, F., E. Talstra,** and **M. Vervenne.** *Instrumenta Biblica 1: Exodus.* Materials in Automatic Text Processing. Pts. I, II. Amsterdam: Turnhout, VU Boekhandel/Uitgeverij Brepols, 1983. **Quell, G.,** ed. *Exodus et Leviticus: Biblia Hebraica Stuttgartensia 2.* Ed. K. Elliger and W. Rudolph. Stuttgart: Württembergische Bibelanstalt, 1973. **Rahlfs, A.,** ed. *Septuaginta,* 6th ed. 2 vols. Stuttgart: Privilegierte Württembergische Bibelanstalt, n.d. **Sperber, A.,** ed. *The Bible in Aramaic.* Vol. 1: The Pentateuch According to Targum Onkelos. Leiden: E. J. Brill, 1959. **Weber, R.,** ed. *Biblia Sacra Iuxta Vulgatam Versionem.* 2 vols. Stuttgart: Württembergische Bibelanstalt, 1969. **Weil, G. E.** *Massorah Gedolah Iuxta Codicem Leningradensem B 19a.* Vol. 1. Rome: Pontifical Biblical Institute, 1971.

The task of the author of a volume such as this one, as I have undertaken it, is defined first and last by the need for a careful and sensitive translation of the biblical text, in this case the text of the Book of Exodus preserved by Codex Leningradensis (B19a) as edited by Gottfried Quell and published in 1973 as *Biblia Hebraica Stuttgartensia* 2, and subsequently as a component part of *Biblia Hebraica Stuttgartensia* by the Württembergische Bibelanstalt of Stuttgart. At a number of points in the Hebrew text of Exodus, there are significant variations from the version of the Masoretic text of the Book of Exodus preserved by Codex Leningradensis. Many of these are noted in the critical apparatus of *Biblia Hebraica Stuttgartensia* prepared by Gottfried Quell, along with a great many minor variations as well. Every note in this apparatus has been considered carefully, and those deemed to provide important or, in some cases, merely interesting variations have been noted. Sometimes the notes of the *Masora Parva*, as edited for *BHS* by Gerard Weil, have been of help in this evaluation, and the 4271 lists of the *Masora Magna* of L have also been an asset (see Weil, vol. 1: Catalogi). Wherever a variant reading has been adopted, such a decision is clearly indicated.

The textual notes in *Biblia Hebraica Stuttgartensia* are necessarily limited, however, primarily by a lack of space. For that reason, I have supplemented the information provided by Quell by reference to (1) the text of the Septuagint, in the version based, so far as Exodus is concerned, primarily on Codex Vaticanus (B) and Codex Alexandrinus (A), edited and annotated by Alfred Rahlfs (6th ed.), published by the Württembergische Bibelanstalt; (2) the text of the Latin Vulgate, in the translation generally regarded as Jerome's, edited and annotated from a series of ancient manuscript editions and from the modern critical edition of the Benedictines of the monastery of St. Jerome in Rome by Robert Weber, with the help of B. Fischer, I. Gribomont, H. F. D. Sparks, and W. Thiele, published by the Württembergische Bibelanstalt in 1969; (3) the text of the Samaritan Pentateuch, edited and annotated from an extensive array of handwritten manuscripts by August Freiherrn von Gall and published by Alfred Töpelmann in 1918 (I used the photomechanical edition of 1966); and (4) the text of *The Bible in Aramaic: Volume I, The Pentateuch According to Targum Onkelos*, based primarily, for Genesis 1:1—Leviticus 12, on three manuscripts from the British Museum's Oriental collection (Mss. Or. 2228, 2229, and 2363), edited and annotated by Alexander Sperber, published by E. J. Brill in 1969. This latter text was further supplemented by reference to the translation of two Palestinian Targums (Codex Neofiti 1 in the Vatican Library and Ms. Add. 27031 in the British Museum) by Roger le Déaut, assisted by J. Robert, published in the Sources Chrétiennes series as *Targum du Pentateuque, Tome II*, by Les Éditions du Cerf in 1979.

The texts from Exodus that appear in full or fragmentary form in the Dead Sea Scrolls show little variation of significance from the readings of the Masoretic text. Of the forty-seven passages listed by Fitzmyer (153–54), to which now must be added the verses from Exod 12:43–13:16 and 20:7–12 from phylacteries and mezuzot published in DJD VI, far the majority follow substantially the reading preserved in B 19a. Those that do not are noted at the appropriate places in the commentary below.

The *Veteris Testamenti Concordantiae* of Solomon Mandelkern and *A Concor-*

dance to the Septuagint of Edwin Hatch and Henry A. Redpath were invaluable aids in the crossreferencing of key vocabulary and the attempt to achieve consistency in the translation of words and phrases that recur in a variety of places in the Book of Exodus. Quite late in the preparation of this commentary, there appeared the first of a series of works that promises additional supplementary help to the translator and the exegete. *Instrumenta Biblica 1*, prepared by Ferenc Postma, Eep Talstra, and Marc Vervenne, has presented "materials in automatic text processing" drawn from the *BHS* text of the Book of Exodus. Part II, Concordance, presents "a catalogue of the vocabulary" of Exodus, arranged alphabetically from אָב "father" to תֵּשַׁע "nine," and enabling the translator to determine, for example, that יהוה "Yahweh" occurs 398 times in Exodus, and where (cf. pp. 192–201), or that the preposition כִּי "for" occurs 198 times in Exodus, and where (cf. pp. 226–30). Part I, Morphological, Syntactical and Literary Case Studies, presents a sampling of data generated by computerized morphological and syntactical listings, and a particularly helpful pairing of parallel passages in Exod 25–28 and Exod 36–39. This work, the firstfruits of a joint project of the Centre Informatique et Bible of the Abbey of Maredsous in Belgium and the Werkgroep Information of the Faculty of Theology of the Free University of Amsterdam, appeared late in 1983. It offers the student of the Book of Exodus a mine of conveniently assembled information for analysis and crossreference.

The text of the Book of Exodus has on the whole been well preserved despite its antiquity, no doubt owing chiefly to the fact that much of the book achieved by use what was effectively a canonical status quite early in the history of the growth of the Old Testament. The usual kinds of textual error are to be found in the Hebrew text of Exodus, and some of these are pointed out in the notes that follow the translation below, but a comparison of the significant problems posed here with those present in certain Psalms, or in parts of the Books of Kings, Isaiah, or Ezekiel, for example, indicates that the text of Exodus is remarkably free of serious textual difficulty.

The language of the Book of Exodus is biblical or "classical" Hebrew. For the most part, the Hebrew of Exodus is straightforward and generally devoid of philological and grammatical complication. The major problem posed by the language of Exodus has to do with terms that appear to be quite correctly transmitted, but for which a precise significance is now unknown. There is no large number of these, however, and by far the bulk of the text of Exodus can be translated both clearly and easily. The few obscure terms are discussed in either the notes or the commentary below.

Most of the Book of Exodus is written in prose forms, either as narrative or as lists of apodictic and casuistic laws or as detailed sequences of cultic specification. One consequential section is in poetic form (15:1b–18, 21), and there is one three-line poetic stanza that some translators render as prose (so RSV; Childs, 554). These poems are certainly among the oldest parts of the book, and there is a possibility that some sections now preserved in prose form were originally in poetic form, as for example the decalogue, expanded from its original "ten words," or early recitations of the mighty acts of Yahweh's deliverance from Egypt and sustenance in the wilderness. Indeed, Pss

105:24–45; 106:1–23; and 136:10–16 may provide later examples of such poetic originals.

I have considered the translation of Exodus my primary and central assignment, and I have attempted to make this translation the foundation of everything else in the volume, deleting from my commentary everything that does not bear directly on the translation itself. I have tried indeed to incorporate the essential results of my research and reflection in the translation, so that the central theological emphasis I have referred to is apparent there. Everything else, whether in the notes on the text, in the discussion of the literary form of the text and the traditions that lie behind it, in the commentary on the text, and in the explanation of the essential point of a given pericope, has been dictated and governed by what is in the translation.

My intention has been to present a translation as near as possible to the sense of the text of the Book of Exodus, in clear if sometimes Hebrew-flavored English. I have given special weight to the particles and to the narrative *waw* (the so-called "consecutive" or "conservative" *waw,* for which my title is simply "special *waw*"), because I believe their use in this carefully weighed and redacted text serves more than an incidental purpose. I have translated every proper name in a parenthesis following its first occurrence in the Book of Exodus. I have sought to indicate special emphasis wherever it occurs, as for example with the double use of prepositions or the use of such emphatic particles as גַּם "also" and הִנֵּה "behold." I have endeavored to allow the drama of narrative dialogue to shine through the translation, along with the flashes of humor that sparkle here and there. I have tried to suggest the action-oriented sense of the Hebrew verb system, rather than the Latinized tenses so frequently imposed on a verb system that really includes no sense of time. I have reflected upon the possible meanings of every single word in the Book of Exodus, chosen meanings that seem to me best to translate the liveliness of the text, and then attempted as much as possible to render the same Hebrew word throughout the translation by the same English word, noting any significant departures from this rule. I have avoided paraphrase, that bane of the reader attempting to hear the original voice of any text, except in those few cases where a literal translation simply made no sense. Such instances are clearly indicated in the notes. I have sought to achieve a translation that suggests the oral flow and cadence of the Hebrew text, and for that reason I suggest that the translation be read aloud, with careful attention to punctuation. The narrative sections of the Book of Exodus, in particular, appear to have been composed with hearing rather than reading in mind.

My attempt, in sum, has been to hear the ancient voice of a living faith speaking in this marvelous theological narrative, and to transmit that voice as clearly as I can to my own time and context. My ambition has been to provide a translation that is not only the center and the anchor of my commentary treatment, but one which in itself is a summary of a commentary that is in turn a sampling of a far wider and more extensive range of questions and proposed answers. Thus the translation is both the beginning and the objective of this volume, the distillation of a lengthy period of work and reflection on the text of the Book of Exodus.

4. THE SHAPE AND THE CONTENT OF EXODUS

The outline of the Book of Exodus is deceptively simple, given the complexity of the book's contents. I have divided the text into three major parts on the basis of the location of the people of Israel in the narrative sequence, so:

Part One: Israel in Egypt (1:1–13:16)
Part Two: Israel in the Wilderness (13:17–18:27)
Part Three: Israel at Sinai (19:1–40:38)

Part One is then subdivided into three major sections, each with a varied number of pericopae: Section I, The Progeny of Israel, The Persecution and the Deliverer, Exod 1:1–2:25, is comprised of seven pericopae; Section II, The Call of the Deliverer, His Commission, and His Obedience, Exod 3:1–7:7, is comprised of ten pericopae; and Section III, The Ten Mighty Acts and the Exodus: the Proof of Yahweh's Presence, Exod 7:8–13:16, is comprised of seventeen pericopae.

Part Two, the briefest of the three major divisions, has no subsections, only eleven pericopae, the last of which, The Beginning of Israel's Legal System, Exod 18:13–27, probably belongs somewhere in the third major division (see below, pp. 240–43).

Part Three is subdivided into four major sections, each with a varied number of pericopae: Section I, The Advent of Yahweh's Presence and the Making of the Covenant, Exod 19:1–24:18, is comprised of six pericopae; Section II, Yahweh's Instructions for the Media of Worship, Exod 25:1–31:18, is comprised of sixteen pericopae; Section III, Israel's First Disobedience and Its Aftermath, Exod 32:1–34:35, is comprised of eight pericopae; and Section IV, Israel's Obedience of Yahweh's Instructions, Exodus 35:1–40:38, is comprised of eight pericopae.

The full outline I have followed can be seen in the Contents. It is an outline that emerges from the text, rather than one superimposed upon it, and it gives some indication of the whole Book of Exodus as a unified composite moving from the promise and the proof of Yahweh's Presence to the revelation and advent of that Presence, incorporating the involvement of that Presence in the solemnization of covenant relationship, recalling the threatened withdrawal of the Presence because of disobedience, and presenting with relief the reconciliation of Yahweh's Presence and his settlement in Israel's midst.

5. THE DEVELOPMENT OF COMMENTARIES ON EXODUS

Bibliography

Beer, G. *Exodus.* HAT. Tübingen: Verlag J. C. B. Mohr, 1939. **Cassuto, U.** *A Commentary on the Book of Exodus.* Jerusalem: Magnes Press, 1967. **Childs, B. S.** *Exodus.* OTL. Philadelphia: Westminster Press, 1974. ———. "Interpretation in Faith: The Theological Responsibility of an Old Testament Commentary." *Int* 18 (1964) 432–49. **Clements, R. E.** *Exodus.* CBC. Cambridge: University Press, 1972. **Davies, G. H.** *Exodus.* TBC. London: SCM Press, 1967. **Driver, S. R.** *The Book of Exodus.* CBSC. Cambridge: University Press, 1953. **Ellison, H. L.** *Exodus.* DSB. Philadelphia: Westminster Press, 1982. **Gispen, W. H.** *Exodus.* BSC. Grand Rapids: Zondervan Publishing House, 1982. **Greenberg, M.** *Understanding Exodus.* Melton Research Center Series, vol. 2, pt 1. New York: Behrman House, 1969. **Hyatt, J. P.** *Exodus.* NCB. London: Oliphants, 1971. **Knight, G. A. F.** *Theology as Narration: A Commentary on the Book of Exodus.* Edinburgh: Handsel Press, 1976. **Lowenstamm, S. E.** *The Tradition of Exodus in Its Development.* 2d edition. Jerusalem: Magnes Press, 1972. Heb., with a brief summary in Eng. **McNeile, A. H.** *The Book of Exodus.* WC. London: Methuen and Co., 1908. **Noth, M.** *Exodus.* OTL. Philadelphia: Westminster Press, 1962. **Schmidt, W. H.** *Exodus.* BKAT II, 1, 2, 3. Neukirchen-Vluyn: Neukirchener Verlag, 1974, 1977, 1983. **Wharton, J. A.** "Splendid Failure or Flawed Success?" *Int* 29 (1975) 266–76.

In the list of abbreviations, and in the bibliography to this final section of the Introduction, I have listed the standard works of reference and commentaries that have been of invaluable help to me in my study of the Book of Exodus, many of them for a number of years. In the commentary, these works are cited only by the author's last name and the relevant page references. They are not listed in the bibliographies preceding the individual pericopae in the commentary, because to have done so would have added unnecessary length to the volume. When two or more works by the same author are cited in the same section, a work from these general bibliographies will be listed only by the author's last name, and the additional work or works will be listed by a shortened form of the title of the work. I have listed no work, either in the general bibliographies or in the more specific bibliographies preceding the individual sections of the commentary, which is not cited directly in the commentary. The works in the table of abbreviations and in the bibliographies in this Introduction have for the most part been cited repeatedly.

The Book of Exodus has not lacked good commentaries from the time of the fathers of the Church to the present day (for a helpful list of commentaries predating the nineteenth century, see Childs, xxi–xxiii). The rise of literary critical approaches to the study of the Bible in the second half of the nineteenth century began a tradition of intense interest in the books of the Pentateuch, an interest that continues unabated to this very day, albeit with important shifts of subject and motive. The Book of Exodus has received more of this attention than any other pentateuchal book except the Book of Genesis, and nearly every major commentary set published in the past one hundred and fifty years has included a consequential volume on Exodus. The notable exception to this record is the International Critical Commentary of T. and T. Clark of Edinburgh, which never presented an Exodus commentary.

The standard commentaries on Exodus have tended to summarize the scholarly opinion of their time, and to be governed, even limited, by the translations upon which they were based. Early in this century, the commentary of A. H. McNeile (WC, 1908) and the commentary of S. R. Driver (CBSC, 1911), both based on the English Revised Version of 1884, displayed in the margins by the biblical text what their authors judged to be the allocation

of each verse to the appropriate documentary source. They gave a good bit
of space, in introductory and excursus sections, to what were believed to
be assumed historical, geographical, and parallel literary connections.

By 1939, when the excellent commentary of Georg Beer (HAT) was published, there was a bit less certainty in the matter of the sources, a bit more
tentativeness about matters historical and geographical, and Beer commented
on his own translation, in a fresh and pointed manner. Twenty years later,
Martin Noth (ATD) published a commentary on his translation of Exodus,
a volume published in English translation in 1962 (OTL), somewhat unfortunately carrying a slightly adapted RSV text, instead of a translation of Noth's
own rendering. Noth differentiated JE from P by differing margins (differing
typefaces in the English translation), and secondary material by brackets,
but the interest in and assurance about source-literary questions is less prominent still, and Noth gave virtually no space to historical matters. The attention
of commentaries on the Book of Exodus was being drawn more and more
by the text itself and was being determined less and less by considerations
taken to that text from nonbiblical interests.

In 1951, Umberto Cassuto published in Hebrew a massive commentary
on Exodus, intermingling an explanatory narrative with the Hebrew text,
assuming an ancient heroic poem as *the* principle source of the book, and
appealing for a consideration of "the book before us." In 1967, this work
was translated by I. Abrahams, who adapted the RSV, JPS, Moffatt's *New Translation of the Bible* and renderings of his own for the biblical text. It presents a
treatment in dramatic contrast to the modern commentaries preceding it,
not only in format, but also in its emphasis on an Exodus that, though combined from a variety of traditions, is nonetheless regarded as a unified work
in its own right, and one that deserves to be considered in its final form.
Cassuto's contribution is not without its flaws, but it deserves more consideration than it has had. Some of its implications have been helpfully explored
by S. E. Loewenstamm's *The Tradition of the Exodus in Its Development* (1972),
and in the very helpful but unfortunately incomplete *Understanding Exodus*
(1969) of Moshe Greenberg.

G. Henton Davis in 1967 gave us a compact commentary (TBC) on the
RSV text, following a standard source-literary critical approach to the text
and giving only minimal and passing attention to historical and geographic
matters, but emphasizing the theological unity of Exodus by reference to
"the theme of the Presence of God." The stark simplicity of this striking
conclusion remains another important contribution to an understanding of
the Book of Exodus for what it is, as a unified composite, rather than for
what it may once have been, as a series of parts.

J. P. Hyatt's *Exodus* (NCB, 1971), also based on the RSV text, marks a
return to the earlier commentary form typified by McNeile and Driver, both
as regards source-literary analysis and also as regards attention to historical
and geographical allusion and extended excursuses. Hyatt's treatment is
a good one, if somewhat old-fashioned, and its chief advance is a summary of traditio-historical approaches that bring balance to source and form
analysis.

A stimulating and influential next step in Exodus commentary was taken in 1974 with the appearance of Brevard S. Childs's *The Book of Exodus: A Critical, Theological Commentary*, a unique second commentary on a single book in a single series (OTL). Childs undertook in this volume to do more than any commentator on an OT book has done heretofore, particularly in the address of "the final shape of the text" (xiv), in a consideration of the treatment of Exodus by the writers of the New Testament and by both Christian and Jewish exegetes through history, and in theological reflection on Exodus as Holy Scripture within a Christian context. Childs's commentary is on his own translation of the Hebrew text of Exodus, accompanied by both text-critical and philological annotation. He has given careful but not excessive attention to source and form-critical questions, and has helpfully surveyed traditio-historical theories. He has entirely abandoned the usual introductory survey of the contents of Exodus and the special problems facing a commentator, and he has largely ignored historical and geographical discourse, I think correctly so. Childs has given us a new kind of commentary (cf. Wharton, 266–76, and Childs's own commentary manifesto in *Int* 18 [1964] 432–49) and in doing so has raised a series of important questions about what is and is not a part of the commentator's task. He has clearly attempted more than can be fully achieved in a single volume and by a single scholar, but he has also achieved more than many would have thought possible. By the encyclopedic sweep of his review, he has moved Exodus commentary to another stage in its evolution, particularly in his insistence that the "final" Exodus, the canonical Exodus, be taken as seriously as it stands as it has been studied in dissection.

More massive still than Childs's volume, in prospect, is the *Exodus* of Werner H. Schmidt (BKAT II) of which thus far only three 80-page fascicles have appeared, giving Schmidt's translation, with extensive bibliography, notes, and commentary, of Exodus 1:1–4:31. The format of the BKAT series more or less insures that this treatment will be a "standard" commentary, and the pace at which it is appearing (II:1, 1974; II:2, 1977; II:3, 1983) suggests that it will be a long time coming to completion. Thus far, it breaks no new ground but provides reference survey of previous work on Exodus, with much attention to source-literary, form- and tradition-critical, and historical and geographical questions.

New commentaries on the Book of Exodus and translations of older ones will certainly continue to appear, not least because of the essential importance of the account Exodus presents for an understanding of the OT and of the Bible as a whole. Some of these will represent basic information in traditional ways, as for example the *Exodus* of R. E. Clements on the text of the NEB (CBC, 1972) or the *Exodus* of H. L. Ellison on the text of the RSV (DSB, 1982) or the translation of the *Exodus* by W. H. Gispen (BSC, 1982), incorporating in its English format the text of the NIV (Gispen's Dutch Commentary, which appeared in KVHS in 1951, was on his own translation). Some of them will take new and imaginative approaches, as for example George A. F. Knight's *Theology as Narration: A Commentary on the Book of Exodus* (1976), in which Exodus is presented as "an 'incarnational' theological essay," "virtually a chapter in the history of God" written by "some one person" whom Knight calls "Ex" (ix–xi).

Such preoccupation with Exodus is an inevitability, and it is also to our very great benefit. We have not begun to understand this magnificent book, much less exhaust its treasure. Every additional work it stimulates makes it available, on some level, to that many more members of the human family who are hungry to know the God who comes and who gives himself to us.

When Moses turned aside on Mount Sinai to the bush all aflame that strangely was not being burnt, he came into Yahweh's Presence. From that moment on, Moses found himself in the stretching tension between ineffable mystery and pragmatic daily living. In the Book of Exodus he is presented struggling to convince a frightened and insecure people in a strange place of the reality of a God he himself knows but has not seen. There is little wonder at his asking Yahweh on Sinai, when he had won mercy for a compromised Israel, "Show me, please, your glory" (Exod 33:18).

Such a request, of course, Yahweh does not answer, though he does come to Moses in a theophany of striking and unique revelatory proportions (Exod 34:5–8). After the covenant has been remade, however, and after the instructions concerning the media of worship have all been fully carried out (a point the account repeatedly goes to great trouble to make), when "Moses," as the text says, "completed the work," Yahweh's Presence filled the Tabernacle, and Moses could no longer enter the Tent of Appointed Meeting (Exod 40:34–35). A great satisfaction must have come over Moses then. He still could not see Yahweh, but he knew, for certain, that Yahweh was there.

Anyone who studies the Book of Exodus seriously and with faith will know how Moses felt.

PART ONE

ISRAEL IN EGYPT

(1:1–13:16)

I. *The Progeny of Israel, the Persecution, and the Deliverer (1:1–2:25)*

II. *The Call of the Deliverer, His Commission, and His Obedience (3:1–7:7)*

III. *The Ten Mighty Acts and the Exodus: The Proof of Yahweh's Presence (7:8–13:16)*

I. The Progeny of Israel, the Persecution, and the Deliverer (1:1—2:25)

"And These Are the Names" (1:1-7)

Bibliography

Albright, W. F. "Northwest-Semitic Names in a List of Egyptian Slaves from the Eighteenth Century B.C." *JAOS* 74 (1954) 222–33. **Coats, G. W.** "A Structural Transition in Exodus." *VT* 22 (1972) 129–42. **Cross, F M., Jr.** *The Ancient Library of Qumran and Modern Biblical Studies.* Rev. ed. Grand Rapids: Baker Book House, 1980. **Klein, R. W.** *Textual Criticism of the Old Testament.* Philadelphia: Fortress Press, 1974. **Noth, M.** *Die israelitischen Personennamen im Rahmen der gemeinsemitischen Namengebung.* BWANT III, 10. Stuttgart: Verlag W. Kohlhammer, 1928. **Vriezen, Th. C.** "Exodusstudien Exodus I." *VT* 17 (1967) 334–53.

Translation

[1] *And [a] these are the names of the sons of Israel, the ones who went down into Egypt with Jacob [b]—to a man they went, each with his family:* [2] *Reuben ("Behold, a son!"), Simeon ("He Surely Heard!"), Levi ("Joined") and Judah ("Object of Praise"),* [3] *Issachar ("There is recompense"), Zebulun ("Honored") and Benjamin ("Son of the Right Hand"),* [4] *Dan ("Judge") and Naphtali ("My Wrestling"), Gad ("Good Fortune") and Asher ("Happy One").[a]* [5] *Thus was the full issue of the loins of Jacob seventy [a] souls, since Joseph ("Increasing One") was already in Egypt.[b]*
[6] *In time, Joseph died, and his brothers and indeed that entire generation as well.* [7] *But the sons of Israel were fertile, and so they became a teeming swarm. Indeed, they became so many they were a strength to be reckoned with by their numbers alone. The land was simply filled with them.*

Notes

1.a. LXX and Vg omit this "and," and many translators follow their lead. The "and" is important, however; see *Comment*, below.

1.b. LXX reads ἅμα Ιακωβ τῷ πατρὶ αὐτῶν "with Jacob, their father."

4.a. See n. 5.b.

5.a. LXX gives a total of 75, here and in Gen 46:27, as also does a fragment from Qumran, 4QEx[a] (Cross, 184–85). See Num 26:28–37 and Hyatt, 57. As Klein (15) correctly notes, this alternate number is a "secondary calculation" based on the addition of five more descendants of Ephraim and Manasseh to the original count. MT's "seventy" is the preferred reading.

5.b. LXX locates Ιωσηφ . . . Αἰγύπτῳ "Joseph . . . Egypt," somewhat logically, following the "Asher" of v 4.

Form/Structure/Setting

This opening passage of Exodus functions as a compact transitional unit that summarizes that part of the preceding Genesis narrative that is essential to what follows, states a new and discontinuous situation, and anticipates the progress of the family of Jacob/Israel toward their birth, in exodus and at Sinai, as the people of God.

Source critics have tended to favor the assignment of v 6 to the Yahwist, because of a supposed connection with the final verse of Genesis (Fohrer, 9), or with Exod 1:8 (Vriezen, *VT* 17 [1967] 335). There is no convincing reason for such a division of this unit, however. It is better taken as a carefully composed introductory section from the Priestly source (Noth, 20; Coats, *VT* 22 [1972] 133), strategically placed to afford an ingenious bridge (see *Comment* below).

As such, this passage links both person and purpose in the patriarchal history to person and purpose in the story of the exodus, and it connects the promise of progeny to the patriarchs with the fulfillment of that promise in the patriarchs' greatly multiplied descendants in Egypt. Above all, it combines these themes to impel the narrative forward into the next stage of its development and into the fulfillment of the second part of the promise to the fathers, the promise of land.

Comment

1 The Book of Exodus opens with a phrase that serves also as its Hebrew name: שְׁמוֹת וְאֵלֶּה "And these are the names." This phrase is a carefully chosen and precisely placed connecting link, a bridge from the promise of descendants to Jacob and his sons to a reality of descendants that makes an exodus from Egypt a necessity. Indeed, the first six words of Exod 1:1 are in the Hebrew text an exact quotation of the first six words of Gen 46:8, a clear rhetorical indication of the continuity intended not only in the narrative, but in the underlying theological assertion.

The author of the opening lines of the Book of Exodus quite probably had at hand, in some form, the genealogical list of Gen 46:8–27. There is good reason to suggest that these two passages have the same author, and that an original sequence may have included at least Gen 46:8–27 followed by 47:6–12, 27b–28; then 48:3–7; 49:28–33; 50:12–13; then Exod 1:1–5, 7. The canonical Exodus thus opens with a listing of the essential names of the detailed genealogy of Gen 46:8–27 (the first substantial passage in the patriarchal history from this author after Gen 36:1–37:2a), continues the account of the settlement in Egypt begun in Gen 47:6–12, and amplifies (v 7) the theme of fertility in Egypt introduced in Gen 47:27b and referred to in prospect in Gen 48:3–7.

The narrative regarding Jacob's desire to be buried in Canaan (Gen 49:28–33 and 50:12–13) and the account of the population explosion in the Egyptian delta (Exod 1:7) both point forward to what is to come, just as the summary of the genealogy of Gen 46:8–27 points backward to what has been promised and thence to what has already come to pass in the fulfillment of that promise.

Thus the "and" with which the Hebrew text of the Book of Exodus begins is an indication of an all-important continuity obscured already both by the growth of the closing part of the Book of Genesis and by the division of the text into "books." Though many modern translators follow the lead of

LXX in omitting this copula, to do so is a mistake. The connection of the text of Exodus with what has preceded it must be emphasized, not further obscured.

7 The fertility of the sons of Israel in Egypt is dramatically underscored by the use in v 7 of the verb שׁרץ, which generally refers in the OT to the swarming multiplication of frogs or fish or other animal life. This verb is used in reference to humans only here and in the blessing upon Noah and his sons (Gen 9:1–7; esp. v 7), two passages stressing, for different reasons, an extraordinary increase in numbers. The translation should in each case emphasize the unusual usage: hence, with "sequential" *waw*, "and so they became a teeming swarm." This multiplication is further dramatized by no less than five separate statements of it in this one verse: "fertile . . . swarm . . . so many . . . numbers . . . simply filled."

2–5 A final important connecting link is reflected in the significance of the names of the twelve sons of Jacob, suggested in the parentheses in the *Translation* above. Present in these names, in a manner unfortunately not always apparent, are clues to the important questions connected with tribal biography and the theological descendancy of Israel. Further clues are present, though some of them are also obscure, in the lists of the "Blessing of Jacob" in Gen 49:3–27 and the "Blessing of Moses" in Deut 33:2–29.

These names, in the present arrangement of the biblical text, also provide a point of contact with the "Blessing of Jacob" in Gen 49:3–27. The same twelve names are listed there, though the final eight occur in a different order. In the list in Gen 46:8–27, the final six names appear in an order different from the one in Exod 1. The "Blessing of Jacob," with its intriguing plus-and-minus characterizations of the twelve tribal families, gives us more history than we can understand. Quite possibly its present location in the text may have been suggested by the two lists that now bracket it, in Gen 46 and Exod 1.

The significance of the twelve names in the traditions of the OT is thus one more part of the interweaving of threads that connect the Book of Exodus with what precedes it. References particularly relevant to this significance are as follows:

1. Reuben—from ראה "see" + בֵּן "son," Gen 29:32.
2. Simeon—from שמע "hear" + emphatic ן, Gen 29:33.
3. Levi—possibly from לוה "joined," as husband joined to wife, Gen 29:34; or as servants joined to Aaron, Num 18:2–4.
4. Judah—possibly from hiphil of ידה "give praise, thanks," Gen 29:35, 49:8.
5. Issachar—from יֵשׁ "it is" or אִישׁ "a man" + שָׂכָר "recompense, wage," Gen 30:18. See Albright, *JAOS* 74 (1954) 229 and 231, on name 231.
6. Zebulun—from זבל "honor, exalt" + emphatic ן, Gen 30:20.
7. Benjamin—from בֵּן "son" + יָמִין "the right," Gen 35:18.
8. Dan—from דין "judge," Gen 30:6.
9. Naphtali—from niphal of פתל "twist oneself = wrestle," + pronominal suffix "my," Gen 30:8.
10. Gad—from גָד "good fortune," Gen 30:11; though compare the fascinating play on Gad and the verb גדד "penetrate, attack," and its derivatives גְדוּד and גְדוּדָה in Gen 49:19.

11. Asher—from אשר "go straight on, pronounce happy," Gen 30:13. See Albright, *JAOS* 74 (1954) 227–28, on name 13.
12. Joseph—from יסף "add to, increase," Gen 30:24.

Explanation

The beginning of the Book of Exodus is a continuation, a look at the present, and a hint of what must come. What is continued is the story of Jacob's family, begun in the history of the patriarchs. The naming of the twelve sons is a link with both the past and the future.

The look at the present is in the pointed, almost laconic obituary notice regarding the twelve just named, and indeed all their generation, in its entirety, and in the awed, almost incredulous description of the unusual multiplication of the progeny of those twelve. There is more than a hint of the miraculous in this growth of "seventy souls" into "a teeming swarm," for the author intends that his readers should recall the promise of a vast descendancy to Abraham, Isaac, and Jacob (Gen 17:1–8 or 26:1–5 or 28:13–15, for example). This unnatural family growth is everywhere accounted for in Exodus as God's doing.

In this recollection of God's covenant-promise, however, there is also an allusion to what is to come, for the promise was a promise of land as well as progeny. And with the promise of progeny so wondrously and abundantly fulfilled, the promise of land must not be far from fulfillment. It *cannot* be, since the Egyptian delta is "simply filled" with Israel's descendants. A shadow of what else is to come is present in the reference to the strength such numbers present, as also in the continuing biblical tension between God's promise and the threats that oppose it.

Never very far from such a text is the larger theological purpose underlying all these events and implicit in any account of them. What God is doing with Israel's descendants has meaning for the whole family of humankind.

The New Dynasty   (1:8–14)

Bibliography

Besters, A. " 'Israël' et 'fils d'Israël' dans les livres historiques (Genèse–II Rois)" and "L'expression 'fils d'Israël' en Ex., I–XIV." *RB* 74 (1967) 5–23, 321–55. **Gardiner, A.** *Egyptian Grammar.* 3d ed. rev. London: Oxford University Press, 1957. **Helck, W.** "Ṯkw und die Ramses-Stadt." *VT* 15 (1965) 35–48. **Mendelsohn, I.** "On Corvée Labor in Ancient Canaan and Israel." *BASOR* 167 (1962) 31–35. **Plaut, W. G.** "The Israelites in Pharaoh's Egypt—A Historical Reconstruction." *Judaism* 27 (1978) 40–46. **Redford, D. B.** "Exodus 1:11." *VT* 13 (1963) 401–18.

Translation

[8] *Then a new king came to power over Egypt, one with no experience of Joseph.*
[9] *Thus it was that he said to his people, "Just look: the people of the sons of Israel* [a]

are numerous and so stronger even than we are. ¹⁰*My advice is that we outsmart them before they* ᵃ *become so many that in the event of a war they could join themselves— indeed they could* ᵇ—*with those who hate us to do battle against us. Under such conditions, they might even go up from the land."*

¹¹*So they set in authority over them slave-gang overseers, in order to keep them under control with hard labor. Thus did Israel build supply-cities* ᵃ *for Pharaoh, Pithom, and Raᶜamses.* ᵇ ¹²*Yet even as they heaped hard labor upon them, they became more numerous still and broke through* ᵃ *the limits imposed upon them. And so the Egyptians* ᵇ *came to have a sickening dread because of the presence of the sons of Israel.*

¹³*The Egyptians then forced the sons of Israel to toil more unremitting than ever,* ¹⁴*making their lives utterly bitter with a backbreaking slavery, mixing mortar, and molding bricks, and even doing every kind of field-labor. In all the toil to which they forced them, the Egyptians made them work without relief.* ᵃ

Notes

9.a. The sense of עַם בְּנֵי יִשְׂרָאֵל is virtually "the people, 'sons of Israel.' " The writer has Pharaoh calling the group previously known as "Israel's sons" a people, in parallel to the same usage in reference to his own nation (עַמּוֹ "his people"), because of Israel's consequential growth to a threatening size. See also Besters *RB* 74 (1967) 7, 21–23, 323–26.

10.a. The subjects and verbs referring to Israel in vv 8–12 are sg in MT, but pl in LXX, Tgs, and other versions. The usage is a collective sg, and best rendered in English by pl, as above. Greenberg (*Understanding Exodus*, 20) thinks the usage a device to call attention to the designation, in v 9, of Israel as עַם, "a people."

10.b. Reading (הֵם =) גַם הוּא "indeed they could" as an emphatic coordinate clause.

11.a. LXX πόλεις ὀχυρὰς "fortified cities."

11.b. LXX adds καὶ Ὤν, ἥ ἐστιν Ἡλιούπολις "and On, that is, Heliopolis." See *Comment* below.

12.a. פרץ "burst out, break through." LXX ἴσχυον σφόδρα σφόδρα "grew exceedingly, exceedingly strong." Vg *multiplicabantur* "became great."

12.b. LXX Vg, Tg Onk add this subject, left unstated by MT.

14.a. Lit., "with harsh severity."

Form/Structure/Setting

These seven verses are made a unity by their reference to a common subject, the new situation of Israel in Egypt with the accession of a new dynasty of Egyptian rulers. Vv 8–12 may safely be considered a unit, probably from the Yahwist. Vv 13–14 present a somewhat intensified version of the narrative of the Israelites' forced labor, generally assigned to the Priestly source.

The two parts of this section can easily be separated on stylistic grounds, as for example, by the use of singular pronouns and verbs in vv 9–12, in reference to the collective singular עַם "people," and by the use of plural pronouns and verbs in vv 13–14.

Yet there is more here than two parallel accounts of the same events. Vv 13–14 take the hardship of Israel's forced labor to a more severe level, drama-tizing the need of Israel, and thus increasing the reader's concern that some-thing must be done. This intensification is certainly not coincidental, and it is even possible that these verses were composed for just such a purpose.

Whether that be so or not, these two sections set together present a dramatic and sequentially developed unity.

Comment

8 The action of the first two chapters of the Book of Exodus is dependent upon two historical events, introduced in the order of their importance in the first two sections of chapter one. The first of these is the miraculous multiplication of Jacob/Israel's descendants, mentioned first in 1:7. The second is the rise to power of "a new king" (1:8) which needs to be understood, in Egyptian terms, as the rise of a new dynasty. The text specifies quite explicitly, by the use of the verb יָדַע "know," that this new "king" had no experience of Joseph. Much more than mere acquaintance is meant, for this verb refers to experiential knowledge of the most intimate kind. It is used to describe long-term and deep relationships (e.g., Gen 29:5, 2 Sam 7:20), as a euphemism for sexual intercourse between husband and wife (e.g., Gen 4:1; 1 Sam 1:19), and to refer to the communion between humankind and God that produces a reorientation of life in men and women (e.g., Ezek 24:27; Isa 1:3).

The writer refers to the radically changed situation, the drastic rearrangement that comes not when one king succeeds another king of the same family and with similar policies, but with the rise of a new succession of kings bringing an inevitable set of changes, some real and consequential, and some cosmetic, giving only the appearance of difference. Thus does he add to his reference to "a new king" the important qualification, "one with no experience of Joseph." This new king is the first king of a new dynasty, and thus a king who has no obligation to respect, or even to inform himself of, any commitments to a non-native group within the territory of his reign.

9 The rise of a new dynasty at just the time when Jacob/Israel's progeny had become so numerous brings together the two events that create the context of the early chapters of Exodus. The new king is faced, as every new king always is, with a series of problems, some of which were unnoticed by his predecessors, or were viewed as assets rather than as problems (Gen 47:6). Among the problems of this new king is the large and incredibly prolific colony of foreigners in the delta region, a territory unfashionable to his predecessors, but the very corner of the kingdom in his plans. Thus he must deal with this people and find justification for doing so.

The new king chooses fear as his justifying motive. While it is perhaps a possibility that the "sons of Israel" in the delta may outnumber their Egyptian overlords at the beginning of a relocation there of Egyptian power, the likelier explanation is that the king of Egypt is reported as justifying his severe forced-labor policies by recourse to scare tactics. V 9 does not say "too many and too mighty" (RSV), but "numerous and so stronger," that is, numerous enough to pose an obvious threat.

10 This sense is supported by the king's immediate proposal of a solution. The text reads הָבָה "give, permit" (BDB, 396), plus the hithpael imperfect of חכם "we make ourselves act wisely," to give a tactfully posed suggestion, "My advice is that we outsmart. . . ."

This advice is made urgent not only by the fear that the sons of Israel

might join forces with potential invaders (a curious fear if they were already
literally more numerous than the Egyptians), but also by the still greater
fear that "they might even go up from the land." This latter possibility became
of course a reality, and when it did, it was reported in what is standard rhetoric
for the exodus, אֶרֶץ + מִן + עלה "go up + from + land" (Exod 13:18).
"Land" or "the land" as the king uses it here means "Egyptian territory,"
as the usage in 13:18 shows.

11 The specific territory the king has in mind is indicated not only by
the accounts in Genesis of Israel's settlement in Goshen (chap. 47), but especially by the designation of the supply-cities Pithom and Raᶜamses in the
MT, to which LXX adds "On, which is Heliopolis." These cities were all in
the delta region, and all were associated with the vigorous building and rebuilding projects of the Nineteenth Dynasty.

It is in this note in v 11 that the new king is called "Pharaoh" for the
first time in the ongoing narrative of the Book of Exodus. The Hebrew term
פַּרְעֹה is a transliteration of the Egyptian word *Pr-ᶜ3*, which referred originally
to the royal palace or the king's court, but came by the time of Akhenaten
to be used also as a respectful royal title, and eventually, by the Nineteenth
Dynasty, to be used as it is here (Gardiner, *Egyptian Grammar*, 75).

12 That the Pharaoh's propaganda campaign worked is suggested by the
graphic use of the verb קוץ at the end of v 12; the root means "feel loathing
or abhorrence for." Though MT does not state the subject, the Egyptians
are clearly intended and are specifically added as the subject in an array of
versions.

13–14 The climax of the confrontation of the new king and the incredibly
expanded family of Jacob/Israel is the subjection of that family to slave labor.
This climax is colorfully presented in the two-verse extension, from the Priestly
source, of the narrative of oppression. The "hard labor" of v 11 becomes
the motif of this paragraph and is five times multiplied with "toil unremitting,"
"lives utterly bitter," "backbreaking (lit., "severe") slavery," "toil . . . forced,"
and "work without relief." This chorus of labor is even further augmented
by a specification of expanded duties: to the making of bricks and the mixing
of mortar is added every imaginable field-task, as a filler for any possible
spare moments. Plaut (*Judaism* 27 [1978] 45–46) has surveyed the midrash
on Israel's hard labor in Egypt and suggests that the Egyptian oppression
deliberately "reduced a proud people to willing serfs, cogs in the machine
of state," and that Moses was able to persuade only "one fiftieth" of Israel
to depart their slavery.

Explanation

As the opening section of the Book of Exodus establishes continuity with
the theological history of the fathers and describes their descendants' situation
in the intervening years, so this second section focuses upon two radical
changes in that situation as a means of moving the narrative forward to its
major goal, the advent of God and the birth of his people.

The first change, described in the closing verse of the first section, is followed immediately by the second change, introduced in the first verse of the second section. God himself is responsible for the first change, and his wonderful multiplication of the family of Jacob/Israel is only the beginning of the fulfillment of half of his promise to the fathers. The second change, at least under the aegis of his authority, will function as a needed catalyst for the fulfillment of the second half of that promise. Like their descendants many years later in Babylon, descendants who began the process of bringing together the canonical Book of Exodus, these people of Israel in Egypt would be reluctant to leave Egypt without good cause.

So the writer tells us about a new dynasty, one that introduced for the benefit of its own grandiose purpose repressive policies that made life in Egypt unbearable for the sons of Israel. This was done with the excuse of keeping under control this foreign people, and in an attempt to discourage their child-bearing.

The Pharaoh's "outsmarting" of the people of Israel happens also to have provided a cheap source of labor for his renovation of the Nile delta. The importance of this theme to the narrative's purpose is made clear by the paragraph (vv 13–14) piling up descriptions of the indescribable and inhumane extent of the forced toil. We are not only given to know that some relief *must* come, we are compelled to long for it, even as we abhor such treatment of human beings.

Yet locked away in the middle of this narrative is the assurance that the growth of this people, now the major reason for their misery, cannot be stemmed (v 12). God is in it, and he is bringing his own purpose inexorably to fulfillment. No Pharaoh, and not even the people of Israel themselves, can alter this growth. Thus the situation is bound to grow more terrible still, for God will not go back on his promise, and a new Pharaoh cannot afford to be wrong.

The Pharaoh's Genocide *(1:15–22)*

Bibliography

Albright, W. F. "Northwest-Semitic Names in a List of Egyptian Slaves from the Eighteenth Century B.C." *JAOS* 74 (1954) 222–33. **Auvray, P.** *Initiation à l'hébreu biblique.* Paris: Desclée, 1955. **Bottéro, J.** *Le problème des Habiru à la 4ᵉ recontre assyriologique internationale.* Cahiers de la Société Asiatique XII. Paris: Imprimerie Nationale, 1954. **Brongers, H. A.,** and **A. S. van der Woude.** "Wat Is De Betekenis van 'Ābanāyîm in Exodus 1:16?" *NedTTs* 20 (1965–1966) 241–54. **Cohen, A.** "Studies in Hebrew Lexicography." *AJSL* 40 (1924) 153–85. **Driver, G. R.** "Hebrew Mothers." *ZAW* 67 (1955) 246–48. **Exum, J. C.** " 'You shall let every daughter live': A Study of Exodus 1:8–2:10." *Semeia* 28 (1983) 63–82. **Lewy, J.** "Origin and Signification of the Biblical Term 'Hebrew'," *HUCA* 28 (1957) 1–13. **Tsevat, M.** "Some Biblical Notes." *HUCA* 24 (1952–53) 107–14. **Wolff, H. W.** "The Elohistic Fragments in the Pentateuch." *The Vitality of Old Testament Traditions.* W. Brueggemann and H. W. Wolff, eds. Atlanta: John Knox Press, 1975. 41–82, 138–40.

Translation

¹⁵ Still not satisfied, ᵃ the king of Egypt said to the Hebrew midwives, one of whom was named Shiphrah ("Fair One"), and the second of whom was named Puah ("Fragrant One"), ¹⁶ "In your midwifery to the Hebrew women, take care to determine the sex of the infant: ᵃ if it is a son, kill him instantly; ᵇ if however it is a daughter, she may live."

¹⁷ But the midwives believed ᵃ in God, and they would not do what the king of Egypt had told them to do. Rather did they help the male children live. ¹⁸ For this reason the king of Egypt ᵃ summoned the midwives and said to them, "On what authority have you done such a thing, that you would permit the male children to live?" ¹⁹ Thinking fast, ᵃ the midwives said to Pharaoh, "We couldn't help it, because unlike Egyptian women, the Hebrew women are robust ᵇ—in fact, before the midwife can get to them, they have already delivered their babies!"

²⁰ Thus did God favor the midwives. And the people of Israel ᵃ became more numerous still and so, increasingly, very strong. ²¹ Because the midwives believed in God, he provided them families.

²² The Pharaoh's next move was to command the whole of his people thus: "Every son born to the Hebrews ᵃ you must pitch into the river Nile; every daughter may be permitted to live."

Notes

15.a. The verb "said" is preceded by the special *waw*, to give what Auvray (*L'hebreu biblique*, 54–55, ¶ 80–82) calls "le mode consécutif." This narrative consecution is shown in this context by the phrase "Still not satisfied."

16.a. MT וראיתן על האבנים "and you look upon the stones." LXX and related versions (cf. Vg) have καὶ ὦσιν πρὸς τῷ τίκτειν "when they are about to drop the child," an interpretive paraphrase.

16.b. "Instantly" is a suggestion of the context and the special *waw*.

17.a. The verb is ירא "fear," in the sense of "reverence, hold in respectful awe." It is used frequently in the OT to describe the reverence for God that governs life and action.

18.a. SamPent פרעה "Pharaoh."

19.a. A suggestion of the continuity of the narrative indicated by the special *waw*.

19.b. Lit., "full of life," חָיוֹת Driver, *ZAW* 67 (1955) 247–48, suggests the pointing חָיּוֹת and translates "prolific."

20.a. "Of Israel" is not in MT, but the context justifies the addition, for clarity. SamPent, some other ancient versions read the verb רבב as a pl.

22.a. "To the Hebrews" is an addition of LXX, SamPent, Tg Onk, Tg Ps-J.

Form/Structure/Setting

There is considerable variance of opinion among source critics concerning which verses in this section are to be attributed to the Yahwist, and which to the Elohist. Most recent critics favor the Elohist as the author of all (Hyatt, 56) or most of the section (excepting v 22; Childs, 7, incorrectly says Noth assigns vv 15–20 to J, but Noth, 23, states that vv 15–21 are "to be taken as a fragment of E"); most older critics tend to divide the narrative between J and E, with E predominating. Fohrer (*Überlieferung*, 11–17, 124–25) assigns vv 15–21 parenthetically to his early Nomadic source (N) and sees it as having been added to Exodus during its redaction.

The evidence for separating this section into such component strands is very thin, however, and clues for speculation about its earlier "nomadic" or "lay" origin are sheer guesswork. It is far simpler and probably no less accurate to think of the section as an EJ amalgam bound together by the single subject of the Pharaoh's genocide. Even if the reference to death by drowning in v 22 once involved a separate version of the means of genocide, it functions now as a sequential step, replacing the unsuccessful plan employing the midwives. (Cf. Schmidt, 16–21, 45–46).

Comment

15–19 The failure of the Pharaoh's plan to control the strength and growth of the children of Israel by a savage workload is made clear not by a direct statement but by his move to a secretive but murderous "plan B," and following further failure, to a still more drastic and violent "plan C."

Essential to plan B is the cooperation of the midwives, who are not only pointedly called "Hebrew," but are given "perfectly good Northwest-Semitic names of women from the first half of the second millennium" B.C. (Albright, *JAOS* 74 [1954] 233). No reason is given to justify the Pharaoh's expectations of these midwives. Perhaps the summons by so powerful a figure was calculated to frighten the women. There is no good evidence for making them out to be *Egyptian*, as some have done (Rudolph, *Elohist*, 3, or Greenberg, *Hab/piru*, 26–27), and the unlikeliness of the Pharaoh's plan is shown by the midwives' sparing of the Hebrew boys and their witty excuse when confronted with their failure.

17–18 Still more to the point is the midwives' belief in God, whose will was for them thus far more important than any orders a Pharaoh could give. Not surprisingly, they not only refused to obey the Pharaoh's command, but they also worked against it. וַתְּחַיֶּיןָ אֶת־הַיְלָדִים "Rather they helped the male children live" suggests, at least, a redoubled effort to help the little boys survive the dangers of birth. It is against such a context of the survival of the male babies, and perhaps even a decline in the usual infant mortality, that the second summons of the Pharaoh and his outraged accusation (מַדּוּעַ "Just why . . ." or "On what account . . .") must be understood. And this defiance of the Pharaoh by the midwives, as secret as the plan of Pharaoh that they were frustrating, is the basis of God's doing good to them (v 20), and making "houses," establishing families for them (v 21). Wolff (*Vitality* 73–74) treats the midwives' "fear" of God, and God's consequent blessing upon them, as typical of the Elohist's primary theological motif. Exum (*Semeia* 28 [1983] 70–82) suggests that the story of the midwives is part of a marked focus on women at the beginning of Exodus.

The key word of the Pharaoh's instruction to the midwives, apart from his order of genocide, is אָבְנָיִם, literally, "stones" (see n. 16.a). This word occurs in the OT only here and in Jer 18:3, where it refers to stones, apparently a pair of them, employed by a potter at his craft. Despite many ingenious interpretations, the most frequent of which is "birthstool" (see especially the elaborate theory of Cassuto, 14, and the dialogue of Brongers and van der Woude, *NedTTs* 20 [1965–66] 247–49, 252–54); the best translation remains "stones," as a euphemism for "testicles." The root of the noun is certainly "stone," and its form is clearly dual, thus signifying a pair. Given the point of Pharaoh's instruction, the determination of the sex of the infant at the moment of birth, the term is best understood as a euphemism, in use to this day, for the male genitalia (cf. Cohen, *AJSL* 40 [1924] 157–59; and Tsevat, *HUCA* 24 [1952–53] 109–10, who proposes, in part on the basis of the text of Isa 65:3 in 1QIsa[a], "the female sex organs").

19 The quick reply of the midwives to Pharaoh's question is tinged with wit. Not only are the Hebrew women "robust," delivering and caring for their babies themselves with a minimum of bother and self-indulgence—the Egyptian women are just the opposite. The suggestion is that these Hebrew midwives attended both Hebrew *and* Egyptian births, or at the very least that the Hebrew women were more vigorous and healthy than any of the women of the Pharaoh's experience.

It is in this section that the word עִבְרִי "Hebrew" is used for the first time (vv 15 and 16) in reference to the family of Jacob/Israel. The term is employed in the narrative of the oppression only as a somewhat derisive epithet intelligible to the Egyptians, one the Israelites would not use among themselves.

20–22 The reference in v 20 to the continuing multiplication of the people of Israel seems almost certainly to be an interruption of the statement regarding God's favor towards the believing midwives, though it is a logical one, giving the inevitable conclusion to the failure of the Pharaoh's plan B. A more logical sequence would place this statement between vv 21 and 22, but logic is only rarely an editorial virture.

22 Thus plan C must be brought into play—genocide by the drowning of the male infants, the deed to be carried out not by Hebrew functionaries whose loyalty is suspect, but by the entire Egyptian populace (כָּל־עַמּוֹ) of Pharaoh's land. Such a policy, if practiced, would in time have reduced the Hebrew work force, but would also have ended the population explosion and, in due course, would have exterminated the family of Jacob/Israel entirely.

The difference in the three plans of the Pharaoh, especially as regards the results of plan A vis-à-vis plans B and C, has led some commentators to propose differing traditions of a single plan of Pharaoh for the Israelites. While this is at least possible, the three "plans" are presented in sequence in MT, and are therefore best read that way, with genocide by drowning being the "ultimate" solution, put into effect when other plans have failed. This third move of the Pharaoh, introduced so abruptly and stated without elaboration, thus becomes both the climax of the narrative of the oppression and the catalyst for the arrival of the delivering hero, Moses.

Explanation

The key to an understanding of these narratives of the Pharaoh's attempts at genocide is theological, as is the purpose for which they have been brought into sequence. As vv 7, 9, 12, and 20b make plain, what is taking place in the family of Jacob/Israel is of God. The promise to the fathers is in view, both the half that is well on the way to fulfillment and the half that is yet to come to pass.

The larger context of the narrative, from Gen 12 forward to this point, confirms such a purpose, and the account of the midwives makes it unmistakably clear. Before this section, God has not been mentioned once in Exodus. Here he is mentioned twice as the object of the midwives' faith and once as the establisher of blessing upon them. Just as Abraham's faith was reckoned to him as righteousness (Gen 15:6), so the midwives' reverence for God, insuring the protection of his purpose in Israel, became a means of blessing for them.

As the first two plans of Pharaoh have been brought to defeat, so also is the ominous third plan, and for that matter, any further plans as well. God is responsible for the growth of Israel in Egypt, and therefore no plan and no force can succeed in ending or even slowing that growth. As fearful as the shocking plan C is, we can be certain that it, too, will not work.

Any speculation about how many midwives are represented by Shiphrah and Puah, or how many pregnant Israelite women there were if there were but two midwives is, of course, irrelevant. The midwives, their number, and their professional activity are not the point here. What is the point is the midwives' faith and its effects for Israel and for the midwives themselves.

Indeed, this sequence functions to assure us that God is present in Egypt and that his purpose there is certain. The question with which the first chapter of Exodus leaves us is not "If?" but "How?"

The Birth of a Deliverer (2:1–10)

Bibliography

Barthélemy, D., *et al. Preliminary and Interim Report on the Hebrew Old Testament Text Project: The Pentateuch.* London: United Bible Societies, 1974. **Childs, B. S.** "The Birth of Moses." *JBL* 84 (1965) 109–22. **Cornelius, F.** "Moses urkundlich." *ZAW* 78 (1966) 75–78. **Exum, J. C.** " 'You shall let every daughter live': A Study of Exodus 1:8– 2:10." *Semeia* 28 (1983) 63–82. **Feilchenfeldt, W.** "Die Entpersönlichung Moses in der Bible und ihre Bedeutung." *ZAW* 64 (1952) 156–78. **Griffiths, J. G.** "The Egyptian Derivation of the Name Moses." *JNES* 12 (1953) 225–31. **Meek, T. J.** *Hebrew Origins.* TB 69. New York: Harper and Brothers, 1960. **Porter, J. R.** *Moses and Monarchy.* Oxford: Basil Blackwell, 1963. **Redford, D. B.** "The Literary Motif of the Exposed Child." *Numen* 14 (1967) 209–28. **Widengren, G.** "What Do We Know About Moses?" *Proclamation and Presence.* Ed. John I Durham and J. R. Porter. Macon, GA: Mercer Univ. Press, new corr. ed., 1983. 21–47.

Translation

¹ *Coincident with these events* ᵃ *a man* ᵇ *of the family of Levi had taken to wife a young woman* ᶜ *who was also Levite.* ² *The wife became pregnant and gave birth to a son. When she saw that he was a healthy child, she hid him as one would*

hide a treasure, ª *for a three-month period.* ³ *Then, when she was no longer able to hide him away, she* ª *got for him a papyrus-reed container, waterproofed it with tar and pitch, put the boy into it, and put it into the reeds at the edge of the river Nile.* ⁴ *Next, his sister* ª *took up a position* ᵇ *some distance away, to learn what would happen to him.*

⁵ *Meanwhile, Pharaoh's daughter came down to bathe beside the river Nile. Her attendants strolled along the river's banks. When the princess* ª *saw the container in the middle of the reeds, she sent her handmaiden down to fetch it.* ⁶ *When she opened it, she saw him, the little boy* ª *Understandably,* ᵇ *the lad was weeping,* ᶜ *and her heart went out to him. She said, "This boy is a Hebrew child!"*

⁷ *Just then, his sister called out to Pharaoh's daughter, "Shall I go and summon for you a wet nurse* ª *from among the Hebrew women to suckle the lad for you?"*

⁸ *Pharaoh's daughter answered her, "Go." So the girl went and summoned the mother* ª *of the boy,* ⁹ *and Pharaoh's daughter said to her, "Take this child with you and suckle him for me. In return, I will pay you a wage." So it was that the woman took the little boy and suckled him.*

¹⁰ *Thus did the boy grow. His mother* ª *brought him frequently to the daughter of the Pharaoh, to whom he was as a son, and she called his name "Moses." "Because," as she put it, "I pulled him from* ᵇ *the water."*

Notes

1.a. Special *waw* with impf of הלך, "go, walk"; "And so he went, a man. . . ."
1.b. The man's name is given, in 6:20, as Amram ("High Father" or "Exalted People"). See Noth, *Personennamen*, 77–78, 145–46.
1.c. בַּת "daughter."
2.a. צפן means "hide" in the sense of treasuring and protecting something of great value.
3.a. LXX ἡ μήτηρ αὐτοῦ SamPent אמו "his mother."
4.a. She is first named, if the same sister is intended, in 15:20, 21: Miriam ("Fatty" from מרא, or "Loved" from an Egyptian root).
4.b. SamPent appears to have the correct hithp form, ותתיצב; cf. GKC § 71.
5.a. Lit., "When she." "The princess," suggested by the context, is added for clarity.
6.a. So reads MT, with an obj pronom suff on the verb "see" *plus* the definite dir obj אֶת הַיֶּלֶד "the male child." It is a nice stylistic touch, and should not be omitted, as it often has been, in both ancient and modern translations. Cf. Barthélemy, *Preliminary and Interim Report*, 89–90.
6.b. וְהִנֵּה "and behold,"
6.c. LXX adds ἐν τῇ θίβει "in the plaited basket."
7.a. אִשָּׁה מֵינֶקֶת "a woman (or wife), a suckle-giving one."
8.a. Her name is given, in 6:20, as Jochebed, either Heb. "Yah is honor" (Meek, *Hebrew Origins*, 97) or, as Noth (*Personennamen*, 111–12) suggests, a name of foreign origin.
10.a. Lit., "she," but this pronoun clearly refers to the boy's mother.
10.b. The Heb verb משה "draw out, pull from," is used here, apparently because of its assonance with the name Moses: מֹשֶׁה־מָשָׁה. For the more likely derivation, see *Comment* below.

Form/Structure/Setting

There is no substantial reason to consider this section in its present form the product of more than one source (as Fohrer does, *Überlieferung,* 18–19, 124). Commentators have generally argued instead about which source should be designated, the Yahwist (e.g., Beer, 12) or the Elohist (e.g., Childs, 7–

8). As Hyatt (63) suggests, this narrative seems more nearly the style of J than of E; but there is no determining evidence.

The more important consideration here is the nature of this account and its connections with the sequences which precede and follow it. Since the work of Hugo Gressmann (*Mose und seine Zeit*, 1913), scholars have been fascinated with the obvious similarities between Exod 2:1–10 and the Legend of Sargon of Akkad (*ANET*[3]), who was also set afloat on a river in a reed and pitch container, rescued (though by a water-drawer, not a princess) and nurtured, and who became in time a mighty hero and king.

Brevard Childs (*JBL* 84 [1965] 109–22) has described this section as a "rags to riches" adaptation, by the circle of the wise men, of a child-exposure motif commonly known in the Ancient Near East. Indeed, D. B. Redford has collected some thirty-two accounts incorporating this motif in the ANE and in the Greco-Roman world.

As intriguing as these parallels certainly are, however, too strict a dependence upon them as *Vorlagen* must be avoided. There can be no question, certainly, of any exposure of the infant Moses. For one thing, there is not even a suggestion here of the divine rescuer so essential in the exposure-of-the-infant-hero motif. For another, the exposure of Moses by a *Hebrew* woman, and by his own mother at that, would turn a positive story, in this context, into negative nonsense.

The form of the story of the birth of Moses is dictated not by an ANE literary type any more than by historical memories, but by the larger theological purpose governing Exod 1 and 2, the sequence dealing with the persecution and the deliverer. While elements of the kind of folk-tale represented by the Sargon legend may well have provided stimulus for the author of this sequence (principally the reed container on the river and its fortuitous discovery by a sympathetic sponsor), his concern was to link the deliverer with the persecution in a dramatic and memorable way. That he did so with no direct mention of God, without bothering with details of name or consistency (vv 1–2 vis-à-vis v 4), and with some fun at the expense of the Egyptians, shows both his skill and his real intention. Indeed, the following section (2:11–15) functions in very much the same way.

The purpose of the three narratives of chap. 2 is to present us with an exceptional deliverer, exceptionally prepared, in the setting of a persecution precipitated by God's fulfillment of the first half of his promise, and in anticipation of his fulfillment of the second half of that promise. By three entirely different devices, these narratives perform a connecting and transitional function. As subsequent sections are to show, God is at no time far from the scene, whether he is mentioned or not.

Comment

1 The Levitical ancestry of Moses is pointedly mentioned as having come to him from *both* his parents, who are said by the priestly source in 6:20 to be nephew and aunt (see n. 6:20.c). Since no other names apart from that of Moses himself are mentioned in Exod 2, this double authentication of Moses' priestly descent, in a non-priestly layer at that, is important. It is an

anticipatory clue to both the stature of Moses and the sacerdotal nature of his leadership as Israel's first great sacral hero (see Porter, *Moses and Monarchy*, 7–28).

Though vv 1–2 do not report as much, the impression is that Moses was the first child born to the Levitical couple, an impression that is complicated by the appearance of an older sister in vv 4 and 7, and of a brother older by three years, Aaron, in later chapters (4:14, 7:7). The first of these two inconsistencies is created only by an impression upon which the text is completely silent; the second is based on information provided by the priestly Aaron-traditions, which have the purpose of pushing Aaron forward.

2–4 The fact that the infant was seen by his mother to be טוֹב "good," that is, healthy, gave her all the more resolve to protect him from the Pharaoh's condemnation of drowning, and so she hid him away quite tenderly with the stealth and care a treasure would demand. When, with the passage of three months, the little boy had grown too active and too noisy to be hidden at home any longer, his mother very cleverly decided to hide her son in the one place no Egyptian would bother to look: in the river Nile itself, exactly where Hebrew boy-babies were supposed to be cast.

With the sparkle of shrewdness that typifies the relationship of the Israelites with their Egyptian neighbors (as opposed to the cruel force of Egyptian bureaucracy) all through the Book of Exodus, Moses' mother thus may be said to have obeyed the Pharaoh's grim command. But she did so with the all-important provision of a papyrus-reed container, carefully waterproofed with "hot tar and pitch." This ark (תֵּבָה, the same word used for Noah's ship, Gen 7, 8, 9) is not a means of exposure but a lovingly made means of salvation, over which a careful watch was to be kept from a distance. Moses' sister is the one guardian mentioned, but others would certainly be assumed, as well as periodic stealthy feedings of the baby and relocations of the container.

5–7 There is no suggestion that the container and its precious cargo was deliberately placed where the Egyptian princess and her party would find it. The implication is that discovery was not a part of the plan, for an Egyptian discovery certainly put the baby in harm's way. The suspense of the discovery is that it was unintended and dangerous. The delight of the discovery is the totally unexpected way it turned out. The climax of the discovery is the quick and bold action of the little boy's sister, who comes forward (with a convenient offer to find a wet nurse) when she sees the princess's reaction to her brother's tears. The involvement of women as the determinative characters throughout this narrative has been emphasized by Exum (*Semeia* 28 [1983] 74–82).

8–9 Thus a second time the shrewdness of Jacob/Israel's house sparkles, for suddenly Moses' mother is delivered from a terrible prison of fear to the security of being paid to nurse and nurture her own son. The medium of death thus becomes for Moses the medium of life. His life is moved from danger to privilege. And delivered from a condemnation to grinding slavery, Moses enjoys the best of both worlds possible to him. It is a supreme use of irony as a teaching tool, the effectiveness of which is made clear by the fact that none of us, having read this account, has ever forgotten it.

10 The name "Moses" is the Hebrew equivalent of the Egyptian noun *ms* "boy-child," from the verb *msỉ* "bear, give birth." This word appears also in Egyptian names, as for example Ptahmose, Tuthmosis, Ahmose, and Harmose. Moses' name, thus transliterated from Egyptian, may very well be a memory, perhaps the most important and best-preserved memory, of the Egyptian backdrop of the oppression (Griffiths, *JNES* 12 [1953] 225, 229–31). The writer of the OT account did not know this. Otherwise, he would not have invented an etymology based on assonance and turned a princess of Egypt into a Hebrew speaker. His case is better made by the facts about Moses' name, of which he was unaware.

Explanation

At center, Exod 2:1–10 presents the story of the birth of God's deliverer, Moses. He is born into peril created by the growth to threatening numbers of the sons of Jacob/Israel, a growth that fulfills God's promise, part one, and makes urgent the fulfillment of God's promise, part two. He is born a sufferer of the very oppression from which he is to deliver Israel, and he is under its ban of death from the moment of his birth.

That his birth is a turning point toward an unseen better future is made clear by the incredible narrative of the first months of his life. To begin with, he survives undetected for three of those months, despite the constant Egyptian surveillance commanded by the Pharaoh (1:22). Then he is spared by being cast onto the very Nile that was to drown him, is treated with maternal kindness by the daughter of the very king who had condemned him and to whose descendants he would become nemesis, and is assigned as a responsibility with pay to the one woman in all the world who most wanted the best for him, his own mother.

The omission of any reference to God in these verses is surely intentional. The author is involving his reader in the conclusion of faith which such a narrative must inevitably suggest. And in doing so, he has Moses in Egypt, in the oppression and out of it at the same time, of the descendancy of Jacob and of the privilege of Egypt, and hence on a collision course that will catapult him—where? The answer to that question, toward which this entire narrative moves, is not long in coming.

Adulthood, Revolt and Flight of the Deliverer (2:11–15)

Bibliography

Childs, B. S. "Moses' Slaying in the Theology of the Two Testaments." *Biblical Theology in Crisis.* Philadelphia: Westminster Press, 1970. 164–83. **Vaux, R. de.** "Sur l'origine kénite ou madianite du Yahvisme." *Eretz-Israel 9.* W. F. Albright vol. Jerusalem: Israel Exploration Society, 1969. 28–32.

Translation

[11] *The days flew by,* [a] *and Moses grew up. He went out one day among his brethren, and saw at first hand* [b] *their oppressive labors. Indeed, he saw an Egyptian man striking a Hebrew man, one from among his brethren.* [12] *So he looked all around, and when he saw nobody, he struck the Egyptian, fatally, and hid his body in the sand.*

[13] *The next day, he went out again and came upon* [a] *two Hebrew men scuffling. He said to the one in the wrong, "Why are you striking your companion?"* [14] *This man* [a] *said, "Who set you as a prince among men* [b] *and a judge over us? Are you to kill me, say,* [c] *as you killed that Egyptian?"* [d] *This struck fear into Moses,* [e] *for he realized* [f] *that the deed was actually known.*

[15] *Then Pharaoh heard about this deed, and so put Moses under a death sentence. Moses thus fled from Pharaoh's jurisdiction, traveling* [a] *to the land of Midian, and camping* [b] *there by a well.*

Notes

11.a. Lit., "And so in those days it was. . . ."

11.b. The verb ראה "see," plus special *waw*. The same construction is used also in the next sentence, where the meaning is obviously an "eye-witness" experience.

13.a. וְהִנֵּה "and behold."

14.a. MT reads וַיֹּאמֶר "And so he said." "This man" is supplied for clarity.

14.b. לְאִישׁ שַׂר is "for a man-prince," and is to be taken, along with "judge," as sarcasm, perhaps reflecting an opinion of Moses' lack of status.

14.c. אֹמֵר "say" is a qal act ptcp following qal inf constr of הרג "kill" plus obj suff, "me," plus independent subj pronoun, "you." This ptcp is to be taken parenthetically, as above; the "you" is the subject of הרג.

14.d. LXX adds ἐχθές "yesterday" to this question, as does Acts 7:28.

14.e. "And so Moses was afraid."

14.f. Lit., "And he said, 'Indeed the deed is known.' " LXX has Moses say Εἰ οὕτως "if so," implying uncertainty about whether the deed is known.

15.a. So Syr. LXX has ὤκησεν "withdrew." MT reads וַיֵּשֶׁב "settled in."

15.b. The verb ישׁב "stay, settle down," here obviously "camp," since Moses' stay at the oasis was a short one.

Form/Structure/Setting

This section, a logical continuation of the one preceding it, is also from the same author. The writer here proceeds to move quickly to the involvement of Moses in the plight of the people, *his* people, whom he is to deliver.

As has been noted already (see *Form/Structure/Setting* on 2:1–10), the main concern here is to present the sequence on the persecution and the deliverer. This concern is a product of the overarching theological purpose linked to God's promise to the fathers and its continuing fulfillment. Thus the writer jumps without a single comment from Moses' infancy and his escape from death in the river Nile to his headlong and impulsive involvement in the plight of his people. We are brought from the first appearance of the deliverer, at his birth, to his espousal in adulthood of his people's agony, *in medias res.*

All that lay between these two events, a period set by tradition as around

40 years in length (42 years according to *Jubilees* 47:1 and 48:1, 40 years according to Acts 7:23–24), as intriguing as it would be to us, is an encumbrance to this writer, and so he omits whatever he knew of it. With the tenacity to the main subject so typical of biblical narrative, he comes directly to Moses' identification with his people, and thence to Moses' flight to the place of his final preparation.

Comment

11   The eagerness of the writer to communicate Moses' identification with his people's plight is shown both by the repetition of the phrase "among his brethren" and also by the pointed use of the uncomfortable word "Hebrew" (see *Comment* on 1:19) with the word "Egyptian." That Moses is not ignorant of his ancestry is made plain by his going out to his people and by his sympathy for their situation. By the use of "Hebrew man" (v 11) and "two Hebrew men" (v 13), the writer may intend to suggest Moses' awkwardness in relation to his own people, because of his association with the Egyptians.

The term סִבְלֹת "hard, oppressive labors" is exactly the term used in 1:11 to describe the slave-labor of the Israelites, and, coupled with וַיַּרְא בְּ "and he saw into," indicates Moses' firsthand exposure to the oppression at its worst.

12–13   The same verb, נכה "strike," is used of the Egyptian hitting the Hebrew in v 11, of Moses hitting the Egyptian in v 12, and of the Hebrew man hitting his companion in v 13. In each case, the verb is in the hiphil stem, and it is best translated by the same English verb. The sense in each instance is probably of a series of blows rather than a single death-dealing blow (Greenberg, *Understanding Exodus*, 45). The point is that there is in the text no suggestion that Moses meant to kill the Egyptian, any more than that the Egyptian or the Hebrew man was attempting to kill his adversary.

13–14   No reason is given for Moses' identification of one of the Hebrew combatants as "in the wrong," רָשָׁע, literally, "the guilty or wicked one" (Childs, *Biblical Theology*, 165, refers to the word as "the technical legal term," but the usage here appears to be more general). The assumption is that the man was the aggressor without obvious justification for being so; hence Moses' interfering "Why?" The quick response Moses gets, apparently from both the Hebrew men ("over us"), underscores in graphic terms his lack of status. The Egyptians do not regard him as one of them (2:6), and he has killed an Egyptian in defense of his own people. But he is unlilke his people, for he is not a slave with them. They resent his high-handed interference in their affairs, and perhaps they fear being punished for his crime. Thus they snarl, "Who made you, only a man, into a prince and a judge over us?"

15   Moses is now alone, cut off from Egyptian hospitality and his own people alike, and the impossibility of his situation in Egypt is deftly spotlighted by the Pharaoh's death sentence in the territory of his authority ("and so Moses fled from Pharaoh's presence"). The deliverer has but a single, unavoidable option: he must flee to a land beyond the Pharaoh's control.

The land to which Moses flees is Midian, the geographic location of which is very vague, both in the OT and outside it (de Vaux, *Eretz Israel*, 29). The biblical Midianites, presented as relations of the sons of Jacob/Israel (see *Comment* on 2:22), appear in various locales, from northeast of the Dead Sea (Num 22 and 25, Judg 6–8) to the desert of Paran southwest of the Dead Sea (1 Kgs 11:14–20), in the vicinity of Kadesh-Barnea (Num 13), to various locales in the Sinai peninsula and beyond it (Ptolemy placed Midian along the eastern shore of the Gulf of Akabah; see *MBA*, map 48, and Hyatt, 66–67).

The Midianites are clearly described in the OT as nomads, and the variety of places in which they turn up affirms this description. It is thus misleading to fix their territory precisely. The narrator's purpose in designating Midian as the land of Moses' retreat is after all not geographic but theological (see *Explanation*, 2:16–22).

Explanation

So Moses comes to the inevitable conflict: Egyptian ways against "Hebrew" ways, the ways of the rulers against the ways of the ruled, oppression for Moses in the freedom of Egypt, and freedom for Moses only in the oppression of the Israelites. By this conflict, Moses is catapulted to the land of Midian, a strange new land (2:22) which is yet somehow an old familiar land, for in that land the God of Moses' father, the God of the patriarchal fathers (3:6), is worshiped.

With this section of his narrative, the redactor has achieved two important purposes: (1) the association of Moses with the agony of his people and (2) the removal of Moses to the land of his final preparation for his work as deliverer, the land of Midian. To that preparation he now turns immediately, and with the beginning of that preparation, he turns also to the beginning of an answer to the question "Why the land of Midian?"

The Deliverer Finds Home   *(2:16–22)*

Bibliography

Albright, W. F. "Jethro, Hobab and Reuel in Early Hebrew Tradition." *CBQ* 25 (1963) 1–11. **Coats, G. W.** "Moses in Midian." *JBL* 92 (1973) 3–10. **Gunneweg, H. J.** "Mose in Midian." *ZTK* 61 (1964) 1–9. **Widengren, G.** "What Do We Know About Moses?" *Proclamation and Presence.* Ed. John I Durham and J. R. Porter. Macon, GA: Mercer Univ. Press, new corr. ed., 1983. 21–47.

Translation

[16] *There was a Midianite priest who had seven daughters, and they came regularly* [a] *to this well,* [b] *drew water, and refilled the troughs so that their father's flock might*

drink. [17] *Unfortunately,* [a] *rough herdsmen also came and usually* [a] *forced the girls and their sheep back. This time, however,* [a] *Moses stood up for them, took up their cause,* [b] *and watered their flock.*

[18] *The girls came to Reuel ("Companion of God"), their father, and he asked them in surprise,* [a] *"Why have you come so early* [b] *today?"* [19] *They replied, "An Egyptian man rescued us from the bullying* [a] *of the herdsmen, and also drew all the water* [b] *for us and gave the flock their drink."* [20] *He immediately asked his daughters, "Where is he? What is this? You have forsaken such a man? Invite him to a meal!"* [a]

[21] *Moses was of course delighted to live with such a man, and Reuel* [a] *in turn gave Moses Zipporah ("Little Bird"), his daughter, as wife.* [b] [22] *In time, she gave birth* [a] *to a son, and Moses* [b] *named him Gershom ("Stranger There"), because he said, "A stranger* [c] *have I been in a land foreign to me."*

Notes

16.a. This continuity is shown by the context and the special *waw*.
16.b. Not in MT; added for clarity.
17.a. See n. 16.a.
17.b. The verb is hiph of ישע "save, rescue" and in the OT is frequently used of God saving his people from their enemies, as in Deut 20:4.
18.a. Surprise is implied by the question itself, מַדּוּעַ "why?" (cf. *Comment* on 1:18) and the reference to the girls' early return.
18.b. Lit., "hastened (piel of מהר) to come (inf constr, בוא)."
19.a. "From the hand, power" of the shepherds.
19.b. The construction is the emphatic דָּלֹה דָּלָה, qal inf abs plus qal pf of דלה "draw water," thus "vigorously drew" or, as above, "drew all. . . ."
20.a. Lit., "Call to him, that he may eat bread."
21.a. MT reads "he." "Reuel," plainly intended, is supplied for clarity.
21.b. An addition of the SamPent (see von Gall, 116, Sec. 3 of apparatus) and LXX.
22.a. LXX adds ἐν γαστρὶ δὲ λαβοῦσα "she received in her belly," i.e., "became pregnant."
22.b. MT reads "he."
22.c. גֵר *ger* "stranger," so that Gershom's name is also given an etymology based on assonance. See *Comment* below, and note the rhetorical link to Gen 23:4.

Form/Structure/Setting

With this third section in the sequence on the deliverer, the narrative moves to the place of Moses' final preparation for his grand task. In style as in vocabulary, this section is like the two that immediately precede it (cf. Beer, 21, and Schmidt, 79–90). As has already been noted, these three sections function as three parts of what is in effect a single narrative. Part one addresses the deliverer's birth into the peril of oppression; part two, the deliverer's identification with his people under oppression; and part three, his discovery of home where he never had been before. Binding the three parts together is the overarching theme of the preparation of the deliverer for his task, itself based, as are the themes of multiplication and oppression, upon the theological foundation of the promise of God to the fathers.

Commentators have often proposed that this "Midianite" section, along with vv 11–15 that lead so inevitably to it, was composed primarily to get Moses to the area of his experience of theophany and call (Noth, 30–35). Coats (*JBL* 92 [1975] 9–10) has argued that the original point of these verses was an explanation of a Moses-Midianite connection through marriage. There is surely something in this suggestion, but more still may be involved. Geography is not the concern, since the Midianites appear to have had no fixed territory (see *Comment* on 2:15) and since the mountain of God was clearly some distance away from the Midianite camp (see *Comment* on 3:1). Nor can relationship alone, specifically the marriage of Moses into a branch of the Midianite family, be the subject, despite the obvious importance of an early and friendly connection of Israel with Midian.

The point, rather, is a theological one, as the writer neatly hints in his very important summary interpretation in v 22. With the Midianites (not "in Midian," as an area), Moses is for the first time in his life at home; for the first time in his life, he is not a foreigner. V 19, with its amusing report of the daughters' flustered first impression of Moses, stands in playful and meaningful contrast with vv 21–22, which present not "an Egyptian man," but a member of the family: by choice, by fatherly (and priestly) acceptance, by marriage, and by the birth of a child.

And why has all this come about? Because of God's purpose, to be sure, but for a more specific reason still: Moses is at home in the author's view because he has come at last to a people who worship the God of his fathers. The Moses-Midian connection is theological. Suggested deftly in this climactic section of the narrative of chap. 2, that connection will be affirmed in chaps. 3–4 and 18.

Comment

16   The priesthood of Moses' Midianite father-in-law is an important detail, and so it is established at the very first mention of the Midianites. Indeed, his priestly vocation is more clearly remembered than his name. For while Moses' father-in-law is consistently said to be a priest of Midian, his name is variously given as Reuel (v 18), a name assigned also to the father of Moses' father-in-law in Num 10:29; Jethro ("His Abundance," 3:1; 18:1, 2, and throughout the chapter); Jether ("Abundance, Preeminence") and Jethro in a single verse (4:18; Jether is apparently a textual slip in MT); and Hobab ("Loving, Embracing One," Num 10:29; Judg 4:11).

This confusion is variously explained as reflective of separate sources (Johnson, "Jethro," *IDB* 2:896); as indicative of textual misunderstandings (Noth, *Pentateuchal Traditions*, 183–84), or a mispointing of חתן, giving "father-in-law" instead of a correct "son-in-law" (Albright, *CBQ* 25 [1963] 7); as the result of a mistranslation, "father-in-law" for "brother-in-law" (Moore, *Judges*, ICC [Edinburgh: T. & T. Clark, 1895] 32–33); and as the taking of a clan-name, Reuel, to be a proper name (Albright, *CBQ* 25 [1963] 5–6) or as the use of two or more names for the same individual (Greenberg, *Understanding Exodus*, 47). None of these solutions is entirely satisfactory, and we are thus left with unexplained confusion in the transmission of the name of Moses' father-in-law (cf. Widengren, *Proclamation and Presence*, 28–30), though with no doubt about his priestly role. The name most frequently given to him is Jethro. Indeed, apart from v 18 here, Jethro is the sole name assigned him in the Book of Exodus.

18–19 The seven daughters of this priest are depicted as being so excited by the gallant behavior of Moses at the well that they quite forget their manners and rush home to tell of their adventure without an appropriate response to their champion. They describe Moses to their father as אִישׁ מִצְרִי "an Egyptian man." There is no justification for the frequent assertion that they knew Moses to be Egyptian by his clothing. What the daughters say is rather the writer's attempt to link the two contexts of his narrative, and, as has been noted already, to contrast what Moses has seemed to be, to his own people in Egypt, for example (2:14), with what he really is.

20 Jethro's response to his daughters is a delightfully witty and realistic narrative touch. Three questions in quick succession depict his incredulity, his astonishment, and his shocked disappointment. Then, as though catching his breath, he barks out a command to the daughters to do what they should have done, with no need for prompting from him.

21–22 The narrator leaps from Jethro's invitation, presumably delivered by his daughters, through Moses' settlement, marriage, and fatherhood, to Moses' retrospective interpretation of it all in the naming of his son. He establishes immediately Moses' great pleasure or eager delight (יאל) in settling down and in remaining to live (ישׁב) with such a man. He demonstrates Jethro's sharing of that delight as he gives Moses his daughter Zipporah in marriage. The explanation Moses gives for the name of his firstborn son then summarizes what is taking place.

This name, Gershom, occurs elsewhere in the OT (e.g., Judg 18:30; 1 Chr 6:1; Ezra 8:2) and is probably derived from גרשׁ "drive, cast out" (BDB, 176–77), signifying "one driven out or thrust forth." The writer, however, has given us a pun and has explained Gershom's name as he did Moses' name (see *Comment* on 2:10), on the basis of assonance of the name with a word that carries the meaning he has in mind. Gershom is thus explained as though it were a compound of גֵּר "stranger" (from גור "sojourn, linger in one's travels") plus שָׁם "there, thither."

The fact that this etymology is probably an incorrect one in no way lessens, however, its value as a key to the intention of the narrative sequence of Exod 2. Indeed, the manner in which such an explanation is given in the service of the writer's point adds to its usefulness for understanding this text far beyond the value of any correct derivation of Gershom's name. It is at least possible that the narrator knew the derivation from גרשׁ (Cassuto, 26, thinks he "undoubtedly knew full well"). Whether he did or not, his real concern is theological assertion, and his choice of the event of Moses' most complete integration into his Midianite family as the setting for this assertion is an inspired one.

So the narrator declares that an invitation to dinner became in turn a visit, a sojourn, a settlement delightful to all parties, involving marriage and then the commingling of blood in the union of childbirth. And at that special moment, Moses gave to the child, a son, the significant summary name "Gershom," the meaning of which, like the meaning of the name of Moses himself, the author is not content to leave to our speculation. His point is far too important.

So the name is connected with "stranger" and "there," and an explanation that connects it with both Moses' past and his new situation is given. The foreign land to which Moses refers must be understood to be Egypt, not Midian, as the commentators generally say. The statement of Moses is "a stranger I have been," הָיִיתִי, not "a stranger I am," אֶהְיֶה. Egypt, the place of Moses' birth, has never been his home, any more than it has been the home of any of the Israelites. There, Moses was a stranger, no matter how familiar to him were that land and the ways of its people. Here, Moses is at home, no matter how unfamiliar to him may be this land and the ways of its people. There, he had been rejected by the Egyptians and even by his kinsmen. Here, he had been received into the innermost circle of a people who had never seen him before. Moses, who had been all his life a stranger there, was here a stranger no longer.

Is it any wonder that Moses should want such a homecoming for his people, foreigners there in Egypt?

Explanation

With this third and climactic section of the narrative of Exod 2, we are brought to the threshold of the real subject of the Book of Exodus. Having prepared Moses in Egypt, having introduced him there to the agony of his people, having removed him to the land of his final preparation for his work as deliverer, the narrator begins to answer the question "Why Midian?" with an assertion placed in the mouth of Moses himself.

Midian, because Midian is home. A loving family is there—a wife and a son, a son whose name both sums up Moses' life to this point and augurs, by his past-oriented explanation, a new and better future. Moses in Egypt was a nonperson, a foreigner without status; here in Midian, where he belongs, and always has belonged, he is at home.

But immediately another question rises: what makes this place the place of belonging? Moses' assertion comes at first glance from the warmth of his domestic happiness. But suddenly we are confronted with a larger context. What has brought about the amazing welcome, the total at-homeness, the "eager delight" of Moses to dwell with this clan among whom Jethro ministers as priest?

The answer to these questions, of course, is to be given fully in Exod 3. Moses has come to a people who not only worship the God of the fathers, but are free to do so. Thus he is at home, because this God is his God. And as this God is also his people's God, Moses is soon to be directed to bring them to a place where they can worship him freely too. For such a narrative we now stand fully prepared.

A Postscript on the Oppression   (*2:23–25*)

Bibliography

Schottroff, W. *"Gedenken" im Alten Orient und im Alten Testament.* WMANT 15. Neukirchen-Vluyn: Neukirchener Verlag, 1964. **Thomas, D. W.** "A Note on וַיֵּדַע אֱלֹהִים in Exod. II.25." *JTS* 49 (1948) 143–44.

Translation

²³ Now while these many days were passing, the king of Egypt died. And the sons of Israel moaned from the agony of their labor ᵃ and cried out in need. Thus did their cry for help go up to God from the agony of their labor. ᵃ ²⁴ And so of course God heard their groaning, and also remembered his covenant with Abraham, with Isaac, and with Jacob. ²⁵ God saw ᵃ the sons of Israel, and so God knew, by experience. ᵇ

Notes

2:23.a. This phrase, מָן־ הָעֲבֹדָה, lit., "from the labor," occurs twice in this verse.
25.a. *BHS* suggests the loss of a word or words here, and notes the addition of "his afflicted condition," by Tg.
25.b. LXX reads καὶ ἐγνώσθη αὐτοῖς "and so he became known to them" instead of "and so ʾElohim knew. . . ." The verb is יָדַע "know experientially," and MT makes perfect sense as it stands.

Form/Structure/Setting

These three verses function in the present sequence of the text of the Book of Exodus as a kind of postscript to the narrative introducing the deliverer, Moses. The redactor thought such a postscript necessary, apparently, because of the length of that narrative sequence and its single preoccupation. He located the postscript here because of the reference in v 22 to Egypt, the land in which Moses had been a stranger, and because of the call narrative which continues the story of Moses with such special emphasis upon his role as the deliverer.

The postscript appears to have come from the Priestly source, with the exception of its very first sentence, usually assigned to the Yahwist (see Noth, *Pentateuchal Traditions*, 30) and sometimes connected with 4:19–20 (Schmidt, 88–89). This first sentence is an attempt to connect the preparation of the deliverer with the calling of the deliverer by revealing that the king who sought his life was no longer a reason for him to stay away from Egypt. The sentences that follow refer both backward and forward to the terrible oppression of the sons of Israel and, still further backward and forward, to the promise to the fathers and to the fulfillment of that promise through Moses.

Thus whatever the sources of this three-verse postscript, its present form is dictated by what precedes and follows it, and it serves quite effectively as a transition.

Comment

23 The reference in v 22 to Egypt as the land strange to Moses, in which he had lived as a foreigner, is further confirmed by the placement of this postscript, with its references to the death of the king of Egypt who had condemned Moses and the multiplied suffering of the people of Israel in oppressive servitude. The latter is graphically depicted by a piling up of terms for their agony and their cries of distress: הָעֲבֹדָה "agonized labor, forced servitude" (v 23b, twice); אנח "groan, sigh in grief" (v 23b); זעק "cry, call out," (v 23b); שַׁוְעָה "cry for help" (v 23b); נְאָקָה "groaning" (v 24).

24–25 These assorted cries, moans, sighs and protests were of course directed to God, as Deut 26:7 (where the verb is צעק "cry," a parallel of זעק) expressly says, and as God's hearing of the crying and as his seeing of the sons of Israel and his experiencing of their suffering shows. D. Winton Thomas (*JTS* 49 [1948] 143–44) rendered the verbs שמע "hear"—ראה "see"—ידע "know" in this context so: "hear-favorably"—"look with kindness"—"cared for, kept in mind," especially in view of the occurrence of the second two in Ps 31:7 [8].

Most significant of all is the specific reference in v 24b to the covenant promise to the fathers Abraham, Isaac, and Jacob. This covenant promise has been implicit throughout these first two introductory and transitional chapters of the Book of Exodus, and here, at the most appropriate possible point, it is mentioned outright, with each of the patriarchal fathers pointedly named. Just as these two chapters are begun with the names of the descendants of the fathers, in and through which the first part of the covenant-promise has been fulfilled, so they are closed with the names of the fathers themselves, a reminder that God remembers the whole of his promise. Thus is the fulfillment of the second part of the promise anticipated by a reference to the fathers to whom it was made.

Explanation

This brief postscript serves as the concluding bracket of an introductory sequence of transitional narratives. The opening bracket is 1:1–7, the listing of the names of the sons of Israel, whose father, grandfather, and great-grandfather are named here. In between these two brackets are the narratives of the rise of the new dynasty, the genocidal plans of the new Pharaoh, and the birth, adulthood, revolt, flight, and homecoming of the deliverer.

Just as the opening bracket provides a look at past, present, and future, so also does this closing bracket: the past is the promise to the three great fathers; the present is the death of the king of Egypt and the continuation of the oppression, with no letup, under his successor; the future is the next step, implied in the important assertion that God remembered (v 24; cf. Schottroff, *"Gedenken,"* 202–17). Although this postscript must certainly interrupt the sequential narrative flow of the story of the book of Exodus, it does so with a telling emphasis upon what that story is all about.

II.   The Call of the Deliverer, His Commission, and His Obedience   (3:1—7:7)

Theophany and Call   (3:1–12)

Bibliography

Alt, A. "The God of the Fathers." *Essays on Old Testament History and Religion.* Oxford: Basil Blackwell, 1966. 3–77. **Baker, J.** "Moses and the Burning Bush." *ExpTim* 76 (1964–1965) 307–8. **Besters, A.** "L'expression 'fils d'Israel' en Ex., I–XIV." *RB* 74 (1967) 321–55. **Davies, G. I.** "Hagar, El-Ḥeğra and the Location of Mount Sinai." *VT* 22 (1972) 152–63. **Freedman, D. N.** "The Burning Bush." *Bib* 50 (1969) 245–46. **Habel, N.** "The Form and Significance of the Call Narratives." *ZAW* 77 (1965) 297–323. **Hoffner, H. A.** "The Hittites and Hurrians." *Peoples of Old Testament Times.* Ed. D. J. Wiseman. Oxford: Clarendon Press, 1973. 197–228. **Hyatt, J. P.** "YHWH as 'the God of My Father.' " *VT* 5 (1955) 130–36. **Jeremias, J.** *Theophanie.* WMANT 10. Neukirchen-Vluyn: Neukirchener Verlag, 1965. **Kuntz, J. K.** *The Self-Revelation of God.* Philadelphia: Westminster Press, 1967. **Liverani, M.** "The Amorites." *Peoples of Old Testament Times.* Ed. D. J. Wiseman. Oxford: Clarendon Press, 1973. 100–133. **Millard, A. R.** "The Canaanites." *Peoples of Old Testament Times.* Ed. D. J. Wiseman. Oxford: Clarendon Press, 1973. 29–52. **Muilenburg, J.** "The Linguistic and Rhetorical usages of the Particle כִּי in the Old Testament." *HUCA* 32 (1961) 135–60. **Oesterley, W. O. E.** "The Burning Bush." *ExpTim* 18 (1906–1907) 510–12. **Preuss, H. D.** " 'Ich will mit dir sein.' " *ZAW* 80 (1968) 139–73. **Rad, G. von.** "Beobachtungen an der Moseerzählung." *EvT* 31 (1971) 579–88. **Richter, W.** *Die sogennanten vorprophetischen Berufungsberichte.* Eine literaturwissenschaftliche Studie zu 1 Sam 9, 1–10, 16, Ex 3f. und Ri 6, 11b–17. FRLANT 101. Göttingen: Vandenhoeck & Ruprecht, 1970. **Skipwith, G. H.** "The Burning Bush and the Garden of Eden: a Study in Comparative Mythology." *JQR* 10 (orig. ser., 1898) 489–502. **Smith, W. R.** *The Religion of the Semites.* New York: The Meridian Library, 1956. **Tournay, R.** "Le nom du 'buisson ardent.' " *VT* 7 (1957) 410–13. **Wiseman, D. J.** "Introduction: Peoples and Nations." *Peoples of Old Testament Times.* Oxford: At the Clarendon Press, 1973. xv–xxi. **Young, E. J.** "The Call of Moses." *WTJ* 29 (1966–1967) 117–35 and 30 (1967–1968) 1–23. **Zimmerli, W.** "The Form-Criticism and Tradition-History of the Prophetic Call Narratives." *Ezekiel 1.* Hermeneia. Philadelphia: Fortress Press, 1979. 97–100. ———. "Ich bin Jahwe." *Gottes Offenbarung.* Munich: Chr. Kaiser Verlag, 1969. 11–40. Also in *I Am Yahweh.* Atlanta: John Knox Press, 1983. 1–28. ———. *Old Testament Theology in Outline.* Atlanta: John Knox Press, 1978.

Translation

¹ *And Moses was grazing the flock of Jethro ("His Abundance") his wife's father, a priest of Midian, driving the flock well into* ª *the wilderness, when he came to the mountain of God,* ᵇ *Horeb* ᶜ *("Desolate Waste"). * ² *Suddenly there appeared to him the messenger of Yahweh in a blaze of fire from the middle of a thornbush. He looked*

in amazement: ª *the thornbush, enveloped in the flame, was still the thornbush— none of it was destroyed!* ³ *So Moses said, "I have got to go over and take a look at this unusual sight! Why is the thornbush not burning up?"*

⁴ *Yahweh* ª *saw that he had gone over to look, and so God called out to him from the middle of the thornbush, saying, "Moses! Moses!" He replied, "I am here."*

⁵ *Then he said, "Do not approach here! Slip your sandals off your feet, because the place on which you are standing is holy ground!"* ⁶ *Next he said, "I am the God of your father,* ª *the God of Abraham, the God of Isaac, and the God of Jacob." Thus Moses covered his face, because he feared to look* ᵇ *toward this God.* ᶜ

⁷ *Yahweh then said, "I have seen clearly* ª *the humiliation of my people in Egypt, and I have heard their cry of distress at the pressure of their work-bosses. Indeed I know their pain.* ⁸ *Thus I have come down* ª *to snatch them from the power of the Egyptians and to bring them forth from that land to a good and roomy land, to a land gushing with milk and honey,* ᵇ *to the place of the Canaanites, and the Hittites, and the Amorites, and the Perizzites,* ᶜ *and the Hivites, and the Jebusites.* ⁹ *Take note now: the distress-cry of the sons of Israel has reached me, and I have also seen the oppression with which the Egyptians are squeezing them.* ¹⁰ *So go now—and I will send you forth to Pharaoh, and you* ª *will bring my people, the sons of Israel, out from Egypt."*

¹¹ *But Moses answered God, "Who am I,* ª *that I am to go along to Pharaoh, that I am to bring the sons of Israel forth out of Egypt?"* ¹² *He* ª *immediately replied, "The point is,* ᵇ *I* AMᶜ *with you. The proof of this fact, that I* ᵈ *have sent you forth, will be plain in this sign:* ᵉ *in your bringing the people forth from Egypt, you all shall become servants of God* ᶠ *on this very mountain."*

Notes

1.a. אַחַר, lit., "behind."

1.b. LXX omits "of God."

1.c. חֹרֵבָה "Horeb-ward," so possibly "in the direction of Horeb."

2.a. "And he looked and behold. . . ."

4.a. SamPent reads אלהים "God" here. LXX here agrees with MT, but also reads κύριος (= Yahweh) with "called out" later in the verse, where MT has אֱלֹהִים "God." Vg does not employ a 2d subj and so reads *Dominus vocavit* "the Lord called out."

6.a. MT is sg, as LXX. Some versions have the more usual "fathers," as e.g., SamPent (followed by NEB) and Acts 7:32. See *Comment* below.

6.b. נבט can mean "gaze," almost "gawk."

6.c. Lit., "the God"; also in v 12. אֱלֹהִים with the def art occurs many times in the OT, nearly 30× in Exodus, generally to signify *the* God of Israel (cf. BDB, 43–44, ¶3, and Mandelkern, 1:89–91).

7.a. רָאֹה רָאִיתִי, lit., "Looking I have looked."

8.a. ירד "descend, go down" from a height is the same verb used of God in Gen 11:5, 7. SamPent gives the verb a cohortative form.

8.b. The phrase is used nearly 20× in the OT to suggest the plenty of Canaan as the land of promise.

8.c. SamPent הגרגשי and LXX add Γεργεσαίων "the Girgashites" here and in v 17.

10.a. So LXX, Vg, SamPent. MT has the impv form הוֹצֵא "bring."

11.a. Reading the independent pers pronoun אָנֹכִי "I" as emphatic with the two 1st pers verb forms that follow.

12.a. LXX adds ὁ θεὸς Μωυσεῖ λέγων "God [spoke] to Moses, saying."

12.b. כִּי lit., "for, because." See Muilenburg, *HUCA* 32 (1961) 135–49.

12.c. On אֶהְיֶה "I am" cf. v 14, and see *Comment* below.

12.d. Emphasis on the subj is made clear by the use of אֲנֹכִי "I" in addition to the pronoun "I" with the verb.

12.e. Lit., "And this will be for you the sign that *I. . . .*"

12.f. See n. 6.c.

Form/Structure/Setting

These verses have for a long time been recognized generally as an amalgam of theophany and call narrative from the Yahwist and the Elohist (Beer, 12; Noth, *Pentateuchal Traditions*, 30 and 36; Fohrer, *Überlieferung*, 124; for a more complex reanalysis, see Fuss, *Deuteronomistische Pentateuchredaktion*, 21–99), albeit an amalgam with some obvious seams. In v 4, for example, both Yahweh and Elohim occur in successive clauses of the same sentence. At the end of v 1, most of which can be assigned to the Yahwist, Horeb, the Elohist's name for the mount of the theophany, is used.

What is more important than the analysis of this section into its constituent sources, however, is an understanding of the text in its present sequence. Why was a composite made, and why does the section bring together theophany and call?

These questions are best answered in reverse order. Theophany and call are brought together in the narrative dealing with Moses for the same reason they are brought together in the narrative dealing with Israel at Sinai. Theophany describes the advent of God's presence; call describes the opportunity of response to that Presence. Theophany provides both stimulus and authority for response; response, despite a choice, is virtually inevitable following theophany.

This pattern is repeated at a number of places in the OT, usually with certain characteristic elaborations, and it has been studied in detail, most notably by Zimmerli, Habel, and Richter. These studies have generally approached the theophany-call sequence from the perspective of the call, however, particularly that of the prophets. Zimmerli (*Ezekiel 1*, 97–100), for example, sees two forms of call narrative: a Jeremiah-Moses type, involving divine manifestation to the person called, the reluctance of that person, and an answer to the reluctance in promises and signs; and a Micaiah-Isaiah type involving a vision of God enthroned and announcing his word to his heavenly council. Zimmerli (100) applies this second type to the account of the call of Saul/Paul in Acts 9, 22, and 26 in a fascinating manner.

Habel analyzes the form in still greater detail, dividing it into such components as divine confrontation, introductory word, commission, objection, reassurance, and sign (*ZAW* 77 [1965] 298–316). He notes, quite correctly, that it has "a significant pre-prophetic history" (305). This history Habel then connects somewhat vaguely to a form employed by "ambassadors or messengers on a special mission" (322–23).

As instructive as these analyses are, however, they are too rigidly conceived in relation to the call and message components of the theophany-call sequence and too closely connected to prophetic traditions. Fuller attention is needed upon a much broader Presence-response pattern, of which the theophany-call sequence of Exodus 3–4 and 19–24 is a basic and often-reflected manifestation.

Indeed, the experience of Moses in 3:1–12 is an exact foreshadowing of the experience of Israel, first in Egypt, then in the deprivation of the wilderness, and finally at Sinai. In each of these narratives, the Presence-response pattern is fundamental. In the climactic narrative of the Book of Exodus (perhaps also the climactic narrative of the entire OT), chaps. 19:1–20:20 and 24:1–11, this pattern is the shaping factor. It is at least possible that such a pattern, which is basic in the oldest traditions of Israel's relationship with God (i.e., the exodus-Sinai experience and in the patriarchal narratives), basic in the great confessions of worship preserved in the Psalms, basic in the experience and in the proclamation of the prophets, basic in the theological presuppositions of the great historiographers, and basic even in the catechetical didacticism of the wise teachers, is the seminal point-of-origin for the call-narratives of the OT.

The section at hand thus presents theophany and call together because each inevitably presupposes and suggests the other. Both were undoubtedly present in the narratives of the Yahwist and the Elohist, as in every other narrative dealing with Moses and the exodus, as a fundamental stratum. At few points could this pattern more appropriately surface than in the account of Moses' own experience of Presence and response. The redactor labored to produce a composite of the sources at his disposal that would make this basic assertion as plain as possible.

Comment

1   At the beginning of the account of the most momentous experience of his life, Moses is presented not only as not seeking such an experience, but as totally oblivious even to the possibility of the confrontation that is to follow. That he may have had some preparation for such an experience is strongly suggested by the pointed and hardly necessary reference to Jethro's vocation as a priest (see below on 18:1–12). But Moses' concern was the sustenance of his father-in-law's flock. That he was in charge of this flock and clearly at some considerable distance from Jethro's camp is yet another indication of Moses' complete integration into his Midianite family, for the family's flock was the family's capital.

As Tg Onk suggests, Moses appears to have been ranging far in search of grazing. He had driven the sheep well into the wilderness, perhaps even "beyond" or "behind" his customary routes. The whole impression is of a completely new and strange and distant place, one outside familiar Midianite territory. There is no hint that Jethro knew of this mountain of God, or indeed that anyone else, ever before, had experienced it as such. That the urgent point of this passage is theology and not geography is made clear by the fact that neither here nor anywhere else in the OT is the location of the mountain preserved or, for that matter, even considered important (cf. Zenger, *Israel am Sinai,* 118–26). The sole geographic inference in this passage is that the mountain was beyond the customary Midianite grazing area; RSV's "to the west side of the wilderness" is misleading.

2–3   The messenger of Yahweh, מַלְאַךְ יהוה, is not an "angel" in the sense in which "angel" is now generally understood. As often in the OT

(Gen 18, Judg 6), there is in this passage a fluid interchange between symbol, representative, and God himself. In the composite form of the present text, Moses sees the symbol ("a blaze of fire") and hears Yahweh (vv 4–6, 7–10, 12). Only we are told that Yahweh's messenger appeared to him. For the redactor, there was no inconsistency: the addition of Elohim (v 4) to the messenger, the fire, and Yahweh of v 2 simply provided four designations of the same and single reality.

The blaze of fire that attracted Moses' attention is of course the theophanic fire, one of the recurring symbols of God's advent in the OT (Exod 19; Ps 18; cf. Jeremias, *Theophanie*, 56–66, Kuntz, *Self-Revelation*, 138–47). This is why the bush is not consumed, as Moses quickly discovers. The endless conjectures about the nature of the bush (Smith, *Religion*, 193–94; Skipwith, *JQR* 10 [1898] 489–502) are pointless. As Tournay has shown (*VT* 7[1957] 410–13), no specific identification of סְנֶה "thornbush" can be made. What is important is the nature of the fire as theophanic fire (and not St. Elmo's fire or volcanic gases; Gressmann, *Mose und seine Zeit*, 26–29). The bush itself is mentioned only once more in the OT, in Deut 33:16, a text that may mark the start of exaggeration of the role of the bush by referring to the "good will of the one dwelling in the thornbush." But the fire is mentioned, directly and indirectly, no less than five times in vv 2 and 3 alone: "blaze of fire"— "enveloped in flame"—"not destroyed" (literally, "not eaten up")—"unusual sight"—"not burning up."

4–5 When Moses moves closer for a look at this remarkable fire, Yahweh, awaiting such an inevitable reaction, calls out to him מִתּוֹךְ הַסְּנֶה "from the middle of the thornbush," the same phrase precisely as in v 2, there locating "the flame of fire." In addition, the verb forbidding too close an approach by Moses, קרב "approach," is frequently used in the OT as a technical term to describe an approach to the Presence of God in worship, or to seek an oracle. Finally, in the ultimate certification of a theophanic site, a place where God is present, Moses is told that he stands now on holy ground, and so must remove his shoes in reverence.

6 Upon the basis of such a careful delineation of the nature of Moses' experience as a theophanic encounter, the God who is manifesting himself is also identified with equal precision. That such an identification should be thought necessary indicates not so much the narrator's acknowledgement that there was more than one possibility as it indicates their concern that there be no doubt in the reader's mind about the identity of the God who spoke to Moses. This is made plain by the exactitude with which the identification is made. Moses is told first that he is being addressed by "the God of his father." The word "father" is pointedly singular (cf. Gen 26:24; 31:5; 43:23; Exod 15:2; 18:4) despite the various (and unjustified) attempts to make it plural. What Moses is told must therefore be understood as a means of connecting the speaking deity with the faith of Moses' family in Egypt. Then Moses is told that this God who addresses him is also the God of the three great patriarchal fathers—Abraham, Isaac, and Jacob/Israel himself—a linking of the speaking deity with the faith of Moses' people, the sons of Israel.

That Moses understood these connections is made clear by his reaction. Where before he continued, albeit in awe, to gaze at the bush, he now covered his face, afraid to stare at God, who is referred to, in view of the revelation of his identity, as הָאֱלֹהִים "the God." As Alt (*Essays*, 10–15) long ago pointed out, this passage and others like it are conscious attempts to identify Yahweh and the God (or gods; *Essays*, 54–61) of the fathers as one and the same. The accuracy of this suggestion is affirmed by Moses' immediate response once he understands that the deity appearing to him in the theophanic fire is his own God, the god of his father and the God of *the* fathers.

7–9 The theophany thus having been described, the call is introduced, first with a review of the plight of the sons of Israel in Egypt. Yahweh states that he has watched the oppression of Israel for a long time and has heard the people's cry of distress. The language of 2:25 is picked up by v 7; Yahweh knows the extent of Israel's need, and the moment for his action on the matter has arrived. The urgency of the need is matched by the power of Yahweh's expression; he has "come down," that is, from the place of his dwelling above the heavens to this place of his appearance to Moses, and he is about "to snatch" his people forth from the grip of Egyptian power. This verb, נצל, means "to tear away from, to snatch forth," often in the OT with overtones of violence in rescue.

Further, this snatching forth will be from a place of restriction and deprivation to a place wide and free, a place of plenty. The rhetoric of the promised fertile land, "a land gushing with milk and honey," is used, and then this land is identified by a list of six peoples (to which list LXX and SamPent add, after Perizzites, "Girgashites"). The Canaanites, the Hittites, and the Amorites were major forces in OT history (see Millard, *Peoples*, 29–52; Hoffner, *Peoples*, 197–228; Liverani, *Peoples*, 100–133). The other three peoples listed and the seventh people added by some versions are minor groups known mostly from the OT (Wiseman, *Peoples*, xv–xvi), unless "Hivites" is an ethnic term for "Hurrian" (Speiser, "Hurrians," *IDB* 2:665).

In the context of Yahweh's speech in vv 7–10, these names are probably intended as designations of a set of geographic boundaries, roughly demarcating a series of external and internal territorial limits. It is now clear that such lists are far more than the general and semiarbitrary lists they have too often been taken to be, but our knowledge of the peoples involved is too incomplete to enable us to understand all that the lists may imply (cf. Wiseman, *Peoples*, xv–xxi, and Speiser, "Man, Ethnic Divisions," *IDB* 3:235–42).

10 The need of Israel reviewed, and his intention stated, Yahweh comes to the point of both his theophany and his address: the call of Moses to be his agent of deliverance. Moses is to go to Egypt, confront the Pharaoh, and bring forth Yahweh's people, specifically and poignantly called "the sons of Israel" (note Besters' theory that this usage is a source-critical clue, *RB* 74 [1967] 326–33).

With this call stated, there is begun in this narrative a brilliant and very significant presentation and explanation of the tetragrammaton, the OT's unique name for the coming and calling God. The vehicle for this narrative sequence is a series of protests from Moses that he should not be the agent of deliverance. The heart of the sequence is a series of *double entendre* plays on the verb היה "to be," from which God's special name is derived. Coupled with this series is an emphatic usage of the first common singular pronoun

"I," a deft reference to the theological rhetoric of God's self-declaratory phrase, "I am Yahweh," so often and so effectively repeated throughout the OT (see especially the studies of Zimmerli, *Gottes Offenbarung*, 11–24, and *Outline*, 17–21).

11–12 In these verses, the presentation of the tetragrammaton is only introduced. Moses objects, מִי אָנֹכִי "Who am I, . . . that I . . . that I . . . ?" and God answers, כִּי אֶהְיֶה עִמָּךְ "the point is, I AM with you." Who Moses is is not the question; it is rather, who is *with* Moses? H. D. Preuss has argued persuasively (*ZAW* 80 [1968] 141–45, 153–55, 171–73) that "I will be with you" is an important, and perhaps an original, theological formula arising from "a nomadic groundstructure of Israelite thought and religious devotion." If Preuss is correct, God's answer to Moses here reflects an extensive and widespread pattern of theological rhetoric, since this phrase, in some form, occurs almost a hundred times in the OT.

Moses' emphatic "I" is echoed by God's emphatic "I," which is immediately reinforced by כִּי אָנֹכִי שְׁלַחְתִּיךְ, literally, "that I have sent you forth." The most important word in the sequence is אֶהְיֶה, translated above I AM. This word will occur again, twice, in the all-important explanation of v 14.

The theophany and call section is closed with a second very important point. God gives a sign in proof of his promised Presence with Moses: when he brings the people forth from Egypt, they shall all, together with Moses, serve him at this very same mountain, this place of advent, call, and promise. This point anticipates (1) Moses' urgent need to bring the sons of Israel to Horeb/Sinai; (2) the guidance of Yahweh through the wilderness; and (3) above all, the theophany and call to covenant of chaps. 19–20 and 24. What Moses has experienced here, Israel will experience here.

Explanation

Exodus 3:1–12 anticipates the two most important sequences in the Book of Exodus. It provides first of all, and most immediately, the introductory context for the revelation of the tetragrammaton and the only explanation of this unique divine name to be found in the OT. It also looks forward, however, to the experience of the sons of Israel at Horeb/Sinai, an experience parallel to the experience there of Moses.

Appropriately, therefore, this section establishes first of all the certainty of the Presence of God in the fire of theophany, in the auditory experience of the identifying and calling word of God, and in the certification of the place as a holy place by virtue of the appearance there of God. This certainty, in turn, establishes the authority for the call of Moses, namely, that God is to be with him in the mission he is to undertake, just as he is with him at this special moment at Horeb/Sinai. And the linking of this experience of Moses with the experience the sons of Israel are yet to have is cleverly made by the sign that is promised as the proof of God's Presence, namely, that the sons of Israel, along with Moses, shall worship God together at this very same mountain.

At an earlier stage in its development, this narrative was probably much briefer and so stood even more obviously as a prelude to the revelation of the special name of God. Its expansion confirms its essential purpose, however, both in the somewhat repetitious statements of Yahweh about the plight of the Israelites and also in the cleverly framed play on the verb "to be" and the pronoun "I," which specifically point to the tetragrammaton and the theological rhetoric surrounding it.

From the next section (3:13–22) forward, much of the narrative of the Book of Exodus is in one way or another a proof of the claim of God's special name. This section, introducing that name, gives us a first glimpse, from several angles, of the essential point of that claim: He is here, really here.

The Name of God and Its Meaning   (3:13–22)

Bibliography

Abba, R. "The Divine Name Yahweh." *JBL* 80 (1961) 320–28. **Albrektson, B.** "On the Syntax of אהיה אשר אהיה in Exodus 3:14." *Words and Meanings*. Ed. P. R. Ackroyd and B. Lindars. Cambridge: University Press, 1968. 15–28. **Albright, W. F.** "Contributions to Biblical Archaeology and Philology: 2. The Divine Name." *JBL* 43 (1924) 370–78. **Alt, A.** "Ein ägyptisches Gegenstück zu Ex. 3:14." *ZAW* 17 (1940–41) 159–60. **Arnold, W. R.** "The Divine Name in Exodus iii. 14." *JBL* 24 (1905) 107–65. **Brownlee, W. H.** "The Ineffable Name of God." *BASOR* 226 (1977) 39–46. **Childs, B. S.** *Memory and Tradition in Israel.* SBT 37. London: SCM Press, 1962. **Coats, G. W.** "Despoiling the Egyptians." *VT* 18 (1968) 450–57. **Cross, F. M., Jr.** "Yahweh and the God of the Patriarchs." *HTR* 55 (1962) 225–59. **Eissfeldt, O.** "Neue Zeugnisse für die Aussprache des Tetragramms als Jahwe." *ZAW* 53 (1935) 59–76. **Freedman, D. N.** "The Name of the God of Moses." *JBL* 79 (1960) 151–56. **Goitein, S. D.** "YHWH the Passionate: the Monotheistic Meaning and Origin of the Name *YHWH.*" *VT* 6 (1956) 1–9. **Herrmann, S.** "Die alttestamentliche Gottesname." *EvT* 26 (1966) 281–93. **Hyatt, J. P.** "Was Yahweh Originally a Creator Deity?" *JBL* 86 (1967) 369–77. **Labuschagne, C. J.** "The Particles הֵן and הִנֵּה." *OTS* 18 (1973) 1–14. **MacLaurin, E. C. B.** "YHWH. The Origin of the Tetragrammaton." *VT* 12 (1962) 439–63. **McCarthy, D. J.** "Exod 3:14: History, Philology and Theology." *CBQ* 40 (1978) 311–22. **Mowinckel, S.** "The Name of the God of Moses." *HUCA* 32 (1961) 121–33. **Murtonen, A.** *A Philological and Literary Treatise on the Old Testament Divine Names* אל, אלוה, אלהים, *and* יהוה. Helsinki: Suomalaisen Kirjallisuuden Seuran Kirjapainon Oy., 1952. 43–92. **Obermann, J.** "The Divine Name *YHWH* in the Light of Recent Discoveries." *JBL* 68 (1949) 301–23. **Radday, Y. T.** "The Spoils of Egypt." *ASTI* 12 (1983) 125–47. **Sandmel, S.** "The Haggada within Scripture." *JBL* 80 (1961) 105–22. **Schild, E.** "On Exodus iii 14—'I Am That I Am.' " *VT* 4 (1954) 296–302. **Terrien, S.** *The Elusive Presence.* San Francisco: Harper & Row, 1978. **Vaux, R. de.** "The Revelation of the Divine name YHWH." *Proclamation and Presence.* eds. John I Durham and J. R. Porter. Richmond: John Knox Press, 1970. 48–75. **Vriezen, T. C.** "'Ehje ʾAšer ʾEhje." *Festschrift Alfred Bertholet.* Tübingen: J. C. B. Mohr, 1950. 498–512. **Williams, A. L.** "The Tetragrammaton: Jahweh, Name or Surrogate?" *ZAW* 54 (1936) 262–69. **Zimmerli, W.** "Ich bin Jahwe," "Erkenntnis Gottes nach dem Buche Ezechiel," "Das Wort des göttlichen Selbsterweises (Erweiswort), eine prophetische Gattung." *Gottes Offenbarung.* Munich: Chr. Kaiser Verlag, 1969. 11–40, 41–119, 120–32. Also in *I Am Yahweh.* Atlanta: John Knox Press, 1982. 1–28, 29–98, 99–110.

Translation

13 *Then Moses asked* ^a *God, "Suppose* ^b *I come to the sons of Israel, and I say to them, 'The God of your fathers has sent me forth to you,' and they ask me, 'What can* He *do?'* ^c*—What am I to say to them?"* ¹⁴ *Thus it was that God answered Moses, "I* AM *the One Who Always Is."* ^a *He went on: "Thus shall you say to the sons of Israel, 'I* AM ^b *has sent me forth to you.'"*

¹⁵ *God said still more* ^a *to Moses: "Speak thus to the sons of Israel: 'Yahweh, the God of your fathers, the God of Abraham, the God of Isaac, and the God of Jacob has sent me forth to you.' This is my name from now on, and this is to bring me to mind generation after generation.* ¹⁶ *Go and bring together the wise old leaders of Israel,* ^a *and tell them, 'Yahweh the God of your fathers appeared to me, the God of Abraham, Isaac and Jacob,* ^b *to say, "I have paid close attention* ^c *to you and to what has been done to you in Egypt,* ¹⁷ *and I say I will bring you up from the humiliation of the Egyptians to the land of the Canaanites, and the Hittites, and the Amorites, and the Perizzites,* ^a *and the Hivites, and the Jebusites, to a land gushing with milk and honey."'*

¹⁸ *"They will listen to your report.* ^a *Then you go, along with the wise old leaders of Israel, to the king of Egypt; and all of you* ^b *tell him, 'Yahweh, the God of the Hebrews, has encountered* ^c *us, and in result, we must ask you please* ^d *to let us go three days' distance into the wilderness, so we may offer sacrifice to Yahweh, our God.'*

¹⁹ *"Now I* ^a *know very well that the king of Egypt will not give you permission to go, not even under the pressure of a strong hand.* ^b ²⁰ *So I will stretch out my hand, and I will strike Egypt with an array* ^a *of my extraordinary deeds that I will accomplish right in Egyptian territory.* ^b *After that, the Pharaoh* ^c *will* drive you out! ²¹ *I will further make this people so likable in the opinion of the Egyptians that when you do go forth, you will not go forth in poverty:* ²² *every housewife will ask from her Egyptian* ^a *neighbor and from any guest in her home* ^b *articles of silver and articles of gold and garments, and you shall dress your sons and your daughters in them* ^c*—in such a manner you will pick the Egyptians clean."* ^d

Notes

13.a. Lit., "said to," with special *waw*.

13.b. הִנֵּה "behold." Cf. Labuschagne, *OTS* 18 (1973) 8–9.

13.c. This question, מַה־שְּׁמוֹ, is lit. "What is his name?" But much more than identity is involved. See *Comment* below.

14.a. "I am the Ising One." See *Comment* below. Cf. LXX Ἐγώ εἰμι ὁ ὤν and Vg *ego sum qui sum*.

14.b. אֶהְיֶה "I AM" as in v 12; see *Comment* above. LXX Ὁ ὤν; Vg *qui est*.

15.a. Special *waw*, showing continuity, plus עוֹד "still, yet."

16.a. Some versions, including SamPent, add בני "the sons of" before ישראל "Israel."

16.b. LXX repeats καὶ θεὸς "and the God of" before Ἰσαακ "Isaac" and Ἰακωβ "Jacob," as in v 15 and often in the OT. So also Vg.

16.c. פָּקֹד פָּקַדְתִּי "observing I have observed."

17.a. See n. 8.c.

18.a. Lit., "to your voice."

18.b. MT has a pl verb, thus referring to Moses *and* the elders telling Pharaoh. Vg and some LXX MSS have a sg verb, obviously in reference to Moses alone.

18.c. קרה "encounter, meet"; LXX, SamPent, Vg read as from קרא "call, summon."

18.d. Cohortative of the verb הלך "go" plus the particle of entreaty, נָא "please" (GKC ¶ 108).

19.a. Emphatic usage, אֲנִי "I" plus 1st pers verb form, יָדַעְתִּי "I know."

19.b. There is no need to alter MT, as many ancient versions (LXX, SamPent, Vg) and modern translations have done. "And not by a strong hand" makes perfect sense, especially when read with the following verse.

20.a. בְּכֹל "with all."

20.b. בְּקִרְבּוֹ "in the middle of it."

20.c. "He." "The Pharaoh" is added from the context, for clarity.

22.a. Added from the context for clarity. SamPent reads ושאל איש מאת רעהו ואשה מאת רעותה "And a man will ask of his neighbor, a woman (or wife) from her neighbor."

22.b. The meaning, apparently, is a request for the loan of these valuable objects, as נצל "pick bare" implies. Compare 12:36–37. BDB (981) even translates שאל as "borrow."

22.c. "In them" is added for clarity, from the context.

22.d. נצל "plunder, strip, pick bare." This verb, here in the piel stem, is used in the hiph stem in v 8 in reference to Yahweh's snatching forth of the Israelites from the Egyptians' power. Radday (*ASTI* 12 [1983] 142–45), in an attempt to remove any notion of stealing from this passage, makes the unlikely proposal that נצל in Exod 3:22 and 12:36 means "free, deliver," and that Israel was freeing Egypt from shame and hatred.

Form/Structure/Setting

These verses, like the preceding section, are an amalgam of EJ source material, with a unity superseding that of either narrative in its original form. Despite the differing presuppositions of the two sources, the two have been forged into a single sequence with a theological point of its own.

The Yahwist records the introduction of the tetragrammaton to the human family early in the primeval history, in the third generation from Adam, the time of Enosh (Gen 4:26), and he uses the special name throughout his narrative. The Elohist, on the other hand, has this name introduced first only to Moses, in his experience of theophany and call at Sinai/Horeb. Yet despite these differences, which are by no means obscured in the composite of Exod 3, the new narrative has an integrity all its own and an impact which since we do not have the original narratives, we may at least imagine, to surpass that of either source by itself.

For this reason, the complicated and subjective attempts to separate Exod 3 into its constituent sources, attempts that have been prodded by ingenious theories into many blind alleys, are best set aside in favor of the amalgam of the text at hand. This is especially important here because the composite account, by its synthetic form, is a far more significant key to the intention of the Book of Exodus than the separate sources could ever be, even if we could reconstruct them completely.

The motif of authority is determinative in the composite here, just as theophany and call determine the form of the first section of this chapter. To that end, originally separate material on the revelation and explanation of God's special name has been combined with material describing Yahweh's commission of Moses (vv 13–15). That commission has been expanded beyond a report of theophany and call (v 16), in the composite form recorded in Exod 3, to include the themes of exodus-deliverance (vv 17, 20), worship-service at Sinai/Horeb (v 18), confrontation of a vacillating Pharaoh (vv 19–20), the mighty wonders that prove the presence and the supreme power of Yahweh (v 20), and the enrichment of Israel at the Egyptians' expense (vv 21–22).

These verses are variously assigned by the source critics, not only because of the alternation of the names for God, but also because of this array of themes and the repetitive and somewhat choppy manner in which they are introduced. Beer (12), for example, assigns vv 13–15 to E, E¹ and Eˢ, 16–20 to J², and 21–22 to J¹; Fohrer (*Überlieferung*, 125) gives vv 13–15 to E, 16–20 to J, and 21–22 to N (his "Nomadic" source); and Noth (*Pentateuchal Traditions*, 267), proposes vv 13–15 to be from E and vv 16–22, from J. The obvious conclusion of such divisions, that the section before us is a composite, is completely accurate. But once again, why was the composite made, and what is its binding emphasis? What gives the section its form?

The answer to these questions can be given in a single word: authority. The essential question of Moses after the theophany and call will become the essential question of Israel after their own call in Egypt, as indeed after their own experience of theophany and invitation (Presence and response again) at Sinai/Horeb. Is it possible? How can it be? Who can do it? What proof do we have? These are versions of a single question, the answer to which gives this section its form. The array of motifs brought together here answers, in one way or another, this central and fundamental inquiry, singled out quite accurately as the one that humankind must always ask. The redactor's composite is nothing short of brilliant.

Comment

13 Moses' first question following the confrontation of theophany and call was "Who am *I*?" (v 11). When God by-passed this question with the more important information that he intended to be present with Moses (v 12), Moses turned then to his second question, "Who are *you?*" The continuity of this sequence is plain not only in its logic, but also in its reference to the God of the fathers and in the terse summary of the call. Moses says, in effect, "If *I* address the sons of Israel in *your* name, since my lack of status is well known to them, they will understandably want to know about *you.*"

So they will ask, מַה־שְּׁמוֹ, literally, "What is his name?" This question has little to do, however, with identity, just as Moses' parallel question in v 11 can have little to do with identity. Moses himself was satisfied by the identification "the God of your father, the God of Abraham, the God of Isaac, and the God of Jacob" (v 6). That identification is linked specifically with Moses' family in Egypt, and the clear assumption of this whole narrative is that such an identification would be understandable also to the sons of Israel in bondage there.

The question of the origins of Yahwism and the beliefs and practices of Israel in Egypt are really quite beside the point here. This text is supremely a theological text, one of the most theological texts in the entire Bible, and long discourses on the relative influence of patriarchal faith or Kenite practices miss the point. The terrible situation of the Israelites in Egypt, described in such pained terms over and over again in the first three chapters of Exodus, provides a dramatic setting for an important statement about the God of the fathers, who is now to become the God of Israel.

The God of the fathers, in various times and places and under various conditions, had proved himself to the fathers. But Egypt and the bondage there present a new situation. Egypt is a world power. The Israelites in slavery are in no way the peers of their oppressors, as the fathers had been the peers of their neighbors and even their enemies. Indeed, the plight of the Israelites in Egypt is entirely unparalleled in the history of the fathers, who had to contend with local groups, local rulers, and local gods. The Egyptians possessed, or were possessed by, an extensive pantheon of gods exerting a cooperative lordship over every aspect of life and granting international influence to Egyptian power. Indeed, the Pharaoh himself, the king whom Moses was to confront and whom Israel was to defy, claimed divine descent.

It is against such a setting, so carefully provided in the repeated references to the agonized suffering of the Israelites, that the question Moses raises has to be interpreted. The question also must be interpreted in the light of the larger significance of the Hebrew word שֵׁם "name." This word, according to BDB (1028), is a "designation of God, specific. of Yahweh . . . ; = his reputation, fame . . . ; especially as embodying the (revealed) character of Yahweh."

What Moses asks, then, has to do with whether God can accomplish what he is promising. What is there in his reputation (see Num 6:27; Deut 12:5, 11; 16:2–6; Pss 8:1, 74:7; Amos 5:8, 9:5–6; Jer 33:2) that lends credibility to the claim in his call? How, suddenly, can he be expected to deal with a host of powerful Egyptian deities against whom, across so many years, he has apparently won no victory for his people? The Israelites in Egypt, oppressed savagely across many years and crying out with no letup to their God, have every reason to want to know, "What can He do? "—or perhaps better, "What *can* He do?"

14 Only an understanding of the meaning of the question of v 13 in its setting makes the much-discussed answer to it clear. The answer Moses receives is not, by any stretch of the imagination, a name. It is an assertion of authority, a confession of an essential reality, and thus an entirely appropriate response to the question Moses poses.

The range of interpretations of this response, from ancient to modern times, is nearly endless, as such survey articles as the ones by Arnold, Vriezen, MacLaurin, de Vaux, and Brownlee show. Some proposals, that the response is meant to be vague and evasive (Beer, 29; MacLaurin, *VT* 12 [1962] 460–62; Terrien, *Elusive Presence*, 119), for example, or a sly joke (Sandmel, *JBL* 80 [1961] 113–14) miss entirely the reason for the response as well as for the question that elicits it. Other proposals, which involve an alteration of the text as it stands (Arnold, *JBL* 24 [1905] 162–63; Obermann, *JBL* 68 [1949] 306–9, 318–23; Albright, *JBL* 43 [1924] 370–78), are unjustified. Not even the change of the person of the pronoun of the second אֶהְיֶה "I am" from a first to a third person pronoun (so LXX in ancient times; Schild, *VT* 4 [1954] 302, in contemporary times) is justified.

When Moses poses the question of the probability, even the possibility of the realization of the prospect God is holding out for the sons of Israel, oppressed as they are in Egypt, he is given an answer both profound and specifically to the point. That answer must be read not only in the context of the three-verse segment (vv 13–15) in which it is nestled, but in the context of the remainder of Exod 3, and indeed the remainder of the narrative sequence of the entire book, anticipated in 3:16–22.

אֶהְיֶה אֲשֶׁר אֶהְיֶה "I AM that I AM," replies God. The verbs are first person common qal imperfects of the verb היה "to be," connoting continuing, unfinished action: "I am being that I am being," or "I am the Is-ing One," that is, "the One Who Always Is." Not conceptual being, being in the abstract, but active being, is the intent of this reply. It is a reply that suggests that it is inappropriate to refer to God as "was" or as "will be," for the reality of this active existence can be suggested only by the present: "is" or "is-ing," "Always Is," or "Am."

A strong supportive argument for taking this answer quite literally is provided by the אֶהְיֶה that anticipates it in v 12, and by the אֶהְיֶה that immediately follows it in v 14. God has answered Moses' protest of his own inadequacy with the assertion אֶהְיֶה עִמָּךְ "I AM with you." He now answers Moses' question about the authority for the command of exodus with the declaration אֶהְיֶה אֲשֶׁר אֶהְיֶה "I AM always I AM," and then says immediately to Moses that he must tell the sons of Israel אֶהְיֶה שְׁלָחַנִי אֲלֵיכֶם "I AM has sent me forth to you."

A further argument for such a reading, a very extensive one, is provided by the manner in which the Book of Exodus develops the narrative of Advent and Response, as well as by the extensive rhetoric of which the tetragrammaton is the center: "I am Yahweh" (intriguingly posed by de Vaux, *Proclamation and Presence*, 70–71, as the equivalent, and more proper version, of אֶהְיֶה אֲשֶׁר אֶהְיֶה), "I am Yahweh your God," "I am He," "I am first, also I am last" (cf. Zimmerli, *Gottes Offenbarung*, 11–17, 98–107, 120–32; Abba, *JBL* 80 [1961] 324–28). The high point of this rhetoric is reached in Isa 52:6, "Indeed will my people know from experience my name (שֵׁם) in that day, indeed, for I am He, the One who speaks out 'Here I am!' "

15 Upon the foundation laid by this declaration, אֶהְיֶה "I AM," repeated four times in succession (v 12, once; v 13, three times), the special name of God, יהוה "Yahweh," is revealed. This multiplication of the verb from which the name is drawn adds impact to the redactor's confessional point. As McCarthy (*CBQ* 40[1978] 316) has suggested, "the spell of the repetition" itself establishes the connection between יהוה and היה.

Far more than a simple connection is in view here, however. The repetition of these "I AM" verbs, as awkward as it may appear, is entirely intentional. The redactor's point is just too important to be missed, and so he has labored to make it obvious: Yahweh Is. However absent he may have seemed to the oppressed Israelites in Egypt, as to the later generations for whom the Book of Exodus was compiled, Yahweh Is, and his Is-ness means Presence. That is true here and in chaps. 19–20 and 33–34, the other major chapters on Presence in which the special name "Yahweh" is emphasized (see below on 20:2 and 33:18–34:9) and with which this chapter and chap. 4 must be read. This God who is present, this God who *Is*, this Yahweh, is one and the same as the God of the fathers (see above *Comment* on v 6).

Thus the name "Yahweh," defined in terms of active being or Presence (cf. Abba, *JBL* 80 [1961] 326–28), is the name by which God is to be known henceforth forever. It is to be his זֵכֶר "remembrance," literally, that which is to make his Presence a reality to the generations to come. The significance of the use of this term in the verse establishing for Israel Yahweh as God's name in perpetuity must not be overlooked. Schottroff ("*Gedenken,*" 291–99) has described the use of זֵכֶר as a synonym for שֵׁם "name" and has noted also that in cultic contexts זֵכֶר is equivalent to the name of Yahweh pronounced, proclaimed out loud (cf. Childs, *Memory and Tradition,* 70–73). Of an array of passages that have a bearing on this point, especially important are Exod 33:19; 34:6–8; Num 6:22–27; and Ps 111:4, which reads זכר עשה לנפלאתיו "Remembrance (bringing Yahweh to mind by pronouncing his special name?) creates his extraordinary deeds."

16–17 V 16 again makes the all-important connection of Yahweh with the God of the fathers and uses niphal of ראה "to see," as did v 2, to describe the theophany, here as the appearance of Yahweh, there as the appearance of Yahweh's messenger. The two are understood as one and the same (see *Comment* on 3:2–3). "I have seen clearly," v 7, becomes "I have paid close attention" here, and v 17 is very close to v 8.

18 To the Pharaoh, Yahweh is to be identified as "Yahweh, the God of the Hebrews" (see *Comment* on 1:19); Moses and the elders are to call him "Yahweh, our God." This contrast is a skillful anticipation of the dramatic contrast between the respective situations of the Egyptians and the Israelites during the sequence of Yahweh's mighty acts and the Pharaoh's progressively changed attitude towards Yahweh. In this speech, the first reference is made to a journey of three days' distance for the purpose of sacrifice to Yahweh. The reference is not of course to Horeb/Sinai nor to any other appointed place; possibly, only a general destination beyond the border of the delta region is intended (see *Comment* on 13:17–14:4).

19–20 The first reference to the proof of Yahweh's Presence in Egypt is made in vv 19–20, in which Yahweh reports that he knows even as he commands Moses and the elders to ask the Pharaoh's permission to make a religious journey that such a request will be denied. The Pharaoh will have no thought of granting such a wish and could not even be forced to do so by any power men could muster. Thus will Yahweh bring *his* power into action and will strike (נכה as in 2:12, 13) Egypt with a series of extraordinary deeds. The term נִפְלָאוֹת "extraordinary deeds" is a key word in the theological rhetoric of the proof of Yahweh's Presence (note its use in Ps 111:4, cited above). This will be done, moreover, not in territory identified with Yahweh, but בְּקִרְבּוֹ "in its midst," in Egypt's "own backyard." And the result of *this* display of power will be not just the desired permission; the Pharaoh will "hurl" or "drive" (piel שׁלח) them out in his eagerness to be rid of them *and* their God. It is a marvelous summary of the whole "plague" sequence.

21–22 Finally in this anticipatory section, the theme of the plundering of the Egyptians is introduced. It also functions as a description of Yahweh's triumph over Egypt and everything Egyptian, and it has been appended here by the compiler of this narrative, admittedly in a somewhat awkward manner (Fohrer, *Überlieferung,* 29–30, 82; Coats, *VT* 18 [1968] 450–451), to complete the introduction of major themes related to the proof of Yahweh's Presence.

Like the other themes on this subject, it is treated more fully at the appropriate spot in the narrative sequence (11:2–3 and 12:35–36). To have omitted it here would have meant a break in an otherwise consistent pattern.

Explanation

Just as the amalgam of 3:1–12 presents the related narratives of theophany and call, so the amalgam of 3:13–22 presents the related narratives on the revelation of the special name of God and the explanation, with illustrations, of the meaning of that name. These two sections, along with 4:1–17, constitute a unit on Moses' experience of theophany, call, and commission, to which yet another unit on the same subject has been added to the narrative of Exodus at a later point (6:2–7:7). Vv 1–12 record God's advent and call, and they close with the promise to Moses of God's Presence. Vv 13–22 follow the direction of this introduction and stress the truth of this promise in the most fundamental way, by tying it to the unique and special name of God, Yahweh.

This name is not given until it has been explained, in a logical response to the question Moses asks (albeit on behalf of the sons of Israel in Egypt). The question raises the issue of authority. The reply asserts that authority in terms of an active Presence, "Is-ing." The name Yahweh, in effect the equivalent of that reply, is then given.

This name is twice stated to be the equivalent of "God of the Fathers," guaranteeing a continuity of the most ancient religious traditions of the sons of Israel. And then the authority upon which the promise of Presence has been made, explained in the repeated use of the verb אֶהְיֶה "I AM'" and symbolized, even made present and real by the name "Yahweh," is illustrated by the introduction of the themes that will provide in the narrative to come the proof of Yahweh's active Presence. These themes are (1) the request for permission to worship; (2) confrontation with Pharaoh; (3) the series of extraordinary deeds in Egypt, the unlikeliest of places for such deeds by a "foreign" God; (4) the plundering of a marvelously gullible Egyptian populace; and (5) the sum of them all, the exodus itself.

With the name "Yahweh" revealed and explained and with the proof of this explanation illustrated, at least in prospect, Moses can have no further question about *God's* authority. The narrative deals next with Moses' own authority, and how that is to be made clear.

The Signs of Moses' Authority   (4:1–9)

Bibliography

Gross, H. "Der Glaube an Mose nach Exodus (4.14.19)," *Wort-Gebot-Glaube.* Ed. J. J. Stamm, E. Jenni, H. J. Stoebe. ATANT 59. Zürich: Zwingli Verlag, 1970. 57–65. **Gunkel, H.** *Genesis,* 7th ed. Göttingen: Vandenhoeck & Ruprecht, 1966. **Hulse, E. V.** "The Nature of Biblical 'Leprosy' and the Use of Alternative Medical Terms in Modern Translations of the Bible" *PEQ* 107 (1975) 87–105. **Pfeiffer, E.** "Glaube im Alten Testament" *ZAW* 71 (1959) 151–64. **Sawyer, J. F. A.** "A Note on the Etymology of Ṣāraᶜat." *VT* 26 (1976) 241–45.

Translation

¹ *But Moses replied, saying, "Look here, they won't trust me, and they won't pay attention to my report, for they will say, 'Yahweh* ᵃ *has not appeared to you' "* ² *So Yahweh said to him, "What is that in your hand?" He responded, "A staff."* ᵃ ³ *Then Yahweh* ᵃ *said, "Throw it down onto the ground." He threw it down onto the ground, and it turned into* ᵇ *a serpent! Moses ran away from it.*

⁴*Then Yahweh said to Moses, "Reach out your hand and catch* ᵃ *it by the tail." So he reached out his hand and snatched* ᵇ *it, and it turned into* ᶜ *a staff again, right in his palm!* ⁵ *"On this account,* ᵃ *they will believe that Yahweh,* ᵇ *the God of their fathers, the God of Abraham, the God of Isaac, and the God of Jacob has appeared to you."*

⁶*Once more,* ᵃ *Yahweh spoke to him: "Just place* ᵇ *your hand against your chest, inside your garment."* ᶜ *He placed his hand against his chest, inside his garment, then withdrew it, and look!—his hand, infected with a skin disease,* ᵈ *was peeling and flaking!* ᵉ ⁷ *When Yahweh* ᵃ *said, "Return your hand to your chest, inside your garment," he did so, then withdrew it,* ᵇ *and look!—it was healthy again, as the rest of his flesh."*

⁸*"If it happens* ᵃ *that they will not trust* ᵇ *you, and be convinced by the evidence of the first sign,* ᶜ *they may trust the evidence of the following sign.* ⁹ *If it happens that they have no trust in either of these two signs and they will not be convinced by your report, then dip up some water from the Nile and pour it onto the dry earth: the water that you dip up from the Nile will turn into* ᵃ *blood on the dry earth."*

Notes

1.a. LXX has ὁ θεός "God" instead of Κύριος "Lord" = "Yahweh," and adds "what am I to say to them?" at the end of this sentence.

2.a. מַטֶּה "staff" comes from נטה "stretch out, extend," and can even mean a tree limb or other stick used as a walking staff and shepherd's tool.

3.a. MT reads simply "he." As the reference is clearly to Yahweh, this name is added for clarity.

3.b. וַיְהִי, "and it was, became."

4.a. The verb is qal of אחז "take hold of, grasp, take possession of" (cf. 2 Sam 6:6, in reference to Uzzah "catching" the unsteady ark, or 1 Kgs 6:6 and 10, in reference to timbers "catching hold," that is, being supported by a wall).

4.b. The verb is hiph of חזק "seize violently, snatch, grab cautiously" (cf. 1 Sam 17:35, in reference to David grabbing a bear or a lion "by his whiskers" [probably = "his bottom jaw"], or Deut 22:25, in reference to an attacker seizing a young woman).

4.c. See n. 3.b.

5.a. למען here is the equivalent of "in the face of such evidence."

5.b. "Yahweh" is not in LXX.

6.a. Special *waw* with the verb, plus עוֹד "again, still."

6.b. הָבָא-נָא hiph בוא "bring in, bring near, put" + particle of entreaty נָא "please": "Do bring near" or "Now put."

6.c. חיק lit. means "bosom," but with the connotation of an emotion in one's breast or an object against one's chest, inside and hidden by the folds of a garment.

6.d. צרעת (the form in this verse is מְצֹרַעַת, a pual ptcp of צרע) has generally been translated "leprosy," but the symptoms described in Lev 13 and 14 do not fit Hansen's disease, the leprosy of our day. צרעת appears rather to have been a general term, descriptive of a variety of skin diseases and disorders. See Sawyer, *VT* 26 (1976) 245. LXX omits.

6.e. MT reads כַּשָּׁלֶג, lit., "as the snow," to which most translators add "white." Hulse (*PEQ* 107 [1975] 92–93, 103) has shown, however, that the comparison with snow refers not to whiteness, which is after all not mentioned in this text (as, for example, in Isa 1:18), but to the flaking of peeling skin, as with psoriasis and related skin diseases.

7.a. See n. 3.a.

7.b. The phrase "your [his] hand to your [his] chest, inside your [his] garment" is repeated, in full, three times in this verse, twice with "return," once with "withdraw." The second and third occurrences are compressed above to "he did so, then withdrew it," though it should be noted that the almost tedious repetition would add to the drama and suspense of the "sign."

8.a. וְהָיָה אִם־לֹא, lit., "and it is, if not."

8.b. The verb is hiph of אמן "believe, trust." I have translated the same verb "believe" in v 5; it occurs once in v 1, three times in vv 8, 9. On the meaning of this verb followed by לְ as in vv 1, 8, 9 here, see Pfeiffer, *ZAW* 71 (1959) 153–56.

8.c. Lit., "if they will not hear the voice of the first sign. . . ."

9.a. See n. 3.b.

Form/Structure/Setting

These verses are generally attributed to the Yahwist (though Fohrer, *Überlieferung,* 29–30, assigns them to his Nomadic source) and regarded as coming from a single hand. There is little reason to doubt that they are a unity, at least, but the section they comprise can only be understood in relation to the larger sequence of which it is an integral part.

As theophany and call (3:1–12) have been followed by assertion and illustration of God's authority (3:13–22), so now the compiler addresses the question of Moses' authority and how that authority is to be made credible. When Moses disavowed his own adequacy for the task to which God was calling him (3:11), God promised to be present with him (3:12). Then Moses logically asked what that Presence would mean (3:13), and God explained, giving him the special name symbolizing that explanation with its every pronunciation (3:14), and relating the new name to the earlier designation, the God of the Fathers (3:15).

Next God commanded Moses to get on with his task (3:16–17), assuring him that the leaders of the Israelites would hear him out (3:18), and even sketching out the sequence of events that would then unfold (3:19–22) by which the divine authority and Presence would be further established. It is this assurance, mentioned so briefly at the beginning of 3:18 and so easily passed by, that becomes the formative point of departure for the first section of chap. 4. God said, "They will listen to your report" (3:18a), and then proceeded to give his explanation and his illustrations. As if to shut out all this proof, Moses seizes upon the assurance and doubts it entirely: "Look here, they won't believe me [or trust me], and they won't pay attention [listen] to my report!" (4:1ab).

With that startling denial of an assertion God himself has made, the frame of this section is set. God must show Moses that the elders *will* hear him, and why. And this he proceeds to do by the introduction of three signs, intended to convince *any* skeptic, including of course even Moses himself, who is presented here as the first of the skeptics.

The point of this section is Moses' authority, and its form is dictated by the gathering of the signs of that authority, as an answer to Moses' protest that he will not be believed.

Comment

1 The hiphil of אמן "trust," which occurs five times in this section (vv 1, 5, 8, 9), is a key to the issue posed by the section. As Weiser ("πιστεύω," *TDNT* 6:186–90) has shown, it involves more than mere acceptance of fact and includes overtones of confidence built on relationship (cf. also Pfeiffer, *ZAW* 71 [1959] 162–64). What Moses must report to the Israelites in Egypt will have to be accepted or rejected by them on subjective grounds, as they obviously will have had no opportunity to share or even to verify the experiences of theophany and commission Moses will describe to them. Their belief of his report must therefore be based on trust, on a confidence in the reporter which gains acceptance for his report. Such a trust, Moses objects, they will not have. His status with his own people was questionable to begin with (see *Comment* on 3:11–12). A fugitive with a clouded reputation, he had left Egypt under sentence of death, and he had been away for a long time. How could they trust him? Thus how could they believe him?

The answer to these questions, of course, is a negative one. Incredible reports based solely upon the claims of men are not to be accepted. Indeed, hiphil occurrences of אמן "trust" which do not in some way involve God are generally negative and are set in a context of skepticism (cf. Jepsen, *TDOT* 1:300–303). This is exactly the point of this sequence on the authority of Moses' claims. Moses has a strong argument. The people will *not* believe him, for they have no basis for trusting him.

2 Even Yahweh acknowledges the validity of Moses' claim, for he provides Moses with three signs of authority, each of them a divinely empowered wonder. And so the point is made: it is not by any authority of Moses that what is taking place will be made effective, but through the authority of God himself, an authority that Moses merely reports and represents. The real hero of this call and commission is not Moses, but God. And the trust that will produce belief must be placed not in Moses, but in God. Moses is but the medium of the message (though compare Gross, *Wort-Gebot-Glaube*, 57–65, for the interesting theory of a "double-predication: 'Servant-God' ").

3–4 The first authenticating sign, the staff changed into a serpent, is a variation of the ancient staff-and-serpent symbolism most widely known to us in the Aesculapian insignia, on which the serpent twines around the staff. Quite widely in the ANE, the serpent was a symbol of special wisdom, fertility, and healing. In Egypt in particular, serpents were worshipped. This latter point is worth noting in view of the fact that this sign occurs in the OT only in connection with the exodus from Egypt.

The word used for serpent is נחש (though compare the different usage of 7:9), which Bodenheimer ("Serpent," *IDB* 4:289) says was a general term applied to all serpents, all of which were probably considered poisonous and therefore dangerous. Moses certainly considered the staff-become-serpent menacing, since he fled from it. Indeed, the narrator has delightfully suggested Moses' fear by his use of verbs in v 4: Yahweh tells Moses to "take hold of" the snake's tail with his hand, a hold which leaves him almost completely vulnerable to the snake's fangs. Moses, with understandable apprehension, does what most of us would do under such circumstances: instead of "taking hold of" the serpent's tail, he "snatched at it," "grabbed it cautiously," and no doubt with gritting teeth. Without being directly mentioned at all, the relief of Moses when the snake became a staff again is made almost palpable by this clever use of verbs.

5–7 This sign alone, says Yahweh, will bring the Israelites to a trusting belief in the report of Moses. But without rejoinder from Moses, Yahweh moves immediately to the second sign, the sign of the hand instantly diseased and instantly healed. Unlike the sign of the staff, which is repeated by Moses and Aaron before Pharaoh and his court (7:8–13), this sign does not turn up again in the narrative of the Book of Exodus. A variation of it appears in Num 12:9–15, where Miriam is punished by Yahweh for rebelling, along with Aaron, against the authority of Moses, and that reference may explain the omission of this sign from the narratives of Moses' experience with the elders and with Pharaoh.

The diseases of the skin designated by the general term צרעת are closely connected in the OT with the judgment-touching of Yahweh (see the "Torah on צרעת," Lev 13 and 14; 2 Kgs 5:19–27; 15:4–5; 2 Chr 26:16–21). While Moses' experience here appears to be only a sign, though perhaps with overtones of judgment for disbelief and continued resistance, Miriam's infection in Num 12 (see Hulse, *PEQ* 107 [1975] 93), both much more extensive *and* longer lasting, is clearly a judgment of Yahweh. That narrative and the general association of צרעת "skin disease" with divine judgment may have eliminated an account of the infection of Moses, even as a sign, in the presence of Pharaoh and his court, particularly as Moses came more and more to be revered as *the* hero of early Israelite faith.

It is this religious connotation of the צרעת skin disorders, and the fact that they and the opprobrium of judgment they carried were potentially infectious upon the slightest, even secondary, tactile contact, that made them so fearful. The infected person was pronounced unclean (טמא), and his uncleanness was considered so contagious that he was required to identify himself by dress and by cry and to dwell in seclusion (Lev 13:45–46). Anyone reading the account of this second sign would be horrified not only at the thought of the great *Moses* being so afflicted, but would shudder once at the thought of his infected hand and twice at the command that such a hand should be placed against the unprotected chest inside one's garments. Again, the sense of relief, this time at the report of Moses' hand being restored to health, would be palpable.

8–9 But Yahweh has yet a third authenticating sign to present. Allowing for the possibility that the first and then even the second of the signs may be inadequate, Yahweh gives instructions for a sign which will turn out to be the first of the ten mighty acts, the changing of water from the River Nile into blood. Of the three signs given to Moses, this one remains unperformed as a sign of Moses' authority. It is presented here as a sign upon which Moses can depend if the first two signs do not convince Moses' audience in Egypt, named in 3:15, though not in chap. 4, as "the sons of Israel."

The word אות "sign" refers in theological contexts to something resulting from an act of God and designed to demonstrate far more than the effect or phenomenon produced by the "sign" itself (see Gunkel, *Genesis*, 150, on the "sign" of the rainbow, Gen 9:12–17). The word is often used in connection with the exodus, and in particular in reference to the so-called "plagues," which are more accurately called "proving acts."

The purpose of the first two signs, which are performed first for Moses' own benefit, is to establish Moses' credibility as God's messenger and deliverer. They are what Helfmeyer ("אוֹת," *TDOT* 1:176–79, 183–85) has called "faith signs," signs designed to "establish" Moses' "legitimacy as one sent from God" and to "guarantee the reliability of the message with which he is sent to the Israelites" (171). But they are more, still: these two signs lead to the third, not performed here, and not specifically called a "sign" in Exod 4. That sign, like the two that precede it here and the nine that are to follow it in Egypt, is to a single end: the proof of the powerful Presence of God.

Explanation

With God's authority having been explained to Moses in 3:13–22, the theme of Moses' authority and how it is to be symbolized is broached in this section. But the real subject is still God's authority. For what Moses is able to do, he is enabled to do by God. The staff is Moses' staff, but what happens to the staff is clearly from Yahweh. The hand is Moses' hand, but what happens to that hand is also clearly from Yahweh. The water in the River Nile, which Yahweh will use to his purpose, also belongs to Yahweh, and what happens to it is the work of his power.

Following closely upon the account of Yahweh's theophany and call, and the revelation of God's special name and the explanation and illustration of its meaning, there comes this section introducing virtually the whole of the remaining narrative of the Book of Exodus. Israel must believe Moses as Moses must believe Yahweh. As Moses is to be the medium of the message to Israel, so Israel is to be the medium of the message to the world (19:4–6). And the message? It is that God *Is,* and so is actively present in a world that belongs to him.

Moses' protest that the Israelites will not believe is a summary of one side of the remaining narrative of Exodus. The other side is summarized by Yahweh's signs, established to make sure that Israel *will* believe. From this point forward, every line of the narrative of the Book of Exodus is in one way or another a development of these two sides, which are held in a marvelous tension, right to the narrative's very end. The doubt/fear/rebellion of Moses/the Pharaoh/the Egyptians/Israel becomes the occasion for Yahweh's proving/redeeming/judging/forgiving action. And the reality of his Presence is established again and again.

The Mouth of Moses (4:10–17)

Bibliography

Anderson, B. W. "Translator's Supplement: Analytical Outline of the Pentateuch," in M. Noth, *A History of Pentateuchal Traditions.* Englewood Cliffs, NJ: Prentice-Hall, 1972. 261–76. **Beegle, D. M.** *Moses, the Servant of Yahweh.* Grand Rapids: Wm. B. Eerdmans, 1972. **Cody, A.** *A History of the Old Testament Priesthood.* AnBib 35. Rome: Pontifical Biblical Institute, 1969. **Habel, N.** "The Form and Significance of the Call Narratives." *ZAW* 77 (1965) 297–323. **Lachs, S. T.** "Exodus IV 11: Evidence for an Emendation." *VT* 26 (1976) 249–50. **North, F. S.** "Aaron's Rise in Prestige." *ZAW* 66 (1954) 191–99. **Noth, M.** *Die Israelitischen Personnennamen in Rahmen der gemeinsemitischen Namengebung.* BWANT III, 10. Stuttgart: Verlag W. Kohlhammer, 1928. **Porter, J. R.** *Moses and Monarchy.* Oxford: Basil Blackwell, 1963. **Speier, S.** "פקח Ex. IV 11." *VT* 10 (1960) 347. **Westphal, G.** "Aaron und die Aaroniden." *ZAW* 26 (1906) 201–30. **Widengren, G.** "What Do We Know About Moses?" *Proclamation and Presence.* New corr. ed. John I Durham and J. R. Porter. Macon: Mercer University Press, 1983. 21–47.

Translation

¹⁰ *Yet Moses said to Yahweh, "Pardon, Lord,* [a] *I am no man of words—I never have been, nor have I become so, in spite of all you have said to your servant* [b]*—for I am heavy of lip and thick of tongue."* ¹¹ *So Yahweh said to him, "Who put a mouth on a man? Who makes him* [a] *mute or deaf or able to see or blind? Is it not I, Yahweh?* [b] ¹² *Now get going, and I* [a] *AM with your mouth, and I will instruct you as to what you must* [b] *speak."* ¹³ *Thus Moses* [a] *then said, "Pardon, Lord; please send anybody you want to send."* [b]

¹⁴ *Then Yahweh was vexed with Moses, and so he said, "Is there not Aaron,* [a] *your brother, the Levite? I know that he is an eloquent speaker—and look! Here he is, coming out to meet you, and he will be delighted to see you.* ¹⁵ *You will speak to him, and put the words into his mouth. And I* [a] *AM with your mouth and with his mouth, and I will instruct you both as to what you are to do.* [b] ¹⁶ *He* [a] *will speak in your behalf to the people, and so it will work out* [b] *that he* [a] *will be as a mouth to you, and you* [a] *will be as a god to him.*

¹⁷ *"This staff you will hold firmly in your hand, and with it you shall do the signs."*

Notes

10.a. בי אדני "Pardon, Lord." Vg omits "to Yahweh" and reads simply *ait Moyses: obsecro Domine* "Moses said, 'I pray, Lord'." LXX has Κύριος "Lord" in both places.

10.b. There is here an important threefold repetition of גם which following the negative לא means "neither/nor"; lit., "neither from yesterday (= heretofore) nor from day before yesterday (= the recent past) nor from now (= the present)."

11.a. Lit., "render, set." The verb is שים/שום as in Yahweh's first question.

11.b. LXXᴮ and minuscule codices have "I God." Some other LXX MSS read "I Yahweh (Κύριος) God."

12.a. The usage is emphatic: אנכי "I" in addition to the first common singular verb.

12.b. Piel דבר "speak," without the frequent אמר "say" clause following, and following hiph ירה "instruct," taken here as a true intensive.

13.a. Lit., "he said." "Moses" is added for clarity.

13.b. Lit., "send, please, by a hand you will send."

14.a. The name "Aaron" apparently has no Heb. meaning (Widengren, *Proclamation and Presence*, 31). It seems to be a foreign name, perhaps Egyptian in derivation (Noth, *Personennamen*, 63).

15.a. See n. 12.a.

15.b. The verb, עשׂה "do, make," has a "paragogic" or emphatic ן (GKC 47m; cf. S. R. Driver, *Notes on the Hebrew Text and the Topography of the Books of Samuel*, 2d ed. [Oxford: Clarendon Press, 1913] 30–31), thus "are to do," in the sense of a specific command. *Masora magna* lists (Weil, 47–48, no. 396) 14 occurrences of this form of עשׂה in the OT, including one more in Exodus (20:23).

16.a. Emphatic usage, with independent pers pronoun plus the subj pronoun with the verb form.

16.b. וְהָיָה "and it will be, will come to pass."

Form/Structure/Setting

This section is a somewhat uneasy composite dealing with a further protest by Moses of his inadequacy for the task to which God has called him. Since his first and general confession of inadequacy (3:11) has been answered by God's promise to be with him (3:12), and since his questions about both God's authority (3:13) and his own authority (4:1) have been fully answered (3:14–22; 4:2–9), Moses turns to a more specific personal complaint: he is a poor speaker (4:10).

This complaint becomes for the redactor the basis for two answers from Yahweh, one which asserts again the promise of his equipping Presence (vv 11–12) and one which introduces Aaron as Moses' spokesman (vv 14–16). These two answers do not complement one another, though some translations attempt to link them by paraphrasing v 13 (RSV, Childs, 49). Then to confuse the sequence further, a kind of postscript (v 17) again mentioning the staff is added. This time, the staff is presented as the symbol of God's Presence with Moses, first of all in the hands of Aaron (7:8–12, 19–21, 8:1–2 [5–6]), then in the hands of Moses (9:22–26; 10:13–15; 14:15–18; 17:5–6).

The assignment of these verses to the usual sources offers no help, since the absence of clear source-critical clues further confuses the issue. Beer (12) and Fohrer (*Überlieferung*, 124) assign these verses to E, for example, but Hyatt (71) and Anderson-Noth (*Pentateuchal Traditions*, 267) to J, except for v 17, which they give to E. Most commentators refer to the "secondary" nature of vv 13–16.

What we have in spite of all these difficulties is the form of the text as it has come to us, and in a purposeful order that must be considered a part of the implication of this section as it stands. Even though it is very likely that the Aaron verses represent a subsequent layer inserted into the narrative as a part of a much later pro-Aaron campaign, the sequence of the narrative as it stands is significant also.

The oldest version of this protest of Moses may have ended with Moses' acquiescence following the additional strong reassertion of Yahweh's promise of Presence. Such an answer by Moses which recognizes also that Yahweh is at the center of all these events is suggested, at least, by v 13, and is hardly the surly or diffident reply it has been made out to be.

The Aaron verses were perhaps added to this older material because they too provide a solution to Moses' further protest, and at that a similar kind of answer. Aaron is pointedly called not just Moses' brother, but the Levite (v 14)—that is to say, he is both set apart for and is a symbol of Yahweh's real Presence. The emphasis here, as in vv 11–12, is upon *Yahweh's* being with Moses' mouth *and* Aaron's mouth. Indeed, the wording of vv 12 and 15 on this point is identical.

Finally, the postscript about the staff (v 17) may have been included both as a means of reasserting the authority of Moses granted by Yahweh's Presence and also as a glance forward to what is to come when this staff is wielded by both Moses *and* Aaron.

Thus two apparently (and originally) different answers to one question are in the present composite spliced into what amounts to a single answer in two versions.

Comment

10 Moses' protest that he is not a "man of words" is keyed both to what Yahweh has asked him to do and to the larger contexts of prophetic (Beegle, *Moses,* 76–80) and perhaps even royal (Porter, *Moses and Monarchy,* 8–11) symbolism. What Moses is to undertake involves above all a persuasive communication of what has happened to him and is about to happen to the sons of Israel, to the elders, the people, and to Pharaoh and the Egyptians. Moses claims inadequacy in speech, and his claim is wittily, perhaps even disrespectfully comprehensive: his condition, he says, is one of long standing, persistent right up to the moment of this confrontation with Yahweh, and still just as much in evidence. One almost has the impression that Moses is producing a last and best excuse, playing a trump card, pushing his argument as far as it will go. In effect, he says, "You are indeed all that you claim. But I am the same old Moses, 'heavy-lipped and thick-tongued.'" Literally, Moses claims to have a heavy (כבד) mouth and a heavy tongue.

This claim of inadequacy is a recurring one in OT passages having to do with God's call and commission (cf., e.g., Judg 6:14–15; 1 Sam 10:20–24; 1 Kgs 3:5–9; Isa 6:5–8; Jer 1:4–10; see also Habel, *ZAW* 77 [1965] 316–23). Whatever its connection to prophetic and royal traditions of the word and the messenger, its more important rootage is in the OT pattern of the weak become strong, the least become great, the mean become mighty, the last become first (cf., e.g, Judg 6:11–24; 1 Sam 16:1–13; 17:19–54; Amos 7:14–15; Isa 6:1–13; Jer 1:4–19; and even Isa 52:13–53:12). This pattern is a metaphor of theological assertion in the Bible, and everywhere it occurs, its fundamental message is the same: God's word, God's rule, God's teaching, God's deliverance come not from man, no matter who that man may be, but from God. Even the election of Israel makes this point. Indeed that election is probably the most convincing of all the occurrences of the pattern.

11–12 Yahweh's answer to Moses' protest shows the protest to be not only invalid, but irrelevant. Once more (3:12, 14–15), Yahweh declares to Moses the promise of the Presence that makes all the difference: אהיה עם־פיך "*I* AM with your mouth." This same declaration is repeated in the

Aaron-section (vv 14–16) with regard to both Moses' mouth *and* Aaron's mouth (v 15). Indeed, it is the important motif that makes the two answers to Moses' complaint one answer. What Moses and Aaron are to say and how they are to say it, in the accomplishment of *Yahweh's* purpose, will be to Yahweh's credit, not theirs. At the crucial moments he will be with them, working out his purpose.

This underlying theme is, of course, the key to v 11. Yahweh has made the mouth of man, and Yahweh withholds or gives the ability to communicate. אלם "mute" literally means "tongue-tied," that is, able to understand but not able to speak, which is what Moses is claiming about himself. With this condition deafness is compared, and parallel to this pair is set their visual counterpart, פקח, literally, "having open eyes" (but perhaps not using them?), and the opposite, blindness (cf. Speier, *VT* 10 [1960] 347). There is thus no need to consider פקח "seeing" out of place in this sequence and in need of emendation (as, e.g., to פסח "lame"; Lachs, *VT* 26 [1976] 249–50). The sequence is carefully designed, with Moses' protest as a point of departure, to declare yet again that *Yahweh* will be present with Moses and will see that both Moses' mouth and his own plan work properly.

13 Thus to Yahweh's repeated and emphatic assertion of Presence, "*I AM* with (or *I* will take care of) your mouth," and his promise to teach or reveal to (hiphil of ירה) Moses what he is to speak, Moses replies with deferential resignation, "Sorry, Lord—pray send whomever you want to send." This verse makes perfect sense as it stands if it is taken as a response to vv 11–12 instead of as a transition to vv 14–16, which supply a similar response, though one adding Aaron to the narrative. This addition is the contribution of a later hand, and its insertion here and elsewhere creates a variety of problems of sequence, not least of which is the problem of who owns and who wields the staff symbolizing God's power.

14–17 The difference in the role of Aaron in the narrative portions of the Book of Exodus and in the texts that are concerned primarily with cultic matters, in the Books of Leviticus and Numbers as well as Exodus, is well known and much studied (cf. Cody, *OT Priesthood*, 146–74). It has occasioned a series of theories, dealing with the triumph of an Aaronide priesthood over an earlier Zadokite priesthood (North, *ZAW* 66 [1954] 191–99); the early role of the Aaronides as the keepers of a calf-cult at Bethel (Mauch, "Aaron," *IDB* 1:1–2); the difference between a tribe of Levi and a levitical priesthood (Westphal, *ZAW* 26 [1906] 227–30); and even the "two Aarons" of the Bible, Aaron the "co-leader" and Aaron the preeminent priest (Rivkin, "Aaron, Aaronides," *IDBSup*, 1–3).

A theory generally accepted in most of this research concerning Aaron is that a wide recognition of Aaron as the priest *par excellence* came late in OT history, certainly after the Exile, but far enough ahead of the final formation of the books of the tetrateuch to permit the insertion of pro-Aaron material at selected appropriate points. The section at hand presents such a point, though one at which the role of Aaron is promoted not exclusively, but in association with and clearly secondary to that of Moses.

Thus Aaron is presented as Moses' brother; he is expressly called הלוי "the Levite" in a manner suggesting more than mere tribal ancestry; and he is promised, as Moses is, Yahweh's Presence with his mouth and Yahweh's instruction as to what he is to speak. Even so, in order that Moses' own preeminence not be compromised, Aaron is put in a relationship to him clearly similar to the relationship Moses has to Yahweh: Moses will speak to Aaron, and put the message into his mouth; Yahweh will be with *both* mouths, instruct *both* servants; and Aaron's speaking will be *for* Moses—*he* will function as Moses' mouth, and Moses will be as a god (or God: לאלהים) to him. It is a remarkable struggle with the tension between the two figures, and one that leaves no doubt about Aaron's submission to Moses, just as the preceding paragraph leaves no doubt about Moses' submission to Yahweh.

The resolution of the Moses-Aaron tension helped to locate this passage here instead of somewhere else, and made possible, perhaps even necessary, the assertion of Yahweh's Presence. The postscript about the staff, which may originally have come after what is now v 13, stands as an ambiguous conclusion to the expanded section, and is equally applicable to both Moses and Aaron as wielders of the staff symbolizing Yahweh's power.

Explanation

What this section comes finally to say to us about the mouth of Moses is that Yahweh who made it and who makes it work will be present with it and will instruct its speaking. Even when Aaron speaks as Moses' mouth, this will no less be so. Moses' specific reference to a particular weakness is beside the point, irrelevant to the subject.

That subject is Yahweh and Yahweh's Presence. Moses' lack of eloquence, or for that matter, Aaron's abundance of it, are not the point. Yahweh, the "I AM," is with Moses and with Moses' mouth, with Aaron's mouth, and he will also be with the sons of Israel in Egypt as with the Pharaoh and his people, to see his purpose brought to fulfillment.

The mouth of Moses may well be heavy and clumsy, slow and halting in speech. It would not matter if it were dumb altogether, and Aaron's mouth, as well. Yahweh will be there, and Yahweh will take responsibility for both the message and the messengers. The staff in the hands of Moses and Aaron is a symbol of this powerful Presence.

The Deliverer Goes to Egypt   (4:18–31)

Bibliography

Auerbach, E. *Moses.* Detroit: Wayne State University Press, 1975. **Beltz, W.** "Religionsgeschichtliche Marginalie zu Ex. 4:24–26." *ZAW* 87 (1975) 209–11. **Dumbrell, W.** "Exodus 4:24–26: A Textual Re-examination" *HTR* 65 (1972) 285–90. **Durham, J. I** שָׁלוֹם and the Presence of God" *Proclamation and Presence.* New corr. ed. Ed. J. I Durham and J. R. Porter. Macon: Mercer University Press, 1983. 272–93. **Gunkel, H.** "Über die Beschneidung im A.T." *Archiv für Papyrusforschung* II, 1 (1902) 13–21.

Hehn, J. "Der 'Blutsbräutigam' Ex 4:24–26." *ZAW* 50 (1932) 1–8. **Junker, H.** "Der Blutbräutigam." *Alttestamentliche Studien.* BBB 1. Bonn: Peter Hanstein Verlag, 1950. 120–28. **Kosmala, H.** "The 'Bloody Husband.'" *VT* 12 (1962) 14–28. **Meyer, E.** *Die Israeliten und ihre Nachbarstämme.* Halle: Verlag von Max Niemeyer, 1906. **Mitchell, T. C.** "The Meaning of the Noun *ḤTN* in the Old Testament." *VT* 19 (1969) 93–112. **Morgenstern, J.** "The 'Bloody Husband' (?) (Exod. 4:24–26) Once Again." *HUCA* 34 (1963) 35–70. **Pedersen, J.** "Passahfest und Passahlegende." *ZAW* 52 (1934) 161–75. **Rost, L.** "Weidewechsel und Altisraelitischer Festkalendar." *ZDPV* 66 (1943) 205–15. **Sasson, J. M.** "Circumcision in the Ancient Near East." *JBL* 85 (1966) 473–76. **Schmid, H.** "Mose, Der Blutbräutigam." *Judaica* 21 (1965) 113–18. **Vermes, G.** "Baptism and Jewish Exegesis: New Light from Ancient Sources." *NTS* 4 (1958) 308–19. **Vriezen, T. C.** *An Outline of Old Testament Theology.* Boston: Charles T. Branford Co., 1958. **Wellhausen, J.** *Prolegomena to the History of Ancient Israel.* New York: Meridian Books, 1957.

Translation

¹⁸ *So Moses went back to Jethro,* [a] *his father-in-law, and said to him, "Give me leave to return, please, to my brethren who are in Egypt, that I may see if they are still alive." Jethro replied to Moses, "Go, with my blessing!"* [b]
¹⁹ *Then Yahweh said to Moses in Midian,* [a] *"Get back to Egypt, for all the men who sought your life are dead."* ²⁰ *Thus Moses took his wife and his sons and seated them upon the ass.* [a] *And he returned to the land of Egypt. And Moses carried in his hand the staff of God.* ²¹ *So Yahweh said to Moses, "When you go back to Egypt, take seriously* [a] *all the wondrous deeds* [b] *that I have given you power to do, and do them in the presence of Pharaoh. And I will make his heart obstinate,* [c] *and he will not send out the people.* ²² *So you say to Pharaoh, 'Thus says Yahweh, "My son, my firstborn, is Israel;* ²³ *and I say to you, send out my son,* [a] *that he may worship me. Should you refuse to send him out, beware:* [b] *I will kill your son, your firstborn!"'"* [c]
²⁴ *And it happened* [a] *en route, at the* [b] *lodging place, that Yahweh* [c] *encountered* [d] *him and sought to put him to death.* ²⁵ *So Zipporah seized a flintknife and cut off the foreskin of her son and touched his* [a] *genitals,* [b] *saying as she did so, "For a bridegroom of blood you are to me!"* [c]
²⁶ *Thus did he sink back from him.* [a] *At that point, she said "a bridegroom of blood," with reference to the circumcision.* [b]
²⁷ *Then* [a] *Yahweh said to Aaron, "Go to meet Moses in the direction of the wilderness." So he went and thus met him at the mountain of God, and he kissed him.* ²⁸ *Moses reported to Aaron all the words of Yahweh that he had sent him,* [a] *and all the signs that he had commanded him.* [b]
²⁹ *Next Moses went,* [a] *and Aaron, and they brought together all the wise old leaders of the sons of Israel.* ³⁰ *Then Aaron spoke all the words that Yahweh had spoken to Moses, and did the signs before the very eyes of the people.* ³¹ *So the people believed.* [a] *And they understood* [b] *that Yahweh had observed* [c] *the sons of Israel, and that he had seen their humiliation. Thus did they bow down and worship.*

Notes

18.a. MT has יתר "Jether" here, but the more usual יתרו "Jethro" later in this verse. "Jether" occurs nowhere else, and seems to be a textual variation. LXX, SamPent, and Vg have the usual word for Jethro. See *Comment* on 2:16.

18.b. Lit., "Go, with fulfillment." The word is שָׁלוֹם, which means "completion, peace," in the sense of achieving God's purpose, and implies, in such contexts, the blessing of the Presence of God. See Durham, *Proclamation and Presence,* 277–93.

19.a. See *Form/Structure/Setting* on 2:16–22.

20.a. There is almost certainly a gap here, as both this sentence and the next appear to belong to separate contexts, and pose together a *non sequitur.*

21.a. Lit., "look at," so "consider." The verb is ראה (BDB, 907 § 7a).

21.b. המופתים "portents, wonders," a stronger term than אוֹתֹת "signs."

21.c. This statement is not to be taken in an adversative, but a complementary sense. Both Moses *and* Yahweh have a part to play in the events to take place in Egypt, and their actions are interlocked, not in opposition. See *Comment* below.

23.a. LXX has τὸν λαόν μου "my people" instead of "my son." See MT at 5:1.

23.b. הנה "behold, look out!"

23.c. The reference to Pharaoh's son, his firstborn, is precisely (and deliberately) parallel to the reference to Israel as Yahweh's son, his firstborn.

24.a. וַיְהִי lit., "and so it was."

24.b. "Lodging-place" is definite, probably in reference to a specific location, identified perhaps in the original setting of vv 24–26.

24.c. LXX reads ἄγγελος κυρίου "angel of the Lord (= Yahweh)" instead of "Yahweh," a reading followed by Tg Onk. Aquila has ὁ θεός "God."

24.d. פגש "encounter," a synonym of פגע (see Exod 5:3), implies, as that verb does, a meeting or encounter of consequence.

25.a. The general assumption is that this 3d pers masc pronoun and the one appended to the verb "encountered" have Moses as their antecedent, because of the context of the passage and the reference to Zipporah. Moses is nowhere named in vv 24–26, however, and the pronouns are ambiguous in view of the presence of a second male.

25.b. Lit., "feet," here used as a euphemism for the genitals, as in Isa 6:2; 7:20; Ezek 16:25, Deut 28:57.

25.c. LXX, taking "feet" literally, has Zipporah falling in supplication πρὸς τοὺς πόδας "at the feet" (there is no "his" as in MT, though the context here and a similar usage in Esth 8:3 would suggest Yahweh's "feet"), and then saying, Ἔστη τὸ αἷμα τῆς περιτομῆς τοῦ παιδίου μου "It stands, the blood of my son's circumcision." See Kosmala, *VT* 12 (1962) 27–28.

26.a. SamPent reads ממנה "from her."

26.b. LXX repeats here the statement of Zipporah at the end of v 25, though LXX[B] omits v 26 altogether.

27.a. Once again, a *non sequitur.* This verse would seem to fit better before v 14.

28.a. there is no need to introduce here an idea of words of commission, or to insert a "with which," as RSV does. The text says plainly what it means; the words Moses has are Yahweh's message, not his. See *Comment* on 4:11–12.

28.b. Syr, Tg Ps-J add "to do, perform," but to do so disrupts the balance of the statement and is in any case unnecessary.

29.a. SamPent, Syr have a pl verb.

31.a. On אמן "believe" see n. 4:8.b above. SamPent and Syr read this verb as pl.

31.b. Lit., "heard," שמע, here meaning "realized." LXX reads καὶ ἐχάρη "and were joyful."

31.c. פקד "visit, attend to, inspect with care." Cf. 3:16.

Form/Structure/Setting

As in the preceding section, so here too we are faced with a somewhat disjointed composite. It includes (1) what appears to be the beginning of a conclusion to Yahweh's command in v 12, one that stops short of the journey to Egypt (v 18); (2) yet another command by Yahweh that Moses return to Egypt, this time with information about conditions there, a brief report of the return, a repetition of some of the instructions given already, and further details about what Moses is to say to the Pharaoh, with a hint, at least, of what he can expect in return (vv 19–23); (3) a strange narrative of fearsome difficulty in the journey (vv 24–26); (4) a report of the wilderness rendezvous with Aaron (vv 27–28); and (5) an account of the arrival of Moses and Aaron in Egypt, with the first response of the sons of Israel to their report (vv 29–31).

The general theme binding this somewhat wide range of material together is the return to Egypt of Moses the deliverer. That theme functions as a kind of nucleus around which a series of narratives, originally separate, has been loosely gathered. The allocation of these narratives to the tetrateuchal sources from which they may be assumed to have come offers little help for an understanding of the form or purpose of this sequence as it stands in the received text. To begin with, such an allocation is both difficult and tentative, as the widely variant opinions of the source critics indicate (for example: Beer [12] J¹: 18b–26, 30b, 31a; J²: 18a, 29, 31b; E and E¹: 27, 28, 30a; Hyatt [84–85] J: 19–20a, 22–26, 29–31; E: 18, 20b, 21, 27–28; Fohrer [*Überlieferung* 124] J: 18, 19, 31b; E: 20b–23, 27–28, 30a; N: 19–20a, 24–26, 30b–31a). Further, this kind of division of the text, though it may isolate discrepancies of sequence, fragments still more an already loose unity, and so winds up raising more questions than it answers. Whatever their context of origin, these narrative fragments have been brought together in one place, and the resultant sequence must claim our first consideration.

Why have we such a sequence, in which the obvious is mixed with the strange, in which points made previously are made over again, and from which details we are curious to have are omitted altogether? For example: Did Moses' family accompany him to Egypt or not? Why did Yahweh "attack" Moses on that journey, and who touched whom where with what? Why is this kind of information left out, while other information is repeated? Given the nature of the biblical narrative as canonical scripture, we cannot assume any part of it, however obscure, to be in the text without purpose.

The section at hand is best understood as a collection of narrative bits and pieces connected with Moses' return to Egypt. The compiler has brought these together in a transitional sequence, the primary purpose of which is first to move Moses from Sinai/Horeb back to his home in Midian and then to the community of the Israelites in the Egyptian Delta. That sequence has been augmented by the repetition of details given already, the statement of new but related details, material connected with circumcision, and material connected with Aaron.

The basic purpose of the section is to move Moses from Sinai to Egypt. And to that end, the compiler has brought together narrative fragments that can be connected somehow with that transition. It is possible that these fragments were all that he had and that their discontinuity dictates the form of their presentation. This is one of the loosest sequences in the entire Book of Exodus.

Comment

18–19   Finally persuaded that he himself must return to Egypt to deliver Yahweh's message and present Yahweh's deeds of deliverance to Israel in bondage, Moses logically goes home to Jethro's camp, there to ask permission for the journey. Moses' coming to Jethro with this request is an important indication of his identification with his Midianite home. Moses' reference to his "brethren who are in Egypt" is an important indication of his memory of his roots. And Moses' stated reason for going, "that I may see whether they are still alive," is a clue both to the passage of time and to the severity of the Egyptian oppression. In view of the narrative of chap. 18, it seems curious that Moses is not reported having shared with Jethro his real mission in Egypt and, for that matter, that Jethro is satisfied with such a general explanation for so undoubtedly hazardous a trip proposed so suddenly. We can only guess, again in view of 18:9–12, whether the blessing Jethro utters upon Moses and his journey suggests a fuller knowledge of Yahweh and his plan than the text of v 18 here suggests.

The additional command of Yahweh to Moses to return to Egypt does not logically follow the meeting with Jethro, and it may well be a part of an original sequence of command and persuasion (cf. 3:10, 16–18; 4:8–9, 12, 15–17). It is justified here by the information that those who formerly sought Moses' life (because of his capital crime?) are now dead (cf. 2:15, 23).

20 The three statements of v 20 represent three entirely separate narrative strands, each of them connected with the return to Egypt, but each of them concerned with a separate aspect of that return: the care and location of Moses' family, the return itself, and the bringing to Egypt of the increasingly important "staff of God."

The reference to Moses' placing his wife and sons upon an ass has frequently been taken, along with the statement of vv 24–26, as an indication that he took his family with him for a part of the journey to Egypt. As they are never mentioned in Egypt or at any point on the return trip to Sinai, and as they are clearly in Jethro's care when Moses returns to Midianite territory (18:2–6), this assumption has little support, none in fact beyond the statement of v 24. Only once in Exodus is a second son of Moses named (18:4; elsewhere in the OT only by the Chronicler: 1 Chr 23:15, 17), and in view of 2:22 and 4:25, the reference in v 20 to "sons" may well be premature, a reflection of the later narrative of 18:2–4. The sentence in v 20, even in the light of vv 24–26, may imply no more than that Moses took leave of his wife and one son at the outset of his dangerous journey to Egypt.

The return itself, as is indicated by a singular pronominal subject, involves Moses alone. This reference in v 20 is probably the most ancient statement of the return. In view of the ambiguity of v 29 and the apparent insertion of Aaron's name, it may be better to say that this is the only specific reference to the return itself.

The staff, which began as Moses' tool of shepherdry (4:2), becomes in v 20 what it is to be for the remainder of the Book of Exodus, the staff of God. This reference to Moses carrying it "in his hand" to Egypt is an important linking of the "signs" at Sinai to the "signs and wonders" in Egypt, the greatest of which, of course, are the ten mighty acts, only anticipated in Yahweh's dialogue with Moses at Sinai.

21–23 This reference to the staff, though separate from what precedes and follows it, provides a point of departure for a section that deftly moves from the signs at Sinai to the wondrous deeds in Egypt and anticipates not only the need for them (proof of Yahweh's powerful Presence, called for by the Pharaoh's divinely induced obstinacy) but the last and most awesome of them.

Moses is told to take these "wondrous deeds" seriously, just as Yahweh clearly does. Heretofore called אותות "signs" (vv 8, 9, 17) and נפלאות "extraordinary deeds" (3:20), these proving actions are now called מופתים "wondrous deeds" for the first time (cf. 7:3, 9; 11:9, 10). Moses is then told, in a marvelous summary of both the purpose and range of the signs and the mighty acts, that Yahweh will be working through both him *and* the Pharaoh to establish irrevocably the powerful reality of his Presence. Through Moses, Yahweh will work the wondrous deeds in the very presence of Pharaoh. Through Pharaoh he will multiply the number of the deeds, prolong their sequence, and heighten their impact by postponing the moment of Pharaoh's unqualified belief (v 21). This statement anticipates what has frequently been called the "hardening of the heart" motif, a dramatic device by which the mighty-act narratives of chaps. 7–12 are moved forward (see further *Comment* below).

The proving deeds themselves are bracketed (1) by the reference to what Moses has been empowered to do *before* Pharaoh at the outset of the sequence (the signs, then the first of the so-called "plagues," v 21); and (2) by the reference to what Yahweh will himself do *to* the Pharaoh at the close of the sequence (the death of the firstborn, v 23). In a brilliant pairing of the themes of Israel's election and the ultimate defeat of the Egyptian oppressors, Israel is declared to be Yahweh's own firstborn son (v 22), and Pharaoh's firstborn son is threatened with death, should Pharaoh be disobedient to Yahweh's request (v 23). Inserted between these two great themes, there is a glimmer of the exodus itself in the request that Yahweh's son be sent out, so that he might worship his divine father (v 23). Israel is lovingly called "my son, my firstborn," and the Pharaoh's son, in an exact parallel, is poignantly called "your son, your firstborn."

The theory of Noth (*Pentateuchal Traditions*, 66–70)—that the death of Egypt's firstborn, itself an outgrowth of Passover legendry, was the point of departure for the development of the "plague" narratives, a kind of "first" plague which remained, as the narratives grew, the last and most important of the plagues—is neither proved nor disproved by v 23. The death of the firstborn is mentioned here because it is the final of the mighty acts, just as the "wondrous deeds" Moses is to perform are mentioned as the logical beginning of the entire sequence. Vv 22–23 are an ingeniously compact preview of election, exodus, and triumphant proof-of-Presence.

24–26   These verses are among the most difficult in the Book of Exodus, not in terms of their translation, which is quite straightforward, but in terms of their meaning and their location in this particular context. From ancient (see the review of Vermes, *NTS* 4 [1958] 309–18) to modern times (see the review of Morgenstern, *HUCA* 34 [1963] 35–46), a wide range of interpretations, both fanciful and plausible, has emerged. Some of these have involved the alteration of the text, without justification, to support a given interpretation. Others have imposed wildly improbable theories designed to explain the difficulties of the passage. Most of them have been aided and abetted by the ambiguity of subject and object in the section. Moses can only be assumed to be one of the actors, since he is never mentioned by name; and the antecedents of the subject and object pronouns are far from clear. The interpreter is further blocked by the problem of the meaning and application of the obscure phrase "bridegroom of blood," which appears in both v 25 and v 26.

Thus Moses is said to have had no part at all in this narrative (Kosmala, *VT* 12 [1962] 18–25, who thinks it a Midianite narrative; cf. Schmid, *Judaica* 21 [1965] 115–18) or at most only the part of "a passive and helpless witness" (Morgenstern, *HUCA* 34 [1963] 66–70, who thinks it "a part of the Kenite Code"). Zipporah is said (Meyer, *Israeliten*, 59; Gressmann, *Mose und seine Zeit*, 55–61) to have moved to avert (1) a fatal attack on Moses by a demon, later displaced by Yahweh, demanding the right of first intercourse with a virgin wife on the wedding night; or (2) an attack upon Gershom (Fohrer, *Überlieferung* 45–48, Cassuto, 59–61) because he had not been circumcised; or (3) even an attack upon Moses (Hyatt, 87) for the same reason. The passage is said to be the most ancient description of circumcision in the Bible (Beltz, *ZAW* 87 [1975] 209–10]; an etiology for circumcision (Beer, 39; Auerbach, *Moses*, 49); and a justification for the change of circumcision from a rite performed on adult males just before marriage to one performed on boys soon after birth (Gunkel, *Archiv für Papyrusforschung* 2/1 [1902] 17–18) or even at puberty (Buber, *Moses* [Oxford: East and West Library, 1946], 56; Wellhausen, *Prolegomena*, 340–41). Vriezen (*Outline*, 155, n.5), following a suggestion of Beer (39), even thinks of the narrative as one in which Yahweh is not an enemy, but one who "thwarts" Moses to give him "his means of grace (circumcision as a protective sign of the Covenant)." Hehn (*ZAW* 50 [1932] 4–8) argued that the different reading of LXX in vv 25 and 26 arose from a different Hebrew *Vorlage*, and Junker (*Studien*, 122–28), that the LXX translator understood the Hebrew original differently on the basis of his view of the significance of circumcision; Dumbrell has contended (*HTR* 65 [1972] 288–90) that the LXX translator consciously altered a Hebrew original he found difficult, either for theological or linguistic reasons.

Given the strangeness and ambiguity of these three verses, such differing and imaginative interpretations are likely to be multiplied, with even stranger and more ambiguous results. Yet what can be said of the passage *as* it stands in Exodus, and, just as important, *where* it stands in Exodus? To begin with, the main point of this brief narrative is clearly circumcision, and at that, a specific circumcision. Childs (100–101) is quite correct to argue that the etiology of circumcision in Israel, often offered as the reason for the inclusion of this section, is not in view here. And whatever "demonic" roots this narrative may once have had, if indeed there ever were such, are now completely absent. Yahweh is plainly named as the one who meets his male quarry with intentions the narrator viewed as deadly. One could wish this quarry had been as clearly indicated as is the attacker.

Whatever the narrative's origin and whatever its original context and its meaning in that context, these verses must be understood now in their present context. The editor who assembled the sequence of which they are nearly

the middle component must have understood them as both adding to that
sequence and as gaining specific clarity from it. That being so, it is hardly
reasonable to claim that anyone except Moses is the object of Yahweh's en-
countering action. Moses is the center of Yahweh's concern everywhere else
in the section, even in the intrusive verses involving Aaron. The sudden
emergence to the forefront of Moses' son would make no sense whatever
in such a sequence.

The reason for this attack, as the redactor's explanatory note in v 26b
makes clear, is that Moses had not previously been circumcised. The difficulty
of such a conclusion for the later generations of Jewish scholars, who proved
themselves capable of contending that Moses, along with other great OT
heroes, was born circumcised (Vermes, *NTS* 4 [1958] 314–15), has made it
difficult also for a great many Christian scholars. But no other explanation
of this passage in this context answers more questions than it raises.

Sasson (*JBL* 85 [1966] 473–74) has pointed out convincingly that Egyptian
circumcision was not only performed on adults, but was, by comparison with
Hebrew circumcision, merely a partial circumcision. Indeed, he contends
(475–76) that circumcision may well have come to Egypt from North Syria,
where it was practiced early in the third millenium B.C. For whatever reasons,
the compiler who set vv 24–26 in their present context had apparently reached
a conclusion confirmed by these facts. Perhaps he combined the abnormal
circumstances by which the infant Moses had to be hidden away at birth
with some knowledge of the Egyptian practice and even a belief that the
circumcision of infant boys was a late development in Israel's life. Quite
possibly, he too was searching for some reason for Yahweh's serious encounter. Whatever the case, he clearly believed that Moses was uncircumcised
and that Yahweh determined to stop him en route to Egypt for that reason.

Zipporah, the only person available to perform the rite, seizes the manda-
tory flint cutting tool (Josh 5:2–9; cf. Sasson, *JBL* 85 [1966] 474) and circum-
cises not Moses, who would have been temporarily incapacitated by the surgery
(cf. Gen 34:18–31) at a crucial time when he could no longer delay his journey,
but her son. For the child, who was not to make the journey to Egypt in
any case, the effects of the circumcision would be less problematic. To
transfer the effect of the rite, Zipporah touched the severed foreskin of her
son to the genitals of Moses, intoning as she did so the ancient formula
recalling circumcision as a premarital rite: "For a bridegroom of blood you
are to me!" This ancient phrase, as Mitchell [*VT* 19 [1969] 94–105, 111–
12) has demonstrated, is a phrase of marital relationship—and it was already
old enough at the time of the compilation of this sequence to require a
specific comment by the redactor that the context of reference for the phrase
was circumcision (v 26b). The final establishment of circumcision as the crucial
point of these verses is of course that Zipporah's action worked and that
Yahweh thus "fell back" or "backed off" from Moses.

The point at issue in vv 24–26 is thus that Moses had not been circumcised
or, at best, had received only the partial circumcision of the Egyptians, referred
to in Josh 5:9 as a "disgrace" or "reproach" (חרפה). A comparable memory
for the compiler of this section may indeed have been the one recorded
now in Josh 5:2–9, which reports the circumcision of all those born in the

wilderness following the exodus who had not been circumcised and so had to be before the crossing of the Jordan for the conquest and settlement of the promised land.

At the beginning of Moses' special mission for Yahweh, this omission, or perhaps this "Egyptian disgrace," had to be remedied. Vv 24–26 pose the problem and describe its immediate and surely temporary remedy. The language of v 24, "sought to put him to death," may reflect an earlier layer of the story, but here it describes the seriousness of the crisis and indicates dramatically that Yahweh is still very much in charge. The language may be compared to the language of the account of the testing of Abraham's faith (Gen 22:2) or of the struggle of Jacob at Jabbok (Gen 32:22–32). Zipporah's reaction to the crisis is a vicarious circumcision of Moses to prevent his being painfully crippled at the beginning of the most important undertaking of his life. And what Zipporah says is the ritual statement which accompanied the premarital circumcision as a declaration to a young man's in-laws that he was of an age appropriate for marriage. The "bridegroom of blood" of circumcision was being prepared to become a bridegroom of a bride. Perhaps there was a similar ritual statement in the wedding ceremony. To the redactor who included this narrative in Exod 4, this ritual phrase was already arcane enough to require the explanation he appended at v 26b.

27–28 The instruction of Yahweh to Aaron would of course seem to fit the narrative sequence of the Book of Exodus better at an earlier point in chap. 4, before v 14, as would the account of the meeting of Moses and Aaron. The Aaron-references are intrusive to the Exodus narrative and are the work of one of the latest of the editorial hands. These verses are added here in the Moses-to-Egypt collection to make it also an Aaron-to-Egypt collection, one which makes Aaron party to both the words of Yahweh and the signs of his Presence, even though Aaron receives both the words and the report of the signs from Moses, who is clearly, after Yahweh, the primary figure.

29–30 The final section of this loosely knit sequence describes the first meeting of Moses (and the added Aaron) with both the leaders of Israel and the people themselves. Nothing is said of the trip from the wilderness of Midian to the delta of Egypt apart from the brief statement in v 20 that Moses made the journey. In view of what we have been told already, it is almost startling to discover Aaron not only speaking the words Moses has given him from Yahweh, but also performing the signs (אוֹתֹת, v 30). These statements, too, belong to the pro-Aaron insertions.

31 The conclusion to the "Deliverer to Egypt" section is a conclusion as well to the "credibility of Moses" motif that threads through the whole of chap. 4 (vv 1, 5, 8–9, 15, 17, 21, 23) and a further amplification of the "proof of Presence" motif that was introduced in 3:19–20 and is to become the crucial center of the mighty-act narratives of chaps. 7–12. The people, whom Moses had declared would *not* believe, now believe (v 31). But their belief is based not on Moses, but upon Yahweh's words and Yahweh's signs, as it should be. This is made dramatically plain by Israel's reaction—they understand Yahweh to have observed their plight sympathetically and to have learned of their oppression at first hand. Thus the people do not acclaim

Moses (or Aaron), or celebrate his (their) presence. Neither Moses nor Aaron is even mentioned, for they should not be. Unlike their modern counterparts, who either worship or denigrate the messenger and idolize but ignore the message, the Israelites bowed down and worshiped neither the messengers *nor* the message, but Yahweh.

Explanation

Thus at last Moses obeys the call and commission of Yahweh. The point of this collection of narrative threads concerning the deliverer's return to Egypt is precisely that obedience. Though they restate motifs introduced already and anticipate others yet to be introduced, and though they include some strange and ambiguous references, the overall impulse of these narrative bits and pieces is the return of Moses, and secondarily, of Aaron, to Egypt and the oppressive bondage of Israel there.

After the excitement and drama of the theophany of Yahweh, his call and commission of Moses, his revelation of his unique name, and the tension-filled dialogue between Yahweh intent on his purpose and Moses afraid and reluctant to go, this account of Moses' obedience and the actual return to Egypt seems both anticlimactic and pallid. But we must not forget in our curiosity about the details of the story that this is first of all a theological account, and that all other considerations must remain secondary, if indeed they are included at all.

Exod 4:18–31 is a transitional section, one designed to move the action of the theological account of the birth of Yahweh's people from one great arena, Sinai, to another, Egypt, in a declaratory preparation for the great act of deliverance that will bring the action back to Sinai again for its great climax. To accomplish this purpose, the compiler of this section has brought together every reference to the return to Egypt available to him, altogether at least seven of them, and then has described a first appearance of Moses before the elders and the people of Israel, a meeting that results in the people's belief in Yahweh's Presence with them and their worship of him.

Though the people are to have doubts again, doubts that can be removed only by signs and mighty acts and powerful words far beyond Moses' first presentation, their initial belief is a confirmation of Yahweh's prediction (vv 5, 8–9) over against all Moses' misgivings. V 31 thus constitutes a positive conclusion to the narrative of chaps. 3–4, just as vv 21–23 anticipate the doubts and the proofs that are yet to come. Above all, v 31 ends a sequence that began with Yahweh present with Moses by a report that the people to whom Moses had come believed, following his presentation to them, that Yahweh was present also with them. This belief led then, as it would later, to their worship.

The First Confrontation with Pharaoh: Moses and Aaron   (5:1–14)

Bibliography

Daiches, S. "The Meaning of עם הארץ in the Old Testament." *JTS* 30 (1929) 245–49. **McCarthy, D. J.** "Plagues and Sea of Reeds: Exodus 5:1–14." *JBL* 85 (1966) 137–58. **Nims, C. F.** "Bricks without Straw?" *BA* 13 (1950) 22–28. **Rost, L.** "Die Bezeichnungen für Land und Volk im Alten Testament." *Das Kleine Credo und Andere Studien Zum Alten Testament.* Heidelberg: Quelle & Meyer, 1965. 76–101. **Vaux, R. de.** *Ancient Israel.* London: Darton, Longman & Todd, 1961. **Westermann, C.** *Basic Forms of Prophetic Speech.* Philadelphia: Westminster Press, 1967. **Zeitlin, S.** "The Am haarez." *JQR* 23 (1932) 45–61.

Translation

[1] *After this, then, Moses and Aaron came and said to Pharaoh, "Thus says Yahweh, God of Israel, 'Send out my people, so that they may make a pilgrimage [a] to me in the wilderness.'"* [2] *But Pharaoh replied, "Who is Yahweh, [a] that I should pay attention to his voice, and so send out Israel? I have no knowledge of Yahweh, and Israel, I am not about [b] to send out!"* [3] *Thus did they respond, "The God of the Hebrews has come upon us unexpectedly [a]—please let us make a three-day journey into the wilderness, and offer sacrifice to Yahweh [b] our God, that he might not send disaster [c] upon us, by plague or by sword."*

[4] *Then the king of Egypt said to them, "Why, Moses and Aaron, do you distract [a] the people from their work? Get on with your heavy duties!" [b]* [5] *Pharaoh further said, "Look here, these peasants [a] are now a horde, [b] and you are causing them to neglect [c] their heavy duties."*

[6] *So Pharaoh that very day gave orders to the work-bosses [a] over the people, and to their section-leaders [b] as well, specifying:* [7] *"You are not to keep gathering [a] straw to give to the people for brick-making as you have done up to now. [b] They [c] can go and gather straw for themselves.* [8] *And the quota of bricks which they have produced up to now you shall hold as a requirement over them [a]—you are not to reduce it, because they are loafing! Indeed they have pled, [b] 'Let us go to sacrifice to our God.'* [9] *Let the labor be heavy upon such [a] men, and they will have their hands full, [b] and perhaps [c] they will not pay attention to false reports!"*

[10] *Thus the work-bosses of the people and their section-leaders went out [a] and said to the people, "Thus says Pharaoh, 'I am through providing you straw.* [11] *You go get straw for yourselves, wherever you find it—for your slave labor will not be lightened one bit!'"* [12] *So the people scattered [a] into the whole of the land of Egypt to gather wind-blown stubble [b] for straw.* [13] *And the work-bosses pressed hard, saying, "Finish your work on schedule, [a] just as when the straw was in hand." [b]* [14] *And the section leaders of the sons of Israel, set in authority over them by Pharaoh's work-bosses, were whipped [a] and questioned, "Why have you not completed your assigned limit [b] of brick-making, as you have done up until yesterday and today?" [c]*

Notes

1.a. The verb חגג emphasizes a religious journey to an appointed place more than it signifies a "feast."

2.a. LXX has ἔστιν "is he" instead of "Yahweh," though G^A has θεός "God."

2.b. וגם "and moreover."

3.a. קרא "encounter, befall"; BDB (897) note: *Niph.* "meet unexpectedly."

3.b. LXX does not have Yahweh (κύριος).

3.c. פגע, lit., "fall upon, encounter, assail."

4.a. פרע, hiph, "cause to refrain"; SamPent reads פרד "separate," to mean "keep the people from their work."

4.b. סבלות "heavy duties"; cf. *Comment* on 2:11.

5.a. עם הארץ lit., "the people of the land" (cf. de Vaux, (*Ancient Israel,* 71, "the common people").

5.b. SamPent reads "Look here, they are of greater number than the people of the land."

5.c. The verb is hiph of שבת "cause to stop their work."

6.a. Qal active ptcp from נגש "press, drive, oppress."

6.b. שטר "organizer, sub-official, minor authority."

7.a. תאספון, generally translated as from יסף "add to, increase," with inf following, as here, "to do something again or more." The expected form would however be תסיפון (so SamPent תוסיפון). The form in MT appears to be confused with אסף "gather, collect and bring, take away." The *Masora Magna* (Weil, 52, no. 430) lists four occurrences of תספון in the OT, only one of which, this one, is written with א. This א is either a scribal slip, or the form should be taken as from אסף and pointed תֶאֱסְפוּן, qal impf. That reading has been followed in the translation above.

7.b. "As yesterday and the day before."

7.c. Emphasis indicated by the independent pers pronoun הֵם plus the 3d pers pl pronoun ending on the verbs.

8.a. "You shall place, set it upon them."

8.b. צעק "cry, call out (in distress)," here in a participial form.

9.a. Lit., "the men."

9.b. ויעשו־בה "and they will do it," = "be busy with it." Several versions, including LXX and Syr, read this verb וישעו from שעה "regard, gaze with interest, pay attention to," the same as the final verb in this verse.

9.c. The negative particle is אל, "denying . . . not objectively as a fact (like לא, οὐ), but subjectively, as a wish (like μή)," (BDB, 39). SamPent has לא instead of אל.

10.a. LXX reads here as at the beginning of v 13, אוץ "press hard, rush."

12.a. Hiph פוץ "scatter." There is no need to read this verb as a passive, as for example RSV does, but BDB, 807.

12.b. Both the verb and the noun are derived from a root, קשש, which appears to signify "dried-out chaff, worthless stubble, trash."

13.a. Lit., "A day's thing in its day."

13.b. SamPent adds נתן לכם "was given to you."

14.a. The verb נכה "whip" is that used in 2:11, 12, 13, to refer to the blows of an Egyptian, Moses, and a Hebrew; see *Comment* on 2:11–13.

14.b. The term here is חק "something prescribed, assigned task," rather than מתכנת "quota, measurement," as in v 8.

14.c. MT reads כתמול שלשם גם־תמול גם־היום, lit. "as yesterday and the day before, both yesterday and the day (= today)." "Both yesterday" is omitted by LXX, but SamPent has the full sequence.

Form/Structure/Setting

Exod 5:1–6:1 deals by and large with a single subject, albeit from two perspectives. That subject is the confrontation between Israel in Egyptian bondage and the one Egyptian who exercises an ultimate control over that bondage, the Pharaoh of Egypt. The two perspectives are: (1) that of the interceding people, represented by Moses (and Aaron) and then their section-leaders, and (2) that of the Pharaoh, who refuses to grant any concessions and uses his position of force ruthlessly.

Source-critics have generally assigned most of this chapter to the Yahwist, though a notable exception to this position is Fohrer (*Überlieferung*, 55–58, 124), who gives about a fourth of the verses to the Elohist, and lists vv 22–23 as from an early layer of tradition common to both J and E. There has been some speculation (e.g., Noth, 53) about the variant titles "Pharaoh" (vv 1,2,5,6, etc.) and "the king of Egypt" (v 4), and some talk of doublets (so Hyatt, 89: v 3 = vv 1–2, v 5 = v 4; cf. Noth, 52–53), but it is clear that this chapter is for the most part a unity that extends through 6:1. It is also clear that the compositor of this sequence of verses has gone to some trouble to present a single narrative with rising tension, one that introduces (cf. McCarthy, *JBL* 85 [1966] 140–42) the great proof-of-Presence sequence of the ten mighty acts of Yahweh by getting things off to a difficult start.

Moses, accompanied by Aaron, delivers Yahweh's message (3:18) to Pharaoh with straightforward boldness (v 1). Well might he have expected, as do we, an immediate permission for Israel to make the requested pilgrimage. But not so—the Pharaoh is blasphemously sarcastic in his refusal and moves immediately to make the position of the sons of Israel more difficult still. Moses is taken aback, so much so that he is lost in the shuffle of commands and counter-pleas that follow, and appears again only at the end of the sequence, and lamely, as unwilling or not permitted to confront the Pharaoh again and as the butt of the people's resentment at their newest difficulties. Only when he echoes to Yahweh their complaint to him do we receive the key to the form of this entire sequence. With a subtle change of the agent of Israel's difficulty (cf. v 21 with vv 22–23), Moses anticipates the reply of God (6:1) which makes the reasons for this curious beginning plain.

It is not Moses, it is not Israel, it is not Pharaoh who has the authority to bring deliverance. Only Yahweh has that authority, as is now, at long last, about to be made irrevocably clear. Exod 5:1–6:1 is the fleshing out of 3:18–20, and at once the prologue to the proof-of-Presence sequence of 7:8–12:36 (McCarthy, *JBL* 85 [1966] 149, 155–56, argues that 5:1–6:1 is introductory to a sequence continued in 7:8–10:27 plus 14:1–31). Moses seems ineffective here not because he was absent from the most ancient layer of tradition, as Noth argues (*Pentateuchal Traditions*, 71, 156–75), but because the Pharaoh and the Egyptians and even the people of Israel must be seen as entirely doubtful about Yahweh and the prospect of any exodus from Egypt. For that matter, Yahweh seems ineffective too, until the very end of the section.

Thus the form of 5:1–6:1 is set by its purpose, the preparation of the reader for the great sequence to follow, a sequence that now begins at 7:8 but originally must immediately have followed what is now 5:1–6:1 (see *Form/Structure/Setting* on 7:8–13). The division of this section into two parts, 5:1–14 and 5:15–6:1, is made according to the two major stages of the first confrontation with Pharaoh, the stage in which it is initiated by Moses and the stage in which it is intensified by the complaints of the section-leaders. This is a division for convenience of what amounts to a single section into two complementary parts.

Comment

1 Moses' first approach to the Pharaoh is authoritative and direct, and begun (as he was instructed in 4:22) with the messenger formula ("Thus says Yahweh . . .") so well-known in the prophetic books of the OT (see Westermann, *Basic Forms,* 98–106). His request is in accord with the command of 3:18, and stated more specifically than the instruction of 4:23, the primary purpose of which was the introduction of the contrasting themes of Israel's election and the death of the first born of Egypt. There is no mention here of a three-day journey; the request is for permission to undertake a religious pilgrimage, at the command of Yahweh.

The almost arrogant confidence of this approach is as deliberate as it is dramatic. It graphically presents a Moses euphoric over the quick success of his presentation to the Israelites, and it sets up the context for the Pharaoh's shattering and sarcastic reply and the devastating and extensive lesson he must be taught in result. This sequence is sensitively and realistically written, to introduce a conflict that is not only inevitable but is also the pivotal didactic instrument of the entire sequence, 5:1–6:1, 7:8–12:36. This is what a confident Moses, naïvely hopeful of a quick success, *would* have said in a first interview with a Pharaoh, and this is how a Pharaoh *would* have replied. We are drawn into the drama by the brilliance of its presentation, quite apart from the message within it.

2–3 Pharaoh must consider the command absurd. He has no experience of any Yahweh, thus no reason to pay any mind to what he says, and of all the actions he is likely to undertake, sending out Israel is *not* one of them. This king of Egypt is presented as a no-nonsense ruler, completely sure of himself, whose time is being wasted.

The first result of Pharaoh's decisive and unyielding response, however, is the demoralization of Moses and Aaron. Whatever the original reference of v 3, if in fact the verse is older than its present context, it has been marvelously woven into this sequence as the chagrined reply of the erstwhile deliverer and his assistant. They are outclassed and overwhelmed by this Pharaoh: since he knows no Yahweh, they now refer to "the God of the Hebrews" (see *Comment* on 1:19); apologetically they explain that the command to pilgrimage was quite unexpected; they return to the three-day limit for the trip; and they plead fear of Yahweh's reprisal, which would of course mean a loss to Pharaoh greater than the loss of three days' work. There is no hint now of any command; their confidence is gone, and they are begging favors from a powerful superior.

4–5 The section continues in much the same vein. Pharaoh accuses Moses and Aaron of "distracting" the people, causing them to neglect duties that he admits are "heavy," even "oppressive," but which they must "get on with." He refers to the people as עם הארץ, literally, "the people of the land." This phrase is variously interpreted as referring to farmers (Zeitlin, *JQR* 23 [1932] 45–46, "in the early tannaitic literature"), the free occupants of a specific territory (Rost, *Das Kleine Credo,* 89–93), "the owners of the land, . . . the leaders, the representatives of the people" (Daiches, *JTS* 30 [1929] 245). In the Judaism of the first century A.D. and following, the phrase was used to refer with disdain to the uneducated, the "common" people (by an evolution traced in detail by Zeitlin), and that usage has often affected its translation in the OT.

The fact that only some such translation makes sense in the text of v 5, where the עַם הָאָרֶץ can hardly be "landed gentry," has led many commentators (so Beer, 38; Childs, 105) to prefer the reading of the Samaritan Pentateuch, which inserts מִן "from" before עַם "people," thus making the Egyptians the people of the land, whom the Israelites have come to outnumber (literally, are "more numerous than"). Such a reading, however, is misleading—the Israelites, despite their miraculous multiplication, are not likely to have outnumbered their Egyptian oppressors (see *Comment* on 1:8). Nor is this reading necessary. The Pharaoh's speech reeks with sarcasm, and עַם הָאָרֶץ has been given to him here just as "Hebrew women" has in 1:16, as a phrase of derision. Thus MT should be taken as correct, and עַם הָאָרֶץ should be read in the sense it came to have, a sense always implicit, "land-people, working people," and so, in the translation above, "peasants."

6–9 The severity of the Pharaoh's take-charge position is further emphasized by his immediate order down through the ranks to the sons of Israel at the bottom of all the echelons of command. They must have too much time on their hands if they can plan a religious pilgrimage; that time can be removed by an expansion of their responsibility. This logic is consonant with that of 1:9–11, whereby Pharaoh sought to control the Israelite birth rate by giving the Israelites a wearying work load. Of course, neither plan can succeed, for the longing for a pilgrimage, like the astonishing increase in population, is from Yahweh.

The expansion of responsibility involves the denial to the Israelites of an important raw material of their Egyptian brick-making, תֶבֶן "chopped straw." This is not to be taken to mean, as it sometimes has been (see the survey of Nims, *BA* 13 [1950] 22–23), that they were now to make bricks without any straw. As the text plainly says, this order increased the heavy work of Israel: they were strictly commanded to make the usual daily quota of bricks, while gathering for themselves the straw necessary to their task wherever they could find it (vv 7 and 10–11). This essential ingredient had previously been provided them. The people's obedience of this command makes plain what an additional burden it was: they "scattered" over "the whole of the land of Egypt" in their search, and they had to make do not with תֶבֶן, the chopped straw prepared for the purpose of brick-making (see Nims, *BA* 13 [1950] 24–27), but with קַשׁ, trashy stubble blown about by the wind (v 12).

10–14 The bureaucracy by which Pharaoh's order is carried out is realistic both in organization and operation. Egyptian נֹגְשִׂים "work-bosses" and Hebrew שֹׁטְרִים "section-leaders" receive the order (vv 6–9) and pass it along to the people (vv 10–11). The work-bosses press the section-leaders, who press their people. And when the quota is not met, these section-leaders, given their authority by the Egyptian work-bosses, are whipped and interrogated (v 14). Thus was set in motion the protest which worked its way back through this bureaucratic sieve to Pharaoh, the account of which continues this chapter.

Explanation

The first confrontation with the Pharaoh of Egypt is not to be understood in isolation from 7:8–12:36, the sequence of Yahweh's ten mighty and proving acts to which it is introductory. This account is wonderfully written to depict a powerful Pharaoh impervious to any human challenge or plea and immovable by any force save one.

Moses and Aaron are no match for him. Their obvious embarrassment, so skillfully suggested by the contrast between vv 1 and 3, and by vv 20–23 to come, is a part of the design of the passage. The bureaucracy, at both its Egyptian and its Hebrew levels, is totally submissive to him, whatever his unreasonable commands. This fact is cleverly presented by the rapid passing of the command and the immediate attempt to fulfill it, without protest, until it proves impossible.

And as for Yahweh, this Pharaoh knows nothing about him and does not care to. As the chapter unfolds, we find ourselves longing to see such a ruler educated from such ignorance and humbled in the process. And thus is the writer's point made, his purpose achieved. This Pharaoh, so unreasonable with men and so stingy with straw, is about to be shown up before Yahweh as no more than a man of straw.

The First Confrontation with Pharaoh: Israel's Protest (5:15–6:1)

Bibliography

Erman, A. *Life in Ancient Egypt.* London: Macmillan and Co., 1894. **McCarthy, D. J.** "Plagues and Sea of Reeds: Exodus 5–14." *JBL* 85 (1966) 137–58.

Translation

[15] *So the section-leaders of the sons of Israel came and protested* [a] *to Pharaoh, saying, "Why have you thus punished* [b] *your servants?* [16] *Straw is not provided your servants, yet, 'Bricks!' they say to us; 'make them!' And just look:* [a] *your servants are whipped,* [b] *but you and your people are at fault."* [c] [17] *Pharaoh* [a] *shouted,* [b] *"Lazy* [c] *is what you are, lazy you are indeed, saying, 'Let us go; let us offer sacrifice to Yahweh,'* [d] [18] *Now go get to work! Straw will not be provided you, and you will produce* [a] *the full measure* [b] *of bricks!"*

[19] *Now the section-leaders of the sons of Israel saw themselves in a difficult spot,* [a] *having to say,* [b] *"You are not to reduce* [c] *your daily output of bricks."* [20] *Thus they hurried to confront* [a] *Moses and Aaron, who stood waiting to meet them as they left their encounter with Pharaoh.* [21] *They said to them, "Yahweh consider you both and make a judgment, inasmuch as you have made us disgusting* [a] *in the opinion of Pharaoh and in the opinion of his advisers,* [b] *giving them a good excuse to massacre us."* [c]

²² *So Moses turned on* ᵃ *Yahweh and said, "Lord,* ᵇ *why have you done harm to this people? Why have you sent me here for this?* ᶜ ²³ *From the minute I came to Pharaoh to deliver your message,* ᵃ *he has hurt* ᵇ *this people, and you have not even begun to rescue your people!"* ⁶:¹ *But Yahweh answered Moses, "You are now* ᵃ *about to see what I am doing* ᵇ *to Pharaoh, because with a forceful hand, he will send them forth, and with a forceful hand,* ᶜ *he will drive them from his land."*

Notes

15.a. Lit., "cried out, made a clamor," צעק.

15.b. תעשה כה "done thus," which in the context = "punished."

16.a. והנה "and behold."

16.b. See n. 5:14.a.

16.c. MT has וְחָטָאת עַמֶּךָ, "and you sin (or are at fault), your people," reading the verb form as qal pf, 2d pers fem sg. The pointing וְחָטָאתָ) would give a 2d pers masc form, more appropriate to the masc עַ, but still difficult, because of the 2d pers. LXX and Syr take the verb thus, reading Pharaoh as its subj, and "your people" as its obj, to give ἀδικήσεις οὖν τὸν λαόν σου "you are harming [sinning against] your people" (by depriving them of needed bricks). Cassuto (71) suggests amusingly that the section-leaders *meant* וְחָטָאתָ אַתָּה ("*you* are to blame" for the shortfall of bricks), but lost their nerve, swallowed the end of the verb, and added עַמֶּךָ "your people." The text as it stands does not make sense in a literal reading, but the sense of the section-leaders' complaint is reasonably clear: *they* have had to take the punishment for a shortfall in brick production which is the fault of Pharaoh and those who have carried out his order to end the supply of chopped straw and to require the Israelite brickmakers to provide their own straw. I propose above therefore the reading וְחָטָאתָ וְעַמֶּךָ "but you and your people are at fault."

17.a. "Pharaoh" is added, for clarity. So Syr, which reads "Thus Pharaoh said to them, ..."

17.b. The verb is אמר "say," thus, lit., "said, replied." The reading above is an attempt to render this verb with special *waw* in the context of what the Pharaoh could only consider an insolent protest.

17.c. The emphasis on נרפים "idle, lazy," in its two occurrences in this verse is shown by its position at the first of both the clauses in which it occurs.

17.d. LXX, Tg Ps-J add τῷ θεῷ ἡμῶν "our God."

18.a. Lit., "give," נתן.

18.b תכן "measure," by comparison with the related term מתכנת "quota," of v 8 (both words are derived from תכן "measure, regulate"), and with חק "assigned limit," of v 14.

19.a. ברע, lit., "in evil, calamity, harm's way."

19.b לֵאמֹר—this qal inf constr means lit. "to say." It is often taken to refer to what was said to the section-leaders by Pharaoh and his advisers (so NEB, JB). Though the absence of any pronouns makes the infinitive ambiguous, it is certainly not a passive inf, "were told." It is better therefore to read the inf as referring to what the section-leaders must now say to their own people. This is what has put them into a difficult spot.

19.c. SamPent reads יגרע to give "your daily output is not to be reduced ."

20.a. The verb is פגע "encounter, fall upon, attack," here with special *waw* and followed by the sign of the def obj before Moses and before Aaron.

21.a. Lit., "made our fragrance stink," so, "made us *persona non grata."*

21.b. עֲבָדָיו, lit., "his servants," the same term the section-leaders use of themselves in vv 15–17, but here obviously in a different sense.

21.c. Lit., "to give a sword into their hand to kill us." SamPent has ידו "his hand."

22.a. Or turned אֶל "toward." For אֶל as "against" or "upon," see BDB, 40 ¶ 4, and the references cited there.

22.b. LXXᴮ adds δέομαι "I pray" after "Lord."

22.c. Or, "Why now have you sent me here?" See BDB, 261 ¶ e.

23.a. Lit., "to speak (piel of דבר) in your name (or authority—שם)."

23.b. Hiph of רעע "cause harm to, do injury, hurt."

6:1.a. SamPent reads this עתה "now" as אתה "you" to give an emphasis on Moses as the one who is to see. The reading of MT is preferable, however, and better suited to the context.

1.b. אֶעֱשֶׂה, qal impf of עשׂה, "do, make," generally translated here as a future, is better read as present. The process of defeating the Pharaoh and proving Yahweh's Presence is already well under way.

1.c. LXX reads rather ἐν βραχίονι ὑψηλῷ "with arm raised up."

Form/Structure/Setting

5:15–6:1 form the conclusion to the section introducing the proof-of-Presence sequence of 7:8–12:36. For a discussion of the form of this introductory unit, see *Form/Structure/Setting* on 5:1–14.

Comment

15 The "section-leaders of the sons of Israel," themselves apparently Israelites given minor supervisory responsibility by the Egyptian work-bosses (Erman, *Life in Ancient Egypt*, 123–29), found themselves caught in the middle between the impossible orders given them by their Egyptian superiors and their own people who were unable to keep up their brick quotas and gather the straw necessary to their task. When they were whipped for a failure they had no power to prevent and interrogated about a command they knew could not be kept, they felt unjustly handled, and they took their protest straight to Pharaoh himself.

The bluntness of their approach to Pharaoh is a parallel to the bold first approach of Moses and Aaron, and a continuation of the brilliant presentation of this narrative. It is pointless to debate whether such minor officials could have had access to a Pharaoh, and whether, with such access, they would so have addressed so august a leader (McNeile, 32; Hyatt, 91). Such considerations miss entirely the point of this carefully composed introduction, which has to do with the kind of king the Pharaoh is, as a device for declaring the kind of God Yahweh is. The purpose of this account is to present an impossible Pharaoh, a powerful and absolute ruler against whom no man can stand, whose will no group of men can successfully deny. No men, and no group of men can resist him—but Yahweh?

16–18 When the section-leaders recount their plight and present their unquestionably just case, topped off with the frank assertion that the real reason for the disruption of the brick supply is the order of Pharaoh and the enforcement of that order by the work-bosses, the Pharaoh will not brook their complaints. He accuses them of laziness (as he accused the people in v 8; the same word, נרפים "lazy," is used three times in vv 8 and 17), and he reaffirms his order; the usual number of bricks must be produced, without an on-site supply of straw (v 18). Pharaoh will hear them no further, and the section leaders withdraw in frustration and dismay, as did Moses and Aaron.

19–21 It is at this point, indeed, that the two approaches of the first confrontation of Pharaoh are drawn together, for the demoralized section-leaders seek out the demoralized Moses and Aaron. There is little basis for the conjecture that two separate confrontations are apparent in this narrative, or that the Moses/Aaron confrontation with which the chapter begins is super-imposed upon a real confrontation led by representatives of the sons of Israel (Hyatt, 89, and especially Noth, 52–56). The sequence as it now stands clearly presents the two approaches as successive levels of a single request and its issue, as the words and reactions of the involved parties and then above all the rendezvous of the section-leaders with Moses and Aaron (vv 20–21) show.

The fact that Moses and Aaron did not return to Pharaoh to present the complaint caused by their original request is a further indication of the severity of their failure, an indication augmented by the section-leaders' rush to confront Moses and Aaron after their own rebuff by Pharaoh. The obvious intent of the section-leaders' visit to Pharaoh was to undo the harm brought upon Israel, and themselves in particular, by the intercession of Moses and Aaron. Their first move following their own failure, quite naturally, was to turn on Moses and Aaron, who are reported to be waiting to meet them, no doubt with some hopes concerning their mission.

If there were such hopes, they were dashed immediately and conclusively. The section-leaders fix the blame for their plight, and their people's, squarely on Moses and Aaron, and they ask Yahweh himself to render upon them a studied judgment for having brought them from a difficult but secure enslavement to a situation in which their very lives are in jeopardy (v 21). This complaint, though its reference to "massacre," given the Pharaoh's words and his own best interest, appears to be a dramatic exaggeration, unites the failure of the two levels of approach to Pharaoh and recalls Moses' complaints and questions at the flaming bush, especially the question about Yahweh's ability or authority to carry out his claim (see 3:11–4:17, and the treatment of those verses above).

22–23 Thus did Moses "turn on" Yahweh, with words that reflect not only the section-leaders' disappointment and frustration, but his own. As Moses has been accused of bringing the sons of Israel into still deeper difficulty, so now he accuses Yahweh, who had prompted him to confront the Pharaoh and who had even told him what to say (3:18 and 5:1), of doing harm (v 22) instead of the good he had promised. Moses' mission, from his first effort to fulfill it, had provoked the Pharaoh to hurt the people, and the promised exodus is farther than ever from reality. Not only has Yahweh not begun it, he has made its very possibility more remote than ever (v 23).

There is in these words of Moses a subtle shift of the responsibility for the new trouble of Israel. Even the section-leaders, whose suffering has been greatest, blame Moses and Aaron for their new troubles: "*you* (plural, הבאשתם) have made us disgusting" (v 21). But Moses blames Yahweh: "*you* have done harm, *you* have sent, following *your* message Pharaoh has hurt, *you* have not even begun to rescue" (נצל, hiphil infinitive absolute plus hiphil perfect, second masculine singular). In this masterful way, we are brought to the point of what seems to be a narrative of the complete and abject failure of Yahweh's plan to rescue his firstborn, Israel, from the bondage of Egypt.

6:1 The whole of chap. 5 must be read indeed in the light of the response of Yahweh to Moses' fearful and angry protest. What Moses thinks has not begun has indeed begun, as he is now soon to see; Yahweh's work on Pharaoh is already under way. It began with the confrontation by Moses himself, to which Pharaoh responded with such sarcastic arrogance. What Yahweh is doing to Pharaoh will be all the more plain to Moses and to Israel because of the "complete" and "final" refusal Pharaoh has made to Yahweh's command, delivered by Moses.

What has happened, though Moses has not realized it, is of Yahweh. The Pharaoh's recalcitrance is but one ingredient in Yahweh's plan, and one which he will amplify for his purpose (4:21; 7:3–5; 9:12; 10:1–2; and so on). What Yahweh is doing to Pharaoh will cause him, in due course, to reverse his refusal, as his ignorance about Yahweh will have been remedied. Though he has declared he will not send Israel out (5:2), he will do so, with a hand of force; in fact, he will drive them forth with that hand of force (cf. 3:19–20).

6:1, the final verse of the narrative that begins at 5:1, thus explains the sequence that has preceded it and connects it, as the prologue it is (McCarthy, *JBL* 85 [1966] 137–42), to the proof-of-Presence sequence by which Yahweh demonstrates his Presence in 7:8–12:36. What has appeared to Moses and the Israelites as a serious deterioration of an already bad situation has been instead a careful preparation for what is to come, an anticipation of the hardening-of-the-mind-of-Pharaoh motif, against which the all-controlling and powerful Presence of Yahweh will be seen in dramatic relief. The dispirited Moses *and* the people of Israel, not to mention the Pharaoh of Egypt and all his people, are now about to see what Yahweh is doing already.

Explanation

The first confrontation with Pharaoh, in both of its levels (5:1–14, Moses and Aaron; 5:15–21, the section-leaders of Israel), is shown by the interpretation given it in 5:22–6:1 to be an introduction of what is to come. In the present arrangement of the text of Exodus, the flow of the proof-of-Presence sequence is interrupted by the insertion of 6:2–7:7, a parallel account of the call and commission of Moses. At an earlier stage in the evolution of the Book of Exodus, however, the prologue now contained in 5:1—6:1 must have been followed immediately by the narrative of the sequential mighty acts proving Yahweh's Presence, a narrative intensified by the vacillation of an increasingly weakening Pharaoh, whose mind must finally be "hardened" by Yahweh so that the "proofs" may be carried through to their climax.

The manner in which the major themes of 7:8–12:36 are all anticipated in this prologue, and indeed the presentation in it of the dramatic structure of the proof-of-Presence sequence, a commanding Yahweh and a resisting Pharaoh, make the connection between the two plain. And equally clear in 5:1–6:1 is the entirely subsidiary role Moses always has in relation to Yahweh. Here, Moses and Aaron fail to accomplish what they had hoped to bring about; at the end, the experience threatens to undo Moses until Yahweh assures him that he is already at work. So also in 7:8–12:36: whatever Moses says or does, and Aaron too for that matter, the source of every accomplishment and the authority for every word that counts is always and only Yahweh.

From the outset, the essential purpose of this narrative is to make plain the real and active Presence of the incomparable Yahweh. In the lengthy sequence begun by 5:1–6:1, the medium of this declaration is a contest between Yahweh and the ruler of the nation supreme in the Near East, the nation that holds Yahweh's special people in a laborious bondage. This contest becomes the fundamental didactic device of Part One of the Book of Exodus, Israel in Egypt (1:1–13:16).

The Covenant Promise to the Fathers and Yahweh's Rescue (6:2–13)

Bibliography

Albright, W. F. *From the Stone Age to Christianity.* 2d ed. Garden City, NJ: Doubleday and Co., 1957. 246–49. **Cross, F. M.** "Yahweh and the God of the Patriarchs." *HTR* 55 (1962) 225–59. **Elliger, K.** "Ich bin der Herr—euer Gott." *Kleine Schriften zum Alten Testament.* TBÜ 32. Munich: Chr. Kaiser Verlag, 1966. 211–31. **Johnson, A. R.** "The Primary Meaning of אל." *Congress Volume: Copenhagen, 1953.* VTSup 1. Leiden: E. J. Brill, 1953. 67–77. **Labuschagne, C. J.** "The Emphasizing Particle *Gam* and Its Connotations." *Studia Biblica et Semitica.* Wageningen: H. Veenman and Sons, 1966. 193–203. **Lehmann, M. R.** "Biblical Oaths." *ZAW* 81 (1969) 74–92. **Lohfink, N.** "Die priesterschriftliche Abwertung der Tradition von der Offenbarung des Jahwenamens an Mose." *Bib* 49 (1968) 1–8. **MacLaurin, E. C. B.** "Shaddai." *AbrN* 3 (1961–1962) 99–118. **McCarthy, D. J.** "Plagues and Sea of Reeds: Exodus 5–14." *JBL* 85 (1966) 137–58. **Mowinckel, S.** "The Name of the God of Moses." *HUCA* 32 (1961) 121–33. **Ogden, G. S.** "Moses and Cyrus: Literary Affinities between the Priestly Presentation of Moses in Exodus vi–viii and the Cyrus Song in Isaiah xliv 24–xlv 13." *VT* 28 (1978) 195–203. **Oliva, M.** "Revelación del nombre de Yahveh en la 'Historia sacerdotal': Ex 6, 2–8." *Bib* 52 (1971) 1–19. **Rendtorff, R.** "The concept of Revelation." *Revelation as History.* Ed. W. Pannenberg. New York: Macmillan, 1968. 25–53. **Sandmel, S.** "Genesis 4:26b." *HUCA* 32 (1961) 19–29. **Ska, J.-L.** "La place d'Ex 6:2–8 dans la narration de l'exode." *ZAW* 94 (1982) 530–48. **Stamm, J. J.** *Erlösen und Vergeben im Alten Testament.* Bern: A. Francke Verlag, 1940. **Wilson, R. D.** "Critical Note on Exodus VI 3." *PTR* 22 (1924) 108–19. **Wimmer, J. F.** "Tradition Reinterpreted in Ex 6, 2–7, 7." *Augustinianum* 7 (1967) 407–18. **Zimmerli, W.** "Ich bin Jahwe"; "Erkenntnis Gottes nach dem Buche Ezechiel"; "Das Wort des göttlichen Selbsterweises (Erweiswort), eine prophetische Gattung." *Gottes Offenbarung.* Munich: Kaiser Verlag, 1968. 11–40, 41–119, 120–32. Also in *I am Yahweh.* Atlanta: John Knox Press, 1982. 1–28, 29–98, 99–110.

Translation

²*Then did God* ᵃ *speak to Moses, saying to him, "I am Yahweh.* ³*I appeared to Abraham, to Isaac, and to Jacob as* ᵃ *'God All-Powerful,'* ᵇ *and my name Yahweh I did not reveal* ᶜ *to them.* ⁴*Indeed, I set up my covenant with them, to give to them the land of Canaan, the land of their wanderings, in which they dwelled as foreigners.* ᵃ
⁵*"I have myself* ᵃ *heard the groaning of the sons of Israel whom the Egyptians*

have forced into slavery, and so I have remembered my covenant. ⁶ Therefore ^a say *to the sons of Israel, 'I am Yahweh. And I will bring you forth from the crush* ^b *of the oppressive labors of the Egyptians, and I will snatch you forth from slavery to them,* ^c *and I will act as your rescuing kinsman,* ^d *with arm stretched out and with great deeds of vindication.* ^e ⁷ I will single you out ^a *as a people for myself, and I will be for you God, and you will know by experience* ^b *that I am Yahweh your God, the one who has brought you forth from the crush of the oppressive labors of the Egyptians.* ⁸ I will bring you to the land which I swore with hand raised up to *give to Abraham, to Isaac, and to Jacob. I will give it to you as an inherited possession.* ^a *I am Yahweh.' '"*

⁹ *So Moses repeated these words* ^a *to the sons of Israel. But they paid no attention to Moses, because they were dispirited and worn out by the severity of their slavery.* ^b

¹⁰ *Again Yahweh spoke to Moses, to say.* ¹¹ *"Go, speak to Pharaoh, king of Egypt, and he will send forth* ^a *the sons of Israel from his land."* ¹² *So Moses spoke to Yahweh's face,* ^a *saying, "Now look* ^b—*the sons of Israel paid no attention to me. How is Pharaoh going to pay attention to me, especially with my stumbling speech?"* ^c ¹³ *Thus Yahweh spoke to Moses and to Aaron, and ordered them, concerning the sons of Israel and* ^a *concerning Pharaoh, king of Egypt, to bring forth the sons of Israel from the land of Egypt.*

Notes

2.a. A number of versions, including SamPent and Vg, read "Yahweh" here. A Cairo Geniza fragment has "Elohim" twice.

3.a. MT has בְּ, lit., "in," in this phrase = "in the person of."

3.b. For אֵל שַׁדָּי "God All-Powerful," see Gen 17:1; 28:3; 35:11; 48:3, all verses usually assigned to P; and 43:14, usually assigned to J. LXX reads θεὸς ὢν αὐτῶν "as their God."

3.c. On niph of ידע "know," see *Comment* on 1:8. LXX has οὐκ ἐδήλωσα, Vg *non indicavi* which mean "I did not disclose."

4.a. גּור "sojourn, dwell," as an outsider, a transient, even for a long period of time.

5.a. This emphasis is shown by the use of the independent pers pronoun אֲנִי "I" plus the 1st pers common form of שׁמע "hear," and also by the use of גַּ "also," introductory particle the "primary function" of which is emphasis (so Labuschagne, *Studia Biblica* 194; BDB, 169).

6.a. LXX has βάδιζε εἰπὸν "Go, speak. . . ."

6.b. Lit., "from underneath."

6.c. "From their slavery."

6.d. The verb is גאל "redeem," which as Johnson (VTSup 1:76) and others (Ringgren, *TDOT* 2:351–52, 354) have shown, involves protection, redemption by one obligated through relational ties.

6.e. See n. 7:4.c and *Comment* on 7:4.

7.a. לקח "take, receive, take in marriage, select, choose," followed by אתכם "you," dir obj; and לי לעם "for myself for a people."

7.b. Qal of ידע "know."

8.a. מורשה, from ירשׁ, "take possession of, inherit, claim as a right."

9.a. Lit., "so Moses spoke thus" with special *waw.*

9.b. Lit., "they did not hear Moses from [on account of] shortness of spirit and from [on account of] hard slavery."

11.a וַיְשַׁלַּח , a 3d masc sg piel impf of שׁלח "send" with a conjunctive *waw,* generally translated as a subordinate clause, and often as an inf (so RSV, NEB); here lit. as a coordinate result clause, a translation affirmed by the following verse.

12.a. So lit., לִפְנֵי יהוה "to Yahweh's face" can also mean "in Yahweh's Presence," but it surely signifies more than RSV's oversimple "to the LORD."

12.b. הן "behold."

12.c. "And I, uncircumcised of lips."

13.a. LXX omits "concerning . . . and," to read just "ordered them concerning Pharaoh. . . ."

Form/Structure/Setting

The sequence at hand is the first part of an extended section of material (6:2–7:13) widely acknowledged to have come from the Priestly source. Indeed, it is the first consequential section from this source to this point in the text of the Book of Exodus, and it is itself a composite, a block of narrative presenting several episodes, into which an extended genealogy (6:14–25) has been set with some care.

Apart from the narrative of the ten mighty acts in 7:8–12:36, itself the most carefully wrought composite sequence in the Book of Exodus, the material from the Priestly source stands for the most part in extended sections like this one (see especially chaps. 25–31 and 35–40). This fact and the generally obvious manner in which the Priestly material is inserted elsewhere, along with the assumption from the days of Wellhausen forward that P is the latest and last of the sources, have led source-critics to suppose an assembly of pentateuchal, or more recently, tetrateuchal books by Priestly hands.

Such a supposition is, however, a considerable simplification of a very complex process. There is in the Priestly material both early and late content, narrative and cultic and legal literature from virtually the full range of the literary history of the OT. The present sequence alone is sufficient to indicate that the Priestly material is in itself composite in nature, by the manner in which the genealogical list of 6:14–25 is inserted into a narrative which is then adjusted because of the insertion. Of the three tetrateuchal "sources," J, E, and P, P is much less a "source" than it is a collection of material from a wide range of periods, reflecting a number of continuing priestly concerns.

The manner in which this Priestly material appears in the final form of the text of Exodus suggests not so much a "source" assembled late in the growth of the material incorporated into the book as it does a parallel collection of materials. Such a collection was probably begun as early as the collections of J and E, was extant and growing alongside them and then beyond them, and was incorporated into the tetrateuchal books more obviously and more *en bloc* form as a parallel account, rather than as a supplementary account. There was thus no attempt by the redactor(s) who put together the sequence of Exodus to reconcile differences in detail any more than there was an attempt to homogenize style and vocabulary. The unity of these separate layers of material was, like the purpose that brought them together, theological. And the key to an understanding of their message and the manner in which they work lies finally not in literary approaches, as helpful to the process of study as they may be, but in the theological impulse of the text in the form in which we have it, not in a form in which we can only suppose that text to have existed.

Exod 6:2–7:13 is the block of Priestly material concerned with (1) the revelation of the special name "Yahweh" (6:2–4); (2) the covenant-promise to the fathers being brought to fulfillment in the exodus (6:5–8); (3) the oppression of Israel (6:5–6, 9); (4) the call of Moses and Aaron (6:6a, 10–13, 26–27); (5) the genealogy of Moses and Aaron (6:14–25); (6) the anticipation of the sequence of the mighty acts and the hardening-of-the-mind motif (6:28–7:7); and (7) a prologue to the mighty acts in the rod and snake miracle (7:8–13), a prologue that belongs more to what follows than to what precedes it, but is by origin a part of the Priestly collection. Indeed McCarthy (*JBL* 85 [1966] 142–56) has argued cleverly, if not entirely convincingly, that 7:8–10:27 forms with 5:1–6:1 and 14:1–31 a composite literary complex separate from 6:2–7:7, 11:1–12:42, each with "its own characteristic phrases and its own conception of the why and the how of the exodus."

6:2–13 must be seen as an integral part of one of three large sections of Priestly material in the Book of Exodus, and as the beginning of a narrative recording a parallel version of the revelation of the tetragrammaton, and of the call and commission of Moses and Aaron. It is not an account that can be said to supplement the account of Exod 3, 4, and 5. For one thing, it is far briefer, and for another, it reflects an entirely different emphasis. The theophany, so dramatic an element of that account, is altogether missing here, as is an explanation of the special name "Yahweh." The long dialogue between Yahweh and Moses, the important vehicle of Yahweh's revelation in that account, is compressed to the barest minimum here, and there is no reference at all to any signs of Moses' authority. And Aaron, so clearly an addition to the earlier narrative, is more carefully integrated here, especially by the addition of the genealogy appended to this section and interrupting the narrative sequence. Indeed, this interruption necessitates the inclusion of a recapitulation (vv 26–30) of the narrative preceding the genealogy (especially vv 10–13).

The form of this section is dictated in part by the larger sequence of which it is the initial component and in part by its purpose. It was not composed to record a second call and commission of Moses, dwelling now in Egypt and depressed by the failure of the first confrontation of the Pharaoh. Ska (*ZAW* 94 [1982] 537–48) has proposed that 6:2–8 presents a new start for God's liberation of Israel after Moses' initial failure. There is no basis for the often repeated claim of commentators (e.g., Beer, 43, who refers to "the new theophany"; Noth, 59; Hyatt, 93) that this call took place in Egypt, in contrast to an earlier one in Midian or at Sinai. The reference in v 28 is too far removed from the narrative of vv 2–13 to be of help, and the context of chap. 5 does not necessarily apply to this narrative.

No location is specified for the events of vv 2–13, as details of place, time, and sequence are irrelevant to this writer's purpose. He is concerned to identify Yahweh as the God of the patriarchal fathers, just as 3:6, 13, 15, 16 do, and to make plain that the covenant made with those fathers is not only still in effect, but about to be brought to fulfillment (cf. Ska, *ZAW* 94 [1982] 544). His statement of the authority of this covenant is the self-proclamatory formula, "I am Yahweh," repeated four times (vv 2, 6, 7, 8) in this passage. And his central concern is to link that covenant to the exodus about to take place. Nothing that does not serve this purpose, in the necessary context of the oppression in Egypt, is included. Thus the narrative is pared to its barest essentials.

Comment

There is no inference in vv 2–13 of a theophany. We are told only that Yahweh spoke to Moses twice (vv 2–8, 10–11) to Moses and Aaron once (v 13), and that Moses spoke with some agitation to Yahweh once (v 12).

2 It is not absolutely clear that the self-declaration אני יהוה "I am Yahweh" in v 2 is the initial revelation of the tetragrammaton. V 3 indicates only that the special name was not revealed to the fathers. As from this point forward the Priestly materials take great care to use the name "Yahweh," however, the general assumption is that this passage contains the report in the Priestly materials of the revelation of the tetragrammaton. The most that can be said with any certainty is that this sequence is as near to such a report as we get in the Priestly materials of the tetrateuch.

This ambiguity may however be intentional. More important to the purpose of this section, at least as it stands now, is the presentation of the autokerygmatic formula, אני יהוה "I am Yahweh," in particular because of its close connection with the covenant. Both the revelation and the explanation of the special name Yahweh were reported in chap. 3. The compiler of the Book of Exodus was here concerned, therefore, with something else; it is even possible that he may have omitted a fuller account in the Priestly materials of the moment of revelation, so carefully presented in the JE amalgam of chap. 3.

Both Zimmerli and Elliger have made special studies of the phrase אני יהוה in its various forms. Zimmerli (*Gottes Offenbarung*, 14) calls it a "self-presentation formula," and even goes so far as to say (20), "All that Yahweh had to say and to declare to his people appears to be a development of the fundamental assertion: 'I am Yahweh.'" He contends, indeed, that the usage of this formula in this passage, in the Priestly literature elsewhere in the Pentateuch, and in the Holiness Code suggests that the formula may be primarily a Priestly formula (12–24).

Elliger (*Kleine Schriften*, 213–16) speaks of אני יהוה as a "primary formula," a "self-declaratory formula," a "holiness or sublimeness formula" to which אלהיך "your God" may be added to create a "saving-history or grace-formula," the first, Law (*Gesetz*), the second, Gospel (*Evangelium*), as for example in Lev 18–20. He sees both "self-attestation formulas" as connected in a special way with Yahweh's deeds of power on behalf of his people, whether in deeds of power against non-Israelites, or in acts of deliverance or even punishment for those Yahweh has claimed as his own (227–31). The range of use of these formulas in the OT suggests to Elliger that the fundamental meaning common to all the occurrences was accented in different ways in varied contexts and that finally it is not possible to trace the formula to a single point of origin (230–31, and especially n. 59, containing Elliger's reaction to Zimmerli's article "Ich bin Jahwe").

Zimmerli has also analyzed in some detail the occurrences of the אני יהוה formula in what he calls the "proof-saying" (*Gottes Offenbarung*, 120–32), particularly in the repeated occurrences of the "recognition-formula," "that they (you) may know that I am Yahweh" in the Book of Ezekiel (42–54), and he has concluded that Yahweh's deeds are held up as proof that he is and does what is claimed in his special name.

The אֲנִי יהוה "I am Yahweh" formula occurs outside chap. 6 at a number of points in Exodus; note for example: 7:15, 17; 8:18 [22]; 10:2; 12:12; 14:4, 18; 15:26; 16:12; 20:2; 29:46; 31:3. In the prologue to the ten commandments (20:2) it serves as a kind of justifying reason for the statement of the commandments and for obedience to them. And it is in the context of that usage that the four occurrences of the formula here (vv 2, 6, 7, 8) may best be understood. The special name יהוה "Yahweh" is defined, in its only explanation in the entire OT, as an assertion of the reality of the active existence of Israel's God (3:13–14). אֲנִי יהוה is above all a confession of authority, the authority of the real and effective Presence of Yahweh who rescues, sustains, calls, and, on the basis of all that, expects a positive response from humankind. As such, the formula is a basic element in the theological rhetoric connected with the special name "Yahweh," which is a confession in and of itself.

The revelation of Exod 6:2–13, therefore, is not the revelation of a theophany, either in Egypt or at Sinai. Nor is it, necessarily, even a first revelation of the tetragrammaton, the presentation of what Mowinckel (*HUCA* 32 [1961] 121) called "an unhistorical theological theory of P's." The keys to this passage are precisely (1) the fourfold occurrence of the autoconfessional phrase אֲנִי יהוה; (2) the repeated references to the covenant relationship (vv 4, 5, 6, 7, 8); and (3) the four references to the forthcoming mighty acts in Israel's behalf, including above all the exodus itself (vv 6, 7, 11, 13, referred to in retrospect in the parallel of 20:2; cf. Wimmer, *Augustinianum* 7 [1967] 414–16).

The redactor who set these lines into their present context was not concerned with theophany. Indeed he was only a little concerned with the call of Moses and either less concerned, or not concerned at all, with the moment of the revelation of the tetragrammaton. His interest was in a special relationship, as old as the patriarchal fathers, as real as Israel's need in bondage, whether Egyptian or Assyrian or Babylonian or, for that matter, even Greek or Roman bondage, and as guaranteed as Israel's response to the active Presence of God could make it. The authority for the relationship, first, last, from past through future, was Yahweh who Is. The demonstration of that authority was his mighty deeds, hinted at here, and shortly to be described in detail. And the purpose of the relationship lay ahead, in a promised land in which Israel would come to be something special in the purpose of the God who Is, Yahweh.

3 The reference to אֶל שַׁדָּי *El Shaddai* "God All-Powerful" as a name of God used by the patriarchal fathers is continuous with the narrative of Gen 17, also generally acknowledged as a product of the Priestly circle (Gunkel, *Genesis*, 264–67; von Rad, *Genesis*, rev. ed., OTL [Philadelphia: Westminster, 1972], 197–99), and, like the passage at hand, a sequence intimately connected with the covenant between Yahweh/*El Shaddai* and Israel. In both passages, *El Shaddai* is given as a name by which Yahweh was known to Abraham, Isaac, and Jacob.

The biblical occurrences of the name *Shaddai* have been carefully surveyed by MacLaurin (*AbrN* 3 [1961–62] 99–112), who has concluded that "Shaddai's primary character is one of power and military prowess" (103), and that for "the Hebrews," his "predominant characteristic" was his covenant-making with men (102). The meaning of the name is still uncertain, despite considerable work. The theory of Albright (*Stone Age*, 246–49) that the name has to do with mountain(s), to which Cross (*HTR* 55 [1962] 244–50) has added that the mountain so referred to is "the cosmic mountain, the *Weltberg*," has been widely accepted. Equally convincing, however, is the connection of the name with power and strength (cf. MacLaurin, *AbrN* 3 [1961–62] 108–15; Wilson, *PTR* 22 [1924] 113–14).

What is of greater import here is the identification of Yahweh with the God of the patriarchs, whatever the name or names by which they called him, and the connection of the covenant made with them in the rescue and resettlement of their descendants, which is about to take place. Lohfink (*Bib* 49 [1968] 1–8) has argued that the roots of the covenant lie in the traditions about a covenant with Abraham, and that the Priestly writers sought to deemphasize the tradition of the revelation of the name of Yahweh to Moses as the crucial covenantal foundation. Too much has been made (Rendtorff, *Revelation as History*, 29–33) of P's unveiling of the tetragrammaton here as something new, the opening of a higher stage in Israel's theological development, in part because of too strict a pressing of parallels between this sequence on Moses' call and commission and the earlier one in chaps. 3 and 4. There is not here, as in that passage (*pace* Childs, 114–16) a discussion of the meaning of the special name "Yahweh." Following the equation of Yahweh and *El Shaddai* in vv 2–3, an equation made necessary by the emphasis the Priestly writers consider essential, this sequence moves immediately to the emphasis on Yahweh's covenant and what its fulfillment means to Israel in Egypt.

It may therefore be more accurate to think of the Priestly writers as following their own and different emphasis, producing a parallel sequence never intended to match the sequence in chaps. 3 and 4, and not so much deemphasizing another line of approach or departing from it as taking up their own special concern, Yahweh's fulfillment of his covenant promises, no doubt seen by them as a convincing basis for Israel's fulfillment of their promises in covenant. Not the least of the merits of such a view is the elimination of the supposed "conflicts" of Gen 4:26 and Exod 3:13–14 with the present passage (Sandmel, *HUCA* 32 [1961] 19–29). Each facet of the account of God's revelation of himself may thus be permitted to reflect the light of man's perception of his Presence in its own distinct way. We should always keep in mind the diversity of our own perceptions of God and not demand of the biblical thinkers a unanimity of experience and a logicality of expression we ourselves cannot demonstrate.

4–5 Thus by reference to the covenant with the fathers the Priestly narrative introduces a sequence begun by the Yahwist with the theophany of the flaming bush, including in the process the important historical memory that the fathers honored Yahweh by other names. Three essential details are then quickly noted: (1) the covenant included a promise of land; (2) that land was the land of their transient life, between the river-basin of Mesopotamia and the river-basin of Egypt; and (3) the oppression by the Egyptians, which necessitates the next stage in the fulfillment of the covenant, has served also as a reminder of it.

6–8 As Yahweh's name, describing his nature as an active, present God, has served as a declaration of the authority Moses sought during his experience of call at Sinai (3:13–17), so now that name, as part of the self-proclamatory assertion "I am Yahweh," serves as the guarantee of the promise of deliverance, which it precedes (v 6) and concludes (v 8; cf. Oliva, *Bib* 52 [1971] 2–5, 13–19, and Ogden, *VT* 28 [1978] 198–99). The covenant Yahweh has made is stressed not only by the reference to the deliverance about to take place ("bring you forth . . . snatch you forth"), but also by Yahweh's claim that he is to act as "a rescuing kinsman" (a usage which, as Stamm, *Erlösen und Vergeben*, 36–39 notes, is also connected with the patriarchal fathers), and by his "singling them out" for himself to be their God (cf. 19:5).

This rescue will mean more than mere deliverance, however, for it will be a rescue that will teach Israel by experience the truth of the claim made in the name "Yahweh" and in the statement "I am Yahweh." The deliverance will be followed, further, by the fulfillment of the second major part of the covenant-promise, the gift of the land of Canaan, the land of wandering existence for the fathers, now to be a homeland for the descendants, and so an inheritance of the promise. That promise, indeed, Yahweh swore—"I lifted my hand to give . . . ," apparently an example, by effect and by symbol if the statement is to be taken literally, of what Lehmann (*ZAW* 81 [1969] 83–84) has described as an oath based on blessing. And the authority for the fulfillment of the promise, again, is "I am Yahweh."

9–13   With no more than a laconic note that Moses reported these powerful words of Yahweh, we are told that the sons of Israel were simply too dejected and worn out by the slavery they had had to endure to take any notice of Moses *or* the words he quoted. Such a notice seems strange indeed until it is seen as the transition to what follows: Yahweh now commands Moses to address the Pharaoh himself, so that *he* will respond (vv 10–11), and Moses objects (v 12).

This is Moses' only protest in this Priestly account of his commission, and it focuses upon the unlikeliness of success for such a petition, and only secondarily on his limitation as a speaker. But this too is a transitional verse. Yahweh's next word to Moses is a word also to Aaron, who appears in this sequence for the first time, and it is not a word of explanation or comfort or further revelation: it is a command. They are to get on with bringing forth the sons of Israel from the land of Egypt.

Explanation

The interpretation of Exod 6:2–13 has often been deflected by too close a connection with chaps. 4 and 5. In both passages, it is true, the call and commission of Moses provide a framework for a narrative that has to do with what Yahweh has promised and what Yahweh is about to do, with both promise and action founded on the kind of God Yahweh is.

But there the correspondence ends, for the most part. The essential features of chaps. 3 and 4, theophany in relation to call, the revelation and explanation of the special name "Yahweh," the signs of Moses' authority, the provision of a "mouth" for Moses, and the movement of Moses from Midian to Egypt, are either lacking altogether or are present only by inference in 6:2–13. Whether any of these subjects was dealt with in sections from the Priestly source which have been omitted from the composite of the final text of Exodus is a moot question. They are not present now, and 6:2–13 as it stands is clearly concerned with another, if parallel, emphasis.

That emphasis, so essential a part of the Priestly conception of the relationship of Israel and Yahweh, is the covenant. What Yahweh has done and is doing and what Israel is doing and must do might be said to be the fundamental theme of the three substantial Priestly sections of the Book of Exodus. Here, at the beginning of the first of those sections, that double motif is sounded clearly and dramatically. It is sounded by a reference to the promise of Yahweh to the fathers, who knew him by other names. It is sounded by a reference to the land of the fathers' sojourning now about to become the possession by inheritance of their descendants. It is sounded by a reference to the deliverance about to take place, a rescue made as necessary by Yahweh's obligation as a redeeming kinsman as by the dire need of the people of Israel. It is sounded by an anticipation of the election of the Israelites to a new status as the people of God, soon to take place at Sinai. And it is sounded in the justifying and authorizing self-confession of the "I am Yahweh" sentence, repeated four times in a sequence of five verses.

The appropriateness of such a beginning to the first lengthy sequence of Priestly material in Exodus may be seen not only in the persistent emphasis throughout the Priestly literature upon what Israel is to become because Yahweh is what he is. It may be seen also in the sequences to follow in the Book of Exodus as a whole, so often preoccupied, in one way or another, with that same theme. Thus the genealogy of Moses and Aaron, the anticipation of the mighty acts, and above all the instructions pursuant to the personnel, the symbols, and the implements of Israel's worship are all tied to this theme. But so also are the proof-of-Presence narratives, the Sinai theophany and covenant accounts, and the climactic account of Israel's first disobedience and the renewal of the covenant.

Israel is indeed called to a covenant of being because Yahweh Is. That covenant was anticipated by the·covenant with the fathers. It is about to be made possible by a deliverance and a gift of land made necessary by the covenant with the fathers. And for the Priestly narrators, its continuance, once it has been made, is a matter of primary obligation tied to Israel's very existence as a people.

The Genealogy of Aaron and Moses   (6:14–27)

Bibliography

Cody, A. *A History of Old Testament Priesthood.* AnBib 25. Rome: Pontifical Biblical Institute, 1969. **Gray, G. B.** *Studies in Hebrew Proper Names.* London: Adam and Charles Black, 1896. **Liver, J.** "Korah, Dathan and Abiram." *Studies in the Bible.* Scripta Hierosolymitana 8. Ed. Chaim Rabin. Jerusalem: Magnes Press, 1961. 189–217. **Möhlenbrink, K.** "Die Levitischen Überlieferungen des Alten Testaments." *ZAW* 52 (1934) 184–231. **North, F. S.** "Aaron's Rise in Prestige." *ZAW* 66 (1954) 191–99. **Westphal, G.** "Aaron und die Aaroniden." *ZAW* 26 (1906) 201–30.

Translation

¹⁴ *These are the heads* ᵃ *of their fathers' families: the sons of Reuben, Israel's first born, are Chanoch ("Trained" or "Dedicated")* ᵇ *and Pallu ("Extraordinary"), Chetsron ("Village-Dweller") and Karmi ("My Vinekeeper"). These are the family-divisions* ᶜ *of Reuben.* ¹⁵ *And the sons of Simeon are Yemuel* ᵃ *(? "El's Sea") and Yamin ("Right Hand") and Ohad (?) and Yachin ("He Makes Firm") and Tsochar* ᵇ *("Tawny Skin") and Shaul ("Asked For, Prayer's Answer"), son of the Canaanite woman. These are the family-divisions of Simeon.* ¹⁶ *And these are the names of the sons of Levi, by their successive generations: Gershon ("Cast-Out" or "Driven Off") and Qehat (? "Blunt One") and Merari ("Bitter One"). Levi lived one hundred and thirty-seven years.*

¹⁷ *The sons of Gershon* ᵃ *are Libni (? "My Whiteness") and Shimei ("My Report") by their successive generations.* ¹⁸ *And the sons of Qehat are Amram ("Exalted People")* ᵃ *and Yitshar ("First Oil") and Chebron ("Uniter") and Uzziel ("My Might Is El"). Qehat lived one hundred and thirty-three years.* ᵇ ¹⁹ *And the sons of Merari are Machli ("Marrow to Me") and Mushi (? "My Feeling" or "My Departure"). These are the family-divisions of Levi, by their successive generations.*

²⁰ *Now Amram married* ᵃ *Yochebed ("Yahweh's Honor"),* ᵇ *his aunt,* ᶜ *and in time, she gave birth to Aaron and to Moses.* ᵈ *Amram lived one hundred and thirty-seven* ᵉ *years.* ²¹ *And the sons of Yitshar are Qorach ("Baldy") and Nepheg ("Clumsy" or "Idle") and Zikri ("My Remembrance").* ²² *And the sons of Uzziel are Mishael* ᵃ *("Who Is That Is God?") and Eltsaphan* ᵇ *("God Has Treasured") and Sitri ("My Hiding Place").*

²³ *Now Aaron married Elisheva ("My God Is Seven" = "Completion," or "My God Is Sworn" = "Bound by His Oath"), Aminadab's ("My People Is Generous") daughter, Nachshon's ("Snake"* ᵃ*) sister, and in time, she gave birth to Nadav ("Generous") and to Abihu ("My Father Is He"), to Eleazar ("God Has Aided") and to Itamar ("Region of Palms").*

²⁴ *And Qorach's sons are Assir ("Captive") and Elqanah ("God Has Created") and Abiasaph* ᵃ *("My Father Has Gathered Together"). These are the family-divisions of the Qorachites.*

²⁵ *And Eleazar, Aaron's son, married one of Putiel's (?)* ᵃ *daughters, and in time, she gave birth to Pinchas ("Mouth of?"* ᵇ*). These are the heads of the Levitical fathers' family divisions.* ²⁶ *This is the Aaron and the Moses to whom Yahweh said, "Bring forth the sons of Israel from the land of Egypt by their organized divisions."* ᵃ ²⁷ *They were the ones who spoke to Pharaoh, king of Egypt, to bring forth the sons of Israel from Egypt,* ᵃ *this very Moses and Aaron.* ᵇ

Notes

14.a. ראש refers to the male in charge of a family or clan, usually the oldest living father, lit., as in contemporary usage, the "head of the household."

14.b. The translations suggested for this and the other names that occur for the first time in Exodus in this genealogy are based on the apparent etymology of the names, and are tentative.

14.c. משפחה designates a technical subdivision of a tribe into the clans that make it up, theoretically by family branches.

15.a. LXX ᴮ reads Ιεμιηλ "Jemiel."

15.b. SamPent has צהר, perhaps "Bright Light."

17.a. LXX transliterates this name Γεδσων "Gedson."

18.a. See n. 2:1.b.
18.b. LXX has ἑκατὸν τριάκοντα "one hundred and thirty."
20.a. Lit., "took, selected . . . to himself for a wife."
20.b. On the difficulty of the spelling of this name, see Widengren, *Proclamation and Presence*, 34–35. Noth, *Personennamen*, 111, doubts that it should be connected with Yahweh, and proposes instead a possible Egyptian origin.
20.c. MT here has דדתו "his aunt." Num 26:59 notes that Yochebed was a daughter of Levi, born in Egypt, thus indicating that Amram married his father's sister, his grandfather's daughter. LXX reads here, instead of "his aunt," "daughter of the brother of his father," but reads Num 26:59 as MT does.
20.d. Some MSS of SamPent and LXX add Μαριαμ "Miriam" here, in accord with Num 26:59.
20.e. SamPent has "one hundred and thirty-six years," as do some LXX and Old Latin MSS. Noth (*Personennamen*, 227) includes this name in his list of names reflecting bodily weakness or indolence.
22.a. This name is missing from the basic text of LXX and from the Old Latin text.
22.b. SamPent אליצפן and Syr read *Elitsaphan*, "My God Has Treasured," as does Num 3:30.
23.a. Noth (*Personennamen*, 230) and Gray (*Proper Names*, 91) list this name in their respective lists of names derived from animals.
24.a. SamPent has אביסף, apparently the אֶבְיָסָף "Ebiasaph" of 1 Chr 6:8, 22 and 9:19.
25.a. Noth (*Personennamen*, 63) considered this name a hybrid form built on an Egyptian word plus a Hebrew word (אֵל). *Masora parva* indicates that the name occurs nowhere else in the OT. Hyatt (96) translates it "he whom El gave."
25.b. BDB (810) proposes an Egyptian name, "Pe-nehasi, the negro." Hyatt (96) reads "the Nubian."
26.a. עַל־צִבְאֹתָם "according to their armies or hosts" is a technical term of organization, primarily, in the OT, for military purposes. Here, the reference seems to be to a logistical apportionment of the sons of Israel by tribal and clan subdivision.
27.a. SamPent has מאֶרֶץ מצְרים "from the land of Egypt" as do some LXX MSS.
27.b. LXX reads Ααρων καὶ Μωυσῆς "Aaron and Moses."

Form/Structure/Setting

The form of this section is dictated in part by the setting in which it occurs (see *Form/Structure/Setting* on 6:2–13) and in part by its purpose, which is to trace the ancestry, primarily of Aaron and then (of necessity) of Moses back to the immediate family of Jacob/Israel. The section has been carefully woven into the narrative from the Priestly circle, beginning at the first mention of Aaron (v 13), and ending with both a justification for its inclusion (vv 26–27) and a partially verbatim recapitulation of the narrative account at the point of its interruption (vv 28–30).

The concern of the section is obviously genealogical, and it is thus reflective of the well-known interest of the Priestly circle in what Robert North ("Theology of the Chronicler," *JBL* 82 [1963] 370–72) has called "legitimacy," that is, having the right people in the right place at the right time. But the care with which this sequence is inserted into the narrative, the point at which it is located, and above all the manner in which it is focused, by and large on one person, Aaron, make it by form what must be called an adapted genealogy, the intention of which is the legitimation of Aaron.

This purpose accounts for the lopsidedness of the section and for its inclusion of a series of names that occur in only a few places, or even nowhere else in the OT, but are nevertheless somehow important to the special position of Aaron. It also accounts for what appears to be a partial listing, both of

the twelve trives named in Exod 1:1–5, and also of the generations of two
of the three tribes mentioned in vv 14–16 of this section.

Thus this sequence is best thought of not as "a great secondary insertion"
(Noth, 58), but as a piece specially composed, albeit perhaps from fuller
genealogical lists (cf. Möhlenbrink, *ZAW* 52 [1934] 187–97), for the single
purpose of authenticating Aaron, and for this specific spot in this particular
narrative. In any setting other than one presenting Aaron as a leader of
special importance, it would make little sense.

Comment

14–16 This genealogical list begins at the same point in the pre-history
of the people of Israel and with the same order in listing the sons of Jacob/
Israel as does the list at the beginning of the Book of Exodus (see also Gen
49). Reuben, the firstborn, and four sons of his first generation, then Simeon
and six sons of his first generation, then Levi and three sons of his first
generation, are all listed. Of Reuben and Simeon and their ten sons no more
is said here. The ten sons are listed in the genealogy of Gen 46 (see vv 9–
10); eight of them (excepting Ohad and Tsochar) are listed in the genealogy
of Num 26 (see vv 5, 6, 8, 12, 13), and seven of them (excepting the two
absent from Num 26, plus Yachin) are listed in the genealogy of the Chronicler
(see 1 Chr 4:24—and note the additional sons of Simeon listed there—and
5:3). These first two sons of Jacob/Israel and the beginnings of their descendancy are included at the beginning of a genealogy of an important segment
of the descendancy of Levi to place the family of Levi in its appropriate
position of honor in the tribal biography. Levi is described as the third-born
son of Jacob/Israel by Leah, the first wife to bear him children (see Gen
35:22b–26, and cf. Cassuto, 84–85).

17–25 The sons of the three sons of Levi's first generation are next listed
(though compare Num 26:57–58, which suggests a different descendancy;
see Liver, *Studies*, 211–14), the eight grandsons of Levi. Of their descendants,
only the two sons of Amram, the three sons of Yitshar, and the three sons
of Uzziel are mentioned. Of these eight great-grandsons of Levi, two (Nepheg
and Zikri) are not otherwise mentioned in the OT (though there are other
persons so named). Aaron is mentioned before Moses as a son of Amram,
and Aaron's wife, four of his sons and one of his grandsons are named,
though none of Moses' family is mentioned. Finally, three sons of Qorach,
Aaron's cousin, are named, one of whom (Elqanah) is not mentioned again
in the OT.

The reason for the inclusion of the line of Aaron through the beginning
of the second generation beyond him is obvious enough, since Aaron is the
reason for this adapted genealogy in the first place. The reason for the inclusion of the first generation of his cousin Qorach is not so clear (note Möhlenbrink, *ZAW* 52 [1934] 221–22). Since Qorach led, or was at least involved
in a rebellion against Moses' authority (Num 16:1–35), his three obscure
sons may be listed here alongside Aaron's two famous (Eleazar and Itamar;
see Westphal, *ZAW* 26 [1906] 222–25) and two infamous (Nadav and Abihu)
sons by way of comparison complimentary to Aaron. As Cody (*Priesthood*,
161–65, 170–74) has shown, in the later genealogies (e.g., 1 Chr 6:1–15 [16–

30]), Aaron and his priestly line are separated from the line of Qehat, though Qorach is not. At some point in the development of the Priestly genealogy, and for some reason, there emerged an effort to discredit Qorach and his sons, an effort intriguingly connected by Jacob Liver (*Studies,* 208–14) with a Levitical revolt against the power of an entrenched priestly group in Jerusalem in the time of Solomon or "even" David. Though the listing of vv 14–25 here predates (Möhlenbrink, *ZAW* 52 [1934] 205–11) that attempt, the sons of Qorach are even here not the important line.

Apart from the note that Simeon's son Shaul was born of a Canaanite woman (v 15), a detail included probably because of its peculiarity, the only women mentioned in this genealogy are, significantly, Aaron's mother (v 20), Aaron's wife (v 23), and Aaron's daughter-in-law, the wife of Eleazar (v 25). Marriage to the sister of one's father is expressly forbidden by Lev 18:12, but a desire to provide a pure Levitical line for Moses and Aaron has apparently overridden (or even preceded) that stricture in the marriage of Amram to Yochebed. Aaron's wife is from the tribe of Judah (Num 1:7), and her brother is mentioned because of his significant leadership in that tribe (Num 2:3–4, 7:12–17, 10:14).

26–27 This preoccupation of the genealogy with Aaron and those connected with him in varying ways is pointedly reflected in the reversal of the usual and expected order of the names "Moses and Aaron" to "Aaron and Moses" in v 26, as in the LXX's translation of v 27, and so perhaps in the Hebrew *Vorlage* of that verse. That Moses is included in this genealogy at all is almost certainly the result of the connection to him of Aaron in another and probably still earlier attempt to promote Aaron as the preeminent Levite (Westphal, *ZAW* 26 [1906] 230). At this stage in the development of the Book of Exodus, Moses would surely have needed no legitimation. Not so Aaron, whose role was still being debated as the tetrateuchal books reached final form (cf. F. S. North, *ZAW* 66 [1954] 191–99).

Thus the Priestly writers assembled and wove into the text of their first extended sequence in the Book of Exodus a carefully drawn justification of Aaron as a figure of great importance to the events taking place in Egypt. The fact that even here Aaron appears as an add-on figure makes all the more clear the secondary nature of the Aaron traditions. It also explains why he is such a here-and-there character in the Book of Exodus, and why he of all persons can be presented both as the custodian of the revelation concerned with Israel's worship and also as a leading figure in Israel's first great apostasy and their first breaking of Yahweh's covenant expectations (see *Comment* on 32:1–6, 21–32).

The function of vv 26–27 is a statement of the purpose of the genealogy, and this function is served in an emphatic fashion: "This is the Aaron and the Moses . . . this very Moses and Aaron." They are the two to whom Yahweh spoke (the reference, of course, is to v 13, since everywhere else so far Yahweh has spoken to Moses alone about the exodus), and they are the two who were to approach both the people of Israel and the Pharaoh.

Explanation

The purpose of the genealogy of 6:14–25 is thus the authentication of Aaron as nobly descended from Jacob/Israel through his third son, Levi, and thus as a worthy partner for Moses in the momentous negotiations about to take place in Egypt. Vv 26–27, which make this purpose clear, are stretched a bit, necessarily so, to include Moses, but Moses' position was in no jeopardy, and the priestly circle, by the thoroughness with which it seeks to push Aaron forward here, reveals that Aaron's position *was* in some jeopardy, at least at the point at which this genealogy was composed.

Even so, the larger frame of reference, the Book of Exodus as it stands before us, must be kept constantly in view as any smaller segment is considered. From that perspective, this genealogy may be seen as an attempt to set both Aaron *and* Moses firmly within the special descendancy of Jacob/Israel's third son, Levi, the ancestor of the line of those who handle holy things and mediate Yahweh's words of expectation and judgment. While the original purpose of the passage may have been legitimation, its purpose in its present setting is the celebration of the descendancy of the promise.

A Preview of the Proof-of-Presence Sequence (6:28–7:7)

Bibliography

Cazelles, H., Gelin, A. *et al. Moïse, l'homme de l'alliance.* Paris: Desclée & Cie, 1955.
Daiches, D. *Moses: The Man and His Vision.* New York: Praeger Publishers, 1975.

Translation

[28] *Now when Yahweh spoke to Moses in the land of Egypt,* [29] *Yahweh spoke to Moses to say, "I am Yahweh. Speak to Pharaoh, king of Egypt, everything that I speak to you."* [30] *So Moses said to Yahweh's face,* [a] *"Now, look—I am a clumsy speaker: just how is Pharaoh going to pay attention to me?"*

[7:1] *So Yahweh said to Moses, "You must understand* [a] *that I will make you a god so far as Pharaoh is concerned,* [b] *and Aaron your brother will be your prophet.* [2] *You are to speak all that I order you to speak,* [a] *and Aaron your brother is to speak to Pharaoh, and he will send forth the sons of Israel from his land.* [3] *At the same time,* [a] *I* [b] *will make Pharaoh stubborn-minded,* [c] *then pile up* [d] *signs and wondrous deeds in the land of Egypt;* [4] *Pharaoh will pay no attention to you, and thus will I set my hand* [a] *against Egypt, and I will bring forth my organized divisions,* [b] *my people the sons of Israel, from the land of Egypt with great deeds of vindication.* [c] [5] *So shall the Egyptians* [a] *know by experience that I am Yahweh, when I stretch forth my hand against Egypt and bring forth* [b] *the sons of Israel from the midst of them."*

[6] *Thus Moses and Aaron set about doing as Yahweh ordered them; they did it to the letter.* [a] [7] *Moses was eighty and Aaron was eighty-three when they spoke to Pharaoh.*

Notes

30.a. Vv 29 and 30 are a recapitulation, following the genealogy (6:14–25) and its justification (6:27–28), of vv 11 and 12. This phrase is repeated verbatim; see n. 6:12.b.

7:1.a. The impv רְאֵה lit. means "see here," "look now," as in the contemporary use of this verb, urging the perception or understanding of a given point or situation.

1.b Lit., "I give you, a god, to Pharaoh."

2.a. Emphasis is shown by the use of the independent personal pronoun אתה, doubling the "you" of the verb form תדבר "you speak." "To speak" is added following the verb "order" for clarity of flow in the translation.

3.a. Lit., ואני is "and I" or even "then I." The narrative of the events these verses anticipate makes abundantly plain, however, that the negotiations of Moses and Aaron, the stiffening of Pharaoh's resolve, and Yahweh's mighty deeds belong together as coordinate actions, not in line as sequential events.

3.b. Emphasis is again shown by the addition of the independent personal pronoun, and the emphatic usage parallels and complements that of v 2: *"You* are to speak, . . . *I* will make Pharaoh. . . ."

3.c. Lit., "heart" is the obj of this verb (קשה "be hard"), as it is also of the hiph of חזק "make obstinate," of 4:21; but as is well known, לב refers to "heart" as the center of reason and intelligence, in contemporary usage, "mind," and not to "heart" as the center of the emotions.

3.d. Hiph of רבה means "increase greatly, multiply," the number of something.

4.a. Or "power, strength," יד.

4.b. The same term as in 6:26; see n. 6:26.a.

4.c. שפטים, from שפט "to judge," and of God especially, "to give vindicating judgment," in the Psalms particularly, often as he comes in theophany. SamPent reads במשפטים, perhaps a slight tempering of MT, which is therefore preferable.

5.a. LXX πάντες οἱ Αἰγύπτιοι and SamPent כל מצרים read "all Egypt"; Barthélemy (*Preliminary and Interim Report*, 97–98) advocates "Egypt" as a collective subj with the pl verb. מִצְרַיִם can be translated either way, however, and "Egyptians" gives a smoother reading, because of the second occurrence of this proper name later in the verse.

5.b. SamPent adds עמי "my people" at this point.

6.a. Lit., "yes (indeed) they did."

Form/Structure/Setting

These verses are an integral part of the large composite from the priestly circle, 6:2–7:13, described more fully above. They function, indeed, as a kind of conclusion to this composite, with its concentration upon the impending rescue of Yahweh, guaranteed by his covenant-promise to the fathers, to be announced by his special servants Moses and Aaron, but to be brought about by his own active involvement.

Vv 28–30 pick up and continue the narrative sequence of the composite, following the interruption the genealogy justifying Aaron as an equal partner with Moses. 7:1–5 then provides (through the vehicle of Yahweh's response to the question of Moses raised first in 6:12, then repeated in 6:30) what amounts to a theological explanation of the entire sequence of the mighty acts which will bring the promise of deliverance to reality. This response of Yahweh reaches back to the covenant promise to the fathers through Moses' involvement (and Aaron's) in bringing that promise to fulfillment (vv 1–2) and reaches forward to the exodus through Yahweh's explanation of how he will bring about that exodus and prove his Presence in Egypt at the same time. 7:6–7 concludes the section and the larger priestly composite with a laconic statement that Moses and Aaron carried out their orders exactly and with a note as to their ages at the time.

The connection of 6:28–7:7 with what precedes it in the composite is shown not only by the continuation of the narrative with which the composite begins (6:2–13), but even more by the amplification of the theme of Yahweh's self-declaration to the sons of Israel (6:6–8) to include also his self-declaration to Pharaoh and to Egypt (7:3–5). And the connection of this preview of what is to come with what follows it, in the prologue to the mighty-act sequence (7:8–13), is shown by the introduction there of what is anticipated here.

Comment

28–30   The question of Moses as to whether the Pharaoh of Egypt can be expected to pay any attention to him is another variation of the motif reflected in 3:11–12, 13–14, 19–20; 4:1, 8–9, 10–12; and 5:22–6:1. And the only reasonable answer to this question here, as in its earlier forms ("Who am I?" 3:11; "they won't trust me," 4:1; "I am heavy of lip and thick of tongue," 4:10; "Why have you sent me here for *this*?" 5:22), is a negative one. It is *not* Moses who will make things happen in Egypt, or who will be trusted to bring powerful deliverance, or whose own eloquence or lack of eloquence will matter at all, or whose coming to Pharaoh will inspire respect and receive attention. The determining Presence will be Yahweh's.

This theme so permeates all the sequences in which Moses is significantly involved in the Book of Exodus that one can only suppose it to be a deliberate reflection of a specific and theological emphasis upon Yahweh as the only prime mover in the narratives of revelation and deliverance, and even of the offering of covenant. We have allowed centuries of the glorification of Moses (surveyed in detail by Cazelles, Gelin, et al., *Moïse, l'homme de l'alliance,* and more briefly by Daiches, *Moses,* 233–56), begun even in the biblical period, to color overmuch our interpretation of the Exodus narratives. We need to note with more precision the amount of attention really given to Moses, how flawed a hero he actually is, how often his involvement is a kind of springboard for an emphasis on the activity of real consequence—the activity of Yahweh—and how at every crucial point, the presence of Moses is either forgotten or at least obscured by the Presence of Yahweh.

7:1–5   Thus a question of Moses is once again an opening for an assertion of Yahweh that makes clear that Moses (and this time, Aaron as well) is but an instrument of *God's* activity. By the technique used so effectively in the Book of Job, Moses' question is not really answered—not as he has asked it. Instead, Moses is given a new perspective on what is about to happen. Getting Pharaoh's attention is not his task; he is ordered rather to speak what Yahweh speaks. Yahweh has plans of his own for getting and holding Pharaoh's attention.

That Moses is to be a god to Pharaoh will be Yahweh's doing, not his, and Yahweh will bring that about through a combination of word and deed, both originating in himself. Moses is to speak what Yahweh speaks, and Aaron, in turn, is to communicate that message to Pharaoh. Then Yahweh will act, and lest the Pharaoh pay too much attention too soon and come prematurely to less than an unquestioning belief, he will harden the Pharaoh's resistance so that he *will* pay no attention to Moses and so bring about Yahweh's rescue of the Israelites in such manner as to provoke even the Egyptians to belief. Moses is entirely right to suppose the Pharaoh will be indifferent to him. But that is not a problem of any consequence: Yahweh is concerned to bring the Pharaoh to an experiential knowledge of *his* powerful Presence, not of Moses' truthfulness or Aaron's eloquence.

The assertion that Moses is to be made a god (אלהים) to Pharaoh, and that Aaron will function as his prophet (נביא "spokesman," Hyatt, 101) is to be understood as a credit to Yahweh and not to Moses or to Aaron. What is to bring this about is described in vv 2–5: Moses is to speak what Yahweh speaks, and Yahweh will act in accord with his own speaking. Thus Moses will appear to Pharaoh as no one else ever has, "given," as he will be, as "a god" to Pharaoh by Yahweh's words, words delivered by Moses with Aaron's help, and confirmed by Yahweh's deeds.

Once again, as in 4:21 and 6:1, Yahweh makes it clear that both Moses (and in this passage also Aaron) and Pharaoh are to be instruments in the proof of his Presence. Moses is ordered to speak to Pharaoh (through Aaron and with Aaron's help) what Yahweh has spoken to him, and Pharaoh will be made stubborn-minded, so that the mighty deeds of proof may be multiplied and their impact heightened (cf. Greenberg, *Understanding Exodus*, 138–40). Of the three verbs used with Yahweh as subject in the presentation of the "hardening-of-the-heart" motif, two are used only once: hiphil of קשה "make hard, severe, stubborn" in v 3 here, and hiphil of כבד "make heavy, insensitive, unresponsive" in 10:1. Moses, Yahweh says emphatically (*"you"* v 2), is to do his part by speaking what he is ordered to speak; Yahweh will see that Pharaoh does *his* part by making his mind stubborn, an assertion also made emphatically and set forth as an action that is to parallel Moses' speaking ("At the same time, *I,*" v 3).

Thus Yahweh is orchestrating, in a combination of opposing and unlikely forces, a deliverance that will above all be a proof of his active Presence. A reluctant Moses, an unbelieving Pharaoh, a crushed and dispirited Israel, a proud and ruling Egyptian people, a non-nation against the greatest of nations, are brought together, and the opposing sides are set still more firmly in their respective ways, so that the proof of Yahweh's Presence, which is to turn everything upside down, may be established irrevocably. Even as Moses and Aaron speak Yahweh's words of command to Pharaoh, Yahweh will increase Pharaoh's resistance, thus creating an impasse.

His preparation made, Yahweh will then "pile up" in the land of the impasse "signs and wondrous deeds," which are to function as convincing proofs and palpable reminders (Helfmeyer, "אות," *TDOT* 1:168–70), the telling climax of which will be the exodus itself, brought about "with great deeds of vindication." The specific allusion of this term, שפטים "vindication," is probably the death of Egypt's firstborn, as its use in 12:12 and Num 33:4 confirms. But its repeated use (ten times) in the Book of Ezekiel to refer to a variety of Yahweh's judgments (see Ezek 14:21) may suggest that it is inclusive of all the mighty deeds in Egypt and perhaps also of the rescue of Israel and the defeat of Egypt at the sea. Zimmerli (*Ezekiel 1,* Hermeneia [Philadelphia: Fortress Press, 1979], 315) calls the term "a word characteristic of Ezekiel and P," and its primary use in reference to acts of Yahweh give שפטים the sense of "proving and vindicating deeds" suggested in the *Translation* above and at 6:6.

The climax of all this preparation, and of this entire sequence of Yahweh's word followed by Yahweh's deed, is in its own way an ultimate vindication, for with the bringing forth of the Israelites from "the midst" of Egypt, that is, from a position entirely favorable to Egyptian power, the Egyptians will know by experience (as the Israelites will, 6:6–7) that "I am Yahweh." (See *Comment* on 6:2; Helfmeyer, *TDOT* 1:171.)

6–7 The brief report that Moses and Aaron did exactly as Yahweh had ordered is a reference to the first confrontation with Pharaoh, reported in detail in 5:1–5, a passage that reflects, along with its sequels in 5:6–9 and 5:10–21, the motif of the resistance of Pharaoh and the resultant early failure of Israel's cause, whether pled by Moses and Aaron or by the Hebrew section-leaders. And the added note about the relative ages of Moses and Aaron when they began their negotiations with Pharaoh, though it fits the information given by Deut 34:7, as Noth (61) points out, and though it conforms to the tradition that Aaron was the elder brother (note the order of the names in 6:20), serves above all to conclude this compilation from the Priestly circle, begun at 6:2, with a moving dignity. Moses and Aaron have earned the right to some respect by virtue of their survival to the age of experienced wisdom.

Explanation

In a remarkable way, 6:28–7:7 sums up the narrative of the Book of Exodus from 5:1 forward and previews the narrative to come through 13:16 at least, and perhaps even through chaps. 14 and 15. This section is above all a theological explanation for the sequence of the mighty acts as a proof-of-Presence sequence. It answers in advance of their raising the questions of why Yahweh did the mighty deeds, of how the Pharaoh could hold out so long, of why there was a "piling up" of signs and wondrous deeds. As at so many other points in the biblical narrative (Gen 22:1, for example, or Job 1 and 2), we are told what is going to happen and what the event means before it unfolds.

But the section also makes unquestionably clear, immediately following the genealogy documenting the importance of Aaron and the preceding section describing (albeit more indirectly than directly) Moses' call and commission, exactly the position of Moses and Aaron in all that is about to unfold. They are God's servants, the medium of his preparatory word, but what they are, they are by his action. What is about to be accomplished, therefore, he will accomplish. Not only is the Pharaoh justified to pay them no attention, the attention Yahweh begins to attract will at first be deflected so that the lesson to be taught may be driven home with all the greater impact. Yahweh's sovereignty is such that he will bring not merely Moses and Aaron but Pharaoh, the Egyptians, and even the natural world into the process of the lesson he is about to teach and the work he is about to do.

It is difficult indeed to conclude that such a section has fallen into the text of the Book of Exodus at precisely the appropriate point by the coincidental shuffle of a redactor's snippets. Exod 6:28–7:7, in this location, is a case in point for the importance of the text of the Book of Exodus in the form in which we have it—admittedly a compilation, but one put together with great care and in a manner that can tell us much about the meaning of the whole as well as of its parts.

III. The Ten Mighty Acts and the Exodus: The Proof of Yahweh's Presence (7:8–13:16)

The Miracle of the Rod and the Monstrous Snake: A Prologue to the Ten Mighty Acts (7:8–13)

Bibliography

Labuschagne, C. J. "The Emphasizing Particle *Gam* and Its Connotations." *Studia Biblica et Semitica*. Wageningen: H. Veenman and Sons, 1966. 193–203. **Redford, D. B.** *A Study of the Biblical Story of Joseph*. VTSup 20, Leiden: E. J. Brill, 1970. **Stadelmann, L. I. J.** *The Hebrew Conception of the World*. AnBib 39. Rome Pontifical Biblical Institute, 1970. **Vergote, J.** *Joseph en Égypte: Génèse ch. 37–50 à la lumière des études égyptologiques récentes*. Louvain: Publications Universitaires. 1959.

Translation

⁸ *Then Yahweh said this* ᵃ *to Moses and to Aaron:* ⁹ *"When Pharaoh speaks to you to say, 'Make* ᵃ *yourselves* ᵇ *a wondrous deed,' then you say to Aaron, 'Take your staff and fling it down right in front of Pharaoh.' It will turn into* ᶜ *a monstrous snake."* ᵈ

¹⁰ *When Moses and Aaron came before* ᵃ *Pharaoh, they did exactly as Yahweh had ordered. Aaron threw down* ᵇ *his staff right in front of Pharaoh and right in front of his court,* ᶜ *and immediately it turned into a monstrous snake.* ¹¹ *So Pharaoh, in a countermove,* ᵃ *called the wise scholars and the magicians, and then they* ᵇ *too, the learned men* ᶜ *of Egypt, did the same thing* ᵈ *by their arcane arts.* ᵉ ¹² *Everybody threw down his staff, and they all* ᵃ *turned into monstrous snakes. Then, suddenly, Aaron's staff gobbled up all their staffs!*

¹³ *But the mind of Pharaoh was unchanged.* ᵃ *He paid no attention to them, just as Yahweh had predicted.* ᵇ

Notes

8.a. לאמר "to say"; so translated in the next verse following ידבר "he speaks."

9.a. "Give," נתן. Pharaoh enjoins Moses and Aaron to give credence to what they say with some sign of the power of the God they claim.

9.b. LXX ἡμῖν reads "us" and Syr *lj* read "me" rather than "yourselves," and LXX σημεῖον ἤ and SamPent או אות add "a sign or" before "a wondrous deed."

9.c. SamPent adds special *waw* to the יהי of MT, to give "then, immediately it will turn into. . . ."

9.d. תנין as opposed to the נחש of 4:3. The "serpent" of that account becomes an even more frightening reptile here. Cassuto (94) even translates תנין "crocodile."

10.a. MT reads אל "to, toward"; LXX ἐναντίον and SamPent have לפני "right in front of," as does MT v 9.

10.b. Hiph of שלך, translated "fling down" in the context of v 9.

10.c. Lit., "his servants."

11.a. Special *waw* plus גם "also," an adverbial particle which has a correlative, and even an adversative, usage; see BDB, 169 §§ 4, 5. Cf. also Labuschagne, *Studia* 197–98, who maintains that גם here is an emphasizing particle connected with the subj and designed "to express correspondence"; he reads, "And Pharaoh in his turn summoned. . . ."

11.b. Emphasis is indicated by the independent pers pronoun with גם "also," in addition to the 3d pers pl pronoun with the verb.

11.c. חרטמים implies, by its derivation from חרט, one who is skilled in the use of a stylus or other tools for writing and engraving; hence the general translation "learned men," embracing both the "wise scholars" and the "magicians" mentioned earlier in the verse. Cf. Vergote, *Joseph en Egypte*, 66–73; Redford, *Biblical Story*, 49, 203–4.

11.d. כן "did *thus*."

11.e. לָהֶטִים is apparently related to לוט "wrap completely, cover fully," and signifies mysterious learning, secret lore.

12.a. "All" is suggested by the pl verb and by the context.

13.a. Lit., "the heart of Pharaoh remained firm, grew strong."

13.b. דִּבֶּר "had spoken."

Form/Structure/Setting

This brief section is from the priestly circle and is a part of the block of Priestly material that extends without interruption from 6:2 through 7:13 (see *Form/Structure/Setting* on 6:2–13). Its association with that block, however, is a kinship more of origin than of subject. By content, the section is drawn to the third major complex of the Book of Exodus in its present form, the complex dealing with the ten mighty acts demonstrating Yahweh's Presence, and with the exodus itself, the climactic proof of that Presence.

These six verses function as a prologue to the mighty-acts sequence. The section preceding them, 6:28–7:7, previews that sequence as a whole by providing a theological explanation of the events narrated by it. 7:8–13 function as a prologue by their single emphasis upon the miraculous as the medium of Yahweh's proof of his Presence. The preceding section (6:28–7:7) is broad in scope and inclusive; this one is focused on a single aspect of what is to follow, and so is exclusive. The preceding section provides a conclusion to the narrative that begins with 6:2, and by its emphasis on the proof of Yahweh's Presence to Pharaoh and to the Egyptians, a transition to the great sequence setting forth that proof in detail, 7:8–13:16. The section at hand functions both as a transitional section and a prologue. It provides a transition from the account of the instructions regarding the proof to the Pharaoh to the beginning of that proof, and it provides a prologue by its focus on miracle as the medium of that proof.

One wonders whether 7:8–13 was originally located in the Priestly compilation following 6:2–7:7, and what may have been the form and sequence of the Priestly narrative following these verses before that narrative was fragmented and spliced into the compilation of the Book of Exodus. Given the Priestly affection for the dramatically miraculous, it is possible that these verses originally functioned much as they do now, as transition and prologue, in particular as prologue to a sequence in which the miraculous was even more dominant than it is in the sequence preserved in the received text. Whatever the accuracy of such a suggestion, the appropriateness of the location of these verses as prologue to the great proof-of-Presence sequence is clear, and the chord they strike must be heard throughout that sequence: the reality and power of Yahweh's Presence is demonstrated to Pharaoh and to the Egyptians by the miraculous.

Comment

8–9 For the first time in the narrative thus far, the suggestion is made that Pharaoh will request a wondrous deed as a vindication of the authority Moses and Aaron are claiming. Such a request may be implicit in Pharaoh's sarcastic question, "Who is Yahweh?" (5:2), but it is not anticipated in the earlier narrative on the changing of the staff (4:1–5), where this sign is given along with two more as proof of Moses' authority for the sons of Israel. There is no need to emend the text of v 9 to have Pharaoh asking this wondrous deed for himself and his court (see n. 9.b above). Moses and Aaron are to do this miracle for themselves, as a means of establishing their own credibility.

In 4:3, the staff of Moses was changed into a נָחָשׁ, a serpent probably regarded as dangerous. Moses ran away from it, then "snatched" at it very cautiously. Here (vv 9, 10, 12), a staff now referred to as Aaron's (vv 9 and 10) turns into a תַּנִּין. This word too is generally translated "serpent," but as it clearly designates a different kind of reptile, the term should be rendered differently. Apart from its three occurrences here, תַּנִּין occurs in the OT a dozen times (Lisowsky, 1525; Mandelkern, 1249, lists eleven occurrences) and refers in most of these occurrences (Gen 1:21; Pss 74:13; 148:7; Isa 27:1, where both terms occur, and 51:9; Jer 51:34; Ezek 29:3; 32:2; Job 7:12) to a reptile of terrifying size, a sea-monster, even a dragon (so perhaps LXX, which reads δράκων here, ὄφις in 4:3). A crocodile may be the point of departure for the Ezekiel references (Eichrodt, *Ezekiel,* OTL [Philadelphia: Westminster, 1970], 403, 432–33), but there is at least a suggestion of the primordial monster of the deep in the background of these and other usages (Stadelmann, *Hebrew Conception,* 20–27). At the very least, a snake of awesome appearance and perhaps size seems intended here, a "frightful" or "monstrous" snake.

10–12 The report that Pharaoh's "learned men" (cf. Redford, *Biblical Story,* 204) are able to duplicate this wondrous deed is by no means to be taken as an indication that what is described here is nothing more than fancy sleight-of-hand, making "a snake go rigid by pressing on a nerve at the back of its neck" (Knight, 53, who adds, "Aaron evidently knew the trick"). All such attempts to find "naturalistic" explanations for the wondrous deeds of the Book of Exodus, along with designs on "what *really* happened," are not only misleading and impossible, but irrelevant as well. The whole point of this prologue is its miraculous element. The narrator goes to great trouble to make plain that Pharaoh had to call in the best he had to match the wondrous deed of Moses and Aaron: "wise scholars," "magicians," "learned men," with "arcane arts."

Even then, however, Yahweh's men had the best and last and triumphant word. In the delightfully funny v 12, when "everybody" throws down his staff and Pharaoh's palace is about to be overrun with monstrous snakes, we are told that "Aaron's staff" (not, significantly, "Aaron's monstrous snake") "gobbled up" or "gulped down" everybody else's staff. Pharaoh and his best minds are by no means presented as inept or lacking in power. Quite the contrary, they are formidable, a force to be reckoned with. But when they come up against Yahweh, they are outdone. This point is reiterated ever more forcefully throughout the proof-of-Presence sequence.

13 With the awesome potential of the two opposing forces thus illustrated and the inevitable conclusion of the confrontation already clearly anticipated, this prologue is brought to a close by a restatement of the foil against which the entire sequence of the mighty acts is parried and sharpened. Gobbling staff or no gobbling staff, and with the requested wondrous deed ignored, Pharaoh remains unconvinced. His mind is unmoved. He pays no attention to Moses and Aaron. Yahweh had said that he would not. And in that closing reminder, Yahweh's own role in Pharaoh's intransigence is subtly anticipated.

Explanation

The point of this brief section is that Yahweh's proof of his powerful Presence to the Pharaoh and thus to the Pharaoh's Egypt will be miraculous in nature. The miracle of the rod transformed into a monstrous snake is not called an אות "sign," as the rod turned into a serpent was (4:8–9), but a מופת "wondrous deed." And confronted by such a wondrous deed, Pharaoh calls in his best, apparently all of them, to match the deed by their own secret lore. This they proceed to do, but not quite, for Aaron's staff gulps down their staffs.

These lines sparkle with the humor of such a scene, in the delivery of Pharaoh's challenge; in the flinging down of one staff, then many; in the proliferation of monstrous snakes; and in the wolfing down of all the copycat snakes by their original. This humor, indeed, may be a part of the creation of an unforgettable scene for a didactic purpose. The proof Moses has wanted, the proof Moses has said Israel will need and Pharaoh will need, the proof which at the opening of this section Pharaoh himself asks for is now about to be given.

This proof is introduced here by a scene telling us that (1) the proof will be so extraordinary a display of Yahweh's power that it can only be understood as miracle; (2) the proof will be matched to begin with by Pharaoh's own considerable power, a power that will nonetheless be outdistanced, then overwhelmed; and (3) the proof will be resisted by Pharaoh, in the face of reason. The introduction ends on this latter note, having raised neatly the questions of how Pharaoh can resist and how long Pharaoh will hold out.

Like the proof-of-Presence sequence it introduces, the impulse of this brief section is theological, and the theological message it bears is so crucial that, in the sequence to follow, it must be made and then remade and emphasized by every conceivable means of making it memorable. Egypt becomes a stage, and Pharaoh a villain. Israel is the rapt audience. And there the metaphor breaks down, for Yahweh is not playing, or performing; he is simply being himself and keeping his promises, and he will not be finished until all who doubt believe completely.

So marvelously matched to the proof-of-Presence sequence of 7:14–13:16 is this prologue that it is easy to imagine its having been composed for the purpose. While that speculation cannot be confirmed, the location of such a section in such a place as such a prologue can be seen as nothing less than an exemplary display of compositional skill.

The First Mighty Act (7:14–25)

Bibliography

Hort, G. "The Plagues of Egypt." *ZAW* 69 (1957) 84–103. **Labuschagne, C. J.** "The Emphasizing Particle *Gam* and Its Connotations." *Studia Biblica et Semitica*. Wageningen: H. Veenman and Sons, 1966. 193–203. **McCarthy, D. J.** "Moses' Dealings with Pharaoh: Ex 7,8–10,27." *CBQ* 27 (1965) 336–47. ———. "Plagues and Sea of Reeds: Exodus 5–14." *JBL* 85 (1966) 137–58. **Winnett, F. V.** *The Mosaic Tradition*. Toronto: University of Toronto Press, 1949.

Translation

[14] *So Yahweh said to Moses, "The mind of Pharaoh is heavy and dull;* [a] *he refuses to send out the people.* [15] *Go along to Pharaoh in the morning, just when* [a] *he is going out toward the water. Take a position where you can intercept him* [b] *upon the bank of the Nile, and take in your hand the staff that was changed into a serpent.* [16] *Say to him, 'Yahweh the God of the Hebrews sent me to you to say, "Send out my people, in order that they may worship me* [a] *in the wilderness. And look here, you have still not obeyed this order.* [b] [17] *Thus does Yahweh say, 'In this are you to know by experience that I am Yahweh: see now, I will strike with the staff that is in my hand against the water of the Nile, and it will be changed into blood;* [18] *the fish in the Nile will die and the Nile will become putrid and the Egyptians will be too repulsed* [a] *to drink water from the Nile.' " ' "* [b]

[19] *Yahweh said further to Moses, "Say to Aaron, 'Take your staff and thrust out your hand against the waters of Egypt: against their streams, against their irrigation-channels,* [a] *against their marsh-basins,* [b] *and against all their stores of water,* [c] *so that all the water* [d] *will become blood. Blood will be everywhere* [e] *in the land of Egypt, even in wooden containers and stone containers.' "*

[20] *Thus Moses and Aaron did exactly as Yahweh had ordered, and Yahweh* [a] *raised high the staff and struck the water of the Nile before the very eyes of Pharaoh and before the very eyes of his court, so that all the water of the Nile was changed into blood.* [21] *Then the fish in the Nile died, and the Nile turned putrid, and the Egyptians were not able to drink water from the Nile. And sure enough,* [a] *there was blood everywhere in Egypt.* [22] *The learned men of Egypt, however, did the same thing by their arcane arts.* [a]

So Pharaoh's mind was again obstinate; he paid no attention to them, just as Yahweh had predicted. [23] *Pharaoh turned his back on them,* [a] *entered his palace,* [b] *and put the whole business out of his mind.* [c]

[24] *The Egyptian people meanwhile searched* [a] *all around the Nile for drinking water, because they could not bring themselves to drink from the water of the Nile.* [25] *Seven days came and went* [a] *following Yahweh's blow against the Nile.*

Notes

14.a. כבד "heavy and dull." The point of this "heaviness" is Pharaoh's insensitivity; his לב "mind," the seat of his process of understanding, is a kind of leaden lump, says Yahweh.

15.a. MT has הנה "behold" followed by the qal ptcp יֹצֵא "going." SamPent, LXX add הוא "him" between these two words, to give "behold him going out."

15.b. נצב means to "take up a stand, station oneself" for some specific purpose. See BDB, 662 § 1.a, and the references cited there.

16.a. עבד "serve."

16.b. Lit., "And behold, you have not heard up until now."

18.a. לאה means "to weary of, to become reluctant to do" something; the point here is that the Egyptians will not be able even to force themselves to drink such polluted and stinking water.

18.b. SamPent adds "So Moses and Aaron went to Pharaoh and they said to him, 'Yahweh the God of the Hebrews has sent us to you to say . . .'" and continues with a verbatim repetition of vv 16b–18.

19.a. יְאֹר appears to be a loan-word from Egyptian, and to refer to a channel for Nile water, a canal as opposed to a tributary-stream.

19.b. The cognate terms and the usage of אגם suggest swampy pools, marshland where papyrus and other aquatic plants grow.

19.c. By derivation, מקוה implies collected water, reserved or set aside for particular purposes.

19.d. וְיִהְיוּ־דָם, lit., "and they (the 'waters' just listed) will become blood."

19.e. Lit., "and blood will be in all of the land of Egypt." SamPent ויהי הדם divides the words at a different place.

20.a. MT has "he," but Yahweh is apparently the subj of the hiph of רום "raise high," and is thus inserted above for clarity. LXX ῥάβδῳ and SamPent מטהו attempt to resolve the ambiguity by reading "his staff," making Moses or Aaron the subject.

21.a. Special *waw* plus יִהְיֶה "it was," to give the apocopated form וַיְהִי "and sure enough, there was."

22.a. See nn. 11.c,d,e above.

23.a. The verb is פנה "turn," to which פנים "face," is related. The context makes clear the direction of Pharaoh's turning.

23.b. "His house."

23.c. "And he did not set his mind (לב) even to this." The particle is גם "even, also," here as elsewhere used for emphasis, as Labuschagne (*Studia*, 193–203) shows.

24.a. חפר "search" may also mean "dig," in reference to a shallow well or pit, but the emphasis here appears to be on an increasingly urgent search for some unchanged, unpolluted water.

25.a. The verb is niph of מלא "filled up, accomplished." It is sg in MT, thus taking the days as a collective whole. SamPent makes the verb pl, thus taking the days individually.

Form/Structure/Setting

The form of this first of the mighty acts accounts is composite. Two of the three tetrateuchal sources, J and P, are clearly in evidence, and most commentators who write from a source-critical perspective find E also, though in a "fragmentary" manner (e.g., Beer, 45, 47–48; Fohrer, *Überlieferung*, 70–72; Childs, 137–38; the major exception is Noth, 69–70).

This composite is not without its problems, some of which are produced by the fact that it is a composite. These have often been pointed out (whose is the plague-bringing rod? how much water became blood? where did the Egyptian learned men find unchanged water for *their* wonder-working? *etc.*), and have in fact been posed as clear evidence of the source-strata within the composite. To a degree, this becomes a self-serving argument.

There can hardly be any disputing the existence of separate traditions reporting the mighty acts designed to demonstrate Yahweh's powerful Presence, and differences in detail between such separate traditions are inevitable. There are undoubted discrepancies, certainly, between the impression these traditions would have left in their earliest forms and the impact of the composite they make up in the text of Exodus. But we must keep two points clearly in view: (1) variant traditions have been woven together here to present a brilliant narrative sequence with a single unmistakable emphasis; (2) the array of diversity in detail within this narrative sequence cannot be there by accident, given the obvious skill of the compositor(s) who put together the sequence.

As intriguing as the differences within this unified narrative are, the question of why they have been permitted to remain, given the clear and single purpose of the sequence as it stands, may be even more intriguing still. The discussion of the so-called "plague" sequence has been too preoccupied with the variations within the narrative as clues to its documents of origin, and not enough concerned with the wholeness of the narrative (cf. McCarthy, *CBQ* 27 [1965] 336–38 and *JBL* 85 [1966] 138–41), which incorporates such variations quite consciously and still presents a single emphasis.

The form of the mighty-act sequence is best understood from the end product we have at hand; it can only partially be understood from component parts we can reconstruct, at best, by a pastiche of fragments and conjecture. Despite the excesses of his argument and the unacceptability of his emphasis on a late Deuteronomistic composite, Rolf Rendtorff (*Überlieferungsgeschichtliche Problem*, 147–73) has raised some very important questions about the usual post-Wellhausenist approach to the composition of Tetrateuch/Pentateuch.

The account of the first mighty act, in Exodus 7:14–25, is perhaps the best section in the mighty act sequence to illustrate this point, a point vital to the interpretation of the entire sequence. Of the ten mighty acts, only the first and the tenth are reported by composites made up from all three tetrateuchal sources, J, E, and P. Since the account of the tenth mighty act is unique as both a part of the narrative as a whole and also as separate in important ways from the sequence of the first nine (see *Form/Structure/Setting* on 12:29–36), the account of the first mighty act stands as a kind of paradigm of the first nine.

That Exodus 7:14–25 includes information from both J and P, as these are usually described, and that this information presents some divergence of detail, cannot be doubted. The case for material from E, as Noth's objections (68–70) have shown, is much less certain, but still plausible enough to persuade a majority of the critical commentators. The divisions of Fohrer (*Überlieferung*, 70, 125) are typical:

```
J:  vv 14–15a   16–17a   18                  21a        24–25
E:            15b       17b        20aβb            23
P:                             19–20aα      21b–22
```

At the same time, the unified and sequential form of this account, especially as it is seen alongside the accounts which follow it, and as an integral part of the whole they present, has led some commentators to elaborate theories of a unity of form in which variations and the sources posed to express them are to be regarded as conjectured impositions. Typical here are Cassuto's (92–93) theory of three cycles of plagues within which five pairs of plagues are to be discovered, and Winnett's (*Mosaic Tradition*, 3–15) theory of stylistic arrangement involving in each plague "an Introductory Formula, a Central Core and a Concluding Formula."

A proper approach to the composite narrative of the mighty acts of Yahweh in Egypt cannot be made on the basis of such an either/or option. Separate traditions regarding the mighty acts are clearly present, as is an overarching pattern of arrangement. Neither must be pressed, however, either to the exclusion of the other or to a degree that superimposes upon the text something clearly not in it. Formulaic patterns can easily become as wildly speculative and as absurd as fragment-hypotheses.

The form of the mighty-act accounts may be seen to be determined by two factors: (1) the traditional material, in both oral and written form, which the compositor of the text of Exodus had at hand; (2) his purpose in composition. The first of the mighty act accounts illustrates this suggestion. There is a variance between the conception of the miracle of the changing of the water to blood as a sign of authority involving a dipping of water (4:9), as a mighty act involving the water of the Nile only (7:17–18, 20), and as a mighty act involving all the water everywhere in Egypt (vv 19, 21). There is a variance in who wields the staff that brings on the miraculous transformation, whether Moses (vv 14–16) or Aaron (v 19) or even Yahweh (vv 17, 20). There may be a variance in what constitutes the pollution of the Nile; McCarthy (*CBQ* 27 [1965] 337) sees two possibilities, Fohrer (*Überlieferung*, 63) proposes three.

But there is also here a clear movement toward an unachieved goal, the proof to Pharaoh and his people and by implication, perhaps, to Israel as well, that Yahweh is indeed both present and powerful. The careful reader of the narrative of the Book of Exodus, moving *seriatim* from 1:1 to this point is not surprised at the disbelief of Pharaoh. Not only has Yahweh predicted it (note 3:19; 4:21–22; 5:2; 6:1; 7:3–5, 13, 22), he has taken responsibility for it in advance and will continue to do so throughout the mighty act sequence. Yahweh's purpose cannot be said to be that of convincing Pharaoh and his people that he is the supreme deity. If that were so, all his efforts would have to be pronounced a failure, even by the unapologetically biased account of the OT. Yahweh's purpose, rather, is to convince the Israelites of the reality of his claims of power and Presence. And this is the purpose too of the compositor of Exodus as we know it—a purpose that has determined, along with the traditional material available to him, the form of his narrative.

That form is largely unaffected by any interest in an all-inclusive or fully homogenized account. The compositor's intention is aided by the variety of traditions, which are for him but the separate facets of a single stone. His intention is to describe Yahweh's validation of Yahweh's own claim, and with the enthusiasm of a believer he uses every argument available to him.

Comment

14 The report of Yahweh to Moses that Pharaoh's mind is כבד "heavy and dull," quite literally like a lump of lead, must be understood, in the context of the mighty act sequence and indeed in the context of the anticipation of that sequence, to be more than a mere announcement of additional difficulty. Every reference to the stubborn, obstinate, dull, hardened mind of Pharaoh must be seen against the backdrop of the entire mighty-act sequence, and every one of them, if only by general implication, reflects Yahweh's involvement. V 14 is thus tantamount to a report by Yahweh that "all is in readiness" for the proof of Presence to begin.

15 Speculation about the hygienic or religious reasons for Pharaoh's morning visit to the River Nile, though frequently undertaken by commentators, is not only useless but also a distraction. The substance of the mighty act at hand is the water of the Nile, referred to specifically no less than seven times in these twelve verses. This, surely, is the necessary point of Yahweh's instruction to Moses: he must intercept Pharaoh exactly where the substance for Yahweh's mighty act is at hand. Given the nature of the miracle, the place is unavoidable.

16–17 The staff can clearly be seen as a symbol of the power and authority of Yahweh. Moses is told by Yahweh to take it along to the meeting with Pharaoh, to announce to Pharaoh formally what everyone knows already, and then to deliver (complete with a messenger-formula) a prophetic word: Yahweh himself will strike (נכה) the Nile waters with the staff in *his* hand, and those waters will become blood. דם "blood" refers only to blood in the OT, whether of men or of animals, and vv 17, 19, and 20 do not say that the Nile waters were turned into something as red as blood, or even into a liquid that looked like blood, but quite directly and without qualification, into blood.

The whole point of this narrative, as of the additional mighty-act narratives that follow it, is the miraculous nature of an act for which Yahweh is given unequivocal responsibility. V 17 asserts and v 20 at least implies that it was *Yahweh* who struck the waters of the Nile. The action of Moses and/or Aaron, armed with the staff (or staffs) symbolizing Yahweh's authorizing power, is symbolic of what was really happening. And the effect of Yahweh's blow is that the Nile turns into דם "blood," not into the muddy or algae-laden and thus red-looking water the "naturalistic" commentators never tire of suggesting (see most fully, Hort, *ZAW* 69 [1957] 87–95). We simply must never lose sight of the fact that the mighty-act narratives are theological accounts, not phenomenological reports. Yahweh struck the Nile, and instantaneously, "before the very eyes of" Pharaoh and his court, it changed into blood. Whatever the difficulties such an assertion may pose for the readers of another age, they must not be allowed to diffuse or even to alter what the text actually says, for that inevitably either obscures or removes entirely the real point of the narrative in the first place.

18–21 In the composite of the present text, the changing of the water of the Nile sets off a chain reaction of unpleasant consequences. The transformed water is inhospitable to the fish of the Nile. They die and begin to decompose. The water-become-blood turns putrid. The Egyptians cannot bring themselves to drink such water. While it is logical to assume that the tradition of such a blow against Egypt expanded and intensified with age, an assumption often supported by reference to this first mighty-act report, we must again take seriously the composite account as we have it as the only form of the narrative about which we can be completely sure. Whatever the separate layers may originally have said about what water and how much water was changed into blood, the composite at hand presents, in effect, an initial transformation of the Nile following a blow struck by Yahweh (vv 17–18, 20) and a subsequent blow struck by Aaron (v 19; Moses *and* Aaron, v 20a), changing the remainder of the water in Egypt, both channeled and stored. Vv 17–19 anticipate this two-stage transformation; vv 20–21 report its accomplishment, finishing with the summary-declaration, "And sure enough, there was blood everywhere in Egypt."

22–23 Immediately following this summary statement, there comes the surprising report that the learned men of Egypt proceeded to do "the same thing": וַיַּעֲשׂוּ־כֵן "and then they did thus." Given the context, כֵן "the same thing, thus," must refer to the follow-up action of Moses and Aaron, the transformation not of the Nile waters already transformed by Yahweh, but the transformation of channeled or stored water, the source of which is not specified. What is especially important about this brief notice is (1) the status it assigns to the learned men of Egypt, as worthy opponents, and (2) the fact that these wizards only duplicate what Moses and Aaron have done, and make no attempt to *undo* the disgusting pollution of the Nile. The most that can be said for *their* miracle-working is that it is a copy of what Moses and Aaron have accomplished and that it actually makes matters worse for their master and their people.

We are not to conclude, therefore, that Pharaoh's obstinacy is a result of the duplication by his learned men of the action of Moses and Aaron. Yahweh has predicted that obstinacy (vv 22b, 23), and as we come increasingly to learn, he is himself responsible for it.

The River Nile as blood is mentioned in a catalog of catastrophe describing the disastrous conditions in Egypt in the period of transition from the Old Kingdom to the Middle Kingdom (*ca.* 2300–2250 B.C.). The copy of the text in which we know this catalog dates, interestingly enough, from the period between 1350 and 1100 B.C., the period in which the exodus almost certainly took place. The pertinent lines read as follows:

> WHY REALLY, the River is blood.
> If one drinks of it,
>   one rejects (it) as human
>   and thirsts for water   (*ANET*³, 441, ii 10).

No more can be made of this than that such a condition describes a time of chaos and distress. One cannot even say whether the usage is in some sense metaphorical. What is important is that the description of a time of serious reverse includes such language, and that such a text was current in the general period of the exodus. The changing of the River Nile to blood may even have been a rhetorical formula for a terrible judgment upon Egypt.

Whether that is the case or not, the language in the composite at hand appears both to have been taken quite literally and also to have represented a blow that resulted in a temporary condition of the Nile.

The Egyptians are depicted as searching everywhere, and feverishly, for potable water. No hint of whether they were successful is given, and there is no suggestion as to whether the Israelites also suffered or were somehow excluded from the blow. With the passage of seven days, the effects of Yahweh's blow apparently passed, for the pollution of the Nile is not mentioned again in the narrative of the mighty acts (cf. also Pss 78:44 and 105:29).

Explanation

Each of the first nine of the mighty-act accounts may be said to have the same fundamental point, expressed in much the same way. That point, concisely summarized, is that Yahweh powerfully demonstrates his Presence to a Pharaoh prevented from believing so that Israel may come to full belief.

As we know from the preview to the proof-of-Presence sequence, Yahweh intends that the Egyptians shall know by experience that he is Yahweh, but that preview states quite specifically that such knowledge will come to them in Yahweh's bringing forth of the children of Israel from their midst (7:4–5). In the prologue to the narrative of the mighty acts, Pharaoh asks for a wondrous deed as an authentication not of Yahweh, but of Moses and Aaron (7:8–9). The wondrous deed is given (7:10), and only partially matched by Pharaoh's learned men (7:11–12), but Pharaoh remains unimpressed by Moses and Aaron, and oblivious of Yahweh. The section at hand begins with Pharaoh heavy and dull of mind, refusing to send out the Israelites (7:14), and ends with Pharaoh turning his back on Moses and Aaron, dismissing the whole affair from his mind (7:23), while his people search feverishly for some water they can drink (7:24). Of the difficult situation of the Israelites in Egypt, nothing has changed. If anything, they are worse off than ever.

To whom, then, has the power of Yahweh's Presence proven anything? Moses and Aaron clearly believed already—else why would they have obeyed Yahweh's orders? The belief of the people of Israel is never mentioned in the narrative of the first nine of Yahweh's mighty acts, and it is only implied in the account of the tenth mighty act, in the complex of inserted liturgical material (see *Form/Structure/Setting* on 12:1–13, 14–20, and 21–28). The belief of Pharaoh is mentioned directly or indirectly in each of the mighty-act narratives, but though Pharaoh comes to an altered attitude toward Yahweh's powerful Presence, he never *believes* in him. McCarthy's theory (*CBQ* 27 [1965] 345) that the "plagues" "come close" to a purpose of producing "a conversion in Pharaoh" is not sustained by the text. Pharaoh never comes to belief, and the most that can be said of his people is that they come to a fearful respect.

Who, then, is left? For whose faith has the composite of the mighty-act narrative been assembled? And to whom are these narratives directed? There can be but a single answer to these questions, an answer that stands forth

more clearly with each successive narrative of the ten. The mighty-act accounts
are written from faith to faith. They were compiled that the generations of
Israel to come might know that Yahweh Is, and so know also the redemption
of exodus, whatever their bondage.

The Second Mighty Act   (7:26–8:11 [8:1–15])

Bibliography

Dijk, H. J. van "A Neglected Connotation of Three Hebrew Verbs." *VT* 18 (1968)
16–30. **Frankfort, H.** *Ancient Egyptian Religion.* New York: Harper & Brothers, 1961.
Loewenstamm, S. E. "The Number of Plagues in Psalm 105." *Bib* 52 (1971) 34–38.
Margulis, B. "The Plagues Tradition in Ps 105." *Bib* 50 (1969) 491–96. **Skehan,
P. W.** "Exodus in the Samaritan Recension from Qumran." *JBL* 74 (1955)
182–87.

Translation

26 [8:1]*Next Yahweh said to Moses, "Go to Pharaoh and say to him, 'Thus says
Yahweh, "Send out my people in order that they may worship me.* 27 [8:2]*Should you
refuse to do so, look out:* a *I will level a blow* b *at the whole of your territory with
frogs.* c 28 [8:3]*The Nile will be aswarm with frogs, and they will leave the river* a
and come into your house, b *right into your bedroom and even up onto your bed,
and into the houses* c *of the members of your court and onto your people, and even
into your cooking-places* d *and mixing-bowls.* e 29 [8:4]*Onto you yourself and onto your
people* a *and onto all the members of your court the frogs will leap." ' "* b

8:1 [5]*So Yahweh said to Moses, "Say to Aaron, 'Thrust out your hand with your
staff against the streams, against the irrigation-channels,* a *and against the marsh-
basins,* b *and bring up the frogs against the land of Egypt.' "* 2 [6]*Thus Aaron thrust
out his hand against the waters of Egypt, and sure enough* a *the frogs* b *came up
and spread over the land of Egypt.* 3 [7]*Then the learned men of Egypt* a *did the same
thing by their arcane arts, and so they brought up the frogs against the land of
Egypt.*

4 [8]*Now concerned,* a *Pharaoh summoned Moses and Aaron, and said, "Pray* b
*to Yahweh, that he may remove the frogs from me and from my people; then I will
send* c *the people out, and they shall sacrifice to Yahweh."* 5 [9]*Moses replied* a *to
Pharaoh, "Just set the time* b *when I am to pray in your behalf, and on behalf of
the members of your court and your people, to cut off the frogs from you* c *and from
your house, that in the Nile only they will remain."* d 6 [10]*He answered,* a *"Tomorrow!"*
So Moses b *said, "Just as you say, so will it be,* c *in order that you may know by
experience that none is comparable to Yahweh our God!* d 7 [11]*The frogs will leave
you and your house,* a *and the members of your court and your people; in the Nile
only will they remain."*

8 [12]*Then Moses and Aaron left Pharaoh's court* a *and Moses proceeded* b *to cry*

out to Yahweh concerning the frogs that he had set against Pharaoh. c 9 [13] *So Yahweh answered Moses' prayer,* a *and the frogs beswarming the houses and the yards and the fields died.* 10 [14] *They piled them up, pile after pile, until the land was heavy with the smell of them.* a 11 [15] *The minute* a *Pharaoh saw that there was an end to the frogs,* b *however, he steeled* c *his mind and would pay no attention to them, just as Yahweh had predicted.*

Notes

27 [8:2].a. הִנֵּה "behold."

27 [8:2].b. נגף most often depicts a blow, either in a physical or a metaphorical sense. It is used particularly of the action of Yahweh, and never, in the OT, of any other deity.

27 [8:2].c. צפרדע "frogs" is used as both a masc pl (7:27, 28, 29, 8:1, 3, 4, 5, 7, 8, 9) and a fem sg collective (8:2) noun in this sequence. It is derived from צפר "peep," and may therefore be an onomatopoeic name, in reference to the "peeping" sound of newly hatched frogs.

28 [8:3].a. Lit., "they will go up," read in the context above "leave the river," for clarity.

28 [8:3].b. LXX has pl, "houses, bedrooms, beds"; SamPent has "house," but pl of the other two nouns.

28 [8:3].c. MT has בית "house," but the pl "houses" of SamPent and LXX fits better with עבדיך "your servants" following.

28 [8:3].d. תנור "cooking-place" is a portable container for fire; cf. Gen 15:17; Ps 21:10 [9]; Hos 7:4, Isa 31:9; apparently it could function also as a kind of oven.

28 [8:3].e. See esp. Exod 12:34; Deut 28:5, 17.

29 [8:4].a. LXX has the more logical order, with λαόν "people" last, and without כל "all" before עבדיך "your servants"; Syr reads כל before "people."

29 [8:4].b. "Will go up," עלה. SamPent adds a lengthy verse summarizing the account to this point. Skehan (186) infers the inclusion of the same expansion in 4QExª.

8:1 [5].a. See above, n. 7:19.a.

1 [5].b. See above, n. 7:19.b.

2 [6].a. Special *waw*.

2 [6].b. צפרדע "frogs" is fem sg collective here as the two fem sg verbs before and after it make clear.

3 [7].a. "Of Egypt" is added from the context for clarity; cf. 7:11.

4 [8].a. Special *waw*, in the context of Pharaoh's request.

4 [8].b. LXX adds περὶ ἐμοῦ "for me." Cf. MT at 8:24 and LXX at 9:28.

4 [8].c. This verb is made emphatic by the addition of cohortative ה. See GKC ¶ 48c, e.

5 [9].a. אמר "say" plus special *waw*.

5 [9].b. Lit., "Please yourself over me as to the time," a statement not so much in deference as in confidence.

5 [9].c. LXX adds καὶ ἀπὸ τοῦ λαοῦ σου "and from your people."

5 [9].d. This last clause is missing from Syr.

6 [10].a. אמר "say" plus special *waw*.

6 [10].b. "Moses" added from the context, for clarity.

6 [10].c. Lit., "in accord with your word."

6 [10].d. LXX reads ὅτι οὐκ ἔστιν ἄλλος πλὴν κυρίου "that there is none besides Yahweh."

7 [11].a. LXX adds here καὶ ἐκ τῶν ἐπαύλεων "and your outbuildings," or as MT in v 9, "yards."

8 [12].a. Lit., "went out from with Pharaoh."

8 [12].b. Special *waw*.

8 [12].c. "That he had put with reference to Pharaoh." Cf. van Dijk, *VT* 18 [1968] 27–30.

9 [13].a. Lit., "did as the word of Moses."

10 [14].a. Lit., "and then the land stank."

11 [15].a. Special *waw*.

11 [15].b. רוחה means "relief, enlarging, respite." It is rendered in the context above, "end to the frogs."

11 [15].c. Hiph of כבד "cause to be heavy, dull, insensitive." MT employs the inf abs; SamPent has 3d masc sg hiph impf.

Form/Structure/Setting

The report of the second mighty act of Yahweh is, like the report of the first one, a composite report. Its seams are not so numerous and so obvious, and only two sources can be posited, J and P, but the addition of Aaron as an agent (8:1–3) and the expansion of the water sources for the miraculous multiplication of the frogs (7:28 vis-à-vis 8:1–2) are alone enough to indicate at least two layers of tradition. The source-critics have been in general agreement for some decades now on the division of this narrative. Beer in 1939 (49), Noth in 1959 (75), Fohrer in 1964 (*Überlieferung*, 70) and Childs in 1974 (131) suggested substantially identical patterns of division: 8:1–3 and 11aβ b to P, the remainder to J (though Fohrer thinks 7:28–29 is an "addition" [*Überlieferung*, 125]).

Here again, however, the whole is far more than a mere sum of its parts. The composite is designed to say more than either of the two traditions by themselves or laid together as two traditions reporting a single narrative sequence. The redactor who produced this amalgam did so without regard to discrepancies of minor detail and sequence. His intention, rather, was to produce a single account suggesting the impact of a mighty act that reached right into Pharaoh's palace, an account giving Yahweh an unqualified triumph, and one in which Moses is presented as Yahweh's representative and spokesman.

The same mingling of traditional material and purpose that dictated the form of the first mighty act account is also determinative here. The same general outline present in the other eight of the first nine mighty-act accounts is present, and what might be called the recurring rhetoric of the mighty acts is fully in evidence. Indeed this narrative, as is true of each of the first nine mighty-act narratives, may be said to have a common form as a mighty-act report: a composite form as a mingling of traditions originally separate, and a combinant form as a part of the larger and longer proof-of-Presence narrative.

A mighty act involving frogs is mentioned both in Ps 78:45 and in Ps 105:30. In each of these references, the term for "frogs" is the same as in this section in Exodus. Ps 105:30 refers to the teeming (שׁרץ) of the frogs and to their intrusion even into the royal chambers, thus conforming to the references in Exod 7:26–8:11. Ps 78:45 refers to the frogs "devastating" or "destroying" (hiphil of שׁחת) the Egyptians, an apparent expansion of the tradition reflected in the Book of Exodus (Durham, "Psalms," *BBC* 4 [Nashville: Broadman, 1971], 332).

This variance has led Loewenstamm (*Bib* 52 [1971] 35–36) to suggest that Ps 105 stands in an "intermediate position" in the development of the tradition, from the Exodus account to that of Ps 78. Indeed, Loewenstamm goes on to argue (37–38) that Ps 105 preserves "a separate form of the plague tradition," one reflecting a "poetic tradition" antedating the Pentateuch.

B. Margulis (*Bib* 50 [1969] 491–96) takes the view that Ps 105 is based on the Exodus narrative, and reflects some revision of that narrative, an argument he sustains by a reconstruction based on the psalm scroll from Qumran's Cave 11 (11QPs^a).

While neither of these two theories can be proven, they yet demonstrate the growth within the OT itself of both the content and the organization of the mighty-act traditions. Not only can the form of the mighty-act narratives be seen to be an evolved form, the number and sequence of the mighty acts themselves is also revealed as variable at different stages (and perhaps in different centers) of the growth of the OT (see *Form/Structure/Setting* on 7:14–25).

Comment

With this second in the sequence of Yahweh's mighty acts in Egypt, Moses is told for the first time to warn Pharaoh (7:27, "look out") of the consequences of continuing intractability. In the prologue to the mighty-act sequence, Pharaoh was simply presented with a wondrous deed (7:8–10). In the first mighty act, he was given a prediction of a demonstration of Yahweh's power (7:17–18). But here for the first time, he is given a warning, and here for the first time, the effects of the mighty act reach his own person. It is at least beside the point to contend, as some commentators do, that the first "plague" is more serious and a greater threat than the second. The mighty acts are not weighted from mild to serious, and the application to their sequence of "logical" patterns of increased or decreased power or intensity of effect is misleading. Each of the accounts is to the same end, and their cumulative effect is a magnification of repetition, not increasing degree. The special feature of the second mighty act, apart from its medium, is the warning and the fact that the Pharaoh actually feels its effect in his house and upon his person.

26–29 [8:1–4] The warning to be delivered to Pharaoh by Moses is not reported in the composite of MT as having been delivered, as for example the prediction of the first mighty act is (7:20, though cf. SamPent 7:29b, which does make such a report). The report of the summons of the mighty act (7:26–28) and the description of its results (7:29) effectively lead us to assume this delivery. The warning anticipates not a "plague," as such translations as RSV, NEB and JB suggest, but a "striking" or "smiting," qal active participle נֹגֵף. The most frequent use of this verb and its two noun derivatives is in reference to Yahweh's striking of blows against nations or individuals whom he is for some reason punishing. Eighteen of the forty-five OT occurrences of נֹגֵף make such a reference (see, e.g., Exod 32:35; Judg 20:35; 1 Sam 25:38; 2 Chr 21:14, 18), as do thirty of the thirty-three occurrences of the two derivatives, נֶגֶף and מַגֵּפָה, both of which are best translated "blow," "hitting." "Plague" is a far more general term than נֹגֵף suggests, and it may imply to the modern reader disease on a widespread and uncontrolled scale.

The effects of this threatened blow of Yahweh are described with some wit and in convincing detail. The Nile will be teeming with frogs, as Egypt's Delta teems with Israelites, and by the same power (שָׁרַץ "teem" is the verb both here in v 28 and in 1:7). They will swarm up from the river into the Egyptians' living quarters. Nobody will escape their incessant "peeping" and their slimy hopping. In a typically Hebrew list, ordered by priority of position,

Pharaoh is mentioned first, then the members of his cabinet, then the ordinary Egyptians (7:28; 8:5). These frogs will get into *everything*, from the most private chambers and even the beds in them, to the utensils where food is prepared and the oven-stoves where it is cooked. These references to sleeping places and cooking places are a graphic description of the extent of the blow, a description amusingly augmented by the mental picture of frogs leaping up onto Pharaoh's own person and the proud persons of the members of his cabinet as well.

8:1–2 [5–6] The introduction of Aaron into this narrative brings the sole mention of the staff symbolizing Yahweh's power and authority in the account of the second mighty act. The instruction of Yahweh in this Priestly tradition of the second mighty act is more detailed than the statement of v 28, but it is in no way contradictory of that statement. In addition to the waters of the Nile, the waters of streams and irrigation canals and river marshes will be media for the miraculous crop of frogs. Aaron's commanded and symbolic move brought on Yahweh's blow.

3 [7] The action of the learned men of Egypt, by which still more frogs were added to the frog infestation can hardly have brought any cheer to the befrogged Pharaoh or his court. V 3 is an obvious parallel to 7:11–12 and 22, and it is significant here as in 7:14–25 that the Egyptian wizards make no attempt to *reduce* the effects of Yahweh's acts; they can indeed only multiply them. One wonders, indeed, if in the original traditions these Egyptian learned men attempted to reverse the effect of Yahweh's mighty acts, and against his awesome power could succeed only in multiplying that effect, the very opposite of what they set out to do. The merit of such a suggestion is that it makes sense of the "magic" of the learned men of Egypt, which in each case only makes the situation worse. The obvious flaw in the suggestion is that it is without basis in the text of Exodus as we know it.

Some commentators (e.g., Cassuto, 101, or Hyatt, 108) suggest in the manipulation by Yahweh of the frogs a defeat of Hekt, the frog-headed goddess who assisted her husband Khnum in bringing men into being (Frankfort, *Egyptian Religion,* 15 and 85). The second mighty act would thus be a frustration, at the very least, of the life-giving process in Egypt. While such symbolism is possible, given the Egyptian context of the mighty-act sequence, it is not to be pressed. For one thing, it assumes more knowledge of Egyptian totemic theology than the collectors and readers of the mighty-act sequence are likely to have had; for another, it draws implications about the second of the mighty acts that are nowhere suggested in Exodus or anywhere else in the OT.

4 [8] With this second of the mighty acts, Pharaoh for the first time is concerned, to such an extent that he asks Moses to pray to Yahweh for the removal of the frogs, adding emphatically that he will send the people of Israel forth for their religious observance when the frogs are taken away. The verb for "pray" in vv 4 and 5 is עתר, used in the OT only of the supplication of God. Pharaoh is thus represented as giving at least a tacit acknowledgment of the Yahweh he has earlier claimed not to know (ידע, 5:2).

5–7 [9–11] The reply of Moses to this request of Pharaoh is a bold display of confidence; not only will he so pray, he is so sure of the effectiveness of such a prayer that he gives Pharaoh the privilege of setting the time for it, and hence the time for the removal of the frogs. Why Pharaoh specified "tomorrow" (8:6) instead of "right now" is unclear. It cannot be that Pharaoh was "hoping" the frogs would leave by themselves within that period (Knight, 61–62) or that "tomorrow" was "the earliest possible time" (Cassuto, 103). Perhaps the specification of such a time is intended to show Pharaoh's skepticism. Obviously so many frogs could not be removed by human means; otherwise Pharaoh would have ordered the removal himself. "Tomorrow" would allow Moses ample time to prepare for such a special prayer, but no time to plan and carry out any trickery.

Moses, however, is not daunted. It will be just as Pharaoh has specified: the frogs will leave every place except the Nile, where they belong, and all to the end that Pharaoh may know by experience (cf. 5:2) the incomparability of Yahweh, God of Israel.

8–11[12–15] The report that Moses began to cry out (צעק) to Yahweh immediately after his departure, with Aaron, from Pharaoh's court is reflective more of the composite nature of this narrative than of any attempt by Moses to ignore Pharaoh's timetable.

The answer to Moses' prayer was immediate, and it must have prompted in Pharaoh a wish that he had been more specific about the means and timing of the frogs' removal. Yahweh's solution was to put them to death, and their rotting carcasses, heaped into piles, sent a terrible stench throughout the land. One could argue that such a further pollution prompted Pharaoh to go back on his promise to send the people of Israel out of the land, but Pharaoh's change of mind is virtually predetermined. Yahweh has predicted it, because Yahweh is prompting it. Whether Pharaoh steels his mind as here, or whether Yahweh makes Pharaoh's mind obstinate, as in 9:12, Yahweh is using Pharaoh, who finally will not fully believe, as a teaching tool for Israel. We have been told as much in 4:21, in a passage encapsulating both the wondrous signs and the mighty acts and stating their purpose.

Explanation

This second of the mighty act accounts is thus a further statement of the point of the first account, the point shared by each of the first nine mighty-act accounts. Here, the motif of the Pharaoh's disbelief is intensified by his apparent capitulation under pressure, a capitulation quickly reversed when the pressure is removed. Just as Pharaoh could not control the population explosion of the Israelites in the Delta of Egypt, even though he wanted to, so here he cannot come to a cooperative belief, even should he want to. Yahweh's hand is in these matters from the start and throughout and to the end that *Israel* might believe—not Pharaoh and not the nation of Egypt.

The entire mighty-act sequence increasingly demonstrates this point, and the assumption that Pharaoh or his people are the real objects of Yahweh's powerful deeds in Egypt makes Yahweh out to be unthinkably and cruelly arbitrary and the whole mighty-act sequence to be both ineffective and irrelevant. The center of purpose of each of these narratives and of all of them together is Israel, the community of faith.

In this narrative, the quasi-comical picture of frogs hopping everywhere, even onto the mighty king of Egypt himself, and Moses' mock-deference in allowing Pharaoh himself to set the time for the frogs' removal, present clearly the message that Yahweh is in charge in the very territory of the Pharaoh's own supremacy. Everything occurs as Moses predicts, except one thing: Pharaoh does not come, by the experience, to a convincing knowledge of the incomparability of Yahweh. But then, as 8:11 makes clear, that was an expectation of Moses, not of Yahweh.

The Third Mighty Act (8:12–15 [16–19])

Bibliography

Couroyer, B. "Le 'doigt de Dieu' (Exode, VIII, 15)." *RB* 63 (1956) 481–95. **Greenberg, M.** "The Redaction of the Plague Narrative in Exodus." *Near Eastern Studies in Honor of W. F. Albright.* Ed. H. Goedicke. Baltimore: Johns Hopkins Press, 1971. 243–52. **Hort, G.** "The Plagues of Egypt." *ZAW* 69 (1957) 84–103; 70 (1958) 48–59. **Loewenstamm, S. E.** "The Number of Plagues in Psalm 105." *Bib* 52 (1971) 34–38. ———. מסורת יציאת מצרים בהשתלשלותה. Jerusalem: at the Magnes Press, 1965.

Translation

12 [16] *Next, Yahweh said to Moses, "Say to Aaron, 'Thrust out your staff* [a] *and strike the loose soil of the earth, and it will turn into* [b] *a swarm of gnats* [c] *blanketing the whole of Egypt.' "* [d] 13 [17] *They did just as Yahweh ordered:* [a] *Aaron thrust out his hand with his staff and struck the loose soil of the earth, and instantly* [b] *it turned into the swarm of gnats, on man and on animal alike. All the loose soil of the earth turned into a swarm of gnats blanketing the whole of Egypt.*

14 [18] *The learned men of Egypt* [a] *then attempted* [b] *by their arcane arts to produce* [c] *the swarm of gnats, but they were not able to do it. Even so, the swarm of gnats was on man and on animal alike.* 15 [19] *Then the learned men said to Pharaoh, "This is an act* [a] *of a god." But Pharaoh's mind remained obstinate, and he would pay no attention to them, just as Yahweh had predicted.*

Notes

12[16].a. SamPent has ידך במטך "your hand with your staff."
12[16].b. Lit., "and it will be," וְהָיָה . SamPent has ויהי, special *waw* with impf of היה.
12[16].c. LXX adds ἔν τε τοῖς ἀνθρώποις καὶ ἐν τοῖς τετράποσιν "upon man and upon animal alike," as in vv 13, 14.
12[16].d. Lit., "in all of the land of Egypt."
13[17].a. This phrase, obviously referring to both Moses and Aaron, is lacking in LXX.
13[17].b. Special *waw*.
14[18].a. The reference is clearly the same as in 7:11 and 22; "of Egypt" is thus added above for clarity.
14[18].b. ויעשׂו־כן, lit., "then they did the same."
14[18].c. להוציא "to cause to go forth."
15[19].a. Lit., "the finger (אצבע) of a god."

Form/Structure/Setting

This brief, compact account of the third of the mighty acts, unlike the two accounts preceding it, is not a composite. Along with the account of the sixth of the mighty acts, this account is usually assigned wholly to the Priestly source (e.g., Beer, 51, and 53; Fohrer, *Überlieferung,* 70–71 [N.B. an error, IV for VI on p. 71]; Hyatt, 109–11 and 115–16), though Greenberg (*Near Eastern Studies,* 245–52) prefers a "tradition-complex" labeled "B," which viewed the "plagues" as "demonstrations of God's power," and Loewenstamm sets forth a theory of an array of traditions amalgamated under the aegis of three motifs (מסורת, ii–v, 25–76). Many commentators consider this third mighty-act account simply a variant of the fourth mighty-act account that follows it (e.g., Rylaarsdam, *IB* 1:900; Hyatt, 110–11), and Noth (76–79) actually treats the two accounts together, as a single mighty act, a procedure that Loewenstamm (*Bib* 52 [1971] 34–38) supports on the basis of the text of Ps 105:31.

One point of importance for the resolution of this problem is the difference between the terms כֵּן כַּנָּם (כִּנָּם, כִּנִּים, BDB, 487) and עָרֹב. כנם is variously rendered "gnats, swarm of gnats, lice, mosquitoes, maggots." The harvester gnat (*Chironomidae*), the *Anopheles* mosquito, and the sandfly (*Psychodidae*) have all been proposed as possibilities (Frerichs, "Gnat," *IDB* 2:403). עָרֹב appears to be a more general term, derived from ערב "mix" and referring to a "mixture" or "swarm" of flying insects; thus עָרֹב is generally translated "flies." JB translates עָרֹב by "gadflies," and some commentators refer to stinging flies (Honeycutt, *BBC* 1:356; Driver, 66–67), the biting fly *Stomoxys calcitrans* (Hort, *ZAW* 69 [1957] 99, 101–3), and even the devouring scarab beetle (Knight, 63–64). The עָרֹב is not said in the account of the fourth mighty act to bite or sting, however; Exod 8:20 [24] says that the land was "devastated" or "ruined" (שחת) by it, a term used in Ps 78:45 of the effect upon the Egyptians of the frogs, while the עָרֹב is said, in that same verse, to have "eaten" (אכל) them. The use of both terms in Ps 105:31 is not much help, since עָרֹב could obviously include כנם as flying insects, and the parallelism is not necessarily synonymous.

A second point of importance, that both the third and the fourth mighty-act accounts appear to be each from a single source, both describing an act of Yahweh involving insects, is also inconclusive. The more detailed account of 8:16–28 is the one that uses the more general term עָרֹב, while the compact account at hand uses the specific term כנם. Though there are additional noncomposite mighty-act accounts (9:1–7; 9:8–12, sixth and seventh of the mighty acts), there are not two additional accounts so similar in theme.

In sum, one has to admit that there is not in these accounts themselves, or in any other passage in the OT sufficient evidence for sustaining either argument, that Exod 8:12–15 and 8:16–28 are two accounts of the same mighty act or separate accounts of two successive (or at least different) mighty acts.

We are thus left with the overall sequence of the ancient proof-of-Presence compilation, a sequence in which, everywhere else, parallel accounts of the same mighty act have been combined, and a sequence which not only drew upon a number of traditions but apparently left some unmentioned (see *Form/*

Structure/Setting on 7:14–25 and 7:26–8:11). In that compilation, which is itself far the most ancient commentary on the mighty-act sequence we have, the כנם "gnats" mighty act and the ערב "swarm of insects" mighty act appear to be separate, with the second of them a more devastating threat than the first.

The section at hand probably describes therefore a separate mighty act, one reported entirely in the characteristic style of the Priestly circle, a discomfiting divine act more akin to the unpleasant multiplication of the frogs than to the devastation of the swarming of a horrible mixture of flying insects. Whatever may be the irrecoverable foundation sequence of the proof-of-Presence acts, the sequence of the text at hand is plain, and in the absence of conclusive evidence, it is best treated as it stands—or, in this instance, appears to stand.

Comment

12–13 [16–17]   Yahweh's instruction through Moses to Aaron that he is to strike the עפר, the loose topsoil or surface-dirt of the land of Egypt, is probably to be understood as a symbol of both the endless number of the gnats and their universal extent. As the water of Egypt was changed to blood, so the loose dirt, not just "dust," is now to be changed to a swarm of gnats that will cover the whole of Egypt just as the loose soil of the earth does. No locale where there is loose soil is to escape (another point of contrast with the following account, involving the ערב "swarm of insects").

Without a report of any confrontation with Pharaoh, the narrative moves instead directly to the obedience first of Moses, then of Aaron, and to the immediate result, the swarming upon humans and animals alike of gnats.

14–15 [18–19]   As in the first two instances of mighty action, the learned men of Egypt attempt to duplicate the marvel, but this time, they fail to do so. Not only can they not reverse the miracle, they cannot now even copy it, as heretofore they have done. Thus the Egyptian wonderworkers declare to Pharaoh that they are up against a god (*Elohim*, 8:15). This assertion should not be taken as an indication that the previous mighty acts were regarded by these learned men as mere tricks or sleight-of-hand. From the first, the learned men are presented as worthy opponents (see *Comment* on 7:22–23). They would no doubt have been regarded, just as were Moses and Aaron, as representatives or extensions of the power of deity. But with this third of the mighty acts, they confess themselves, and thus the power they represent, as outdistanced.

The statement of the learned men of Egypt, אצבע אלהים הוא, literally, "Elohim's finger, this!" has been taken by Couroyer (*RB* 63 [1956] 483) as unique in its reference to the "finger" as opposed to the more usual reference to the "hand" of God. Couroyer distinguishes between texts that speak of the "fingers" of God (as Ps 8:3) and those that speak of the "finger" of God (as here, and in Deut 9:10), and he proposes (487) that the phrase, spoken by the Egyptian wizards, may be of Egyptian origin. He then concludes (487–90), from references in Egyptian texts, that the "finger of Elohim" refers to Aaron's staff, by which the loose soil is turned by a blow into the swarm of gnats. הוּא "this" comes thus to refer not to the mighty act of Yahweh, but to the staff that brings on that act. And *Elohim,* Couroyer concludes (491), may refer not to Yahweh, or to any specific deity, but simply to divinity in general: "god," not "God."

Couroyer's theory is interesting, but his support for it is not conclusive. The idea that the phrase "finger of god (God)" refers literally to the staff of Aaron which the learned men of Egypt have watched in increasing awe (491–92) is only arbitrarily supported. But Couroyer may be correct in his suggestion that the Egyptian wizards are declaring to Pharaoh the presence in this miracle of divine power without confessing a belief in Yahweh, the God Moses and Aaron represent. The statement of the learned men is perhaps not the surrender it has often been made out to be, but instead a declaration to Pharaoh that God or a god, perhaps even one of Egypt's gods, is responsible for what has taken place.

This information, however, has no effect on Pharaoh. His mind remains obstinate, and he pays no attention to his learned men now, any more than he has earlier to Moses and Aaron (here not in his presence, as before).

Explanation

The new element introduced in the account of the third of the mighty acts is the realization by Pharaoh's learned men that God or a god is in the midst of what is happening in Egypt. In the first two mighty act accounts, Moses and Aaron represented Yahweh, as the learned men represented their gods. But with the terrifying swarm of gnats, which they cannot remove or control or even copy, these learned men declare for the first time, "This is an act of a god."

This difference is a difference of nearness. For the first time, the Egyptians, in the person of those most likely to be the first to know such a thing, move a step toward the recognition of the one fact the entire mighty-act sequence is designed to prove: that Yahweh, the God of the Israelites, is himself powerfully present right in their midst, precisely where their own gods manifest *their* greatest strength. And though it is probable that the Egyptian learned men are to be understood at best as making a declaration that is far short of a surrender, they have nevertheless been shaken, and their arrogant defense for the first time shows a crack.

Perhaps the most that can be said of Pharaoh and the Egyptians, even at the end of the proof-of-Presence sequence and following its full cumulative effect is that they admit the existence of Yahweh and the reality of his powerful Presence. They do not come, even according to the OT's accounting, to a belief in him that changes anything more than their policy toward the Israelites, and even on that subject they remain ambiguous and mercurial right to the very end.

There is thus a kind of theological realism in the arrangement of the proof-of-Presence sequence, a realism reflected both in the primary purpose of the mighty acts, the proof of Yahweh's Presence to the sons of Israel, and also in the clear suggestion that the Egyptians, though shaken, never really come to faith in Yahweh as *their* God, only to the admission of his powerful

Presence as *Israel's* God. The first hint of this realism is the manner in which the learned men of Egypt are represented in the first two of the mighty-act accounts. They are not mere magicians, the clever tricksters they have sometimes been represented to be, but worthy opponents who are able to match the miracles wrought by Yahweh through Moses and Aaron. There is no attempt in Exodus to discredit these learned men, for discrediting them means discrediting Moses and Aaron and hence Yahweh. On the contrary, they are taken very seriously, and the move is to outdo them, *not* to undo them.

The second manifestation of this theological realism is the admission by the learned men, when they are first outdone here in the third of the mighty acts, that "this is an act of a god!" Even if their reference is to their own deity, or to one of their own deities, the declaration is no less significant, for they are acknowledging themselves outdistanced by a divine power manifested through two men their Pharaoh has refused to take seriously. The context of their assertion makes plain that its reference is not to the miracle of the gnat-swarm (in which case the assertion should have come after 8:13 [17]) but to their inability to copy that miracle, for the assertion (8:15 [19]) follows the report of their failure (8:14 [18]).

There are further reflections of this theological realism in the proof-of-Presence sequence, and these will be noted as they occur; but perhaps the most telling evidence of it to this point is the refusal of the narrator of Exod 8:12–15 [16–19] to give in to the temptation to have the learned men of Egypt say, "This is an act of Yahweh!" What they *do* say is far more likely what they *would* have said: "This is an act of a god!"

The Fourth Mighty Act   (8:16–28 [20–32])

Bibliography

Albright, W. F. "New Light on Early Recensions of the Hebrew Bible." *BASOR* 140 (1955) 27–35. **Davies, G. I.** The Hebrew Text of Exodus VIII 19—An Emendation." *VT* 24 (1974) 489–92. **Gardiner, A. H.** "The Geography of the Exodus: An Answer to Professor Naville and Others." *JEA* 10 (1924) 87–96. ———. "The Supposed Egyptian Equivalent of the name of Goshen." *JEA* 5 (1918) 218–23. **Ginzberg, L.** *Legends of the Jews.* New York: Simon and Schuster, 1961. **Greenberg, M.** "The Thematic Unity of Exodus III–XI." *Fourth World Congress of Jewish Studies: Papers*, Vol. 1. Jerusalem: World Union of Jewish Studies, 1967. 151–54. **Labuschagne, C. J.** "The Emphasizing Particle *Gam* and Its Connections." *Studia Biblica et Semitica.* Wageningen: H. Veenman and Sons, 1966. 193–203. ———. "The Particles הֵן and הִנֵּה." *OTS* 18 (1973) 1–14. **MacIntosh, A. A.** "Exodus VIII 19, District Redemption and the Hebrew Roots פדה and פדד." *VT* 21 (1971) 548–55. **McCarthy, D. J.** "Moses' Dealings with Pharaoh: Ex 7,8–10,27." *CBQ* 27 (1965) 336–47. **Naville, E.** "The Geography of the Exodus." *JEA* 10 (1924) 18–39. **Nötscher, F.** "Zum Emphatischen Lamed." *VT* 3 (1953) 372–80. **Philo.** *De Vita Mosis in Philo*, VI. LCL. Cambridge, MA: Harvard University Press, 1935. 273–595.

Translation

16 [20] *Next, Yahweh said to Moses, "Get up early in the morning, and take a*
position ^a *where you cannot miss Pharaoh,* ^b *just as he is going out toward the water;* ^c
then say to him, 'Thus says Yahweh, "Send out my people, in order that they may
worship me. ^d 17 [21] *If you do not send out my people, look out: I will send forth* ^a
against you and against the members of your court and against your people and
against your houses a mixed swarm of flying insects. ^b *The Egyptians' houses will be*
full of these flying insects, and even the very ground will be covered with them. ^c
18 [22] *Yet on that day I will separate the land of Goshen, where my people remain.*
There will not be there any swarm of insects, so that you may know by experience
that I am Yahweh, right in the heart of the land. 19 [23] *I will set a protecting shield* ^a
between my people and your people. Tomorrow this sign will arrive." ' " ^b

20 [24] *So Yahweh did exactly that.* ^a *A thick* ^b *swarm of flying insects came* ^c *into*
Pharaoh's palace, into the mansions of the members of his court, and into the whole
land of Egypt. The land was devastated by the presence of this swarm.

21 [25] *Once again concerned,* ^a *Pharaoh summoned Moses and Aaron, and said,*
"Go along and offer sacrifices to your god in this land." 22 [26] *But Moses replied,*
"It would not be proper to do that, because we will offer sacrifices to Yahweh our
God that the Egyptians will find objectionable; if we offer such sacrifices before the
very eyes of the Egyptians, won't they stone us to death? ^a 23 [27] *We must rather go*
along three days' journey into the wilderness and there offer sacrifice to Yahweh our
God, just as he is telling ^a *us."*

24 [28] *Then Pharaoh responded, "I* ^a *will send you out, and you will offer sacrifices*
to Yahweh your god in the wilderness; just don't go any great ^b *distance away. Pray* ^c
in my behalf." ^d

25 [29] *Moses replied, "I am going straight out* ^a *from your presence to pray to*
Yahweh, ^b *and the swarm of flying insects will leave Pharaoh,* ^c *and the members of*
his court, and his people, tomorrow. Just let Pharaoh not multiply deceit by not
sending out the people to offer sacrifices to Yahweh."

26 [30] *So Moses went forth from Pharaoh's presence and prayed to Yahweh.* ^a
27 [31] *And Yahweh did what Moses prayed he would do,* ^a *and took the swarm of*
flying insects from Pharaoh, the members of his court, and his people.

28 [32] *Not one insect was left. Once again, however,* ^a *Pharaoh steeled* ^b *his mind,*
this time as well, and he would not send out the people.

Notes

16[20].a. See n. 7:15.b.

16[20].b. Lit., "before Pharaoh's face," or "right in front of Pharaoh."

16[20].c. See n. 7:15.a.

16[20].d. LXX adds εν τῇ ἐρήμῳ "in the wilderness," in accord with MT at 7:16. Cf. also
5:1 and 8:24.

17[21].a. Lit., "look at me sending forth."

17[21].b. On ערב "swarm of insects," see *Form/Structure/Setting* on 8:12–15[16–19].

17[21].c. Lit., "The Egyptians' houses will be full . . . and also the ground that they are
upon." Cf. Labuschagne, *Studia,* 199–203.

19[23].a. Reading פרדת from פרד "divide, separate," instead of MT's פדת from פדה "ransom, redeem, save." Though פרדה "separation, shield" does not occur in the Hebrew of the
OT, the verb from which it may be derived does, more than 25 times. פְּדוּת "ransom" occurs
only 4 times, including this occurrence, and can be made to fit the context here only by a

complete and arbitrary change of its clear meaning. The emendation to פרדת is a suggestion of Davies (*VT* 24 [1974] 491–92), who explains פדה as a corruption by haplogr (the similarity, in this instance, of ר and ד). For a review of the traditional position and an alternative suggestion, see MacIntosh, *VT* 21 (1971) 548–55. By its "Factor 8, misunderstanding of linguistic data," the *Preliminary and Interim Report* (99–100) of the United Bible Societies stays with the פדה of MT, with the explanation that "this deliverance will distinguish my people from your people"— a circumlocution the text and the context will not sustain. LXX reads διαστολήν "distinction"; Vg *divisionem* "division."

19[23].b. Lit., "this sign will be." To this, LXX adds ἐπὶ τῆς γῆς "upon the land."

20[24].a. Special *waw* + עשה + כן: "So Yahweh did yes, thus."

20[24].b. כבד "heavy," to which SamPent adds מאד "very, exceedingly."

20[24].c. Syr and Tg Onq have "so he (Yahweh) brought."

21[25].a. Special *waw* in this context.

22[26].a. The negative is lacking in LXX, Syr, Vg, thus turning the verse into an assertion ending with "they will stone us to death." Labuschagne (*Studia*, 10–11) argues against deletion of the negative on the basis of the presence of הן "behold" as a conj followed by an interrogative clause. Notscher (*VT* 3 [1953] 375) argues that לא "not" here is an emphatic usage of ל "to" giving "an affirmative sense" to the statement: "Die Ägypter werden uns *gewiss* steinigen."

23[27].a. Or "as he tells us, is saying to us"; the instruction has been given already, repeatedly. There is thus no reason to translate the impf יאמר "he says" as a fut tense verb.

24[28].a. The "I" is made emphatic by the use of the independent personal pronoun אנכי plus the 1st pers verb form.

24[28].b. Hiph inf constr plus hiph impf of רחק "make distance, go from."

24[28].c. LXX adds οὖν "therefore, please."

24[28].d. LXX adds πρὸς κύριον "to Yahweh" as in v 4 and 9:28.

25[29].a. Lit., "Look, I am going out from with you."

25[29].b. LXX has θεόν "God" instead of "Yahweh."

25[29].c. LXX has ἀπὸ σοῦ "from you" instead of "from Pharaoh," and σου "your" instead of "his" with "court" and "people."

26[30].a. See n. 25.b.

27[31].a. Lit., "as the word of Moses."

28[32].a. Special *waw* in this context, followed by גם "also." Cf. Labuschagne, *Studia*, 202–3.

28[32].b. Hiph of כבד "cause to be heavy, dull insensitive." Cf. above, n. 11.c.

Form/Structure/Setting

The account of the fourth mighty act is, like the account preceding it, an apparent unity, and one generally attributed to the Yahwist (so, e.g., McNeile, 51–52, Hyatt, 111–15). Noth (76–79) thinks of it as a J version of the "plague" described by P in vv 12–15[16–19], the two narratives side by side making up a composite consisting of two accounts of the same mighty act. This argument cannot, however, be sustained, and for the reasons set forth above (*Form/Structure/Setting* on 8:12–15) it is best to consider the two accounts separate narratives of two mighty acts, at the very least by the time the proof-of-Presence sequence was brought together in its present order.

The similarity of the sequence of this mighty-act account to that of the first (7:14–25) and the seventh (9:13–35) mighty-act accounts, along with the like parallels in the other accounts, has led to a series of theories about a cyclical arrangement or a grouping of accounts based on certain recurring features (see, e.g., Greenberg, *Fourth World Congress*, 153–54, and much more fully, *Understanding*, 169–82; Cassuto, 92–93; McCarthy, *CBQ* 27 [1965] 341–44). As ingenious as these theories are, however, the very fact that they all begin with the same original and all end with a different pattern suggests either that they are making too much of inevitable similarities or that they are approaching these similarities from the wrong perspective.

There may be some truth in both of these suggestions. As Childs quite correctly says (150), ". . . it is difficult to determine how much sense for symmetry was intended by the final redactor and how much is accidental," and the wide variation in the patterns suggested tends to support the alternative of accident as opposed to the alternative of intention. A still more important consideration may be that of perspective: if the points of similarity are viewed not from the outside, as clues to formal and parallel patterns, but from the inside, as indicative of an inventory of what may be called mighty-act rhetoric, they may perhaps be seen more as evidence of the long accumulation of mighty-act tradition than as the formal characteristics of cyclical or counterpointed arrangement.

The one common denominator of all the mighty-act narratives is their purpose in proving Yahweh's Presence, in establishing both the validity of the claim of "Is-ness" made by the tetragrammaton and also the authority of the command to both Pharaoh and Israel. But expressive of that purpose, and so an inevitable outgrowth of that common denominator, is the special language of the mighty-act narratives, a language of both concept and deed, of both context and symbol. So the hardening of Pharaoh's mind, the bringing and the ending of the specific mighty acts, the necessary occasions and places of confrontation with Pharaoh, the authorizing staff, all gave rise to a pointed and loaded mighty-act rhetoric. This rhetoric, further, was a common stock from which all the narrators drew, and would immediately have been understood by all who were in any meaningful way party to the tradition. It necessarily dictates much of the form of the report of the mighty acts in the proof-of-Presence sequence, and it may suggest, when viewed from the outside, patterns of arrangement not actually present.

Thus the form of this fourth mighty-act account, itself a unity, can be parallel to that of the first account, clearly a composite. The parallels are created by a common purpose and the language expressive of that one purpose. The additional elements in this account, the exclusion of the land of Goshen (v 18[22]) and the flexibility of Pharaoh (vv 21 and 24[25, 28]), may be seen therefore as logical and appropriate additions to the traditions, not as variations in established patterns. And the form of this account, as of the other mighty act narratives, emerges more from the mighty-act rhetoric and the confession of faith that gave rise to it than from any overarching and recurring formula.

Comment

The command of Yahweh in Exod 7:15 that Moses should intercept Pharaoh "in the morning, just when he is going out toward the water," a command that specifies "the bank of the Nile" as the place of confrontation, bears a logical connection with the first of the mighty acts, which has as its substance the waters of Egypt, to begin with, apparently, the water of the Nile.

16–20[20–24] No substance for the swarm of flying insects of the fourth mighty act is specified, and the command of v 16 that Moses "get up early" (hiphil of שׁכם), a new element in the instruction, and that he intercept Pharaoh as he goes "toward the water," is probably best taken as a rhetorical provision of a setting, perhaps a reflection of the first mighty-act account, and not as a reference to some "standing custom" (Driver, 59). The instruction to "get up early" is repeated verbatim in 9:13, the opening sentence of the seventh mighty-act account, but there is no reference there to any water, or to any movement of Pharaoh. Yet Moses is in that instance, as in these other two, to "take a position" in Pharaoh's presence. The similarity in the three separate instructions is rhetorical, and probably an evidence that they come from the same source. The differences in them are also important, for they reflect an adaptation of a single setting, necessary in the first instance, to two additional instances in which a specific setting within Egypt is unnecessary.

The ערב "mixed swarm of flying insects" (LXX κυνόμυιαν "dog-fly, i.e., shameless fly" (Liddell-Scott, Greek-English Lexicon [Oxford: Clarendon, 1968] 1010), dramatically described by Philo (De Vita Mosis I, xxiii, 130–32) and transformed in Haggadic legend into "a mixed horde of wild animals, lions, bears, wolves, and panthers, and . . . many birds of prey" (Ginzberg, Legends, 335–36) is best taken as a general term, referring to a terrifying collection of insects. They are said in Ps 78:45, but not here, to have "eaten" the Egyptians. They are clearly regarded as a miracle of Yahweh, both by the suddenness of their arrival and by their endless number, and also by the equal suddenness and completeness of their departure (vv 26–27[30–31]). So similarly, their absence from the land of Goshen, where Yahweh's people are, is regarded as miraculous.

Goshen has generally been connected with the eastern half of the Delta region of Egypt, in the main because of references in Gen 46:28–29, 33–34; and 47:1–6, 11. Joseph is said to have given his father Israel and his brothers "land of their own in the land of Egypt, in the best (מיטב) of the land, in the land of Rameses (רעמסס, in Genesis an anachronism), just as Pharaoh had ordered" (Gen 47:11), and the context makes clear that this is at least inclusive of Goshen. A variety of attempts to locate Goshen more specifically, either in terms of Egyptian texts (Naville, JEA 10 [1924] 19–32; Gardiner, JEA 5 [1918] 218–23, and JEA 10 [1924] 94–95) or the LXX references to "Gesem of Arabia" in Gen 45:10 and 46:34 (Albright, BASOR 140 [1955] 31), have proven inconclusive (cf. Lambdin, "Goshen," IDB 2:442).

The exclusion of Goshen from the visit of the swarm of flying insects, whatever relief it may have meant for the sons of Israel there, is said specifically to be to the end that Pharaoh might come by experience to know that Yahweh is a reality and "right in the heart of the land," that is, in Egypt itself. The admission by Pharaoh that the "Hebrews" might have their own god in their own land is one thing—an admission that he exists even in Egypt's land is something else. The rendering of some translators (e.g., RSV; Cassuto, 108), "in the midst of the earth," obscures this point and is misleading. Once again, it is not Pharaoh's "conversion" that is in view, but his acknowledgement that Yahweh *is*, and to that end, Yahweh interposes a barrier, a protecting shield, between his people and the insect-covered Egyptians.

21–24[25–28]   Once more, as when the frogs filled the land, Pharaoh becomes concerned and offers an opportunity for sacrifices "in this land." The opportunity offered in 8:4 is less specific, though the piel שלח at least implies a sacrifice beyond the land. To this offer, however, Moses raises a question of discretion. The Egyptians, he says, will find the sacrifices offered to Yahweh תועבת "objectionable."

Exactly the same term is used, in Gen 43:32, of the Egyptians' attitude toward dining with Hebrews, and in Gen 46:34, of the Egyptians' opinion of the Hebrews' vocation as shepherds. What in particular may be objectionable about the Hebrews' sacrifices is not said. Given the references in Genesis and the reflections in Exodus of the virulence of Egyptian oppression, we might easily conclude a general Egyptian antipathy toward all things Israelite.

Pharaoh indeed is apparently convinced by the argument of Moses that Hebrew sacrifices right in front of the Egyptians could well lead to violence, and he accepts the condition that Moses and his people should do what Yahweh is saying to them, by indicating without demurrer, and emphatically, that he will himself send them forth from the land to their religious duty to Yahweh their god. To this assertion, Pharaoh adds two conditions, or at least a condition and a request: they are not to go a great distance, and Moses must pray on his behalf, apparently for the removal of the thick swarm of insects.

25–28 [29–32] The second of these conditions Moses agrees to meet, without reference to the first. Then he states a condition of his own: the Pharaoh is not this time to go back on his word. Moses is as good as his word, and Yahweh answers Moses' prayer fully, removing even the last insect. But once again, Pharaoh breaks *his* word, steels his mind, and refuses to send Israel forth. By now we are not surprised. Though we are not here reminded of Yahweh's prediction of this intransigence, as at the end of the second (8:11) and third (8:15) mighty-act accounts, we are increasingly aware of its inevitability, throughout the proof-of-Presence sequence.

Explanation

Once more, then, the recurring point of the mighty-act narratives is made. Yahweh *is* what his name claims him to be, and he *is* that in Egypt, in Pharaoh's own territory, in the houses of his cabinet and his people, and under the very noses of Pharaoh's own gods.

What is new in this fourth of the mighty acts, apart from the nature of the miracle itself, is the separation of the land of Goshen from the effects of miracle (there has been no mention of Goshen's fate in the earlier accounts), the negotiations between Pharaoh and Moses, with each of them setting conditions, and the allusion to the antipathy of the Egyptians to Israelite worhsip (or to Israelite ways, and to Israelites in general).

But the point remains the same. Yahweh *is* in Egypt. Pharaoh will see that Yahweh *is*, and *is* in Egypt, both by what he does and also by where he does it. But so also will Israel, the real pupils, see the point. For they, Yahweh's own people, are the ones who are spared the devastation of the thick swarm of flying insects. And in the end, though Pharaoh sees enough to negotiate, he does not see enough to believe. Nor does he, ever, as the further mighty acts reveal.

The Fifth Mighty Act (9:1–7)

Bibliography

Hort, G. "The Plagues of Egypt." *ZAW* 69 (1957) 84–103. **Loewenstamm, S. E.**
מסורת יציאת מצרים בהשתלשלותה. Jerusalem: at the Magnes Press, 1965. **Ogden,
G. S.** "Notes on the Use of היה in Exodus IX 3." *VT* 17 (1967) 483–84.

Translation

¹*Next, Yahweh said to Moses, "Go to Pharaoh and speak to him: 'Thus says
Yahweh, God of the Hebrews, "Send out my people in order that they may worship
me. *²*For should you refuse to do so,* ᵃ *and once again tighten your grip on them,
³ look out—the hand of Yahweh will be* ᵃ *against your livestock* ᵇ *in the pasture, against
the horses, against the he-asses, against the camels, against the herd* ᶜ *and against
the flock:* ᶜ *a decimating* ᵈ *epidemic.* ⁴*Yet Yahweh* ᵃ *will separate the livestock of Israel
from the livestock of the Egyptians, and no animal* ᵇ *belonging to the sons of Israel
will die."'"*
⁵*Then Yahweh set a specific time, saying, "Tomorrow Yahweh will do this deed* ᵃ
in the land." ⁶*And sure enough,* ᵃ *Yahweh did this deed, beginning the next day.* ᵇ
*In consequence, all the Egyptians' livestock died; but of the livestock of the sons of
Israel, not a single animal* ᶜ *died.* ⁷*Yet when Pharaoh sent out* ᵃ *and saw* ᵇ *that not
even a single animal from the livestock of* ᶜ *Israel had died, Pharaoh's mind remained
heavy and dull,* ᵈ *and he did* not *send out the people.*

Notes

2.a. Lit., "For if you refuse to send out."
3.a. *Masora parva* notes that the qal ptcp of היה "be" occurs only here in the OT, and SamPent
has the qal pf form, הָיָה. Ogden (*VT* 17 [1967] 484) has proposed that the usage of the participle
here is reflective of a pattern followed uniformly in the first, second, fifth, seventh, and eighth
mighty-act accounts.
3.b. מקנה "livestock" is a collective term, referring generally to domesticated grazing animals,
as the list of v 3 shows.
3.c. בקר and צאן are also general terms, the first referring to herd-animals such as cows
and horses, the second referring to flock-animals such as sheep and goats.
3.d. Lit., "a very heavy (or severe) epidemic."
4.a. LXX continues in 1st pers here, and uses a somewhat different expression, καὶ παραδοξάσω
ἐγὼ ἐν τῷ καιρῷ ἐκείνῳ "And I will make an extraordinary (lit., a paradoxical) distinction in
that time. . . ."
4.b. דָּבָר "thing."
5.a. The word here and in v 6 is also דָּבָר "thing"; in an unpointed text, however, these
consonants could be read דֶּבֶר "epidemic," a more specific vocalization.
6.a. Special *waw* in this context.
6.b. "From the next day," thus giving an impression of the start of an epidemic lasting
through some days.
6.c. "One, a single one."
7.a. The verb שלח "send out" here, in apparent reference to servants or even soldiers of
Pharaoh, presents a dramatic parallel with Yahweh's command ("Send out my people," v 1),
contrasting whom Pharaoh does and does not "send out" (שלח is used twice in v 7). LXX
reads altogether differently, ἰδὼν δὲ φαραω "Pharaoh saw."
7.b. והנה "and behold."

7.c. SamPent, LXX, and some Tg MSS (see Déaut, *Targum*, 67, British Museum Add. 27031) add "the sons of" here.

7.d. כבד "heavy and dull," as in 7:14; qal pf there, qal impf with special *waw* here; cf. n. 7:14.a.

Form/Structure/Setting

Source-critics generally have assigned this fifth mighty-act account to the Yahwist (so, e.g., Beer, 52–53, "J²"; Fohrer, *Überlieferung*, 70–73). The general features of J narration are present, and the section is clearly uniform in style. The account is more compact than any other all-J-mighty-act narrative, and some commentators use this fact and various supposed "discrepancies" as indications of important shifts in layer in the traditions underlying the mighty-act accounts. Noth (79), for example, thinks this account is "a secondary addition" to J, set forth in J's pattern.

The difficulty with such proposals is that they must speculate a non-extant original form from which the extant narratives can be seen to deviate. The proposals themselves, as helpful as they sometimes are in illuminating specific details, reveal their own limitation by the wide divergency between them. To date they have not produced any agreed-upon original pattern, even in the most general terms. Nor are the motifs of Loewenstamm (מסורת, ii–v, 25–79) or the cycles of Cassuto (92–131) or the sets of Greenberg (*Understanding*, 169–92) any less contrived than the patterns based on source criticism. They too provide not a single schema, but as many schemata as there are theorists.

What we must keep in mind is not a series of carefully controlled variations of several themes and forms, but a series of somewhat haphazard variations on a single theme, all drawn to a common general form from at least several circles of tradition. The mighty-act accounts were a long while growing (and in some cases reducing) into the form in which we know them. They came to that form in the service not of the integrity of their source-traditions, but in the service of their single theme, the proof of Yahweh's active Presence.

Thus this fifth of the mighty-act accounts, wholly from J, is closer in form and closer in literal phrasing to the second account in 7:26–8:11 [8:1–15], a JP composite, than to the fourth account immediately preceding it (8:16–28 [20–32]), generally agreed also to have come solely from J. The common denominator, once again, is the purpose of the accounts and the rhetoric giving exposition to that purpose.

The major peculiarity of the form in which this fifth mighty-act account is presented is the shift from the first to the third person in Yahweh's speech to Moses, from vv 1–2 into v 3 and especially v 4. It is, of course, possible to speculate that vv 1–2, spoken to Moses, were followed by an account of Moses' repetition of Yahweh's words to Pharaoh, and that v 4 and even v 5b originally represented further explanations by Moses, who logically referred to Yahweh in the third person. But such an "original" account, we do not have; and in the account in hand, what we do have is Yahweh referring to himself first in the first person, then in the third person, a style of which there are ample examples in the OT.

Comment

1-4 Yahweh's command to Moses in v 1 as well as the command he is to pass along to Pharaoh, including also the first part of the warning of v 2, is a duplicate of 7:26-27a, except for the use of דבר "speak" instead of אמר "say" and the addition of "God of the Hebrews" and the deictic particle כי "for." Pharaoh is then warned that, if he should again "tighten his grip" on the Israelites, literally, "make strength against them," Yahweh intends to bring a decimating epidemic against the domesticated livestock of Egypt.

יד "hand" is often used in the OT in reference to strength or power, especially in reference to God (over 200 times in the OT; see van der Woude, *THAT* 1:672-74). The reference in v 3 adds impact to Yahweh's warning in a context that implies his thinning patience with Pharaoh and a concurrent intensification of the effect of the mighty acts (cf. Greenberg, *Understanding*, 170-71).

Hyatt (114) surveys the plausibility of the presence in Egypt of the animals listed in v 3 at any period to which the oppression and the exodus can reasonably be assigned. The mention of the camel, in particular, has been widely questioned as an anachronistic reference. As intriguing as such discussions are, however, they are misleading, for they imply a historical motivation that is lacking in these theological narratives. As Hyatt notes, the list itself may reflect the time at which the account was written. To this we might add also the growth of the tradition to that point, and the time should by now have arrived when all this could simply be assumed.

The decimating epidemic has been identified by Hort (*ZAW* 69 [1957] 100-101) as *B. anthracis*, brought on by the frog carcasses left by the second mighty act and affecting only unstabled animals (thus sparing some Egyptian animals for the seventh mighty act, and the stabled [?] Israelite animals altogether). This kind of wild speculation is also misleading, and not alone because of its absurdity. Worse still is its discrediting of the theological tenor of the biblical narrative, which will admit no naturalistic and hence nonmiraculous "explanations." The epidemic is, as the text plainly says, the work of Yahweh's hand; so also is the protection of the Israelite livestock.

5-7 As in the fourth mighty act (8:19b), so here too, the next day is set for the arrival of the blow against Egypt. ממחרת "from the next day" implies only the start on the morrow of the דָּבָר, a term that is used in the OT only of epidemic as an act of God's powerful judgment (Mayer, TDOT 3:126-27).

The sparing of the Israelite livestock (vv 4, 6, 7) is, like the exclusion from Goshen of the thick swarm of flying insects (8:18-19[22-23]), a further miracle of Yahweh. When the epidemic arrives, Pharaoh sends out to Goshen to check on this further exclusion, and his discovery that it is a fact strengthens instead of weakens his resolve to keep his hold on Israel. The juxtaposition of שלח "send out" in reference to Pharaoh sending his representatives *to* Goshen with שלח in reference to Pharaoh not sending Israel *from* Goshen is a deft stylistic touch, one that leaves us once more in the suspense of an inevitable "What next?"

Explanation

There is no new element in this fifth of the mighty-act reports apart from the statement in v 7 that Pharaoh sent out to Goshen to check on the predicted exclusion of Israel's livestock from the decimating epidemic. In the only other mighty act in which Goshen has been mentioned thus far—the fourth, involving the "mixed swarm of flying insects" (8:16–28)—there is no reference to any such curiosity on Pharaoh's part, even though it would be logical to assume.

The point of this fifth mighty-act account is of course the same as that of the four preceding it, the proof of Yahweh's Presence. That point is sharpened still further here, however, by the Pharaoh's skepticism in sending out to Goshen to determine that the Israelite livestock really has been spared, and by his reaction of redoubled stubbornness in the face of what should have been a convincing enhancement by confirmation of the miracle. That the epidemic should come with such sweeping devastation is one thing; that the livestock of Israel in Goshen should be spared is another; but that Pharaoh should *still* be heavy and dull of mind, in the fact of such a double demonstration, is an enigma until we remember Yahweh's recurring prediction of Pharaoh's intransigence (3:19–20; 4:21; 7:13; etc.) and Yahweh's continuing involvement in Pharaoh's reaction (7:3–5, 22; 8:11; etc.). Then we can understand why Pharaoh would send out those whom he had no need to send out, his factfinders to Goshen, and refuse to send out those whom Yahweh had commanded him to send out, the sons of Israel to their religious commitment.

The Sixth Mighty Act   (9:8–12)

Bibliography

Gressmann, H. *Die Anfänge Israels.* Göttingen: Vandenhoeck und Ruprecht, 1922. **Hort, G.** "The Plagues of Egypt." *ZAW* 69 (1957) 84–103; 70 (1958) 48–59. **Wilson, R. R.** "The Hardening of Pharaoh's Heart." *CBQ* 41 (1979) 18–36.

Translation

⁸ *Next, Yahweh said to Moses and to Aaron, "Scoop up* [a] *for yourselves double handfuls of furnace-ash;* [b] *Moses is to fling it heavenward in full sight of* [c] *Pharaoh.* [d] ⁹ *It will become a dust settling upon the entire land of Egypt and will infect* [a] *man and beast with inflamed swellings* [b] *breaking into septic sores,* [c] *everywhere in Egypt."*
¹⁰ *They thus scooped up the furnace-ash, and standing right in front of* [a] *Pharaoh, Moses flung it heavenward; it immediately* [b] *caused* [c] *inflamed swellings breaking into* [d] *septic sores, on man and on beast.* ¹¹ *The learned men* [a] *were no longer able to stand up to Moses* [b] *because of the infection of* [c] *the inflamed swellings, for they afflicted* [d] *the learned men along with all the Egyptians.*

¹² *Yet Yahweh made obstinate the mind of Pharaoh, so he paid no attention to them, just as Yahweh had predicted* ᵃ *to Moses.* ᵇ

Notes

8.a. Qal impv לְקַח "take, take in hand," rendered here in the context of the מְלֹא "full" and the dual חָפְנֵיכֶם "the hollow of your hands" that follow.

8.b. פִּיחַ, a derivative of פּוּחַ "blow, puff," refers probably to the fine powdery ash left by a thorough burning, and כִּבְשָׁן, as the additional reference of Gen 19:28 and Exod 19:18 suggest, is a furnace, or even kiln (cf. Funk, "Brickkiln," *IDB* 1:446, and "Furnace," *IDB* 2:330), producing thick columns of smoke reminiscent of the destruction of Sodom and Gomorrah and the Sinai theophany.

8.c. "To the eyes of Pharaoh."

8.d. LXX adds καὶ ἐναντίον τῶν θεραπόντων αὐτοῦ "and in front of his servants."

9.a. Lit., "will be upon (or against) man and beast."

9.b. שְׁחִין apparently comes from a root meaning "hot, inflamed" (cf. BDB, 1006), and its usage in Isa 38:21; Deut 28:27; Lev 13:18–20; and Job 2:7 implies a somewhat stronger term than the usual "boil"; so "inflamed swellings," "angry boils."

9.c. פֹּרֵחַ אֲבַעְבֻּעֹת is difficult, because the second and determining word occurs only in vv 9 and 10 of this passage. פָּרַח means "break out, spread," and perhaps in such a context, even "drain, suppurate." אֲבַעְבֻּעֹת are "blisters, sores, boils," and these two words with the preceding שְׁחִין "inflamed swellings" suggest the contextual translation "septic, putrefying sores." Pope (*Job*, AB 15 [Garden City, NJ: Doubleday, 1965] 21) refers to שְׁחִין here as a "boil" or "botch" breaking out into "pustules," posing the meaning "a boil which becomes ulcerous and leaves a deep scar." LXX has ἕλκη φλυκτίδες ἀναζέουσαι "blistered, boiling ulcers," and adds "upon man and upon animal alike" as it does in 8:12–14.

10.a. See n. 8.c.

10.b. Special *waw* in this context.

10.c. "Became," הָיָה.

10.d. The word order differs in this second occurrence, with פֹּרֵחַ "septic" coming last; Syr reads וַיִּפְרַח instead of פֹּרֵחַ, but the end result is the same.

11.a. See n. 7:11.c.

11.b. Lit., "to the face of, before Moses," and so rendered above in the sense of "stand in opposition to, hold one's own with."

11.c. Lit., "from the face or presence of."

11.d. Lit., "were on," הָיָה. The verb is sg in Hebrew, here as elsewhere in the passage; שְׁחִין "inflamed swellings" is a collective sg noun.

12.a. This closing statement, "so he . . ." is the same in 7:13; 8:11, 15.

12.b. LXX omits this final "to Moses."

Form/Structure/Setting

This sixth of the mighty-act accounts, like the third, is generally assigned to the priestly stratum (see above, *Form/Structure/Setting* on 8:12–15[16–19]. The two accounts are the briefest of all the accounts (four verses and five verses, respectively), and are the only mighty-act accounts assigned exclusively to P. They both display the unique priestly interest in the learned men of Egypt (compare 7:11, 22; 8:3, 14[7, 18]), the general priestly sequence, and the priestly inclusion of Aaron.

In the account at hand, however, Aaron's role in the execution of the instructions of Yahweh is minimal. He merely scoops up a double handful of furnace-ash, apparently, though the text does not say so, as an additional supply of ash for Moses to fling heavenward. This reduction in the role of Aaron is all the more interesting in a priestly section, and it should be taken as a caution against a tendency in the form-critical treatment of the mighty-act accounts to present too standardized a narrative pattern for each of the respective sources (so Driver, 55–59; Fohrer, *Überlieferung*, 62–70; and, to a lesser degree, Childs, 133–41). It may also reflect here the strength of the tradition associating Moses alone with the more severe mighty acts. In this account, for the first time, Yahweh is said explicitly to be responsible for Pharaoh's resistance (v 12), and from this point forward in the narrative sequence of the mighty acts, Aaron does not appear in an active role: he is mentioned either as merely present (9:27; 10:3; cf. v 6; 10:16; 12:1, etc.), or in such summary-verses as 11:10 and 12:28.

R. R. Wilson has argued (*CBQ* 41 [1979] 29–36) that in P, the hardening-of-the-heart motif is connected with the vocabulary and the theology of Yahweh's holy war against Egypt, and that it serves both a unifying function, in the redaction of the narrative of Exodus, and a didactic-theological function, as a call of Israel to obedience. It is well known that the motif occurs in each of the major source-layers reflected in the mighty-act accounts. While this motif *may* help to unify these accounts, however, and *may* also have fulfilled a didactic function, its primary function is neither literary nor didactic, but theological. Indeed, the motif is far more understandable as a theological assertion linked to the overall theme of the mighty-act compilation: the proof of Yahweh's Presence. As such, it unifies the layers within the composite and within the successive mighty-act accounts as well, because it makes always and everywhere the same point in much the same way: Yahweh *Is*, as he has claimed; and he *Is* powerfully Present.

Comment

8–9 Yahweh's instruction to Moses and to Aaron here, as in 8:12, includes no words of warning to Pharaoh. As in that miracle of the swarm of gnats, so here there is no threat of what is to come for a lack of obedience, though Moses is told in this instance to perform the disaster-bringing action in full view of Pharaoh. No such restriction of place is mentioned in the instruction to Aaron in 8:12, and this detail, so pointedly included, functions in connection with the assertion of v 12 as a declaration of Yahweh's undeniable involvement.

There is no obvious link between the furnace-ash flung toward the sky and the settling dust that brings infection. Hugo Gressmann translated פיח "soot," and linked the blackness of the soot to the darkness of the ninth mighty act (*Die Anfänge Israels*, 43, 46), but there is no basis for such a proposal, or even for such a translation. The word occurs only in this passage (vv 8, 10) in the OT, and the root from which it is derived and the context alike require a powdery substance that can be scooped up in the "hands'-hollow" from a furnace—ash seems a more likely possibility than soot.

The furnace-ash cast heavenward in front of Pharaoh appears to be a symbol of the infectious dust (אבק, a synonym of עפר, takes on such a meaning only here and, possibly, in Deut 28:24; cf. 28:27) which settles down from heaven (again cf. Deut 28:15–35, esp. v 24) onto the whole land. The disease caused by this infectious dust has been frequently identified as "skin anthrax" (Hort, *ZAW* 69 [1957] 101–3, appears to be the source of the most recent repetitions of this diagnosis). The disease, interestingly called "inflammed swellings of Egypt" in Deut 28:27, cannot be identified, of course, and attempts to make such identifications serve only to obscure the miraculous nature of the mighty act. Like the horrendous illness of Job, which amasses a terrifying array of dreadful symptoms (compare Rowley, "The Book of Job and Its Meaning," *From Moses to Qumran* [New York: Association Press, 1963] 143–44), the point of these awkwardly described "inflammed swellings breaking into septic sores" has much to do with theology and little to do with medicine.

The speculation that this sixth mighty act is somehow a variant account of the one preceding it and the question whether there would be any animals left outside Goshen for this infection (cf. Rylaarsdam, "Exodus," *IB* 1:903; Hyatt, 115) are likewise beside the point at hand. Even the terminology employed in the two accounts, מקנה "livestock" (9:3–4, 6–7) and בהמה "beast" (vv 9–10) denies a discrepancy; the former refers to domesticated grazing animals of the species listed in 9:3, the latter to beasts of all kinds (BDB, 96–97). But more important still is the cumulative sequence of theological assertion. The point of these narratives, both singly and in compilation, is not animal husbandry and stylistic verisimilitude, but their declaration of the Is-ness of Yahweh.

10–11 As in the previous accounts, the obedience of Yahweh's instructions by Moses (and, secondarily, by Aaron) leads immediately to the result predicted. In this account, the learned men of Egypt appear for the fifth and final time, and here they not only cannot reverse or duplicate the mighty act, they suffer its effect so severely that they can offer no resistance of any kind. G. Hort (*ZAW* 69 [1957] 101) reads עמד "stand" literally and in comparison with Deut 28:7–35 to mean that the disease affected "principally . . . the legs and feet" so that the learned men are reported to be unable to stand up. The more probable meaning, reflected in the translation above, is that the learned men, afflicted as were their countrymen, no longer had any will to oppose or resist Moses and his God.

12 It may well be in the light of this most serious setback to the Egyptians up to this point in the mighty-act sequence, as Pharaoh is left alone before Moses, that Yahweh's involvement in Pharaoh's resistance comes for the first time to be stated explicitly. In 8:15, following their failure to produce a swarm of gnats, the learned men of Egypt confessed themselves outdistanced in the presence of a divine power: "this is an act of a god." Pharaoh ignored them; his mind "remained obstinate." Here, these same learned men, afflicted along with all Egyptians, have no will to further resistance. It is difficult to imagine how Pharaoh could have held out so long, and inconceivable that he could hold out any longer, and so, at the ideal point, we are told plainly what has been implicit all along (cf. *Comment* on 3:19–20 and 4:21): Yahweh has made obstinate the mind of Pharaoh.

Explanation

Yet again the recurring motif of the proof-of-Presence sequence is sounded. Yahweh Is, and Yahweh Is in Egypt; Yahweh Is, and Yahweh Is responsible for the affliction of an Egypt whose Pharaoh remains intractable. Here, for the first time, the inevitable complete defeat of the learned men of Egypt is announced; they are no longer able to offer any resistance, diseased as they are along with the rest of their countrymen. And here for the first time there is an explicit assertion of Yahweh's responsibility for the Pharaoh's strange stubbornness, a responsibility implicit in the composite Exodus from 3:19–20 following, inferred by 4:21, 6:1, 7:13 and in each of the first five mighty-act accounts, and plainly asserted in 7:3–5.

Again in the eighth (10:20) and ninth (10:27) mighty-act accounts, Yahweh is said to "make obstinate" the mind of Pharaoh, as in the prologue to the tenth mighty act (11:10) and the prologue to the account of Yahweh's rescue at the sea (14:4, 8). Only once more, in the conclusion of the seventh mighty-act account (9:35), is the responsibility for Pharaoh's obstinacy left unassigned, while in 9:34, Pharaoh is said to have "made heavy and dull" (hiphil of כבד) his mind and that of his courtiers.

Whatever may have been the original implication of the varied expressions of the motif of Pharaoh's obstinacy, with their varied vocabulary and differences about the cause of his stubbornness, the clear implication of the composite presented to us in Exodus is that Yahweh is in every case the prime mover in this matter. We are told as much in anticipation of the proof-of-Presence sequence, in the prologue that begins it, and in the dramatic victory that concludes it, the final triumph over Pharaoh and Egypt at the sea. Every mighty act must be read within such a bracketing, and so every stubborn reversal of promise by Pharaoh, like every reversal of the welfare of his country, must be recognized to be the work of Yahweh.

Such an implication is made all the more clear by the first specific declaration, within the mighty-act sequence itself, that Yahweh himself has "made obstinate" the mind and intention of Pharaoh (9:12), for the declaration comes precisely at the point in the sequence when any other explanation is no longer possible.

The Seventh Mighty Act (9:13–35)

Bibliography

Couroyer, B. "Un Égyptianisme biblique: 'depuis la fondation de l'Égypte.' " *RB* 67 (1960) 42–48. **Labuschagne, C. J.** *The Incomparability of Yahweh in the Old Testament.* POS 5. Leiden: E. J. Brill, 1966. **Thomas, D. W.** "A Consideration of Some Unusual Ways of Expressing the Superlative in Hebrew." *VT* 3 (1953) 209–24.

Translation

[13] *Next, Yahweh said to Moses, "Get up early in the morning, and take a position* [a] *where you cannot miss Pharaoh,* [b] *and you say to him, 'Thus says Yahweh, the God of the Hebrews, "Send out my people, in order that they may worship me,* [14] *because now* [a] *I will send my whole arsenal of blows* [b] *against* [c] *your mind, against the members of your court, and against your people, to the end that you may know by experience*

that there is none like me in the whole earth. ¹⁵*Indeed* ^a *now I will let loose my power* ^b *and strike you and your people with total* ^c *epidemic, so complete* ^d *that you will be effaced from the earth!* ¹⁶*In fact* ^a *for this one reason alone will I cause you still to stand firm, to the end that I show you my strength, in result of which my name will be celebrated* ^b *throughout the earth.*

¹⁷ *"You are still tyrannizing my people, refusing* ^a *to send them out.* ¹⁸*Just watch me send a downpour of very heavy hail this time tomorrow, the like of which has never fallen* ^a *in Egypt from the day of its beginning to this moment.* ¹⁹*Send out now, bring your livestock and everything you own that is out in the open* ^a *into a protected place: every man and beast left* ^b *out in the open, not gathered into the shelter of home,* ^c *and onto which the hail falls, will die."' "*

²⁰*Those members of Pharaoh's court* ^a *who had respect for Yahweh's word set their servants and their livestock in flight toward the shelter of home.* ²¹*Those who had no confidence in* ^a *Yahweh's word left their servants and their livestock loose out in the open.*

²²*Then Yahweh said to Moses, "Thrust out your hand against the heavens, and there will be hail throughout the land of Egypt, upon man and upon beast, and upon every crop* ^a *in the land of Egypt."* ²³*So Moses thrust forth his staff* ^a *against the heavens, and Yahweh loosed* ^b *thunderclaps and hail, and lightning licking earthwards.* ^c *Indeed Yahweh poured* ^d *hail upon the land of Egypt.* ²⁴*There was hail,* ^a *and lightning cracking back and forth* ^b *through the midst of the very heavy hail, the like of which had never fallen anywhere in the land of Egypt* ^c *from the beginning of the nation.* ²⁵*The hail battered the entire land of Egypt, everything out in the open, from man to beast and every crop—indeed, the hail hit and shattered the unprotected trees.* ^a ²⁶*In the land of Goshen alone, where the sons of Israel were, was there no hail.*

²⁷*Thus Pharaoh sent anxiously,* ^a *summoned Moses and Aaron, and said to them, "I have been wrong* ^b *this time. Yahweh is the righteous one; I and my people are the guilty ones.* ²⁸*Pray* ^a *to Yahweh. Enough of God's thunderclaps and hail!* ^b *I will* ^c *send you out; you shall certainly stay no longer."* ^d ²⁹*Moses answered him, "As I depart the city, I will open my hands in prayer* ^a *to Yahweh: the thunderclaps will stop instantly,* ^b *and the hail will fall* ^c *no more, so that you may know by experience that the earth belongs to Yahweh.* ³⁰*You and the members of your court, I know,* ^a *have yet no sense of awe in* ^b *the Presence of Yahweh God."*

^{31a}*The growing flax and the standing barley were* ^b *beaten to the ground,* ^c *for the barley was coming to head and the flax was coming to bud.* ^d ³²*The wheat and the spelt were not beaten down, because they had not yet sprouted.* ^a

³³*So Moses then went out from Pharaoh's presence,* ^a *departed* ^b *the city, and opened his hands in prayer to Yahweh: immediately* ^c *the thunderclaps and the hail stopped, and rain* ^d *inundated the earth no longer.* ^e ³⁴*Yet Pharaoh, seeing that the rain and the hail and the thunderclaps stopped, gave in once more to wrongheadedness,* ^a *and so steeled his mind; he did, and the members of his court did.* ^b ³⁵*Thus Pharaoh's mind remained unchanged,* ^a *and he did not send out the Israelites, as Yahweh had predicted through Moses.* ^b

Notes

13.a. See n. 7:15.b.
13.b. See n. 8:16.b.

14.a. בְּפַעַם הַזֹּאת "in this stroke, at this time," translated above as an emphatic usage.

14.b. כָּל־מַגֵּפֹתַי "all my smitings, strikings, plagues." The pl form of מַגֵּפָה is used only here in the OT.

14.c. MT has אֶל "toward, against"; SamPent reads עַל "upon, against."

15.a. כִּי עַתָּה, lit., "because now." There is no basis in the text for RSV's and NEB's "by now" followed by the conditional "could."

15.b. יָדִי "my hand."

15.c. בַּדֶּבֶר "with *the* epidemic, plague, pestilence." I read the def art here as giving the sense of "epidemic *par excellence,* the epidemic of epidemics."

15.d. Special *waw* with כחד "efface, destroy," in this context.

16.a. וְאוּלָם "and indeed, but indeed," an adverb with an adversative sense, qualifying the sweeping assertion of v 15.

16.b. Piel סְפֵּר "to declare over and over, recount again and again."

17.a. לְבִלְתִּי "in order not to. . . ."

18.a. Lit., "which has not been (הָיָה) as like it in Egypt."

19.a. Lit., "in the field," that is, "out-of-doors."

19.b. יִמָּצֵא "found."

19.c. Lit., "not gathered homewards."

20.a. "The one respecting the word of Yahweh from (= among) the servants of Pharaoh."

21.a. Lit., "And the one who did not set his mind toward [SamPent "upon"] the word of Yahweh."

22.a. כָל־עֵשֶׂב הַשָּׂדֶה "every growth, herb of the field."

23.a. LXX reads χεῖρα "hand."

23.b. נתן "gave."

23.c. Lit., "fire was going earthwards."

23.d. Hiph מטר "rain," plus special *waw.*

24.a. SamPent הברד and LXX ἡ χάλαζα read "the hail."

24.b. וְאֵשׁ מִתְלַקַּחַת "and fire seizing or snatching at itself," a graphic description of the play of lightning bolts seeking ground.

24.c. Lit., "in the whole land of Egypt." SamPent במצרים and LXX ἐν Αἰγύπτῳ have only "in Egypt."

25.a. Lit., "every tree of the field."

27.a. שלח "send" with special *waw* in this context.

27.b. חָטָאתִי "I have missed the way, gone wrong, sinned," though "sinned" is probably an over-translation in this instance.

28.a. LXX adds οὖν περὶ ἐμοῦ "therefore for me" here; cf. 8:4, 24.

28.b. Lit., "and surely from being thunderclaps of God and hail," to which LXXᴬ adds καὶ πῦρ "and fire."

28.c. וַאֲשַׁלְּחָה "I will send" is a cohortative indicating determination; cf. GKC § 48*cde.* SamPent has simply וְאַשְׁלַח.

28.d. The verb יסף "add" ends with paragogic *nun,* indicating "marked emphasis" (GKC, § 47*m*) so, lit., "and certainly you will not add to standing, delaying (עמד)."

29.a. אֶפְרֹשׂ אֶת־כַּפַּי "I will spread out my palms," one of several OT idioms for prayer.

29.b. חדל "stop" with paragogic *nun;* see n.28.d.

29.c. Lit., "will be (הָיָה) no more." LXX adds καὶ ὁ ὑετός "and the heavy rain" following "the hail" in this verse; cf. MT v 33.

30.a. This emphasis is shown by the separating accent *zāqēp̄ magnum* on יָדַע "know."

30.b. מִפְּנֵי "from the Presence of. . . ."

31.a. Vv 31–32, a parenthetic note about the damage sustained by the growing crops and avoided by those still germinating, are perhaps displaced in their present location, and might better be read following v 25.

31.b. 3rd pers fem sg נכה "beat" connected to each of the two subjs separately: ". . . flax was . . . barley was. . . ."

31.c. "To the ground" is added for clarity. נכה means "strike, smite down," etc.

31.d. גבעל "bud" occurs only here in the OT; the text literally says "the barley fresh [making grain] and the flax bud."

32.a. אֲפִילֹת is a fem pl adj meaning "concealed, in the dark," and so, perhaps, not yet showing above ground.

33.a. מֵעִם פַּרְעֹה "from with Pharaoh."

33.b. The single verb for both clauses is ויצא "went out"; "departed" is added above for clarity.

33.c. Special *waw* in context.

33.d. SamPent and LXX have "the rain."

33.e. Niph נתך "was not poured out earthward."

34.a. Lit., "he added to sinning," in consequence of the cessation of the hail and lightning, as the special *waw* with יסף "add" shows.

34.b. Lit., "he and his servants."

35.a. Cf. 7:13, 22; and 8:15.

35.b. ביד משה "by Moses' hand, power."

Form/Structure/Setting

The account of the seventh of the mighty acts in the proof-of-Presence sequence is the longest of the mighty-act accounts, and of them all, the composite that is most awkwardly assembled. It begins with a somewhat typical instruction of Yahweh to Moses (v 13), but moves then to what has often been taken to be an explanation of the entire mighty act sequence (vv 14–16), includes the report of a special provision for those Egyptians who have come to have reverence for Yahweh's word (vv 19–21), and, quite clearly out of sequence, a parenthetic explanation of why some crops were destroyed by the hail while others were not (vv 31–32).

Not surprisingly, the length and patchwork appearance of this sequence have led to an array of opinion among source critics. Noth, who doubts the presence of Elohistic material in the mighty-act narratives (69–70), assigns the account mostly to the Yahwist, with some incomplete sentences from P: vv 22, 23aα, and 35 (80). B. Anderson ("Analytical Outline of the Pentateuch," in Noth's *Pentateuchal Traditions*, 268) assigns the account entirely to the Yahwist. Fohrer (*Überlieferung* 70, 124) finds nothing here from the Priestly source, but assigns vv 22–23aα, 24a (N.B., typographical error on p. 70), 25b, and 35 to the Elohist. Others ascribe the section to all three of these sources (Hyatt [117]: J, vv 13, 17–21; JE, vv 27–35; EJ, vv 22–26; P, vv 14–16); to the three sources plus a redactor (so Beer [12, 53–54]; J², vv 13, 14–16, 17–18, 19–21ᴿ, 23αβ–24, 26, 27 [deleting "and Aaron"]–30, 31–32ᴿ, 33, 34; E, vv 22–23aα, 25, 35a; P, v 35bᴿ); or to the three sources plus "glosses" (Childs [131, 141–42, 158–59]: J, vv 13, 17–18, 23b, 24b, 25b, 26–30, 33–34; E, vv 22–23a, 25a, 35a; JE, v 24a; P, v 35b; "Additions": vv 14–16, 19–21, 31–32).

The fact that there is so wide a divergence of opinion in the source-division of the seventh of the mighty-act accounts underscores both its somewhat patchy appearance and also the fragility of an over-precise assignment of verses and verse-fragments to specific sources without strong evidence for doing so. Once again, the single absolute certainty is the compilation at hand in the received text, beyond which, in the case of the obvious composite, it is possible to look with any assurance only in broad and general ways.

Such a broad look at the section in hand reveals that the dominant source, the one governing the shape of the pericope, is J. Into J's account, additional material has been inserted, probably from P, and from a source or sources concerned with explanatory annotation. There is no clear evidence establishing the presence of E, and the presence of P is only slightly more assured. The most that can be said with any degree of assurance is that this longest of the mighty-act narratives is a compilation built on a foundational account from the Yahwist, expanded more than once by explanatory additions from later hands, one of which (vv 31–32) has been inserted awkwardly into the sequence at the wrong spot. This clumsiness may suggest a later disruption of a sequence originally as smooth at least as the other compilations among the mighty-act accounts. Without question, this composite, like the others, is governed in its form by the availability of varying traditions brought together in the service of a single purpose (see *Form/Structure/Setting* on 7:14–25).

Comment

13–16 The reference to "Moses taking a position" from which his interception of Pharaoh will be guaranteed and the opening words of the message he is to deliver to Pharaoh are very close to parts of 7:15–16 and 8:16, both of which also may be assigned to the Yahwist. What follows this, however, is unique in the mighty-act accounts, however it is understood, whether as an explanation of the number of the mighty acts (Childs, 158), as "an apology for all of the plagues" (Hyatt, 118), or as an announcement of a terrible intensification of the force and effect of the mighty acts leading up to the last of them affecting the Egyptians, the death of their first-born and the deliverance at the sea (cf. Cassuto, 115–16).

The translations generally (RSV, NEB, JB, RV) render v 15 as a conditional statement, giving the sense of what Yahweh *could* do or *could* have done had he chosen to, and leading to the rationale as to why he did not so do. There is in the text, however, no suggestion of conditionality. None of the usual terms or circumlocutions of conditional expression are present (cf. GKC, ¶ 106*p*, ¶ 112*ff-mm*, ¶ 159*a-k*), nor is there anything in the wider context of the account to suggest a conditional sense.

Yahweh is depicted instructing Moses to report to Pharaoh (in a speech begun with an authenticating messenger-formula) not what he could have done or might do, but what he is doing and is about to do (cf. KJV). This sense is made plain not only by the absence of any conditional terms and syntax, but by the emphatic *"now"* (בפעם הזאת) of v 14 and by the "indeed now" (כי עתה) of v 15, as well as by the assertion in v 17 that Pharaoh continues to tyrannize the sons of Israel and persists in his refusal to obey Yahweh's command.

Verses 14–16, as they stand now in the composite account of the seventh mighty act, are directed forward, first of all to the mighty act immediately at hand, and second, to the cumulative impact of the concluding mighty acts, especially the terrible darkness, the death of the first born, and the decisive victory at the sea. In this seventh mighty act, for the first time Egyptian lives are lost; in the eighth mighty act, the last remnants of life-sustaining food are destroyed; in the ninth mighty act, the very source of light and life in Egypt, the sun-god Kephri-Re-Atum (see *ANET*[3], 12–14), is overpowered; and in the tenth mighty act, any ordered future that Egypt might have is cut off in the death of the first born. Thus Yahweh tells Moses to say most appropriately to Pharaoh that he is now sending his "whole arsenal of blows" and now loosing his "power" to strike Pharaoh and his people with "*the* epidemic," the ultimate raining of blows so complete that Pharaoh will be effaced from the earth. In the context of the mighty acts that follow and bring the proof-of-Presence sequence to a conclusion, that is exactly what comes to pass.

All this is to the end, still, that Pharaoh, his court, and his people may know by experience both that Yahweh *Is,* and that Yahweh is incomparable in the whole earth (v 15; cf. Labuschagne, *Incomparability of Yahweh,* 74–76). At this point, however, a new element is introduced. Not only is Israel to have proof of Yahweh's Presence in the mighty acts, and not only are Pharaoh and the Egyptians to come to know therefrom that he really *is;* Pharaoh is by Yahweh "caused to stand firm" (hiphil of עמד), both sustained and kept stubborn, and shown (hiphil of ראה) Yahweh's strength that as a result Yahweh's name (= Yahweh's Presence) "will be declared over and over again" (piel of ספר) throughout the whole earth.

17–19 The context for this awesome pronouncement, as for the devastating seventh mighty act that follows it (and the still more dreadful mighty acts following the seventh) is provided by the important linking verse, 17. Pharaoh continues still to lord it over (hithpael of סלל) Yahweh's people, that is, to tyrannize them, and to refuse to send them out of Egypt. And though we know why this is so, even if Pharaoh does not, it nonetheless makes the mighty acts that follow an inevitability.

The "downpour of very heavy hail" (vv 18, 24) mixed with lightning licking back and forth onto the earth (vv 23, 24) and rain (v 33) does not yield itself to the kind of meteorological explanation Hort (*ZAW* 70 [1958] 48–49) and Knight (73–74) provide. The point of the repeated descriptions of the storm, which may suggest layers in the composite, is not its naturalness but its unnaturalness as a supernatural phenomenon. No earthly hailstorm could ever be like this. The recurring thunderclaps (vv 23, 28, 29, 33, 34, קלת "voices"; cf. Ps 29), the lightning darting back and forth (vv 23, 24, אש "fire"; cf. Ps 18 and Thomas, *VT* 3 [1953] 210, 214–15), and the severity of the storm (vv 18–19, 23–26) all suggest the advent of Yahweh in theophany (cf. Durham, "Psalms," *BBC* 4:202–3) and thus the Presence of Yahweh in a more dramatic and intense coming than anywhere in the mighty-act sequence to this point.

B. Couroyer has argued (*RB* 67 [1960] 42–46) convincingly that the phrase in v 18 referring to the day of the "foundation" or "beginning" of Egypt is Egyptian in origin, on the basis of its recurrence in Egyptian texts of all periods and its usage in the OT in reference to the founding of a nation only here. Normally in the OT, the verb יסד and its derivatives refer to the foundation of a building of some kind, especially the Temple of Yahweh (Isa 44:28; 1 Kgs 5:31 [17]). The phrase in v 24, "from that time it [Egypt] was being [or "becoming," היתה] a people," Couroyer holds (46–48) to be an equivalent expression, not attested so far (as of 1960) in Egyptian texts, and referring to that ancient time when the nation was founded and the people and the government were organized.

The warning of Yahweh to Pharaoh that he and his people should take precautions to protect both themselves and their livestock from the death-dealing hail is without parallel in the entire proof-of-Presence sequence. It stands as a further indication of the fatal seriousness of the last four mighty-act accounts and is a further confirmation of the context of the awesome pronouncement of vv 14–15, described above. For the first time, a mighty act is to bring not just annoyance, not just physical reverse, but death—and so Yahweh gives a warning.

20–26 The report of this warning and the news that some members of Pharaoh's court take it seriously, while some do not, serve both to intensify the gathering suspense of the narrative and to indicate a further weakening of any possible human basis Pharaoh could have for further resistance.

No account of Moses' actual confrontation of Pharaoh with the warning of vv 13–19 is given, though the presence of such a report in any original sequence seems a safe assumption. The composite at hand moves directly from the end of the warning to the reaction of the members of Pharaoh's court who were privy to whatever Pharaoh learned, and to the command of Yahweh to Moses to bring on the fierce storm of terrible hail by thrusting out his hand "against" (על) the heavens. What Moses thrusts forth, according to MT, is his "staff" (v 23); LXX reads "hand" here, as in v 22. This variation is not substantial enough to suggest an insertion from the Elohist, as Hyatt (119) does. The storm that follows this action is of supernatural intensity and dimension, as noted above, not only in its combination of thunder and the continual play of lightning with a battering (נכה) heavy hail, but also in the exclusion of Goshen. Even the trees were shattered, a statement again reminiscent of the language of theophanic advent (cf. Ps 29:5, 9), so of course any unprotected crops were destroyed utterly.

31–32 The technical explanatory note specifying the crops that were leveled and those that escaped would logically fall within, or following, the statement contained in what is now v 25.

27–30 As in the accounts of the second (8:4 [8]) and fourth (8:21 [25]) mighty acts, so here Pharaoh summons Moses (and Aaron), this time for the first time admitting to culpability on his part and his people's part. Given the context, it is probably too much to have Pharaoh confessing sin. חטא should be taken in its more general sense, "to miss the mark, go wrong," and רשעים as a reference to "guilt," even "criminal wrong," rather than to "evil." Pharaoh is admitting to mistake, and even unfairness, but he must not be thought to be coming to abject repentance and pious belief. As the continuation of the narrative shows, his remorse is short-lived and is no more than another ruse to get relief.

Once more (as in 8:4, 24 [8, 28], Pharaoh requests prayer and promises to send Israel ("you" in v 28 is masculine plural) out. Moses (there is no mention of Aaron beyond the ולאהרן, "and (to) Aaron" of v 27) promises to pray, and he predicts an end to the storm so that Pharaoh may know at first hand that the world is Yahweh's. He also expresses an understandable skepticism about any real reverence for Yahweh on the part of Pharaoh or his court.

33–35 Thus again Moses prays for an end to a mighty act, an end that comes immediately. Rain is mentioned for the first time as a part of the terrible storm of the seventh mighty act, yet another indication of layers in the account.

Once more also Pharaoh, relieved of the oppression of Yahweh's mighty act, added to his accumulation of wrongness. He "steeled his mind" (hiphil כבד), as did his courtiers, excluding perhaps—the account is not specific— those who had saved their livestock by respecting Yahweh's word (v 20). As before, Pharaoh's mind remained unchanged, and immediately following this astounding, almost unbelievable assertion, we are given a reminder as to how this could be: Yahweh has predicted this intractability; we recall, of course, that Yahweh is behind it.

Explanation

The new element in the account of the seventh of Yahweh's mighty acts in proof of his Presence, an element that turns not only this act but the ones following it toward the conclusion of the mighty acts in Egypt, is death among the Egyptians. The terrible hailstorm deals death as well as destruction and discomfort, and so it points forward to the three additional life-threatening mighty acts in Egypt, as well as to the terrible rout at the sea.

This new element is dramatically highlighted by the new intensity of Yahweh's warning, by the provision of instructions of safety for the members of Pharaoh's court who have respect for Yahweh's word, by the supernatural and theophanic dimensions of the terrible storm, by the dreadful devastation of the storm itself, and by Pharaoh's admission of culpability in himself and in the members of his council. Each of these highlighting motifs, each in its own way also unique in the mighty-act sequence to this point, is directly related to what may be called first death in Egypt in the intensification of Yahweh's proof.

With this awesome intensification, Pharaoh admits more clearly than ever that Yahweh Is, and even that Yahweh Is right, but he does not admit Yahweh's command to his list of things to do. Even though he has himself promised to send Israel out, fulfilling Yahweh's prediction of 3:19–20 and reversing his own declaration of 5:2, and despite the fearful theophanic hailstorm, he goes back on his word and remains as firm in his disobedience as ever. We know that there can be but one explanation of such unbelievable, even inhuman, resistance.

Thus the seventh mighty act sets things in motion for the end of the proof-of-Presence sequence. From this point forward, events can move in only one terrible direction. We have passed the point of return. And the compilers of the Book of Exodus leave us with a haunting question: if Pharaoh can admit Yahweh Is, and still be stubborn, how about the Israelites?

The Eighth Mighty Act (10:1–20)

Bibliography

Andersen, F. I., and **D. N. Freedman.** *Hosea.* AB 24. Garden City, NY: Doubleday, 1980. **Childs, B. S.** "A Study of the Formula, 'Until this Day.'" *JBL* 82 (1963) 279–92. **Dhorme, E.** *L'emploi métaphorique de noms de parties du corps en Hébreu et en Akkadien.* Paris: Librairie Orientaliste Paul Geuthner, 1923. **Hort, G.** "The Plagues of Egypt, II." *ZAW* 70 (1958) 48–59. **Weiss, R.** "A Note on אַתָּה in Ex 10, 11." *ZAW* 76 (1964) 188.

Translation

[1] *Next, Yahweh said to Moses, "Go to Pharaoh—because I[a] have made heavy and dull both his mind and the minds of the members of his court, to the end that I be taken seriously[b] through[c] these signs of mine right in their own territory,[d]* [2] *and to the end that you[a] may recount again and again[b] in the hearing of your son and your grandson that I amused myself aggravating[c] the Egyptians, and that I set my signs against[d] them in order that you may know by experience that I am Yahweh."[e]*
[3] *So Moses came, and Aaron,[a] to Pharaoh. They said to him, "Thus says Yahweh, the God of the Hebrews, 'Just how long[b] will you resist being submissive in my Presence?[c] Send out my people, so that they may worship me,* [4] *for should you refuse to send out my people, look out: I will bring[a] a locust-swarm against your territory[b] tomorrow.* [5] *This swarm[a] will blanket the surface[b] of the earth, and the earth will no longer be visible;[c] it will eat up the scraps of the crops left to you from the hailstorm, and all the sprouts beginning to grow again on the trees[d] out in the open.[e]* [6] *The locusts will fill your houses and the houses of all the members of your court and the houses of all the Egyptians. It will be like nothing your fathers or your fathers' fathers have seen any time in their lives.'"[a] Then he turned,[b] and left Pharaoh's presence.*
[7] *Immediately,[a] Pharaoh's courtiers asked him, "Just how long is this impasse[b] to bring ruin upon us?[c] Send out the men,[d] so that they can worship Yahweh their god.[e] Have you still not seen[f] that Egypt is destroyed?"* [8] *Quickly then,[a] Moses was brought back, and Aaron,[b] to Pharaoh, who said to them, "Go along, worship Yahweh your god. Exactly who[c] will be going?"* [9] *Moses replied, "With our young men and with our old men, we will go; with our sons and with our daughters, with our flocks and with our herds we will go, for we are committed to[a] a pilgrimage-worship[b] of Yahweh."* [10] *But he responded, " 'Yahweh'[a] will indeed be with you when I send out you and your toddlers[b]—look here, you are up to no good![c]* [11] *No, indeed![a] The able-bodied men may go and worship 'Yahweh,' for that is what you claim to be seeking!"[b] Then he[c] threw them out from Pharaoh's presence.*
[12] *So Yahweh said to Moses, "Thrust out your hand against the land of Egypt to bring[a] the locust-swarm: it will fly up against the land of Egypt and eat up every crop of the land,[b] everything the hail left alive."* [13] *Moses thus thrust forth his staff[a] against the land of Egypt,[b] and Yahweh directed an easterly[c] wind onto the land all that day and all night. When the morning came, the easterly wind had blown up[d] the locust-swarm.* [14] *This swarm flew up against the whole land of Egypt, and then alighted right to the very borders of the country.[a] Such a very heavy swarm*

of locusts had never been before, and was never to come again; [15] *indeed it blanketed
the surface of the whole earth, so that the earth was stripped bare,* [a] *and ate up all
the vegetation of the earth and all the fruit of the trees that had survived the hail.* [b]
*No green sprig was left, either on a tree or of the field-crops, in the whole of the
land of Egypt.*

[16] *As quickly as possible,* [a] *Pharaoh summoned Moses and Aaron, then said, "I
have wronged Yahweh your god and you.* [17] *Now tolerate,* [a] *please, my guilt, just
this once, and pray to Yahweh your god that he may remove from upon me only
this death."*

[18] *Thus Moses* [a] *went out of Pharaoh's presence and prayed to Yahweh.* [b] [19] *Yahweh
in turn diverted a very strong sea wind,* [a] *which stirred* [b] *up the locust swarm and
blew it into the Sea of Reeds. Not one locust remained, within any of the borders of
Egypt.* [20] *Yahweh once more made Pharaoh's mind obstinate, however, and he did
not send out the sons of Israel.*

Notes

1.a. This emphasis is made clear by the use of the independent personal pronoun אני "I"
in addition to the 1st pers hiph form of כבד "make heavy and dull."

1.b. The verb is שׁית "put, fix, appoint, set," and the form is qal pass ptcp plus the 1st
com sg pronom suff (cf. Jer 31:21), lit., "the establishment, authentication of me." Note that
LXX reads differently, "so that these signs may happen in sequence to them."

1.c. אתתי אלה, lit., "these my signs." "Through" is added on the basis of the context, for
clarity.

1.d. בקרבו "in his midst," read as a pl by LXX, Syr, Tg Onq, and Tg Ps-J.

2.a. The person of the verb is sg in Heb., an indication that Moses alone is addressed as
the beginner of the tradition of recounting.

2.b. Piel ספר "recount," here suggesting iteration. LXX has διηγήσησθε "describe in detail."

2.c. Hithp of עלל, implying self-diversion, occupying oneself, and with the prep בְּ "in, with"
following, doing so with or even against someone or something else. Cf. Num 22:29; 1 Sam
31:4; Jer 38:19; Judg 19:25.

2.d. The prep, again, is בְּ "in, with" and this clause too is governed by the particle אֵת־,
indicating that this assertion also is to be a part of the account Moses is to repeat to the generations
following. The syntactical emphasis is on "my signs," which comes first in the clause.

2.e. SamPent adds אלהיכם "your God" and a lengthy summary.

3.a. The sg form of the verb and the position of Aaron's name in the sentence suggest
that here, as elsewhere, Aaron is a later insertion into the narrative.

3.b. "Until when?," in this context expressed with growing impatience.

3.c. Lit., "Until when will you refuse to be bowed down from my face (מפני)?"

4.a. Lit., "Behold me causing to come tomorrow. . . ."

4.b. LXX adds ταύτην τὴν ὥραν "at this hour."

5.a. Lit., "it." "This swarm" is added for clarity.

5.b. Here and in v 15 below, the expression is "cover, conceal the eye of the earth." Cf.
BDB, 744–45 § 4.

5.c. Lit., "And one will not be able to see the earth."

5.d. SamPent reads כל עשב הארץ ואת כל פרי העץ "every plant of the earth and the fruit
of every tree. . . ."

5.e. See above, n. 9:19.a.

6.a. Lit., "They will not have seen, your fathers and the fathers of your fathers from the
day of their being upon the land to this day." On עד היום הזה "to this day" see Childs, *JBL*
82 [1963] 280–81.

6.b. This verb and the one following are sg in MT, a further indication of the extraneous
nature of the Aaron-references in vv 3, 8, and perhaps in 16. Syr gives the pl form to both
verbs here.

7.a. Special *waw* in this context.

7.b. Lit., "Until when is it to be, this." זֶה "this" refers to the continuing and mounting frustration between Moses, reporting Yahweh's commands and threats, and Pharaoh, resisting, seeming to give in, then resisting with greater vigor still. The conflict leads only to more suffering for Egypt, and so can be termed an impasse.

7.c. מוקש "ruin" a noun derived from יקש "set a trap, arrange a lure to destruction," refers here to the decimation of Egypt and its people the impasse is bringing.

7.d. את־האנשים "the men" is to be taken in this context as referring to the able-bodied men, the husbands and fathers who will not leave their wives and children except temporarily. Cf., e.g., Gen 3:6; Lev 21:7; Judg 13:6; 1 Sam 25:19.

7.e. Lower case is used with "god" when the Egyptians speak of Yahweh, whom they do not worship.

7.f. הטרם תדע "Do you yet not know by experience . . . ?"

8.a. See n. 7.a.

8.b. See n. 3.a.

8.c. מי ומי "who, and who?" i.e., "identify precisely the ones to go."

9.a. Lit., "for Yahweh's pilgrimage-worship is for us (לנו)."

9.b. חג־יהוה "pilgrimage-worship of Yahweh" occurs only 3 other times in the OT (Lev 23:39; Judg 21:19; Hos 9:5), and in every instance refers to an occasion of worship, a religious festival, involving pilgrimage to an appointed place. Cf. also חג ליהוה "pilgrimage-worship to Yahweh," Exod 13:6.

10.a. "Yahweh" is set off by quotation marks to indicate the sarcasm and irony of Pharaoh's reply, which in Hebrew is a play on the verb היה "be" and the tetragrammaton derived from it. Pharaoh says, "the 'being one,' yes, will *be* with you (יהי כן יהוה עמכם) when I send out": one prospect, in a word, is as unlikely as the other.

10.b. טף is related to טפף "take quick little steps, toddle along," and refers here as elsewhere to small children.

10.c. "For evil [mischief, wrong רעה] is before your face."

11.a. The SamPent reads לכן "for yes, therefore," instead of לא כן "no, yes," or "no, indeed." לא כן occurs 19 × in the OT (see Weil, 53:436), and every case, as here, communicates an emphatic negative. MT is surely right.

11.b. אתה "that, it" refers here to Pharaoh's interpretation of what Moses appears to be requesting (permitted by his concession in this verse), as opposed to what he clearly believes Moses really has in mind (v 10); so "claim to be seeking," above, for the piel ptcp מְבַקְשִׁים. Cf. GKC ¶ 135p, and note also the different view of Weiss (*ZAW* 76 [1964] 188), who argues that כי אתה "for that" should be read כי את ה' "for Yahweh" with ה' understood as an abbreviation of the tetragrammaton, a proposal both unlikely and unnecessary.

11.c. SamPent, LXX, Syr read "they."

12.a. בארבה lit. means "with, in, by, through the locust-swarm." BDB (91, in a special note) suggests "with," "the locusts being conceived as implicit in Moses' hand," and proposes the substitution of ל for ב, to give "for, to, in the direction of, with reference to the locust-swarm." While the usage is unusual, however, the text need not be emended (cf. also Barthélemy, *et al.*, *Preliminary and Interim Report*, 102) to give a sensible translation. "In, through" in such a context would signify "bring."

12.b. SamPent ואת כל פרי העץ and LXX καὶ πάντα τὸν καρπὸν τῶν ξύλων add "and the fruit of every tree. . . ."

13.a. SamPent and some minuscule codices of LXX read "hand" here, as we should expect on the basis of v 12.

13.b. LXX has εἰς τὸν οὐρανόν "towards the heaven" instead of "against . . . Egypt."

13.c. As BDB (870) notes, this could mean the fierce and hot desert wind, the "sirocco."

13.d. נשא "raise up, carry, lift, take away."

14.a. Lit., "In every boundary, territory of Egypt."

15.a. Reading וַתֶּחְשַׂף from חשׂף "strip off, make bare," for וַתֶּחְשַׁךְ from חשׁך "be dark, grow dark." Only one real consonantal change is required for this emendation, the substitution of final ף for the similar final ך. Though a niph form of חשׂף is not attested in MT, such a reading better fits into the context. Reading the text as it stands gives "so that the earth grew dark," i.e., from its blanket of locusts. LXX reads καὶ ἐφϑάρη "and it was ruined."

15.b. Lit., "that the hail left remaining."

16.a. מהר "hasten" plus special *waw* in this context.

17.a. The full idiom, as in Num 6:26, would be נשׂא פנים "lift up face" with regard to Pharaoh's guilt, a sign of favor in spite of short-coming (see Dhorme, *L'emploi métaphorique*, 46–49). Here, in a compression of the idiom, Pharaoh asks that his wrong or guilt be lifted up, i.e., disregarded just this time. "Tolerate" is masc sg in MT, pl in SamPent and LXX.

18.a. "He." Moses is obviously intended, and his name, added here for clarity, is included by LXX, Syr, and some Vg MSS (so Cavensis and Sixto-Clementina).

18.b. LXX has θεόν "God."

19.a. רוח־ים "sea wind" could of course be "westerly wind." Cf. Hort's translation (ZAW 70 [1958] 51), "north wind."

19.b. As in v 13 (see n. 13.d above), the verb is נשׂא "raise up."

Form/Structure/Setting

The narrative of the devastating swarm of locusts, though it is but three verses shorter than the long composite immediately preceding it, is much less awkwardly put together. This narrative appears to have come for the most part from a single source, generally agreed by the commentators to be J. Noth (82), for example, finds J in the "forefront," with "fragments of a P variant" here and there (vv 12, 13aα, 20), and Anderson (in Noth's *Pentateuchal Traditions*, 268) assigns the account solely to J. Rylaarsdam ("Exodus," *IB* 1:907) finds "bits of E" (vv 12–13a, 20) inserted into J, and Hyatt (121–22), E (vv 12–13a, 14a, 15b, 20) and a Deuteronomic redaction (vv 1b–2) grafted into the "basic source," J. Beer (55) assigned vv 12, 13aα, 14aα, and 15a to E, the rest to J², but Beer's *das übrige* includes vv 24–26, 28–29 (see also Beer, 57–58), a division followed also by Fohrer (*Überlieferung*, 65, n. 17, 70–72). Beer and Fohrer take this view on the theory that J knew nothing of a darkness-plague and that 10:17 indicates J's understanding that the terrible swarm of locusts was the last in the sequence of Yahweh's mighty acts.

Once again, however, the composite sequence of the mighty acts must be considered of first importance, both because that is the sequence in hand, on whose existence and shape we do not therefore need to speculate, and also because that sequence has its own purposeful form. Whatever the Yahwist may or may not have included in *his* narrative of the mighty acts and however many inconsistencies and *non sequiturs* there may be in the sequence before us, we have the latter in the received text in its canonical form. The Yahwist's narrative we have only in pieces, and at that only in *some* of its pieces, and those in obvious disarray.

The form of this eighth of the mighty-act accounts is dictated, as is the form of each of the others, by the same proof-of-Presence motif that is the key signature of the entire mighty-act sequence (see *Form/Structure/Setting* on 7:14–25). Any discrepancies it may contain are not of such significance as to disrupt an overarching and inexorable movement. There is a dramatic intensification in the narrative of the mighty acts with the first loss of Egyptian life to the shattering hailstorm, and a rush forward from that seventh mighty act through this one, and the ninth, to the last of them involving the Egyptians, the death of the firstborn and the deliverance of Israel at the sea.

Even if 10:24–26, 28–29 belonged originally to the Yahwist's account of this eighth mighty act, as Beer and Fohrer hold, these verses nevertheless belong now, quite clearly, to the composite account of the ninth mighty act. 10:1–20 is thus best taken as an inclusive unit, set off by the same beginning and ending devices as all the other mighty-act accounts.

Comment

The eighth of the mighty acts, like the one that precedes it and the two that follow it, is life-threatening to the Egyptians. As the seventh mighty act brought death to those who took no shelter before the onslaught of the shattering hailstorm and threatened death by the destruction of the growing crops, so this one complements and then confirms the threat of death by the destruction of every remaining scrap of the battered but still growing crops.

1–2 Thus again at the very outset of the narrative, there is set an explanation of what is taking place. Yahweh quite emphatically takes responsibility for Pharaoh's otherwise incredible stubbornness and once again (as in 9:14–16) gives his reason for doing so. He wants his existence to be plain to Pharaoh and his court, literally to "authenticate" himself by means of the mighty acts and in the last place where they might expect him to be with any power—in their very midst. Yet Yahweh has a higher objective still— the proof of his existence to Israel, both the Israel at hand and the Israel yet to be. Again, as throughout the proof-of-Presence sequence, there is a difference in the intended effect of the mighty act upon the Egyptians, who are to be brought to the point where they will take Yahweh and his demands seriously, in their own territory, and upon the Israelites, who are to know by experience that he is all that he claims to be down all the generations. Of special interest is the pointed emphasis upon Moses as the one who is to begin the practice of recounting (2d person singular piel imperfect תְּסַפֵּר) the firsthand report of Yahweh's self-proof in his treatment of the Egyptians, a recounting to be carried from generation to generation to bring Israel experiential knowledge of Yahweh as reality. At its simplest level, this assertion lies at the root of the tradition connecting Moses with the narrative of the Book of Exodus. At a far more profound level, it is an assertion encapsulating the process of oral transmission that is at the foundation of the entire Bible, one of a series of important glimpses at the generation of the testimony of faith through the reporting and the accumulation of eyewitness accounts.

3–6 As in 9:17, Moses' exasperation with Pharaoh's vacillations is suggested, this time more keenly than ever (see nn. 3.b, 3.c). As in each mighty-act account in which Pharaoh is actually confronted (whether the confrontation is commanded only, or carried out, or both), Yahweh's command is given, and the consequences for disobeying that command are set forth. The consequences, this time, are a locust-swarm of supernatural density and a resultant destruction of every last remaining prospect of food for the future of Egypt. This awful swarm and its dreadful effect are described in vivid detail, and much is made of the fact that nothing in any way comparable to such a visitation has ever occurred before. This is a point insufficiently noted by such interpreters as Hort (*ZAW* 70 [1958] 49–50), who attempt a naturalistic explanation even of the "mass invasion" of the locusts. The narrative of the eighth of the mighty acts goes to considerable lengths to deny the very possibility of any naturalistic explanation, even one of quite extraordinary dimensions (vv 5–6, 7, 12–15), noting indeed (v 14) that such a visitation of locusts not only never had been, but was never to be again. This locust-swarm is not a mere nuisance, as the abundance of frogs was, or a painful inconvenience, as the swarm of flying insects was, but a life-endangering disaster that makes the starvation of the Egyptian people a terrible probability.

7–9 His prediction made, Moses turns abruptly and leaves Pharaoh and his courtiers to ponder it, as they do immediately and with some anxiety, a further indication of the seriousness of this blow, for in no previous instance have Pharaoh's advisers acted so. The passion of the courtiers' appeal to Pharaoh has a note of accusation in it, an implication that *his* resistance is creating the impasse and bringing on the ruin of Egypt, and more than a hint that he has not counted the cost of his pride. Their plea to Pharaoh, "Send out the men [האנשים]," is best taken to mean the adult males (cf. 23:17, 34:23), and not just Moses and Aaron (as Greenberg, e.g., suggests, 163–64).

Under the pressure of his advisers, Pharaoh thus summons Moses to return to the court. Aaron is, here as elsewhere, a later insertion into the narrative. For the first time, Pharaoh gives in to Yahweh's command, but with a suspicion couched in both a question and a qualification (vv 8, 11). מי ומי, asks Pharaoh, "Who and who" are to undertake this religious journey? Moses' reply is direct and uncompromising: everybody is going, and they will take with them their property—"with our flocks and with our herds." The point of this language and of Moses' necessarily inflexible position, is that the worship Yahweh has commanded cannot be qualified in any manner. All Israel must make the pilgrimage and share the experience of the worship of Yahweh, young and old, male and female alike. They are to give themselves to this experience fully, without any distraction posed by anyone or anything left behind. The pilgrimage-worship is to be total, not token, in dimension. Hosea (5:6) picks up this language and gives it a sardonic twist: the total pilgrimage of the harlot-Israel of his time will fail, because Yahweh will have drawn away (חלץ) from them (cf. Andersen-Freedman, *Hosea*, AB 24 [Garden City, NY: Doubleday, 1980] 394). Such an idiomatic understanding of the phrase "flocks and herds" is helpful also to the understanding of the shortage of food experienced by Israel in the wilderness a short time later.

10–11 Moses' firmness serves, however, to confirm Pharaoh's suspicions, in actuality quite accurate ones, that the "pilgrimage" is really a flight. Thus does he rail out, in a sarcastic and quite clever word-play on the meaning of the tetragrammaton, " 'Yahweh' will indeed *be* with you when I fall for such a request as that!" Not yet has Pharaoh come to believe that any "One who always Is" can at last get the best of him, a point which this arrogant play on the name Yahweh makes with brilliant deftness. Thus Moses is accused of "no good, mischief" (רעה), told that the most that is to be conceded is that the able-bodied men may go to worship "Yahweh," and thrown out. The suspicion Pharaoh already has is confirmed by the unusual nature of Moses' request, that all people and property go on the sort of pilgrimage worship generally required only of men (23:17)—though the attribution of such detailed knowledge to an Egyptian Pharaoh is one of many special touches underscoring the theological nature of the narrative sections of the Book of Exodus.

12–15 Since Pharaoh's limited concession amounts to yet another refusal, Yahweh commands a Moses, whom we can imagine to have been eagerly ready, to bring on the locust-swarm. Again the severity of the effect of this mighty act is stressed, first in prediction, then in description. Yahweh's action is described not as creating the locust-swarm, either from dust or any other substance at hand, but rather he sends a strong easterly wind which rounds up the locusts in a day and a night and blows them across into Egypt from the Sinai peninsula. They cover the land of Egypt from border to border. No mention is made of Goshen, but the locust swarm would pose no threat to the people of Israel, who are shortly to be gone in any case. Again the incredible extent of the locust-swarm is stressed, and their life-threatening decimation of the living food supply is described in detail.

16–17 The fearful peril into which Egypt is plunged by such a situation is further dramatized by Pharaoh's immediate response. "As quickly as possible," he summons Moses (Aaron is, as everywhere else, a later insertion into the narrative), and admits that he has "wronged" (חטא) both Moses' God Yahweh and Moses himself. We are left to assume what this wrong is, in specific terms, but vv 10–11 leave us with the impression that the "wrong" was Pharaoh's angry suspicion of Moses' motives and his peremptory ejection of Moses from his presence. Pharaoh is thus represented as asking, in the idiom of the priestly blessing of Num 6:26, that his "guilt" (חטאתי) be "lifted up, raised," and not held against him, thus "tolerated." His tone here, by contrast to his earlier arrogant fury, is conciliatory, and almost pleading: "please . . . this once . . . pray . . . only."

Pharaoh indeed has not been in such straits before. Not even had the terrible destruction of the hailstorm, the mighty act that took the first Egyptian lives, stirred in him such panic, for once ended, the hailstorm left hope amidst destruction in the living men, animals, and crops. These locusts, however, were systematically and thoroughly cutting off Egypt's future. The only word for it is Pharaoh's chilling description: המות הזה "this death," a still further echo of the frightening prospect brought by the worst of the mighty acts to this point.

18–20 Once more, then, Moses prays to Yahweh, and once more Yahweh answers his prayer for the relief of Egypt. The locust swarm is removed as it was collected and brought, by the movement of a wind, described this time as רוח־ים חזק מאד "a very strong sea wind."

רוח־ים is often translated "west wind," because of the orientation of the land of Israel to the Mediterranean Sea to the west. As the sea is not to the west of Egypt, however, the more literal translation above is preferable. The locust swarm is blown by this wind into the ים סוף "Sea of Reeds," the sea which Israel is later to cross in exodus from Egypt, and the miraculous nature of the mighty act is emphasized by the pointed statement that every single locust was removed from the whole territory of Egypt.

Yahweh's proof of his Presence in Egypt was not yet at an end, however.

And so once again, he made Pharaoh obstinate-minded: even after the removal of the locust swarm, Pharaoh proved intractable yet again.

Explanation

From the terrible theophanic hailstorm in which Egyptian lives are first taken, this eighth mighty-act narrative moves forward with the supernatural locust swarm to a set of circumstances in which all Egyptian lives are threatened. The pace of events appears to have quickened; the seriousness of the proving deeds has intensified. Pharaoh and his advisers have lost some of their cocky arrogance; the patience of both Moses and his God, Yahweh, is clearly wearing thin. The whole impression is of an accelerating rush toward some awful resolution to the impasse, a resolution that will at last mean freedom for the Israelites but terrible consequences for Pharaoh and his Egyptians.

The tenor of the proof-of-Presence sequence has moved from contest to increasingly difficult defeat to death, and now, to a prospect of extermination by starvation. The resistance of Pharaoh has moved from proud and resolute leadership to courageous perseverance to petulant stubbornness to a kind of sick denial to an obstinancy beyond any human explanation. Israel, we may only presume, must witness all this with a steadily growing reverence for a God whose claim of Presence has been cumulatively established.

There is a gripping sense of increasing desperation on the part of all the protagonists, except for Yahweh alone. He quite plainly knows what he is about, and we ourselves are drawn ever more surely and swiftly, along with Israel, into a sharing of some part, at least of that knowledge.

Above all, there is in this composite in its context a sense of growing urgency. Pharaoh's attitude and that of the members of his court, alongside the increased severity of the mighty acts, make it plain that we have moved beyond the point of return. And at both the beginning and end of this section (vv 1–2 and 20), we are told quite explicitly who is in charge of these events, and why.

The Ninth Mighty Act   (10:21–29)

Bibliography

Frankfort, H. *Ancient Egyptian Religion.* New York: Harper and Brothers, 1961. **Halevi, Z'ev ben Shimon.** *Kabbalah and Exodus.* Boulder, CO: Shambhala Publications, 1980. **Hort, G.** "The Plagues of Egypt," II. *ZAW* 70 (1958) 48–59. **Labuschagne, C. J.** "The Emphasizing Particle *Gam* and Its Connotations." *Studia Biblica et Semitica.* Wageningen: H. Veenman and Sons, 1966. **Rüger, H. P.** "Zum Text von Sir 40:10 und Ex 10:21." *ZAW* 82 (1970) 103–9.

Translation

[21] *Next, Yahweh said to Moses, "Thrust out your hand against the heavens, and there will be darkness upon the land of Egypt, a darkness so thick people will have*

to feel their way around." [a] [22] *Thus Moses thrust out his hand against the heavens, and immediately* [a] *there was eerie darkness* [b] *in the whole land of Egypt, three days in duration.* [23] *No man could see his neighbor, and no man could dispel the darkness* [a] *for three days. All the sons of Israel, however, had light in their dwelling-places.*

[24] *So Pharaoh summoned Moses,* [a] *then said, "Go ahead—worship Yahweh.* [b] *Just leave behind your flocks and your herds; even your toddlers may go along with you."* [25] *Moses replied, however, "You must also make it possible for us to make* [a] *sacrifices and offerings to Yahweh our God.* [26] *Even our livestock is to go with us; not a hoof is to remain here, for from our own possessions* [a] *we must take the means of the worship* [b] *of Yahweh our God, and we* [c] *have no way of knowing* [d] *what is to be the means of our worship of Yahweh until we come there."*

[27] *At that very moment,* [a] *Yahweh made Pharaoh's mind obstinate, and he did not consent to their going out.* [28] *Indeed, Pharaoh said to him, "Get out!* [a] *Be sure for your own good that you never again look upon my face,* [b] *for on the day you see my face, you will die!"* [29] *Moses retorted,* [a] *"Whatever you say* [b]*—I will not again see your face!"*

Notes

21.a. וימש חשך, lit., "and darkness will cause to grope," read above as "a darkness . . . way around" for clarity. The verb משש is used also of Laban feeling about in Jacob's tents (Gen 31:34) and groping through Jacob's packed-up goods (Gen 31:37) in search of his missing Teraphim, and of the blind "feeling around anxiously" (Deut 28:29).

22.a. Special *waw* in this context.

22.b. חשך אפלה is "darkness of calamity," quite lit., the darkness of a supernatural gloom or danger. LXX adds θύελλα "storm, squall," to give "darkness, a storm upon . . . ."

23.a. Lit., "no man could stand up, rise up, from under it"; no man could counteract its effect.

24.a. LXX and Vg add "and Aaron." SamPent has אל־משה ואהרן "to Moses and to Aaron."

24.b. LXX, Syr add "your God."

25.a. LXX, Vg read "you are to give us"; see *Comment.*

26.a. ממנו "from it," in reference to the livestock, the Israelites' own property, and "wealth." Moses' point is consistent with the requirements of worship specified throughout the OT: the sacrifice or offering must be costly to the worshiper, must be his own gift.

26.b. לעבד את־יהוה "to serve Yahweh," is employed consistently through the mighty act sequence in this sense.

26.c. Emphatic usage, expressed by the independent pers pronoun plus the 1st com pl form of the verb ידע "know by experience."

26.d. Lit., "we do not know."

27.a. Special *waw* plus piel of חזק "make obstinate."

28.a. Lit., "Get from upon me!"

28.b. L reads אֶל "toward," thus "guard yourself toward you adding to see my face." But MSS published by Kennicott, de Rossi, and Ginsburg read אַל "not," thus "guard yourself that you not add . . ." which is the more probable reading.

29.a. Special *waw* plus אמר "say" in this context.

29.b. כן דברת "Thus, yes, you have spoken."

Form/Structure/Setting

The abrupt beginning and the strange sequence of this ninth of the mighty-act accounts have led commentators to the opinion that it is an incomplete composite, even an amalgam, including material that belongs to a separate mighty-act narrative altogether. The account opens with Yahweh's command to Moses to bring on the terrible darkness, without the usual confrontation, command, and warning of Pharaoh. Indeed, the first part of 10:21 is nearly identical in wording (only the sign of the definite object, את, is missing before ידך "your hand" here) to the first part of 9:22, which is the *tenth* verse of the narrative of the eighth mighty-act account.

Further, this account moves from the command and arrival of the terrible darkness (vv 21–23) to negotiations so unsuccessful that Pharaoh breaks them off utterly and forever, on pain of death to Moses (vv 24–29). Missing is the usual verbal relenting of Pharaoh, heretofore withdrawn with the hardening of his mind. Indeed, Yahweh hardens Pharaoh's mind as the negotiations are in progress, and the inevitable result is furious and total impasse and an irreconcilable break between the two primary negotiators, Pharaoh and Moses.

As noted already (cf. *Form/Structure/Setting* on 10:1–20) some critics attempt to explain this unusual sequence by relocating parts of this account. Fohrer (*Überlieferung*, 63, 70), e.g., assigns vv 24–26, 28–29 to J's account of the eighth mighty act, as does Hyatt (125–26), on the view that J produced no narrative of a mighty act involving darkness. Both Fohrer and Hyatt follow the lead of Beer (55–58), and all three assign vv 21–23 and 27 to E, who alone, by their view, preserved an account of a mighty act that brought darkness. Noth (83–84), on the other hand, finds "elements of a short P version in 10:21 f., 27" into which the J material has been amalgamated.

Additional difficulties are posed by the specific notation (vv 22–23) that the terrible darkness is to last for three days; by the ambiguity of the time of Pharaoh's summons of Moses (v 24), whether it was during the darkness or following it; and by the implication of 11:7–8 that, even after the unconditional finality of 10:27–29, Moses is once again facing Pharaoh (see below). Greenberg, who does not follow a source-documentary approach, even proposes (*Understanding Exodus*, 165–92) the reading of 10:21–29; 11:4–8, then 11:1–3 and 11:9–10 in sequence, according to an elaborate theory by which "the substance of the plagues" is contained in "two sets of three plagues each," "capped" by the climactic death of the firstborn of Egypt.

The possibilities are many, of course, and are limited finally only by the extent to which their speculation reaches. The more complicated and apparently disjointed the sequence, however, the more we must remind ourselves of the integrity of the text in its canonical form. These compilations cannot have been made arbitrarily, with no thought to the point and impression they would present. They are deliberate, and they are what we have in hand from a time far closer to the events and a living theological interpretation of them than any speculation about them and any rearrangement of them can possibly be. Once again, it is important that we begin and end with what we have in certainty, and we must remember that however valuable speculation is about what these texts may once have been, we are not to lose sight of their impact and meaning *as they stand,* in the canonical form of the received text.

The unusual sequence of this account of the ninth mighty act is dictated by its content. The terrible darkness, despite the fact that it causes no death and is of prescribed duration, is presented as the most fearful and ominous of the mighty acts in the sequence to this point. The proof-of-Presence sequence rushes forward with quickened pace from the seventh mighty act to its terrible climax, and with this ninth mighty act, at least in the compilation before us, the usual protocols are dispensed with entirely. The warnings to Pharaoh have had no effect heretofore; this time, there is no warning. The terrible darkness falls suddenly, with paralyzing density. In the context of all that has happened, and in view of the fact that the Israelites have light still, there can be no doubt about the nature of the darkness and its source.

Thus Pharaoh summons Moses yet again, makes a "final" offer, is rejected, and, once more made obstinate by Yahweh, erupts in a violent fury. Moses responds in kind and stalks out. Human negotiation is brought to an abrupt end. Yahweh must become the prime mover, and this he does. From this point forward, Moses recedes even further from the center of the narrative.

The form of the ninth mighty-act account thus is an accurate reflection of the agitation and the penultimate crisis it presents. It is a compilation to this very end, and this is a fact the search for its sources must not be allowed to obscure.

Comment

21–23 The darkness that Yahweh brings upon the signal of Moses' thrust-out hand must be understood as entirely supernatural if the point and the position of the ninth of the mighty acts are to be appreciated. This is not a *khamsin*, even of such extraordinary dimension and effect as the one imagined by Hort (ZAW 70 [1958] 52–54), nor is there any basis in the narrative for describing what occurs here as an eclipse of the sun (Knight, 79–80).

This darkness is inexplicable, comparable to nothing the Egyptians or the Israelites have ever before known, so thick as to suggest palpability, and "eerie," heavy with impending calamity. וימש חשך has been variously translated as darkness that could be "felt" or "touched." H. P. Rüger has reviewed (ZAW 82 [1970] 108–9) a series of suggested emendations, and proposed from the occurrence of תמוש in Sir 40:10 and cognate usage in Mishnaic Hebrew and Arabic that וימש חשך in v 21 should here be considered a "doublet" with ויהי חשך in v 22b, and read "and darkness will arrive" following "stick out your hand that darkness. . . ." As Rüger proposes, "darkness" is the subject of the verb משש "grope," but as that verb is pointed in MT as a 3d person masculine singular hiphil imperfect, the text quite literally says "and darkness will cause groping," that is, the darkness will be so thick as to require people to feel their way about.

This darkness is חשך־אפלה "eerie darkness," the darkness of calamity, quite probably divine calamity. Most of the occurrences of אפלה refer to the unnatural and fearsome darkness of the Day of Yahweh (cf. Isa 8:22; Joel 2:1; Zeph 1:15; see also Deut 28:29; Amos 5:20; Isa 58:10; 59:9). It is unquestionably a supernatural darkness, thus all the more terrible and frightening. No man could see the person next to him, and no man could do anything to cancel or ward off the thick darkness. Only the sons of Israel

had any light at all, and that in their מושבות "dwelling places," probably
to be taken, as Hyatt (127) suggests, as their very houses.

24 Faced with so obvious and frightening an act of the God of the "Hebrews," Pharaoh commands the presence of Moses. His fullest capitulation,
the release of all but the Israelite livestock without restriction as to the place
or the duration of their pilgrimage, can be understood only in the context
of a mighty act far worse than anything that has happened before. This calami-
tous darkness is precisely that, for it has shut out the sun's rays, Egypt's
chief source of creative life (cf. Frankfort, *Egyptian Religion*, 14–22). Chap.
17 of *The book of the Dead* includes these words (*ANET³*, 4):

> *"I am he among the gods who cannot be repulsed."*
> *Who is he? He is Atum, who is in his sun disc.*
> *(Another Version: He is Re, when he arises on the eastern horizon of heaven.)*

Commenting on these lines, translator John A. Wilson (*ANET³*, 4, n. 9)
has written, "The eternally rising sun cannot be destroyed." So all Egyptians
believed, above all the supposedly divine Pharaoh. But when for three days
the eternally rising sun made no appearance, and that in the aftermath of
the killing hail and the decimating locusts, fear was as thick as the darkness,
and Pharaoh had to act. Thus were given the sudden call for Moses and
the order of release which held back only livestock. Pharaoh is depicted attempting to hold onto one last fragment of pride, and even an earnest of
the return of the "Hebrews" from their pilgrimage-worship.

25–26 Moses, however, has tasted triumph, and in any case he cannot
leave behind the property from which the Israelites must take their expressions
of worship. Labuschagne's translation (*Studia*, 202) of וגם . . . גם in this
sequence to mean that Moses is asking Pharaoh for animals for the sacrifices
of the pilgrimage-worship in addition to the release of Israelites' own livestock
is unacceptable. So also is the subjunctive circumlocution of Hyatt (127).
"Make it possible for us" is literally "give into our hands" in terms of granting
authority over (cf. Judg 9:19; Deut 24:1–4) and thus, here, making possible
the Israelites' worship by sacrifice in the release to them of their own animals.

This point is all the more important in view of Moses' argument that the
means of their worship must come from their own possessions, a requirement
to be made more specific upon their arrival at the place of pilgrimage, as
opposed to animals they might locate and pick up, somehow, along the way.
Such sacrifices would be no sacrifices, because they would cost the sons of
Israel nothing.

27–28 Pharaoh's own response to this reasonable request, which would
nevertheless be suspected by a skeptical and misunderstanding foreigner, is
not given. Immediately, we are told, Yahweh made Pharaoh's mind once
more obstinate to the release of the "Hebrews," and he flew into an uncon-
trollable rage. This rage, like Pharaoh's intransigence following earlier promises he had made, and like the frightening and supernatural darkness, can
only be from Yahweh. No other explanation is possible under the circumstances.

29 Moses takes Pharaoh at his word. In a response tinged with the irony of the knowledge that Pharaoh himself may very well yet ask for him to come back, Moses responds to Pharaoh's command of banishment, "Just as you say!"

Explanation

The point of this ninth of the mighty-act accounts is made in part by the location of the account, in part by the serious calamity of unbroken darkness in a land so accustomed to and dependent upon the sun as Egypt, and in part by the altogether supernatural aspect of the eerie darkness that cannot be dispelled yet does not somehow afflict the sons of Israel in their dwelling places. Following upon the supernatural hailstorm that beats the standing crops into pulp and the supernatural locust swarm that devours what is left to sprout and grow, this darkness blocking out the sun is an awesome threat of total and final extinction. The Kabbalists, for all their allegorical excesses, interpreted the ninth mighty act accurately when they described it as "the curtailment of the *Hokhmah* or the life force" (Halevi, *Kabbalah and Exodus*, 73).

This point is reinforced by the unusual form of the narrative setting it forth, a form that disregards the usual sequence and presents an account tumbling over itself with urgency and alarm. What has been taken by some critics as evidence of patchy editorial work and an inconsistent text may be in fact an entirely deliberate attempt to present the high tension of the continuing confrontations of Moses and Pharaoh coming to climax in frustrating impasse and failure.

Still further reinforcement is provided by the language of the account, which describes the darkness as impenetrably thick and completely resistant to the Egyptians' light and as retreating before the Israelites' light. It is language used in an array of passages to refer to the supernatural judgment-darkness of the Day of Yahweh. Insufficient emphasis has been placed on this language and upon the darkness as entirely unnatural and related to the move of Yahweh toward a settlement of the issue of the freedom of the Israelites in the climactic mighty act of the proof of this Presence in Egypt.

Indeed, the complete breakdown of the negotiations between Moses and Pharaoh needs to be seen as the intended catalyst to the tenth and final mighty act in Egypt. For the first time, Yahweh moves to make Pharaoh obstinate *during* the negotiations. Heretofore he has made Pharaoh stubborn *after* he has agreed to Moses' demands, after Yahweh's mighty action has ceased and before Moses can leave with the sons of Israel. This time, Yahweh causes Pharaoh to turn obstinate during the negotiations themselves, to grow angry, and to banish Moses on pain of death. No further human mediation is possible. Moses' attempts on Israel's behalf have failed utterly because of Yahweh's own intrusions into Pharaoh's decision-making. Now Moses cannot even attempt further negotiations. The Israelites are not only no nearer freedom, they are farther from it than ever.

There is no longer any place to turn, no longer anyone to whom petition can be made, no longer anyone to do the turning and the petitioning. As happens so often in the biblical narrative, every human endeavor stands exhausted, and every apparent alternative has been used without success. What is left? What can even God do? The dream of freedom lies smashed. Yahweh's deliverer may have difficulty delivering even himself. All Yahweh's promises remain unfulfilled. He has proved his Presence, but to what avail? The expectations of the Israelites have been brought to nothing.

The moment is like that of the scattering and the confusion of Babel, like the moment of the command to Abraham to sacrifice Isaac on Moriah, like the moment of the destruction of Jerusalem in 586 B.C., and like the moment of the death of Jesus on the cross. Nothing more can be done, clearly. Yet the promises are promises of *God,* so how *can* nothing more be done?

In this stark contradiction, the point of this special section is to be seen, and we are made ready for what is to come.

The Tenth Mighty Act Anticipated   (*11:1–10*)

Bibliography

Coats, G. W. "Despoiling the Egyptians." *VT* 18 (1968) 450–57. **Durham, J. I.** *The Senses Touch, Taste, and Smell in Old Testament Religion.* Unpublished D.Phil. thesis, University of Oxford, 1963. **Fensham, F. C.** "The Dog in Ex. XI 7." *VT* 16 (1966) 504–7. **Morgenstern, J.** "The Despoiling of the Egyptians." *JBL* 68 (1949) 1–28. **Thomas, D. W.** "*KELEBH* 'Dog': Its Origin and Some Usages of It in the Old Testament." *VT* 10 (1960) 410–27.

Translation

[1]*Next, Yahweh said to Moses, "One final* [a] *stroke of judgment* [b] *will I bring upon Pharaoh and upon Egypt: after that, he will send you out from there without any restrictions.* [c] *In fact, he will throw you out of Egypt.* [d] [2]*Speak promptly, instruct* [a] *the people to ask, each man and woman of their neighbors, articles of silver and gold."* [b] [3]*Then Yahweh gave* [a] *the people credibility* [b] *in the opinion of the Egyptians.* [c] *The man Moses also was very great in the land of Egypt, in the opinion of the members of Pharaoh's court and in the opinion of the people.*

[4]*So Moses said, "Thus says Yahweh, 'Around the middle of the night, I will go out into the midst of the Egyptians.* [5]*All the firstborn of the land of Egypt will die, from the firstborn of Pharaoh, the occupant of the royal throne, to the firstborn of the servant-girl who grinds with* [a] *the hand-mill, and all the first-born of the cattle as well.* [b] [6]*There will be a great cry of anguish* [a] *through the whole land of Egypt, unlike* [b] *any that has ever been heard or that is ever to be heard again.* [c] [7]*As regards the sons of Israel, however, not even a dog shall show malice* [a] *towards either man or beast,* [b] *so that you may know without question* [c] *that Yahweh has separated* [d] *Israel from the Egyptians.'* [8]*And all these members of your court will flock to me and prostrate themselves in homage before me, saying, 'Go out, you and all the people who follow after you.' Then will I indeed go out." With that, Moses* [a] *went out from Pharaoh's presence burning with anger.*

⁹ *Then Yahweh said to Moses, "Pharaoh will pay no attention to you: my purpose* ᵇ *is that my wondrous deeds may be many in the land of Egypt."* ¹⁰ *So Moses and Aaron did all these wondrous deeds in Pharaoh's presence, and Yahweh made Pharaoh's heart obstinate, and he did not send out the sons of Israel from his land.*

Notes

1.a. אֶחָד . . . עוֹד "yet one, still one"; the context suggests "one final."

1.b. נגע "stroke" occurs 77× in the OT, 62× in reference to the "touch-mark of skin-disease" (see above, n. 4:6.d.) regarded as the result of Yahweh's judgment, and 15× in reference to various kinds of "touching" in judgment. The term is used only here in reference to any of the mighty acts, and in this context suggests something more than the general word "plague." See Durham, *Touch, Taste, and Smell,* 30–47.

1.c. כשלחו כלה, "as for his sending, it is complete." LXX reads כלה with גרש יגרש "he will throw you out": σὺν παντὶ ἐκβαλεῖ ὑμᾶς ἐκβολῇ "with everything he will throw you out." כשלחו, the Masoretic tradition of L notes, occurs only here in the OT, and the unusual syntax of the verse has led to a variety of interpretations, ancient *and* modern (cf. NEB; Morgenstern, *JBL* 68 [1949] 1–5). The clear point of the narrative, however, is a *complete* exodus; heretofore Pharaoh has been willing to permit only a partial going out, *sans* family or *sans* cattle. Yahweh now announces an exodus without limitations, exactly what the tenth mighty act brings about.

1.d. The emphasis is indicated by the use of the inf abs with the piel of גרש "drive out," by itself a verb indicating violent action. See BDB, 176.

2.a. Lit., "Pray speak into the ears of the people." Moses is to be sure the people understand what is clearly a strange request.

2.b. In 3:22 and 12:35, שמלת "garments" is added to "articles of silver and gold," and LXX and SamPent include "garments" here.

3.a. SamPent begins the verse with a 1st pers verb and has Yahweh giving an extended summary of his tenth mighty act.

3.b. חן "grace, favor," here an attractiveness or trustworthiness that renders the Egyptians willing to part with their valuables.

3.c. Both SamPent and LXX add "so they gave what was requested."

5.a. אשר אחר "who is behind" the pair of stones of a grinding-mill (cf. *ANEP,* 46, no. 149). The servant-girl grinding grain for bread represents the opposite pole of human existence from the Pharaoh, enthroned in power. Note "The Instruction of the Vizier Ptah-Hotep," 11. 50–65 (*ANET*³, 412).

5.b. Domesticated animals, thus personal property, are in view here. SamPent עד בכור כל בהמה and LXX ἕως πρωτοτόκου παντὸς κτήνους read "right up to the firstborn of all the cattle."

6.a. See Ps 9:13[12]; Isa 5:7; Job 27:9; 1 Sam 4:14; and BDB, 858.

6.b. כָּמֹהוּ, lit., "the like of him," masc sg pronom suff. צעקה "cry of anguish" is a fem noun, and the two verbs in this sequence are fem sg. SamPent and some Masoretic notes (see Cassuto, 133) read כָּמֹהָ for this reason, but the change is unnecessary. The reference is to the cry of anguish but also to the whole context prompting it, so the use of the broader masc suff.

6.c. The text reads lit. "the like of it has not been [niph pf of היה] and the like of it will not cause to add [increase, hiph impf of יסף]."

7.a. A dog (or a man, Josh 10:21) "sharpening his tongue" describes an attitude of malice and opposition much like the expressions "he curled his lip" and "he bared his teeth." There is no support for the view of Fensham (*VT* 16 [1966] 505–7) that the expression is a curse involving the licking of the blood and the flesh of a vanquished enemy.

7.b. בהמה "beast" is used here in its collective sense (BDB, 96) to represent the other end of the gamut of Israelite life, "from man all the way to beast."

7.c. This emphasis is indicated not only by the use of ידע "know," but also by the addition of *nun paragogicum* (see GKC § 47m). SamPent and LXX make it sg, without the *nun*. MT's pl suggests these words are addressed to Pharaoh and his court.

7.d. SamPent has יפלא "he worked a wonder" instead of יפלה "he separated," thus "Yahweh has worked a wonder between the Egyptians and Israel."

8.a. MT has "he." Moses is clearly the antecedent of this pronoun; thus his name is added above for clarity.

9.a. לְמַעַן "in order that, so that."

Form/Structure/Setting

This section, like the one before it, is a composite. Three sources are represented, two of them announcing the final and most devastating blow in the sequence of mighty acts in Egypt. Once again, the disjointedness of the pericope must not be allowed to obscure the reason for its presentation in the form before us. The purpose of this section is twofold: the introduction of the tenth mighty act and the instruction for the despoiling of Israel's Egyptian neighbors, anticipated in 3:21–22. The arrangement of this section must be seen not only as dictated by the flow of the narrative to follow, but also by the complex interweaving of the narratives of the tenth mighty act and the exodus from Egypt with the cultic and narrative material dealing with Passover.

The proposed rearrangements of this material (see *Form/Structure/Setting* on 10:1–20, 21–29), interesting enough as studies of the content and sequence of some of the sources reflected in the Book of Exodus, almost invariably serve to deflect attention from the more important matter at hand: an understanding of the text in its composite form.

Source critics have generally divided Exod 11 into three sections, each from a different source: vv 1–3 are assigned to E, vv 4–8 to J, vv 9–10 to P (Beer, 12, 58; Fohrer assigns v 1 to E, vv 2–3 to his "nomadic" source, *Überlieferung* 60–62, 72–73, 81–85, 124; Hyatt, 129; Childs, 131). These divisions are obvious ones, but the content of the three sections is less clearly complementary than in the previous mighty-act composites.

Indeed, each section within this composite has its own and separate purpose. This fact, along with the movement into the foreground of the action of Yahweh and the insertion into the larger narrative of the specification of the sacral commemoration of the exodus from Egypt, has made necessary an alteration of the form of the mighty-act narrative that has been followed generally up to this point.

The first section (vv 1–3) thus deals primarily with the "despoiling theme," a variation on the theme of the triumph of Yahweh over Egypt and Egypt's gods. The mention of the tenth mighty act here (v 1) is necessary as the basis for the despoiling story and the exodus, without which the despoiling could not occur. The second section (vv 4–8) deals primarily with the tenth mighty act and its result. The address of these verses at first seems ambiguous. The obvious address of the instructions of v 2 to Israel and the plural verb ("so that you may know") of v 7 have led some interpreters (Noth, 94) to think of Moses as speaking here to Israel as well. Vv 7–8 make clear, however, that Pharaoh is being addressed, by the contrast of the fate of the Israelites with that of the Egyptians, by the reference to the members of Pharaoh's court, and by the report of Moses' angry departure from Pharaoh's presence. The third section (vv 9–10) is a kind of summary review, as before, indicating by the hardening of the heart motif the reason for the array of mighty acts and for their failure to this point, and anticipating the movement of Yahweh into prominence.

Together, these three sections provide a skillful transition from the first nine mighty-act accounts, in which Moses (with the addition of "and Aaron") is presented as Yahweh's prophetic messenger, to the account of the all-important tenth mighty act, in which Yahweh acts for himself. Indeed, from this point forward, Yahweh is increasingly in the foreground, and Moses is increasingly in the background until the rebellion of Israel and its aftermath, in chaps. 32–34.

Further, Exod 11 sums up as it looks forward (compare v 1 with vv 9–10), and provides the necessary foundation for the Priestly material on Passover given immediately in chap. 12. The unity of this sequence is thus provided above all by its location between the preparatory first nine mighty acts and the climactic tenth mighty act and the exodus which that act makes possible. The number of the mighty acts in the separate sequences of the sources, their order, and their emphasis are not questions to be addressed to the composite that presents them as ten, in a succession of rising disaster and with the single emphasis of the proof of Yahweh's powerful Presence. What is most important about Exod 11 is its suggestion as a whole, and not its confusion in parts.

Comment

1 The reference to "yet another" or "one final" blow against the Egyptians, one Yahweh himself is to bring and one that will prompt Pharaoh to *compel* Israel by force to leave Egypt, has been anticipated in the narrative of Exodus at 3:19–20 and 6:1. When, in the sequence of the mighty acts, Pharaoh has shown any willingness to compromise, he has done so each time with restrictions wholly unacceptable to Yahweh and therefore to Moses. This time, Yahweh declares, there will be no restrictions, and Pharaoh will be so eager to be rid of the Israelites that he will literally drive them out of the country. In an intriguing juxtaposition of themes, however, the narrative of chap. 11 makes plain that Pharaoh's new reasonableness is divinely wrought. When he has begun to come around prematurely, Yahweh has stiffened his resolve (v 10); now Yahweh will cause him to send Israel forth urgently, not only with all that is rightly theirs, but with some Egyptian valuables as well.

2 Thus the Israelites are to be instructed to ask of their neighbors, both male and female, articles of silver and gold. The use of רֵעַ "friend, companion, neighbor" does not imply that the Israelites are no longer living separately from the Egyptians, as Noth (93) suggests. Nor does the general term כְּלִי "article, vessel, object" suggest jewelry, as both RSV and NEB propose. The object of the request the Israelites are to make is a further humbling of Pharaoh and the gods who are supposed to be looking after his people and his country. Not just jewelry, but any objects of value, prized possessions of silver and gold, and, according to 3:22 and 12:35, even clothing would do.

3 Yahweh, in a further display of his complete control over the situation, will lead the Egyptians, who have wanted to be rid of the Israelites, to have favor towards them now, just as Pharaoh, who has wanted to keep them in Egypt, will וח come to want them gone. Yahweh, granting the Israelites]ח "grace, favor" in the Egyptians' eyes, would make them credible, thus persons to be trusted with precious possessions. Given the consistent OT picture of antipathy towards the Israelites by the Egyptians, even in the days of Joseph's ascendancy (Gen 43:32; 46:34), this gift of credibility is all the more miraculous.

2–3   The theft of the Egyptians' valuables by the Israelites has been the occasion of an amusing array of theories and excuses. Childs (175–77) handily summarizes the apologetical arguments from Hellenistic times forward, arguments still pressed with only minor variations. Daube (*Exodus Pattern*, 55–72), for example, justifies this taking of Egyptian valuables as the payment ("fitting out") due a released slave; Knight (82–83) considers it a payment ("conscience money") in part for the Israelites' labor on Egyptian building projects across many years; Coats (*VT* 18 [1968] 453–57) thinks of the despoiling as a deception (לאשׁ "ask" of v 2 = borrow with expectation of return) linked to a tradition of exodus by stealth, now obscured; Morgenstern (*JBL* 68 [1949] 1–5, 17–28), beginning with an alteration of the text of v 1 suggested first by M. van Hoonacker and followed by NEB, concluded that the "despoiling" was incidental to a deception which required that the Israelite women go forth to a festal dance arrayed as brides in finery that included "something borrowed."

These excuses and theories, however ingenious, are unnecessary. Each of the four occurrences of the "despoiling" narrative in the OT (Exod 3:19–22; 11:2–3; 12:35–36; Ps 105:36–38) makes plain that the Egyptians give their precious possessions to the Israelites gladly, because of Yahweh's intervention. There is no hint of any deception, any "borrowing" with even an implied promise of a return of the borrowed items. לאשׁ "ask" alone does not suggest such a meaning (cf. BDB, 981). The Israelites "ask," and the Egyptians, in a kind of trance of affection and trust caused by Yahweh, freely give. The Egyptians thus are "picked clean" (3:22 and 12:36) by Israel as a result of yet another action by Yahweh in behalf of his people, demonstrating the power of his Presence. For the narrators who composed these texts, this act of Yahweh, as an act of Yahweh, needed no further justification, only proclamation.

The mention of Yahweh's gift of credibility to Israel prompts a summary comment on the esteem in which Moses is now held throughout Egypt by the people both high and low. The phrase "the man Moses," used in a similar though even broader accolade in Num 12:3, appears to present Moses with an aura of awe.

4   The prediction of the tenth of the mighty acts is made abruptly, without the usual introductory address to Moses or the usual account of Moses' movement to intercept Pharaoh. This abruptness creates an ambiguity of context that is resolved only by vv 7–8 and suggests the excision for some reason of the beginning of the narrative. Various attempts have been made to reconstruct this beginning, either by the assumption that 11:4–8 is a continuation of the narrative of 10:21–29 or by the provision of some other introductory section. Morgenstern, following H. Holzinger, suggested (*JBL* 68 [1949] 19–

21), the relocation at this point of 4:22–23. That passage, however, is better left in its present location, in which it serves a quite definite function (see *Comment* on 4:22–23). The probability is that the original introduction to 11:4–8 was omitted on purpose in the combination of the array of themes now surrounding the tenth mighty act.

5 The more immediate agency of Yahweh in the terrible events at hand is emphasized by the assertion "I will go out into the midst of the Egyptians." The full range of the Egyptian populace is to be affected by this going out, and this fact is dramatized by the juxtaposition of the highest in the land, Pharaoh on his royal throne, with the lowest in the land, the servant-girl pulverizing grain with two stones, as by the addition of stock-animals, thus including any who have property but no children.

6 The cry of anguish sent up by this decimation will be unique, just as the disaster will be unique. This language is reminiscent of 9:18, 24, in reference to the "very heavy hail," and of 10:6, 14, in reference to the "locust-swarm." The hailstorm was unparalleled in the history of Egypt as a nation; the locust-swarm was unparalleled in the experience of the Egyptians to the third generation back, and would never come in such density again; the death of the firstborn would bring a cry of anguish throughout Egypt that had never been and would never be matched. These comments intensify the final mighty acts, the last of them most of all.

7 Against such a tragic backdrop, the Israelites will remain unharmed and undisturbed. Not even the empty snarl of a dog will interrupt the quiet of the Israelite settlement, while among the Egyptians the air will be torn by the piercing cries of lament. Again there is a graphic contrast. As Winton Thomas demonstrated (*VT* 10 [1960] 415–17, 426–27), כלב "dog," in the *vox populi* of Israel, is a "vile and contemptible animal," "despised and generally wretched." The malice of a dog would therefore be occasion for little alarm, yet not even that shall come against Israel, while the Egyptians are suffering the loss of their future. Among the Egyptians is an unparalleled wail of anguish; among the Israelites, silence. All this is to the end that the Egyptians may know the power of Yahweh and where his favor rests.

8 This separation will be so clear and its terrible implication so unmistakable that the members of Pharaoh's council will come to Moses in homage and plead with him to leave and to take all his people with him. It is a terrible prediction, delivered as a triumphant challenge. Thus bowed to and begged, says Moses, "I will indeed go out." No response of Pharaoh is recorded. Instead, the narrator gives the impression of an angry Moses stalking out, leaving an awed Pharaoh in stunned silence.

9–10 The concluding paragraph of this chapter is generally assigned to P, and so is taken by Noth (94–97) to go with the section on Passover that follows. These two verses belong here, however, as the important summary of the foregoing sequence of mighty acts, the explanation of why they did not achieve their purpose, and the justification of what now is about to come.

Explanation

Exod 11 is above all a preparatory transition, from the cumulative proof-of-Presence sequence in Egypt to its climactic end. To this point, Moses (sometimes with Aaron added) has served as Yahweh's prophetic spokesman and as the agent of Yahweh's wonders. As we have been told all along, however, and as we are told again now (vv 9–10), Yahweh has himself blocked any success his efforts through Moses might have achieved. He is ready now to step onto the scene himself. Moses makes the announcement and gives the instructions, nothing more.

What is to come upon Pharaoh and his land now, Yahweh himself will bring. Any resistance the Egyptians might yet have will be cancelled by Yahweh's gift of credibility or favor to Israel. Then Egypt's firstborn will die, and Pharaoh and all who advise him will want the Israelites and Moses to be gone.

The transition is not only suggested by prediction, instruction, and retrospect, it is dramatized by these implicit and explicit pairings: an unrestricted exodus with Pharaoh's earlier restrictive proposals; an expulsion of the Israelites from Egypt with an earlier refusal to let them go; a giving of valuable possessions to a people heretofore treated only as cheap labor; a striking of every Egyptian household, from highest to lowest, with Israel unharmed; the agonizing cry of loss throughout Egypt with the silence of security among the Israelites in Goshen; and complete esteem for Moses in contrast to an earlier treatment of rejection.

With the end of this transitional composite, the way has been prepared for the tenth of the mighty acts, for the exodus it will make possible, and for the Passover celebration by which Israel is to be taught to remember them both.

Yahweh's Passover   (12:1–13)

Bibliography

Alter, R. *The Art of Biblical Narrative.* New York: Basic Books, 1981. **Beer, G.** "Miscellen. 2. Die Bitterkräuter beim Paschafest." *ZAW* 31 (1911) 152–53. ———. *Pesachim (Ostern):* Text, Übersetzung und Eklärung. Giessen: A. Töpelmann, 1912. **Haag, H.** *Vom alten zum neuen Pascha.* SBS 49. Stuttgart: Verlag Kath. Bibelwerk, 1971. **Keel, O.** "Erwägungen zum Sitz im Leben des vormosaischen Pascha und zur Etymologie von פֶּסַח." *ZAW* 84 (1972) 414–34. **Laaf, P.** *Die Pascha-Feier Israels.* Bonn: P. Hanstein, 1970. **McKay, J. W.** "The Date of Passover and Its Significance." *ZAW* 84 (1972) 435–47. **Oesterley, W. O. E.** *The Sacred Dance.* New York: Macmillan, 1923. **Pedersen, J.** "Passahfest und Passahlegende." *ZAW* 52 (1934) 161–75. **Segal, J. B.** *The Hebrew Passover from the Earliest Times to A.D. 70.* London: Oxford University Press, 1970. **Seters, J. van.** "The Place of the Yahwist in the History of Passover and Massot." *ZAW* 95 (1983) 167–82. **Vaux, R. de.** *Ancient Israel, Vol. 1: Social Institutions.* New York: McGraw-Hill, 1965. ———. *Studies in Old Testament Sacrifice.* Cardiff: University of Wales Press, 1964.

Translation

[1] *Next, Yahweh said this* [a] *to Moses and to Aaron, in the land of Egypt:* [2] *"This month is to be for you the lead* [a] *month. It is for you the first of the year's months.*

³ *Speak to the entire congregation of* ᵃ *Israel to say that on the tenth of this month they shall take for themselves, each man, as a head of a family,* ᵇ *an animal of the flock* ᶜ—*one flock-animal per household.* ⁴ *If the household is too small for a flock-animal, the family-head* ᵃ *and his neighbor nearest to his household shall take together, in accord with the number* ᵇ *of their two households,* ᶜ *each as much as his family can eat: so shall you apportion the flock-animal.*

⁵ *"The flock-animal you take shall be the best,* ᵃ *a yearling male. You shall take it from either the lambs* ᵇ *or the goats.* ⁶ *It shall remain in your special care until the fourteenth day of this month; then all the assembly of the congregation* ᵃ *of Israel shall slaughter it in the evening before dark.* ᵇ ⁷ *They shall take some of the blood, and smear it upon the two doorposts and the lintel they support,* ᵃ *thus marking* ᵇ *the houses in which they shall eat the animal* ᶜ *chosen and kept.*

⁸ *"They shall eat the flesh, roasted over fire, during that night, and they shall eat it with unleavened bread cakes and bitter herbs.* ⁹ *You are not to eat any of it raw or soaked or boiled in water, but roasted over fire—its head along with its legs and its entrails.* ᵃ ¹⁰ *You shall leave none of it until morning:* ᵃ *any remnant of it you shall burn before morning in the fire.*

¹¹ *"In this way you shall eat it: dressed for travel,* ᵃ *your sandals on your feet, your walking-stick* ᵇ *in your hand. Further, you shall eat it anxiously.* ᶜ *It is Yahweh's Passover.* ¹² *I will pass through the land of Egypt in that night, and I will strike a fatal blow* ᵃ *against all the firstborn of the land of Egypt, the firstborn of mankind and cattle alike. Against all the gods of Egypt, I will bring judgments. I am Yahweh.*

¹³ *"The blood is to be for your protection,* ᵃ *a sign upon the houses where you are; I will see the blood, and I will pass over you. There will be no smiting of destruction* ᵇ *against you when I strike my fatal blow against the land of Egypt."*

Notes

1.a. לאמר. the Hebrew idiom is lit. "said . . . to say."

2.a. ראש חדשים "head" or "first" of the "new moons," i.e., lunar months.

3.a. SamPent, LXX, Vg, Syr, Tg Neofiti I (Déaut, 82) add "the sons of."

3.b. לבית אבת, lit., "according to the fathers' family," i.e., per household with a male in charge, as the further qualification of שה לבית "one flock-animal per household" and v 4 show.

3.c. שה includes any flock-animal, here either a lamb or a kid, as v 5 makes clear. Cf. BDB, 961.

4.a. MT has הוא "he"; the family head is clearly intended, and so substituted above.

4.b. SamPent reads "numbers."

4.c. במכסת נפשת "according to the counting of persons."

5.a. תמים "sound, whole," not crippled or marred in any way and so of less value.

5.b. SamPent has הכשבים, the transposed form of MT's הכבשים "the lambs."

6.a. עדת "congregation," is lacking in Vg and the fragmentary texts from the Cairo Geniza. See also n. 3.a above.

6.b. בין הערבים "between the pair of evenings," either the evening before and the evening of the fourteenth day, or the "pair" suggested by sunset and then dark. Note Exod 30:8. Cf. BDB, 788, and GKC, § 88m.

7.a. "They support" is added for clarity, on the basis of the probable meaning of משקוף, the "roof" of the door and its casing. Cf. BDB, 1054.

7.b. על "upon" the house.

7.c. אתו "it," referring to the flock-animal, is the dir obj of "eat" in MT.

9.a. קרבו "its inward parts," internal organs, viscera.

10.a. LXX here adds Καὶ ὀστοῦν οὐ συντρίψετε ἀπ' αὐτοῦ "and you shall not break a bone of it."

11.a. מתניכם חגרים "your loins girded," i.e., "your skirts hitched up," to make rapid and strenuous movement possible. See BDB, 291, 608.

11.b. מַקֵּל, a different word for "staff" or "branch" or "rod" (BDB, 596), no doubt deliberately chosen to avoid any confusion with the מַטֶּה of Moses and Aaron, Exod 4:20, 7:19, 14:16, though note also Hos 4:12. SamPent reads "walking-sticks."

11.c. חִפָּזוֹן "anxiously" suggests urgent hurry, action with alarm. Cf. the usage of the verb form, חפז, in 2 Sam 4:4; 2 Kgs 7:15; Ps 116:11.

12.a. The verb is נכה "strike," used some 75× in the OT of Yahweh's "smiting" in judgment, always with violent, and sometimes, as here, fatal results. See Durham, *Touch, Taste and Smell*, 68–78.

13.a. לכם "for you," i.e., for the Israelites' benefit.

13.b. נֶגֶף לְמַשְׁחִית "smiting of destruction": the noun נֶגֶף refers in the OT only to Yahweh's "hitting" or "smiting," always, as here, with disastrous effect. See Durham, *Touch, Taste and Smell*, 65–68.

Form/Structure/Setting

This section, like the two that follow it, constitutes an intrusion into the narrative of the tenth mighty act. The account of the final proof of Yahweh's Presence in Egypt has been expanded by a series of instructions related to cultic requirements designed to commemorate that proof and the freedom it purchased. The first such series has to do with the annual keeping of Yahweh's Passover (vv 1–13, the section at hand); the second has to do with the annual feast of unleavened bread (vv 14–20); the third relates the symbols of Yahweh's Passover more directly to the narrative of the tenth mighty act (vv 21–28). Implicit throughout the instructions is the important justification for the consecration of the firstborn.

Quite understandably, such a complex assemblage of diverse though related material has led to an equally diverse set of opinions concerning the sources whence these instructions are derived. The section before us, for example, has been assigned to P (e.g., Beer, 60–61, who includes v 14, and who considers vv 21–27 a parallel version from J¹ and Rᴰ; and Noth, 94–96). Childs (184–85), on the other hand, has "tentatively" proposed assigning vv 2–23 to J, though without setting forth satisfactory reasons for doing so (Childs, 191–94; cf. van Seters, *ZAW* 95 [1983] 172–75). Others (e.g., Fohrer, *Überlieferung*, 87–89) propose the admixture of yet other source material (N, Fohrer's "nomadic" source), or dismiss altogether the source documentary approach in favor of a theory of compilation reflecting the chronological "evolution" of the Passover ritual (Segal, *Hebrew Passover*, 42–77).

Though Segal goes too far in his dismissal of the source documents, his emphasis on the greater importance of the composite that stands in the MT of Exod 12 is a correct one. The assignment of portions of the text to sub-sources is a speculation, even when it is a well-informed one. The text at hand is always a certainty, and has been brought to its canonical form for specific theological and cultic reasons, even though they may no longer be recoverable. Attempts to determine the correct source-criticism of a pericope may be suggestive of these reasons, and therefore quite helpful, but these attempts must not be permitted to obscure the form and the thrust of the pericope as a whole.

Exod 12:1–13 may most reasonably be assigned to P, as also may the section following, vv 14–20. This opinion is based on the content of the two sections and the manner in which they sharply interrupt the narrative into which they have been set. The principle by which they have been set into place is illustrated more obviously by the large parallel insertions of Exod 25–31 and 35–40. It is the principle by which cultic requirements are set into the narrative that justifies them, by which ritual expectations are rooted in the story that explains them. What strikes us as disunified, a patchwork, must be seen in terms of the purpose suggested in the compilation before us, rather than in terms of our own expectation of a logical and coherent sequence. As Robert Alter (*Art,* 133) has so aptly put it, "The confused textual patchwork that scholarship has often found . . . may prove upon further scrutiny to be purposeful pattern."

Exod 12 is the result of such a pattern. Read in its context, this chapter both interrupts (vv 1–28) and continues (vv 29–42) the narrative without which the requirement of Yahweh's Passover and the feast of unleavened bread would be arbitrary and puzzling, and as provincial as their probable origin (see *Comment* on vv 8–10, 15, below). The form of the chapter is thus determined largely by the sections it inserts into the narrative. The form of vv 1–13 is determined by specifications essential to the celebration of Yahweh's Passover.

Comment

2   The reference to the Passover month as the "lead month," "the first of the year's months" is best understood as a *double entendre.* On the one hand, the statement may be connected with an annual calendar, but on the other hand, it is surely an affirmation of the theological importance of Yahweh's Passover. There is here, quite significantly, no mention of the name of a specific month, as there is in 23:15 and 34:18, e.g., in connection with the feast of unleavened bread, and in Deut 16:1, in connection with Passover itself. The elaborate discussions of the calendar of pre-exilic and post-exilic times (e.g., de Vaux, *Ancient Israel,* 178–79; Cassuto, 136–37) cannot be applied to this text except as it is considered in relation to these other more specific references.

The more important emphasis of this verse therefore is its insistence upon Yahweh's Passover as a commemoration of Israel's beginning as a people freed by Yahweh. The Passover month is the "head" of the months not primarily as the first month of the year in a calendar, either a "civil" calendar or a "religious" calendar, but because it is the month during which the Israelites remembered and so actualized their redemption. Its association with the spring of the year may originally have come from the nomadic context in which the Passover appears to be rooted. J. W. McKay (*ZAW* 84 [1972] 438–46) has argued that no precise date for the celebration, beyond "the spring month," was fixed prior to the exilic and post-exilic periods, at which time the night of the fourteenth Nisan was pinpointed because it was the eve of the spring equinox in the Babylonian calendar adopted by the Priestly circle.

3–6   The general specification "flock-animal," a deliberate attempt to provide a broad source for the Passover sacrifice, must not be obscured by the specific translation "lamb" (e.g., RSV), as v 5 makes clear. Two considerations are of utmost importance in the selection of this animal. One is that the animal be apportioned among a group of people large enough to consume it entirely, or as nearly so as possible (cf. v 10). The other is that the animal selected be the best the worshipers could afford, an animal selected with care and guarded (שׁמר) conscientiously from the moment of its selection on the tenth day until the moment of its slaughter on the fourteenth. That slaughter was to take place between sunset and dark, and it marked the beginning of the Passover.

7–10 Some of the blood of this sacrifice was to be smeared upon the entry-way, the door-frame, of the houses of the Israelite worshipers, thus marking them as Israelite. The animal's flesh, thoroughly cooked by roasting, was to be eaten entirely by the worshipers, along with unleavened cakes and bitter herbs. Any remnant of the animal, along with its inedible parts, had to be burned with fire before the morning of the next day.

All these specifications, none of which has any obvious connection with the exodus itself, and only one of which, the apotropaic use of the blood, has any link to the tenth mighty act, have suggested to commentators the mingling of an ancient ceremony with a new context. So Beer (*Pesachim,* 9–40) and de Vaux (*Studies,* 2–12), among many (more recently, Laaf, Haag, Keel), have argued that the ritual described in Exod 12 suggests a nomadic or semi-nomadic milieu, in which fertility of the flocks and the availability of suitable grazing are of uppermost concern. With the new start brought by the exodus, the old ceremony, now given a new set of meanings, became symbolic of that new start.

Thus the sacrificial flock-animal became a gift of gratitude and a catalyst of family communion instead of an offering of pacification. Its blood became a mark of protection instead of an apotropaic charm. The unleavened bread cakes and bitter herbs eaten with the sacrifice became reminders of haste and the suffering of bondage instead of symbols of purity and protection against demonic spirits (Beer, *ZAW* 31 [1911] 152–53). Even so, features of the earlier ceremony remained, with no apparent new meaning: the roasting of the flock-animal whole, and the eating or burning of it before the next morning.

11–12 This new significance for the ancient feast was then further enhanced in practice by the specification of the manner in which the flock-animal was to be eaten. Those consuming the meat were not to be in the relaxed dress of home, but in traveling attire; not at ease around a table, but with walking-stick in hand; not in calm security, but in haste, with anxiety. And finally, the reason for the new meaning: the meal is "Yahweh's Passover"; it is to be taken in the night of his passing through the land of Egypt to strike the fatal blow that is the tenth of the mighty acts, the death of Egypt's firstborn. This blow is specified as a defeat of all the gods of Egypt, and the instructions for it are ended with the autokerygmatic declaration found so often in the Holiness Code of Lev 17–26 and the Book of Ezekiel: "I am Yahweh," "I am the One Who Always Is" (see *Comment* on 6:1–13).

13 Appended to the end of these instructions for Yahweh's Passover is an explanation of the significance, in this new context, of the smearing of the blood of the sacrificial animal. This explanation is another indication of the reapplication of the old symbolism, and perhaps seemed necessary to the Priestly redactor because of the uniqueness of the blood ritual described in the instruction of v 7. There is no further reference to such a ritual anywhere in the OT, and only one other ritual even resembling this one is mentioned in the OT: in the ceremony of atonement for the Temple, described in Ezek 45:18–20, the priest puts (נתן) the blood of a bull-calf, on the doorpost of the Temple and on the doorpost of the inner court gate.

The explanation indicates that the blood is a protective sign: Yahweh, upon seeing it, will "pass over" the Israelites and so spare them from the fatal blow he is about to strike against Egypt. The verb "pass over" is פסח, and it is this explanation of the purpose of that blood that gives the ritual of commemoration its name, פֶּסַח "Passover." Various attempts have been made to assign a meaning to this noun by etymology. These attempts are surveyed by Segal and Laaf, and none of them has proved satisfactory. The most familiar of them, that פסח means "limp, hobble, hop," has been connected both with a limping dance performed in connection with the פסח ritual (Oesterley, *Sacred Dance,* 50–51; Pedersen, *ZAW* 52 [1934] 167) and also with the leaping of a destroyer-demon in the "pre-Mosaic" פסח ritual (Keel, *ZAW* 84 [1972] 428–34).

In fact, it is not possible to establish any convincing connection of פסח with a verb root that provides a clue to the ritual it describes, given only the OT references we have. The best clue we have may be the verse at hand, which uses פסח to describe Yahweh sparing by "passing over" the houses of the Israelites marked with sacrificial blood. The name פסח "Passover," used of the ritual and of the sacrificial animal, may simply be taken from the verb describing Yahweh's protection of his own people, whom he is about to deliver, in a separation similar to that mentioned in the fourth, fifth, seventh and ninth of the mighty acts. Isa 31:5, which employs פסח in such a sense, may well be a reflection of exodus-Passover traditions.

Explanation

Exod 12:1–13 is an intrusion into the narrative of the tenth mighty act, the death of the firstborn of Egypt. The Priestly redactors who set it here did so because of their need to establish the authority of the ritual commemorating the exodus-deliverance the tenth mighty act effected. This is virtually a standard procedure of the Priestly redactors, nowhere practiced more obviously than in the Book of Exodus.

The purpose of this section can be seen in its location as well as in its content. Yahweh's "passing over" of Israel occurs as a further proof of his powerful Presence in the land of Egypt. The instructions for "Yahweh's Passover" therefore must be given in the context of the events they are to call to mind. Discussions of the historicity of this material (e.g., Hyatt, 144–46) are beside the point as well as necessarily inconclusive. What we have before us is theological narrative, attested as such as it is expanded by the specification of interpretative and actualizing acts of ritual worship. Though a history certainly lies behind the narrative, and for that matter the ritual as well, it is history as a point of departure for a theological confession that imparts to the history a transcendent meaning it could not otherwise have.

The authority for both the narrative and the ritual, indeed the reason for both, is stated by the simple assertion at the end of this section, just before the appendix explaining the significance of the blood and perhaps the name "Passover": "I am Yahweh." That is what the exodus and the Passover worship commemorating it are about.

Yahweh's "Reminder": Unleavened Bread (12:14–20)

Bibliography

Ackroyd, P. R. "The Meaning of Hebrew DOR Considered." *JSS* 13 (1968) 3–10. **Kraus, H.-J.** "Zur Geschichte des Passah-Massot-Festes im Alten Testament." *EvT* 18 (1958) 47–67. **Kutsch, E.** "Erwägungen zur Geschichte der Passafeier und des Massotfestes." *ZTK* 55 (1958) 1–36. **McEvenue, S. E.** *The Narrative Style of the Priestly Writer.* AnBib 50. Rome: Biblical Institute Press, 1971. **May, H. G.** "The Relation of the Passover to the Festival of Unleavened Cakes." *JBL* 55 (1936) 65–82. **Neuberg, F. J.** "An Unrecognised Meaning of Hebrew DOR." *JNES* 9 (1950) 215–17. **Vaux, R. de.** *Ancient Israel, Vol. 1: Social Institutions, Vol. 2: Religious Institutions.* New York: McGraw-Hill, 1965. **Welch, A. C.** "On the Method of Celebrating Passover." *ZAW* 45 (1927) 24–29.

Translation

14 *"This day is to be for you a day for remembering.*[a] *You are to observe it, a day sacred*[b] *to Yahweh, generation after generation: you shall observe it as a requirement*[c] *forever.* 15 *For seven days you shall eat unleavened bread cakes. In fact,*[a] *on the first of those days, you shall remove all*[b] *leaven from your houses, because anyone who eats anything leavened, from the first day through*[c] *the seventh day, that person is to be excluded from Israel.*

16 *"On the first day you are to gather for special worship,*[a] *and on the seventh day as well.*[b] *All work is to cease*[c] *on those days. Only what is to be eaten*[d] *by any person, that alone may have any work from you.* 17 *You are to keep the festival*[a] *of unleavened bread cakes, because on this very day I brought you in great numbers out of the land of Egypt. You are to keep*[b] *this day, further, generation after generation, a requirement forever.*

18 *"On the fourteenth day of the lead*[a] *month, in the evening, you shall eat unleavened bread cakes, and you shall eat them*[b] *until the twenty-first day of that month, in the evening.* 19 *Seven days, leaven is not to be found in your houses, because anyone eating anything leavened will be excluded then and there*[a] *from the congregation of Israel, whether he is a newcomer*[b] *or a native in the land.* 20 *You shall eat nothing leavened. In all your dwelling-places, you shall eat unleavened bread cakes."*

Notes

14.a. לְזִכָּרוֹן "for remembering" has the significance here of an anniversary, but still more, suggests the cultic emphasis upon the exodus deliverance as a present-tense event, an event of continuing effectiveness. See further Schottroff, *"Gedenken,"* 314–17, or Childs, *Memory and Tradition*, 66–70.

14.b. As a חג "religious festival" or "pilgrim-feast"; BDB, 290–91.

14.c. חק here is a "sacred statute," a perpetual requirement of members of Israel's community in faith.

15.a. אך "in fact" is an emphatic and demonstrative adverb. Cf. BDB, 36.

15.b. MT reads simply שאר "leaven"; "all" is added above as plainly intended in the context following אך "in fact," for clarity.

15.c. עד "until, up to," here obviously means "through"; so vv 15 and 19. BDB, 723–25.

16.a. מקרא־קדש, lit., a "holy calling-together," so BDB, 896: "term. techn. in P for religious gathering on Sabbath and certain sacred days."

16.b. MT repeats מקרא־קדש "holy calling-together."

16.c. לא־יעשה "is not to be done."

16.d. LXX has instead ποιηθήσεται "is to be done," i.e., is essential.

17.a. MT reads simply המצות "the unleavened bread cakes." SamPent has המצוה "the commandment"; LXX τὴν ἐντολὴν ταύτην "this commandment."

17.b. LXX has ποιήσετε "do" again.

18.a. See n. 12:2.a.

18.b. "And you shall eat them" is added for clarity.

19.a. MT has הנפש ההוא "that person" here, as in v 15.

19.b. גר "newcomer" is a temporary resident, even a "tourist," or one who has newly come to the community and is without family claims. Cf. BDB, 158.

Form/Structure/Setting

These verses are a continuation of the Priestly instructions that have been inserted into the narrative of the tenth mighty act following the first account (a prediction) of the events the instructions are designed to call to mind and so to faith. As to style, they are typical of a priestly manner of presentation that may be called both precise and repetitious (McEvenue, *Narrative Style*, 1–22). As to form, they show that tendentious quality that is usually the result of P's attempts to set forth instructions and regulations in a narrative framework. Since ritual concerns are the primary matter, the narrative never has any real chance and almost always sounds wooden, unreal. This kind of narrative form is dictated by the context into which the material is set, not by the material itself. The form, of necessity, is an artificial medium for the content it transmits.

In the present text of Exodus, vv 14–20 are of a piece with vv 1–13, the whole bound together as a series of instructions having to do with the keeping of Yahweh's Passover. In fact, the very different nature and origin of the instructions recorded in these verses makes clear that two separate sets of instructions, representing two originally separate sets of ritual, have here been brought together in a sequence linked by a verse (14) that refers both to Passover Day and the first day of seven days of eating unleavened bread cakes. This verse has, in consequence, been taken both with the first set of instructions (JB) and also with the second set of instructions (NEB). In fact, it belongs to and links them both.

Comment

14 "This day" refers in general terms, in the broader context of chap. 12, to the day of exodus brought about by the tenth mighty act, the death of Egypt's firstborn. Set here, in this link-verse, the phrase refers to both the Passover evening and the first day of the seven-day period of the eating of unleavened bread cakes, since the two overlap (cf. de Vaux, *Ancient Israel*, 181–82). The day is a day for "actualizing," or making contemporary the event of the exodus deliverance. It was set aside by Yahweh as a holy day, the keeping of which was to be required of Israel generation after generation (לדרתיכם), or even, as Neuberg (*JNES* 9 [1950] 215–17) and Ackroyd (*JSS* 13 [1968] 3–10) have argued, from one liturgical community to the next.

15 One means of such "actualization" was Yahweh's Passover; another was the eating, across a seven-day period, of unleavened bread cakes. Both the symbolism and the duration of Passover as an evening meal to be taken by families in anxious preparation for departure are consonant with the narrative into which the instructions for the ritual are set. A seven-day festival of unleavened bread cakes will not fit the context of such a narrative, however. Quite clearly, a ritual observance from another context has here been placed by the Priestly redactors into a narrative sequence where it is an illogical element. The question is, why?

This question has been answered in a diverse variety of ways, as comparison of the positions taken by such authors as Welch, May, Segal, Kraus, and Kutsch makes plain. They argue, for example, that (1) Exod 12:1–28 and 13:1–16 link three duplicate sets of laws, including one from the Northern Kingdom and one from the Southern Kingdom, all connected with "Yahweh's dealings with Israel at the Exodus" (Welch, *ZAW* 45 [1927] 27–29); (2) the festival of unleavened bread cakes was the earlier of the two ritual commemorations—the exodus was remembered in pre-exilic Israel by the sacrifice and redemption of the first born as "an occasional ceremony," and Exod 12:1–28 belongs wholly to P, is postexilic, and perhaps composed with the diaspora in view (May, *JBL* 55 [1936] 65–74); (3) "the Pesaḥ and the Maṣṣoth festival" were from the beginning "a single festival," "Pesaḥ" opening the week brought to conclusion by "Maṣṣoth," a week beginning and ending with a "holy convocation" at the local sanctuary (Segal, *Hebrew Passover*, 174–80); (4) the festival of unleavened bread cakes and the "archaic Passover practices" were combined in pre-exilic Israel and linked to both the exodus and the crossing of the Jordan in worship at the sanctuary at Gilgal, so Josh 5:1–12 (Kraus, *EvT* 18 [1958] 65–67); and (5) the festival of unleavened bread cakes and Passover were joined for the first time during the exile, from which period also Josh 5:10–12 dates, thus providing no support for the view of Kraus (Kutsch, *ZTK* 55 [1958] 34–35).

All of these suggestions, along with most of the variations upon them, begin with the same basic information. That they end with such divergent explanations indicates the difficulty of finding a satisfactory reason for the assemblage of this material as a continuous narrative. A look at the material against the context within which it was brought together suggests that this sequence has been produced for liturgical purposes, not for narrative purposes. The fact that liturgical material has been set into a narrative frame must not be allowed to set us onto a wrong path. What we have here is a briefer example of what we have in Exod 25–31 and 35–40, also liturgical material that cannot belong to the narrative sequence into which it has been set.

Just as Passover has connections with a flock-animal sacrifice predating it, so also the ritual eating of unleavened bread cakes was first practiced in a setting having nothing to do with the exodus and the tenth mighty act. Eating unleavened bread cakes with the Passover meal is one thing, but a seven-day observance is something else altogether. The "festival" of unleavened bread cakes is rooted, in all likelihood, in an agricultural celebration connected with grain harvesting, specifically the beginning of the grain harvest (cf. de Vaux, *Ancient Israel*, 490–91). As such a festival fell of necessity into the same time-period as Passover, the two were combined at some point between the settlement of Israel in Canaan and the exile into Babylon. Thus the impressive features of two ancient religious observances, one nomadic and one agricultural, were redefined and united in the development of the ritual symbolizing Israel's beginning as a people chosen by Yahweh.

15, 19–20 The prohibition against "leaven" has to do with the purity of the newly ground grain, whether offered to Yahweh or eaten in his Presence in expression of gratitude. There may also be undertones of suspicion of the process of fermentation that leaven promotes, though the avoidance of leaven at the Passover meal was connected as well with the need for haste in the preparations for departure (v 39). The penalty for the violation of this restriction, exclusion from the community of Israel, suggests a level of jeopardy far more serious than a need for haste in the preparation of a meal.

16–18 The liturgical provisions of the combination festival described in Exod 12:1–20 specify a special day of worship at the beginning and at the end of the festival period. On these two days, no work but that involved in the necessary preparation of food could be done. The two days serve to bracket a seven-day sequence whose sole purpose, according to Exod 12, was the commemoration of the tenth mighty act and the exodus it brought about. Whatever the origin of what came to be Passover and the festival of unleavened bread cakes, the two occasions of worship came to be joined together as commemorative of the greatest departure of Israel's history. Their celebration was expanded, finally to a seven-day festival begun and ended with a day devoted as exclusively to worship as was the Sabbath itself. Just when the combination was made, we can only speculate; de Vaux (*Ancient Israel*, 488–93) argues for the time of Josiah. Following that junction, there occurred the expansion of what had been two separate occasions of worship into two days, and over the course of time, into seven days of worship. The presentation here of the expanded event, identified so specifically with the exodus from Egypt (vv 14 and 17), is a reflection of the celebration in its most fully evolved OT form.

Explanation

Nowhere else in the OT is the festival of unleavened bread cakes so closely connected with the exodus deliverance as here in Exod 12. The same can be said of course for Passover, and the connection is quite deliberately effected by the insertion into a narrative sequence of two sets of liturgical specification. The point of the connection, and the reason for the insertion, is the provision of authoritative and didactic means of bringing the exodus deliverance into the experience of the Israel of the generations beyond settlement and the unified monarchy.

The liturgical specifications governing the festival of unleavened bread cakes, particularly in their somewhat repetitive sequence in Exod 12:14–20, seem more than a little fossilized in an existence all their own. Thus these verses are set here and connected by statement (vv 14 and 17) as by context with the all-important event that the worship they specify is supposed to bring to mind. They are therefore not only an indicator of the importance of the exodus to Israel's faith, but also an object-lesson in the interrelation of theological narrative and liturgical requirement.

Israel's Protection   (12:21–28)

Bibliography

Crowfoot, G. M., and L. Baldensperger. "Hyssop." *PEQ* 63 (1931) 89–98. Gray, G. B. *Sacrifice in the Old Testament.* New York: KTAV, 1971. Honeyman, A. M. "Hebrew סף 'Basin, Goblet.'" *JTS* 37 (1936) 56–59. Lohfink, N. *Das Hauptgebot.* AnBib 20. Rome: Instituto Biblico e Pontificio, 1963. Loza, J. "Les Catéchèses Étiologiques dans l'Ancien Testament." *RB* 78 (1971) 481–500. Meyer, E. *Die Israeliten und Ihre Nachbarstamme.* Halle, 1906. Noth, M. "Die Vergegenwärtigung des Alten Testaments in der Verkündigung." *EvT* 12 (1952 / 1953) 6–17. ET in *Essays on Old Testament Hermeneutics.* C. Westermann, ed. Richmond: John Knox Press, 1963. 76–88. Seters, J. van. "The Place of the Yahwist in the History of Passover and Massot." *ZAW* 95 (1983) 167–82. Soggin, J. A. "Kultätiologische Sagen und Katechese im Hexateuch." *VT* 10 (1960) 341–47. Trumbull, H. C. *The Threshold Covenant.* Edinburgh: T. & T. Clark, 1896.

Translation

[21] So Moses called together [a] all the elders [b] of Israel, and said to them, "Separate [c] and take [d] for yourselves flock-animals by family-divisions; [e] then slaughter the Passover animal. [22] Take a bundle of hyssop and dip it in the blood that is in the basin; [a] then smear [b] the upper beam over the door and the two side-posts of the door with the blood that is in the basin. Not [c] one of you is to go out the door of his house until morning. [23] Yahweh will move through to level a blow [a] at the Egyptians, and he will see the blood upon the upper beam and the two side-posts of the door, and Yahweh will pass over the door and will not permit the destroyer to come in to your houses to level a blow.

[24] "You are to abide by this command, as a requirement of you and of your sons in perpetuity. [25] When, in due course, you enter the land that Yahweh will give to you, just as he promised, there too [a] you shall abide by this obligation. [b] [26] When your sons say to you, 'What is this obligation to which you are committed?,' [27] then you shall say, 'It is the Passover sacrifice to Yahweh, recalling that [a] he passed over the houses of the sons of Israel in Egypt when he leveled his blow at the Egyptians and protected [b] our houses.' "

[28] So the people bowed down and worshiped. Then the sons of Israel dispersed [a] and did just as Yahweh had commanded Moses and Aaron—indeed, they did.

Notes

21.a. קרא "call together" has the sense of "summon" in this context (BDB, 895–96).
21.b. LXX and Vg add "of the sons of" (υἱῶν, *filiorum*).
21.c. The verb משׁך "separate" signifies the drawing or "cutting-out" of the animal selected from the flock as a whole.
21.d. Syr reads *b'ql sbw* "quickly choose."
21.e. See n. 6:14.c.
22.a. סף "basin" has also been understood as the threshold or doorsill, perhaps carved out to provide a shallow container for the blood of the Passover animal. LXX may have understood it so: παρὰ τὴν θύραν "beside the door." Rylaarsdam ("Exodus," *IB* 1:923) follows such a reading, given an elaborate rationale by Trumbull (see *Threshold Covenant*, esp. 203–12). Note BDB, 706. Syr reads "in the blood of the sheep" instead.
22.b. The verb is hiph pf נגע "touch"; in this context, in reference to the spreading of the blood with a hyssop-bundle, it describes an application, a daubing, a smearing, a spattering.
22.c. SamPent has אל for MT לא.
23.a. See n. 7:27.b.
25.a. Special *waw* with perfect שׁמר "keep, abide by."
25.b. עבדה "obligation" refers to the heavy and oppressive labor of the Egyptian bondage in Exod 1:14; 2:23; 5:9, 11; 6:6, 9; etc. Here, in a clever rhetorical contrast, it refers to Israel's service in the worship of Yahweh, an obligation of a very different sort. SamPent adds here בחדשׁ הזה "in this month."
27.a. אשׁר "that"; "recalling" is added from the context (note vv 14–17) for clarity.
27.b. נצל "protect" refers also, and frequently, to the "snatching forth," the rescue of Israel from Pharaoh's slavery.
28.a. הלך "disperse" plus special *waw* here provides the second bracket of the pair begun by the "called together" of v 21.

Form/Structure/Setting

The mixture of narrative and liturgical material characteristic of the account of the tenth mighty act is continued in this section, but with a difference. Here the events that have been predicted (chap. 11) are actually set in motion as steps are taken to protect Israel from the impending terrible devastation. The narrative of Moses' instructions is interrupted, however, by an interpretation of the blood ritual for the generations yet to come (vv 24–27a), then concluded twice (vv 27b and 28). Still further complexity is introduced by the differences between the instructions Moses gives here and those given to him for transmission in vv 1–20.

The usual resolution of these problems has been achieved by source analysis. Vv 21–23 and the final sentence of v 27 have been assigned to J (Noth, 97–98; Hyatt, 131, 136–37); vv 24–27a to a Deuteronomic redactor (Hyatt, 137; Childs, 184) and a supplementer (Noth, 97, because of the singular pronominal suffix "you" in v 24b); and v 28 to P (Noth, 97; Hyatt, 137; Childs, 184). In such an explanation, v 27b is the conclusion to the J account of vv 21–23, and v 28 is the conclusion to the P account of vv 1–20. The inserted material of vv 24–27a has generally been assigned to the Deuteronomic circle, or at least to an editor influenced by the Deuteronomic style and vocabulary. Lohfink, however, has isolated a series of words and phrases (*Hauptgebot*, 121–22) with which he argues convincingly that these verses are "nicht-deuteronomisch." Van Seters (*ZAW* 95 [1983] 172–75) has assigned the whole of 12:1–28 to P.

As so often in Exodus, the composite of the text at hand needs to be seen in its wholeness, possessing an integrity all its own quite apart from the integrity of the sources that make it up. As Childs has written (199–200), there is "an inner coherence in the present structure" of the sequence. This narrative does not purport to be a transmission by Moses to the people of Israel of the liturgical instructions of Yahweh to Moses on the Passover and the festival of unleavened bread cakes. The subject here is the protection of Israel from the decimation of the tenth mighty act. That protection in itself becomes a medium of memory and celebration for future generations, a fact attested by the command that it be kept as a requirement in perpetuity.

Once again, narrative has become the framework for liturgical material, in part as that material has itself been given at least a semi-narrative form. The form of this section has been dictated by this combination, and the section has been delimited by the assembly (v 21) and dispersal (v 28) of the Israelites, instructed through their elders, then sent to follow those instructions as the tenth mighty act gets under way. The inconsistencies in the narrative—for example, the elders called and the people dispersed, or the people bowing for worship without having previously been mentioned in the sequence—are inevitable in a composite and of little consequence to the point of the narrative, which is Israel's protection against the powerful force Yahweh is about to unleash.

Comment

21 Moses' instruction to the elders that they "separate" a flock-animal from the animals available is consonant with the instructions of Exod 12:3–5, though the emphasis differs. Here it is on allocation of the animals by family branches rather than on assembling a group large enough to consume the roasted carcass. In the former sequence, preparedness for the impending departure is the point. Here, protection from the terrible force about to be unleashed is in view: thus there is concern that each family of each clan of each tribe be accounted for and protected.

22–23 Hyssop here, as in the ritual for the lustration of a leper who has been healed (Lev 14:1–9), is a means of smearing the blood of a sacrificial victim. The additional references of Num 19:1–10 and Ps 51:9[7] imply that hyssop had a special role in ceremonies of cleansing, but the OT references are too sparse in both their number and their information to afford either a clear picture of the exact significance or a clear identification of the plant being mentioned. Crowfoot and Baldensperger contended (*PEQ* 63 [1931] 89–91) that it was "*za'tar,*" a marjoram (*Origanum Maru, L.*), and functioned as an aspergillum which also slowed the clotting of the blood of the Passover ritual, largely on the basis of their observation of the use of this plant by the Samaritans in their Passover worship (in April, 1930).

The reference to "the blood that is in the basin" into which the bundle of hyssop is to be dipped seems to suggest a longer narrative of instruction, one that may have made clear just what kind of basin was to be used and where it was to be placed. As the text now stands, this סַף could be either a basin or some other movable container, or even a part of the threshold or sill of a doorway, an ambiguity that has given rise to the theory that the blood in "a hollow place" in the threshold was an invitation to Yahweh to "covenant cross" as an "honored guest" of the family within (Trumbull, *Threshold Covenant*, 203–12). A. M. Honeyman has argued (*JTS* 37 [1936] 59), though unconvincingly, that סף can never mean "basin" but can only signify "threshold, sill" in Exod 12:22.

There is really very little basis for such speculation about the blood in the basin, wherever it was located, but the significance of the blood smeared upon the lintel and the side-posts of the door is clearly protective. No one was to leave the house during the night of Passover, and within the house, each Israelite was protected, apparently by Yahweh himself, who would see the blood and bar entry to the destroyer making rounds at his command (cf. v 13). This משחית "destroyer" has been variously held to be a death angel acting in Yahweh's service (cf. 2 Sam 24:15–17; 2 Kgs 19:32–37), a kind of extension of Yahweh himself, or a primitive demon either opposed or replaced by Yahweh (Meyer, *Israeliten*, 38; Gressmann, *Mose und seine Zeit*, 104; Gray, *Sacrifice*, 364–65). Once again, the information in the OT is too sketchy for any detailed conclusions, but the repeated assertion that the blow to come is to be leveled by Yahweh and the clear statement of this verse that Yahweh "will not permit" the destroyer to enter the Israelite houses suggests that in the composite at hand the destroyer was considered Yahweh's emissary.

24–27 The instruction that the Israelites are to "abide by this command . . . in perpetuity" would seem, by its location, to apply to the ritual of Israel's protection involving the Passover blood. In such a case, the smearing of the blood would be continued year after year, beyond any need for the protection it symbolized, as a means of confession to successive generations. In fact, the wording of the response to the inquiry of the children concerning the meaning of this worship (v 27a) gives the instruction a wider application, to the tenth mighty act as a whole. The statement "It is the Passover sacrifice" brings to mind both Israel protected and Egypt smitten.

The didactic language of these verses is not Deuteronomistic, as Lohfink (*Hauptgebot*, 116–19) has correctly maintained. It belongs rather to an instructional, catechetical style that the Deuteronomists inherited and brought to a level of application all their own. The same technique was inherited by the "wisdom" teachers and brought to the very different kind of application apparent in Proverbs. Martin Noth (*EvT* 12 [1952 / 53] 9–10) has named this technique aptly—*Vergegenwärtigung*, "representation" or "actualization." Quite simply, it amounts to an attempt to make the past present, to teach through a repetition that aims to create experience rather than simply transmit information. The brilliant use of the technique by the Deuteronomic and Deuteronomistic theologians has prompted too often the assignment of any passage appearing to employ it, as here, to one of those circles. To do so, however, in a passage such as Exod 12:26–27a, is surely a mistake, not least because it suggests so late a date for material that must obviously have been extant and in active use much earlier. J. A. Soggin (*VT* 10 [1960] 341–47) has discussed these verses and others as cultic catechism, and J. Loza (*RB* 78 [1971] 481–87, 491–99) has analyzed the same passages in detail as etiological catechism paralleled in the treaties of Esarhaddon and in the *Sfire stelae*, "deeply rooted in a living tradition, probably a cultic one" (496).

In both vv 25 and 26, עבדה, the noun that frequently describes (see n. 12:25.b.) the difficult labor of Egyptian bondage, is used in reference to Israel's worshipful service of Yahweh in the "obligation" of Passover. This clever rhetorical touch makes graphic the difference between what is done in slavery by force and what is done in freedom by commitment.

28 Thus provided with a means of protecting themselves from the decimation about to fall, the people of Israel bow in worship. Then, according to the sequence of the composite describing the signs of protection, they scatter to follow the instructions they have received, in this reference all of the instructions regarding Passover.

Explanation

In a variation of the theme of Yahweh's separation of his people from the damage of the harmful and fearful mighty acts, the account of the final and most devastating of those mighty acts includes a means of the protection of the families of Israel. This composite is approached altogether too literally by those who argue that the protection of the Israelite households by the sign of the blood of the Passover victim introduces an element of inconsistency (so Fohrer, *Überlieferung*, 79–86, who assigns these verses to his Nomadic source). Yahweh is to move through *Egypt*, not just parts of Egypt, and the point of the protective sign as of the mighty act itself is the proof of Yahweh's powerful Presence.

Once again, we are given liturgical material intrusive to the narrative sequence into which it has been placed. But it has been placed there as a means of dramatizing that narrative, as a means of contemporizing it, and as a means of turning it into a confession of faith. Yahweh, proving his Presence to his people, was about to provide freedom for them by a mighty blow from which he was solicitous to give them protection. Yahweh present, freeing, protecting is the subject of the larger narrative and liturgical composite designed above all to make, to sustain, and to continue a confessional assertion. This section is devoted primarily to Yahweh's protection.

The Tenth Mighty Act　　(*12:29–36*)

Bibliography

Brichto, H. C. *The Problem of "Curse" in the Hebrew Bible.* JBLMS 12. Philadelphia: Society of Biblical Literature and Exegesis, 1963. **Coats, G.** "Despoiling the Egyptians." *VT* 18 (1968) 450–57. **Morgenstern, J.** "The Despoiling of the Egyptians." *JBL* 68 (1949) 1–28.

Translation

²⁹*Thus it was that in the middle of the night Yahweh struck a fatal blow against all the firstborn in the land of Egypt, from the firstborn of Pharaoh, the occupant*

of the royal throne, ᵃ *to the firstborn of the prisoner in jail,* ᵇ *and all the firstborn of the cattle.* ³⁰ *Pharaoh rose urgently* ᵃ *in the night, he* ᵇ *and all the members of his court and all the Egyptians. There was a great cry of anguish throughout Egypt,* ᶜ *for there was no family* ᵈ *where there was no one dead.*

³¹ *Pharaoh* ᵃ *summoned Moses and Aaron in the night, then said,* ᵇ *"Get going!* ᶜ *Go out from the midst of my people, not just you, but the sons of Israel as well!* ᵈ *Go along* ᵉ *and worship Yahweh in accord with your demand!* ᶠ ³² *Take your flocks and even* ᵃ *your herds, just as you have demanded, only go! And you, bless even* ᵃ *me."*

³³ *The Egyptians, meanwhile, pressed the people to hurry their going out from the land—for they said, "All of us will be dead."* ³⁴ *So the people took up their dough before it could rise;* ᵃ *their breadboards were wrapped up in their coats and carried upon their backs.* ᵇ ³⁵ *The Israelites also did as Moses had instructed: they asked of the Egyptians articles of silver, articles of gold, and garments,* ᵃ ³⁶ *and Yahweh gave the people credibility* ᵃ *in the opinion of the Egyptians, so that they gave these things. In this manner,* ᵇ *they picked the Egyptians clean.* ᶜ

Notes

29.a. Cf. 11:5. Here, as there, the text has "Pharaoh the one sitting upon his throne," a phrase that clearly refers to the zenith of power and position in the land.

29.b. בבית הבור "in the house of the pit," signifying a place of confinement, a prison or even a dungeon (BDB, 92).

30.a. Special *waw* in this context.

30.b. "He" is lacking in LXX and Vg.

30.c. LXX has ἐν πάσῃ γῇ Αἰγύπτῳ "in all the land of Egypt."

30.d. בית "house."

31.a. MT has "he." "Pharaoh" is clearly intended, and is added above for clarity. LXX, Syr, Vg Editio Clementina include the word "Pharaoh."

31.b. LXX adds αὐτοῖς "to them."

31.c. The impv form of קום, meaning "rise up to go" (cf. BDB, 878).

31.d. On this use of גם . . . . גם "not just . . . but . . . as well" in vv 31–32, see Labuschagne, *Studia*, 199–203.

31.e. Impv הלך. This series of three verbs depicting going, קום "get going," יצא "go out," and הלך "go along," all impvs, gives a graphic sense of Pharaoh's rising panic and urgency.

31.f. Piel inf constr of דבר "speak."

32.a. See n. 31.e.

34.a. חמץ "be sour, leavened," (BDB, 329); the dough was not given time to ferment.

34.b. Or "shoulders" (BDB, 1014). This is probably no more than a description of their mode of transporting the dough from which the bread of the next meals would be made. Cassuto's (146) theory that the wrapping and carrying of the dough against the body was an attempt to hasten its rising is unlikely, as v 39 makes clear.

35.a. See n. 11:2.b.

36.a. See n. 11:3.b.

36.b. Special *waw*.

36.c. See n. 3:22.d.

Form/Structure/Setting

The actual arrival of the tenth of the mighty acts is described succinctly in a composite usually assigned to J (vv 29–34, the death of Egypt's firstborn) and E (vv 35–36, the "despoiling" of the Egyptians). Amidst the complexity of all the liturgical material that has been added to the narrative of this climactic and determinative mighty act, the account itself seems almost too brief.

This brevity may, however, be a deliberate feature of the larger composite presented by Exodus. The entire sequence of the mighty acts leans towards this conclusive proof of Yahweh's Presence. Anticipated even before the beginning of the mighty-act sequence, in 3:20–22 and in 4:21–23, and insinuated throughout the sequence in the hardening-of-the-heart motif, this final mighty act is effectively recounted in so stark and brief a form.

The assignment of vv 35–36 to E is based on little more than the theory that E is *the* tetrateuchal source for the "despoiling" tradition. There has been much speculation about the incorporation of ancient traditions into J, and even the "preliterary fusion of traditions incorporated without concern for tensions into J" (Coats, *VT* 18 [1968] 450). In fact there is no decisive evidence for the assignment of the "despoiling" accounts to one source, excluding any others. It is for this reason that Exod 12:35–36 is assigned both to E (Driver, 99–100; Hyatt, 137–38; Childs, "may be," 184), and to J (Beer, "J¹" 68; Morgenstern, *JBL* 68 [1949] 27; Noth, 98–99; Coats, *VT* 18 [1968] 450–51).

The form of the section at hand is set by the need to bring together three motifs, each of which declares conclusively the powerful Presence of Yahweh in Egypt, and the utter capitulation of Pharaoh. The first of these is the arrival of the predicted tenth mighty act (vv 29–30); the second is the urgent order of Pharaoh that Moses and his people leave, on *their* terms, but as quickly as possible (vv 31–32); the third is the equal urgency of the Egyptians to be rid of the Israelites, to which an etiology of the use of unleavened bread at Passover and the despoiling story have been logically attached. The original context of these various narratives is indeterminate. Their impact, in the tight combination of this pericope, is dramatic.

Comment

29–30 The announcement of the death of Egypt's firstborn differs in the expression of the range of its effect from the prediction of 11:5. The "servant-girl who grinds with the hand-mill" is replaced here by someone even farther down the social scale from Pharaoh exalted on his throne, "the prisoner in jail." There is a contrast also between a Pharaoh who knew nothing of Yahweh at the first encounter with Moses (5:2) and who now rises urgently in the middle of the night, along with his court, because of the powerful action of Yahweh throughout the land of Egypt. The "great cry of anguish" described in 11:6 as unprecedented and unrepeatable is even more chilling here by virtue of the terrible assertion that every Egyptian family was touched by death.

31–32 The summons of Moses and Aaron by Pharaoh under these catastrophic circumstances is not to be considered evidence of a separate tradition because 10:28–29 represent Moses' "final" audience with Pharaoh. The summons here is all the more dramatic a representation of Pharaoh's complete defeat by virtue of that earlier reference. At the end of the ninth mighty act, Pharaoh is still resistant, even though he is so under Yahweh's influence; in the awful aftermath of the tenth mighty act, Pharaoh's resistance is gone. He reverses his own order and summons Moses to come to him. When Moses arrives (Aaron here as elsewhere in Exodus is an addition to the narrative), Pharaoh blurts out a series of three imperatives, each a different verb for "go," and beginning with Moses, he orders every Israelite and everything Israelite out of Egypt. "Get up, get out, go on," he says, "take along and go on!" "*You* get out; and not you alone, but the Israelites as well; go along and worship Yahweh, and take flocks and herds alike; just go, Go, GO!" This series of five imperative verbs, three meaning "go" (הלך is used twice) and one meaning "take," coupled with five usages of the emphatic particle גם "also" (cf. Labuschagne, *Studia* 195–202), marvelously depicts a Pharaoh whose reserve of pride is gone, who must do everything necessary to have done with Moses and Israel and the Yahweh who wants them for his own. As Yahweh has said, the time would come when Pharaoh would "drive" or "hurl" them out (3:20 and 6:1). That time had now arrived.

This convincing sequence is then brilliantly capped by the ultimate capitulation of the Pharaoh who had claimed ignorance of Yahweh, then had sought to match Yahweh's mighty deeds, and then had withdrawn his promises nearly as soon as they were made. Pharaoh at last asks Moses and Aaron for the blessing of Yahweh. The verb, this time, is not an imperative. Pharaoh is quite beyond any resistance, and his request is that the terrible curse that has fallen be effective no longer (cf. Brichto, *"Curse,"* 10). Yahweh has proved his Presence and his power, and there is no need further to stiffen Pharaoh's resolve. The exodus, so long awaited, will be delayed no longer.

33 Pharaoh's order that Moses and his people leave Egypt is paralleled by the pressure upon Israel of Pharaoh's people. They "make strong, urge" the people to hurry their departure, and they do so because this final mighty act is of them all the most threatening to life. The three mighty acts preceding this one each threatened the Egyptians with the fear of death (see *Comment* on 10:14–16) but this final blow brought death itself into every Egyptian family (v 30), and the Egyptians quite reasonably felt that if these Israelites were restrained any longer, no Egyptian would be left alive.

34 The point thus graphically made that nothing remains to hold them back any longer, the people of Israel, already forewarned (11:1, 12:11–12), are prepared to set off immediately. They have only to scoop up the dough laid out for the next day's bread, pack the bowls or boards in which or onto which it had been left, take up their other goods, and leave. The word בָּצֵק "dough" is a cognate of בצק, a verb that means "swell." The dough for a day's bread was mixed and allowed to stand before it was baked, so that it could "leaven," that is, rise from the yeast in a pinch of the previous day's bread (Ross, "Bread," *IDB* 1:462). In this instance, apparently, the dough was prepared and left to rise through the night, a process that was interrupted when the dough had to be disturbed for the abrupt departure. The mixing boards, or bowls, presumably with the dough on or in them still, were wrapped and carried in readiness for the next meal, whenever and wherever it might be, but the dough, so disturbed, would not rise, and so would have to be eaten unleavened, as bread that did not rise (see 12:39).

This narrative about the dough thus effectively presents two points: (1) that when the moment of release finally comes, the people of Israel leave Egypt in a great hurry; (2) that the eating of unleavened bread in the worship of Passover had its origin in this hasty departure and forever symbolized it in a manner arresting even to children.

35–36 The taking by the Israelites of their Egyptian oppressors' valuables, anticipated in Exod 3:19–22 and 11:2–3, is here reported without elaboration. This "despoiling" is made possible by Yahweh's gift of grace to Israel, an aura of credibility which made the Egyptians trust them and want to give them articles of silver, gold, and clothing. That the Egyptians could so be "picked clean" is another testimony of Yahweh's triumph over Pharaoh and all his gods and wizards.

Explanation

This brief account of the tenth of the mighty acts of Yahweh in Egypt brings together a series of themes introduced here and there within a sequence that had actually begun in the promise of the proof of Presence made to Moses in Exod 3. Yahweh has proved himself in Egypt to Israel, to the Egyptian populace, to the royal wizards and courtiers, and finally to the powerful Pharaoh himself. He has pressed that proof beyond the boundaries a human resistance would have set, by hardening Pharaoh's resolve. He has taught Pharaoh, who claimed never to have heard of him, that he is present, and powerfully so, to such an extent that Pharaoh comes at last to ask Yahweh's blessing as a means of curbing any further reach of the disaster that threatened Egypt's future through the death of the next generation.

Every Egyptian is affected and threatened by this last of the final acts. So Pharaoh, his resolve no longer strengthened by Yahweh, surrenders, commands Moses to get out, with all Israel and with all things Israelite. The Egyptians urge departure upon the people of Israel. Thus the slaves and prisoners are not only set free but driven out, as Yahweh had predicted, laden with the gifts of an Egyptian populace glad to be rid of them, at whatever price. With a deft recapitulation of major themes, proof of Presence, defeat of Pharaoh and his gods, the cancellation of the bondage by those who had opposed it, the complete humiliation of Pharaoh and his people, the actual beginning of the move toward exodus has at long last been reached. This compact section, ringing with a staccato rhythm of commands and bustling with a departure upon the instant, brings to a close the longest single section in the entire Book of Exodus, the section proving the claim of the special name "Yahweh."

The Exodus from Egypt *(12:37–50)*

Bibliography

Alt, A. "Die Deltaresidenz der Ramessiden." *Kleine Schriften zur Geschichte des Volkes Israel,* vol. 3. Munich: C. H. Beck'sche Verlagsbuchhandlung, 1959. 176–85. **Davies, G. I.** "The Wilderness Itineraries and the Composition of the Pentateuch." *VT* 33

(1983) 1–13. **Dussaud, R.** *Les origines cananéennes du sacrifice Israelite.* 2d ed. Paris: Presses Universitaires de France, 1941. **Helck, W.** *"T*kw und die Ramses-Stadt." *VT* 15 (1965) 35–48. **Laaf, P.** *Die Pascha-Feier Israels.* Bonn: P. Hanstein, 1970. **Lucas, A.** "The Number of Israelites at the Exodus." *PEQ* 75 (1944) 164–68. **Mendenhall, G. E.** "The Census Lists of Numbers 1 and 26." *JBL* 77 (1958) 52–66. **Noth, M.** "The 'Re-presentation' of the Old Testament in Proclamation." *Essays on Old Testament Hermeneutics.* Ed. C. Westermann. Richmond: John Knox Press, 1963. 76–88. **Redford, D. B.** "Exodus I 11." *VT* 13 (1963) 401–18. **Scheiber, A.** " 'Ihr Sollt Kein Bein dran Zerbrechen.' " *VT* 13 (1963) 95–97.

Translation

³⁷ *So the sons of Israel set out from Rameses towards Succoth, some* ᵃ *six hundred thousand able-bodied men,* ᵇ *not counting women and children.* ᶜ ³⁸ *A large and motley group went along with them as well, and flocks and herds, a* ᵃ *great number of domestic animals.* ³⁹ *At their first stop,* ᵃ *they baked the dough which they had brought from Egypt into round, flat, unleavened bread-cakes* ᵇ—*it had not risen,* ᶜ *because they were pushed out of Egypt and had no chance to linger; indeed they had packed no food for themselves.*

⁴⁰ *The period of the residence of the sons of Israel,* ᵃ *in Egypt* ᵇ *was four hundred and thirty years.* ⁴¹ *Indeed, it was at the end of the four hundred and thirty years, on the very last day,* ᵃ *that they came out, all Yahweh's hosts, from the land of Egypt.* ⁴² *It was a night* ᵃ *of keepings for Yahweh, to bring them out from the land of Egypt—so it is, this night for Yahweh, a night* ᵇ *of keepings for all the sons of Israel, generation after generation.*

⁴³ *Therefore Yahweh said to Moses and to Aaron, "This is the requirement* ᵃ *of the Passover: anyone outside the covenant* ᵇ *shall not eat it.* ⁴⁴ *Any man's slave, bought and paid for,* ᵃ *when you have circumcised him, may then eat it.* ⁴⁵ *A transient or a hired hand is not to eat it.* ⁴⁶ *In one house,* ᵃ *it is to be eaten; you are not to take any* ᵇ *of the meat outside the house, and you are not to break any bone in it.* ⁴⁷ *The entire congregation of* ᵃ *Israel is to keep this requirement.* ᵇ ⁴⁸ *And when an outsider is visiting with you and he wants to do Passover for Yahweh, when every male of his family* ᵃ *is circumcised, then he may come near to do it. He is like one of the land's own.* ᵇ *But no one uncircumcised is to eat it.* ⁴⁹ *There is a single law for the native-born and for the outsider come to visit in your midst."*

⁵⁰ *And all* ᵃ *the sons of Israel did as Yahweh commanded Moses and Aaron— indeed, they did.* ⁵¹ *And in that very day Yahweh brought the sons of Israel out from Egypt together with their hosts.* ᵃ

Notes

37.a. כְּ used "quantitatively . . . = about" (BDB, 453).
37.b. רַגְלִי הַגְּבָרִים refers to "strong men on foot," here the protecting, fighting force of Israel; cf. BDB, 150, 920.
37.c. See Cassuto, 125.
38.a. LXX, Vg insert "and."
39.a. Special *waw* in this context, and in relation to vv 33–34.
39.b. עֻגֹת מַצּוֹת: the addition of עֻגֹת "disc, round cake" to מַצּוֹת "unleavened bread cake" suggests a flat cake instead of the loaf or pone, the "risen" cake the Israelites had intended to prepare.

39.c. See nn. 12:34.a, b.

40.a. SamPent אבתם and LXX^A οι πατερες αυτων add here "and their fathers."

40.b. SamPent adds בארץ כנען ובארץ מצרים "in the land of Canaan and in the land of Egypt," as does LXX, but in reverse order.

41.a. בעצם היום הזה lit. means "in that very same day" (BDB, 783); the reference here is clearly the end of the Egyptian sojourn and the day of exodus.

42.a. MT has the constr ליל "night of" at the beginning of v 42; SamPent has the abs לילה "night" at the end of v 41. LXX^A omits "night" altogether.

42.b. "A night" is added here for clarity; שמרים "watchings," vigils," is rendered "keepings" in its two occurrences in this verse to signify the fulfillment of commitments first by Yahweh and then by Israel in succession.

43.a. See n. 12:14.c.

43.b. כל־בן־נכר "every foreign son" here clearly refers to anyone, whatever his land, who is not a member of the covenant community of Israel.

44.a. מקנת־כסף "a purchase of money." SamPent has כספו "of his money."

46.a. Or perhaps even "in a single family," בבית אחד.

46.b. מן־הבשר "from the flesh."

47.a. LXX and Vg add "of the sons of" (υἱῶν, filiorum).

47.b. יעשו אתו "do it"; "requirement" is added here (see v 43) for clarity.

48.a. לו, lit., "belonging to him."

48.b. כאזרח הארץ "as a native of the land."

50.a. "All" is not in LXX or the Cairo Geniza fragment of Exodus.

51.a. על here is taken in its sense of "addition to" (BDB, 755), and "hosts" may be understood broadly in reference to the great number of Israelites (as in v 41), and more specifically, in reference to the Israelite families now at last accompanying the able-bodied men. The more specific reference to tribal organization may also be present (see n. 6:26.a).

Form/Structure/Setting

The kernel of this section is the account of Israel's movement of exodus, the first leg of the actual journey toward freedom. That account, set forth in vv 37–39, has been assigned generally to J, though Davies (*VT* 33 [1983] 5–13) has argued that 12:37 is dependent upon Num 33 and is the insertion of "a redactor in the Deuteronomistic tradition." Following this narrative, there is a kind of reflective miscellany, vv 40–51, dealing successively with the chronological extent of the period of Israel's stay in Egypt (vv 40–41), the commitments called forth from Israel because Yahweh had kept his commitments (v 41), additional details concerning who is to have a part in keeping those commitments (vv 43–49), and reporting Israel's first obedience to Yahweh's requirements (v 50), and, again, the exodus itself, this time as effected by Yahweh (v 51). This miscellany, which in its present location seems almost to be both musing and additional requirements prompted by the final arrival of the exodus so long awaited, is usually assigned to P (so Beer, 68–71; Anderson, in Noth, *Pentateuchal Traditions,* 269; Hyatt, 139–41) though sometimes to layers of tradition within the Priestly source (Laaf, *Pascha-Feier,* 10–15).

Some commentators (e.g., Hyatt, 137, 140; Childs, 184) reckon vv 40–51 to be the continuation, along with v 28, of a Priestly narrative of the tenth mighty act, Passover, and exodus begun in 12:1–20. In such a view, the P narrative has been broken up for distribution at appropriate points in a composite of narrative and liturgical material connected with the tenth mighty act, Passover, and exodus.

As always, however, the resultant composite is more important than speculation, however informative, about the way the narrative came together. Here,
as throughout Exodus, we have a narrative framework into which has been
inserted important theological confession and liturgical instruction designed
to re-present or contemporize a foundational experience in Israel's faith (cf.
Noth, *OT Hermeneutics*, 80–82). In an entirely logical sequence, the first reference to the actual movement of exodus prompts reminiscence about the stay
in Egypt, an assertion that Yahweh kept his promises right on schedule, and
some instructions about who is and who is not to take part in the continuation
of the event through its ritual celebration.

Comment

37 The specification of the direction of the exodus journey "from Rameses
in the direction of Succoth" was no doubt intended to locate the movement
of the first stage of Israel's journey from the Egyptian Delta. Unfortunately,
the note no longer serves its original purpose, because of the uncertainty
in identifying the two places mentioned. Alt (*Kleine Schriften* 3:176–85) summarized the data available up to 1954, and more recently Herrmann (*Israel in
Egypt*, 23–28) and Hyatt (59–60) have reviewed the location of Delta place-
names mentioned in the OT, but any precise plotting of the route of Israel
in exodus remains impossible.

The Hebrew transcription of the Egyptian name *Pr-R^cmśśw* differs in this
verse, in Gen 47:11, and in Num 33:3, 5 from Exod 1:11. Here and in Genesis
and Numbers it is רַעְמְסֵס. In 1:11, it is רַעַמְסֵס. This variation is probably
indicative of differences in the oral transmission of place-names in an unfamiliar language. The full name of the city, according to Herrmann (*Israel in
Egypt*, 27) was "House of Ramesses, beloved of Amun, great in victorious
might." Alt argued (*Kleine Schriften* 3:181–85) that the name may have represented a large capital city area in the nineteenth dynasty, a view followed
by Herrmann (26–27). Redford has argued (*VT* 13 [1963] 412–18) that the
OT references to רעמסס "Rameses" are all from P, indicate a transcription
from Greek, not Egyptian, and are therefore a late addition to the exodus
tradition. He is opposed in this view by Helck (*VT* 15 [1965] 41–48).

Succoth has been connected with the Pithom of 1:11, with a region, and
with Tell el-Maskhuta in the Wadi Tumilat (see the summary of Hyatt, 59–
60, and cf. Helck, *VT* 15 [1965] 35–40). Certainty remains elusive, but there
is little reason to doubt that this note originally marked a specific route
now lost to us, a route to the east and out of Egypt by the most direct possible path.

The number of "able-bodied men" leaving Egypt also presents difficulty,
not least in the number six hundred thousand, as so many able-bodied men
would suggest a total company of two (Knight, 94) to three (Beer, 68–69)
million. As so vast a company cannot fit what we know even of the biblical
context of the narratives of Genesis and Exodus (Lucas, *PEQ* 75 [1944] 164–
68), a series of explanations of the figure has been offered. Mendenhall (*JBL*
77 [1958] 60–66), for example, refining a suggestion made by W. M. Flinders
Petrie in 1906, has argued from the comparable references in Num 1 and

26 that the word אֶלֶף should be read not as the number "thousand," but as the designation of a tribal subsection determined by the size of a given tribe. This use of the term was not understood in post-exilic times, in which the military units were defined according to a monarchical pattern as comprised of units of one thousand. The older understanding of אֶלֶף, according to Mendenhall, would give a translation here of around five thousand able-bodied men (*not* 2500, as Knight, 94, says). Beer (69), to cite another example, proposed that the number "about six hundred thousand" was arrived at by Gematria, the equivalence of the letters of the phrase בְּנֵי יִשְׂרָאֵל "sons of Israel" with their numerical equivalents. Such an equation yields the number 603,551, remarkably close to the 603,550 of Num 1:46, and even the 601,730 of Num 26:51 and the "about" 600,000 here.

Neither of these suggestions is entirely convincing, in part because they are such obvious attempts to reduce what is clearly a straightforward number to a manageable size. Other approaches attempt to take the number as it stands, either as an outright exaggeration (Hyatt, 139) or as an accurate representation of the number of Israelite fighting men at the time of the composition of J (cf. G. H. Davies, 117). These latter interpretations are preferable.

38   The tradition of a "motley group" accompanying the Israelites in their exodus may well be an accurate reflection of a process referred to also in the narratives of conquest and settlement (e.g., Josh 9:3–21 and 24:14–28). That there were many who became Israelite by theological rather than biological descendancy is many times referred to in the OT and is the occasion for such requirements as those set forth in vv 43–49 of this composite.

39   V 39 is the conclusion to the narrative of the dough disturbed before it could rise (vv 33–34) and the end of an etiology for the use of unleavened bread in the worship of Passover. The departure from Egypt had come so abruptly that the only food at hand at the Israelites' first stop, still in Egyptian territory, was the dough they had scooped up on their way out. This they baked, unrisen, into flat cakes.

40–42   The account of the actual departure, so long awaited and so dramatically prepared for, provides an appropriate place for an appendix on the time spent in Egypt. The figure given here for that stay, four hundred and thirty years, is at variance with the figures given in other passages (four generations, Gen 15:16; four hundred years, Gen 15:13), and thus it too has been the subject of considerable interpretation. Cassuto (85–87) has an elaborate theory based on units derived from a sexagesimal system that connects v 40 to the ages of Levi, Kohath, and Amram in Exod 6:16, 18, and 20. He arrives at the correct total, but by a method that seems dictated by the answer. Other explanations pose the need for a long period, a generation of a hundred years, or even apply the four hundred and thirty years to the period in Egypt *and* Canaan from Abraham's arrival there (a solution applied by the reading of the SamPent and LXX; see n. 40.b.). No explanation thus far advanced, however, gives a satisfactory accounting of the number four hundred and thirty. It may have been exaggerated for the same reason as the number given in v 37, or even because of the inflated number there.

What is more to the point is that Yahweh kept his promise, precisely on schedule on the very last night of the long period of the sojourn in Egypt, to bring out his "hosts," his "organized divisions" (see above, n. 6:26.a.). "Hosts" very probably has a double meaning: in general, the great number of Israelites fulfilling Yahweh's promise of progeny to the fathers; specifically, the organization of the Israelites into a traveling—and fighting—force. The "very last day" is the end of the long period, the four generations. Yahweh made that night a "keepings" (שִׁמֻּרִים) night—a night when he kept his promises of release and protection and freedom and movement of his multiplied people toward the land he had promised them. In response, the Israelites were to make that night a "keepings" night for Yahweh, a night when they would keep *their* promises of remembrance, generation following generation. The juxtaposition of the two occurrences of שִׁמֻּרִים "keepings" (a word occurring nowhere else in the OT), once in reference to Yahweh's keeping and once in reference to Israel's keeping, is a brilliant rhetorical touch.

43–49 The reference to requirements to be kept at Passover, in the context of Israel's going forth into a world of many peoples and accompanied by a "motley group" at that, provides a natural location for the important specification that only members of the covenant community are eligible for Passover worship. The criterion for this membership is circumcision. Slaves bought and paid for, that is, owned outright and without question, must be circumcised before they can keep Passover. Those passing through, even those engaged for temporary work, are not to keep Passover. An outsider may be allowed to keep Passover only if he and his entire family are circumcised, that is, admitted to the covenant community. One rule applies to all: circumcision.

Further, the meal of remembrance is to be eaten inside, in the one house selected for a gathering of smaller families (Exod 12:4). None of the meat is to be taken outside, where someone uncircumcised would have access to it. No bone of the sacrificial animal is to be broken, to ensure that the meat will remain inside, in the one house set apart for the worship of remembrance (so Dussaud, *Les origines,* 211), and perhaps as a symbol of the unity of the family worshiping (Noth, 101) and even of the covenant community. Scheiber (*VT* 13 [1963] 95–97), commenting on collections of unbroken animal bones discovered in excavations at Qumran, has called this verse, along with Num 9:12, "pre-Mosaic instructions," the significance of which is apotropaic. He cites *Jub.* 49:13 as an interpretation of this practice, and notes that it was observed by a wide and intercontinental array of "primitive peoples."

50–51 The appendices of Passover requirements, in themselves repetitive, are summed up with a typical Priestly assertion of obedience and a further reference to Yahweh's bringing-out right on time.

Explanation

The exodus itself, long awaited by Israel, much postponed by Pharaoh, and carefully prepared by Yahweh, is the point of this section. The pericope functions as a kind of conclusion to the longest narrative complex within the Book of Exodus, a complex begun with the account of the call of Moses in chaps. 3 and 4 and anticipated by the conditions of bondage and suffering described in chaps. 1 and 2. Though much liturgical material has encrusted this narrative in its present form, both before and after the report of the exodus itself, the narrative, which is after all the stimulus for the commemorative liturgy, shines through still, and even with an enhanced lustre.

The numbers (of able-bodied men departing, of years spent in Egypt) and the requirements (circumcision, the separation of the Passover ritual as private worship) are an enhancement of a great event, an event made concrete by the mention of a point of departure and a specific route. The emphasis upon Yahweh's own timetable for this event, read in the light of the precision of the abrupt departure on the very last night of such a lengthy residence and against the backdrop of Yahweh's hardening of Pharaoh's heart, suggests the transcendent effectiveness of the event, which becomes exodus for every believing Israelite of whatever generation.

What gives a literary appearance of hodge-podge dimensions, a narrative onto which has been loaded a miscellany of cultic requirements, then, has a somewhat different theological appearance as the testimony of a night of keepings *by* Yahweh, to be made real to successive generations by the specification of a night of keepings *for* Yahweh. What Yahweh did in Egypt he did for all Israel, in every generation. That each generation might know that, the confession of what *he* did is here extended by the requirement of what *they* are to do, once yearly, on a night that is different from all other nights.

The Ritual Testimony of the Exodus　　*(13:1–16)*

Bibliography

Brekelmans, C. "Die sogenannten deuteronomischen Elemente in Gen.-Num. Ein Beitrag zur Vorgeschichte des Deuteronomiums." *Volume du Congrès: Genève*. VTSup 15. Leiden: E. J. Brill, 1965. 90–96. **Caloz, M.** "Exode, XIII, 3–16 et son rapport au Deutéronome." *RB* 75 (1968) 5–62, plus two appendices. **Lohfink, N.** *Das Hauptgebot.* AnBib 20. Rome: Instituto Biblico e Pontificio, 1963. **Loza, J.** "Les catéchèses étiologiques dans l'Ancien Testament." *RB* 78 (1971) 481–500. **Muilenburg, J.** "Form Criticism and Beyond." *JBL* 88 (1969) 1–18. **Seters, J. van.** "The Place of the Yahwist in the History of Passover and Massot." *ZAW* 95 (1983) 167–82. **Skehan, P. W.**, and **J. T. Milik.** *Qumran Grotte 4: II (4Q128–4Q157).* Oxford: At the Clarendon Press, 1977. **Soggin, J. A.** "Kultätiologische Sagen und Katechese im Hexateuch." *VT* 10 (1960) 341–47. **Speiser, E. A.** "ṬWṬPT." *JQR* 48 (1957–58) 208–17. **Vaux, R. de.** *Ancient Israel, Vol. 1: Social Institutions.* New York: McGraw-Hill, 1965.

Translation

¹ *Then Yahweh spoke to Moses as follows:* ² *"Set apart for me all firstborn. Every life that opens the womb* ᵃ *among the sons of Israel, whether human or animal, is mine."*

³ *So Moses said to the people, "Keep in mind this day in which you went out from Egypt,* ᵃ *from the non-status of slaves, because by strength of power* ᵇ *Yahweh brought you out thence. Nothing leavened is to be eaten.* ⁴ *The day* ᵃ *you are going*

out is in the month of the green grain. [b] [5] *It is necessary,* [a] *when Yahweh* [b] *brings you into the land of the Canaanites, and the Hittites, and the Amorites,* [c] *and the Hivites, and the Jebusites, the land that* [d] *he promised by oath* [e] *to your fathers to give to you, a land gushing with milk and honey, that you worship in this manner* [f] *in this month:* [6] *seven* [a] *days you are to eat unleavened bread cakes, and on the seventh day there is to be special worship* [b] *to Yahweh.* [7] *Unleavened bread cakes are to be eaten for seven days, and no leaven is to be seen in your possession.* [a] *Leaven is not to be seen* [b] *in your possession* [c] *anywhere within your borders.* [8] *You shall explain to your son on that day as follows: 'This is because of what Yahweh did for me in my coming out of Egypt.'* [9] *And it is to be for you a sign upon your hand* [a] *and a reminder between your eyes, in order that the instruction of Yahweh may be in your speech,* [b] *because with a strong power Yahweh has brought you forth from Egypt.* [10] *So you are to keep this requirement* [a] *at its scheduled time year after year.*

[11] *"It is necessary, when Yahweh* [a] *brings you into the land of the Canaanites, in accord with his promise by oath to you and to your fathers, and gives it to you,* [12] *that you commit* [a] *to Yahweh every life that opens the womb. Every firstborn animal* [b] *that belongs to you, all the males, go to Yahweh.* [c] [13] *Every firstborn he-ass* [a] *you shall replace* [b] *with an animal from the flock; if you do not replace it, then you are to break its neck. Every firstborn human among your sons you must replace.* [14] *It is necessary,* [a] *when your son asks you, in due course, 'What is this?' that you say to him, 'With a strong power, Yahweh brought us out from Egypt, from the non-status of slaves.* [15] *For when Pharaoh was stubborn-minded about sending us forth, then Yahweh killed all the firstborn of the land of Egypt, from human firstborn to the firstborn of the domesticated animals. For that reason, I am sacrificing to Yahweh all the males that open the womb, except all my firstborn sons,* [a] *whom I am replacing.'* [16] *And it is* [a] *to be for a sign upon your hand and for bands* [b] *between your eyes that with a strong power Yahweh brought us out from Egypt.''*

Notes

2.a. פטר כל־רחם "that which opens every womb."

3.a. LXX, Syr, SamPent add "from the land of."

3.b. בחזק יד "by strength of power" (cf. BDB, 390).

4.a. SamPent concludes v 3 with היום "the day," and begins this sentence with אתם יצאים "you are going out."

4.b. אביב "green grain," from אבב, is descriptive of the fresh green barley forming heads of grain. See 9:31–32 and BDB, 1.

5.a. היה "be" plus special *waw.*

5.b. SamPent, LXX, Tg Ps-J add "your God."

5.c. SamPent adds והפרזי והגרגשי "and the Perizzites and the Girgashites" as does LXX, though in reverse order. 4Q128 *verso* (DJD VI, 51, ll. 54–55) has "the Amorites, the Perizzites, the Hivites, the Jebusites, the Girgashites." Cf. Exod 3:17.

5.d. MT has only אשר "that"; "the land" clearly intended, is added above for clarity.

5.e. BDB, 989.

5.f. ועבדת את־העבדה הזאת "and you serve this service"; cf. BDB, 712–13, 715.

6.a. SamPent and LXX read "six."

6.b. See n. 10:9.b.

7.a. לך "to you"; note BDB, 512–13.

7.b. LXX has ἔσται "is to belong" instead of יֵרָאֶה "to be seen."

7.c. ולא־יראה לך שאר "leaven is not to be seen in your possession" is lacking in Syr.

9.a. SamPent reads ידיך "your hands" and begins the verse והיו "and they are."

9.b. Or "mouth" (BDB, 804–5).

10.a. See n. 12:15.b.

11.a. SamPent and LXX add "your God" (אֱלֹהֶיךָ‎, ὁ Θεός σου).

12.a. The verb, hiph of עבר‎, has the sense "to cause something to pass to," in this case into Yahweh's possession and use. Driver (108) speculates a connection with the practice of child-sacrifice by Israel's neighbors; note 2 Kgs 16:3; Ezek 20:31.

12.b. וְכָל־פֶּטֶר שֶׁגֶר‎ "and every offspring that opens." Cassuto (153) takes שֶׁגֶר‎ "offspring" here to refer to the רֶחֶם‎ "womb" of animals. Cf. BDB, שֶׁגֶר‎, 993. The meaning is clear, even if שֶׁגֶר‎ is taken to mean "animal offspring."

12.c. לַיהוה‎ "to Yahweh"; LXX, Tg Onk, Vg insert "set aside, consecrate."

13.a. LXX μήτραν and Tg Ps-J add "womb," and Syr has bwkr' dkr' pṭḥ rḥm' "firstborn male opening the womb." MT has simply וְכָל־פֶּטֶר חֲמֹר‎ "and every he-ass that opens."

13.b. פדה‎ "buy" or "ransom" at a price or by a substitute agreed upon.

14.a. MT has וְהָיָה כִּי‎ (special waw) "it is necessary when"; Syr and the Cairo Geniza fragment have simply "and when."

15.a. The Qumran text adds אָדָם בִּבְנֵי‎ "human sons."

16.a. SamPent has וְהָיוּ‎ "and they are," as in v 9 above.

16.b. טוֹטָפֹת‎ "bands" functions here as זִכָּרוֹן‎ "reminder" does in v. 9. We may misunderstand the significance of the word, on the basis of the later literal use of it to refer to the phylactery. See Speiser, JQR 48 (1957/58) 208–9.

16.c. SamPent, LXX read "you."

Form/Structure/Setting

The stimulus for this section is the narrative of the sparing of the firstborn of Israel in the decimation of the tenth mighty act upon Egypt. That connection then logically becomes a basis for the inclusion of further instructions, somewhat differently phrased, regarding the ritual commemoration of the exodus. The layers in the section (vv 1–2; 3–4; 6–10; 11–16) are obvious. Yet there is also a single purpose for this collection of material, the ritual commemoration of the exodus, as a means of making it an experience real to the generations to come.

Quite apart from the subjects dealt with here, there are obvious stylistic differences, on the basis of which, in recent years, vv 1–2 have been assigned to P and vv 3–16 to D or a Deuteronomic redactor (Rylaarsdam, "Exodus," IB 1:923–28; Fohrer, Überlieferung, 86–87; Hyatt, 141–44; Childs, 184). There are, however, departures from such an attribution: Noth (101) contended that the entire section is deuteronomistic; Clements (78) assigns the entire section to J (cf. van Seters, ZAW 95 [1983] 175–76, who assigns 13:3–16 to a "post-Deuteronomic and exilic" J); Loza (RB 78 [1971] 481–83, 487–88) has singled out the catechetical element of vv 8, 9, 14, and 16 as indicative of the relation of some of this material to a north Levitical provenance, perhaps at the sanctuaries of Shechem and Gilgal.

The most elaborate analysis of the verses usually connected in some way with deuteronomic or deuteronomistic circles, vv 3–16, has been made by Masséo Caloz. Following the three criteria set forth by Brekelmans (Volume du Congrès, 93–96) for the separation of predeuteronomic texts from texts truly deuteronomic or deuteronomistic, Caloz (RB 75 [1968] 8–23) makes a careful study of the vocabulary of vv 3–16 and concludes that the largest number of words in recurring use is "pre-dtr": 16 words used a total of 59 times. The words singled out in his analysis are then sought (23–43) in other pentateuchal sources; E, P, J, Eissfeldt's Laienquelle, Deuteronomy and the Deuteronomistic History. A further comparison of the formula-phrases of

Exod 13:3–16 with the formula-phrases of Deuteronomy (43–54), and a comparison of what is said in these verses with what is said elsewhere in the OT on the subject of unleavened bread cakes and the requirement of the firstborn (55–61), lead Caloz to the conclusion that Exod 13:3–16 is predeuteronomic, to be placed before the Josianic reform (62), and perhaps can be linked to the "more ancient traditions, J and E."

As noted above (*Comment* on 12:24–27), the didactic language of such passages belongs to a style inherited not only by the Deuteronomists, but by other oral-literary circles as well. Caloz is undoubtedly correct in his basic conclusion, as also are Lohfink, Soggin, and Loza. The evidence of what James Muilenburg (*JBL* 88 [1969] 1–18) called "rhetorical criticism," essentially what these scholars, in varying ways, have been doing, must lead us to less provincial conclusions about the sources of both the vocabulary and the traditions that make up the rich tapestry that is the OT.

What binds this section together is not vocabulary or style, but the need to provide a ritual testimony to the divine rescue that is the exodus. That single theme is the nucleus around which are gathered here two sections (vv 1–2, 11–16) on the requirement of the firstborn, and perhaps two (note the change from singular verbs in vv 3–4 to plural verbs in vv 5–10) on unleavened bread. Into these sections have been threaded the motifs of the ritual calendar (vv 4, 5, 10), possession of the land promised by oath (vv 5, 11), instruction in the faith of the generations yet to come (vv 8–10, 14–15), substitutionary sacrifice (vv 13–15), and actualizing symbol (vv 9, 16). And all of this, far from the miscellany it has sometimes been held to be, is drawn together by a single intention: to make the parents' exodus also the children's exodus.

Comment

1–2 The view of Childs (202–4) that 13:1–2 serves as a "superscription" to vv 3–16, one "patterned after 12:1–20," is not entirely convincing, not least because vv 1–2 refer not at all to the concern of the first eight of the fourteen verses that follow. That concern, the eating of unleavened bread cakes in commemoration of the tenth mighty act and the exodus made possible by it, has been given extensive attention in the composite of Exodus already (12:14–20, 33–34, 39). The concern of vv 11–16 is new in the sequence of the composite, and so it is the subject of v 2. The reason for the strange order is the redactor's desire to bring together a variety of ritual devices rooted in a common purpose: the actualization of the exodus-deliverance. The listing of these devices is begun both in a reference to their divine authority (they are instructions of Yahweh, passed along by Moses) and by the introduction of the motif of the dedication of the firstborn of Israel, saved by Yahweh from the decimation of the tenth plague. The parallels between vv 3–10 and 11–16, instructively listed by Childs (203), are testimony to the single purpose of this sequence rather than an indication that vv 1–2 are "a heading" to all that follows.

3 The motif of remembering begins both of the sections of Exodus devoted to the preparation and eating of unleavened bread cakes (see 12:14 and n. 12:14.a). Whatever they may become in the better times ahead, the people of Israel are never to forget what they were. Their plight in Egypt is described graphically as בית עבדים, literally, "house of slaves," read above "the non-status of slaves" (cf. BDB, 713). Their rescue from that plight, they must recall, was made possible only by the strength of Yahweh's power, attested by the whole range of the proof-of-Presence sequence of the ten mighty acts.

4–5 The time of the exodus, referred to in a neat *double entendre* in 12:2 (see above) as "the lead month," is here set in "the month of the green grain," the first month in the Canaanite calendar, אביב "Abib" (de Vaux, *Ancient Israel*, 183–84). The place of the future celebration of the exodus is set by a reference to the promise of land to the fathers, a promise now about to be fulfilled and so mentioned here as a confessional link with both the past and the future. The peoples listed are peoples with whom the Israelites had to reckon repeatedly in conquest and settlement. There are many such lists in the OT, and the peoples listed vary from passage to passage and even in version to version (see n. 5.c above). The authority for the future celebration is the command of Yahweh himself, והיה "and it shall be," "it is necessary. . . ."

6–10 The differences between the instructions given here and those given in Exod 12:14–20 are not substantial: seven days of eating unleavened bread cakes are mentioned in both passages; the special worship of the first day is not mentioned here; the perpetual nature of the observance is mentioned in both passages, and its significance is linked to the exodus experience, though only here is a catechetical explanation given and only here are reminding symbols mentioned. The strict prohibition of leaven is made very clear in both passages, though a penalty for being found with leaven is given only in the former passage.

9, 16 The references to reminding symbols, "a sign" אות and "a reminder" זכרון (v 9), and "a sign" and "bands" טוטפות (v 16) are ambiguous. Deut 6:8–9 and 11:18–20 can much more easily be taken in literal reference to the small containers of key verses and the leather bands used by orthodox Jews at their devotions even in our own time. Hyatt (143–44) thinks the references of vv 9 and 16 are "to be taken figuratively." Speiser has argued (*JQR* 48 [1957–58] 210) that the three OT references to טוטפת should be pointed as singulars, טוֹטֶפֶת, instead of plurals, טוֹטפֹת, as in MT, and he has speculated (211–17) an etymology that would connect טוֹטֶפֶת with protective symbols. Speiser insisted upon the "strictly hypothetical character" (216) of his proposal, but the gist of his argument too is that the references at hand are metaphorical and not to be taken, as they came to be in Judaism, to indicate physical symbols. The antecedent of the "it" at the beginning of both vv 9 and 16 remains unclear, but the instruction concerning the unleavened bread cakes and the instruction concerning the firstborn are probably what is to serve as the "sign," the "reminder," and the "bands." Indeed the substitution of "bands" in v 16 for "reminder" in v 9 may serve not as a movement away from metaphor to a symbol, but as an extension of the metaphor by reference to some physical object, just as a strong person may be referred to as "a brick" or "a rock."

11–13 Much as the sacrifice of the Passover flock-animal is given an etiology in the meal commanded on the eve of the departure from Egypt, and as the eating of the unleavened bread cakes is given an etiology in the experience of hasty departure in exodus, so the requirement of the dedication of Israel's firstborn is given an etiology in the tenth mighty act that made exodus a possibility. This paragraph is introduced (v 11) as is the requirement of the eating of unleavened bread cakes (v 5), though more compactly. Along with v 2, v 12 specifies that all firstborn, "every life that opens the womb," of man or of animal, belongs to Yahweh. As this requirement is first stated, it appears to be without exception. Conditions are therefore introduced, first of all excepting female offspring, and second of all allowing substitutions, both for the he-ass and for the human males. Both these exceptions are apparently for practical reasons; there is no firm OT evidence (see Lev 11:1–8) that the he-ass was considered unclean—it was a valuable burden carrier (note Exod 9:3). The animal could be "ransomed, replaced" (פדה) by a flock-animal, or it could be destroyed (not sacrificed). The firstborn human male was to be replaced, but at what cost this text does not say (nor does Exod 34:20).

14–15 This instruction too is justified in catechetical fashion and as founded on the experience of exodus-deliverance. Yahweh's decimation of all of the firstborn of Egypt, prompted by Pharaoh's stubborn-mindedness, necessitated the sparing of all of the firstborn of Israel, who, having thus been saved by him, belong to him. Thus each Israelite livestock-owner and father must offer to Yahweh or replace every firstborn male. The antiquity of such a custom, even in relation to human sacrifice, has prompted considerable comment, but speculation is rife, and fact is elusive. The practice is probably older than the exodus and much wider than Israel's commitment to it, just as a spring lambing festival may lie behind Passover (see *Comment* on 12:8–10), and just as a grain-harvesting festival may lie behind the eating of unleavened bread cakes over a seven-day period (see *Comment* on 12:15). What is of primary importance to an understanding of Exodus, however, is the use to which the ritual involving the firstborn of animal and man have been put in the exodus composite.

Explanation

This section, for all its apparent multiplicity, has finally a single point, the actualization to the generations yet to come of the experience of the exodus. The medium of this actualization is ritual, founded in various dimensions of the exodus experience itself and made authoritative as Yahweh's own command. Part of what Yahweh had promised the fathers—the multiplication of progeny—had been fulfilled before the exodus; indeed, that fulfillment had made necessary the exodus. The further part of that promise—the wide and spacious land "gushing" with milk and honey—was now about to be fulfilled. That further promise is itself cleverly brought to mind by the stipulation of these rituals of actualization as necessary when the Israelites shall come into that promised land.

Thus are requirements of recollection set—specified acts at a specified time, rituals carefully controlled, rituals for which even the explanations are givens. The impression is present, at least, that the questions to be raised by the generations to come are set questions, as they indeed are in the celebration of Passover to this day. All that is set forth here is to the single end that those who are to come may know the exodus, by taste and by feel, by cost and by result, as an experience of their own as equally as an experience of their fathers. And so they await the time, then taste the bread and give Yahweh his due, explain it all to the ones who must remember to those after them, and thus experience the freedom to glorify Yahweh in service that is their heritage.

PART TWO
ISRAEL IN THE WILDERNESS
(13:17–18:27)

The Route of the Exodus   (13:17–14:4)

Bibliography

Aharoni, Y. *The Land of the Bible.* Philadelphia: Westminster Press, 1967. **Albright, W. F.** "Baal-Zephon." *Festschrift Alfred Bertholet.* Tübingen: J. C. B. Mohr (Paul Siebeck), 1950. 1–14. **Batto, B. F.** "The Reed Sea: Requiescat in Pace." *JBL* 102 (1983) 27–35. **Cazelles, H.** "Les localisations de L'Exode et la critique littéraire." *RB* 62 (1955) 321–64. **Davies, G. I.** "The Wilderness Itineraries and the Composition of the Pentateuch." *VT* 33 (1983) 1–13. **Eissfeldt, O.** *Baal Zaphon, Zeus Kasios und der Durchzug der Israeliten durchs Meer.* Halle: Max Niemeyer Verlag, 1932. **Gardiner, A. H.** "The Ancient Military Road Between Egypt and Palestine." *JEA* 6 (1920) 99–116. **Haran, M.** "The Exodus." IDBSup, 304–10. **Krahmalkov, C. R.** "A Critique of Professor Goedicke's Exodus Theories." *BARev* 7 (1981) 51–54. **Kuntz, J. K.** *The Self-Revelation of God.* Philadelphia: Westminster Press, 1967. **Muilenburg, J.** "The Linguistic and Rhetorical Usage of the Particle כִּי in the OT." *HUCA* 32 (1961) 135–60. **Noth, M.** "Der Schauplatz des Meereswunders." *Festschrift Otto Eissfeldt.* Halle: Max Niemeyer Verlag, 1947. 181–90. **Rabenau, K. von.** "Die beiden Erzählungen vom Schilfmeerwunder in Exod. 13:17–14:31." *Theologische Versuche,* vol. 1. P. Watzel and G. Schille, eds. Berlin: Evangelische Verlagsanstalt, 1966. 9–29. **Shanks, H.** "The Exodus and the Crossing of the Red Sea, According to Hans Goedicke." *BARev* 7 (1981) 42–50. **Terrien, S.** *The Elusive Presence.* San Francisco: Harper & Row, 1978. **Volz, P.** "Grundsätzliches zur elohistischen Frage." *Der Elohist als Erzähler.* Giessen: Verlag von Alfred Töpelmann, 1933. 1–142. **Wolff, H. W.** "Zur Thematik der elohistischen Fragmente im Pentateuch." *EvT* 29 (1969) 59–72. ET: *Interpretation* 26 (1972) 158–73.

Translation

[17] *Now when Pharaoh sent the people out, God did not guide them by the route of the land of the Philistines, in spite of the directness of that way,* [a] *for God said, "The people may well change their minds,* [b] *if they encounter* [c] *fighting, and turn back toward Egypt."* [18] *So God turned the people toward the wilderness via the "sea of rushes." The sons of Israel went up from the land of Egypt ready for battle.* [a]

[19] *Moses also* [a] *took with him Joseph's bones, for Joseph* [b] *had made the sons of Israel swear unconditionally,* [c] *saying, "God* [d] *will come to you, without a doubt* [e]*— then you are to bring up my bones from here with you."*

[20] *Thus they set out from Succoth and made camp at Etham, on the outskirts of the wilderness.* [21] *Yahweh* [a] *preceded them in the daytime in a column of cloud to guide them on the route, and in the nighttime in a column of fire to give them light; thus they could travel* [b] *day and night.* [22] *He did not take away* [a] *from in front of the people the column of cloud in the daytime or the column of fire in the nighttime.*

[14:1] *Then, Yahweh spoke to Moses as follows:* [a] [2] *"Speak to the sons of Israel so that they turn back and make camp in front of Pi-hahiroth,* [a] *between Migdol and the sea, in front of Baal Zephon. You are to make camp opposite it, on the edge of the sea.* [3] *Pharaoh will conclude* [a] *that* [b] *the sons of Israel are turning one way and then another in confusion in the land, that the wilderness has blocked their exodus.* [c] [4] *Then I will make Pharaoh's mind obstinate; he will come chasing after them, and I will win myself glory over Pharaoh and all his force, so that the Egyptians will know by experience that I am Yahweh." So they did as Yahweh instructed.* [a]

Notes

17.a. כִּי קָרוֹב הוּא followed by כִּי אָמַר, lit., "for near it [was], for he said. . . ." כִּי . . . כִּי here has an adversative sense; see BDB, 474, and Muilenburg, *HUCA* 32 (1961) 135–39, 159–60.

17.b. כִּי אָמַר פֶּן "for he said, Lest" is an idiom, "implying always that some precaution has been taken to avert the dreaded contingency" (BDB, 814). Niph of נחם "change their minds" means lit. "to sorrow oneself," and so "to rue" something: BDB, 636–37.

17.c. רָאה "see," here as experience: BDB, 307.

18.a. LXX has πέμπτη δὲ γενεᾷ "in the fifth generation." Cassuto (156) argues from the Arabic usage of a similar word that חֲמֻשִׁים means "in proper military formation." Cf. BDB 331–32, and also 301, for the suggestion that חֲמֻשִׁים may be a qal pass pcp of חוּשׁ, and so mean "hastening."

19.a. Special *waw*.

19.b. MT has "he"; "Joseph" is the clear antecedent of this pronoun, and so is added above for clarity. SamPent and some LXX MSS make this addition.

19.c. Hiph inf abs of שׁבע "swear."

19.d. LXX has κύριος = Yahweh.

19.e. Qal inf abs of פקד "come to."

21.a. LXX has ὁ Θεὸς "God."

21.b. MT has לָלֶכֶת "for going."

22.a. יָמִישׁ "take away" can also be read with the column of cloud and the column of fire as subj, but in the context, Yahweh is the more logical choice. Cf. the references listed in the *masora magna* of L (Weil, 363, no. 3293). SamPent has יָמוּשׁ, qal impf instead of MT's hiph impf.

14:1.a. This verse is the same as 13:1.

2.a. LXX has τῆς ἐπαύλεως "the unwalled village" (Liddell-Scott, *Greek-English Lexicon*, 611). *BHS* wonders whether this is the Greek equivalent of the חצרות "Hazeroth" of Num 11:35; 33:17, 18; and Deut 1:1.

3.a. אָמַר "he will say," with special *waw;* cf. BDB, 55–56.

3.b. LXX reads ἐρεῖ φαραω τῷ λαῷ αὐτοῦ Οἱ υἱοὶ Ισραηλ "Pharaoh will say to his people, 'The sons of Israel.'"

3.c. סָגַר עֲלֵיהֶם "has shut in upon them."

4.a. וַיַּעֲשׂוּ־כֵן "so they did thus."

Form/Structure/Setting

This section, a composite of information from at least two, and perhaps three, tetrateuchal sources, has as a major concern Israel's route in exodus as planned and revealed by Yahweh. The division of these verses into source-strata has been done on the basis of the shift in the use of the names "Elohim" (vv 17–19) and "Yahweh" (vv 20–22; 14:1–4), the reference to Joseph's desire to have his bones returned to the promised land (v 19; cf. Gen 50:24–25), the difference in the reasons given for the route to be followed (13:17–18 vis-à-vis 14:1–3), and the introduction of the guiding columns of cloud and fire (13:20–22).

The presence of J (13:20–22) and P (14:1–4) has been a matter of general agreement for many years, though note the view of Davies (*VT* 33 [1983] 5–13) that 13:20 and other itinerary-notices are the insertions of a Deutero-nomistic redactor. The presence of E (13:17–19, according to Beer, 74; Hyatt, 147) has been disputed since the work of Volz and has generally been reckoned to remain in Genesis and Exodus in very fragmentary form. Some scholars have reassigned verses to earlier *Ur*-sources (so Fohrer [*Überlieferung*, 98–99,

124–25] gives 14:1–3 to his nomadic source, N, and 14:4 to a supplememtal
hand), but others (Noth, 104–6; Childs, 218–21; and especially von Rabenau,
Theologische Versuche, 9–14) have argued even more persuasively that P is very
much present.

The combination of varied material dealing with the route of the exodus
in the section at hand is not to be doubted. The theories about the original
provenance of that material are necessarily highly subjective, and finally give
only a limited illumination to the meaning of the text in its canonical form.
As intriguing as speculation may be about the E that once was (Wolff, *EvT*
29 [1969] 59–72), Rendtorff (*Überlieferungsgeschichtliche Problem* 1–28, 147–73)
has performed a service in pointing out the topheaviness of the structure
that has been erected on the theory of the source-documentary hypothesis,
and we must always accord the text in its redacted form an integrity of
its own.

Thus the present section may be seen as an assemblage of tradition about
a route for the exodus so apparently eccentric as to have had necessarily
some purpose beyond a mere departure from Egyptian territory. That purpose
is suggested in this composite, both by the recurring insistence that God/
Yahweh laid out the route and guided the Israelites in it, and also by the
anticipation of what is to come in the autokerygmatic assertion of 14:4, so
reminiscent of the יהוה אני כי "that I am Yahweh" sentences in the Book
of Ezekiel. The form of this section is thus set by two interlocked themes:
the route of the exodus and the guidance of Israel in that route by Yahweh.
These two themes, in turn, provide an introduction to the motifs of deliverance
and glorification that are the interest of the next three sections to come.

Comment

17 The use in this verse of the piel of שלח in reference to Pharaoh's
"sending," literally, "hurling, driving" the people of Israel forth from his
battered land, is an important rhetorical connection with Exod 3:20, where
the same verb is used, also in the piel stem, in Yahweh's prediction to Moses
of the proof-of-Presence sequence. As Yahweh has said, no human force
could bend the proud king of the proudest kingdom. Under the power of
Yahweh's hand, however, Pharaoh has become an enthusiastic participant
in the exodus, not only permitting but demanding, even forcing it.

That some historical event lies at the root of this narrative seems a certainty;
yet despite many ingenious attempts to find extrabiblical reference to even
one of the events mentioned in the exodus sequence, no convincing equivalence has thus far been established. The most recent such attempt, that of
Hans Goedicke (Shanks, *BAR* 7 [1981] 42–50; Krahmalkov, *BAR* 7 [1981]
51–54), involves redating even the century of the exodus, to "the early morning hours of a spring day in 1477 B.C." (Shanks, 42). Previous attempts have
set the time of the exodus at various periods in three separate centuries
(fifteenth, fourteenth and thirteenth centuries B.C.) and have placed the route
of the exodus at various locations across 250 miles, north to south.

The single most convincing biblical testimony to the historical rootage
of the exodus experience is the formative and extensive influence of exodus

faith upon the theology of the OT. Second only to that massive testimony, however, is the preoccupation of this composite with the route the people of Israel took to the border of Egypt at the edge of the wilderness. This route is given for a theological reason, as is nearly all the information in Exodus, or for that matter in the OT and even in the Bible itself. But it is too erratic a route to have been invented, and the continuing debate about its exact location has given too little attention to the assertion that God/ Yahweh determined the route as a ruse by which he might get further glory at Pharaoh's expense—a point made explicit by the summary statement of 14:1–4, the latest layer in the composite in its present form.

The major difficulty in plotting the route of the exodus lies not in the lack of information supplied in Exodus, but in our ignorance of the identification and correct location of the places listed in Exod 13:17–18, 20; and 14:2. Of the many attempts to fix these sites, none has produced more than speculative success, as the summaries of Eissfeldt, Cazelles, Aharoni, and Haran show. The best we can do, with any assurance, is to plot the general directions of Israel's departure. This uncertainty about the geography of the exodus is not, however, an obstacle of major dimensions to our understanding of the narrative of the exodus, the point of which is theology, and not geography.

18 One key to the understanding of this theology is the assertion that Elohim "God" guided (נחה) them. A deliberate contrast is made between the direct and therefore logical route east, "the route of the land of the Philistines" and the way in which Yahweh instead led Israel, a route in the direction of the wilderness via the ים־סוף "sea of rushes." The reason given for this longer route is that the more direct path would probably lead to conflict that could prove so discouraging to Israel that they might turn back to Egypt. This reason can be documented from Egyptian records from the time of Seti I and Rameses II (Aharoni, *The Land*, 41–49). There was a well-fortified military road on the direct route from the Egyptian Delta into Canaan (Gardiner, *JEA* 6 [1920] 99–116), and though it is referred to in v 17 by its later name, "the route . . . of the Philistines," this is certainly the route Elohim guides Israel to avoid.

The turn toward the wilderness by way of the "sea of rushes" is a turn to another easterly, or even a southeasterly, direction. This "sea of rushes" has traditionally been read as "Red Sea" under the influence of LXX and Vg and because of the proximity of the Red Sea to the most popular location of Sinai. B. F. Batto has argued (*JBL* 102 [1983] 30–35) that the traditional identification is a correct one, exactly what "P consciously intended." This "sea" has not, however, been identified with any certainty, though virtually every body of water and marshland between and including the Mediterranean and the Red Sea has been proposed in the scholarly discussion. The more circuitous route specified in vv 17–18 avoided the certainty of conflict offered by the fortified *Via Maris*, but afforded still the danger of some unknown opposition. The Israelites go forth therefore in fighting formation, that is, with the armed men in the vanguard, their more vulnerable dependents in the protection of their lead.

19 The report that Moses kept Israel's oath to Joseph by bringing Joseph's bones out of Egypt with Israel in exodus is virtually a verbatim repetition of the account of Joseph's requirement of the oath in Gen 50:25. Its location here is a somewhat arbitrary interruption of the narrative of the route of the exodus. Even so, the report serves the double function of fulfilling the expectation raised by Gen 50:25 and of asserting yet again that Elohim has made possible the exodus of Israel.

20–22 Succoth (see *Comment* on 12:37) and Etham (Cazelles, *RB* 62 [1955] 354–60) remain uncertainties, in spite of continuing attempts at location. That they were "on the outskirts of the wilderness" implies, at least, the east-southeasterly direction of v 18. The Israelites were headed out of Egypt by as direct as possible a route which would not offer an armed resistance. They were guided in this choice by Yahweh's own Presence, symbolized by the theophanic fire (Kuntz, *Self-Revelation of God*, 96–100; Terrien, *Elusive Presence*, 109–12, 149–51), seen as a column of cloud in daylight and as a column of fire at night. What Moses had experienced at the thornbush aflame but unconsumed (3:2–3) Israel now experienced in exodus. Both experiences stand as an augury of what is to come in the great theophany of Exod 19–20. The assertion that Yahweh did not remove these symbols of his guiding Presence is an indication of his continuing nearness to Israel from the time of the mighty acts to the rebellion of the golden calf. This motif of Yahweh's guiding Presence in the wilderness is, like the notice about Joseph's bones, an interruption of the narrative account of the route of the exodus. Unlike that interruption, however, this one is essential to the narrative: Israel cannot head into the dangerous expanse of the wilderness, as Yahweh is directing, without Yahweh's guidance.

14:1–2 This reference to the special guidance of Yahweh is followed immediately in the present composite by an account of a further and still more eccentric change of route by Yahweh. Moses is instructed to have Israel turn yet again, apparently back toward Egyptian territory, and to pitch camp for the third time since their departure (Succoth, 12:37, 39; Etham, 13:20), at a site in front of Pi-hahiroth and Baal *Zephon*, between Migdol and "the sea." Indeed, their camp is to be "on the edge of the sea." The purpose of so precise a location, one that provides no less than *four* points of reference, not only suggests a historical base for the exodus route described in this narrative, but also implies that the directions so specified are important for an understanding of the narrative. Once again, our vision of the picture set forth with such precision is clouded by an inability to identify with any assurance the places listed. Noth's argument (*Festschrift Otto Eissfeldt*, 181–90) that the information of these verses is too late to be of any value is not convincing, since P could have had little reason to invent what is apparently a meandering route.

Our difficulty lies not in the uncertainty of the names, but in our uncertainty about the locations to which they refer. Cazelles (*RB* 62 [1955] 350–52) wonders whether "Pi-hahiroth" should be understood as the "mouth (?) of Hirôt," as a river or a canal. "Migdol" as a name for more than one Egyptian fortified town is attested in Egyptian sources (Gardiner, *JEA* 6 [1920] 103–6). "Baal Zephon," generally located in the vicinity of Lake Sirbonis (though see Albright, *Festschrift A. Bertholet*, 1–14, for a different view), is described by Eissfeldt (*Baal Zaphon*, 48–71) and Herrmann (*Israel in Egypt*, 59–63) chiefly on the basis of classical texts as an ideal spot for the events of Exod 14.

Yet all of this information, interesting though it is, gives us no more specific a location than Exodus does.

3 The best clue we have to the route of Israel's exodus from Egypt has to do finally not with its location, but with its purpose. The route from the Egyptian Delta to the border of the wilderness was plain enough to the editor who brought together Exod 13:17–18, 20–22; and 14:1–2. That editor included precise details of location because they made his point more clearly, just as the redactor who set the superscription to the Book of Amos intended to fix the date of his collection by reference to a memorable earthquake *we* can no longer remember. But the compiler of this pericope has made even plainer the purpose that his geographical information, lost on us, was intended to illustrate. Yahweh guided his people away from the shortest and most logical route and into an eccentric series of turns designed to depict confusion, first of all because of an intention to trick and then to defeat Pharaoh, and second, because he was not ready in any case to take his people on to the land he had promised them.

4 This purpose, and indeed the entire route-of-exodus composite, is thus handily summed up by ידע כי אני יהוה "know that I am Yahweh." Yahweh's intention in the meandering route of Israel is to "win glory," literally, "be made an honored one" by Pharaoh's defeat, so that the Egyptians will know at first hand that Yahweh is indeed what and who he has claimed to be.

Explanation

The first section of the second major division of Exodus thus functions as a kind of précis to the division as a whole. Everything that occurs in Exod 13:17–18:27 wins Yahweh glory in one way or another: the victory at the sea most of all, of course; but also the provision for Israel in the wilderness; the defeat of Israel's enemies, the Amalekites; and the guidance toward Sinai and into a divinely founded system of principles for life in covenant together with Yahweh.

The fundamental point of this section is that Yahweh guides Israel in exodus. His guidance is plain and continual. He sets a puzzling route no man would have thought of, to confuse Pharaoh by an appearance of confusion and to win further and final glory for himself at Pharaoh's expense. Once more, Pharaoh and his Egyptians are to become a medium for a theological message. Yahweh's guidance must be seen not primarily as guidance *from* something, but instead as guidance *toward* something. In this section, it is guidance not toward Sinai or any other place of desert rendezvous but toward a final great moment of victory over Pharaoh, toward the greatest of all the self-proving mighty acts. In the sections following that great victory, it is guidance toward the place of Yahweh's great giving of himself to all of Israel.

Yahweh's first intention was to give the appearance that Israel, fearful of the main road, then fearful of the wilderness, was starting first one way and then another, not knowing where to turn and so a ready prey for recapture or destruction. Yahweh's second intention was to lure the Egyptians into a trap, first by making Pharaoh's mind obstinate once again, and then by defeating Pharaoh and his forces, who were certain to come down in vengeance upon an apparently helpless and muddled Israel.

The Pursuit of Pharaoh   (14:5–20)

Bibliography

Ap-Thomas, D. R. "All the King's Horses?" *Proclamation and Presence.* Ed. J. I Durham and J. R. Porter. New corr. ed. Macon, GA: Mercer University Press, 1983. 135–51. **Coats, G. W.** *Rebellion in the Wilderness.* Nashville: Abingdon Press, 1968. **DeVries, S. J.** "The Origin of the Murmuring Tradition." *JBL* 87 (1968) 51–58. **Speiser, E. A.** "An Angelic 'Curse': Exodus 14:20." *Oriental and Biblical Studies.* Ed. J. J. Finkelstein and M. Greenberg. Philadelphia: University of Pennsylvania Press, 1967. 108–12. Also *JAOS* 80 (1960) 198–200. **Yadin, Y.** *The Art of Warfare in Biblical Lands.* New York: McGraw-Hill, 1963.

Translation

[5] *Now when it was reported to the king of Egypt that the people had fled, Pharaoh and the members of his court had a change of heart toward the people, and they said, "What is this we have done, that we have sent [a] Israel forth from enslavement to us?"* [6] *Then he hooked up his chariot and arrayed his forces [a] with him:* [7] *he took six hundred crack [a] chariots, then all the Egyptian chariots, each one with its own commander.*

[8] *Thus Yahweh made obstinate the mind of Pharaoh, king of Egypt, so that he chased after the sons of Israel; but the sons of Israel went out disregarding Pharaoh's attitude. [a]* [9] *The Egyptians chased after them, then caught up with them settled for the night [a] by the sea—all the horses and chariotry [b] of Pharaoh, his riders, [c] his infantry, [d] by Pi-hahiroth, [e] in front of Baal Zephon.*

[10] *As Pharaoh made his approach, [a] the sons of Israel looked up, [b] and there were [c] the Egyptians, bearing down upon them! [d] They were scared witless, [e] and they cried out, the sons of Israel, to Yahweh.* [11] *They said to Moses, "Is there some shortage of graves in Egypt that you have carried us away to die in the wilderness? What is this you have done to us in bringing us forth from Egypt?* [12] *Is this pursuit [a] not the very thing we spoke to you about in Egypt, when we said, 'Stop bothering us, and let us slave for the Egyptians, for it is better for us to be slaves to the Egyptians than for us to die in the wilderness!'"*

[13] *But Moses replied to the people, "Don't be afraid—stand your ground, and see Yahweh's salvation, that he will do for you this day: as for the Egyptians whom you see here now, [a] you will not see them again, not ever.* [14] *Yahweh will do battle on your behalf; you need only to keep quiet."*

[15] *Then Yahweh [a] said to Moses, "What are you crying out to me for? Speak to the sons of Israel, that they should get on with their journey.* [16] *You raise up your staff, and thrust out your hand over the sea and cleave it apart, that the sons of Israel may come through the middle of the sea on dry ground.* [17] *As for me, just watch me [a] making the Egyptians' minds obstinate, so that they will come after them, enabling me to win myself glory [b] over Pharaoh and over all his infantry, over his chariotry and over his riders.* [18] *Thus the Egyptians [a] will know by experience that I am Yahweh, in my winning glory for myself over Pharaoh and over his chariotry and over his riders."*

[19] *Next, the attendant [a] of God set out, the one who goes in front of the company [b]*

of Israel; this time, [c] *he went* behind *them, and the pillar of cloud set out from in front of them to stand in readiness* [d] *behind them.* [20] *Indeed, it came between the company of the Egyptians and the company of Israel: there was the cloud and the darkness—there was no other light in the night.* [a] *So neither force* [b] *drew near to the other, the whole night through.*

Notes

5.a. LXX adds τοὺς υἱοὺς "the sons of."

6.a. עמו לקח "his people he took"; on עם "people" as a fighting force or band, see BDB, 766.

7.a. Qal pass ptcp of בחר "choose," select."

8.a. ביד רמה "with a high hand"; cf. Num 15:30; 33:3.

9.a. חנה "encamp, settle at"; "for the night" is added in this context.

9.b. רכב "chariot": see BDB, 939, and cf. v 23. *BHS* notes that the text here may be corrupt on the basis of the reading of v 23.

9.c. See Ap-Thomas (*Proclamation and Presence,* 135–51) for an extensive review of פרש "rider," and the proposal that the original and specific meaning of the word is "mare."

9.d. חיל "army, strength, force" can hardly mean anything else in this context.

9.e. See n. 14:2.a.

10.a. Hiph of קרב "draw near": see BDB, 898.

10.b. SamPent adds ויראו "and they saw."

10.c. והנה "and behold."

10.d. נסע "pull up, set out on a journey, march (BDB, 652) after them." LXX, Syr, Tg Onk, Tg Ps-J have a pl ptcp. Vg omits the word altogether.

10.e. "They were very frightened," וייראו מאד.

12.a. Since the imminent arrival of Pharaoh and his force is the clear cause of the Israelites' distress, "pursuit" is added above for clarity.

13.a. היום "this day," again.

15.a. Syr begins this verse with "Then Moses cried out to Yahweh," thus resolving the *non sequitur* of the verse as it stands in MT. Such an insertion, however, may not be necessary. See *Comment* below.

17.a. Lit., "And I, behold me making obstinate. . . ."

17.b. Lit., "And I will win myself glory."

18.a. LXX and SamPent read "all the Egyptians" (πάντες οἱ Αἰγύπτιοι, כל מצרים).

19.a. מלאך "messenger, minister," from לאך. The usual "angel" is a somewhat misleading translation, because of the context surrounding it after centuries of Christian art.

19.b. מחנה "company" could also suggest "encampment" in this sequence.

19.c. Special *waw.*

19.d. עמד "stand," see BDB, 763–65.

20.a. MT has ויהי הענן והחשך ויאר את־הלילה "and there was the cloud and the darkness, and it illumined the night." I have attempted to take the text as it stands—the only light the night had was the opaque light of the cloud, the guide not for the night but for the day. LXX has a different reading, καὶ ἐγένετο σκότος καὶ γνόφος καὶ διῆλθεν ἡ νύξ "and there was gloom and darkness, and the night passed." Cassuto (167) understands the reference to light as indicating that the pillar of fire was on the Israelites' side of the cloud and the darkness, a speculation with no support in the text. JPS emends the verb to ארר "cast a spell," and reads "the cloud with the darkness . . . cast a spell upon the night. . . ." So also Speiser, *Oriental and Biblical Studies* 108–12. See further in *Comment* below.

20.b. Lit., זה אל־זה "this one to that one."

Form/Structure/Setting

That this section dealing with Pharaoh's pursuit of Israel is a composite of narrative drawn from at least two sources has been generally argued for many years. Most literary critics, indeed, have found three sources here. The major point of disagreement has been the identification of the sources. A minor point of difference has been the allocation of the various strata in the composite to the sources identified within it. Some scholars (so Beer, 76–77, and Noth, 104–6, 111–20) believe that J, E, and P are each represented. Others (so Fohrer, *Überlieferung*, 98–109) would eliminate P in favor of other possibilities (Fohrer: N), and there is disagreement about just what, if anything, is to be assigned to E. Few sections in Exodus have been divided into as many fragments as this one (cf. Beer, 12, and the detailed and conflicting summaries of Noth, 104–6, and Childs, 218–21).

Upon careful analysis, some of the reasons for this fragmentation, turning upon *non sequitur,* vocabulary, and the appearance of motifs held to be characteristic, begin to look not only very subjective, but also somewhat arbitrary. This, indeed, accounts for the considerable differences in source analysis from critic to critic. The evidence for any precise analysis is too ambiguous. The most we can say with any assurance is that the section is a composite, one of the more carefully molded composites in Exodus, and that an exact division of this material into its constituent layers is impossible, given only the information we have in the OT. Too much of the source criticism of such composites is done by a search for differences, some real, some imagined. Not enough attention is given to the thematic unity that brings the undoubted literary diversity together.

Exod 14:5–20 is bound together by the theme, Pharaoh's pursuit of Israel. This pursuit is represented primarily as set up by Yahweh, just as the resistance of Pharaoh to the persuasion of the mighty acts is set up by Yahweh. Indeed the pursuit by Pharaoh is as much a part of Yahweh's plan as were those mighty acts and the proof-of-Presence lesson taught by them. The route of Israel in exodus is determined by this plan, as is Pharaoh's otherwise inexplicable change of heart and his pursuit, so totally unexpected by the people of Israel. Israel's alarm and anxious protest set up an occasion for the obviously didactic interpretation of what is about to follow—the final and greatest of all the lessons to be taught Israel at the Egyptians' expense.

Within the composite, three major and related subjects are presented: (1) the change of mind by Pharaoh, accounted for by Yahweh's injection of a further dose of obstinacy, and the ensuing pursuit of Israel (vv 5–9); (2) Israel's alarmed protest at such an unimagined and frightening turn of events, and the assurances of both Yahweh and Moses that all will be well (vv 10–18); and (3) the interposition of Yahweh's guarding protection for his people (vv 19–20). Though any precise division of these three subsections into the sources from which they are drawn is not possible, this general guide may be suggested: vv 5–7 are from JE; vv 8–9, P; vv 10–14, JE; vv 15–18, P; and vv 19–20, JE. A more exact division is not possible, and even this general allocation must be kept secondary to the more important composite impression of the text in its final form.

Comment

5–9   The assumption that a narrative of a secret flight from Egypt is reflected in the reference to the report to Pharaoh of Israel's exodus and his "change of heart" is without any foundation in the text. The reaction of Pharaoh and the members of his cabinet to the result of what they have permitted in the panic of catastrophe is entirely logical. Fear and the shock of grief are now replaced by practical considerations. An important source of cheap labor is rapidly getting beyond reach. Perhaps even anger is implicit in the response of Pharaoh and his court to a flight that cannot be any surprise to them. Knowing something will come and actually experiencing it are quite different to us, and this important difference is skillfully represented by this narrative. That such is the case in this sequence is made clear by the interpretation presented in the report of Yahweh's part in Pharaoh's change of heart. Once again, Yahweh turns Pharaoh's mind towards obstinacy. The Israelites, by contrast, are leaving the land with no regard for what is going on in Pharaoh's mind. Their departure "with a high hand" is not to be considered an act of defiance (so Knight, 101), but an act of assurance. As vv 10–12 show, the Israelites thought themselves beyond Pharaoh's interest and reach.

His mind changed by Yahweh, however, Pharaoh plunges into a headlong pursuit of the people he had not only released but had driven out. He harnesses his own chariot, and takes "his people with him." V 7 makes plain that the "people" he took were his fighting force; that verse is not a doublet, as some critics have maintained; it is rather a description of the organization of the pursuit force. Pharaoh surrounded himself with his "select" or "crack" charioteers, those who could be counted on to hold formation and obey orders (cf. Yadin's account of the battle of Kadesh on the Orontes, *Art of Warfare*, 103–10). This vanguard force was then supported by a larger random force, each chariot of which was manned by three charioteers, one of whom was שָׁלִישׁ "commander" whose title is derived from the word for "three, third." This arrangement is amply depicted in Egyptian wall paintings and reliefs from the period of the exodus (Yadin, 86–90, 104–5, 239). The implication is that the select chariots were under a direct chain of command from Pharaoh and that the larger chariot force operated independently, each unit under its own commander. These details about the size and efficient organization of Pharaoh's force are a further means of adding both to the despair of Israel's virtually defenseless plight and also to the luster of the victory Yahweh is to win for them. They are details reinforced by the report that the Egyptians located exactly the Israelite encampment (note 14:2, 9), and by the addition to the description of Pharaoh's force of both riders and foot-soldiers.

10–12 The reaction of Israel to the appearance of so formidable a force is understandable in view of their apparent assumption that they were rid of Pharaoh (v 8) and the entirely reasonable judgment that they have no chance of defending themselves (vv 11–12) against such a massive onslaught. They are frightened into a panic, and they cry out to Yahweh and protest to Moses. What they said to Yahweh (as also what Moses said to Yahweh, v 15) is not recorded, but their protest to Moses is both poignant and humorous, and an anticipation of the murmuring and rebellion motif to come in the narratives of the wilderness journeys, in both Exodus and Numbers (cf. Coats, *Rebellion*, 21–43; De Vries, *JBL* 87 [1968] 51–58). The reference by the protesting Israelites to their fear of such a pursuit and of death in the wilderness when Moses arrived in Egypt with a proposal of exodus is only generally reflected, if indeed it is reflected at all, in Exod 5:20–21. It is, however, a logical reply to such a proposal, before the sequence of the mighty acts of Yahweh in Egypt. Following that sequence, and after the exodus itself has been under way for three days, the sudden appearance of Pharaoh and his force is as surprising as it is appalling, and the three questions fired at Moses are a graphic representation of the Israelites' panic and distress.

13–14 Moses' reply to the complaint of Israel is unruffled. He ignores their sarcastic attack on his leadership and their justification of themselves by blaming him. He commands them to set aside the fear demoralizing them, to stand firm where they are, and to witness Yahweh's imminent salvation. They have seen the Egyptians pursuing and feared greatly: they are now to see Yahweh's deliverance and believe with an equal intensity. This contrast is deftly made by the declaration that the Egyptians whom they see, and who are the cause of their great fear, they will soon "add to seeing" no more, forever—an ominous anticipation of the medium of the victory to come. Seeing, then not seeing; not seeing, then seeing are to be, furthermore, the extent of their activity. Yahweh is going to do their fighting (an anticipation of Exod 15:3). In addition to watching, they have only to keep quiet. The victory will be gained wholly by Yahweh, for the reason that is stated explicitly in v 18. Israel's quietude suggests not only nonintervention but also the sanctity of Yahweh-war as a religious and confessional event.

15 Yahweh's inquiry to Moses is a *non sequitur* to the narrative preceding it, as no cry of Moses to Yahweh has been reported in MT. The inclusion by Syr of the report that such a cry was made is probably an attempt to resolve this problem, but since the cry itself is not recorded, the attempt is not convincing. We may imagine a protest of Moses to Yahweh following the people's attack on him (vv 11–12), but such a protest would need logically to fall before Moses' reply in vv 13–14, and that in turn would create difficulty with the sequence of vv 15–18. The inquiry of v 15 is best left in its present location and assumed to be a response to a complaint of Moses that is now lost. What follows the inquiry, Yahweh's instruction to Moses, and through Moses, to Israel, fits the sequence perfectly.

16–18 Israel, then, is to continue the exodus. To make that possible, Moses is to raise his staff and thrust out his hand over the sea, which will then split apart, enabling Israel to cross the sea on יבשה "dry ground" or "solid ground" (cf. Jonah 1:13; 2:11; where the term means "shore," as opposed to "sea"). Yahweh, then, will make all the pursuing Egyptians as obstinate as he has made their Pharaoh, so that they will continue their pursuit. Next, he will "win glory," "honor," even "reputation" for himself by the defeat of Pharaoh and his entire force. The purpose of this victory is Yahweh's proof-of-his-Presence, and so the defeat of the Egyptians at the sea is consonant in intention with their defeat in Egypt. The route of Israel and the minds of Pharaoh and his force will have been guided toward such an end.

19–20 The location of Israel (v 2) and of Egypt (v 9) in approximately the same place at the same time, presumably when darkness is hampering the movement of both, poses the need of a separation of some sort. This separation is provided by God's guiding messenger, מלאך האלהים "attendant of God," who moves from a position before the people to one behind them, and by the guiding pillar of cloud, the symbol by day (Exod 13:21–22) of Yahweh's leadership, which also takes up a place between Israel and the Egyptians. This מלאך "attendant" has not before been mentioned in the narrative of Exodus (though cf. 32:34); מלאך האלהים has generally been thought to be E's term for the symbol of God's guidance of Israel.

The pillar of cloud, however, is the symbol of Yahweh's guidance of Israel not by night but by day. Here, that same pillar of cloud, in the company of God's attendant (מלאך), is moved in the nighttime to a position behind Israel. To what end? The answer to this inquiry is given by the assertion of v 20. The pillar of cloud came between the company of Israel and that of the Egyptians to obscure their view of, and therefore their access to, each other. "There was the cloud and the darkness"; the pillar of fire, which normally provided light at night, was absent. The pillar of cloud, which only added to the obscurity of the darkness, "was the light" for that night. The statement is a deliberate contrast: the day's guide takes the place of the night's light. In this composite, the מלאך stands guard, and the guiding cloud for the day becomes a blocking cloud in the night. The closing statement of v 20 affirms such a reading: through the entire night, neither side came near to the other.

Explanation

Just as Israel is guided in an eccentric route to a place precisely located, so also are Pharaoh and his magnificently disciplined fighting force guided to the very same place. Yahweh directed Israel to the edge of the sea, and he made obstinate the mind of Pharaoh so that he would pursue Israel there. As Yahweh made provision for Israel to cross the sea blocking the way of exodus, so also he made obstinate the minds of Pharaoh's force, so that they would attempt the otherwise unthinkable maneuver of pursuing a company on foot through the middle of a sea, however strangely it may have opened itself. In a final testimony of Yahweh's orchestration of the entire affair, the two forces are miraculously partitioned off from one another, until Yahweh is ready to fight Israel's fight in the place of his choosing, on his schedule, in the open light of day where the defeat and its making can clearly be seen by all.

The point of the pursuit by Pharaoh is the further and final mighty act of Yahweh for Israel and against their Egyptian oppressors. This composite presents that point by the dramatic arrangement of three scenes: Pharaoh's change of mind and his powerful pursuit; Israel's frightened reaction and Yahweh's response; and the postponement through the night of the moment of deliverance by miraculous means.

Not only is Israel thus prepared for deliverance to come at the sea; by such a testimony, the Israel of the generations to come is also prepared for an array of deliverances from an array of oppressors.

Yahweh's Deliverance at the Sea (14:21–31)

Bibliography

Eakin, F. E., Jr. "The Reed Sea and Baalism." *JBL* 86 (1967) 378–84. **Gross, H.** "Der Glaube an Mose nach Exodus (4.14.19)." *Wort-Gebot-Glaube.* Ed. J. J. Stamm, E. Jenni, H. J. Stoebe. Zürich: Zwingli Verlag, 1970. 57–65. **Hay, L. S.** "What Really Happened at the Sea of Reeds?" *JBL* 83 (1964) 397–403. **Kuntz, J. K.** *The Self-Revelation of God.* Philadelphia: Westminster Press, 1967. **Mann, T. W.** *Divine Presence and Guidance in Israelite Traditions: The Typology of Exaltation.* Baltimore: Johns Hopkins University Press, 1977. **Muilenburg, J.** *The Way of Israel.* London: Routledge & Kegan Paul, 1962. **Robinson, T. H.** "Der Durchzug durch das Rote Meer." *ZAW* 51 (1933) 170–73.

Translation

²¹ *When Moses stretched forth his hand over the sea, Yahweh manipulated* ᵃ *the sea with a gale* ᵇ *from the east all through the night, so that he changed* ᶜ *the sea into solid ground: the waters were cleaved apart.* ²² *The sons of Israel then went through the middle of the sea on dry ground—the waters were to them as a wall to their right and to their left.* ²³ *The Egyptians pursued, going after them, all the horses of Pharaoh, his chariotry, and his riders, right into the middle of the sea.* ²⁴ *So it was, when daylight came,* ᵃ *that Yahweh looked down towards* ᵇ *the Egyptian force from* ᶜ *a pillar of fire and cloud, and he threw the Egyptian force into complete disarray.* ᵈ ²⁵ *He misguided* ᵃ *their chariots' wheels, so that they were very difficult to drive. Thus the Egyptians said, "Let us take flight from the presence of Israel, because Yahweh is fighting for them against Egypt."* ᵇ

²⁶ *Next, Yahweh said to Moses, "Stretch forth your hand over the sea, then the waters will rush back* ᵃ *upon the Egyptians, upon their chariotry, upon their riders."* ²⁷ *Moses once again* ᵃ *stretched forth his hand over the sea, and the sea rushed back, as morning brightened,* ᵇ *to its proper place.* ᶜ *The Egyptians, taking flight,* ᵈ *met it head-on. Thus Yahweh scattered* ᵉ *the Egyptians in the middle of the sea.* ²⁸ *As the waters rushed back, they covered the chariotry and the riders belonging to the entire force of Pharaoh that had gone after Israel* ᵃ *into the sea. Not even one of them was left.* ²⁹ *The sons of Israel, by contrast, walked on dry ground through the middle of the sea; the waters to them were as a wall to their right and to their left.* ᵃ

³⁰ *Thus did Yahweh rescue Israel that day from the power* ᵃ *of the Egyptians. Israel saw the Egyptians dead upon the edge of the sea,* ³¹ *and Israel saw the great power that Yahweh unleashed* ᵃ *against the Egyptians. So the people were in awe of Yahweh—and in consequence, they put their trust in Yahweh* ᵇ *and in Moses, his servant.*

Notes

21.a. Hiph impf הלך "cause to go, lead, guide, channel."

21.b. ברוח קדים עזה "by a strong east wind."

21.c. The verb is שׂום "put, set, establish, appoint."

24.a. באשמרת הבקר "in the morning watch," here taken as the period when the morning became light enough for Israel and the Egyptians to see.

24.b. SamPent and LXX have "upon" (על, ἐπί).

24.c. The prep is ב "in." Cassuto (169) translates it "through." Other translators move the phrase back in the sentence to Yahweh (so RSV). The syntax of MT is better left as it is, however, and "a pillar of fire and cloud" taken here as elsewhere as a theophanic symbol of Yahweh's guiding and protecting Presence.

24.d. המם "make a noise, cause confusion, disturb, discomfit noisily": cf. BDB, 243. There is implicit in this verb a confusion aided by distracting noise.

25.a. סור "turn aside, push from the way, path." See BDB, 693–94. LXX has συνέδησεν, a reading paralleled by Syr and SamPent אסר and meaning "bind, imprison, bog down."

25.b. L has no *soph pasuq* at the end of v 25, but as there is a פ before v 26 and as other texts have *soph pasuq*, its absence is best regarded an error.

26.a. The verb is שוב "turn back, return," translated "rush back" in this context; cf. BDB, 996–1000.

27.a. Special *waw* in this context.

27.b. לפנות בקר the "turning, approach, arrival, facing of morning"; cf. BDB, 815.

27.c. לאיתנו "to its steady flow, its permanent, usual place." BDB, 450–51.

27.d. Instead of נוס "take flight," SamPent has נסע "moving forward."

27.e. נער "shake, shake loose, off." BDB (654) cites the usage in Ps 109:23 as "sim. of perishing helplessly."

28.a. MT has "them," but the antecedent is clearly Israel, thus the reading above.

29.a. See n. 25.b. above; there is a similar omission here.

30.a. יד lit., "hand," also means "strength, power," even "possession"; cf. BDB, 388–91. The use of this noun in reference to the Egyptians here and to Yahweh in the next verse provides a neat rhetorical contrast.

31.a. עשה, lit., "made, did, performed."

31.b. LXX reads τῷ Θεῷ "in God."

Form/Structure/Setting

The narrative account of Yahweh's deliverance of Israel at the sea is, like the preparatory accounts preceding it in 13:17–14:4 and 14:5–20, a composite. That such is the case, given the pivotal importance of the deliverance at the sea, is not surprising. That the narrative is not more complex than it is, and that it appears to contain material for the most part from only two sources *is* surprising, for the same reason. Though fragments of this pericope have sometimes been assigned to E (so Noth, 117; Childs, 220, v 25a), for the most part this section is given to J and to P (see *contra*, Beer, 12, 76–78), with P dominating in a fairly close interweaving of the two sources.

The governing factor in this sequence is of course Yahweh's rescue, which comes in two parts. The first of these is the entrapment of the Egyptian force in the midst of a miraculously divided sea into which the Egyptians are lured by a fleeing Israel and driven (14:8, 17) by Yahweh. The second is the overwhelming of that same force by the sea rushing back to its customary place. Both these miraculous manipulations of the waters of the sea are effected by Yahweh following a signal Moses has been instructed to give. There is a dramatic build-up of the peril of Israel and the loss of the Egyptians through repeated reference to the units and the extent of the Egyptian force (vv 23, 25, 26, 28), and the play on what Israel is to see and not to see (14:13) is echoed in vv 30–31.

As always, the composite as a whole must be considered of greater importance for an understanding of the meaning of the text than the separate strata that make it up. Despite a seam here and there, the impression left by this section is single: Yahweh, proving his Presence still, rescues his people and decimates a powerful and well-organized Egyptian force with no exertion of effort by Israel.

Comment

21–22 Moses' first act of stretching out his hand over the sea is the execution of the command of Yahweh reported in 14:16. As the text makes plain,
however, it is Yahweh, not Moses, who works the wonder. Calling up a strong
wind (see above, n. 10:13.c and *Comment*), Yahweh cleaves apart the waters
of the sea into two parts, leaving "solid ground" where water had been.
This wind blew all through the night, and when there was sufficient light to
make movement possible (cf. 14:9, 16, 20), Israel continued the journey of
exodus by way of this opening through a barrier that had appeared impassable
(14:1–4, 9–12).

23 The Egyptians, their judgment blunted by Yahweh's infliction upon
them of a further wave of obstinacy (14:17–18), follow headlong with all
their armament into this most unlikely place. The clear impression in the
contrast between a large and disciplined strike force strategically arrayed
and a path strangely opened into ground always covered before with seawater
is that the Egyptians are acting without reason. So, of course, they are, by
divine cause, and the effect of their madness is heightened by the repetition
of their ranks: Pharaoh, horses, chariots, riders—they all went.

24–25 No sooner are they in the trap than Yahweh moves to keep them
there, confusing them and causing the wheels of their chariots to go awry.
Just how this confusion and misguiding was brought about, the text does
not suggest. The arguments that the reference to "a pillar of fire and cloud"
suggests a fearsome thunderstorm (Cassuto, 169–70), a volcanic eruption
(cf. Robinson, *ZAW* 51 [1933] 171–72), a theophany (Hyatt, 154) or even
Sinai traditions (Kuntz, *Self-Revelation*, 82–85, 185–87) are unconvincing. Also
wide of the mark is the theory of Hay (*JBL* 83 [1964] 397–403) that the
account of Yahweh's defeat of the Egyptians is a "fanciful" and "augmented"
version of an "extraordinary" victory achieved by a clever choice of terrain
and a strategic deployment of sure-shot Hebrew archers. The "pillar of fire
and cloud" in these verses, as elsewhere in Exodus, are symbolic of Yahweh's
Presence, and the narrative composite leaves not the smallest doubt about
Yahweh's achievement of the victory over Pharaoh and his forces. The answer
to the question "What Really Happened at the Sea of Reeds?" (Hay, *JBL*
83 [1964] 397) is even less recoverable than the location of the Sea, and in
any case only marginally relevant to the theological point of these verses, a
point made repeatedly, throughout Exod 13:17–15:21: this event is set up,
managed, and brought to its dramatic conclusion by Yahweh, to an end clearly
stated four times (14:4, 13–14, 17–18, 30–31) in this chapter alone. Even
the Egyptians are reported to have taken the point (v 25).

26–28 Yahweh's further instruction to Moses seals the fate of the entrapped Egyptians. The waters diverted from their normal place are loosed
to return to their usual channels. Too late, the Egyptians, stopped in their
headlong pursuit, come to their senses and attempt to fall back. They meet
(קראת) the sea, rushing to return to its proper place, and are overwhelmed,
to a man. So Yahweh scattered (נער) the force so awesome in its ordered
pursuit, buffeting them about in a fool's trap in the midst of the sea, where
no rational force would have ventured.

29 Yet the route so fatal to the Egyptians was a route of deliverance for Israel. They walked as on dry ground, with the waters standing aside for them, a wall to their right and a wall to their left. This language is not conducive to the attempts at naturalistic accounting often pressed upon these verses (cf. *JBL* Hay 83 [1964] 397–98; Eakin, *JBL* 86 [1967] 380–81; the review of de Vaux, *Early History*, 382–83). It is the language, rather, of confession. This victory, like the victories in Egypt, is declared to be Yahweh's victory, Yahweh's alone. What we may make of that is our problem. The compositor who set these lines together was speaking from faith and attempting both to address faith and to stimulate faith (cf. Muilenburg, *Way of Israel*, 48–54). Every tradition employed and virtually every word used are to that end.

30–31 The entire narrative of Exod 13:17–14:29 is thus summarized by the two final verses of Exod 14: *Yahweh* rescued Israel that day from the power of the Egyptians. The manner of his doing it is incidental to the fact that *Yahweh* is the one who made the rescue. Not tides, not storms, not bad planning, not tactical error, not bad luck, or good luck, but *Yahweh*. This repeated declaration of the narrative is made still again in this resounding summary. *Yahweh* did it, and what is more, Israel *saw* (ראה) him do it. They *saw* the bodies of the Egyptians, washed up onto the edge of the sea. They *saw* Yahweh's great power (היד הגדלה) performed against the Egyptian force. And the inevitable result of it all was reverential awe—of Yahweh, and even of his servant Moses.

On this latter point—the presentation of Moses as Yahweh's servant to be trusted—H. Gross (*Wort-Gebot-Glaube*, 57–65) has argued from the occurrences of the hiphil of אמן in Exod 4, 14, and 19 that a special "double-predication," "Servant-God," can be seen here, is reflected elsewhere in the OT (e.g., 2 Chr 20:20) and comes to full fruit in such NT texts as Heb 8:5, John 5:46 and Phil 2:6. While Gross may press his theme a bit far, there can be little doubt that the vindication of Moses as an authority is an important part of the message of this verse. It is, however, a secondary point, not only in importance, given the repeated references in this chapter to Yahweh as the prime mover in the victory at the sea and this single reference to Moses as a figure inspiring confidence, but also in terms of what T. W. Mann (*Divine Presence*, 130–39) has called "the exaltation theme." The exaltation of Moses here is entirely dependent upon the prior exaltation of Yahweh, who has called Moses and given him both authority and special powers. This is true, moreover, throughout Exodus. Indeed, as we shall see in the murmurings in the wilderness and especially in the rebellion of the golden calf, Israel's confidence in Moses dissipates along with their confidence in Yahweh. And whenever confidence in Moses increases, as here and at Sinai, it is because of an action of Yahweh.

Explanation

The point of this section, as also of the one following it, is the glorification of Yahweh for his deliverance of Israel from the final and most serious threat posed by Pharaoh and his people. This glorification is prepared for with a fugal layering, as the narratives of guidance and pursuit, protection and a double entrapment follow one another with a rising intensity. The exhilaration of exodus is followed by the terrible disappointment of freedom lost between the pursuing Egyptians and the impassable sea. Then, from a chaos of recrimination and the certainty of impending death, Yahweh snatches his people forth, turning the very means of *their* entrapment into the medium of the *Egyptians'* entrapment and death.

From the start of the exodus, it becomes clear, Yahweh has orchestrated the entire sequence. He has so guided Israel as to avoid the inevitable but certainly lesser resistance of the coastal road, all the while tempting the Egyptians by an erratic and apparently self-defeating route into a pursuit he both suggests to them and impels them to. When Israel then is presented with a terrifying prospect of conflict and defeat more terrible than anything they could have imagined in the fortified coastal road, and with an advancing force so awesome in array as to make undeniably plain the total hopelessness of any resistance on their part, Yahweh moves. First of all, he reassures and protects them. Second, he manipulates the waters that permit Israel's escape and become the means of the Egyptians' destruction. Then he forces the Egyptians into the trap—there can be no other explanation for their irrational behavior. And finally he scatters the Egyptians in the midst of the sea *they* thought had Israel entrapped, even as Israel crosses through the barrier dry-shod.

The whole affair is such an amazement to all—all, that is, save Yahweh who planned it, that the narrative account of it is ended with an awed assertion of what Israel *saw* that day (cf. Exod 19:4a) and a pointed announcement of their awed belief, in Yahweh first, then in Moses his servant. Events so unexpected, so impossible, left no other choice of interpretation. Yahweh had rescued his people, as he had promised. He must be praised.

The Victory Hymn of Moses and Miriam
(15:1-21)

Bibliography

Albright, W. F. *The Archaeology of Palestine.* London: Penguin Books, 1954. **Bauer, H.** "Die Gottheiten von Ras Schamra." *ZAW* 51 (1933) 81–101. **Bender, A.** "Das Lied Exodus 15." *ZAW* 23 (1903) 1–48. **Clements, R. E.** *God and Temple.* Philadelphia: Fortress Press, 1965. **Clifford, R. J.** *The Cosmic Mountain in Canaan and the Old Testament.* Cambridge: Harvard University Press, 1972. **Cross, F. M., Jr.** "The Song of the Sea and Canaanite Myth." *Canaanite Myth and Hebrew Epic.* Cambridge: Harvard University Press, 1973. 112–44. ——— and **D. N. Freedman.** "The Song of Miriam." *Studies in Ancient Yahwistic Poetry.* SBLDS 21. Missoula, MT: Scholars Press, 1975. 45–65. **Dhorme, E.** *L'emploi métaphorique des noms de parties du corps en hébreu et en akkadien.* Paris: Librairie Orientaliste Paul Geuthner, 1963. **Durham, J. I.** *The Senses Touch, Taste, and Smell in Old Testament Religion.* Unpublished thesis, University of Oxford, 1963. **Freedman, D. N.** "Early Israelite Poetry and Historical Considerations." *Pottery, Poetry, and Prophecy.* Winona Lake, IN: Eisenbrauns, 1980. 167–78. ———. "Strophe and

Meter in Exodus 15." *Pottery, Poetry, and Prophecy.* 187–227. ————. "The Song of the Sea." *Pottery, Poetry, and Prophecy.* 179–86. **Gaster, T. H.** "Notes on 'The Song of the Sea' (Exodus XV)." *ExpTim* 48 (1936–37) 45. **Good, E. M.** "Exodus XV 2." *VT* 20 (1970) 358–59. **Haupt, P.** "Moses' Song of Triumph." *AJSL* 20 (1904) 149–72. **Humbert, P.** " 'Qânâ' en Hébreu Biblique." *Festschrift Alfred Bertholet.* Tübingen: J. C. B. Mohr (Paul Siebeck), 1950. 259–66. **Irwin, W. A.** "Where Shall Wisdom Be Found?" *JBL* 80 (1961) 133–42. **Köhler, L.** "Kleinigkeiten." *ZAW* 52 (1934) 160. **Labuschagne, C. J.** *The Incomparability of Yahweh in the Old Testament.* Leiden: E. J. Brill, 1966. **Loewenstamm, S. E.** " 'The Lord Is My Strength and My Glory.' " *VT* 19 (1969) 464–70. **Lohfink, N.** "The Song of Victory at the Red Sea." *The Christian Meaning of the Old Testament.* Milwaukee: Bruce Publishing Company, 1968. 67–86. **Lys, D.** *Nèphèsh: histoire de l'âme dans la revelation d'Israël.* Paris: Presses Universitaires de France, 1959. **Mowinckel, S.** "Die vermeintliche 'Passahlegende' Ex. 1–15." *ST* 5 (1952) 66. ——————. "Drive and/or Ride in the O.T." *VT* 12 (1962) 278–99. ————. *Psalmenstudien II. Das Thronbesteigungsfest Jahwäs und der Ursprung der Eschatologie.* Amsterdam: Verlag P. Schippers, 1961. ————. *The Psalms in Israel's Worship.* Oxford: Basil Blackwell, 1962. **Muilenburg, J.** "A Liturgy on the Triumphs of Yahweh." *Studia Biblica et Semitica.* Wageningen: H. Veenman & Zonen, 1966. 233–51. **O'Connor, M.** *Hebrew Verse Structure.* Winona Lake, IN: Eisenbrauns, 1980. **Parker, S. B.** "Exodus XV 2 Again." *VT* 21 (1971) 373–79. **Pedersen, J.** *Israel: Its Life and Culture III–IV.* London: Geoffrey Cumberlege, Oxford University Press, 1959. ————. "Passahfest und Passahlegende." *ZAW* 52 (1934) 161–75. **Reymond, P.** *L'Eau, sa Vie, et sa Significa-tion dans L'Ancien Testament.* VTSup 6. Leiden: E. J. Brill, 1958. **Rozelaar, M.** "The Song of the Sea." *VT* 2 (1952) 221–28. **Schmidt, H.** "Das Meerlied. Ex. 15:2–19." *ZAW* 49 (1937) 59–66. **Sendrey, A.** *Music in Ancient Israel.* New York: Philosophical Library, 1969. **Stadelmann, L. I. J.** *The Hebrew Conception of the World.* AnBib 39. Rome: Biblical Institute Press, 1970. **Strauss, H.** "Das Meerlied des Mose—ein 'Sieges-lied' Israels?" *ZAW* 97 (1985) 103–9. **Talmon, S.** "A Case of Abbreviation Resulting in Double Readings." *VT* 4 (1954) 206–8. **Tromp, N. J.** *Primitive Conceptions of Death and the Nether World in the Old Testament.* Rome: Pontifical Biblical Institute, 1969. **Watts, J. D. W.** "The Song of the Sea—Ex. XV." *VT* 7 (1957) 371–80. **Wifall, W.** "The Sea of Reeds as Sheol." *ZAW* 92 (1980) 325–32.

Translation

[1] *At that time, Moses and the sons of Israel sang this song to Yahweh,* [a] *in these words:* [b]

> *"I will sing* [c] *to Yahweh,*
>   *for he has risen proudly:* [d]
> *horse and chariot* [e] *alike*
>   *he has cast into the sea!*
> [2] *My might and song of praise* [a] *is Yah:* [b]
>   *he is salvation for me.*
> *Such* [c] *is my God,*
>   *and I will compliment* [d] *him—*
> *the God of my fathers,*
>   *and I will raise him with praise!* [e]
> [3] *Yahweh is a warrior!* [a]
> *Yahweh is his name!*
> [4] *Pharaoh's chariots and his whole force*
>   *he threw* [a] *into the sea.*

The elite among his commanders ^b
   are sunk down in the 'sea of rushes.'
⁵*Ancient deeps*ᵃ *covered them over—*
   they went down into the depths like stone.
⁶*Your right hand, Yahweh—*
   magnificent in strength!
Your right hand, Yahweh—
   shattering the enemy!
⁷*And in the multiplication of your majesty*
   you throw down those who rise against you—
You send out your burning anger,
   it gobbles them up as a bundle of dry straw! ᵃ
⁸*And in the wind of your anger* ᵃ
   the waters were piled in a heap,
   the currents ᵇ *stood waiting* ᶜ *in a stack,* ᵈ
   the ancient deeps grew solid in the heart of the sea.
⁹*The enemy said,*
  'I will chase after,
   I will catch,
   I will share the plunder,
    my battle-lust ᵃ *will sate itself,*
   I will rid my sword of victims, ᵇ
    my power ᶜ *will possess them by force!'* ᵈ
¹⁰*You blew with your wind—*
   the sea covered them over!
   they sank like lead in the wide ᵃ *waters!*
¹¹*Who is like you among the gods, Yahweh?*
Who is like you,
   magnificent in holiness,
   awesome in praiseworthy deeds, ᵃ
   doing the extraordinary?
¹²*You thrust out your right hand,*
   the earth gulped them down.
¹³*You have guided in your love unchanging*
   this people you have redeemed as kinsmen. ᵃ
You have led ᵉ *them in your might*
   to the dwelling-place of your holiness.
¹⁴*The peoples have heard—they are worried.*
   Anguish has gripped those who live in Philistia.
   ¹⁵*Now the chieftains of Edom are terrified;*
   the leaders of Moab, trembling has gripped them;
   all who live in Canaan are faint with weakness.
¹⁶*Terror and dread have fallen over them—*
   against the greatness of your arm,
   they are struck dumb as stone.
Till your people pass by, Yahweh,
   till this people you have created ᵃ *pass by.*
¹⁷*You will bring them,*
   and you will establish them,
    on the mountain that belongs to you,
     the place fixed for your dwelling
      that you made, Yahweh—

> a holy sanctuary, [a] Lord, [b]
> your hands have made it firm. [c]
> [18] Yahweh reigns forever and without interruption." [a]

[19] When Pharaoh's horses along with his chariotry and his cavalry came into the sea, Yahweh turned back upon them the waters of the sea, while the sons of Israel walked on dry land through the middle of the sea. [20] Then Miriam ("Fat One" or "Loved One" [a]) the prophetess, Aaron's sister, took up in her hand the hand-drum, [b] and all the women went along after her, with hand-drums and dancing. [21] Thus did Miriam sing [a] to them:

> "Sing to Yahweh,
> for he has risen proudly:
> horse and chariot alike
> he has cast into the sea!"

Notes

1.a. LXX has τῷ Θεῷ "to God."

1.b. ויאמרו לאמר "and they said to say."

1.c. Cohortative form, showing determination.

1.d. גאה גאה "he has risen risingly," that is "proudly"; Yahweh has risen to the occasion, vindicating himself and bringing honor to himself by his victory. SamPent reads instead גוי גאה "a people has risen."

1.e. סוס ורכבו "horse and his chariot"; "rider" here would be an anachronism, according to Mowinckel (VT 12 [1962] 278–89).

2.a. זמרת is a song in praise of God; זמר refers to the creation of music in worshipful praise. See BDB, 274; Loewenstamm, VT 19 (1969) 464–68. SamPent and Vg have "my song of praise"; LXX reads σκεπαστής "covering, protection."

2.b. LXX omits "Yah."

2.c. זה "such"; cf. BDB, 260–62.

2.d. נוה is to "beautify, adorn," even "decorate with praise." Cf. BDB, 627. LXX and Vg have "I will glorify him" (δοξάσω αὐτόν, glorificabo eum).

2.e. Polel רום "lift up, exalt," in this context, by praising confession: BDB, 926–27.

3.a. SamPent גבור and Syr have "a mighty hero"; LXX has συντρίβων πολέμους "crushing wars" instead of "man of war."

4.a. ירה "throw, shoot"; cf. רמה "cast, shoot" in v 1.

4.b. These "select commanders" are the best of Pharaoh's officer corps. See Comment on 14:6–7.

5.a. תהמת "ancient deeps" suggests more than "waves" or "floods"; cf. Pss 77:17; 78:15; 106:9; 135:6; Isa 63:13. LXX has ἐκάλυψεν αὐτούς "he [i.e., Yahweh] covered them" with the ancient deeps.

7.a. קש from קשש "gather stubble" and perhaps even "be old, dried out": BDB 905.

8.a. אפיך lit. means "your nostrils." It is a derivative, however, of the verb אנף, used exclusively in the OT of the "snorting anger, violent rage" of God. אף refers to God's anger 177× in the OT, according to BDB (60). See further Durham, Touch, Taste and Smell, 298–307; Dhorme, L'emploi métaphorique, 80–83.

8.b. נזלים from נזל "flow, trickle, run, stream"; this pl ptcp suggests moving, flowing currents within the sea. Cf. BDB, 633.

8.c. נצב means "take a stand, a position, a station," even "stand at attention" for a specific purpose. Cf. BDB, 662.

8.d. כמו־נד "as a heap, rising hill": BDB, 622.

9.a. נפשי "my soul"; on נפש as the "seat of the appetites," see BDB, 660 § 5, and cf. also Lys, Nephesh, 149–50.

9.b. Lit., "I will make empty my sword." The sense is not "draw" by emptying the scabbard (so BDB, 938 § 3), but to clear the sword, by vigorous use, of enemies before it. Thus, giving the context of the usage here, "rid . . . victims." Cf. LXX ἀνελῶ "I will destroy."

9.c. See n. 14:30.a.

9.d. יָרַשׁ, BDB 439 § 1: *"take possession of,* esp. by force."

10.a. אַדִּירִים from אָדַר "wide, great, high, noble, magnificent, majestic"; see BDB, 12.

11.a. Cf. BDB, 239–40.

13.a. See n. 6:6.d.

16.a. On קָנָה as "create," as opposed to the more usual "acquire, purchase," see Humbert, *Festschrift A. Bertholet,* 259–66, and cf. Deut 32:6; Ps 139:13; Prov 8:22.

17.a. Syr reads "your holy sanctuary."

17.b. SamPent and Cairo Geniza read יְהוָה "Yahweh" instead of אֲדֹנָי "Lord" here.

17.c. Syr reads *tgnjhj bʾjdjk* "built by your hands."

18.a. וָעֶד "without interruption" stresses perpetuity, continuousness: BDB, 723.

20.a. See Ross ("Miriam," *IDB* 3:402), who proposes also "one who loves or is loved by Yahweh," and "the wished for child"; and cf. Bauer (*ZAW* 51 [1933] 87, n. 2) who argues for "Wunschkind" on the basis of a similar sounding Arabic word, *'marām.'*

20.b. The תֹף is a small hand-drum, and not a tambourine, which is a sort of hand-drum plus percussive metal discs. The latter instrument developed much beyond OT times. Cf. Sendrey, *Music,* 372–75.

21.a. עָנָה here could also indicate that Miriam "responded to" or "answered" the movement of the women to follow her with her invitation to them to sing.

Form/Structure/Setting

This magnificent poem has been much analyzed, dissected, scanned, and compared with an array of supposed precedent and counterpart works. It has been variously attributed and dated, and forced into a wide variety of forms and *Sitze im Leben.* There have been attempts to determine some parts of it as early and some parts as late, and to describe therefrom an evolution of both its form and its content. None of these attempts has been entirely successful. The best of them have amounted to no more than helpful suggestions, while the worst of them have been fiction bordering fantasy.

Four categories of questions are of primary importance: the form of the poem, the date of the poem, the *Sitz* of the poem, and the source (or sources) of the poem. Difficulties encountered in attempts to deal with these questions have sometimes posed a fifth direction of basic inquiry: is this a single poem, or two or three or even more poems?

The very range of suggestion about the form of this victory poem is an indication of its composite, eclectic nature. A number of scholars, for example, have called this poem a hymn (so Pedersen, *Israel III–IV,* 737; Fohrer, 112–13; Lohfink, *Christian Meaning,* 72–81; Rozelaar, *VT* 2 [1952] 225–28; Watts, *VT* 7 [1957] 371–80: "This amphictyonic hymn"); others, a victory song (Cross, *Canaanite Myth,* 121–23; Freedman, *Pottery, Poetry and Prophecy,* 187–95), "an Ode of Triumph" (Cassuto, 173) or a "liturgy" (Muilenburg, *Studia,* 233–51). Still other scholars have considered it a combination of forms: so, for example, Schmidt (*ZAW* 49 [1937] 59–66), who connected v 1 with v 21 and described the poem as a song of thanksgiving intertwined with a hymn of praise, the former sung by a soloist and antiphonal choirs, the latter by the responding congregation; or Beer (80–84), who described it as a combination of hymnic lines and lines in ballad-style creating a *"Passahkantate";* or Noth (123–26), who thought it a "solo hymn" with which "elements of the thanksgiving form" have been combined.

Such theories, and variations of them, have been much multiplied in the study of Exod 15:1–21. The chief conclusion to be drawn from them is that this poem cannot be made to fit a single form. It is not comparable to any one psalm, or song or hymn, or liturgy known to us anywhere else in the OT or in ANE literature. It is, in Gunkel's terminology, a poem of mixed type. Nor should this be in the least surprising to us in what is so clearly a *pièce d'occasion*. This is a poem stimulated by an exceptional moment in Israel's history, propelled forward by a continuation of the benefit of that moment viewed with believers' faith, and expanded, in time, to include the testimony of additional events seen as continuous by Israel. Its form is inevitably eclectic.

An almost equally wide range of theory has been advanced with regard to the date of the poem, though in general a tendency towards a late dating, characteristic of the first decades of the twentieth century, has been reversed as we have learned more about the Hebrew language in its historical setting. Thus the argument of Adolf Bender (*ZAW* 23 [1903] 46–48) that an artificial antiquing and terms showing the influence of Aramaic set the poem in the postexilic period around 450 B.C., or the argument of Paul Haupt (*AJSL* 20 [1904] 150–58) that the poem, though showing no evidence of "Aramaism," should be considered "a post-Exilic liturgical hymn for the Passover," dated around 350 B.C., have been superseded (though note the suggestion of Strauss, *ZAW* 97 [1985] 103–9, that the poem may have an application to a postexilic context).

The contention more recently is for an earlier date. Cross (*Canaanite Myth* 121–25) has posited a date in the tenth century B.C. for the conversion of the poem from an oral work into a written work, and a date "in the late twelfth or early eleventh century B.C." for its composition. Freedman (*Pottery, Poetry, and Prophecy,* 176–78) has suggested a twelfth-century date for the composition of the poem. Any precise dating is of course impossible, given the evidence available, but there is little reason to deny at least echoes of contemporaneity to the poem, and no avoiding the obvious conclusion that with the passage of time the poem was expanded to incorporate new events important to Israel's faith, related to conquest and settlement.

The *Sitz im Leben* of the poem, despite occasional reference to certain popular or balladic qualities, has by and large been viewed as a *Sitz im Kult.* This suggestion is all but necessitated by the poem itself and affirmed by its prose introduction and conclusion. A frequent suggestion of cultic connection has linked the poem of Exod 15 to the celebration of Passover. Pedersen even argued that the whole sequence of Exod 1–15 is to be understood as a narrative celebration dictated by the Passover feast, intended to historicize Yahweh's struggle against and victory over the opposing power of Pharaoh, and at the same time "the great battle at the beginning of time," when Yahweh "created an ordered world from chaos and slew the chaosdragon" (*ZAW* 52 [1934] 161–75). Exod 15, in Pedersen's view, is a great summary "hymn of triumph" that is "entirely a hymn to the royal temple and its God" (*Israel III–IV,* 728–737). Though Pedersen's theory has stimulated wide comment, it has not gained wide acceptance, in the main because Pedersen was able to present so little in the way of concrete support for his view (cf. Mowinckel, *ST* 5 [1952] 66–88; Noth, *Pentateuchal Traditions,* 66–71).

The connection of Exod 15 with Passover worship has been made with

some frequency (so Beer, 80–84; Hyatt, 162), and the poem has been linked
also to such high cultic celebrations as Mowinckel's Enthronement Festival
(cf. *Das Thronbesteigungsfest Jahwäs,* 111–12; *The Psalms in Israel's Worship* 2:247)
and the "autumnal festival" or the New Year Festival variously proposed
(cf. Muilenburg, *Studia,* 236–37). The most that is to be said with any firm
assurance, however, is that the setting of the poem was Israel's corporate
worship. And the likelihood is that the poem was used on a regular basis,
throughout the cultic year, not just at Passover or at some other holy occasion.
The deliverance the poem celebrates is far too basic to Israel's faith and
far too pervasive in OT theology for so splendid an account of it to have
had so restricted a usage.

Speculation about whether the poem originated with Miriam or with Moses
is futile. The repetition of Miriam's invitation to praise in v 21 as the first
two couplets of the song sung by Moses and the people of Israel in v 1
demonstrates only that the point of departure of the poem is Yahweh's great
delivering victory at the sea. The immediacy of that confession and much
else within the poem makes plausible the suggestion that the beginning point
of the poem was the event itself. The narrative of the poem, which as Childs
(244) quite correctly says has received too little attention, suggests in addition
the growth of the poem in its use across a number of years. Most telling of
all, is the conclusion that no other point and place of origin for the *original*
poem, of which of course the present text is a much expanded and overlaid
version, makes as much sense. V 19, an obvious summary and transition
verse, appears logically to be from the hand of P, probably at the level of
the editorial compilation of Exodus. V 20 is sometimes attributed to the
Yahwist (so Beer, 84: "J¹"; and Hyatt, 169), but as Noth (121–23) has shown,
there is no good reason for doing so.

The poetic form of 15:1b–18 and the couplet of v 21 is too obvious to
be denied. There is a vigorous rhythm in these lines that even translation
does not obscure, so much so that Exod 15 has become a standard example
of early Israelite poetry. A precise analysis of this poem, or for that matter
any other OT poem, remains difficult because of the considerable disagreement and confusion about the bases of Hebrew poetic form. The application
of the quantitative meters of classical poetry and the qualitative meters of
English and European poetry to the poetry of the OT has created more
problems than it has solved, in the main because Hebrew poetry cannot be
made, without alteration, to fit the patterns such application would impose
upon it. Despite many attempts, most notably by Julius Ley, Karl Budde,
Gustav Bickell, Hubert Grimme, and especially Eduard Sievers, no workable
set of metrical patterns for the poetry of the OT has thus far been proposed.

More recent work on Hebrew poetic form has recognized a freer approach
to rhythmic structure, and has measured this structure by counting syllables,
generally the accented syllables only, though more rarely *all* the syllables
(so, for example, Freedman, *Pottery, Poetry and Prophecy,* 179–86). If sufficient
account is taken of the variation in (as well as the purpose of) the Masoretic
systems of accentuation, this technique provides at least a basis of measure,
albeit one that is somewhat flawed. Its use has involved, in the analysis of
Exod 15 (and frequently with other poems as well), a shift from the theory

of longer units (four beat stichoi: cf. Cassuto, "rhythm . . . mainly quaternary," 173; and Noth, 123) to a theory of shorter units (two beat stichoi: cf. Muilenburg, *Studia,* 238, and Cross, *Canaanite Myth,* 125–31).

More recently still, a complete rejection of metrical patterns vis-à-vis OT poetry has been suggested, and the recurring patterns in Hebrew verse have been described as the result of "a system of syntactic constraints" (O'Connor, *Hebrew Verse Structure,* 64–78). A somewhat broader theory, and one more clearly suggested by the flexible variety of OT verse, is the theory of Benjamin Hrushovski ("Prosody, Hebrew," *EncJud* 1200–1201) that the rhythm of biblical Hebrew verse is "semantic-syntactic-accentual," "basically a free rhythm, i.e., a rhythm based on a cluster of changing principles."

The translation above is an attempt at representing the poetry of Exod 15 from such a base of flexibility. Short stichoi and longer stichoi are used in English to suggest both the staccato and the more fluid rhythms of the original, as these rhythms are dictated by syntax, by the presence of accents, and by rhetorical considerations. There is here no attempt to set forth any *system* of versification, as too much attempted systemization has blunted, rather than sensitized, our feel for the poetry of the OT. The attempt rather has been to feel the rhythm of Exod 15:1b–18 and 21, in terms of a brilliant commingling of sense and sound, and to suggest that feeling in the translation as much as possible. The basic units, even in the longer lines, are short, and the mood of the poem is one of ecstatic excitement.

As is implied several times above, this poem is a composite of at least two (vv 1b–12 and vv 13–18) and perhaps three (dividing vv 13–18 into 13a, 14–16 and 13b, 17–18) poems, the first and oldest of them itself a development of the couplet now given twice in Exod 15, in v 1 and in v 21. The subject matter and the form of the poem give some support for such a division. At last, however, this suggestion of the evolution of Exod 15 is necessarily subjective, and must not be allowed to obscure the composite form in the text before us, for the composite has an implication all its own.

Comment

1 The song of praise for Yahweh's victory is addressed to Yahweh, as the hymns of praise and thanksgiving always are in OT worship. Yahweh is both the subject and the object of this psalm; the hymn is about him and to him, both here and in the similar usage of Judg 5:3 (*contra* Freedman, *Pottery, Poetry and Prophecy,* 199). The motif of the praise is stated generally: Yahweh has "indeed risen" to the crisis, to his people's urgent and apparently hopeless cause. This general statement is then given specific definition: Yahweh has cast horse and chariot alike into the sea. As Mowinckel has shown (*VT* 12 [1962] 281–85), the "horse" here is the span-horse; the "chariot," literally the "riding-apparatus" (participle of רכב "drive, ride"); and the phrase "horses and chariots" is the "standing O.T. phrase characterizing human military forces as against God's. . . ."

The subject and object of his song thus set, and his theme thus stated and defined, the poet proceeds to address his theme from a variety of perspectives: his own confession of faith (vv 2–3); a narrative of the victory with allusions to Yahweh's prior victory over the cosmic chaos-waters (vv 4–8); the enemy's arrogant claim (v 9); Yahweh's incomparable deeds and person (vv 10–12); and Yahweh's guidance of his people (v 13) through their enemies (vv 14–16) to the place of their rest because of his rule (vv 17–18).

2 זִמְרָת "song of praise" has been questioned as a *non sequitur* with "my might" since ancient times, as the variant readings of some of the versions show (LXX σκεπαστής "protection"; so Vg MS *Ottobonianus*). Gaster (*ExpTim* 48 [1936–37] 45), Freedman (*Pottery, Poetry, and Prophecy*, 200) and Parker (*VT* 21 [1971] 373–79) argue for זִמְרָה "fortress," "protection," by posing a different root זמר (cf. *HALAT* 263, III *זמר and II זִמְרָה). Loewenstamm (*VT* 19 [1969] 464–68) and Good (*VT* 20 [1970] 358–59) argue for "praise in song" = "glory" and hendiadys, here "my singing about strength." The evidence for posing a root meaning "protection" or "fortress" is not convincing, and the recurrence of the exact phrase in Ps 118:14 and in Isa 12:2 makes unlikely the addition of י to זִמְרָת as proposed by Cross-Freedman (*Studies*, 55) and Talmon (*VT* 4 [1954] 206–8).

יה "Yah," once regarded as an early form of the tetragrammaton (cf. BDB, 219) is now generally considered a later form than יהוה "Yahweh" (de Vaux, *Early History*, 339). Its occurrence here has been cited as evidence of an alteration or even a later insertion of this verse into the poem (Freedman, *Pottery, Poetry, and Prophecy*, 200). V 2 does break the sequence of content between v 1 and vv 3–10, the confessional narrative of Yahweh's defeat of his enemies, but it also serves as a memorable summary of faith and the rationale of the poet for the song about to follow. If it is an addition, it is a functional one, with its declaration that Yahweh is "salvation" and the God of the fathers, eminently worthy of being lifted on praise.

3 There follows a descriptive celebration of Yahweh as victorious deliverer. He is אִישׁ מלחמה, a "man of battle," a "warrior," an undoubtedly authentic epithet the translators of LXX found too embarrassing to keep (and so altered it: συντρίβων πολέμους "crushes wars," a reading out of place in this context). The declaration that his name is Yahweh must be understood in the full sense of the confession the tetragrammaton is (see *Comment* on 3:13–22), and it is at least possible that this declaration here suggested the rhetoric of "the God of my fathers" of (the inserted?) v 2.

4–7 Pharaoh's entire force offered no threat to such a God. He threw them into the sea, along with their "elite commanders," the officers on whom Pharaoh depended for correct judgments in the heat of battle. They were all inundated by the תְּהֹמֹת "ancient deeps," the great primordial ocean waters held in restless impotence by Yahweh save when, as here, he turns them to his purposes (see Tromp, *Primitive Conceptions*, 59–61; Reymond, *L'Eau*, 167–76; 182–94). Yahweh's strong right hand, an OT metaphor for the divine power (cf. Dhorme, *L'emploi métaphorique*, 144–47), has shattered the enemy's pursuing attack, and he has magnified his highness (גָּאוֹן, derivative of גאה, the verb employed in v 1b of the poem; see n. 15:1.d.) by his defeat of those who have risen up (קוּם) against him.

8 The wind that has moved the sea waters out of their channel (cf. 14:21) is described as the wind of Yahweh's anger (literally, his "nostrils"; cf. Dhorme, *L'emploi métaphorique*, 81: ". . . אַף et אפים deviendront synonymes de colère."). There is here a subtle but important shift from "waters" (מִים) and "currents" (נֹזְלִים), neither of which refers to the primordial waters of chaos (cf. Tromp, *Primitive Conceptions,* 64–65; Reymond, *L'Eau,* 70, 178) to "ancient deeps," תְהֹמֹת. The implication, at the very least, is that the visible waters in their everyday flow were thrust aside to make way for the temporary release of the devastating rebellion-waters from their subterranean prison. Then, these same waters, the very symbol of disorder in motion, are "made solid," "stilled" in the middle of the sea (cf. Reymond 69, and n.3).

9 Against this kind of authority, which upon command can stop still the sweeping instability of the primeval deep, requiring it to stand by with "waters" and "currents" till needed, Pharaoh's opposition is held up to ridicule. The device of this ridicule is a series of staccato claims, put into the enemy's mouth, set forth in a rapid succession of phrases very difficult to represent adequately in English:

> *I will chase* after
> *I will catch*
> *I will share* the plunder
> *It will sate itself,* my battle lust ("soul")
> *I will empty* (= "rid of victims") my sword
> *I will possess* them by force, my power ("hand")

10 These claims are arrogant and presumptuous—and futile. Yahweh had but to blow with his wind, and they were all covered, sunk down like lead in the collected waters.

11 Yahweh is thus extolled as incomparable among the אֵלִים "gods," any and all beings for whom divinity is claimed. There is simply none like him, none even approaching an equality with him (cf. Pss 82:6 and 89:7–8; Durham, "Psalms," *BBC* 4 [Nashville: Broadman, 1971] 341, 353–54). He is magnificent in the holiness that sets him apart from all others. Labuschagne (*Incomparability,* 79–80) would emend בַּקֹּדֶשׁ "in holiness" here to בַּקְּדֹשִׁים, following LXX's ἐν ἁγίοις, and read "the proven powerful among the holy ones!" This rendering is without sufficient support, however, and in any case unnecessary. Following the rhetorical question "Who is like . . . ?" (cf. Labuschagne, 16–23), a series of three aspects of Yahweh's incomparability is raised in a further rhetorical question: his magnificent holiness, his praiseworthy deeds, and his extraordinary accomplishments.

12 This incomparability is summed up by a return to the event that inspired the poem, and in a line that rounds off the first part of the poem, the part dealing with Yahweh's victory at the sea. He thrust forth his right hand, and the earth swallowed them. Some scholars (so Tromp, *Primitive Conceptions,* 25–26; Dahood, *Psalms III,* AB 17A [Garden City, NY: Doubleday, 1971] 353–54; cf. Ps 71:20: וּמִתְּהֹמוֹת הָאָרֶץ "and from the depths of the earth") consider "earth" here to be the equivalent of "nether world." Compare the view of Wifall (*ZAW* 92 [1980] 325–32) that the "sea of reeds" is based on Egyptian symbolism, the *Shi-Hor,* equivalent to the Hebrew "Sheol" as a place of death.

13 V 13 begins the second part of the composite poem of Exod 15, or,

if the poem is a composite of three poems, it introduces the two that follow.
Its first couplet refers to the guidance through the wilderness of the people
Yahweh has claimed as his own. Its second couplet refers to Yahweh's leading
of that same people to the place where his holiness dwells. While this latter
reference is ambiguous enough to include either Sinai or Zion or even both
at once, v 17 makes Zion the more probable choice, the more so if v 13
serves, as I am suggesting, as an introduction to parts two (vv 14–16) and
three (vv 17–18) of the composite poem.

14–16 The first of these two motifs, guidance through the wilderness
into the promised land, is represented by a graphic catalog of the fright of
the peoples Israel came to encounter in the journey. The incompleteness
of the list and the inclusion in it of פלשת "Philistia" are not to be taken as
precise indications of the date of this part of the poem, though the poem
from v 13 to the end does not preserve the vigorous and terse rhythmic
feel of the first twelve verses. My suggestion is that parts two and three
were composed later than part one, at a time when "dwellers in Philistia"
was a familiar phrase. But that leaves unanswered, of course, the question
of just how much earlier part one may have been composed.

The fear of the inhabitants of the areas en route to and within Canaan is
a familiar device of the narratives of conquest and settlement (Num 22:2–6;
Josh 2:8–11), and it is used effectively here. The peoples worry, are gripped
by anguish, are terrified, seized with trembling, grow faint with the weakness
of fear, and are altogether overcome with terror and dread before Yahweh's
relentless march with his people: it is an effective description of the growing
paralysis of fear. Before the great power of Yahweh's arm they are literally
petrified with fright: "struck dumb as stone." This condition persists until
Yahweh's people pass by, the people arrestingly described as those whom
Yahweh has created (קנה). As Schmidt ("קנה erwerben," THAT 2:650–59) and
others have shown, this verb, which occurs more than eighty times in the
OT, most often refers to acquiring by effort or payment, as through commer-
cial transaction of some kind. Köhler (ZAW 52 [1934] 160) referred to acquisi-
tion by work and difficulty, even by pain and suffering, citing Gen 31:18 as
a clear example. Humbert (Festschrift A. Bertholet, 259–66) has shown, however,
that in nine OT passages, six of which are "hymnic and cultic" (Exod 15:16;
Deut 32:6; Pss 74:2; 78:54; 139:13; and Prov 8:22), קנה means "create" (cf.
Stadelmann, Hebrew Conception, 6). Irwin's argument (JBL 80 [1961] 135–36,
142) that קנה means not "create," in the sense of "form," but "beget," "become parent of," affirms the sense in which קנה is translated above (cf. Moses
' rhetorical question in Num 11:12, where the verbs הרה "conceive" and ילד
"give birth to" are employed). Yahweh is celebrated as seeing through a
dangerous passage the people whom he has made his own people—he had
"created" them, "conceived" them, they are Israel, whom he calls "my son,
my firstborn" (see Exod 4:22).

17–18 The conclusion of the composite poem of Exod 15 is a terse summary of the end of the exodus. Behind the exodus lies Yahweh's promise
to the fathers of progeny and land. The fulfillment of the first part of that
promise necessitated the exodus, and the exodus in turn necessitated the
keeping of the second part of that promise. V 17, anticipated by v 13b (see

above), refers to what came, in time at least, to be seen as an important goal of the exodus, the settlement of Yahweh in the midst of his special people, themselves settled in the land he both promised and provided. The "mountain" that belongs to Yahweh, to which he "will bring" his people, and around which he "will establish" them, is Mount Zion, the new Sinai. The undoubted rootage of the phrase, "the mountain that belongs to you," in Canaanite theology (Clifford, *Cosmic Mountain,* 131–41), does not guarantee that this reference is earlier than the construction of Solomon's temple and the rise of the Zion theology (see Albright, *Archaeology,* 233), or that it must originally have "meant the hill country of Canaan" and the sanctuary, "probably," at Gilgal (Clifford, *Cosmic Mountain,* 139).

Whatever the time of origin of the phrase, its usage in v 17 is certainly a reference to Zion, as the "holy sanctuary" is a reference to the great temple in Jerusalem (Clements, *God and Temple,* 52–55), and as Yahweh's permanent reign is a reference to the theology of divine sovereignty that became so important in Jerusalem. It is at least a reasonable assumption that this part of the poem of Exod 15, and in all probability the part preceding it, were added to the older hymn of victory at the sea at a time when the sovereignty of Yahweh, his residence upon Zion, and the fright of Israel's enemies as his enemies were important confessional themes. The reference to Yahweh's continuing and uninterruptable rule must certainly be understood in context with Pss 47, 93, 96–99 (see Durham, "Psalms," *BBC* 4: 265–68).

19–21 The fact that the composite poem of Exod 15 ends with two brief sections moving the confessional tradition forward beyond the deliverance at the sea to the wilderness journeys after Sinai, to conquest, settlement, and then to the cult of Yahweh's sovereign Presence in Jerusalem necessitates this transitional summary, probably from the Priestly compiler (cf. the language of 14:29). It is a summary that brings us back to the narrative at hand and so prepares us for the notice in prose of Miriam's song of victory, followed by the song itself. As indicated already, this song, apart from the change in the form of the opening verb (שִׁירוּ "sing!," a 2d person plural command, instead of אָשִׁירָה "I will sing," a 1st person singular assertion) is identical with the song sung by Moses and Israel. There is obviously no basis for the contention that Miriam's song of v 21 antedates by many years the version of it given to Moses and Israel in v 1. Either version could be contemporary with the event; neither version has to be. Miriam is mentioned in Exodus only in these two verses, and she is called first "the prophetess," and then, in what may well be an addition (cf. Noth, 122) to the text, "Aaron's sister."

Explanation

The composite poem of Exod 15:1b–18 may be understood best as the end result of a cumulative hymnic development produced by many occasions of confessional worship re-presenting Yahweh's greatest deliverance of his people and the further acts of provision necessitated by that deliverance. The oldest elements of the composite may certainly be dated, insofar as basic narrative and perhaps also rhetorical terms are concerned, very close to the time of the event itself. Later elements are to be connected both with the expansion of the accounts of the events at the sea and with the celebration of the further deliverances and victories of conquest, settlement, and the rise of the theology of Yahweh's sovereign Presence in Jerusalem-Zion.

The poem as it stands in the text of Exodus thus has neither poetic unity nor chronological unity. The unity it does display is theological. Given the complexity of its tapestry of important themes, its overall emphasis is surprisingly singular: praise of the incomparable Yahweh whose saving Presence rescues, protects and establishes his people. This point is suggested by the exultant couplet which now begins and ends this section of Exodus, and its persistence is emphasized by the reference to the patriarchal fathers at the beginning of the poem and by the reference to the temple of Yahweh and the sovereignty of Yahweh celebrated there at the end of the poem.

Thus the victory hymn of Moses and Miriam is far more than merely a hymn of Yahweh's victory over Pharaoh and his Egyptians in the sea. Its point of departure is that, without question. But the poem of Exod 15 is more a celebration of Yahweh than a celebration of one of his great victories. Indeed, it is more a celebration of Yahweh and the kind of God he is than a celebration of all that Yahweh had done at the sea and would do beyond it, in the wilderness, in Canaan, and in Jerusalem. The poem of Exod 15 celebrates Yahweh present *with* his people and doing *for* them as no other god anywhere and at any time *can* be present to do. As such, it is a kind of summary of the theological base of the whole of the Book of Exodus.

Yahweh's Provision for Israel in the Wilderness: Water (15:22–27)

Bibliography

Aharoni, Y. *The Land of the Bible.* Philadelphia: Westminster Press, 1967. **Coats, G. W.** *Rebellion in the Wilderness.* Nashville: Abingdon Press, 1968. ————. "The Wilderness Itinerary." *CBQ* 34 (1972) 135–52. **Cross, F. M.** "The Priestly Work." *Canaanite Myth and Hebrew Epic.* Cambridge: Harvard University Press, 1973. 295–325. **Davies, G. I.** "The Wilderness Itineraries: A Comparative Study." *TynB* 25 (1974) 46–81. **Greenberg, M.** "נסות in Exodus 20:20 and the Purpose of the Sinaitic Theophany." *JBL* 79 (1960) 273–76. **Hempel, J.** " 'Ich bin der Herr, dein Arzt.' " *TLZ* 82 (1957) 809–26. **Long, B. O.** *The Problem of Etiological Narrative in the Old Testament.* BZAW 108. Berlin: Verlag Alfred Töpelmann, 1968. **Porter, J. R.** "The Role of Kadesh-Barnea in the Narrative of the Exodus." *JTS* 44 (1943) 139–43. **de Vries, S. J.** "The Origin of the Murmuring Tradition." *JBL* 87 (1968) 51–58. **Walsh, J. T.** "From Egypt to Moab. A Source-Critical Analysis of the Wilderness Itinerary." *CBQ* 39 (1977) 20–33.

Translation

²² *Then Moses pressed* ᵃ *Israel on from the "sea of rushes," so that they went out* ᵇ *into the wilderness of Shur ("Wall").* ᶜ *They traveled for three days in the*

wilderness without finding water. ²³ *Then they came to Marah ("Bitter-Place") where* ᵃ
*they were unable to drink water because of its bitterness: indeed, that is the reason
its name is called Marah.* ᵇ ²⁴ *So the people grumbled* ᵃ *against Moses, saying, "What
are we to drink?"* ²⁵ *He* ᵃ *called out to Yahweh for help, whereupon Yahweh directed
him to* ᵇ *a tree: when he cast it into the water, the water became potable. At that
very spot,* ᶜ *he* ᵈ *established for them* ᵉ *a requirement* ᶠ *and a divine guidance,* ᵍ *and
there he put them on trial;* ²⁶ *thus he said, "If you will pay careful attention* ᵃ *to
the voice of Yahweh your God, and do the right thing according to his standard,* ᵇ
and be obedient to ᶜ *his commandments, and meet* ᵈ *all his requirements, all the diseases
that I put upon the Egyptians I will not put upon you: for I am Yahweh your
healer."*
      ²⁷ *Next they came to Elim ("Great Trees"), a place* ᵃ *of twelve springs of water
and seventy date-palms. They pitched camp there, beside the waters.*

Notes

22.a. Hiphil נסע, meaning "cause to pull out, set forth"; cf. the qal ptcp usage in 14:10,
and see n. 14:10.d. above.
22.b. SamPent and LXX have "and he brought him (them) out" (ויוצאהו, ἤγαγεν αὐτοὺς).
22.c. שׁוּר "Shur" is usually understood to be derived from a root meaning "become raised,
excited" (so BDB, 1004) in reference to a "wall" of fortifications mentioned in Egyptian literature
at least from the middle of the twentieth century B.C. (see Aharoni, *Land* 130–31, 178–81). It
is possible, however, that שׁוּר might be derived from a root meaning "traveling" or even one
meaning "watching" (BDB, 1003), and so be the "wilderness of travelers" or the "wilderness
of watchfulness."
23.a. Lit., "and they were not able to drink water from Marah."
23.b. LXX has *Moses* naming the place Μερρα "Marah" because of the bitter waters. Such a
reading is possible, even with the MT of *BHS.*
24.a. The verb is ילון. It is used only of the "murmuring" or "grumbling" of Israel against
their leaders, primarily in the period of Moses' leadership between Egypt and Canaan in Exod
15, 16, and 17, and in Num 14, 16, 17. The one additional context is Joshua's wars of conquest,
Josh 9:18; Ps 59:16 appears to refer to the "roving, prowling, scavenging" of wild dogs, another
meaning of ילון: see BDB 533–34.˙ Cf. Coats, *Rebellion,* 21–28. SamPent reads ילון hiph instead
of MT's וילנ, a niph.
25.a. SamPent, LXX, Vg and Syr add "Moses."
25.b. LXX, Syr, Tg Ps-J, Vg, SamPent all read ראה "caused him to see," instead of MT's
ירה "directed him."
25.c. שׁם, "placed early in sentence for emph": BDB, 1027.
25.d. The context makes clear that the antecedent of this pronoun is Yahweh.
25.e. לו "for him," i.e., Israel, so "them" above, for clarity.
25.f. חק is a prescribed, required, preset obligation or due. See BDB, 349, and n. 5:14.b.
above.
25.g. משׁפט here refers to the divinely guided judgment or case-decision that gave direction
to life in covenant with Yahweh, as in Exod 18:19–26. Note שׁפט in vv 22 and 26.
26.a. אם־שׁמוע תשׁמע "if you will listen listeningly"; cf. Exod. 19:5.
26.b. בעיניו "in his eyes."
26.c. Hiph אזן "cause to hear, listen."
26.d. שׁמר "guard, keep, observe," even "follow." See BDB, 1036–37.
27.a. ושׁם, lit., "and there." SamPent reads ובאילים "and in Elim" instead of ושׁם, as does
Tg MS 27031 (cf. Déaut, 131).

Form/Structure/Setting

      This brief account of the continuation of Israel's journey after the victory
at the sea is at least a composite of motifs. Quite probably, it is also a composite

of source material. The motif of Israel's need for sustenance has been combined with the motifs of Yahweh's provision for his people's need. The motif
of Israel's complaint, or murmuring, has been set alongside the motif of
Yahweh's requirement of his people.

The tendency of the source critics has been to assign different motifs to
different sources, or at least to different layers in the same source. So Driver
(141–44), for example, assigned these verses to E (22–25, 27) and R^JE (26);
Beer (84–87), to J¹ (22a–25a, 27) and R^D (25b–26); Noth (127–29), to P (22aα,
27), J (22βb–25a) and "a deuteronomistic supplement" (25b, 26); and Hyatt
(171–73), to P (22a), J (22b–25a) and R_D (25b–26). This amount of variance
suggests the ambiguity of the evidence for source analysis. There is not here
enough stylistic or thematic data to make precision in the division of this
section a firm possibility. The awkwardness of the sequence (the use of "he"
as subject four times in v 25, twice in reference to Moses, twice in reference to Yahweh, each time without qualification; the introduction of the testing
motif, v 25, followed by a Deuteronomistic-style conditional promise and the
somewhat out-of-place reference to Yahweh the healer, v 26) clearly
suggest a composite of sources, but provide too little information for exact
attribution.

The question of form must once again be focused upon the composite
rather than upon its parts. While typical source interests are certainly present,
and perhaps also etiological (Coats, *Rebellion*, 47–53; Long, *Etiological Narrative*,
10–12) interests, the primary function of the pericope is to present the narrative of the continuation of Israel's journey toward Yahweh's goal, and to
move that narrative forward by reference to Israel's continuing and growing
complaint (see the anticipation of this motif at Exod 5:20–23, 14:10–18; note
also de Vries, *JBL* 87 [1968] 51–52) and Yahweh's continuing and fuller
provision. The form of the section is thus determined more by the purpose
of the composite than by the pieces that make it up. That purpose is not
etiology or the highlighting of the murmuring motif. It is the glorification
of Yahweh who provides for his people, whatever and wherever their need,
Yahweh who is eminently deserving of service and loyalty.

Comment

22   The route of the continuation of Israel's journey in exodus beyond
the barrier of the "sea of rushes" is no more clear to us than their route
through and from the Nile Delta. Once again, the narrators have gone to
some lengths (vv 22, 23, 27, cf. also Num 33) to make the direction of the
journey clear to us, but places and landmarks that were clear to them are
clear to us no longer. Several identifications of Marah and Elim have been
attempted (cf. Hyatt, 172–73), but not one of them is convincing. The location
of Sinai, equally uncertain, is of course a determining factor. If the traditional
view is followed, we must pose a route east, then south from the delta; if
Sinai is located at Kadesh (Porter, *JTS* 44 [1943] 139–43) or in Edom (Seir),
a direction more nearly due east is likely. This question remains unanswered
not only because of the uncertainty surrounding the geography of the places
mentioned, but also because, as the studies of Coats (*CBQ* 34 [1972] 135–

52), Davies (*TynB* 25 [1974] 46–81), Walsh (*CBQ* 39 [1977] 20–33) and Cross (*Canaanite Myth,* 301–21) have shown, there are at least two, and perhaps three travel sequences that give evidence in themselves of some independence from the tetrateuchal sources generally posed. Attempts to unravel and plot these sequences have been unsuccessful because of literary problems as well as because of the lack of geographical information.

23 The first difficulty encountered by Israel beyond the sea is introduced almost immediately: after three days of travel into the wilderness, Moses and his charges had found no water. Water is of course a matter of life and death, nowhere more so than in the dehydrating heat of the desert. The anxiety of the people would of course have been mounting by the hour, and the false relief brought by arrival at a place where there was water unfit to drink would have sharpened that anxiety dramatically. Whatever etiological quality may be present in the narrative of the polluted water of Marah, the "bitter-place," it is far less important (cf. Long, *Etiological Narrative,* 12) to the narrative in its present form than the tragedy apparently unfolding: Israel, miraculously freed and rescued, is now about to perish in the desert for want of water.

24–25 The grumbling of the people against Moses is no surprise, both because of the anticipation of the motif and also because of the terrible circumstances of their plight. Their complaint here serves as the trigger of Yahweh's provision of a solution to their problem. Moses called on Yahweh for help, and Yahweh guided him to a tree, a kind of wood, עץ, that could be used to purify the water. Whether the tree is to be thought of as purifying the water by a chemical reaction, or as a symbol, such as the staff of Moses, of the active power of Yahweh at hand, the text does not make plain. That Yahweh is the source of the miracle of the changed water, there can be no doubt, as the next lines, including a statement of Yahweh, indicate.

The very spot at which their panic of thirst is changed to the contentment of provision becomes the appropriate place for the establishment of expectation and the offering of option. This same sequence is repeated, though on a much larger and more dramatic scale, at Sinai: there the place of Advent in theophany becomes the place of relationship in covenant. So here, as there, Yahweh puts his people to a kind of try-out, or test (נסה). He gives them here an option authenticated by what he has done with the water, as by what had happened to the Egyptians from the fifth of the mighty acts forward. He gives them at Sinai an experience of his Presence at first hand, so that they might have reverence for him (20:20; cf. Greenberg, *JBL* 79 [1960] 273–76).

26 The substance of the option Yahweh offers is set forth in terms of obedience and judgment—the standard accompaniments of OT covenant-making, indeed of covenant-making in the ANE. They are to take his requirement and his guidance seriously, pay close and committed attention to his voice, adopt *his* standard as the measure of what is right, obey *his* commands and meet *his* requirements. He will then spare them the harm of the diseases he heaped upon the Egyptians: he then will *not* put these diseases upon Israel. This statement of the positive response to the positive side of the option implies the negative response to the negative side, punishment for disobedience. But the positive side is emphasized further by the use of the self-proclamatory formula, כִּי אֲנִי יהוה "for I am Yahweh" with רֹפְאֶךָ "your healer" in the place of אֱלֹהֶיךָ "your God." Stoebe ("רפא *heilen*," *THAT* 2:809) calls this a "hymnic" usage, and Hempel (*TLZ* 82 [1957] 809–26) has written a sweeping survey on OT medicine and on Yahweh as the one who strikes dead and heals, considered alongside an array of parallels from the ancient world in which he suggests (823) a series of possibilities for the translation of v 26, ranging from *dein Arzt* "your doctor" as a technical term to *der dich heilende* "the one who heals you" as a broad generalization.

The phrase in which רֹפְאֶךָ is used may, however, suggest more still. The "diseases of Egypt" refer to the mighty acts by which Yahweh made himself known to Israel and to the Egyptians in Egypt. The protection of an obedient Israel from those same diseases is to be a means by which Yahweh is now to make himself known to Israel in the wilderness and beyond. The self-proclamatory phrase אֲנִי יהוה אֱלֹהֶיךָ "I am Yahweh your God," a basic confession of Yahweh's special nature and special relationship thus becomes, with the replacement of אֱלֹהֶיךָ "your God" by רֹפְאֶךָ "your healer," a confession also of special blessing upon those in right relationship with him. The assertion does have a Deuteronomistic ring to it, as scholars have often noted. But its covenantal overtones may be louder even than its Deuteronomistic ones.

27 The crisis past and the option posed, no report of any response is given, appropriately enough in a passage anticipating the great presentation of much the same options, albeit in markedly different form, in Exod 19–24. The people now move on to the pleasant oasis of Elim, a place of abundant waters and date-palms, and there they camp in welcome respite before the most difficult part of the journey they have undertaken. Elim can be located no more certainly than Marah, but the presence of such oases in the wilderness is well established.

Explanation

Yahweh thus provides for the needs of his people: by purifying polluted water, by guiding them through wasteland to an oasis overflowing with both water and fruit. That is the essential point of this section: Yahweh's provision for his people. Set off against that point, as a means of making it all the more obvious, are the motifs of the people's grumbling in their difficulty, the people's obligation, set for them by the Yahweh who also rescues and provides for them, and the confession of Yahweh as healer, both protecting and healing his people from disease.

The composite is built on a sequence of contrasts. The first and governing contrast is Israel's need met by Yahweh's provision. Related to that contrast are these further pairs of opposites: the total lack of water at the beginning of the pericope opposed by the oasis of twelve springs at its end; the bitter water of Marah opposed by the sweet water that Yahweh's guidance (and miracle?) makes of that nonpotable resource; the people's grumbling opposed by Yahweh's provident care of them; their protection and healing opposed by the Egyptians' affliction and illness; and life according to their own disordered whim opposed by Yahweh's ordered standard.

The multiplied effect of these pairings is of course the spotlighting of Yahweh's guiding provision for the people whom he has singled out to special purpose. And this first array of provision in the wilderness is an anticipation of much more, and much greater provision yet to come.

The Grumbling of Israel against Yahweh (16:1–12)

Bibliography

Aharoni, Y. "Kadesh-Barnea and Mount Sinai." *God's Wilderness: Discoveries in Sinai.* B. Rothenberg, Y. Aharoni and A. Hashimshoni. New York: Thomas Nelson & Sons, 1962. 115–70. **Coppens, J.** "Les traditions relatives à la manne dans Exode xvi." *Estudios Eclesiásticos* 34 (1960) 473–89. **Galbiati, E.** *La Struttura letteraria dell' Esodo.* Milan: Edizioni Paoline, 1956. **Malina, B. J.** *The Palestinian Manna Tradition.* Leiden: E. J. Brill, 1968.

Translation

[1] *Next they journeyed forth from Elim and came, the whole company of the sons of Israel, to the wilderness of Sin,* [a] *which is between Elim and Sinai, on the fifteenth day of the second month of their exodus from the land of Egypt.* [2] *There, the whole company of the sons of Israel grumbled* [a] *against Moses and against Aaron in the wilderness.* [3] *The sons of Israel said to them, "Why didn't somebody give us dead into the hand of Yahweh in the land of Egypt, where we had a settled life* [a] *with plenty of meat,* [b] *where we ate bread till we were stuffed? Now* [c] *you have brought us out into this wilderness to kill this whole crowd by starvation!"*

[4] *So Yahweh said to Moses, "Just watch me rain down upon them bread from the heavens—the people are to go out and pick up one day's provision daily; by that requirement,* [a] *I will put them to a trial: will they walk according to my instruction,* [b] *or not?* [5] *On the sixth day, when they process what they have brought in, they will find that it is twice as much as they have gathered day by day."* [6] *Then Moses and Aaron said to all the* [a] *sons of Israel, "At evening you will know by experience that Yahweh has brought you forth from the land of Egypt,* [7] *and at morning you will see Yahweh's glory, in his response* [a] *to your grumbling against Yahweh. What are we, that you have grumbled against us?"* [8] *So Moses said, "When Yahweh gives you in the evening flesh to eat, and bread in the morning until you are stuffed,* [a] *in Yahweh's response to your grumbling which you have grumbled against him,* [b] *what have we to do with that?* [c] *Not against us are your grumblings, but against Yahweh."* [d]

[9] *Then Moses said to Aaron, "Say to the whole company of the sons of Israel, 'Approach the Presence of Yahweh,* [a] *because he has heard your grumblings,'"* [10] *While Aaron was speaking to the whole company of the sons of Israel, they turned toward the wilderness, and there the glory of Yahweh appeared in a cloud.* [11] *At that moment,* [a]

Yahweh spoke to Moses, and said, [12] *"I have heard the grumblings of the sons of Israel—say to them now, 'Between dusk and dawn, you are to eat meat, and in the morning you are to be stuffed with bread; then you will know by experience that I am Yahweh your God.'"*

Notes

1.a. The etymology of סִין "Sin" and סִינָי "Sinai" is not known. The two terms are clearly related, and as Aharoni (*God's Wilderness*, 143) has pointed out, the OT uses no less than five names for parts or all the wilderness of the Sinai peninsula: Zin, Paran, Shur, Sin and Sinai. None of the various attempts to apply these names to specific areas of the Sinai peninsula has been entirely successful, not only because of a lack of specific information, but also because some of these names are used interchangeably in the OT.

2.a. See n. 15:24.a. The verb לון as written here is hiph, "caused grumbling." The Masoretes have vocalized it, however, as niph impf, and it is so read above: lit., the significance is "grumbled themselves."

3.a. בשבתנו "in our dwelling, remaining."

3.b. על־סיר הבשר "upon the pots of flesh."

3.c. כי "for, because."

4.a. למען, lit., "to the intent, in order that."

4.b. בתורתי "to my instruction."

6.a. LXX adds συναγωγήν "company, congregation."

7.a. בשמעו, lit., "in his hearing."

8.a. לשבע "for sating, stuffing."

8.b. LXX has καθ᾿ ἡμῶν "against us."

8.c. The phrase ונחנו מה is the one rendered "what are we?" in v 7. It is varied in translation here because of the context. The meaning of either rendering is the same.

8.d. LXX has κατὰ τοῦ Θεοῦ "against God."

9.a. LXX has τοῦ Θεοῦ "of God."

11.a. Special *waw* in context.

Form/Structure/Setting

The question of the form of this section must be considered against the form of the whole of Exod 16, which is a composite drawn together to present material having to do with Yahweh's provision for his people. Nourishment for the body is provided, in the manna and the quails, and nourishment for the spirit, in the sabbath-rest. This chapter has to be considered alongside Num 11, to which it is parallel in some ways, against which it is different in some ways, and by which it appears to some degree presupposed. A variety of source- and form-critical analyses of the chapter have been made, chiefly on the grounds of linguistic-stylistic and, especially, sequential considerations.

Far the majority of source critics have assigned most of Exod 16 and most of vv 1–12 to the Priestly source, in part on linguistic grounds and in part by comparison with Num 11, which is generally reckoned to be a JE compilation. The most notable exception to this majority view is Wilhelm Rudolph ("*Elohist,*" 34–36), who argues that the "foundation" (*Grundstock*) of the chapter is not P, but J. Generally, vv 4–5 of the first twelve verses of Exod 16 have been assigned to J, and the remainder of the verses to P (so Beer, 87–88; Noth, 131–34; Hyatt, 173; Childs, 274–76).

There is, however, an apparent illogicality of sequence in these twelve verses that the source-critical theories have failed to clarify; this illogicality is presented by the repetition of much of vv 6–8 by vv 9–12, especially in the revelation of Yahweh in a theophanic appearance to Moses, Aaron, and Israel (vv 10–12) of information Moses had already given the people (v 8) along with the prediction of the theophany (vv 6–7). Galbiati (*La Struttura* 164–75), Coppens (*Estudios Eclesiásticos* 34 [1960] 473–89) and Malina (*Manna Tradition*, 1–20) have attempted to set aside source-analysis as an inadequate means of resolving the difficulty, and to provide instead a kind of structural analysis. Malina, for example, posits a synthesis of four narratives in Exodus: a "Moses, Aaron, and the whole congregation" narrative (vv 1–2, 3c, 6–7, 9–10), a "Moses and the children of Israel" narrative (vv 3ab, 11–15, 16b–17a, 21, 31, 35a), a "Moses and they" narrative (vv 4abα, 5, 16a, 17b, 18–20, 22–27, 28–30, 35b), and a "Moses and Aaron" narrative (vv 32–34), plus "glosses" (vv 4bβ, 8, 16aα, 28, 36). The unity of Exod 16, then, is brought about according to a chronological purpose, set by "a Priestly redactor" whose primary interest was "the Sabbath theophany and the Sabbath rest." Childs (276–80) has argued that neither a confusion of the order of the sources in compilation nor the imposition of a preset pattern by the redactor afford an adequate explanation of the sequence of Exod 16. His theory, rather, is that "a traditional sequence," reflected also in Num 14 and 16, makes this sequence understandable. What becomes the governing and important factor in Exod 16 is not logical transition, but the linking, in this order, of murmuring, disputation, theophany, and divine instruction through Moses to Israel.

While each of these approaches sheds some light on the clearly difficult order of Exod 16, vv 1–12 in particular, none of them is entirely satisfactory, not least because they appear a bit too clever, imposing upon the text about as much as they take from it. Two considerations need to be kept firmly in mind: one, that our sense of logic in the organization of a biblical passage may well discover difficulty where none was present to the ancient redactor and his reader; and two, what remains most important, not least because it is all we have with certainty, is the compilation of the text in hand, supposed illogicality and all. Childs takes this quite seriously, and so has given us the most sensitive approach, but his "traditional sequence" may also be an imposition which would come as a surprise to the authors/editors of Exod 16 and Num 14 and 16. A more convincing place for such a pattern to have occurred, surely, would have been Num 11, the chapter most closely parallel to this one, but one in which Childs does not find his "traditional sequence."

My view therefore is that Exod 16:1–12 functions as an introduction to the account of Yahweh's provision for his people of needed food. Its structure is dictated by its purpose, which is to prepare the reader for the more important Presence-demonstrating provision to follow. It is a composite that leans forward, that functions primarily as an anticipation of what is to come. It does this, moreover, by a didactic multiplication of two preparatory themes: Israel's grumbling and Yahweh's authoritative statement of his response to their complaint. Into the combination of these themes have been worked the themes of Israel's obedience or disobedience under pressure (v 4), the keeping of the sabbath (v 5), and the authority of Moses (and Aaron) (vv 7–8), but the important emphasis of the two preparatory themes governs this sequence, even to the point of a didactic repetition which introduces the problems of *non sequitur* that have so troubled the literary critics. As in so many instances in the compiled narrative literature of the OT, purpose takes precedence over logic, and emphasis overrides considerations of sequence.

Comment

1 The report of the movement of "the whole company of the sons of Israel" from the pleasant oasis of Elim into the wilderness of Sin is, like other such references in the narrative of Exodus, an attempt to locate and plot the route of Israel in exodus from Egypt to Sinai, and eventually from Sinai to Canaan. The most extensive such attempt, of course, is Num 33, which lists more than forty places of encampment and "setting-forth." These attempts no longer serve their intended purpose, however, for two reasons at least: one, most of the places listed can no longer be identified; and two, the various references, when brought together, present a conflicting sequence of information. The best interpretation we can manage, with any confidence, is a general plotting of vicinity or area for the movement of Israel in exodus, and even that is fraught with some ambiguity because of the uncertainty with which even the most important of all the places, Sinai, can be located.

Yohanan Aharoni (*God's Wilderness* 117–70), who surveyed the Sinai peninsula along with colleagues from the Hebrew University and Israel's Department of Antiquities in 1956–1957, wrote an extensive and convincing discussion of the problems posed by the places mentioned. He concluded that while Kadesh-Barnea (which *can* be accurately located) was an important center of Israelite life during the wilderness period, and perhaps the Israelites' first major destination in exodus, one of the mountains in the range at the southern end of the Sinai peninsula is almost certainly *the* Sinai / Horeb of Exodus. Aharoni holds (165–70) that Paran was the original name for the whole of the Sinai peninsula; that "Sinai" is mentioned in the OT *only* in reference to the exodus and Yahweh's revelation of his Presence to Israel; that the location of Sinai / Horeb in the southern part of the peninsula is at least as old as the period of the united monarchy of Israel; and that the varied and sometimes apparently conflicting information about Israel's wilderness travels must be understood as the result of an attempt to combine into a single route the traditions of the separate travels of a number of tribal groups. The overlapping areas, the separate but synonymous designations of Exodus, Numbers, and Deuteronomy, may thus be seen to represent accurate memories that were never intended to be taken as a single route, and the major points of gathering for "the whole company of the sons of Israel" may be said to be at least four: the Red Sea, Kadesh-Barnea, Sinai / Horeb, and a ford of the Jordan River just north of the Dead Sea. Of these sites, only one can thus far be located with complete certainty: Kadesh-Barnea.

The notice that a month and a half has elapsed since the departure from Egypt comes as a bit of a surprise, since the only previous notice of the passage of time since the exodus, at 15:22, mentions three days. Here, just six verses farther along in the composite, a month and a half has slipped by. This measure of time has to do, in all probability, with the Priestly circle's liturgical calendar. It functions here, however, as an anticipation of what follows.

2–3 Israel has settled into a routine. The newness of freedom has worn off, and the hardship of wilderness life has set in, and so the people complain against their leaders. Coats (*Rebellion*, 21–28) has made an analysis of the occurrences in the OT of verb or noun forms of לון "grumble" followed by the preposition על "against" and has concluded that this combination, which occurs seven times in five verses (2, 7, 8, 9, 12) of this pericope, is both characteristic of "the murmuring motif" and always involves "a well-defined event." The "event" in this instance, as Coats (87–90) quite correctly points out, is not one that has been, but one that is about to occur. The exaggerated report of "plenty of meat" and "bread till we were stuffed" in Egypt provides a dramatic anticipation of "the coming miracle of meat and bread." It also combines the two gifts of food which appear to have been reported earlier in separate traditions of provision.

This point can be taken a step further still. The hungry complaint of the absence of food in the wilderness, heightened by an all-too-human exaggeration of the diet in Egypt, and reported with an almost humorous irony ("settled life," "plenty of meat," "bread till we were stuffed") is revealingly parallel to the panicky complaint of 14:11–12 that graves were in good supply in Egypt, verses that also serve to anticipate a miraculous intervention of Yahweh (see *Comment* above). There is another parallel in the elaborate description of the delicacies of an Egyptian menu in the complaint against manna in Num 11:4–6. That passage too is oriented toward the miracle to come, the provision of abundant meat by the flocks of quail.

In each of these three instances, a complaint stated with an excess that approaches humor is an anticipation of miraculous provision by Yahweh. Here and in Exod 14, the complaint is directed against Moses (with Aaron added here). In Num 11, no direct address is made, though Moses of course must hear the complaint. In each instance, however, the complaint functions ultimately as a complaint against Yahweh and a wish that the exodus from Egypt had never been made, even to the extent that it might have been prevented by an early death in Egypt (cf. Coats, *Rebellion*, 88–89). As such, all these complaints anticipate not only Yahweh's miraculous and Presence-proving reactions to them, but also Israel's tendency toward the incredible denial that culminates in the orgy of the golden calf. This anticipatory tendency, as noted above, governs this entire section, overriding considerations of logical sequence.

4–5 Thus the complaint of Israel is followed by a word of Yahweh to Moses that anticipates the provision of the manna, the disobedience of some of the people, and the hallowing of the sabbath as a special day of worship and rest. The manna is referred to as לחם "bread." That the reference is to the manna, and not to food in general, including even meat (so Cassuto, 192–93), is made clear by the further reference to a daily gathering, for six days, and in the morning of each day (vv 5, 7, 8, 12). Not only are the Israelites to gather the miracle-bread daily in the morning for six days of the week, they are to pick up only a day's supply on any given day, including the sixth day. Yahweh who provides the bread will provide also for the need of the day of non-harvest. They are to collect no more on the sixth day; what they gather on that day will turn out to be two days' supply when it is prepared for consumption. This assertion, alongside the statement of the miraculous expansion or reduction of the miracle-bread to the quantity of one omer in v 18, suggests an additional dimension of divine provision that is absent from the report of double-harvesting on the sixth day in the Priestly narrative of v 22.

6–8 Moses and Aaron and then Moses alone are next described responding to the complaining Israelites with much the same answer. Yahweh will bring at evening an experience that will prove his Presence in the exodus from Egypt, and in the morning, an experience of his כָּבוֹד, his "glory" = his Presence. These revelations will be his response to Israel's grumblings, identified as grumblings against Yahweh, despite their address. The evening experience is then specified as the provision of meat, the morning revelation as the provision of bread in abundance, and the direction of the grumbling of Israel is stated more pointedly still to be toward Yahweh.

9–12 When this point is made for the third time in a row, it is made in the most authoritative manner possible: by a theophany, in the midst of which Yahweh himself reports that he has received Israel's grumblings. Aaron is instructed by Moses to instruct the people to come near to Yahweh's Presence ("face"). Just how they are to do this is not said: at this point, before the arrival at Sinai, there is no ark, and no mention of the pillar of cloud or the pillar of fire has been made. In response to Aaron's instruction, indeed while he is speaking still, the people turn to face the wilderness. Just what wilderness they face, we are not told, but the fact that Yahweh appears to them there בֶּעָנָן "in a cloud" at least implies the wilderness of Sinai, the place of the greatest theophany.

At the moment of the theophany, Yahweh reports to Moses that he has heard Israel's grumblings, and he gives Moses a message for them. They are to have meat between dusk and dawn and bread in the morning. And the result of it all will be an experiential knowledge that Yahweh is their God. The use in v 12 of the autokerygmatic formula כִּי אֲנִי יהוה אֱלֹהֵיכֶם "that I am Yahweh your God" (see *Comment* on 6:2–13 and 12:12) is a pointed assertion of the movement of the entire provision-in-the-wilderness sequence. Like the mighty-act sequence in Egypt, the deliverance at the sea, and the guidance sequence, so also the provision sequence is to the end that Israel should come to know, on the basis of a firsthand experience, that Yahweh is God, and moreover, that he is Israel's God.

All questions of the logical sequence of this preparatory section have to be set aside as secondary to this major purpose of the composite. So also questions of the interlocking of the sabbath theme, the obedience / disobedience theme, and even the separation of the manna and meat traditions, each of which is an important motif in its own right, must be considered of lesser importance than the sum of the parts they present together. Not even the question of whether this whole narrative might fit better into the post-Sinai narrative (so Hyatt, 174) or the question of how Israel could possibly have doubts at *this* point about Yahweh's involvement with them or his intention to provide and care for them, must be allowed to fragment the impression of the composite as it stands. Israel's grumbling, not unlike Pharaoh's recalcitrance, becomes a foil for Yahweh's display of his provident Presence. And the repetition within this sequence, so often viewed as distraction and a basis for breaking it up, may better be seen as didactic, the multiplication for emphasis of an important preparatory point.

Explanation

What can be taken as a somewhat fragmented and disordered sequence, one characterized by a confusing gathering of themes and by *non sequiturs,* may better be seen as a deliberate sequence, designed to open the reader to several events to come, all of which are to a single end. The grumbling of the whole company of Israel, complaining against Moses, five times referred to in the section, and three times identified as grumbling against Yahweh, becomes the basis for his miracles of provision which demonstrate his Presence. The instructions regarding the use of the provision of food, both as regards the daily gathering of the foodstuff and also as regards the keeping of one day in seven as a special day, anticipate the gifts Yahweh's Presence brings as well as the response Yahweh's Presence invites. And the theophany in the direction of the (deeper) wilderness, with its declaration through Moses to Israel, is an anticipation of the great theophanic experience to come, with its accompanying revelation.

Israel's grumbling thus becomes occasion for a response of Yahweh that gives further proof of his Presence. But the report of the grumbling and the anticipation of Yahweh's response points both to and beyond the provision of food to the provision of Yahweh's supreme revelation of himself in the entire OT.

Yahweh's Provision for Israel in the Wilderness: Food (16:13–36)

Bibliography

Bodenheimer, F. S. "The Manna of Sinai." *BA* 10 (1947) 2–6. Also *BAR* 1:76–80. **Coppens, J.** "Les traditions relatives à la manne dans Exode xvi." *Estudios Eclesiásticos* 34 (1960) 473–89. **DeGuglielmo, A.** "What Was the Manna?" *CBQ* 2 (1940) 112–29. **Feliks, J.** "Wachtel." BHH. Göttingen: Vandenhoeck & Ruprecht, 1966. Col. 2123. **Galbiati, E.** *La Struttura Letteraria del' Esodo.* Milan: Edizioni Paoline, 1956. **Gray, J.** "The Desert Sojourn of the Hebrews and the Sinai-Horeb Tradition." *VT* 4 (1954) 148–54. **Heising, A.** "Exegese und Theologie der Alt- und Neutestamentlichen Speisewunder." *ZKT* 86 (1964) 80–96. **Jacob, B.** *Das Zweite Buch der Torah.* Unpublished MS, assembled posthumously in 1945, available on microfilm in the Library of Congress, and in photocopy at the University of Chicago. **Malina, B. J.** *The Palestinian Manna Tradition.* Leiden: E. J. Brill, 1968. **Noth, M.** *The Old Testament World.* London: Adam & Charles Black, 1966.

Translation

¹³ *That very evening,* ᵃ *therefore, the quails flew up* ᵇ *and blanketed the camp. And in the morning, there was a dewfall all around the camp.* ¹⁴ *When the dewfall evaporated, however, just look: all over the surface of the wilderness were thin flakes, as thin as a layer of frost* ᵃ *upon the earth.* ¹⁵ *Then the sons of Israel saw it, and they said, each man to his neighbor, "What is it?"* ᵃ *For they did not know what it was. So Moses said to them, "It is the food that Yahweh has given to you to eat.* ¹⁶ *This is the instruction* ᵃ *Yahweh gave—'Pick up of it, each man, what you need for food;* ᵇ *you are to take an omer per person, by the count of the persons a man has in his tent.' "* ᶜ

¹⁷ *Thus did the sons of Israel; they picked it up, some a lot and some a little.* ¹⁸ *Then when they measured it by the omer,* ᵃ *the one who took a lot had none too much, and the one who took a little had no shortage. Each had taken only* ᵇ *what he needed for food.* ¹⁹ *Moses said to them, "No man is to leave any of what he has picked up* ᵃ *until the next* ᵇ *morning."* ²⁰ *Some paid no attention to Moses, and they kept some until morning: it became wormy and vile-smelling. So Moses was furious with them.*

²¹ *They picked it up morning after morning, each man what he needed for food. When the sun heated it, it melted away.* ²² *On the sixth day, they picked up double the food, two omers per person, and all the chief men of the company came to report this to Moses.* ²³ *He* ᵃ *said to them, "This is what Yahweh specified: 'The sabbath-keeping of the sabbath holy to Yahweh is tomorrow: what you are going to bake, bake; what you are going to boil, boil. All that is left,* ᵇ *put aside for yourselves to keep until the morning.' "* ᶜ ²⁴ *So they put it aside until morning, just as Moses instructed, and it did not develop a vile smell, nor was there a worm in it.*

²⁵ *Then Moses said, "Eat this today, for this day is the sabbath of Yahweh— today, you will not find it on the ground.* ²⁶ *Six days you are to pick it up, then on the seventh day, a sabbath, there will not be any to pick up."* ᵃ ²⁷ *Yet on the seventh day, some of the people went out to pick it up—of course,* ᵃ *they found none.* ²⁸ *Thus Yahweh said to Moses, "How long will you be lax* ᵃ *about keeping my commands and my instructions?* ²⁹ *Take note* ᵃ *that Yahweh has given you* ᵇ *the sabbath: therefore he gives you on the sixth day two days' food! Stay, each man of you, in your own spot! Do not go out from your place, any man of you, on the seventh* ᶜ *day!"* ³⁰ *So the people ceased attempting to gather on the seventh day.*

³¹ *The family* ᵃ *of Israel came to call* ᵇ *it by the name "manna." It resembled the seed of the coriander plant, was white, and had a taste like flat honeycakes.* ³² *Moses said, "This is the instruction Yahweh gave: 'An omer-measure is to be kept for your descendants, so that they may see the food that I gave you to eat in the wilderness when I* ᵃ *brought you out from the land of Egypt.' "* ³³ *Moses also said to Aaron, "Take a single jar,* ᵃ *and put into it an omer-measure of manna and set it down in Yahweh's* ᵇ *Presence to be kept for your descendants."* ³⁴ *Just as Yahweh instructed Moses, Aaron set the jar* ᵃ *in front of the Testimony* ᵇ *to be kept.* ³⁵ *The sons of Israel ate the manna for forty years, until they came into habitable land; they ate the manna, until they came to the border of the land of Canaan.*

³⁶ *The omer, it should be noted,* ᵃ *is a tenth of an ephah.*

Notes

13.a. בערב ויהי "and thus it was in the evening."

13.b. עלה refers to the sudden appearance of the quails as from nowhere; they suddenly "flew up," as quails do, but this time in vast numbers.

14.a. LXX has ὡσεὶ κόριον λευκὸν ὡσεὶ πάγος "like coriander, white as frost." Cf. 16:31.

15.a. הוא מָן "what is it?" This question and the statement following it are sometimes given as an explanation of the term "manna." So Cassuto, 196.

16.a. הדבר "word, word of command" (BDB, 182) becomes "instruction" in this context.

16.b. אכלו לפי איש "a man according to his eating," i.e., according to the daily requirement, without storing any.

16.c. I.e., the persons for whom he has responsibility, his "house."

18.a. בעמר "by the omer"; the term is used only in this chapter of the OT, and as a quantitative measure amounting to about 2.3 liters. See Sellers, "Weights and Measures," *IDB* 4:835 § h; and BDB, 771.

18.b. No matter how much or how little each man gathered, his harvest was miraculously equated with his need, an omer per person; "only" is thus added above for clarity.

19.a. ממנו, lit., "leave from it."

19.b. The following morning is clearly intended, and so "next."

23.a. LXX (except B), Syr, Vg, Tg Ps-J read "Moses" here. LXXᴮ has κύριος = "Yahweh."

23.b. I.e., all that has been prepared, by baking or by boiling, but not eaten. No allowance is made for manna in its raw, or unprepared form.

23.c. The morning of the next day, the sabbath.

26.a. יהיה־בו לא, lit., "there will not be in it."

27.a. Special *waw*.

28.a. מאנתם lit. means "you refuse"; BDB, 549, suggests also "be distasteful, slothful." The sense above is clearly negligence; disregard as opposed to a willful rebellion, so "lax."

29.a. ראו "see, consider," as BDB notes, 907, "nearly = הַנֵּה."

29.b. LXX adds τὴν ἡμέραν ταύτην "this day."

29.c. SamPent, LXXᶠ, Ethiopic have השבת "the sabbath day."

31.a. בית "house," read בני "sons" by LXX, Syr, some Tg MSS (see Sperber 1:117).

31.b. קרא, with special *waw*.

32.a. LXX has κύριος "when Yahweh (lit., the Lord)."

33.a. LXX, Tg Ps-J (text 27031, Déaut, 139) read στάμνον χρυσοῦν "golden jar."

33.b. LXX has τοῦ θεοῦ "God's."

34.a. The text has "it," but the jar of manna is the clear antecedent of the pronoun, and so "the jar" is added above.

34.b. עדת refers to the Testimony of the Ten Commandments engraved on stone tablets, a symbol of Yahweh's guiding Presence. See BDB, 730. LXXᴮ adds τοῦ θεοῦ "of God" after "Testimony."

36.a. This phrase is added to make clear the intrusive nature of this explanatory note, a probable addition of a later hand.

Form/Structure/Setting

As I have noted already (*Form/Structure/Setting* on 16:1–12), Exod 16 is a composite governed by a "provision" motif: Yahweh provides for his people nourishment for the body in the manna and the quails, and nourishment for the spirit in the sabbath-rest. Vv 1–12 function as an introduction to these provision-narratives by means of two anticipatory themes: Israel's grumbling and Yahweh's own response to Israel's complaints.

The difficulty of any analysis of the sources making up Exod 16 is shown by the divergence of approach from one school of critics to another, especially in the assignment of the bulk of the chapter to both P (the view of the majority of the source critics) and J (so Rudolph, *"Elohist"* 34–36). This difficulty has led, in turn, to a series of proposals moving beyond source analysis to a kind of structural analysis designed to solve the tangle of sequential problems presented by the chapter (so Jacob, *Zweite Buch,* 647–50; Galbiati, *La Struttura,* 164–75; Coppens, *Estudios Eclesiásticos* 34 [1960] 473–89; Malina, *Manna Tradition,* 10–20; see above on 16:1–12). Childs (276–80) has suggested "a traditional sequence," reflected also in Num 14 and 16, as the factor governing the form of Exod 16.

Despite some helpful suggestions, none of these approaches offers an acceptable explanation of the form and the sequence of Exod 16, in part because they operate from assumptions of logical development that may well have been absent from the mind of the ancient redactor and his readers. Our most important clue to an understanding of the form of Exod 16 is not Exod 16 as it might have been but Exod 16 as it is. The form of this chapter is dictated not by a dominating source to which other accounts are supplemental, but by a theme: provision demonstrating Presence. That theme, anticipated by vv 1–12, overrides the sources that present it and any alignment of those sources logical by our Western canons precisely because its theological importance far outweighs considerations of style and sequence. For this same reason, indeed, instructions are repeated, the question of the name "manna" is dealt with twice, the provision of food proving the Presence is three times intertwined with the provision of the day of rest celebrating the Presence, a symbol of Presence yet to be invented, the "Testimony," is introduced, and even several qualifying and time-bridging notes are lovingly added.

The assignment of most of 16:13–36 to P (so Beer, 87–90; Noth, 131–33; Hyatt, 16–17; Childs, 275) with J material interspersed and redactor's comments and a gloss added is the usual source-critical analysis, but any such analysis must not be permitted to obscure the impact of a chapter that is far more in compilation than the sum of its supposed component parts.

Comment

13–14 The anticipation of meat in the evening and bread in the morning raised in vv 8 and 12 is satisfied immediately by this narrative of Yahweh's provision for his grumbling people, and according to a pattern strikingly similar to the prediction-fulfillment sequence of the mighty acts in Egypt, designed also to prove Yahweh's claim of powerful and effective Presence. The very evening of the promise delivered by Yahweh through Moses and Aaron, the quails arrive and the manna falls.

Naturalistic explanations of the quails and the manna abound. The quails are held to be flocks migrating from their winter habitat in Africa, coming to the ground exhausted from their flight (Gray, *VT* 4 [1954] 148–49; McCullough, "Quail," *IDB* 3:973, who cites Aristotle and Tristram; Feliks, *BHH,* col. 2123). The manna is described as the "liquid honeydew excretion" of a number of insects in "dry deserts and steppes" (Bodenheimer, *BA* 10 [1947] 6; cf. DeGuglielmo, *CBQ* 2 [1940] 119–21). While it is entirely possible that such natural phenomena provide a point of departure for the provision narratives, however, the acts of provision are described in Exod 16; Num 11; and Ps 78:23–29 as entirely unnatural, the miraculous actions of a God who proves his Presence by providing for his people's need. The preface to these narratives in vv 1–12 is alone enough to establish their theological intention, but the narratives themselves underscore that intention repeatedly.

The quails are mentioned less in their arrival than in the anticipation of that arrival in vv 8 and 12. After a brief report that they "flew up" and covered the camp (cf. the much fuller account of Num 11:31–35), the narrative moves on to a detailed and repetitive account of the manna, which in turn provides opportunity for an account of the sacred nature of the sabbath day. The connection of the arrival of the manna along with the dewfall (see Noth, *OT World,* 31) further links the manna to the morning and is one of several attempts to describe the manna: it was in "thin flakes" and gave the appearance of a coat of frost, a statement reinforced by the note in v 31 that it was white.

15–16 The Israelites did not know what the strange frostlike material was, so they asked הוּא מָן "what is it?"—a question which then serves as a folk-etymology for the name "manna," in the vernacular, "whazit?" Moses explains that the strange substance is the food (לֶחֶם) of Yahweh's provision, and that Yahweh has specified that no one is to collect more of it than is needed for a day's food, a quantity set at one omer, about two and one-third liters or two quarts, by dry measure, for each member of a given household.

17–18 This specification, however, is miraculously governed, in two ways. No matter how much or how little the men collected, they found themselves when they came to prepare and eat the manna with precisely the amount needed and allowed for the day's food. The amount collected was always the amount specified.

19–21 The second control on the collection of the manna was inherent: the manna had to be eaten the day it was picked up; otherwise it became wormy and putrid. It had to be picked up in the morning before the sun warmed it enough to melt it.

22–24 Both these restrictive measures, miraculously set (cf. Heising, *ZKT* 86 [1964] 80–81), could be miraculously removed, a removal necessitated by the need to keep the sabbath holy to Yahweh. On the sixth day, the collection amounted to two omers per person. This statement in v 22 must be read in the light of the statement of v 5 that the collection of the sixth day was double that of each of the other days. Once again, the control of the amount collected is miraculous (cf. Malina, *Manna Tradition,* 17), but on the sixth day the amount allowed was doubled to provide a quantity of food sufficient also for the sabbath, when there would be no collection. This expansion of the amount alarmed the people's leaders, who were concerned that the one-omer limit was being passed. Moses allayed their fears with the explanation that Yahweh intended and allowed it to be so. They were to prepare it, whether by baking or boiling, and then keep the leftovers to eat on the sabbath. The second control was also miraculously waived: the manna kept over on the sixth day did not spoil.

25–30 The extra collection of the sixth day, and Moses' explanation of it to the anxious chief men gives place to a more detailed account of the provision of Yahweh's sabbath. There is no manna to collect on that day, and those who go out to collect it despite Moses' instruction and assurance of course find none. Their disobedience gives rise to a complaint of Yahweh about laxity in the keeping of his commands. Yahweh's sabbath is his gift to Israel; he provides them on the sixth day with two days' supply of manna, to allow for the seventh day, and so each one is commanded not to stir forth from his place on the seventh day. This time, the instruction is heeded.

Here again, the patterns of belief-disbelief and obedience-disobedience recurrent in the mighty act sequence and indeed in the narrative sequence of the entire Book of Exodus stand out in bold relief. Yahweh proves his Presence by a miraculous provision for a people who then fail to believe and who disregard his clear instruction. Yahweh provides for physical needs each day, only to have some of his people attempt to hoard for the next day. Yahweh provides for the spiritual growth of his people by setting one day apart as special, only to have some lose the benefit by ignoring the day. All this is of course both anticipation and reflection of what is to come in the most important and incredible narrative of them all, in chaps. 19–20, 32–34. Heising (*ZKT* 86 [1964] 83–84) links these contrasts to "the religious intention of J" and to "the basic intention of P's salvation-teaching method." But a larger concept still is clearly operative, one that informs and undergirds not only the individual source accounts, but also the compilation of those accounts into the Book of Exodus.

31 A second time, the manna, designated as so-named by the children of Israel, is described—this time a bit more fully than in v 14. There it is said to have been in the form of thin flakes and to have looked like frost. Here it is said to be white, to look like the seed of the coriander plant ("small, globular, grayish, aromatic seed with ridges," Trever, "Coriander Seed," *IDB* 1:681), and to have a taste like that of flat (and therefore crisp?) honeycakes. Zohary ("Flora," *IDB* 2:289) notes that the likeness of the *Coriandrum sativum* to the manna has to do only with "the size and shape of the seeds."

32–34 A further instruction of Yahweh establishes a further miraculous suspension of the prohibitions concerning manna. One omer, a day's ration for one person, was to be collected and put into a jar as a witness to future generations of Yahweh's provision for his people in the wilderness. This omer could be kept without deterioration, and not only its container but also its location is specified. This location, as critics have frequently pointed out, is anachronistically specified here. "The Testimony" in front of which the jar containing the manna is to be placed is The Testimony of the tables of the Ten Words, or the Ark of the Covenant containing these tables of the Commandments (BDB, 730), and of course, neither tables nor Commandments nor Ark nor Covenant have made an appearance in the Exodus narrative to this point. Neither, for that matter, apart from this passage, has the institution of the Sabbath holy to Yahweh.

These references are set here however for an important theological purpose which overrides considerations of logical and chronological sequence. Yahweh has proved his Presence in his provision for a complaining and disobedient people. That proof, miraculously wrought, must be made plain to the descendants of Israel who have yet to face the struggle of belief. They should share the story of their fathers and also the important evidences of their faith.

Thus is the manna to be kept, one omer of it, one day's supply for one person. It is to be put into a jar and located in a spot before an object anyone reading this passage would know full well. The redactor who made the compilation of Exod 16 was aware of this and was more interested in the proof and its transmission to the generations than in preserving a chronological and consistent sequence.

35–36 Two final notes round out the provision narratives. The first indicates that the manna was at least a part of the Israelite diet until they came to the promised land of Canaan. The second, an unconnected "footnote" or gloss, specifies, as an afterthought the redactor considered important, that an omer is the equivalent of one-tenth of an ephah. Since the ephah, the basic OT measure of solids, is equal to about one-half bushel, an omer would be equal to slightly more than two quarts (Sellers, "Weights and Measures," *IDB* 4:834–35). These quantities are rough estimates, since as de Vaux (*Ancient Israel*, 199–203) has pointed out, our knowledge of ancient Hebrew terms of measurement has too many blank spots. The note of v 36 is an attempt to prevent just such a blank spot, in ancient times.

Explanation

Yahweh's provision for his people is the obvious point of the compilation of Exod 16; and emphasis of that point overrides considerations of logical and chronological sequence in the introductory and theme-setting prologue of vv 1–12 and in the narrative development of these themes in vv 13–36. Further, the redactors of this sequence have gone to great lengths, to stress the comprehensive nature of Yahweh's provision. It is provision in the morning, in the manna, and provision in the evening, in the quails. It is provision for the need for reflection and the strengthening of the spirit, in the sabbath, but that provision is not allowed to set aside the provision of food: the quantity of manna allowed is doubled on the day before the sabbath. It is even provision for the duration of the wilderness experience, for we are expressly told that the Israelites were provided manna until they reached the border of the land promised them, that land described elsewhere as "flowing with milk and honey," where therefore manna would not be needed.

This array of miraculous provision answers more than physical and even spiritual needs. It proves Yahweh's Presence, just as had the mighty acts in Egypt, the deliverance at the Sea, the water miracles, and the guidance through the wilderness. Yahweh is seen as provident, and as compassionately so: he provides for more than the barest needs of subsistence, and he is tolerant of laxity and carelessness concerning his instructions. Yahweh's providence extends also to the descendants of Israel yet to be born: he specified that they be given the opportunity of seeing for themselves how he has provided for their fathers in the barren wilderness.

Over against Yahweh's provision and kindness, however, there is set the contrasting attitude of the Israelites. They grumble and complain; dissatisfied with what they are given, they are always wanting something different or something more; they are disregardful of the instructions given by Yahweh who has freed and is guiding and providing for them; and sometimes they even do the opposite of what they are told.

Thus the pattern is set, and it is increasingly and repeatedly demonstrated. Yahweh is present—powerfully, effectively, beneficently, and convincingly present. But the people of Israel, the recipients of so much of Yahweh's care and the people to whom Yahweh even gives himself are unaccountably insensitive, indifferent, disobedient, and finally overtly rebellious. Exodus is a history of theological relationship written with an incredible tension hovering, the tension of a loving provident God giving himself to a chosen people whose ways reject him. The narratives of Israel in the wilderness are thus a part of an accumulating preparation for the quite unbelievable story of Israel at Sinai.

Israel's Testing of Yahweh and Moses   (17:1-7)

Bibliography

Fritz, V. *Israel in der Wüste. Traditionsgeschichte Untersuchung der Wüstenüberlieferung des Jahwisten.* Marburg: N. G. Elwert Verlag, 1970. **Gemser, B.** "The *Rib*- or Controversy-Pattern in Hebrew Mentality." *Wisdom in Israel and the Ancient Near East.* VTSup 3. Leiden: E. J. Brill, 1955. 120–37. **Gunneweg, A. H. J.** *Leviten und Priester.* FRLANT 89. Göttingen: Vandenhoeck & Ruprecht, 1965. **Lehming, S.** "Massa und Meriba." *ZAW* 73 (1961) 71–77. **Würthwein, E.** "Der Ursprung der prophetischen Gerichtsrede." *ZTK* 48–49 (1951–1952) 1–16.

Translation

[1] *Next, they journeyed forth, the whole company of the sons of Israel, from the wilderness of Sin, setting out as Yahweh directed.* [a] *They pitched camp at Rephidim ("places of spreading out"?), where there was no water for the people to drink.* [2] *So it was that the people became dissatisfied with Moses, and said "Give* [a] *us water, so that we may drink!" But Moses answered them, "Why are you so dissatisfied with me? Why are you putting Yahweh on trial?"* [3] *Still the people were parched for water there, so the people grumbled against Moses, and said, "What is this? You have brought us up from Egypt to kill us,* [a] *along with our sons and our stock, of thirst?"*

[4] *Moses then called out to Yahweh for help, saying, "What am I to do with these people? A little more, and they will be stoning me to death!"* [5] *So Yahweh said to Moses, "Move along in front of the people, and take with you some of the elders of Israel: take in your hand the staff with which you struck the river Nile, and go along.* [6] *When you see me standing* [a] *in front of you, there on a rock in Horeb, then strike the rock, and water will flow forth from it, so that the people can drink." So Moses did exactly that, as the elders of Israel looked on.* [b]

[7] *For that reason,* [a] *he called the name of the place "Massah (Testing) and Meribah (Dissatisfaction)," on account of the dissatisfaction of the sons of Israel and on account of their putting Yahweh to the test, asking, "Is Yahweh present with us, or not?"*

Notes

1.a. יהוה עַל־פִּי, lit., "according to the mouth, word of Yahweh."
2.a. This verb, impv pl in MT, is sg in LXX, Syr, Tg Ps-J, Vg, SamPent.
3.a. אֹתִי "me" is read "us" by LXX, Syr, Vg, Tg Ps-J.
6.a. עֹמֵד הִנְנִי lit., "Behold me standing."
6.b. זִקְנֵי לְעֵינֵי "before the eyes of the elders." LXX adds τῶν υἱῶν "the sons of" after "elders."
7.a. Special *waw*.

Form/Structure/Setting

The composite nature of this section is obvious, with its successive references to the continuation of Israel's route in the wilderness, to a new problem of water supply, to yet another complaint-crisis, and to the two symbolic place-names Massah and Meribah. The literary critics in general have assigned most of this material to J or to E, with the opening geographical note mentioning the wilderness of Sin and Rephidim going to P. So Noth (137–40), for example, assigns v 1abα to P; v 1bβ, v 3 to E; and vv 2, 4–7 to J. Hyatt (179–82) poses a combination of two etiological stories and gets v 1a, P; vv 1b–3 and 7, JE; and vv 4–6, E. There are exceptions to this general pattern, however. Rudolph (*"Elohist,"* 32–33, 36–39, 275), by an involved fragmenting, attributes most of the section to J. Fritz (*Israel in der Wüste,* 10–12, 48–54) proposed P as the determinative source, one supplemented in this section by J.

Other critics make the obvious comparison of this section with Num 20:2–13, and argue that this material should be analyzed by means of traditions bound to place-name etiology. So Coats (*Rebellion,* 53–82), for example, connects Exod 17:1–7 primarily with J; Num 20:1–13 primarily with P; and argues that the Meribah reference is fundamental to the Exodus passage, that the Massah reference is a secondary addition (from Dtr), and that three levels are involved in the growth of the narrative: a Meribah–רִיב wordplay, "a miraculous aid" in the wilderness layer, and "the murmuring motif." All of this, in turn, was joined to a Massah-spring tradition, probably in the Deuteronomistic redaction (62–63, 70–71). Childs (306–7), on the other hand, sees in the Meribah narrative the reflection of his oral "Pattern I" (258)—need, complaint, intercession, miraculous meeting of need—and proposes that the etiology of "Meribah" was an expansion of "the primary tradition" reflected in this pattern.

This multiplicity of opinion about the makeup of Exod 17:1–7 makes clear that the shifts and currents present in this section render any universally acceptable source or tradition analysis an impossibility. The evidence is too ambiguous; the points of departure are too elusive. Wherever and whenever the Meribah theme originated, its occurrence in this passage, as elsewhere in the OT (cf. Num 20:13; Deut 33:8; Pss 95:8; 106:32–33), recalls an experience of Israel's putting Yahweh, and sometimes Moses, to a test of patience. In an interesting variation of this theme, Yahweh tests Israel's faith and loyalty (cf. Ps 81:8 [7]). The testing of Yahweh on the wilderness trek to Sinai is the lodestone of this pericope. To this motif are drawn a variety of memories of such testing, from a variety of the layers of Israel's experience. The end-product, viewed from a literary or even a traditio-analytical perspective, can only give an impression of fragmentation. But seen in the focus of its purpose, Israel's doubting of what should be undoubtable, this section shows a remarkable oneness, admirably summed up in the question of Moses that closes it (v 7).

Comment

1   The note of the continuation of the wilderness journey from Sin to the camp of Rephidim is, like all such references, an attempt to locate the exodus journeying (see *Comment* on 15:22; 16:1), but one that no longer succeeds because of our ignorance of the location of the places named. Exod 19:1-2 and Num 33:15 make Rephidim the last stop before Sinai, and the reference to "a rock in Horeb" in v 6 gives some confirmation to this proximity, but the difficulty of locating Sinai limits the usefulness of this information. The location of the camp at Rephidim, a place where there was no water, no doubt meant that no oasis was within traveling distance of the previous campsite, in the right direction. The obvious reason for the inclusion of such a detail in a theologically oriented narrative, however, is that it becomes the basis for a further miracle of provision demonstrating Yahweh's powerful Presence.

2   This time, though, the proof of the Presence is further dramatized by Israel's doubt of Moses and therefore of Yahweh as well. The motif is a familiar one by this point in the narrative of Exodus, both because of the frequency of its recurrence and because it functions as a dramatic foil for a conclusive proof that Yahweh really is present, and effectively so. Israel thus becomes dissatisfied (ריב) with Moses' leadership and demands that he provide them water to drink. The answer of Moses to the people's fault-finding makes the essential connection and describes the protest for what it is: their dissatisfaction with Moses is an attack on Yahweh.

The key term for this attack in the section at hand is ריב "strive, contend, be dissatisfied or find fault with," a verb from which the noun ריב "dispute, case taken to court" and the name מריבה "Meribah" ("Dissatisfaction-place") are derived. A primary usage of ריב in the OT has to do with formal legal proceedings, as Exod 23:2-3, 6 or Deut 25:1 show. The studies of Köhler (*Deuterojesaja: Stilkritisch Untersucht*, BZAW 37 [Giessen: A. Töpelmann, 1923] 110–20), Begrich (*Studien zu Deuterojesaja*, BWANT 25 [Stuttgart: Kohlhammer Verlag, 1938] 18–31), Würthwein (*ZTK* 48–49 [1951–52] 1–16), and Gemser (*Wisdom in Israel*, 120–37) have surveyed the legal sense of the ריב-family of terms, but they have established also a usage that refers to an informal and prelegal accusation and quarrel (cf. Begrich, 29–31) and even to what Gemser (127–28, 136–37) calls "a frame of mind." In vv 2 and 7 of this section, ריב functions in this prelegal sense, to describe not a formal "suit" against Yahweh, but a complaint, a general protest of dissatisfaction ("outside the legal sphere, to fix blame ['*Vorwürfe machen*']," Würthwein, 4, n.1).

3–6   A second reference to the people's reaction to the dry campsite, perhaps a reflection of another narrative source, uses the verb לון "grumble" (see n. 15:24.a. above), and states the protest in the sarcastic-rhetorical style of 14:11–12 and 16:2–3 (see above). Parched with thirst, the people wonder to Moses' face why he has brought them forth from Egypt to die of thirst, along with their progeny and their livestock. Coats (*Rebellion* 89–90) suggests that here, as in other passages belonging to what he calls "the murmuring motif," the real problem is the exodus itself, with the lack of water (or food) serving as no more than a setting for a protest that Egypt has been left at all. This seems to me to be beyond what these narratives suggest, but there can be no doubt that more is involved in the general dissatisfaction of Israel than water and food, as important as these necessities of life are.

We must remember that the composite before us has a *theological* purpose, and that narrative details of incidents along the way have been included to that end. That point is made dramatically by what follows next. As usual under such circumstances, Moses cries out to Yahweh for help, his cry tinged with the fear that the people may be about to turn on him in violence. The point is that with Moses' authority under question, so also is Yahweh's. Thus it is Yahweh who must provide the solution, and it is Yahweh who does so provide. Moses is instructed to move in front of the people, not away from them, but out where they can see him; and to take with him some of the elders, the wise and trustworthy leaders, as well as the staff with which he struck the river Nile in the first of the mighty acts in Egypt (7:17, 20; cf. also 8:12–13 [16–17]). He is then to go along until he sees a rock Yahweh will designate by "standing" upon it. He is to strike that rock with the staff, and that blow will bring water gushing forth to quench the people's thirst.

Nothing is said of the nature of Yahweh's guiding appearance to Moses; as with the theophany of Exod 3:1–6, apparently only Moses saw it. This appearance is important, however, both for Moses and for the solution to the people's (and therefore Moses') plight: it is the telling proof of Yahweh's Presence which results, once more, in provision for his complaining people. The naturalistic explanations of the water as coming from a spring that flows beneath "a thin layer of rock" (so Cassuto, 202–3) are as misplaced as the attempts at a "logical" accounting for the manna and the quails (see *Comment* on 16:13–24). The whole point of and reason for this narrative is Yahweh's miraculous provision for his people, by supplying water where there was none, from the unlikeliest of all spots, a rock. A specific rock is clearly intended, as the reference to Yahweh standing upon it suggests, rather than "the rocky mass in general" (Driver, 157), and Moses follows his instructions to the letter, watched by the elders who can report the miracle without prejudice.

7 The point of this narrative is underscored by its summary conclusion: Moses names the place "Testing and Dissatisfaction," a name that reverses the sequence of the events, since the dissatisfied people put Yahweh (and Moses) to the test by their complaining, a complaining which posed the unbelievable question, "Is Yahweh present with us, or not?" The scandal of this question of course is that their release and their freedom, their rescue at the sea, their guidance through and sustenance in the wilderness, and their very presence at Rephidim all answered such an inquiry in pointed and unmistakable events. The only unbelievable aspect of the narrative is that the Israelites could possibly ask such a question at such a time, and on the basis of so flimsy a provocation. The question anticipates the terrible doubt of Exod 32, even as it poses, with stark economy, the real basis of the grumbling and contending narratives and the proof-of-Presence narratives preceding them: is Yahweh's claim really demonstrated; is his Presence really proven? The addition in this summary verse of the name מסה "Massah" may be, as Noth (139) and Coats (*Rebellion*, 55–58, 62–71) propose, an addition to the Meribah narrative of a portion of another spring story. If so or if not, the effect of the inclusion of Massah in the name Moses assigns to the miraculous spring is an emphasis upon the unbelievable "trying" of a Yahweh who has proven his power and his Presence over and over again. The combination appears also in Deut 33:8 and Ps 95:8, and with similar effect. The theory of Lehming (*ZAW* 73 [1961] 76–77) that Massah refers originally not to a place at all but to the "testing" of Yahweh's "pious one" ("den du in Versuchung versucht hast") in Deut 33:8 and that it came by a misunderstanding to be regarded as a place name in Exod 17:7 and other passages is not sustained by the evidence (cf. Gunneweg, *Leviten und Priester*, 41–43). Both Massah and Meribah are clearly presented in this passage and elsewhere as place names connected with the testing and complaining traditions.

Explanation

Once more, then, Yahweh provides for the need of his people, this time for the physical need of water. Once more, when a need arises, the Israelites do not wait for it to be met; indeed they do not even assume that it *can* be met. Rather they attack Yahweh and put him on trial by attacking Moses, to put *him* on trial. Their thirst, of course, was real. But infinitely *more* real was the powerful Presence of Yahweh in their midst. The lesser reality they embraced; the more important reality they ignored and doubted: so once more, he dealt with the lesser reality by a demonstration of the greater, underlying reality.

All this is presented not only as a composite of the proof of the Presence in the wilderness by Yahweh's meeting of his people's need; it serves also as an accumulating anticipation of the even greater proof to come, followed, not preceded, by an even greater disbelief. The composite sections of the whole that is the Book of Exodus thus have to be understood not only as self-contained units with an integrity of their own, outweighing the separate directions of the sources that have been used to make them up; they must be seen also as working parts of the larger structure of Exodus, and as part of an inexorable movement to a proof of Yahweh's Presence and a rebellion born of doubt. Such perspectives go a long way toward setting the theological frame and contributing the basic theological rhetoric for the whole OT.

Israel's First Battle: Amalek   (17:8–16)

Bibliography

Childs, B. S. *Memory and Tradition in Israel.* SBT 37. London: SCM Press, 1962. **Gradwohl, R.** "Zum Verständnis von Ex. XVII 15f." *VT* 12 (1962) 491–94. **Grønbaek, J. H.** "Juda und Amalek. Überlieferungsgeschichtliche Erwägungen zu Exodus 17, 8–

16." *ST* 18 (1964) 26–45. **Mölenbrink, K.** "Josua im Pentateuch." *ZAW* 59 (1942–43) 14–58. **Schmid, H.** *Mose: Überlieferung und Geschichte.* BZAW 110. Berlin: Alfred Töpelmann, 1968. **Seebass, H.** *Mose und Aaron, Sinai und Gottesberg.* Bonn: H. Bouvier, 1962.

Translation

⁸ *It was also in Rephidim* ᵃ *that Amalek* (*"Trouble-maker"?*) *came and joined battle with Israel.* ⁹ *Then Moses said to Joshua* (*"Yahweh is deliverance"*), *"Select for us* ᵃ *men,* ᵇ *then go out, join battle with Amalek: tomorrow, I will station myself upon the brow of the hill, with the staff of God in my hand."* ¹⁰ *Joshua did just as Moses instructed him, joining battle with Amalek. Moses, Aaron, and Hur* (*"Child"?*) ᵃ *went up to the brow of the hill.* ¹¹ *And when Moses lifted up his hand,* ᵃ *Israel was stronger; but when he dropped* ᵇ *his hand,* ᵃ *then Amalek was stronger.* ¹² *The hands of Moses grew heavy, and so they took a rock and placed it under him, that he might sit down upon it, and Aaron and Hur, one on either side of him, supported his hands. Thus did his hands hold steady* ᵃ *until sundown,* ¹³ *and consequently, Joshua disabled Amalek and his people* ᵃ *with the sword-blade.* ᵇ

¹⁴ *There Yahweh said to Moses, "Write this as a reminder in the book, and drum it* ᵃ *into Joshua's ears: 'I will utterly efface the recollection of Amalek beneath the heavens!' "* ¹⁵ *Then Moses built an altar,* ᵃ *and named it "Yahweh is my standard."* ¹⁶ *Indeed, he said, "Because* ᵃ *a hand has been against Yah's throne,* ᵇ *there will be battle between Yahweh and Amalek, from one generation to another."*

Notes

8.a. Special *waw* at the beginning plus ברפידם "in Rephidim" at the end of the verse.
9.a. LXX σεαυτῷ and Syr read "for yourself."
9.b. LXX ἄνδρας δυνατούς "strong men, men of ability."
10.a. חור "Hur," according to Noth (*Personennamen*, 221), is "probably a pet name." It might, however, be related to חור "be white, grow pale" and mean "White One" (see BDB, 301) or even to חרר and refer to the Horite or Hurrian people, who originally appear to have been cave dwellers (see BDB, 359–60, and Speiser, "Horite," *IDB* 2:645).
11.a. SamPent reads ידי "hands" here, in agreement with v 12.
11.b. יניח ידו "he caused his hand to rest."
12.a. MT is more graphic still: ויהי ידיו אמונה "and thus his hands were firmness." SamPent, LXX, Tg Onk, Tg Ps-J, Syr read the verb as pl, instead of MT's more general ויהי.
13.a. SamPent adds ויכם "and struck them."
13.b. לפי־חרב "by the sword's mouth."
14.a. ושים "and fix, establish, set."
15.a. LXX adds κυρίῳ "to Yahweh."
16.a. Syr reads הנה "behold," instead of כי "because."
16.b. MT is difficult: כִּי־יָד עַל־כֵּס יָהּ "because a hand has been against (the throne?) of Yah." "Throne" requires כִּסֵּא or כִּסֵּה. The alternate possibility, followed by rsv, is כִּי־יָד עַל־נֵס יָהּ "because a hand has been against the flag of Yah." "Throne" is preferred above, since MT must be emended in any case and since no special flag of Yahweh is known elsewhere in the OT. The Versions generally lean toward "throne"; so SamPent, Syr, Vg. LXX has ἐν χειρὶ κρυφαίᾳ "with a secret hand," used in reference to Yahweh's waging war on Amalek. Tg MS 27031 (Déaut, 145) paraphrases elaborately: "He said, 'Because the Word of Yahweh has sworn by the throne of his Glory that by his Word he will fight against the entire house of Amalek, he will wipe them out for the three generations: this present generation, the generation of the Messiah, and the generation of the world to come.' " The *Preliminary and Interim Report on the Hebrew Old Testament Text Project*, ed. Barthélemy (*Pentateuch*, 110), citing its "Factor 8"

("Misunderstanding of linguistic data") reads "⟨for a hand⟩⟨has been raised⟩ against the throne of the LORD: (⟨therefore there is⟩ war between the LORD and Amalek)."

Form/Structure/Setting

This narrative of Israel's first battle, a conflict with the Amalekites, the descendants of Esau (Gen 36:12, 15–16), appears to serve both as a justification for a continuing enmity and as a further testimony of Yahweh's care for his people, this time by a miraculous enhancement of their fighting ability, clearly linked to his Presence on the field of conflict. The compact and sequential developmment of the narrative suggests that it is a unity, and the literary critics have generally agreed that it is so, without clear consensus about the hand from which it comes. So Beer (92) gives the section mostly to his J[1] (v 14: R[D]); Hyatt (183) prefers E, but also assigns v 14 to "a Deuteronomic redactor"; Davies (145) assigns the entire section "probably" to E; Noth (141), just as tentatively, attributes it to J (though note his *Pentateuchal Traditions*, 120, n. 343), remarking however that it "belongs to the old narrative material"; and Childs (313), also commenting that the "basic story . . . gives the impression of being ancient," assigns the section to no specific source.

Certainly the chief reason for assignment to E, the appearance of מטה האלהים "the staff of Elohim" in v 9, is inconclusive, not least because no further reference to the staff is made. Similarly, the evidence for the supposed antiquity of the narrative is too speculative to permit its attribution to any old narrative source, though a logical suggestion might be the Book of the Wars of Yahweh mentioned in Num 21:14. That this battle with the Amalekites is one of the earliest of the "Wars of Yahweh" after the defeat of the Egyptians at the Sea is suggested both by its occurrence in the Exodus narrative at this point, and also by the persistence of the Amalekite-Israelite enmity throughout the OT (see Landes, "Amalek," *IDB* 1:101–2).

The primary function of this section in its present location is the demonstration of yet another proof and benefit of Yahweh's Presence with Israel. The occasion for the demonstration this time is an attack from the outside instead of an internal complaint. The result, however, is once again an undeniably supernatural intervention of Yahweh. The leader of the military force, Joshua, is given instructions by Moses, the religious-civil leader whose guidance is always from God. The staff of Elohim, the appearance of a symbolic cultic blessing in the lifting of Moses' hands, and the recording of what seems to be a divine curse in perpetuity all have as their primary aim in this context the demonstration of the important theological point that Yahweh is present, when the need arises, to fight alongside and even on behalf of his people.

Thus Joshua, in his first appearance in the OT, is not properly introduced. Neither is Hur, the son of Caleb. And the enmity between Jacob and Esau, carried on in the bitter animosity between the Israelites and the Amalekites, is not given an appropriate explanation. No reason is given for Amalek's attack, and no consequences of the battle are described beyond the essential reference to Amalek's defeat. Everything about the encounter takes second place to its primary point, Yahweh's intervention for Israel, and that point thus dictates the form this section takes.

Comment

8 The reference to Rephidim as the location for the battle with the Amalekites has sometimes been regarded as "out of place" (Noth, 141) and "dependent on v 1" (Hyatt, 183), in part because of the connection of the Amalekites with Kadesh in Gen 14:7 and with the Negeb in general in Num 13:29 and 1 Sam 15:7 and 27:8 and in part because of the placement of Rephidim by the sequence of the narrative of Exodus in proximity to Sinai. None of this information is conclusive, however, and since both Sinai and Rephidim cannot be located, and since the Amalekites appear to have been a nomadic group who roamed Sinai and the Arabah north of Ezion-Geber as well as the Negeb (cf. Landes, "Amalek," *IDB* 1: 101 § 2; Grønbaek, *ST* 18 [1964] 26–29), there is no reason that they could not have turned up on Israel's route toward Sinai, wherever it lay. The conflict may even have been connected with Israel's discovery and use of water in a difficult area where none was known before. After a long history of conflict, the Amalekites are said finally to have been dealt a concluding blow in Hezekiah's time (1 Chr 4:34–43), but as Hyatt (183) points out, their antagonism may be preserved even in the Book of Esther in the designation of the villainous Haman as an Agagite (Esth 3:1), after the most infamous of the Amalekite kings (1 Sam 15). As Grønbaek (29–31, 42–45) has suggested, traditio-historical analysis of this pericope against the other OT references to the Amalekites may reveal the expansion of earlier traditions to accommodate later ones.

9 The attack of Amalek prompts Moses to give instructions that appear to be the result of another cry for help to Yahweh, though such an exchange is missing from the narrative. Joshua is mentioned without elaboration as a military commander clearly subject to Moses' command; note Beer's (92) somewhat Prussian designations: Joshua is "Der eigentliche Heerführer," Moses "der Oberfeldherr." Joshua is clearly understood in this narrative as the younger assistant of Moses and as the military leader he came to be (cf. Exod 32:17). He is presented here as someone we should know already, a fact that may lend further support to the suggestion that this narrative may have come from the collection of Yahweh war-narratives known as the Book of the Wars of Yahweh.

Mölenbrink has made a detailed analysis of the references to Joshua in the Pentateuch in comparison to the Book of Joshua and has posed a *Josuarezension* (20–24) that has inserted Joshua into the Pentateuchal narrative. The oldest stratum of this recension, he holds (*ZAW* 59 [1942–43] 56–58), lies in the story (*Sage*) of the Amalekite war in Exod 17:8–16 and in the Joshua-recension of Num 13–14. This would account for the abrupt introduction of Joshua in some passages outside the Book of Joshua, but it is not sustained by others, in which Joshua is an essential figure (see, for example, Exod 33:11 and Num 11:26–30). The abrupt introduction of Joshua in the passage at hand and in other passages as well may suggest that Joshua's early training as Moses' assistant was too well known to make details necessary, rather than that the Joshua references are secondary (see Good, "Joshua Son of Nun," *IDB* 2:995–96).

Moses' instruction to Joshua to "pick out" (בחר) men reflects the selection of a fighting elite (a motif taken to an almost humorous extreme in Judg 7) from the larger group of Israel. By the time Joshua is ready and moves out with his force, "tomorrow," Moses will take a position overlooking the field of battle, and he will be equipped with "the staff of Elohim." This reference to the staff that is an authenticating symbol of Yahweh's powerful Presence (see *Comment* on 4:2–4; 7:16–17; and *Explanation* on 7:8–13), despite the fact that the staff is not mentioned again in this section, is an indicator of the motif of the narrative: what is about to take place is firmly and surely under Yahweh's control.

10 Joshua carries out his instructions, presumably on the schedule Moses has set, and Moses proceeds to his position, accompanied by both Aaron and Hur. Hur, the son of Caleb and Ephrath and the grandfather of the famous artisan Bezalel (1 Chr 2:19–20), is mentioned along with Aaron as an assistant to Moses also in Exod 24:14. There is probably more to the Aaron-Hur partnership in relation to Moses than we can now recover from the text of the OT. Seebass (*Mose und Aaron,* 25–28) has made the imaginative though undemonstrable proposal that the primary form of the tradition preserved in this narrative involved only Hur and that originally the battle with the Amalekites was fought by Aaron and Hur, who were replaced in the expansion of the tradition by Moses and Joshua.

11–13 The reason for Moses' position on the brow of the hill can be seen in what he does during the battle. Moses lifted his hands, in symbol of the power of Yahweh upon the fighting men of Israel, surely, but in some miraculous way Moses' upraised hands became also conductors of that power. As long as he held his hands up, Israel prevailed in the fight; but when in weariness Moses allowed his hands to drop, the Amalekites prevailed. Noth (142) and Hyatt (184) speak of magic, and Childs (315) aptly cites the parallel of Balaam's involvement in blessing and cursing Israel and Moab (Num 22–24). In fact, the text does not make clear what Moses did, apart from raising his hands, with or without the staff of Elohim (cf. the comment of Schmid, *Mose,* 63). But about Yahweh's consequential involvement in the battle, an involvement closely linked to Moses' raised or lowered hands, there can be no doubt. When Moses through weariness could hold his hands up no longer, Aaron and Hur provided him a rock for a seat and held his hands up for him. His hands were then "firmness itself," right through the daylight fighting hours, and as a direct result, Joshua was able to cripple the Amalekite attack.

14 As a result of this Amalekite attack, and no doubt as well because of the ancient antipathy of Jacob and Esau and the continuing conflict between Israel and Amalek (cf. Grønbaek, *ST* 18 [1964] 31–42), Yahweh required Moses to record in "the book" a promise to destroy Amalek completely that has the effect of a curse. This writing is to serve as a *"Protokoll"* (Schottroff, *"Gedenken"* 305) or a "memorandum" (Childs, *Memory,* 66), but as more still: the writing of a blessing or a curse in the ANE was believed to add to its effectiveness. "The book" in which this writing was to take place is made definite by the article, and apparently a specific book (not, as Cassuto, 206, proposes, an inscription on the altar Moses built) is in view. What this book was we can only guess, but once more the Book of the Wars of Yahweh seems a likely possibility. Since Joshua is in charge of the fighting force, this promissory curse must be "fixed, set," that is, "drummed into" his ears.

15 Moses' construction and naming of an altar apparently commemorating the victory, Yahweh's part in it, and the promissory curse may shed some light also on the relation of Moses' uplifted hands to Yahweh's power strengthening the Israelite forces. Moses named the altar, in commemoration of the defeat of the Amalekites, "Yahweh is my standard." נֵס can mean "signal" as well as "ensign, flag, banner," and BDB (651) renders the word *"standard, as rallying-point"* in this verse. In Ps 60:6, נֵס refers to a flag to which those who revere God can flee for their lives. Ps 74:4 refers to the Babylonian troops setting their own "signs" (אֹתוֹת) as "signs" in Yahweh's Temple as they destroyed it. The Temple was furnished with "signs" or "standards" of Yahweh's Presence and power. The Ark, the Golden Altar and Lampstand, the Table of the Bread of the Presence all were Yahweh's signs of his Presence in Israel's midst. Moses' hands raised aloft on the hill above the Israelite-Amalekite battle may also have served as such a sign, and one emanating power even as they did (e.g., 2 Sam 6:6–15). The sight of Moses so blessing Israel and judging Amalek would symbolize Yahweh, by whom all blessing and all cursing were believed to be empowered; thus the altar was named not "Moses is my standard," or "The staff of Elohim is my standard," but *"Yahweh* is my standard."

16 Such an interpretation may be borne out by the explanation of Moses, though v 16 is complicated by what appears to be a corrupt text at its crucial point. As noted above (n. 16.b.), the reading כְּסֵא יָהּ "throne of Yah" is preferable to the other possibilities, in part because it requires less textual emendation and in part because it better fits the context. The Amalekites have raised a hand against Yahweh's sovereignty, symbolized repeatedly in the OT by reference to his כסה / כסא "throne" (see BDB, 490 § 1b, 491 § 3b), but not against a flag or banner of Yahweh, never mentioned in the OT at all.

Moses' explanatory statement thus becomes a justification for the promissory curse of v 14, repeated as an assertion in v 16. The battle between Yahweh and Amalek will continue across the generations because the Amalekites have raised a hand against Yahweh's throne, that is, they have challenged his sovereignty by attacking his people. The "hand" of v 16 is thus not a *"Votivhand"* on the flagpole of God (Gradwohl, *VT* 12 [1962] 494), guaranteeing the war against Amalek down through the generations; the statement of Moses, in agreement with Yahweh's promissory curse in v 14, refers to a war with Amalek to which Yahweh commits *himself,* not Israel. The "hand" is the power of Amalek in collision course with Yahweh's purpose in his people; and the כִּי "because" clause of this verse functions as the justifying explanation of what Yahweh will do to Amalek in result. Schmid (*Mose,* 63–64) even suggests the combining of "the hand on Yahweh's throne" in v 16 with the "stone seat" in v 12 and the altar-name "Yahweh is my ensign" in v 15 with the "staff of Elohim" in v 9 as conscious efforts of the narrator to incorporate into the Yahwistic tradition elements originally foreign to it.

Such a theory imposes more upon the text than it will sustain, but Schmid's emphasis upon Yahweh as the key figure in the narration is entirely correct.

Explanation

Despite the introduction of special people (Joshua and Hur), special objects (the book containing Yahweh's promissory curse, and the named altar) and special themes (Moses' uplifted hands, Yahweh's continual and eventual war with Amalek, and Yahweh's throne), the central figure in this section is Yahweh, and its central action is his further provision for his people by empowering them to defeat the Amalekites. This point is made at the outset of the narrative by the introduction of Joshua, whose name, significantly, means "Yahweh is deliverance." (This fact may help to account for the abrupt presentation of Joshua here.) The same point is made at the end of the narrative by the specific assertion that *Yahweh*, not Israel, will do battle with Amalek from generation to generation.

In between these two assertions, Yahweh *is* the deliverer. The staff symbolizing his power introduces the sign of Moses' uplifted hands, through which Yahweh's power flows to defeat the Amalekites by a miraculous strengthening of Israel. The divine source of this strength is emphasized by its loss when Moses lowers his hands, and so diverges from the instructions Yahweh has evidently given him. Then it is Yahweh who makes the promissory curse against Amalek, and Yahweh who requires Moses to record this curse in "the book" and to fix it in the consciousness of Joshua, the military leader whose name means "Yahweh is deliverance." And all of this, Moses summarizes by building an altar which he names "*Yahweh* is my standard."

Once more Yahweh has provided for his people. Once more he has promised to continue that provision. And once more Yahweh's Presence has been proven, to Israel *and* to Israel's enemies.

The Rendezvous with Jethro (18:1–12)

Bibliography

Albright, W. F. "Jethro, Hobab and Reuel in Early Hebrew Tradition." *CBQ* 25 (1963) 1–11. **Audet, J. P.** "Esquisse historique du genre littéraire de la 'bénédiction' juive et de l'"eucharistie' chrétienne." *RB* 65 (1958) 371–99. **Bernhardt, K. H.** *Gott und Bild.* Berlin: Evangelische Verlagsanstalt, 1956. **Brekelmans, C. H. W.** "Exodus XVIII and the Origins of Yahwism in Israel." *OTS* 10 (1954) 215–44. **Buber, M.** *Moses: The Revelation and the Covenant.* New York: Harper & Brothers, 1958. **Cody, A.** "Exodus 18, 12: Jethro Accepts a Covenant with the Israelites." *Bib* 49 (1968) 153–66. **Fensham, F. C.** "Did a Treaty Between the Israelites and the Kenites Exist?" *BASOR* 175 (1964) 51–54. **Gray, G. B.** *Sacrifice in the Old Testament.* New York: KTAV, 1971. **Gunneweg, A. H. J.** "Mose in Midian." *ZTK* 61 (1964) 1–9. **Knierim, R.** "Exodus 18 und die Neuordnung der Mosaischen Gerichtsbarkeit." *ZAW* 73 (1961) 146–71. **McKenzie, J. L.** "The Elders in the Old Testament." *Bib* 48 (1959) 522–40. **Meek, T. J.** *Hebrew Origins.* New York: Harper and Brothers, 1960. **Rowley, H. H.** *From Joseph to Joshua.*

London: Published for the British Academy by Oxford University Press, 1950. **Stevenson, W. B.** "Hebrew ʿOlah and Zebach Sacrifices." *Festschrift Alfred Bertholet.* Tübingen: J. C. B. Mohr (Paul Siebeck), 1950, 488–97. **Towner, W. S.** " 'Blessed Be YHWH' and 'Blessed Art Thou, YHWH': the Modulation of a Biblical Formula." *CBQ* 30 (1968) 386–99. **Vaux, R. de.** "Sur l'origine kénite ou madianite du Yahvisme." *Eretz-Israel* 9. Jerusalem: Israel Exploration Society, 1969. 28–32.

Translation

[1] *Now Jethro, priest of Midian, father-in-law of Moses, heard about all that God [a] had done for Moses and his people, Israel—that Yahweh had brought Israel forth from Egypt.* [2] *Jethro, father-in-law of Moses, had taken in Zipporah, Moses' wife, after he had sent her back,[a]* [3] *along with her two sons. The name of one of these boys [a] was Gershom,[b] because Moses [c] said "A stranger have I been in a land foreign to me."* [4] *The name of the other was Eliezer ("My God is help"), because he said,[a] "The God of my father [b] was my help;[c] thus he rescued me from Pharaoh's sword."*
[5] *So Jethro, father-in-law of Moses, came with Moses'[a] sons and his wife to Moses in the wilderness where he was camped, there at the mountain of God.* [6] *He said[a] to Moses, "I, your father-in-law Jethro, have come [b] to you along with your wife, and her two sons with her."* [7] *Thus Moses went forth to meet his father-in-law, and he bowed low [a] and kissed him. Then they inquired, each of the other, how things were,[b] and went into the tent.*
[8] *There, Moses recounted to his father-in-law all that Yahweh had done to Pharaoh and to the Egyptians on behalf of Israel, all the wearying difficulties they had come upon in the journey, and how Yahweh had rescued them every time.[a]* [9] *Jethro was overjoyed at all the good things Yahweh had done for Israel, that he had rescued them from the power of the Egyptians.* [10] *So Jethro said, "Blessed be Yahweh, who has rescued you from the power of the Egyptians and from the power of Pharaoh, who [a] has rescued the people from the domination [b] of the power of the Egyptians.* [11] *Now I know for certain that Yahweh is greater than all the gods, for in this thing they have acted rebelliously against them."[a]* [12] *Then Jethro, father-in-law of Moses, received [a] a whole burnt offering and sacrifices to God, and Aaron came along with all the elders of Israel to eat bread with the father-in-law of Moses in God's Presence.*

Notes

1.a. LXX and the Cairo Geniza text read "Yahweh."
2.a. שִׁלּוּחֶיהָ is a noun derived from the piel of שלח "send away, dismiss," even "divorce." With the 3d fem sg suff here, it refers to Moses sending Zipporah back to Midian at the beginning of the final and most dangerous leg of his return to Egypt. See *Comment* on 4:20. The other two OT occurrences of שלוחים, at 1 Kgs 9:16 and Mic 1:14, suggest here the translation "after her parting [from Moses], after he had sent her back."
3.a. אֲשֶׁר שֵׁם הָאֶחָד, more lit., "concerning whom the name of the one. . . ."
3.b. "Stranger, new-comer there"; on this popular etymology see n. 2:22.c. and *Comment.*
3.c. "Moses" is plainly the subject of אמר "he said," and so is added above for clarity.
4.a. "Because he said" is not repeated in MT.
4.b. אָבִי "father," sg here as also in 3:6; see *Comment* there.
4.c. בְּעֶזְרִי, lit., "being my help"; the ב is the so-called ב *essentiae:* GKC ¶ 119i.
5.a. MT has בניו "his sons"; Moses is, however, clearly the antecedent of "his."
6.a. LXX, Syr read this sequence as a 3d-pers report, "It was said to Moses," necessitating

also the substitution of "Look, behold" for MT's אֲנִי "I." These changes appear to be an attempt to get around the difficulty posed by Jethro's identification of himself to Moses, followed by the verb וַיֵּצֵא "thus he went forth" at the beginning of v 7. Cassuto (215) deals with this problem another way, by assuming the statement to be a message of Jethro sent from the "gateway of the camp . . . through one of the guards." The MT may, however, be read as it stands, without alteration and without such assumptions. It makes perfect sense for Jethro to present himself to Moses with such formality.

6.b. GKC ¶ 116d: "The period of time indicated by a participle active . . . must be inferred from the particular context." See also ¶ 116o.

7.a. SamPent has Jethro bowing before Moses.

7.b. לְשָׁלוֹם "as to welfare."

8.a. "And how . . . every time": special waw in this context.

10.a. This clause is transposed by some translators to v 11: so RSV, NEB. It is omitted altogether by LXX, but kept in the place in which MT has it by other translators: so Vg, JB, JPS. SamPent is identical with MT. The difficulty of v 11 does not provide justification for the deletion of the phrase, however, which makes sense where it stands. Cassuto (216) proposes, perhaps rightly, that the phrase was added, along with the threefold use of נצל "rescue" for emphasis.

10.b. מִתַּחַת "from under, beneath."

11.a. The final clause of the verse is difficult and sometimes regarded obscure, perhaps correctly so. The attempt above is to translate it more or less as it stands, reading "the gods" as the antecedent of "they" and "Israel" as the antecedent of "them," to give the sense that the gods of Egypt, acting as they have against Israel, have been rebelling toward Yahweh, who has in turn proven his superiority by defeating them. This interpretation is of course based on context more than upon the text of the clause. BHS assumes a gap in the text.

12.a. וַיִּקַּח from לָקַח "take, select, get," here read as "receive," in reference to Jethro as the leader of worship who receives the gifts directed to God and presides at their offering. Cf. BDB, 543 § f; and Cody, Bib 49 (1968) 159–61. Vg has obtulit "offered."

Form/Structure/Setting

The nuclear theme of the whole of Exod 18 is the integration of the traditions of the Sarah / Isaac / Jacob / Joseph side of Abraham's family with those of the Keturah / Midian side. Moses, the descendant of the Sarah-Isaac side, becomes the divinely chosen medium of connection with Jethro, the descendant of the Keturah-Midian side. Moses, bereft of his family in Egypt by his flight from the justice of Pharaoh, has found a family in Midian. By one of those remarkable connections so recurrent in the Bible, however, Moses' new family is, in a quite literal sense, just another branch of his old family. And Moses becomes the guide and the bridge-person who links the two parts of the family separated since Abraham's day (Gen 25:1–6).

The central figure of Exod 18 is thus Moses' father-in-law, Jethro, who is presented by the narrative as (1) the caretaker of Moses' wife and two sons during Moses' absence in Egypt, (2) the glad recipient of the report of Yahweh's deliverance of Israel, (3) the confessor of Yahweh's supremacy among all gods, (4) the sacerdotal leader of all present, including even Moses and Aaron, and (5) Moses' counselor in the application to Israel of Yahweh's guidance for living in Covenant.

This collection of motifs around a single and dominant figure gives Exod 18 a kind of unity lacking in most of the narratives of Exodus, or, for that matter, most of the tetrateuch. The commentators have generally accounted for this by assigning Exod 18 to a single source, E (so Beer, 94–95; Hyatt, 186; Noth, 146), or to E with a few notes inserted from J (so Driver, 161–67; Davies, 147; Knight, 125). Childs (322–26) is certainly on a right path, however, in his suggestion that the study of the traditions interwoven in this chapter is of more help than an analysis of sources and suppositional pre-sources.

These traditions, at least as they have been perceived and interpreted, have been the subject of widely divergent theories: (1) the "Kenite" theory of the origin of faith in Yahweh in Israel, which holds that Moses and thus Israel learned about Yahweh from the Midianites, represented particularly by their priest, Jethro (Rowley, *Joseph to Joshua,* 148–61); (2) the theory that Yahweh is new to Jethro, that having been persuaded by the account of Moses, he makes his own confession of faith in Yahweh (cf. Gunneweg, *ZTK* 61 [1964] 1–9; Meek, *Hebrew Origins,* 93–96; Buber, *Moses,* 94–98); (3) the theory that the Israelites and the Midianites, variously connected with the Kenites (as a subtribe; see Bernhardt, *Gott und Bild,* 127, n. 1), had a common faith and entered into a mutually beneficial covenant, a historical event reflected in Exod 18 (Brekelmans, *OTS* 10 [1954] 215–22; Fensham, *BASOR* 175 [1964] 51–54; Cody, *Bib* 49 [1968] 153–66); and (4) the theory that the traditions that surface in Exod 18 are very ancient, have to do with both Midianite and Israelite beginnings (de Vaux, *Eretz-Israel* 9:28–34, and *Early History,* 330–38), and may be more thematic than historical (Knierim, *ZAW* 73 [1961] 146–57).

There is not enough evidence in Exod 18 and in the OT as a whole, for that matter, to confirm or to disprove in detail any of these theories. The best one can make of them involves a sifting that retains, as suggestive, the more reasonable (or less deniable) features of the proposals they make. The notion of a Kenite-Midianite origin for Israel's Yahwism, for example, now seems far too much a theory made of incompatible straws, as does the even more imaginative theory of Jethro's "conversion." A historical Midianite-Israelite covenant-treaty, though certainly not beyond possibility, cannot be sustained from the biblical text. And the ancient themes imbedded in Exod 18 are just as difficult to dig out with any certainty as are the ancient source layers.

Once more, it is far better to take more seriously what we have in hand, the Exod 18 of the received text, than what we can only imagine, the process preceding the canonical forms of the text. And what we have at hand displays a literary and thematic unity virtually unparalleled in the narrative chapters of the Book of Exodus. However this end product began, it functions now as the conclusion of a division in the family of father Abraham, prefigured with the expulsion into nomadism of Cain (Gen 4:10–16), begun with Abraham's dismissal to the east of the sons of Keturah (Gen 25:1–6), confirmed in Abraham's shameful expulsion of his Egyptian wife Hagar and her son Ishmael (Gen 21:8–21), and symbolized most dramatically in the conflict between Jacob and Esau (Gen 25:19–34; 27:1–45; 28:6–9; 32:3–6; 33:1–20).

Cain went to dwell "east of Eden, in the land of wandering" (Gen 4:16) while Seth, the son in Adam's own likeness, his very image (Gen 5:3), remained with his father (Gen 4:25, 5:1–6). Ishmael came to live in the wilderness of Paran (see *Comment* on 16:1), and married a wife from Egypt (Gen 21:21), while Isaac remained with his father and married a wife from the ancestral home to the east, in Mesopotamia (Gen 24:1–10). There is reference to only one further meeting of the two half-brothers—at their father Abraham's burial in the cave of Machpelah (Gen 25:9). After that, Isaac and Ishmael dwelled each in his own lands (Gen 25:11–18). Keturah's sons were sent "easterly, to the land of the east," while Rebekah's son Isaac remained with Abraham (Gen 25:6). Jacob, having returned to the ancestral home for his wives (Gen 28:1–5), refused despite his promise to follow his brother Esau to Seir (Edom), south and east of the Dead Sea, settling rather at Succoth, then Shechem, then Bethel (Gen 33:12–18; 35:5–15). The one further reference to the two brothers in the same passage is a notice that they could not dwell together (Gen 36:6–8).

The medium of the reunion of the family thus torn apart and separated across many generations is Moses, whose presence in Egypt was the result of yet another outburst of family strife (Gen 37), and who is separated from one side of the family by violence and from the other side by the call of Yahweh. The symbol of the Cain/Keturah/Ishmael/Esau side of the family in the chapter of the reunion is of course Jethro; and the symbol of the Seth/Sarah/Isaac/Jacob side is Aaron, accompanied by "all the elders of Israel." Moses, the medium of reunion, belongs to both sides, just as each side comes to belong to the other. For this reason, perhaps, Moses is not mentioned alongside Jethro, Aaron, and the elders in the communion meal of Exod 18:12.

In the light of the importance of this reunion in Exod 18, the question posed by its location may best be considered. As has often been pointed out, Exod 18 is set at the encampment at the mountain of God before Israel has arrived there (18:5 vis-à-vis 19:1, 2), and Moses is at trouble to apply and interpret God's prescriptions and instructions for living in the covenant before they have been given and before the covenant has been offered and then made. Sequential discrepancies of this magnitude cannot have been overlooked by the compilers of Exodus, of course, so some reason must be sought for the location of this chapter just before Exod 19 instead of after chap. 24, when the covenant has been solemnized, or after chap. 34, when the covenant has been renewed and Israel is preparing to leave Sinai, or at some later point in the narrative sequence, at the oasis at Kadesh, or even in Canaan itself. There had to be a reason for the placement of the narrative of this chapter so obviously out of sequence, a reason overriding considerations of logical or chronological order.

The reason was perhaps a thematic one. The compilers of Exodus were for a number of very good reasons eager to have "one" Israel before the momentous events at Sinai. The family that was to be so much fragmented in national schism and an array of captivities, that was often to be divided in matters of belief and commitment (as the messenger-speeches of the prophets are alone sufficient to show), simply had to be one for the advent of Yahweh's presence and the gift of his covenant. Thus does the reunion precede the preparation for the great theophany of Exod 19. In the compilers' view, this reunion was quite possibly the most important preparation of all.

Both the form and the location of Exod 18 are thus set by the theme of reunion, to which Jethro is the central and determinative figure. Vv 1–12 describe the moment and the solemnization of that reunion. Vv 13–27 describe its logical aftermath, a kind of proof that occurs after no other reunion in the OT except the one following Israel's first disobedience, in Exod 34. The fact that Moses "allowed his father-in-law" to return to his own region (v 27) after the events described in Exod 18 has no bearing on the reunion motif, both because it belongs to a later part of the narrative sequence and also because the reunion is far more a theme important to the theological concept of the compilers of Exodus than an event in history.

Comment

1 Jethro is the name given to Moses' father-in-law most often in Exodus, though a variety of names assigned to him in the OT present a somewhat confused picture that cannot be resolved satisfactorily (see *Comment* on 2:16). Albright's theory (*CBQ* 25 [1963] 4–9) that the Reuel of Exod 2:18 is the "clan name of Hobab" (Num 10:29), that Jethro was Moses' father-in-law and that Hobab was his son-in-law and a (Judg 1:16, 4:11) Kenite (= member of a metalworking group of Midianites) cannot be sustained. Both the Kenite-Midianite connection, argued with such assurance for many years, and also the varied attempts to harmonize Jethro-Hobab-Reuel must now be regarded as uncertain. The statement, "_____ heard what _____ had done" is a much-used narrative introduction in the OT and does not therefore imply either an occasion or a messenger for a report.

2–4 The note that Jethro had cared for Zipporah and her sons "after her parting" from Moses is consistent with 4:18–20. The inconsistent note is introduced by 4:24–26, a passage that mentions only one son, Gershom, and presents a full measure of complexity on its own (see above). The name Gershom, "Stranger There," as noted already (*Comment* on 2:22), is best understood as a reference to Moses' life in Egypt, not in Midian, in which he has found a home. Eliezer, "My God is help," is explained by Moses in a manner supporting such an interpretation, because it too, even after so much of Yahweh's help *beyond* Egypt, nevertheless refers also to the rescue from Pharaoh. Here, as in 3:6 and 15:2, Moses refers pointedly to "the God of my father" אבי, a connection of his faith in the wilderness with the faith of his family in Egypt (see *Comment* on 3:6), and an additional allusion to the reunion about to take place.

5–7 "The mountain of God" at which Moses and Israel are camped and to which Jethro comes with Moses' wife and sons is Sinai/Horeb, as the use of the same phrase at 3:1; 4:27; and 24:13 makes clear. Whatever the time of Jethro's rendezvous, the place quite appropriately is the mountain of the supreme revelation of Yahweh's Presence. If indeed this meeting took place after the theophany of chap. 19 and the covenant-making of chap. 24 (see *Form/Structure/Setting*) some more direct reference to those momentous events might be expected here.

Noth (146–47) takes the view that the name "Jethro" was added to an original "father-in-law of Moses," the only designation in vv 13–27, to give the "periphrastic description" of vv 2, 5, 6, and 12. While this is a possibility, this expanded and formal description in the verses describing the reunion may be the quite deliberate device of the narrator/compiler, whose purpose is to leave no ambiguity about Jethro's crucial presence and role. The deference shown Jethro by Moses is completely in keeping with such an interpretation, as also with the leading part played by Jethro throughout the chapter. The formal and public greeting completed, the two men move into the privacy of Moses' tent, where the recital of Yahweh's mighty acts takes place.

8–10 This recital is summarized concisely, with careful reference to the purpose of these mighty acts: Moses recounted what Yahweh had done to Pharaoh and the Egyptians *on behalf of Israel;* he related the "wearying difficulties" of the journey as a means of pointing out how *Yahweh had rescued Israel every time.* Moses' summary is a proof-of-Presence summary, a confession of Yahweh's powerful protection of and provision for Israel. Jethro's joyous response to this recital echoes it with the same pattern, though appropriately in reverse: he rejoices at the good Yahweh has done *for Israel* in his rescue of them from the Egyptians' power, and he declares a blessing upon Yahweh, who had rescued Israel "from the power of the Egyptians," a general reference to Israel's dependent sojourn in a foreign land, "from the power of Pharaoh," perhaps a reference to the slave-labor of the building projects of the nineteenth dynasty, and "from the domination of the power of the Egyptians," perhaps a reference to the persecution that intensified when the question of departing the delta to worship Yahweh was raised. This threefold recital is for emphasis, as Cassuto (216) says, but it is much more a repetition of Moses' confession, a kind of mirror-image of the declaration of the proof of Yahweh's Presence. Towner (*CBQ* 30 [1968] 386–90) has studied the ברוך יהוה "blessed be Yahweh" formula and concluded, rightly so, that it is used "not as prayer but as a kerygmatic utterance" (389), intended "to express joy in God's gracious acts and to proclaim those acts to the world" (387; cf. also Audet, *RB* [1958] 376–81).

11 Jethro's further confession moves from a repetition of Moses' summary to an assertion of his own. He declares his own faith on the basis of his own experience. What Moses has told him, coupled with what he knew already, leads him to conclude on his own (עתה ידעתי "now *I know*") that "Yahweh is greater than all gods." The assumption implicit in this statement is that Jethro believes, as he *has* believed, that Yahweh is a God among gods. He has believed indeed, that Yahweh is greater than the others. Now he has confirmation that in that belief he was right. The second half of v 11, so difficult that it has usually been regarded as incomplete, may give confirmation to this interpretation, despite its obvious difficulty. Jethro's confession of the superiority of Yahweh may be taken as justified by Jethro by reference to what Yahweh has done to the gods of Egypt, who have acted rebelliously in regard to Yahweh by working against his people Israel (עליהם "against them"). This reading must be made against the backdrop of such references to the gods of Egypt as 12:12, 15:11, and to "other gods" in general in 20:3, and with the incompleteness of the latter part of v 11 clearly acknowledged. Its merit, even so, is that it takes the verse as it stands in MT.

12 Following his confession, Jethro presided at a sacrifice, then took part in a communion meal involving Aaron and the elders of Israel as the representatives of Israel. ויקח refers to Jethro's "receiving" or "accepting" the whole burnt offering and the sacrifices, but as the presiding leader of worship and not in token of his acceptance of a covenant (Cody, *Bib* 49 [1968] 159–61) or treaty (Fensham, *BASOR* 175 [1964] 53–54). As in the various orders for sacrifices and offerings in Lev 1–3, Jethro, as presiding priest, receives the gifts that are brought. The details of his preparation and offering of these gifts are of course unnecessary to this narrative, and may simply be assumed. The עלה "whole burnt offering" is appropriately listed first; the זבחים "sacrifices," as offerings partly burned on the altar and partly eaten by the worshipers (Gray, *Sacrifice* 5–6; de Vaux, *Ancient Israel* 2:415–18) are mentioned second. V 12 thus presents an appropriate summary sequence of this narrative. It is entirely unnecessary to assume, as Cody (*Bib* 49 [1968] 162–65) does, that the עלה is a later addition to this text through a priestly "tendency to retouch." As Stevenson (*Festschrift A. Bertholet*, 488–89) has shown, the differing character of these two kinds of sacrifice "led to their frequent association in one ceremonial and made the two words together a fitting expression for sacrifice in general." Such is the case, for example, in 10:25.

This narrative is not to be considered an attempt to insert priestly interests into the text of Exodus, but as an entirely plausible summary account of a very special occasion of reunion, solemnized with the kind of actions in worship that every Israelite would have known. Indeed, we may need to think less of an original narrative expanded by later special interests than of a narrative drawn to present as effectively as possible a deliberate theme or set of themes. The presence of Aaron, to cite a further example, is better thought of in this way than as a later addition to the narrative (so Cody, *Bib* 49 [1968] 163; Noth raises the question, then assigns this verse "to the oldest material" [*Pentateuchal Traditions*, 178–80]). Aaron and "all the elders of Israel" are a further means of depicting a very special occasion.

The elders are the representative extension of the whole people of Israel (cf. McKenzie, *Bib* 48 [1959] 522–23). In this narrative of reunion, it is important to stress that they *all* were there. Aaron accompanies them as their leader (cf. McKenzie, 524–25), since he is, like them, one to whom some of Moses' authority has been delegated. Moses remains the bridge-person, one already belonging to Israel and to Midian. So it is then that the לחם "bread" or "food" of the communion meal is eaten in God's Presence by Aaron and all the elders of Israel on the one side, and no doubt by Jethro, who has received, prepared, and offered it, on the other side. While we may assume the presence also of Moses, already a member of both branches of this family of Abraham, it is Jethro, Aaron, and the elders who are the essential parties of the reunion.

Explanation

The conclusion to generations of division is thus the governing motif of this important section of Exodus. The narrative of Jethro's meeting with Moses may well have belonged originally to a later point in the story of Moses and Israel, after the revelation of Yahweh's commands and the making of the covenant. The importance of the reunion of the two parts of Abraham's family *before* the revelation to Israel at Sinai has, however, overshadowed the importance of this narrative in its proper sequence. Thus the compilers of Exodus have relocated at this point *all* the material having to do with the visit by and the meeting with Jethro, even the account of his counsel to Moses about the administration of Yahweh's instructions for living, logically out of place before Exod 19–24.

The question of those parts of Abraham's family that belonged to the Jacob side but were not involved in the Egyptian sojourn and the exodus experience is not in view here, as it is not in most of the OT. That important reunion, recounted in Josh 23 and 24, is the conclusion to a separation that involves no animosity, though it too, like this one, has a theological point that overrides historical narrative.

Repeatedly in Exodus and in the OT, Israel is described as *one* Israel. "The sons of Israel," "all Israel," and other such phrases abound. In the later confessions of the exodus experience, the rescue from Egypt is described, in faith, as an experience in which all Israel and every Israelite shared (so Deut 6:20–25, to name just one important example). Consistent with this longing for a theological oneness that may well never have been more than a fervent hope, the compilers of Exodus used 18:1–12 to bring back together, immediately before the momentous Sinai revelation and covenant, the two major parts of Abraham's family, which had been separated by strife and greed and jealousy. Moses, as the forerunner who became a member of both halves of the family, was the agent of the reunion. Jethro was the symbol of the nomadic desert side, Aaron and all the elders were the symbol of the settled farming side. And the reunion was an ideal attained by Israel only in faith, and even there, no doubt, only by the greatest of Israel's prophets and teachers.

The Beginning of Israel's Legal System (18:13–27)

Bibliography

Gunneweg, A. H. J. "Mose in Midian." *ZTK* 61 (1964) 1–9. **Hauret, C.** "Moïse était-il prêtre?" *Bib* 40 (1959) 509–21. **Hentschke, R.** *Satzung und Setzender: Eine Beitrag zur israelitischen Rechsterminologie.* BWANT 83. Stuttgart: W. Kohlhammer, 1963. **Herrmann, S.** "Mose." *EvT* 28 (1968) 301–28. **Knierim, R.** "Exodus 18 und die Neuordnung der Mosäischen Gerichtsbarkeit." *ZAW* 73 (1961) 146–71. **Muilenburg, J.** "The Linguistic and Rhetorical Usages of the Particle כי in the Old Testament." *HUCA* 32 (1961) 135–60.

Translation

¹³ *The very next day,* ᵃ *as Moses sat to decide cases for the people* ᵇ *and the people stood waiting for Moses from the morning until the evening,* ¹⁴ *Moses' father-in-law saw all that he was doing for the people, and so said, "What is this business* ᵃ *you*

are doing for the people? For what purpose [b] *are you sitting by yourself, with all the people standing in line* [c] *before you from morning until evening?"* [15] *So Moses replied to his father-in-law, "The reason is that* [a] *the people come to me to make inquiry of God.* [16] *When they have a problem,* [a] *they come to me and I make a decision between a man and his neighbor, so that I may make understandable* [b] *the requirements* [c] *of God and his instructions."*

[17] *Then Moses' father-in-law said to him, "It is not good, the procedure you are following.* [a] [18] *You will exhaust yourself completely, both you yourself and this people along with you, because this work* [a] *is more than you can carry: you are not able to do it by yourself.* [19] *Pay attention to me now: I will give you counsel, and God will be with you. You* [a] *be for the people an advocate before God,* [b] *and you* [a] *bring the* [c] *problems to God.* [20] *You make the requirements* [a] *and the instructions* [b] *clear* [c] *to them, and make understandable to them the manner in which they are to live* [d] *and how they are to conduct themseves.* [e] [21] *You* [a] *also look carefully* [b] *among all the people for men of ability, ones who have reverence for God, men of firmness, ones who hate a dishonest profit, and establish them as leaders over thousands, leaders over hundreds, leaders over fifties, and leaders over tens,* [22] *that they may decide cases for the people on a continuing basis.* [a] *Every complex* [b] *problem they shall bring to you, and every routine* [c] *problem they shall deal with.* [d] *Thus will things be lighter for you: they will carry the load with you.* [23] *If you follow this procedure, as God charges you to do, then you will be able to stand up under the pressure,* [a] *and all this people as well will go to their own place satisfied."* [b]

[24] *So Moses followed the counsel of his father-in-law; indeed he followed it to the letter.* [a] [25] *Moses selected men of ability from the whole of Israel, then set them in charge* [a] *over the people, leaders over thousands, leaders over hundreds, leaders over fifties, and leaders over tens.* [26] *They decided cases for the people on a continuing basis: the difficult problem, they brought straight* [a] *to Moses; every routine problem, they dealt with.*

[27] *Thus Moses took leave* [a] *of his father-in-law, who then went on his way to his own land.*

Notes

13.a. ויהי ממחרת "and so it was, from the following day." The intention is to indicate the day immediately following the reunion and its celebration and to establish this narration as connected with, even as made possible by, that one.

13.b. וישב משה לשפט: "Moses sat to judge" is a bit too formal a rendering, since Moses here is helping the people apply to their lives the principles laid down by Yahweh's covenant expectation. Cf. BDB, 1047.

14.a. הדבר הזה "this matter, affair, thing, action": BDB, 183, IV.

14.b. מדוע "wherefore, on what account, . . . i.e., from what motive?" (BDB, 396).

14.c. Niph ptcp of נצב: "position oneself, take a stand," followed by על "upon" with the person or place of the position. Cf. BDB, 662.

15.a. Moses' reply is introduced by כי "for" in the special deictic sense defined and illustrated by Muilenburg, *HUCA* 32 [1961] 135–36, 142–44.

16.a. דבר "problem, matter, word," seen in vv 14, 16, 17, 18, and 19 in this passage in a wide range of its meanings.

16.b. Hiph of ידע "cause to know, declare," even "explain." Cf. BDB, 394–95.

16.c. חק "requirement"; see n. 15:25.f; and cf. Hentschke, *Satzung und Setzender*, 28–32.

17.a. הדבר אשר אתה עשה, lit., "this business that you are doing."

18.a. See n. 16.a.

19.a. The independent pers pronoun is added to the pronoun of the verb for emphasis.
19.b. היה . . . מול האלהים, lit., "be . . . in front of God," as the people's representative.
See BDB, 557.
19.c. LXX, Syr, Tg Ps-J read "their problems."
20.a. LXX adds τοῦ θεοῦ "of God."
20.b. SamPent reads simply התורה "the instruction"; LXX has "his law."
20.c. Hiph זהר, "explain, instruct, give light, even warn": BDB, 264.
20.d. Lit., "the way in which they are to walk."
20.e. Lit., "the work, doing, which they are to do."
21.a. See n. 19.a.
21.b. The verb is חזה "see, perceive," with discernment or even with a prophet's vision.
See BDB, 302, and *HALAT*, 289, which would add לך "to you" (as do LXX and SamPent)
and read "sich auslesen." The addition is unnecessary, and perhaps even a distortion, but
"choose," especially with perception, is the idea intended.
22.a. בכל־עת "in every time."
22.b. הדבר הגדל "the big matter."
22.c. הדבר הקטן "the small matter."
22.d. ישפטו־הם "*they* shall decide, judge."
23.a. עמד "take a stand, stand firm, stand up to, hold one's own," read in this context
"stand up under the pressure." Cf. BDB, 763–64.
23.b. בשלום "with welfare, completeness," that is, with their conflicts resolved.
24.a. Lit., "and thus [special *waw*] he did everything he said."
25.a. ראשים "heads, choice leaders, chieftains."
26.a. Emphatic usage, indicated by *nun paragogicum*. Cf. GKC, ¶47m.
27.a. שלח "let go, free," BDB 1019 § 3.

Form/Structure/Setting

This section is intimately bound up with the section preceding it, and
the form of chap. 18 as a whole as well as with reference to its two major
parts has been discussed on *Form/Structure/Setting* on 18:1–12. Vv 13–27 follow
the important reunion described in vv 1–2 as both a logical next step and a
conclusion and also, as I have noted above, as a kind of validating proof
that the reconciliation and rejoining of the two parts of Abraham's family,
separated for so long a time, has actually taken place.

A still closer focus on this closing part of chap. 18 reveals, however, that
it is directly linked to the origins of the system by which the requirements
and instructions of Yahweh's covenant were made both accessible to the ordinary Israelite and also applicable to the maze of problems that inevitably
arise in the adjustment of day-to-day existence to a prescribed norm of any
kind. Scholars have commented at length and often quite helpfully on three
aspects of this subject: (1) the role of Moses, as both historical and etiologically
prototypical (Hauret, *Bib* 40 [1959] 516–21); (2) the related subject of the
origin and development of the structure of Israel's legal system (Knierim,
ZAW 73 [1961] 146–71); and (3) the priority and interrelationship of Midianite
and Sinai traditions and their connection with the evolution of the tetrateuch,
and with Exodus in particular (Gunneweg, *ZTK* 61 [1964] 1–9, and, taking
an opposing view, Herrmann, *EvT* 28 [1968] 324–28).

While it is of course impossible to fix with any certainty the origin of the
traditions reflected in the narrative of Exod 18:13–27, the view of Knierim
(*ZAW* 73 [1961] 155–71), based to a considerable degree on 2 Chr 19:5–
11, that they are linked to juridical reforms under Jehoshaphat does not

take seriously enough earlier and more important layers in this account (cf. the review of Childs, 324–26). Gressmann (*Mose und seine Zeit*, 174–75) many years ago argued for a historical base for these verses, and while the exact dimensions of that base remain beyond reach, Gressmann's general argument is correct. The attempt of Beyerlin (*Sinaitic Traditions*, 145–51) to connect 18:13–27 with Kadesh and argue that the "administration of justice in the Yahwistic community" and the decalogue as "the basic law of the Sinaitic covenant" "probably originated" there after an extended pilgrimage to Sinai has won no general support and is in any case unnecessary. No convincing reasons have yet been set forth, despite a number of attempts, for the separation of Israel's beginnings from Sinai, or for the divorce of Sinai traditions from the exodus traditions (cf. Durham, "Credo, Ancient Israelite," *IDBSup*, 197–99).

In the absence of such reasons, the OT's insistent connection of Moses and Israel and Israelite beginnings with Sinai must be taken seriously, at the least on the theological ground from which this insistence emerges. Far too much of the important reason for what Israel is to become and to do—Yahweh's Presence in the midst of the people—is lost otherwise. In the sequence at hand, what is being presented is not a separation of civil administration of justice from a cultic administration (see Knierim, *ZAW* 73 [1961] 157–71), but a quite deliberate attempt to link all law, significantly described here as "requirements and instructions" of God (v 16), to the God with whom the law began, whose Presence in covenant relationship makes it desirable and from whom alone therefore any accurate application of it must come. Whatever additional justifications of Israel's covenant law and its interpretation may have been grafted onto the Sinai narrative (and on this point Knierim's work is quite instructive), we must not lose sight of the foundational Sinai layer which gives rise to all the later possibilities and so determines the form of Exod 18:13–27.

Comment

13 The day immediately following the day of the reunion was *a* day, perhaps the regular day repeated periodically or as necessary, when Moses took his position to receive and to help all who were having difficulty of any kind in the application of the terms of God's covenant to the exigencies of day-to-day living. As noted already (*Form/Structure/Setting* on 18:1–12), the location of this narrative demanded by a logical sequence would be after Exod 24 at the earliest. The need, however, to have the desert family of Abraham reunited with the farming and village family of Abraham *before* the advent of the Presence at Sinai has overridden considerations of logical sequence. The problem of logistics faced by Moses and the people of Israel in this process becomes the point of departure for two motifs: (1) the counsel of Jethro, and (2) the beginning of Israel's legal system.

14–16 Having seen that Moses was rendering a great service to the people, but that the press of people needing to see him kept the people waiting and Moses at work throughout the day, Jethro asks Moses for an explanation, particularly as to why Moses is attempting so essential but demanding a task

alone. Moses' reply, that the people come to him "to make inquiry (דרש)
of God," is his explanation of why he has undertaken the work alone. The
people who come are those who have some question, individually or along
with those with whom they have some dispute, about what God has required
of them for life in the covenant. God is the origin of the requirements and
instructions, so God must give the explanatory application of them, and Moses
is the medium of access by whom the people may approach God with problems
of this kind. Since "the requirements of God and his instructions" are what
Moses must "make understandable" to the people, God is the authority of
each explanation and may need to be consulted. Until this point, no one
but Moses has had the privilege of such consultation.

17–20 The response of Jethro to Moses' explanation is practical: Moses
is wearing out both himself *and* the people, who must wait long hours before
they can see him; but the response is also clearly perceptive of the source
from which the counsel comes. Jethro tells Moses that he will be unable
alone to bear the weight of the work he has undertaken. He then proceeds
to give advice that he represents as no less derived from God than the explanations Moses has been giving the people regarding *their* difficulties: the counsel,
Jethro will give, but it is God who will be with Moses if he follows that
counsel.

The counsel falls into two parts, both of which leave no doubt that God
is the source and the center of what Jethro advocates. Moses, first of all, is
to remain the representative of the people to God: the requirements and
instructions are God's, as are the people who are in covenant with him. It
is thus only fitting that the problems God's people have bringing their lives
into conformity with God's expectations should be brought to God—and
brought by Moses whom God has called to be Israel's leader. The words of
Jethro emphasize this role of Moses, with the double stress on *you* twice in
v 19 and once in v 21. Moses is then to make God's expectations clear to
the people of Israel, and help them to understand the application of these
expectations to their daily living, to the question of how they are to conduct
themselves.

21–22 The second part of Jethro's counsel involves the delegation by
Moses of some responsibility in the matter of hearing the people's problems.
The source of the counsel the people are to receive of course remains God,
and the authority of the guidance they are to receive is also God, for just
as any word given to the people by Moses shall have come from God, so
also any word given to them by those whom Moses chooses shall have come
from the same source. Jethro thus specifies that Moses' selection of helpers
is to be made with great care (almost with reliance upon a visionary perception,
חזה) from the whole of Israel, and is to include only men who are able,
firm, and honest and "who have reverence for God." The men thus chosen
are then to be made leaders over divisions of people, specified on a numerical
basis but with no further criteria, and they are to serve on a continuing basis
as those to whom the people may bring their less complex problems of interpretation of the covenantal directions. When the more difficult problems
come up, these leaders are to bring them to Moses for guidance, a guidance
for which Moses, as the people's representative, could consult Yahweh.

Knierim (*ZAW* 73 [1961] 168–71) may be correct that the division of Israel into companies of "thousands, hundreds, fifties, and tens" has a military derivation (cf. Noth, 150). He (162–67) may even be correct in the theory that there is a connection between Exod 18:13–27 and Jehoshaphat's "military judges" described in 2 Chr 19:5–11. The numerical divisions, in such a case, would amount to an anachronistic attempt to suggest how the leaders selected by Moses functioned in relation to "all Israel." And the linkage with Jehoshaphat's organization would be forward from Exod 18 by way of precedent rather than backward to it by way of etiology. There is no firm evidence, however, that there is in this passage any "division between sacral and 'civic' justice" such as Noth (150) and Knierim (163–67) suggest.

Indeed, there is no division of civil from sacred, or profane from holy, in Israel's thought about and practice of laws of any kind. In Israel as elsewhere in the ANE, all laws were the gift of deity, and obedience of them, finally, amounted to obedience of God or gods. The requirements and instructions Moses' chosen helpers are to promulgate are thus no more "secular" and no less divinely drawn and monitored than are those Moses himself promulgates. Their authority, equally, is God, as is their requirement and their interpretation, whether they are applied by Moses or by the leaders Jethro proposes. The origin and the provenance of the requirements and instructions that are the concern of Exod 18:13–27 are not under question. The only point at issue is how Moses is to manage the interpretation of these requirements and instructions to so large a number of people. As Hentschke (*Satzung und Setzender,* 30–31) has noted, the terms חק "requirement" and תורה "instruction" are "technical terms" for the information gained from the consultation of God concerning matters of right behavior, and as synonymous in meaning with דרך "way" and מעשה "work" in v 20, they are not the language one would expect in the description of "civil law," but are typical of "the deuteronomic sermon."

The reason for this is that the requirements and instructions of both Moses and his chosen leaders are one in source, one in authority, one in direction, one in provenance. Their one difference, as specified in vv 22 and 26, is that the problems the leaders are to deal with are "routine" (קטן "small," vv 22 and 26); those Moses is to take are "complex" (גדל "big," v 22) or "difficult" (קשה "hard," v 26). The further specification that the people come to Moses "to make inquiry of God" (v 15) and that Moses is to "bring the problems to God" (v 19) at least suggests that the difference between the cases handled by the leaders and those handled by Moses is the difference between the situation for which there was some precedent and the situation that was unique. A recurring problem could be met by another application of an interpretation determined and employed already. The essential need in such a case would be for a leader wise enough to know the precedents and understand their application and honest enough to apply them without prejudice. A new problem would demand special wisdom and experience, and in all likelihood, the consultation of God, by holy oracle or by some other means, in order to determine the application of covenant principle to a situation not previously faced. In sum, the difference is the distinction between case-law for which there is precedent and the new case for which the correct application of apodictic principle must be determined.

If this proposal is even remotely appropriate to Exod 18, one might argue that here, even if in somewhat overlaid form, is one of the oldest traditions in the OT of how Israel's legal system began. One would in this case need also to propose that every Israelite law was ideally conceived as beginning in Yahweh, and that the question of covenantal obedience always took precedence, ideally, over all other legal obligations.

23 Jethro completes his counsel to Moses not only with the assurance that the procedure he advises will bring much-needed relief to both Moses and the people, but also with the remarkable assertion that God charges (or "commands, orders," צוה) Moses to follow it. This assertion shows Jethro to be far more than simply the respected patriarch he is ordinarily made out to be. He is functioning toward Moses much as he is telling Moses *he* should function toward the people of Israel. It is not an assertion likely to have been assigned to Jethro at some later time. It belongs to the original layer of tradition in Exod 18 and is another confirmation of the importance of the reunion of the two sides of the one family of Abraham.

24–27 Moses' response to Jethro's counsel is a further indication of its significance *and* its originality. He follows it to the letter, and it works just as Jethro predicted that it would. After an unspecified time, Moses and Jethro part, Jethro to return "to his own land." This reference, which in the present sequence of Exodus has Jethro going just before the great Sinai Revelation, may well be a reflection of the original location of the narrative of Jethro's counsel to Moses regarding God's requirements and instructions. It has been brought to its present location in Exodus by compilers eager to set the reunion narrative before the events at Sinai for theological reasons, which always take precedence over considerations of narrative sequence. Quite possibly, the reunion narrative of vv 1–12 and the narrative of Jethro's counsel may originally have belonged to the Exodus sequence at two different points, the reunion coming before the Sinai advent and covenant, and the counsel of Jethro after it.

Explanation

Exod 18 thus might be called a "Jethro-compilation," consisting as it does of the two principal Jethro-narratives of the OT, one describing the important reunion in which Jethro represents the desert-nomad side of Abraham's family, the other describing the beginning of Israel's legal system. The essential point of the second of these two narratives is that Israel's covenant law has its source in God. He gives it, he provides its authority, and to him therefore Israel must turn to have it interpreted and applied at any point of potential misunderstanding.

Moses is an intermediary in this process, and he is instructed to select with great care men who can assist him in this work, a task too heavy for any one man. But the source of information about God's requirements and instructions remains God who issued the requirements and instructions. On this point, there is never any uncertainty in Exodus, or for that matter in the OT.

This narrative makes clear that Israel's legal system begins where the covenant law begins, in God. God gives the requirements and instructions, and then clarifies and applies them as the need arises. Moses, the principal original figure intermediary to this process, must be joined, for practical reasons, by those who can extend his work. Their responsibility is the reapplication (and no doubt also the collection) of interpretations of God's requirements and instructions given already. And in such a manner, the system of casuistic application of apodictic law given by God may well have been begun. At the very least, the narrative of Exod 18:13–27 is the best picture we have in the OT of how the system worked and a clear designation of God as the authority of both the law and its interpretation.

PART THREE

ISRAEL AT SINAI

19:1–40:38

I. The Advent of Yahweh's Presence and the Making of the Covenant (19:1–24:18)

Israel Prepares for Yahweh's Coming (19:1–15)

Bibliography

Baltzer, K. *The Covenant Formulary.* Philadelphia: Fortress Press, 1971. **Bauer, J. B.** "Drei Tage." *Bib* 39 (1958) 354–58. ———. "Könige und Priester, ein heiliges Volk (Ex 19, 6)." *BZ* 2 (1958) 283–86. **Buber, M.** *Moses: The Revelation and the Covenant.* New York: Harper and Bros., 1958. **Caspari, W.** "Das priestliche Königreich." *TB1* 8 (1929) 105–10. **Driver, S. R.** *A Treatise on the Use of the Tenses in Hebrew.* 3d ed. Oxford: Clarendon Press, 1969. **Fohrer, G.** " 'Priesterliches Königtum,' Ex. 19, 6." *TZ* 19 (1963) 359–62. **Galling, K.** *Die Erwählungstraditionen Israels.* BZAW 48. Giessen: Verlag von Alfred Töpelmann, 1928. **Greenberg, M.** "Hebrew sᵉgulla: Akkadian sikiltu." *JAOS* 71 (1951) 172–74. **Klopfer, R.** "Zur Quellenscheidung in Exod. 19." *ZAW* 18 (1898) 197–235. **Labuschagne, C. J.** "The Emphasizing Particle *Gam* and Its Connotations." *Studia Biblica et Semitica.* Wageningen: H. Veenman & Zonen, 1966. 193–203. **McKenzie, J. L.** "The Elders in the Old Testament." *Bib* 48 (1959) 522–40. **Mendenhall, G. E.** *Law and Covenant in Israel and the Ancient Near East.* Pittsburgh: Presbyterian Board of Colportage, 1955. Also *BA* 17 (1954) 26–46, 49–76. **Moran, W. L.** "A Kingdom of Priests." *The Bible in Current Catholic Thought.* J. L. McKenzie, ed. New York: Herder and Herder, 1962. 7–20. **Muilenburg, J.** "The Linguistic and Rhetorical Usages of the Particle ⟨כי⟩ in the Old Testament." *HUCA* 32 (1961) 135–60. ———. "The Form and Structure of the Covenantal Formulations." *VT* 9 (1959) 347–65. **Newman, M. L., Jr.** *The People of the Covenant.* Nashville: Abingdon Press, 1962. **Scott, R. B. Y.** "A Kingdom of Priests (Exodus xix 6)." *OTS* 8 (1950) 213–19. **Sendrey, A.** *Music in Ancient Israel.* New York: Philosophical Press, 1969. **Wildberger, H.** *Jahwes Eigentumsvolk.* ATANT 37. Zürich: Zwingli Verlag, 1960.

Translation

¹ *In the third month* ᵃ *of the exodus* ᵇ *of the sons of Israel from the land of Egypt, on the very day they came to the wilderness of Sinai—*² *they had journeyed forth from Rephidim and come to the wilderness of Sinai, where they pitched camp:* ᵃ *indeed, Israel had pitched camp in sight of the mountain—*³ *Moses went up towards God.* ᵃ *So Yahweh* ᵇ *called out to him from the mountain,* ᶜ *saying, "This is what you are to say to the family of Jacob and declare to the sons of Israel:* ⁴ *'You yourselves* ᵃ *have seen what I did to the Egyptians, and that I then lifted you upon wings of eagles and brought you to myself.* ⁵ *So now, if you will pay very careful attention* ᵃ *to my voice, and keep my covenant, then you will be my own special treasure* ᵇ *from among all the peoples—for to me belongs the whole earth—*⁶ *and you yourselves will be my own kingdom of priests and holy people.' These are the words that you are to repeat* ᵃ *to the sons of Israel."*

⁷ *So Moses came and summoned the elders of the people.* ᵃ *Then he established as*

authoritative for them ^b *all these words, just as Yahweh had commanded him.* ⁸*All the people responded together, and they said, "Everything Yahweh* ^a *has spoken, we will do." Next, Moses brought back to Yahweh* ^a *what the people had said.*

⁹*Then Yahweh said to Moses, "Pay attention!* ^a *I am coming to you in a thickness of cloud, to the end that the people will hear when I speak with you, and particularly* ^b *so that they will have confidence in you from now on." Then Moses declared* ^c *the words of the people to Yahweh.*

¹⁰*So Yahweh said to Moses, "Go to* ^a *the people, and set them apart for holiness today and tomorrow. They are to wash their clothes.* ¹¹*They are to be completely ready* ^a *by the third day, because on the third day Yahweh will come down, before the eyes of the whole people, onto Mount Sinai.* ¹²*You are to establish boundaries for the people* ^a *all around,* ^b *warning,* ^c *'Be careful about going up onto the mountain, or even touching its outcropping: all who touch the mountain will certainly be executed* ^d*—* ¹³*no hand is to touch him; rather* ^a *is he to be stoned to death* ^b *or mortally shot,* ^b *whether beast or man he is not to live.' With the drawn-out signal of the bell-horn,* ^c *they are to come up to the mountain."*

¹⁴*So Moses went down from the mountain to the people. Then he set the people apart for holiness, and they washed their clothes.* ¹⁵*Next, he said to the people, "Be completely ready by the third day. Do not have intercourse* ^a *with a woman."*

Notes

1.a. בחדש can mean "in the new moon" as well as "in the month," and ביום הזה "in that day, on the very day" is sometimes understood in reference to בחדש and so to specify that Israel reached the Sinai wilderness on the very first day of the third lunar month from the departure from Egypt: so RSV; Cassuto, 223–24; Childs, with some caution, 342. The more precise statement of such references as Num 1:1 and 1 Kgs 12:32 suggests, however, either that an exact reference has been deleted (so Driver, 169; and JB), or that none was intended. ביום הזה is taken above to refer to Moses' action in v 3. The reference to "the third month" is thus read as a more general designation, v 2 is understood as an explanatory parenthesis (perhaps even an insertion), and "on the very day" is an indication of Moses' understandable eagerness to have Israel experience at Sinai the revelation of the Presence he had experienced there.

1.b. לצאת "with the reference to the going out"; translated τῆς ἐξόδου by LXX, this is the verse from which the name Exodus has come, via LXX and Vg, into the English Bible. The only other use of ἐξόδου in LXX Exodus, at 23:16, refers to the "going out" of the year.

2.a. MT has ויחנו במדבר "and then they pitched camp in the wilderness."

3.a. LXX adds τὸ ὄρος, to give "towards the mountain of God."

3.b. LXX, Syr have ὁ θεός "God."

3.c. LXX^B reads τοῦ οὐρανοῦ "from heaven."

4.a. The person of the verb is made emphatic by the addition of אתם "you."

5.a. אם־שמוע תשמעו, lit., "if listening you will listen."

5.b. LXX has λαὸς περιούσιος "peculiar people."

6.a. Piel impf דבר "speak, recount, even speak again and again"; cf. GKC, ¶ 52f, and BDB, 180–81.

7.a. The Cairo Geniza fragment has "Israel" instead of "people."

7.b. וישם לפניהם, lit., "he set, fixed, determined in their presence."

8.a. LXX has ὁ θεός "God."

9.a. הנה "with ref. to the future . . . serves to introduce a solemn or important declaration . . . and is used esp. [so here] with the ptcp.," BDB, 244; cf. Driver, *Hebrew Tenses*, 168–69, ¶ 135, (3).

9.b. וגם "and particularly"; on גם as such an "emphasizing particle," see Labuschagne, *Studia*, 194–201.

9.c. נגד "declare" here parallels the use of the same verb at the end of v 3, and as this sentence is *non sequitur* following v 8 and the earlier part of v 9, it perhaps should be connected with that earlier sequence.

10.a. LXX has Καταβὰς διαμάρτυραι "go down and instruct carefully."

11.a. Niph pl ptcp of כון "be firm, established, fixed, prepared": BDB, 465–66.

12.a. SamPent has ההר "the mountain."

12.b. סביב "circuit, round about," in reference to the circumference of the base of the mountain.

12.c. לאמר "to say, saying," translated "warning" in this context. SamPent reads ואל העם תאמר "and to the people you are to say."

12.d. מות יומת "be put to a violent death"; cf. BDB 559–60 § 2.a. & b.

13.a. כי is "often used adversatively to denote a striking contrast": Muilenburg, *HUCA* 32 [1961] 139.

13.b. Inf abs before the verb, intensifying the verbal idea (cf. GKC, ¶ 113n), in this context indicating stoning/shooting to death.

13.c. משך "draw, drag, prolong, continue" (BDB, 604), in this case the signal of the יבל, described by Sendrey (*Music*, 368–71) as a horn, perhaps even a שופר or a קרן, to which has been added a "metal sound bell" to amplify the resonance of the horn's sound. Thus יבל is rendered "bell-horn" above. ὅταν αἱ φωναὶ καὶ αἱ σάλπιγγες καὶ ἡ νεφέλη ἀπέλθῃ ἀπὸ τοῦ ὄρους "when the sounds [prob. = 'thunder'] and the trumpets and the cloud leave the mountain."

15.a. אל-תגשו אל-אשה, lit., "do not approach, draw near a woman," is here a prohibition of sexual intercourse during a period of cultic purity, in accord with such requirements as those laid down in Lev 15:16–33 and 1 Sam 21:5–7 [4–6].

Form/Structure/Setting

This section is the introduction to what may be called the Sinai narrative sequence. On the basis of what remains of that sequence in the compilation that is Exodus, we may assume a narrative beginning with Israel's long-awaited arrival at Sinai, then going on to include accounts of Yahweh's Advent there, the making of the covenant between Yahweh and Israel, Israel's first disobedience and Yahweh's subsequent judgment, and finally, the renewed covenant and the qualified relationship of the Presence of Yahweh. In analyzing what remains of such a narrative sequence in our canonical Exodus, we can posit, in broad terms, something like this: Exod 19:1–3a, 10–19a; 20:1–21; 24:1–18; 32:1–34:35.

This narrative has been expanded by the accretion of explanatory and qualifying material and by the insertion of blocks of cultic material linked to Sinai for the purpose of establishing their authority. No doubt, the narrative that must originally have existed, even as an early composite, has been considerably pruned, for a variety of reasons. Some of the drama and tension of such an earlier sequence can be recovered by reading the narrative sections *seriatim*, without the cumbrance of the sections applying the covenant requirements and setting forth the media and practices of worship. There is much to be said, indeed, for writing the commentary on this narrative sequence in the order of the events it recounts, and for dealing with the materials that have so obviously been squeezed into it in a separate treatment altogether. Not least of the advantages of such an approach is the recovery of more of the excitement and some of the integrity of the original narrative: Exod 32, for example, just makes more sense read immediately following Exod 24, as does Exod 24 following 20:21.

There are some disadvantages to such a procedure also. An obvious one is the difficulty created by such a disarrangement of the canonical text for the use of a commentary as a ready reference. This is surely an essential function of a commentary, and one considerably complicated by departure from the biblical sequence of a given book. The superb Anchor Bible *Jeremiah* by John Bright (AB 21, Garden City, NY: Doubleday, 1965) is a case in point. Another disadvantage of course is the lack of any firm agreement about where any save the most obvious seams occur. The sections on the media of worship are far easier to detach from the narrative sequence than is the Book of the Covenant, or, even more, the expansions of the Decalogue.

The greatest and most telling disadvantage is that posed by the compromise of the final form of the Book of Exodus. However disruptive that form may be, of whatever narrative sequences we can suppose, it is in fact the one sequence we know without speculation. Though it is an obvious compilation, it is a compilation based on a coherent theological intention, and any understanding of Exodus as a whole, or even in major sections and subsections, must keep the intention in view.

A still further complicating factor is posed by the nature of the narratives themselves: they too are obvious compilations, in some cases so often expanded and contracted that they can no longer be unraveled into the separate strands that made them up. Nowhere in Exodus is this more clearly the case than in the Sinai narrative sequence. The account of Yahweh coming to Israel at Sinai and entering into covenant with Abraham's descendancy is so much at the center of OT theology and faith that it received repeated attention and became perhaps the one most reworked passage in the Bible. This being so, all of the many attempts to dissect the Sinai narrative sequence, either on source-literary or traditio-analytical terms, have produced suggestions only, and in general each suggestion has been opposed by another of equal authority.

This most important of the narrative sequences of Exodus is examined here with the following assumptions: (1) the Advent of Yahweh's Presence at Sinai is the formative event of OT faith; (2) such an event inevitably gave rise to multiple narrative accounts; (3) these accounts were combined and recombined across many years, to produce a series of narratives, of which the Sinai narrative of our Exodus is itself a composite; (4) that composite has a development of expansion and revision all its own, complicated most of all by the insertion and addition of large blocks of covenantal and cultic material authorized by reference to Sinai; and (5) any part of the narrative must be read as a part of the larger sequence, extending from the arrival at Sinai and the establishment there of one kind of relationship with Yahweh to the prelude to the departure from Sinai under a different and tempered kind of relationship with Yahweh.

The key to the Sinai narrative sequence lies in its theological purpose, not in its narrative-source or traditio-historical roots. Indeed, the remarkable way in which those roots have been manipulated has created a quagmire of problems for the literary critic. Though many helpful observations may be harvested from the critical work of more than a century, the sum total of that work is a clear assertion that no literary solution to this complex narrative has been found, with more than a hint that none is likely to be found. Far

too much has been done with and to this material on its way to the form in
which we know it for any such solution to be any longer a realistic possibility.
This accounts for the variety of source assignment among the critics, as it
does for the failure also of the attempts to rearrange the narrative sequence
to explain discrepancies in the movement of Moses up and down Mount
Sinai, or to connect the people's reaction to the theophany in 20:18–21 with
the theophany itself in 19:16–19a.

The form of the entire Sinai narrative sequence has been determined by
a single factor. That factor is also the reason for the attraction into and
onto the Sinai narrative sequence of a variety of material having to do primarily
with the requirements of the covenant and the media of worship, and secondarily, with the special role of Moses and those who extend Moses' contribution.
This factor is of course the gift by Yahweh of his Presence to Israel. From
beginning to end, and in both its positive and its negative features, the Sinai
narrative sequence, and indeed the Book of Exodus of which it is the important
center, is linked to the Advent of Yahweh's Presence to Israel at Sinai. And
that central event, which clearly gave rise to an array of separate narratives,
is here reflected variously in a compilation of at least several of them.

To this larger narrative sequence, then, the compilation of Exod 19:1–15
is introductory. The usual source division of these verses is between J and
E, with an itinerary notice (vv 1–2a) from P and some redaction by D in vv
3b–8. The elaborate analysis of Klopfer (*ZAW* 18 [1898] 197–217), for example, ascribes vv 1–2a to P, vv 2b and 3a to E, v 3bα to "an interpolator,"
vv 3bβ–7a to a Deuteronomistic redactor, vv 7b–8 to J, v 9a, b to J in close
combination with E, and vv 10–15 predominantly to E, with an admixture
of J. Beer (96–97) gives vv 1–2a to P, vv 2b–3a to E¹, vv 3b–8 in their present
form to R^D, v 9 to J², v 10 to E¹, vv 11–13a to J², vv 13b–14 to E¹, and v
15 to J². Noth (154–58) assigns vv 1–2a to P also, then v 2b to "one of the
older sources" ("may be" E, 154), v 3a to E, vv 3b–9 to "a later addition,"
probably from Dtr, vv 10–15 to J. Newman (*People of the Covenant*, 39–
51) attributes vv 2b–6, 10–11a, 14–15 to E; and vv 9a, 11b–13, 7–8, in this
sequence, to J. Hyatt (196–202) ascribes vv 1–2a to P; vv 9a, 10–16a to J;
vv 2b–3a to E; vv 3b–8 to R$_D$; and v 9b he calls a "late addition." Childs
(344–64) gives a good survey of literary-critical and traditio-historical work
from Wellhausen forward, but wisely refrains from any specific source assignment.

The form of Exod 19:1–15 is not determined by the emphasis of a single
literary source, nor by the motif of a growing traditional emphasis. It is set
rather by the supreme event of Exodus, the Advent of Yahweh, which in
the Sinai narrative sequence bends everything else to its purpose and provides
the magnet to which covenantal and cultic materials needing authority are
drawn. The section at hand functions as a two-part introduction to that supreme event, and that is what determines the form it takes. The first part
of that introduction (vv 1–8), the heart of which is the famous "Eagle's Wings"
speech of Yahweh, serves as a general prologue to the entire Sinai narrative
sequence: thus it quite appropriately makes reference to the covenant and
to Israel's role as Yahweh's special people in advance of the events of Exod
20 and 24. The second part of the introduction (vv 9–15) serves as a specific

anticipation of the account of Yahweh's advent itself, in the instruction of the people of Israel to prepare themselves for the experience of the momentous event to come. To these introductory ends, material from several separate narratives may have been combined, but the determining force behind the combination is the great event being introduced.

Comment

1–3a This beginning of the Sinai narrative sequence serves primarily to connect the events about to occur with those already past which were nevertheless always in movement toward Sinai and what would occur there. There is in ביום הזה באו "on the very day they came" (v 1) . . . ומשה עלה "and Moses went up" (v 3) a clear connection with the eagerness of Moses to bring Israel to Sinai and to the experience of Yahweh's Presence *he* had known there: Moses goes up toward God "on the very day" of Israel's arrival at Sinai. The urgency of this completely natural narrative touch has been obscured by the insertion of what amounts to a parenthetic note designed to connect this sequence also with the geographic itinerary of 12:37; 13:20; 14:2; 15:22–23, 27; 16:1; and 17:1. It is possible that this insertion has been made necessary by the relocation of the narrative of chap. 18 described above (*Form/Structure/Setting* on 18:1–12). The disruption of so carefully plotted (see *Comment* on 16:1) a movement toward Sinai prompted the compiler to insert a note reestablishing the sequence of the journey. He set it, appropriately enough, following the very next reference to the wilderness of Sinai, but in so doing created disruption and confusion of his own at the beginning of the Sinai narrative sequence by obscuring the reference of "on the very day."

3b Moses' eager and no doubt apprehensive rush up the mountain where he had experienced Yahweh's Presence is met immediately, in this narrative sequence, by an instruction from Yahweh, who calls out to him "from the mountain." The impression the account leaves is that Yahweh is as eager for Moses and Israel to arrive at Sinai as they are to get there, and he gives Moses a message addressed quite formally to "the family of Jacob" and to "the sons of Israel," that is, to the house and descendancy of Jacob = Israel. As Muilenburg (*VT* 9 [1959] 354) has pointed out, this address of Yahweh to the people via Moses is "probably" of the provenance of "the royal message"; more than a general connection with the pattern of the royal/oracular patterns of Mari or the Hittite kings, however, is apt to be misleading.

4–6 The speech that follows this formal messenger-introduction is a poetic summary of covenant theology, and the careful economy and memorable phrasing of its language suggests that it was a set piece, composed for repeated use at covenant renewal ceremonies. It follows the standard direction of such pieces, both within (see the lengthy list of Muilenburg, *VT* 9 [1959] 355, n. 2) and without (see Mendenhall, *Law and Covenant*, 3–13, 24–35, and Baltzer, *Covenant Formulary*, 9–31) the OT, from the declaration of what Yahweh has done to the specification of the appropriate avenues of response by those for whom he has done it. These verses may very well have been taken from a standard covenant renewal liturgy and woven into the introduction of the

Sinai narrative sequence to serve here the same summary purpose they had
in their original setting, and to provide a familiar and theme-setting point
of contact for the important sequence to follow.

4 Yahweh's reference to what he has done emphasizes that the people
of Israel, for whom he has done it, have experienced it at first hand: They
have seen for themselves (1) what he "did to the Egyptians," a summary of
the entire proof-of-the Presence narrative from the first of the mighty acts
through the deliverance at the sea; (2) that he "lifted them on eagles' wings,"
a summary of the proof of his Presence through the variety of guidance and
provision in the wilderness; and (3) that he has brought them to himself,
to the mountain of his special Presence, to Sinai/Horeb. A fuller application
of the eagles' wings metaphor is made in the "Song of Moses" at Deut 32:11–
12. As Buber (*Moses*, 102) has so poetically shown, the image is one of the
utter dependency of Israel and of the tender and protective care of Yahweh.
The double emphasis of v 4 is that Yahweh has done what has been done
for Israel and that the people have themselves seen and experienced his
mighty work on their behalf.

5 ועתה אם "so now, if" sets the frame for Yahweh's expectation of Israel
in voluntary response. Yahweh is not forcing these people to serve him, as
some conquering king might do; that is but one of the drawbacks of too
close an equation of this and other OT covenant passages with ANE covenant
formulary, both real and conjectured. This "so now, if" is not even the offer
of a "choice between obedience or disobedience," as Muilenburg (*VT* 9 [1959]
353) has suggested. Yahweh is here offering Israel the means of appropriate
response to what he has done for them, if they choose to make it. The correct
comparison is with Josh 24:15, "choose for yourselves this day" (also introduced by אם), rather than with the "you shall . . ." of those who have made
a commitment to Yahweh. What Israel is to do *if* they choose to make a
response to what Yahweh has done is to pay the most careful attention to
his instruction concerning what is expected of them and then to "keep,"
that is, to abide by, the terms of his covenant.

An affirmative response to Yahweh's "if" on the part of the people of
Israel will mean the birth of "Israel" as Yahweh's people. Without that affirmative response, indeed, there would have been only "sons of Israel," the descendants of Jacob. With the affirmative response, "Israel," a community of faith
transcending biological descendancy, could come into being. That community,
an entity new to the narrative of Exodus in its sequential development to
this point, but the entity all the same because of whom and in a sense from
whom Exodus originated, is described here by three separate but interrelated
images. Israel's affirmative response will first of all mean the genesis of a
people who will be Yahweh's own סגלה "special treasure." Greenberg (*JAOS*
71 [1951] 172–74) has linked this word to an Akkadian term, *sikiltu*, which
refers to a personal collection or hoard. The image presented is that of the
unique and exclusive possession, and that image is expanded by what appears
to be an addition ("for to me belongs the whole earth") to suggest the "crown
jewel" of a large collection, the masterwork, the one-of-a-kind piece.

6 The second and third images are introduced, as was Yahweh's statement
of his work for Israel, with an emphatic "you yourselves," a deft underscoring

of the motif of uniqueness stressed by סגלה "special treasure." Such a people will be Yahweh's own ממלכת כהנים "kingdom of priests." This phrase, since it is unique in the OT, has occasioned an array of interpretations, both in the ancient Versions (see Scott, *OTS* 8 [1950] 213–16) and among modern commentators. Scott (216–19) has proposed the meaning "a kingdom set apart like a priesthood," and followed Galling's (*Erwählungstraditionen*, 27) statement that ממלכת כהנים is not a "terminus technicus" but a designation of Israel as those who worship or venerate Yahweh. Bauer (*BZ* 2 [1958] 284–86) reads ממלכת as an absolute rather than construct form, then links it to כהנים to get "kings [who are] priests," or "priestlike kings," whose royalty is an extension of Yahweh's kingship: ממלכת matches the גוי "people" and כהנים the קדוש "holy" of the following phrase. Wildberger (*Jahwes Eigentumsvolk*, 80–95), arguing from 2 Sam 8:18 and 1 Kgs 4:5, takes ממלכת כהנים as an honorific title connecting the lordship of Yahweh over Israel with the lordship of Israel over the nations. Moran (*Current Catholic Thought*, 11–20), following and supplementing Caspari (*TB1* 8 [1929] 105–10), takes the view that ממלכת can mean "king" or "royalty" and ממלכת כהנים, "a royalty of priests," leading the worship of Yahweh's גוי קדוש "holy nation" in "the pre-monarchical period." Fohrer (*TZ* 19 [1963] 359–62) agrees with much of Moran's argument, expanding it from ANE parallels and by reference to grammatical and syntactical arguments, but dating the usage somewhat later.

While the notion of Beer (97) that the root of the idea of the priesthood of all believers lies in this passage goes too far, it is also excessive to claim that v 6 is a reference to a royal elite, whether among kings *or* priests. The phrases "special treasure," "kingdom of priests," and "holy people" are closely related to one another, and although they each refer to the whole of the people who will pay attention to and follow the covenant, they are not to be taken as synonymous, either all three of them or the second two of them. Israel as the "special treasure" is Israel become uniquely Yahweh's prized possession by their commitment to him in covenant. Israel as a "kingdom of priests" is Israel committed to the extension throughout the world of the ministry of Yahweh's Presence. ממלכת here is exactly what it appears to be, a noun in construct relationship with כהנים, and it describes what Israel was always supposed to be: a kingdom run not by politicians depending upon strength and connivance but by priests depending on faith in Yahweh, a servant nation instead of a ruling nation. Israel as a "holy people" then represents a third dimension of what it means to be committed in faith to Yahweh: they are to be a people set apart, different from all other people by what they are and are becoming—a display-people, a showcase to the world of how being in covenant with Yahweh changes a people.

The question of the date of this marvelous summary sequence is unanswerable. In concept, it began evolving with the birth of Israel as a people of faith in covenant with Yahweh. As a summary used in the cultic context of covenant renewal services, it certainly predates the Deuteronomistic period. Whether it also predates the monarchy is unlikely.

7–8 Moses' summons of the elders for his commanded report of Yahweh's words is consonant with their role as the representatives of the people. As McKenzie has shown (*Bib* 4 [1959] 523–24), often when the elders are gathered, the people are addressed. So here, the people, "all . . . together," respond following Moses' explanation ("he established as authoritative for them all these words") that they will do everything Yahweh has said, a statement that may imply more than is specified in the "eagles' wings" summary ("pay very careful attention" and "keep"). Moses then reports the people's response to Yahweh.

9 The logical next step in the narrative is the anticipation of the Advent of Yahweh, in the instructions for the preparation of the people, but what we have instead is a statement of Yahweh to Moses concerning Moses' authentication as a leader in whom the people can have unwavering confidence in time to come. This verse, which includes also another reference to Moses' report to Yahweh of the people's response to his words, is best considered an addition to the earlier versions of this narrative, an addition designed to offset further the negation of the "murmuring" narratives and to augment the role of Moses as the needed intermediary between Yahweh and the people. This theme is secondary, however, to the main concern of Exod 19, the Advent of Yahweh. Indeed it is attracted by the theophany, and by the emphasis throughout the narrative that the theophany was experienced by the whole people. This emphasis may account for the placement of the insertion, immediately before the instruction for the preparation of the people for *their* meeting with Yahweh. It is an insertion of a piece with the verses at the end of chap. 19, in which Aaron also is allowed a special nearness to Yahweh, and at 20:21; 24:1–2, 9–18; 33:11, 17–23; and 34:29–35, and one somewhat out of step with a sequence beginning and ending with the preparation of the people for an experience Moses has had already. The additional reference to Moses' report of the people's words to Yahweh, using דגנ "declare," may possibly be displaced from the end of v 6, where it would fit better; or it may be, as Beer (97) wrote, a repetition of v 8b that should be deleted.

10–12 Following the agreement of the people to hear and keep the covenant of Yahweh and thus to commit themselves to becoming the people so special to him and for him, Yahweh next instructs Moses to prepare them for the theophany to come. He is to "set them apart for holiness," for two days. Not all that this involves is specified, apparently, only that they are to wash their clothes (v 10) and refrain from sexual intercourse (v 15). Moses himself is to set boundaries for the people around the circumference of Sinai, with specific instructions regarding its approach and severe warnings concerning the observance of these boundaries. All preparations are to be made by "the third day," when Yahweh will come down onto Sinai, and—on this the text is emphatic—"before the eyes of the whole people." J. B. Bauer (*Bib* 39 [1958] 354–58), who has examined biblical and extrabiblical references to "the third day," has come to the conclusion that the phrase is a general expression for an interdeterminate brief period of time, as in the contemporary saying "ein 'paar' Tagen." This interpretation does not, however, account for the persistence of the phrase through the whole range of the biblical narrative, in which nearly always it is used with a sense of rising anticipation.

13 The prohibition against touching Mount Sinai, like the prohibition against touching those who have violated that restriction, is based on the belief that holiness, like uncleanness, was infectious through physical contact

(Durham, *Touch, Taste and Smell,* 108–22). With the Advent of Yahweh, Mount Sinai would become holy by virtue of his special Presence there, and that holiness would constitute a danger to all persons and everything forbidden contact with it (cf. 2 Sam 6:6–8 and 1 Chr 13:9–10; see Durham, 229–30). Thus any person or any creature touching any part of the mountain beyond the boundaries that Yahweh has commanded Moses to set is to be stoned or shot (presumably by archers or even by slingers, Judg 20:16) to death.

The signal for the people to come up on the third day to the boundaries set by Moses is to be a sustained blast on the bell-horn, either a ram's horn or some other type of horn whose tone was amplified by the attachment of a metal resonance-bell. The sound produced by this arrangement would probably have been far more piercing and awesome signal than a musical tone.

14–15 Moses took these instructions from Yahweh to the people. He consecrated them for the momentous experience of the third day. As bidden, they washed their clothes. Moses then reminded them of the need to be completely ready by the third day, with the additional instruction that they were not to "come near שׁגַּ to a woman," a euphemism for sexual intercourse. This prohibition is parallel to the prohibition against touching the isolated area of Mount Sinai: a man's semen rendered both the man and the woman with whom he was having intercourse unclean and therefore cultically unacceptable for a specified period (Lev 15:16–18). The reason for this has to do with the holiness of what may be called a life-immanence connected with the Presence of Yahweh (Durham, *Touch, Taste and Smell,* 93–96). The people must take care to be cultically pure by the third day, so that they may have their own part in Yahweh's revelation of his Presence.

Explanation

The twofold introduction to the most important event of Exodus, and even of the OT itself, is thus set forth. There is, first, a prologue to the entire Sinai narrative sequence, in the form of a summary of Yahweh's deeds for Israel and of his hopes for Israel if they choose to make a response to what he has done. There is, second, a narrative of the preparation of Israel for the experience of Yahweh's Presence, to be manifested to them on the third day following the arrival at Sinai. These two sequences are linked by the people's response to what Yahweh has done and said, a response that prompts his further instructions.

There is without question clear evidence in these lines of multiple narratives in compilation. What is most important about them, however, is their focus, which overrides any inconsistencies apparent in them in its emphasis upon the great event about to take place. The first verses of this section suggest that this event is very much *the* act of Yahweh for which all else he has done has been preparatory and toward which all else has been moving. The following verses make plain that Israel has an important part in what Yahweh hopes to do beyond this great event, and beyond even Israel. And the concluding verses make it clear that the sole recipients of the great event to come are the people of Israel: not just to Moses or the elders or any elite company of priests is Yahweh coming on the third day, but to the people of Israel themselves. This emphasis is a studied one, repeated throughout this section, and it is in a way the essential point of a sequence introducing the great event of Exodus, Yahweh's Advent, by stressing the role and the preparation of the people to whom and for whom he comes, the people whose very being is to be related directly to the degree to which they receive or ignore his Presence.

Yahweh Comes to Israel at Sinai   (19:16–25)

Bibliography

Clifford, R. J. *The Cosmic Mountain in Canaan and the Old Testament.* Cambridge: Harvard University Press, 1972. **Jeremias, J.** *Theophanie.* WMANT 10. Neukirchen-Vluyn: Neukirchener Verlag, 1965. **Klopfer, R.** "Zur Quellenscheidung in Exod 19." *ZAW* 18 (1898) 197–235. **Koenig, J.** "Le Sinai, montagne de feu dans un désert de ténèbres." *RHR* 167 (1965) 129–55. **Terrien, S.** *The Elusive Presence.* San Francisco: Harper & Row, 1978. **Vaux, R. de.** "Les Fouilles de Tell El-Far'ah, près Naplouse." *RB* 62 (1955) 541–89. **Weiser, A.** "Zur Frage nach den Beziehungen der Psalmen zum Kult: Die Darstellung der Theophanie in den Psalmen und im Festkult." *Festschrift Alfred Bertholet.* Tubingen: J. C. B. Mohr (Paul Siebeck), 1950. 513–49.

Translation

[16] *And so it was, on the third day, when the morning was breaking,* [a] *that there were rumblings of thunder* [b] *and flashes of lightning, and a heavy cloud upon the mountain. The sound of a ram's horn was very strong,* [c] *so much so* [d] *that all the people in the camp were terrified.* [17] *Then Moses led the people out from the camp to encounter God.* [a] *They took a position at the bottom of the mountain.* [18] *The whole of Mount Sinai was smoking from the Presence* [a] *of Yahweh,* [b] *who came down upon it in the fire—indeed, the smoke of it boiled up like smoke from the pottery-kiln, and the whole mountain shook violently.* [c] [19] *The sound of the ram's horn meanwhile* [a] *was moving,* [b] *and growing very strong.*

|[c] *Moses spoke, and God answered him in a rumble of thunder.* [d]

[20] *Thus Yahweh came down upon Mount Sinai, to the top of the mountain; Yahweh summoned Moses to the top of the mountain, and Moses went up.* [21] *Then Yahweh* [a] *said to Moses, "Go down, caution the people, to keep* [b] *them from pushing through toward Yahweh* [a] *to see: many of them then would fall dead.* [c] [22] *And be sure* [a] *the priests who approach Yahweh* [b] *in ministry* [c] *set themselves apart for holiness, to keep Yahweh from rushing upon them in punishment."* [d]

[23] *So Moses answered Yahweh,* [a] *"The people are not permitted* [b] *to go up Mount Sinai, because you yourself cautioned us, specifying,* [c] *'Establish boundaries for the mountain, and set it apart for holiness.'"* [24] *But Yahweh replied to him, "Get along, go down—then you* [a] *go up, and Aaron along with you: but the priests and the*

people are not to push through ^b *to go up toward Yahweh,* ^c *else he will rush upon them in judgment!"*

|^{25a} *Moses then went down to the people, and said to them. . . .* ^b

Notes

16.a. בהית הבקר "in the happening, being of the morning": note BDB, 90, "Followed by an inf constr, בְּ forms a periphrasis for the gerund, though in English it is commonly rendered by a verb and conj." Cf. also BDB, 224–25.

16.b. קלת, lit., "voices, sounds"; see BDB, 877 § 2.a.b.

16.c. The sound is the amplified sound described above, n. 13.c., and is "very strong" because it is near at hand. Here the instrument is called simply a שפר "ram's horn"; in v 13 it is called a יבל "bell-horn."

16.d. Special *waw* in this context.

17.a. האלהים. The definite form refers to *the* God, "the (true) God," BDB, 43–44 § 3. Cf. Deut 4:35, כי יהוה הוא האלהים "that Yahweh he is the God."

18.a. The sequence of MT emphasizes Presence. Lit., it reads: "from a Presence that came down upon it, Yahweh in the fire." Presence and Yahweh are brought together above to make this emphasis as plain in Eng. as it is in Heb.

18.b. LXX has τὸν θεὸν "God."

18.c. LXX has instead καὶ ἐξέστη πᾶς ὁ λαὸς σφόδρα "and the whole people were utterly astonished."

19.a. See n. 16.d.

19.b. הולך "moving" here needs to be taken literally; the warning sound of the amplified ram's horn is "growing very strong" because it is moving closer to the mountain and to the people to indicate the arriving Presence of Yahweh.

19.c. This sentence is not continuous with what precedes or follows it; see *Form/Structure/ Setting* below.

19.d. בקול "in thunder"; see n. 16.b. But cf. Terrien (*Elusive Presence*, 127): "the meaning of the word *qôl* (vs. 19b), used for the answer of God, is uncertain: it may refer to a thunderstroke or to an articulated voice.

21.a. LXX has ὁ θεός "God."

21.b. פֶּן: "conj. (averting or deprecating)," BDB, 814–15.

21.c. נפל "fall," but in this context, of death brought by judgment: note BDB, 657 § 2.a., "Esp. of violent death (c. 96t.)."

22.a. וגם "and be sure"; cf. Labuschagne, *Studia*, 200–203.

22.b. LXX reads κυρίῳ τῷ θεῷ "Yahweh God."

22.c. נגש "draw near, approach," + אֶל "to" + Yahweh, as here, or מזבח "altar" as in 28:43, has reference to the approach of the priests to Yahweh's Presence in the ministry of worship.

22.d. פרץ "break through, burst upon" refers here and in v 24, as in 2 Sam 5:20 and 6:8; Pss 60:3 [1] and 106:29, to the sudden and violent onslaught of Yahweh in a forewarned judgment.

23.a. LXX has τὸν θεὸν "God."

23.b. יכל "be able, have power," in this verse with "ability . . . dependent on external authority," BDB, 407 § 1.a. The authority here is of course Yahweh, who has forbidden the people access to the mountain.

23.c. לאמר "specifying" in this sequence.

24.a. Emphasis indicated by the independent pers pronoun אתה "you" in addition to the pronoun of the verb.

24.b. Or, "let them not push through"; the neg is אַל.

24.c. LXX reads "God."

25.a. See n. 19.c.

25.b. ויאמר אלהם "and he said to them," often taken as a reference to Moses' report of what Yahweh has just said (so RSV, "and told them"; cf. Cassuto, 234), is taken by Davies (157–58) as referring instead to "the instructions of chaps. 22f." Some translators (NEB, "and spoke to them."; JB, "and spoke to them . . .") understandably leave the matter as vague as the text does. BDB (56) notes: "in all cases usually sq. dir. obj. of words said, Ex 19²⁵ Ju 17² being singular." Noth (160) calls this verse "a fragment." Klopfer (*ZAW* 18 [1898] 230) connects it with vv 21 and 22. What is likely is that at least a summary of Moses' words to the people followed this verb and its indir obj. In the compilation of Exodus, that summary, or even a longer speech, was dropped.

Form/Structure/Setting

This continuation of the Sinai narrative sequence is, like the section preceding it, a compilation, and one that must be read also as a part of that larger sequence. This section, however, contains the beginning of that section of the narrative that is central to the entire sequence, the account of Yahweh's Advent and Yahweh's "ten words." To that central account, the narratives of the preparation of the people (19:9–15) for the theophany and the reaction of the people (20:18–21) to the theophany have been set as brackets. Preceding this bracketed central narrative, there is an introduction (19:1–8) to the Sinai narrative sequence as a whole; following it, there is an account of the aftermath of Advent, with narratives of Covenant-Making (chap. 24), Disobedience (32:1–24), Judgment (32:25–33:17), and Covenant Renewal (33:18–34:35). The energizing nucleus of this entire sequence, however, is the narrative of Yahweh's coming to Israel at Sinai, a narrative of which the ten commandments in their earliest and briefest form were an integral part. Everything preceding this narrative of Advent points to it, in one way or another, from the theophany of Moses' call in chap. 3. Everything following it stems from it: not only is the continuation of the Sinai narrative sequence a sequence turning on Presence and threat of Absence, even the covenant instructions and the symbols and personnel of worship are rooted in the assumptions of Yahweh's Presence. Even in its composite form, the Sinai narrative sequence can be seen to have Yahweh's Presence as a fundamental preoccupation (cf. *Form/Structure/Setting* on 19:1–15).

Given the importance of Yahweh's theophany at Sinai, it is not surprising that the account of it in Exodus is a composite, and a multilayered one at that. What is surprising is that this account is not longer and even more convoluted than it is. The very awesomeness of what ultimately can only be an ineffable experience may help to account for this brevity. Despite an obvious layering of narrative material, the motif of Yahweh's coming to Israel permeates this section: only v 25 makes no reference to it. Onto this motif has been grafted the obvious theme of the exposure of Israel to Yahweh's Presence: vv 16, 17, 21, 22, 23, and 24 are concerned with Israels' experiencing Yahweh's Presence and being protected from it. But into these two unavoidably related themes has been worked a third motif, one in conflict, to a degree, with these two that preceded it. This conflict, indeed, accounts for much of the confusion of Exod 19, most of which comes at the end of this second section of the chapter.

The standard source-critical summaries reflect the problem, but do not solve it. Generally, they have tended to complicate it. The elaborate rearrangement of Klopfer (*ZAW* 18 [1898] 231–35) is a somewhat extreme example of violence to the compilation that is Exod 19, but most literary critics have, like Klopfer, assigned the chapter, including these final ten verses of it, to J and E in all but inseparable quantities. So Beer (96–98): vv 16, 17, 19 go to E[1]; vv 18, 20, 25 to J[2]; vv 21–24 to R[JE]; Noth (158–60): vv 16aα, 18, 20 to J; vv 16aβb, 17, 19 to E; vv 21–25, "secondary additions"; Hyatt (199–203): 16a, 18 to J; 16b–17, 19, 25 to E; 20–24 to J_s, "the J supplementer." As is the case with vv 1–15, these verses also have been too many times overworked to permit any definitive source assignment, and attempts to resolve confusion by this method tend rather to multiply it.

A clearer understanding of the form of this complicated section may come from an identification of the third motif mentioned above, the motif added to the obvious pair of themes, Yahweh's Presence and Israel's experience of that Presence. The obsession of Moses, from his call forward, has been to get Israel to Sinai and to an experience of the Presence he knew there. Most of the narrative of Exodus from chap. 7 to this point has involved the proof to Israel of the Presence of Yahweh in the mighty acts in Egypt, the guidance through the wilderness, the deliverance at the sea, the provision and protection *en route* to Sinai, and the bringing of Israel to himself at Sinai. All the preparation of Israel, finally *at* Sinai, has been to the end that *they,* and no one else, might be "completely ready" to encounter Yahweh on that most important "third day." The boundaries that have been set up are for *Israel's protection* in the midst of an experience of rendezvous. *Israel* is made ready for holiness. *Israel* is commanded to ritual purification and cultic abstinence. *Israel* is brought by Moses from the camp to the perimeters of safety at the base of Sinai, there to meet and be met by Yahweh. Then, suddenly, just at the very moment when the experience of Yahweh so longed for has arrived, Moses, represented throughout the narrative as eagerly longing for Israel to know it, is suddenly thrust into the center as the sacerdotal/prophetic intermediary between Yahweh and his people.

This insertion, barely even anticipated before chap. 19, is one for which the narrative of Exodus to this point is ill prepared, and one which is a diversion of the main track of the narrative, continued with no further reference to Moses until the account of the people's reaction to the theophany of Yahweh in 20:18–21. There, Moses' role as intermediary makes sense, as it does also in the revelation of the special instructions for life and worship in the covenant relationship with Yahweh that follow 20:21 and the making of the covenant in chap. 24.

It may be suggested, therefore, that the emphasis of this section on Moses as intermediary is dislocated; that it belongs more properly to the narrative sequences following 20:21; that the confusing disparity of Moses' trips up and down Sinai can be solved by the movement forward of this material to a setting following the people's request for an intermediary in the meeting of Yahweh; and that the narrative of Exod 19 is best ended at v 19a, to which then Exod 20:1–21 should be read in immediate sequence. The ten commandments (though certainly in a shorter form) belong to the narrative of Yahweh's Advent at Sinai; they represent, along with the thunder and the sound of the ram's horn, the auditory dimension of the Sinai theophany. The motif of Moses as sacerdotal/prophetic intermediary belongs to a later sequence, one following the people's first and unique experience of Yahweh's Presence.

The reason for the placement of vv 19b–25 with the account of Yahweh's Advent to Israel is obvious enough. It is the same motive by which Aaron has been added to the Exodus narrative: the glorification of sacerdotal prerogative, and in Moses' case, prophetic prerogative as well. Yahweh's warning about trespassing on the holy ground of Sinai may also belong to a later narrative context, as for example Exod 24:1–2 or even 32:29–35, relocated here because of its logical bearing on the narrative of the boundaries in 19:12–13. It would in such a case be more than "a later gloss" designed to deal with a question raised in Priestly circles about the approach to Yahweh, and attached here "as a sort of midrash on vv. 12–13a" (Beyerlin, *Sinaitic Traditions*, 8).

Thus the key to this section, as also to the larger narrative sequence of which it is the foundational part, is Yahweh's Advent. A series of traditions reporting that awesome event have been compressed into a single compact, starkly eloquent, sequence. Then into and onto that account has been grafted a narrative designed more to glorify the offices of Moses than Moses himself. The location is perfect, from the point of view of the redactor who added these lines. But for once, the compilation is less than the sum of its parts.

Comment

16–17   The Advent promised "on the third day" begins right on schedule, at daybreak, the reason that Israel had to be "completely ready" by the third day (vv 11, 15). The thunder and lightning and the heavy cloud lowering over the mountain are not to be thought of as reflecting a tradition of Yahweh's appearance in the thick of a thunderstorm, separate from a different and somewhat conflicting account of his appearance in the fire and smoke of some kind of volcanic eruption (e.g., as Newman, *People of the Covenant*, 39–51, and Kuntz, *Self-Revelation of God*, 72–100, suggest). Not only are the layers of the composite of Exod 19 virtually impossible to separate with any such precision, there is not the slightest reason to imagine some unusual thunderstorm or to look for an extinct volcano as a means of locating Sinai (so Koenig, *RHR* 167 [1965] 129–55). The storm and fire imagery of vv 16–19a is one part of an attempt to describe the indescribable experience of the coming of Yahweh. It is language recurrent in OT theophany accounts, and language rooted in Canaanite descriptions of the arrival of deity (cf. Clifford, *Cosmic Mountain* 107–20). The reference to the increasing sound of a ram's horn following each of the two verses using the storm and fire imagery (vv 16, 18) and the reference between those verses to the positioning of Israel binds the verses together into a unity of rising intensity.

After the first rumblings of thunder, the flashing lightning and the breaking day revealed a thick cloud hiding the mountain from view. Before the people could reach the conclusion that what they were hearing and seeing was an ordinary storm, the sound of the ram's horn, so strong as to indicate that it was near at hand, made it clear that the experience of the third day, for which they had prepared, was at hand. The sounding of the ram's horn was a signal that Yahweh was present in the worship of Israel (2 Sam 6:15; Ps

47:6 [5]). Weiser (*Festschrift A. Bertholet*, 523–24) has suggested that the re-sounding trumpet may have been an "intimation of Yahweh's voice" in the cultic re-presentation of theophany, and Beyerlin (*Sinaitic Traditions*, 135–36, also 35–36) has argued that the account of the Sinai theophany "was obviously influenced by a definite cultic usage" in the sounding of a trumpet to signal Yahweh's arrival. There is here no hint about who was sounding the ram's horn, a fact that adds to the awesome mystery of the narrative. The horn was sounded by no one belonging to Israel, not even by Moses.

Whether the sounding of the ram's horn is a feature added to this narrative from later cultic contexts, as Weiser and Beyerlin both suggest, or whether later cultic practice arose from the memory of a fearsome sound at Sinai, is of course now impossible to determine. Nor is the sound to be thought of as the howling of the wind "which resembled the sound of the horn" (Cassuto, 232) or as "a liturgical imitation of the sound of the wind . . . or of thunder" (Clifford, *Cosmic Mountain*, 111–12). The sound, quite explicitly described in v 13 and mentioned in very definite terms in vv 16 and 19, is clearly understood and reported as the signal of the arrival of Yahweh's Presence. Only on such an interpretation do the next two actions make sense: first, the people in the camp literally shake with fear, not a reaction one would expect from a thunderstorm on the mountain, however violent. Second, Moses immediately leads (ויצא) the people forth to encounter (לקראת) God, sta-tioning them at the foot of the mountain before the boundaries designated by Yahweh, who has promised to come on the third day. This too is not an action a thunderstorm would have provoked.

18 With the people in place, the experience intensifies. The entire moun-tain smokes from the Presence of Yahweh descending upon it in fire, the most frequent of all OT symbols of theophany. The smoke boils forth "like smoke from the pottery-kiln," a description that in itself sets aside any image of a volcano in eruption, since "the kiln" is likely to have been a closed kiln with a fire chamber beneath it and with a number of flues to conduct both heat and smoke, much like a modern upright steam boiler (see *CAH, Plates to I & II:* 37a; and de Vaux, *RB* 62 [1955] 557–63). Furthermore, as Terrien notes (*Elusive Presence*, 153, n. 7), the fire, descending, is moving in the wrong direction for a volcano. The fire is the fire of Yahweh's Presence; the smoke is the thick blinding smoke of Isaiah's vision (Isa 6:4), the purpose of which is to obscure what man cannot look upon and live; and the violent quaking of the mountain is the upheaval of the natural world that always accompanies Yahweh's coming (Jeremias, *Theophanie*, 1–16).

19 The description of the intensifying phenomena surrounding Yahweh's Presence following the people's movement to their place calls for a second reference to the identifying signal. The second sounding of the ram's horn brings the reassurance, amidst the tumult of the mountain, that Yahweh is indeed coming. But that reassurance brings a greater fear of a different kind, for the sound is moving closer, growing ever more strong. The description is not of a stationary sound growing louder and louder, but of a moving sound, growing stronger as it comes closer. Yahweh has come. He now is close at hand. The purpose of this narrative is to present an atmosphere electric with Yahweh's Presence.

As noted above (on v 16), the narrative of Yahweh's Advent is best read
directly on from the second reference to the sounding of the ram's horn to
Yahweh's self-declaration at the beginning of Exod 20. Vv 19b–25 belong
to a later section of the larger Sinai narrative sequence, one having to do
with the justification of the Mosaic offices. Such a justification, though obviously important to the priestly/prophetic compilers of Exodus, has no part
in the narrative of Yahweh's coming. The question of where these verses
ought to go opens an array of possibilities, but none of them can be put
forward as definitive.

20–25 The reference to Moses speaking and being answered by God in
thunder, like Yahweh's summons of Moses up to himself on the mountain
and the ensuing dialogue there, would fit more logically at a number of later
points, two of which have already been suggested (p. 270). Since no suggestion
is determinative, these verses are best left in their canonical location, even
though they appear to belong elsewhere. The compiler's reason for placing
them here must primarily have been a desire to avoid any impression that
Israel might approach Yahweh without a priestly/prophetic intermediary; secondarily, the repetition of the instructions about Sinai made holy by Yahweh's
Presence helped to draw vv 20–24 into what is now chap. 19. Both v 19b
and v 25 appear incomplete as they stand; v 19b is *non sequitur* with what
precedes and follows it, and v 25 is clearly the introduction for an address
of Moses that no longer comes after it. This has led some commentators
(so Beyerlin, *Sinaitic Traditions*, 8–9) to propose that vv 19b and 25 belong
together and are the introduction to a message to Israel now missing, but
such a proposal has only a conjectural basis.

20–22 This additional reference to Yahweh's descent onto Mount Sinai
has the appearance of a summary introduction to the dialogue between Yahweh and Moses that follows. There is not evidence in chap. 19 or anywhere
else in Exodus or in the OT to sustain the theory that there are two traditions
of Yahweh's relation to Sinai, in one of which he is somehow "enthroned"
on the mountain, and in the other of which he lives in the heavens and
must come down to the mountain (so Newman, *People of the Covenant*, 46–
48; Hyatt, 202). Yahweh moves where he will, and places become holy, as
in Exod 19, because of his Presence. The composite of Exod 19 reflects
the OT theology of Yahweh's Advent at its foundation, and the emphasis is
on coming, not on residence, and not even on direction of coming (there
is likewise no clear evidence here for the "March in the South" theory of
Clifford, *Cosmic Mountain*, 114–20).

The reference to Yahweh coming down on Sinai connects the dialogue
with Moses to the Sinai/theophany sequence. Moses must then be summoned
"to the top of the mountain," that is, to a place beyond the boundaries,
where the people of Israel are forbidden to go. This move establishes the
uniqueness of Moses' role, a uniqueness immediately reinforced by the repetition of the warning that the people are not to cross the boundaries, even
in the excitement of the visit of Yahweh, in an understandable desire to
see. The result of such a disobedience would be an immediate and fatal
judgment. Even the priests whose ministry requires that they draw near to

Yahweh's Presence are not to do so with impunity; they must set themselves apart for the holiness of such a context, just as the people of Israel have had to do in preparation for the third day. The introduction of the necessity for priests to respect the holiness of Yahweh's Presence, attached to the Sinai narrative as an illustration of the seriousness of the restrictions made necessary by that holiness, is anachronistic even to the sequence of Exodus. It is thus another indication that this narrative, or at least this verse, belongs at a later point.

23–24 Moses' reaction to Yahweh's repeated warning about the boundaries provides a further means of emphasizing both the restrictions regarding the boundaries and the uniqueness of Moses' role. Moses reiterates Yahweh's instruction of v 12, with two shifts: the boundaries are for the mountain rather than for the people, and the mountain, rather than the people, is to be set apart for holiness. The result is the same in either case. Yahweh's reply underscores the special position of Moses; this time Aaron is added, and the priests are included with the people in the ban of any approach beyond the boundaries. Thus Moses and Aaron, and the special intermediary rôles they represent, are made more special still: Moses and Aaron are permitted to come where not even Yahweh's priests, at this point in the Sinai narrative sequence yet non-existent, can go.

Explanation

At last Israel comes to the experience Moses had known on Mount Sinai, the experience toward which he has led them and for which not even what they had seen in Egypt or in their journey could have prepared them. The scene having been laid dramatically by the "eagle's wings" summary and by the instructions and the acts of preparation, Yahweh comes at daybreak on the third day. All the awesome accompaniment of that Advent—the thunder, the lightning, the heavy cloud, the fire, the thick, obscuring smoke and above all the resounding ram's horn moving closer through the opaque covering on the mountain—is a dramatization of *the* event of Exodus and of the OT: Yahweh's coming to his people, gathered by his instruction at the edge of a boundary set for their protection.

This coming is told with the engaging directness of most biblical narrative: Yahweh comes down upon the mountain in the fire. More space is given to the preparation for his coming, and to the listing of the audible and visible effects of his coming, than to the announcement itself. That is without elaboration, for what more can be said than that God, who is holy, comes to his people, who are wholly other than holy? Indeed, the simplicity of the announcement may help to explain the insertion of the additional but misplaced material glorifying Moses' offices by repeating the instructions about the boundaries of holiness and permitting Moses and Aaron to pass them.

That material, however, disrupts a dramatic sequence in which Yahweh comes to his people, then speaks to them. As exciting as is his Advent onto the mountain, more amazing still is his address to all the people waiting, an address in which he gives himself to them more fully still by trusting them to enter into covenant with him. Exod 19 holds but half the theophany; the other half, the completing half, is in Exod 20.

Yahweh's Principles for Life in Covenant (20:1–17)

Bibliography

Alt, A. "Das Verbot des Diebstahls im Dekalog." *Kleine Schriften I.* Munich: C. H. Beck'sche Verlagsbuchhandlung, 1953. 333–40 ————. *Essays on Old Testament History and Religion.* Oxford: Basil Blackwell, 1966. **Alter, R.** *The Art of Biblical Narrative.* New York: Basic Books, 1981. **Andreasen, N.-E. A.** *The Old Testament Sabbath.* SBLDS 7. Missoula, MT: Society of Biblical Literature, 1972. **Andrew, M. E.** "Falsehood and Truth." *Int* 17 (1963) 425–38. **Bernhardt, K.-H.** *Gott und Bild.* Berlin: Evangelische Verlagsanstalt, 1956. **Boecker, H. J.** *Law and the Administration of Justice in the Old Testament and Ancient East.* Minneapolis: Augsburg Publishing House, 1980. ————. *Redeformen des Rechtslebens im Alten Testament.* WMANT 14. Neukirchen-Vluyn: Neukirchener Verlag, 1964. **Brongers, H. A.** "Der Eifer des Herrn Zebaoth." *VT* 13 (1963) 269–84. **Burkitt, F. C.** "The Hebrew Papyrus of the Ten Commandments." *JQR* 15 (1903) 392–408. **Cannon, W. W.** "The Weekly Sabbath." *ZAW* 49 (1931) 325–27. **Coates, J. R.** "'Thou shalt not covet.'" *ZAW* 52 (1934) 238–39. **Elliger, K.** "Ich bin der Herr–euer Gott." *Kleine Schriften zum Alten Testament.* TBü 32. Munich: Chr. Kaiser Verlag, 1966. 211–31. **Fichtner, J.** "Der Begriff des 'Nächsten' im Alten Testament." *Wort und Dienst* 4. Bethel: Verlagshandlung der Anstalt Bethel, 1955. 23–52. **Flusser, D.** "'Do Not Commit Adultery,' 'Do Not Murder.'" *Textus* 4. Ed. S. Talmon. Jerusalem: Magnes Press, 1964. 220–24. **Gamberoni, J.** "Das Elterngebot im Alten Testament." *BZ* 8 (1964) 161–90. **Gerstenberger, E.** "Covenant and Commandment." *JBL* 84 (1965) 38–51. ————. *Wesen und Herkunft des 'Apodiktischen Rechts'* WMANT 20. Neukirchen-Vluyn: Neukirchener Verlag, 1965. **Gese, H.** "Der Dekalog als Ganzheit betrachtet." *ZTK* 64 (1967) 121–38. **Gevirtz, S.** "West Semitic Curses and the Problem of the Origins of Hebrew Law." *VT* 11 (1961) 137–58. **Gottstein, M. H.** "Du sollst nicht stehlen." *TZ* 9 (1953) 394–95. **Gressmann, H.** *Die älteste Geschichtsschreibung und Prophetie Israels.* 2d ed. Göttingen: Vandenhoeck und Ruprecht, 1921. **Grether, O.** *Name und Wort Gottes im Alten Testament.* BZAW 64. Giessen: Verlag von Alfred Töpelmann, 1934. **Gutmann, J.** "The 'Second Commandment' and the Image in Judaism." *HUCA* 32 (1961) 161–74. **Harrelson, W.** *The Ten Commandments and Human Rights.* Philadelphia: Fortress Press, 1980. **Herrmann, J.** "Das zehnte Gebot." *Beiträge zur Religionsgeschichte und Archaeologie Palästinas.* Leipzig: Deichert, 1927. 64–82. **Hillers, D. R.** *Covenant: The History of a Biblical Idea.* Baltimore: Johns Hopkins Press, 1969. **Horst, F.** "Der Diebstahl im Alten Testament." *Gottes Recht.* TBü 12. Munich: Chr. Kaiser Verlag, 1961. 167–75. **Hulst, A. R.** "Bemerkungen zum Sabbatgebot." *Studia Biblica et Semitica.* Wageningen: H. Veenman & Zonen, 1966. 152–64. **Humbert, P.** "La 'femme étrangère' du livre des Proverbes." *RÉtSém* 27 (1937) 49–64. **Hyatt, J. P.** "Moses and the Ethical Decalogue." *Encounter* 26 (1965) 199–206. **Jirku, A.** *Das weltliche Recht im Alten Testament.* Gütersloh: C. Bertelsmann, 1927. **Keszler, W.** "Die Literarische, Historische und Theologische Problematik des Dekalogs." *VT* 7 (1957)

1–16. **Kilian, R.** "Apodiktisches und kasuistisches Recht im Licht ägyptischer Analogien." *BZ* 7 (1963) 185–202. **Klopfenstein, M. A.** *Die Lüge nach dem Alten Testament.* Zürich: Gotthelf-Verlag, 1964. **Knierim, R.** "Das Erste Gebot." *ZAW* 77 (1965) 20–39. **Köhler L.** "Der Dekalog." *TRu* 1 (1929) 161–84. ———. "Justice in the Gate." *Hebrew Man.* Nashville: Abingdon Press, 1956. 127–50. **Kornfeld, W.** "L'adultère dans l'orient antique." *RB* 57 (1950) 92–109. **Kremers, H.** "Die Stellung des Elterngebotes im Dekalog." *EvT* 21 (1961) 145–61. **L'Hour, J.** *Die Ethik der Bundestradition im Alten Testament.* SBS 14. Stuttgart: Verlag Katholisches Bibelwerk, 1967. **Lohfink, N.** "Zur Dekalogfassung von Dt 5." *BZ* 9 (1965) 17–32. **Martin-Achard, R.** *Actualité d'Abraham.* Neuchâtel: Éditions Delachaux et Niestlé, 1969. **Mathys, F.** "Sabbatruhe und Sabbatfest." *TZ* 28 (1972) 241–62. **McCarthy, D. J.** *Old Testament Covenant: A Survey of Current Opinions.* Richmond: John Knox Press, 1972. ———. *Treaty and Covenant.* AnBib 21. Rome: Pontifical Biblical Institute, 1963. **Meek, T. J.** "The Sabbath in the Old Testament." *JBL* 33 (1914) 201–12. **Meinhold, J.** "Zur Sabbathfrage." *ZAW* 48 (1930) 121–38. **Menes, A.** *Die Vorexilischen Gesetze Israels.* BZAW 50. Giessen: Verlag von Alfred Töpelmann, 1928. **Moran, W. L.** "The Conclusion of the Decalogue (Ex 20,17 = Dt 5,21)." *CBQ* 29 (1967) 543–54. ———. "The Scandal of the 'Great Sin' at Ugarit." *JNES* 18 (1959) 280–81. **Morgenstern, J.** "The Oldest Document of the Hexateuch." *HUCA* 4 (1927) 1–138. **Mowinckel, S.** *La décalogue.* Paris: Felix Alcan, 1927. **Muilenburg, J.** "The Linguistic and Rhetorical Usages of the Particle כי in the Old Testament." *HUCA* 32 (1961) ———. "The Speech of Theophany." *Harvard Divinity Bulletin* 28 (1964) 35–47. **Nielsen, E.** *The Ten Commandments in New Perspective.* SBT 2d ser., 7. London: SCM Press, 1968. **North, R.** "The Derivation of Sabbath." *Bib* 36 (1955) 182–201. **Nougayrol, J.** *Le palais royal d'Ugarit.* Vol. III. Mission de Ras Shamra, VI. Paris: Imprimerie Nationale, Librarie C. Klincksieck, 1955. ———. *Le palais royal d'Ugarit,* Vol IV. Mission de Ras Shamra, IX. Paris: Imprimerie Nationale, Librarie C. Klincksieck, 1956. **Obbink, H. Th.** "Jahwebilder." *ZAW* 47 (1929) 264–74. **Pedersen, J.** *Israel, Its Life and Culture,* I–II. London: Oxford University Press, 1959. **Pettinato, G.** *The Archives of Ebla.* Garden City, NJ: Doubleday & Company, Inc., 1981. **Petuchowski, J. J.** "A Note on W. Kessler's 'Problematik des Dekalogs.'" *VT* 7 (1957) 397–98. **Phillips, A.** *Ancient Israel's Criminal Law: A New Approach to the Decalogue.* New York: Schocken Books, 1970. **Phillips, M. L.** "Divine Self-Predication in Deutero-Isaiah." *BR* 16 (1971) 32–51. **Rabast, K.** *Das apodiktische Recht im Deuteronomium und im Heiligkeitsgesetz.* Berlin: Heimat-Dienst Verlag, 1948. **Rabinowitz, J. J.** "The 'Great Sin' in Ancient Egyptian Marriage Contracts." *JNES* 18 (1959) 73. **Rad, G. von.** *Old Testament Theology,* vol 1. Edinburgh: Oliver and Boyd, 1962. **Reicke, B.** *Die Zehn Worte in Geschichte und Gegenwort.* BGBE 13. Tübingen: J. C. B. Mohr, 1973. **Reventlow, H. G.** *Gebot und Predigt im Dekalog.* Gütersloh: Gütersloher Verlagshaus Gerd Mohn, 1962. **Robinson, G.** "The Idea of Rest in the Old Testament and the Search for the Basic Character of the Sabbath." *ZAW* 92 (1980) 32–42. **Rodorf, W.** *Sunday.* Philadelphia: Westminster Press, 1968. **Rowley, H. H.** "Moses and the Decalogue." *Men of God.* London: Thomas Nelson and Sons, 1963. 1–36. **Schmidt, H.** "Mose und der Dekalog." *Eucharisterion.* Festschrift H. Gunkel. Göttingen: Vandenhoeck & Ruprecht, 1923. 78–119. **Schmidt, W. H.** *Das erste Gebot.* Munich: Chr. Kaiser Verlag, 1969. **Schulz, H.** *Das Todesrecht im Alten Testament.* BZAW 114. Berlin: Verlag Alfred Töpelmann, 1969. **Stamm, J. J.** "Dreissig Jahre Dekalogforschung." *TRu* 27 (1961) 189–239, 282–305. ———. "Sprachliche Erwägungen zum Gebot 'Du sollst nicht töten.'" *TZ* 1 (1945) 81–90. **Stamm, J. J.** and **M. E. Andrew.** *The Ten Commandments in Recent Research.* SBT 2d ser. 2. London: SCM Press, 1967. **Staples, W. E.** "The Third Commandment." *JBL* 58 (1939) 325–29. **Stoebe, H. J.** "Das achte Gebot (Ex 20:16)." *Wort und Dienst* 3. Bethel: Verlagshandlung der Anstalt Bethel, 1952. 108–26. **Watts, J. D. W.** "Infinitive Absolute as Imperative and the Interpretation of Exodus 20:8." *ZAW* 74 (1962) 141–

45. **Weidmann, H.** *Die Patriarchen und ihre Religion.* FRLANT 94. Göttingen: Vandenhoeck & Ruprecht, 1968. **Wellhausen, J.** *Die Composition des Hexateuchs und der Historischen Bücher des Alten Testaments.* Berlin: Walter de Gruyter & Co., 1963. ———. *Prolegomena to the History of Ancient Israel.* New York: Meridian Books, 1957. **Zimmerli, W.** "Das Zweite Gebot." *Gottes Offenbarung.* TBü 19. Munich: Chr. Kaiser Verlag, 1969. 234–48. ———. *Grundriss der alttestamentlichen Theologie.* 2d ed. ThW 3. Stuttgart: Verlag W. Kohlhammer, 1975. ———. "Ich bin Jahwe." *Gottes Offenbarung.* TBü 19. Munich: Chr. Kaiser Verlag, 1969. 11–40.

Translation

¹ *Then God* [a] *spoke all these words, saying,*
²"I am Yahweh, your God, who brought you forth
from the land of Egypt,[a]
from the non-status of slaves. [b]
³You[a] are not to have other gods *in my presence.* [b]
⁴You are not to make for yourself a shaped image,
whether [a] *in the form of something*
in the heavens above,
or in the earth underneath,
or in the waters below the earth. [b]
⁵ *You are not to prostrate yourself to them,*
or be enticed to serve them, [a]
because, I, Yahweh your God, am a jealous God,
one who will keep in mind [b] *the fathers' guilt*
against the sons of the third and the fourth generations
of those who hate me,
⁶*yet one who will act with unchanging love* [a]
towards the thousands who love me,
and who keep my commands.
⁷You are not to employ[a] the name of Yahweh
your God to empty purpose,[b]
because Yahweh will not leave unpunished [c]
anyone who employs his name
to empty purpose.
⁸Remember[a] the sabbath day,
to set it apart for holiness. [b]
⁹ *Six days are you to work*
and do all your customary labor: [a]
¹⁰*the seventh day* [a] *is a sabbath of Yahweh your God—*
on that day, [b] *you are to do*
none of your customary labor,
neither you, nor your son, nor your daughter,
your servant, nor your maidservant,
nor your work-animal,
not even the foreigner [c] *who is living with you.* [d]
¹¹ *Indeed,* [a] *in six days Yahweh made*
the heavens and the earth,
the sea and everything in them:
then he rested on the seventh day.
For this reason, Yahweh blessed the sabbath day. [b]
and set it apart for holiness.

¹²Give honor to your father and your mother,
in order that ᵃ *you may surely prolong* ᵇ *your days,*
your days on the promised land ᶜ *that*
Yahweh your God is giving to you.
¹³You are not to kill.ᵃ
¹⁴You are not to commit adultery.
¹⁵You are not to steal.
¹⁶You are not to give against your neighbor
a lying testimony.ᵃ
¹⁷You are not to desire for yourselfᵃ
the houseᵇ of your neighbor;
you are not to desire for yourself
the wife of your neighbor,
nor his servant, ᶜ *nor his maidservant,*
nor his ox, nor his he-ass, ᵈ
nor anything that belongs to your neighbor.

Notes

1.a. LXX has κύριος "Yahweh."

2.a. The words set in bold type represent a suggestion of the early form of the ten commandments. See below, *Form/Structure/Setting.*

2.b. מבית עבדים lit., "from the house of slavery"; see above, *Comment* on 13:3.

3.a. The commandments are addressed to each Israelite individually; the pronom subj are sg throughout the sequence.

3.b. LXX, Syr, Tg Onk, Tg Ps-J have "in addition to me" instead of "in my Presence." This verse is not ended by *soph pasuq* in L, though *soph pasuq* is supplied in a number of MSS.

4.a. ‌} . . . ‌} connecting *"alternative* cases, so that it = *or"* and *"whether . . . or":* BDB, 252 § 1.d.

4.b. See the 2d sentence of n. 3.b.

5.a. Hoph עבד "serve"; cf. BDB, 713.

5.b. פקד "attend to, give heed to, observe, seek out with interest"; see n. 4:31.c.

6.a. עשה חסד "one who does, makes unchanging love."

7.a. נשא "lift, carry, raise, take up"; "= utter," BDB, 670 § 1.b.(7), but far more than just the utterance of Yahweh's name is intended, as important as that is. See *Comment* below.

7.b. לשוא "to the vain nothingness," i.e., the cause that is inconsequential.

7.c. נקה "be clean, empty, exempt from punishment"; here piel; cf. BDB, 667.

8.a. SamPent has שמור "keep, guard." MT's זכור "remember," a qal inf abs, is taken here as an "emphatic imperative," GKC §§ 113y, bb. Note also Watts (*ZAW* 74 [1962] 144–45), who suggests "a kind of gerundive force" for זכר, to give "Remembering . . . to hallow . . ., you shall labour. . . ."

8.b. *Soph pasuq* is missing in L, but supplied in a number of MSS.

9.a. מלאכה "customary labor" refers to the daily work of one's occupation, and also to what might be called the labor of sustenance. *Soph pasuq* is missing again in L.

10.a. The Nash Papyrus reads "in the seventh day."

10.b. This phrase is added above for clarity, since the restrictions listed obviously apply only to the sabbath day. Cf. Nash Papyrus וביום "and in the day" (Burkitt, *JQR* 15 [1903] 395); LXX ἐν αὐτῇν "in it."

10.c. וגרך lit., "and your foreigner." On גר, see n. 12:19.b.

10.d. בשעריך "who is within your gates." The sense is "under your protection, supervision." Cf. LXX, ὁ παροικῶν ἐν σοί "the one dwelling with you." This verse is also without *soph pasuq* in L.

11.a. כי "indeed," taken in its emphatic usage, as "a word of motivation"; see Muilenburg, *HUCA* 32 (1961) 150–57.

11.b. Nash Papyrus (Burkitt, *JQR* 15 [1903] 395), LXX, Syr read "the seventh day."

12.a. Nash Papyrus (Burkitt, *JQR* 15 [1903] 395–96) adds here וייטב לך ולמען "it may go well with you and in order that"; so also LXX.

12.b. Hiph ארך = "cause to be long," + *nun paragogicum*, expressing "marked emphasis"; see GKC ¶ 47m.

12.c. האדמה "ground, land, territory"; "esp of land as promised or given by '׳ to his people = Canaan . . . in all c. 41 t." (BDB 9–10). LXX reads τῆς γῆς τῆς ἀγαθῆς "the good land."

13.a. Nash Papyrus (Burkitt, *JQR* 15 [1903] 394–97) and LXX follow a different order of commandments 6–8, so: vv 14, 15, 13. Luke 18:20 orders commandments 5–9 so: vv 14, 13, 15, 16, 12. Rom 13:9 orders commandments 6–8 and 10 so: vv 14, 13, 15, 17.

16.a. Nash Papyrus (Burkitt, *JQR* 15 [1903] 395) reads עד שוא "empty testimony" instead of עד שקר "lying testimony."

17.a. לא תחמד "you are not to lust for, desire obsessively." The clear implication of this use of חמד is desire for one's own possession or use; thus "for yourself" is added above. See *Comment* below.

17.b. LXX has γυναῖκα "wife" first, οἰκίαν "house" second.

17.c. SamPent, LXX and apparently Nash Papyrus (Burkitt, *JQR* 15 [1903] 395) add "his field" before "servant."

17.d. LXX adds οὔτε παντὸς κτήνους αὐτοῦ "nor any of his livestock."

Form/Structure/Setting

In some ways the single most important point about the canonical form of the Decalogue is not what this section contains but its location. The commandments are given as an integral part of the Sinai narrative sequence, and as an essential segment of the account of Yahweh's presentation of himself to Israel within that sequence. The Decalogue has so often been taken out of this sequence, for liturgical reasons, didactic reasons, and scholarly reasons, that this point has become all too easy to miss. Some literary critics (McNeile, lvi–lxiv, e.g., or Hyatt, 196–97, 217, or Harrelson, *Ten Commandments*, 43–45), indeed, have even suggested the relocation of the Decalogue, assessing it as an uneasy insertion disruptive of the narrative sequence of which it now is a part. Such suggestions are mistaken, however, not alone for the violence they do to an Exodus carefully planned and arranged, for very definite reasons, into the form in which we have received it. The ten commandments must first of all be seen as Exodus presents them, words addressed by Yahweh himself to Israel gathered by his command at the perimeter of holiness about the base of Mount Sinai. They form an essential part of Israel's experience of Yahweh's Advent, and to detach them from the narrative preceding and following them compromises our understanding of both that narrative and the commandments themselves.

With such a point clearly in mind, better consideration can be given to the form of the Decalogue, especially the question whether that form may have been dictated in part by the original purpose of the commandments and in part by continuing application of the principles set forth by them to life lived out in Israel in covenant with Yahweh. At least five aspects of the form the Decalogue has taken need to be considered: (1) the ANE covenantal/legal form to which the commandments are obviously related; (2) the "original" form of the commandments in relation to the "expanded" form that some of them now have; (3) the connection between the commandments and other OT covenantal/legal collections, in particular the Book of the Covenant in Exod 20:22–23:33; (4) the arrangement of the commandments into a sequence coincident with the sequence of the larger narrative of which they are a part; and (5) the "age" of the commandments and the hand by which they have been brought into Exodus.

(1) The ANE covenantal/legal form has been the subject of extensive and continuing research almost since the birth of OT literary criticism in the last half of the nineteenth century. An earlier sensationalism which sought connections of topic and theme between the OT and the literature of Israel's neighbors gave way to a more careful analysis of the material at hand, both within and without the OT, first of all in relation to source-literary questions and then in connection with form-critical inquiry. Of special importance here is the work of Anton Jirku (*Das weltliche Recht,* passim, but see especially 12–16, 150–60), who sought to isolate ten separate kinds of legal formulary in the Pentateuch and proposed that Moses could have put together the ten commandments from a considerable inventory of legal material; Sigmund Mowinckel (*Décalogue,* 114–60), who argued for an old literary form behind the Decalogue and a cultic origin and provenance (his "Enthronement of Yahweh festival") for the Decalogue; Albrecht Alt (*Essays,* 87–132), who divided OT laws into case-laws of the "if-clause" type and apodictic laws of the unconditional "thou shalt" type, the former common to the ANE, the latter uniquely Israelite; George Mendenhall (*Law and Covenant,* 5–41) and Klaus Baltzer, (*Covenant Formulary,* 9–93), both of whom, independently of each other (Baltzer, xi), paralleled the covenant formulary of the Hittites to that of the OT and proposed the derivation of the OT version from Hittite state treaties; and Erhard Gerstenberger (*Wesen,* 23–88), who has shown the casuistic-apodictic categories of Alt to be far too great an oversimplification, has joined other scholars (Gevirtz, *VT* 11 [1961] 137–58; Gese, *ZTK* 64 [1967] 121–38; Kilian, *BZ* 7 [1963] 185–202; Schulz, *Todesrecht*) in pointing out that the apodictic legal form is by no means uniquely Israelite, has introduced a category of "prohibitive" legal statement (*Prohibitivgattung*) closely linked to the curse formula, and has connected OT commandments to the circles of the wise and to the family instead of to the priests and prophets of the cultus (cf. Gerstenberger, *JBL* 84 [1965] 46–51).

Helpful surveys of the work of these scholars and others who have implemented and reacted to their proposals have been made by McCarthy (*Treaty and Covenant* and *Old Testament Covenant*) and Boecker (*Law* and *Redeformen*). The most valuable applications of this research to the Decalogue have been made by Stamm (*TRu* 27 [1961] 189–239, 282–305) and Nielsen (*Ten Commandments*). The work goes on along both form-literary and comparative lines, and the discovery and continuing decipherment of the treaty and legal materials of Ebla (Pettinato, *Archives* 103–5), added to the considerable material already in hand, provides the resources for additional research for some time to come.

Several lessons are clear already, however. One is that Alt's contribution, as valuable as it remains, was far too great an oversimplification of the complexity of both OT and ANE legal material. Another is that Mendenhall's application of Hittite treaty patterns to the covenant passages of the OT was far too rigid, in some instances misleadingly so, despite the obvious value of some of the comparisons made, both by Mendenhall and such scholars as Beyerlin and Baltzer, who followed him closely. Yet another is that too fixed an association of OT law with a single group, whether one has in view the priests (Wellhausen, *Prolegomena*, 392–401), the prophets (Mowinckel) or the wisdom teachers (Gerstenberger) is far too great an oversimplification.

We must view the legal material of the OT against an ANE background of vast proportions, yet known to us still only in a very fragmentary representation. We must think of OT law as the concern of all Israel, of all the leaders of Israel as well as of all Israelites whose commitment in covenant to Yahweh was to live according to *his* standard and *his* instructions. We must consider a variety of literary forms in which the legal material was set, along with a variety of support-devices such as the authorizing prologue and the warning curse, without allowing any of the forms or the support-devices or overarching patterns to become rigid and binding. Our fault so far in the history of the study of OT law has been to see parts of a very fragmented picture as the whole picture and to magnify details of various patterns into a single pattern which then becomes determinative. Most of all, we have to keep in mind the special nature of OT law as liberating law, law as revelation instead of law as restriction, law given by Yahweh to a people wanting to be guided in his way.

Quite apart from their relation to other ANE law, the laws of the Decalogue show a development of their own, the details of which we can only surmise. The references to the commandments as עשרת הדברים "the ten words" in Exod 34:28; Deut 4:13; 10:4 should be taken as an indication of both the number of the commandments and the brevity of the foundational covenant list at a very early stage. Nielsen (*Ten Commandments*, 6–34) has pointed out the tension between a consistent "ten" numbering and the various lists of laws in the OT, and Gerstenberger (*JBL* 84 [1965] 47; *Wesen*, 70–76) has proposed original "groupings of two and three," but these proposals and others like them are highly speculative and do not take seriously enough the OT emphasis on ten as the foundational number.

(2) An array of attempts has been made to "reconstruct" the original form of the commandments; see, for example, Schmidt (*Eucharisterion*, 79–82, 100–107), Rabast (11 commandments, *Das apodiktische Recht*, 35–38), Nielsen (*Ten Commandments*, 84–86); and Harrelson (*Ten Commandments*, 41–42, 207, n. 37). All such attempts are of course speculation; even though the assumption of an original list of very brief commands is probably a correct one, any precise recovery of such an *Ur*-form is not possible, given the information available to us. A principle that should be kept firmly in mind in the study of the development of OT law is that expansion answered specific need: the longest commandments and the most often repeated laws are the ones with which Israel had the greatest difficulty. We may posit as reasonable theory that each of the commandments in the Decalogue should be as brief as the briefest of them, and that any additional length beyond the most succinct possible statement is the result of a special need.

(3) A survey of the OT with the Decalogue in hand reveals additional versions of and references to the Decalogue: Deut 5:6–21, of course, but so also Exod 34:17–26; the "Schechemite Dodecalogue" of Deut 27:15–26 (see von Rad, *OT Theology* 1:190–93, and Harrelson's comparison-table, *Ten Commandments*, 32–33); Ps 15:2–5 (see Mowinckel, *Psalmenstudien V, Segen und Fluch*

[Amsterdam: Schippers, 1961] 55–60; and cf. Ps 24); Lev 19:1–4, 11–19a, 26–37 (cf. von Rad, *Studies in Deuteronomy*, SBT 9 [London: SCM, 1953] 27–31); Ezek 18:5–9 (cf. Köhler, *TRu* 1 [1929] 165–66; Zimmerli, *Ezekiel*, 375–77). There are a number of additional law-lists and some longer collections of legal material that can be linked to the Decalogue: for example, the ten commandments prohibiting sexual abuse in Lev 20:10–21 (cf. von Rad, *Studies*, 31–33, and Harrelson, 35–36, who adds also Lev 18:6–18); the instructions regarding clean and unclean animals, fish and birds in Deut 14:3–21; and above all the entire Holiness Code of Lev 17–26 and the Book of the Covenant of Exod 20:22–23:33.

The designations "ethical Decalogue" and "cultic Decalogue" as applied by earlier commentators (e.g, Wellhausen, *Die Composition*, 329–35, and L'Hour, *Die Ethik* 90–91) to Exod 20:2–17 and 34:17–26 respectively should now be dropped as misleading generalizations, along with the opinion that the first of these two lists is the later of the two (because of a supposed dependence upon the ethical teaching of the great prophets of Israel). The distinction is foreign to the OT and at best irrelevant to the analysis of OT law, and the chronological sequencing is a reflection of the evolutionary synthesis of the Wellhausen school, and so both an oversimplification and an error.

The question of the relationship between the Decalogue and the Book of the Covenant can be answered only in the most general terms, not least because of the differences in form that are readily apparent and the complexity of the arrangement of the Book of the Covenant. That the Book of the Covenant is a disruption of the Sinai narrative sequence, and that many of its laws are more appropriate to the settled life in Canaan than to the nomadic life of the wilderness of Sinai, cannot reasonably be doubted. Even so, the compilers of Exodus have placed this collection where it now stands, between the account of Yahweh coming to Israel and the account of Israel entering into covenant with Yahweh. There must have been some reason for such a placement: what was it?

Answers to this question have ranged from the opinion that the placement of the Book of Covenant was purely arbitrary, even accidental, to the opinion that this material is Mosaic in origin and so falls where it does inevitably. Neither of these extremes is acceptable, however. The first does not take seriously the final form of Exodus as a deliberate arrangement; the second does not take seriously the real contribution of Moses. Some parts of the Book of the Covenant could easily be as old as the Decalogue in its earliest form; other parts reflect periods obviously later. Hillers (*Covenant*, 89–94) has suggested an equivalence between most of the commandments and specific situations covered in the Book of the Covenant or elsewhere in the OT, and some of his connections are undeniable. It may be suggested that what became the Book of the Covenant may have been begun by Moses as an application of the principles for life in covenant with Yahweh given in the Decalogue. To such a collection, the steadily cumulative body of precedent decisions applied by the "men of ability" whom Jethro had counseled Moses to select (Exod 18:21–26) would readily have been drawn. The combined laws, steadily being expanded, reapplied, and supplemented, may very well have been circulated along with the Decalogue they were designed to clarify and apply. Among other things, such a theory would explain the location of the Book of the Covenant at a point following the Sinai theophany and its revelation of the Decalogue (see *Form/Structure/Setting* on 20:22–23:33, and cf. Phillips, *Criminal Law*, 39–40).

(4) The arrangement of the ten commandments into a sequence giving priority to Yahweh before humankind and emphasizing throughout the importance of relationship may well be more than a coincidental parallel to the narrative sequence of which the commandments are now an essential and climactic part. The Sinai narrative sequence also begins with Yahweh, in the one account to which he is most central in the OT, the account of his Advent; and it ends with Israel, attempting to salvage what they can of a covenant shattered by their failure to keep their promises and hoping that Yahweh will fail to keep some of his promises—the statements of penalty for disobedience. The binding motif of the Sinai narrative sequence, similarly, is relationship: Yahweh gives himself in a unique relationship to Israel; the people pledge themselves in unique relationship to Yahweh in return. Indeed, the narrative moves forward on what brings this relationship about, what happens to it, and what saves it when it seemed sure to be lost forever.

More than a suggestion is obviously impossible, but perhaps the sequence of the commandments that stand at the dramatic center of the Sinai narrative sequence is a reflection of, and perhaps even determined by, the order of that narrative. Not alone the principles set forth by the Decalogue, but even the order of those principles may have been shaped by the narrative that now contains them.

(5) The question of the "age" of the ten commandments has been given many answers, ranging from the time of Moses (Gressmann, *Mose*, 471–74, an opinion he later modified in *Die älteste*, 237; Driver, 413–17; Schmidt, *Eucharisterion*, 85–91) to the exilic (Beer, 103–4) or even the postexilic (Hölscher, 129) periods. The trend in recent years has been to date the Decalogue at an earlier rather than a later time, and to argue the "possibility" or the "probability" of a connection with Moses (cf. the extensive review of Rowley, *Men of God*, 1–36, who proposed "a high degree of probability"). This trend is the result of an increasing interest in (a) the Decalogue in its cultic/covenantal setting in ancient Israel (Mowinckel, for example); (b) the form-literary analysis of the Decalogue in relation to the legal forms employed in the OT (so Alt and his followers); (c) the analysis of the Decalogue against the background of ANE treaty patterns (so Mendenhall, Beyerlin); and (d) a move towards a greater acceptance of the narratives and heroes of Israel's early history as historically based (Martin-Achard, Weidmann, e.g.). Any establishment of a precise date for the origin of the ten commandments, or for that matter their successive expansion into the form in which we know them is of course impossible—but we can now be confident of an earlier rather than a later dating.

Equally difficult is the determination of the source from which the Decalogue came into Exodus. The earlier assured opinions that the commandments are from E (Morgenstern, *HUCA* 4 [1927] 1); E + R^D (Driver, 192–200); J^2 + (R^D) R^P (Beer, 12, 98–103) have given way to the view that the Decalogue developed as a unit independent of the standard sources, probably preceding them (at least in its earlier forms), and was incorporated either by them or by the compilers of Exodus into the location it now occupies (so Noth, 153–55; Beyerlin, *Sinaitic Traditions,* 11–12; Hyatt, 197, 207; Childs, 397–401).

Comment

1   As noted above *(Form/Structure/Setting* on 19:16–25), this verse and all that follows it through v 21 is best read in direct sequence to 19:19a, so: "The sound of the ram's horn meanwhile was moving, and growing very strong. Then God spoke all these words, saying, 'I am Yahweh, your God. . . .'" The people, duly prepared, have been brought by Moses to the place appointed for them at the bottom of Sinai, amidst the sounds and sights of Yahweh's impending Advent. This accompaniment to Yahweh's coming is pierced from time to time by the sound of an amplified ram's horn, which is nearer and louder with each successive signal. Then, when the sounding of the ram's horn has reached its most intense level, Yahweh speaks, addressing all the people assembled at the perimeter of holiness around the mountain's base.

This memory of Yahweh speaking from Sinai in the hearing of all the people is common to every account of the Sinai theophany in the OT (see especially Exod 19:9 and 20:18–20; Deut 4:10–14, 32–40; 5:4, 22–27, 9:10; Neh 9:13; cf. Greenberg, "Decalogue," *EncJud:* 1435–38). It is an emphasis integral both to the Sinai narrative sequence and to the larger narrative sequence, which consistently sets Yahweh at the center and leaves no doubt that his proof of his Presence and then his climactic revelation of himself is first and foremost to the people of Israel. Though the tempering of this emphasis began even before Exodus was compiled, specifically in the attempt to emphasize the intermediacy of Moses (see above, on 19:19–25), and has been carried on since by an array of commentators for a variety of reasons, the clear assertion of the basic narrative is that Yahweh's first words to Israel at Sinai were spoken directly by himself to *all* the people, assembled for that very purpose. To deny this emphasis of the Exodus narrative is to make nonsense of some of it and to do great violence to the theological concept set forth by its arrangement, as by its report. Exod 19–20 presents an excellent case, indeed, for what Alter *(Art,* 131–54) has instructively called "composite artistry," a "fullness of statement" that transcends for its own purposes what we may think of as "logical coherence."

2   The autokerygmatic phrase אנכי יהוה "I am Yahweh" is a basic phrase of OT theological rhetoric. It has been carefully studied by both Elliger and Zimmerli, who have referred to it respectively as a "primary formula" *(einfachen Formel,* Elliger, *Kleine Schriften,* 214) and a "self-presentation formula" *(Selbstvorstellungformel,* Zimmerli, *Gottes Offenbarung,* 14). This phrase functions here as it does in Exod 6:2 (see above, and cf. Phillips, *BR* 16 [1971] 36–45), primarily as an assertion of the authority of Yahweh, the "One Who Always Is" (see *Comment* on 3:11–20). Elliger (213–16, 221–23) has suggested that the addition of אלהיך "your God" to אנכי יהוה makes a "holiness or sublimity formula" into a "saving history or grace-formula." The objects of

that salvation-grace, the people of Israel, are reminded by Yahweh's opening words (1) who Yahweh is, by the use of the self-confessional phrase אֲנֹכִי יְהוָה ; (2) who *they* are, by the addition of the self-giving phrase אֱלֹהֶיךָ since Yahweh can only have become *their* God by his act of giving himself; and (3) that these assertions are validated by their completely discontinuous new situation, as a people brought forth from Egypt, and from the non-status of slaves to the status of a people to whom Yahweh has given himself.

This prologue verse thus introduces the ten commandments, a series of principles concerned with relationship with Yahweh and with humankind, by reference to what that relationship has meant, thus far, *for* the people of Israel. Yahweh, who is speaking to them, has given himself to them. He has brought them out from Egypt. He has made them who were no people a people; he has given freedom to those who were slaves. What follows is what the relationship, if it is to be continued, must have *from* the people of Israel. The connection of this verse with the formal prologues of Hittite (or any other) treaty formulary (Beyerlin, *Sinaitic Traditions*, 49–55; Hillers, *Covenant*, 48–52) should be made, if it is made at all, only in the most general terms. Far more is being declared here than any treaty ever claimed, above all in Yahweh's self-revelation and self-giving, neither of which appear to have been motives of any Hittite king. As Muilenburg put it, these "first words" of Yahweh to Israel, "indispensably prior to all that is to follow," are "the center and focus of the whole Pentateuch" and "the very heart of the whole Old Testament," and in connection with what follows them, "the association of proclamation and teaching: *kerugma kai didache*" (*Harvard Divinity Bulletin* 28 [1964] 39–42).

3 The first of the ten commandments is basic to the nine that follow it and to the relationship the Decalogue is designed to insure. It sets forth an expectation of absolute priority, a first and fundamental requirement of those who desire to enter into the covenant relationship with Yahweh. MT reads, literally, "It (or There) is not to be to you (singular) other gods in my Presence." The singular verb and the singular subject and indirect object, along with the plural direct object, "gods," make the application of the command unmistakably clear. There is not to be even one other god (Exod 34:14 even reduces "other gods" to the singular אֵל אַחֵר), each single member of the covenant community is specifically involved, and there is no place where this expectation is invalid, since there is no place from which Yahweh's Presence is barred (so Ps 139).

Zimmerli (*Grundriss*, 100) has contrasted the use in the first commandment of הִיה "be" as opaque and overarching ("unanschaulichen, weitgespannten") alongside the other commandments in which more specific verbs are used to describe the deeds prohibited or commanded. He compares this "unusual" mode of expression with the "absolute commands" of the creator in Gen 1:3, 6, and 14, and suggests that it "obviously represents a final condensation of a foundational proposition." עַל has variously been rendered (cf. Knierim, *ZAW* 77 [1965] 25; Stamm and Andrew, *Ten Commandments*, 79–81) as expressing preference, defiance, proximity, exclusion, opposition, and the like. It is taken above in connection with Yahweh's "face" or "Presence" to refer to Yahweh's Advent to Israel. He has given himself to them, and they are therefore no longer to have any other gods save him. It is possible that "in my Presence" is an expansion of a briefer earlier form; if so, it could be an expansion especially appropriate to the Sinai-Theophany context.

As a survey of other forms of this prohibition (see Knierim *ZAW* 77 [1965] 23–25, for a helpful listing) makes clear, the first commandment is not an assertion of monotheistic conviction, that Yahweh is the only God, and hence the sole choice. The OT makes very clear that such was not the case in the world of ancient Israel. The first commandment, in a sense, was called for by the many gods who demanded of Israel the allegiance Yahweh alone had the right to command. The commandment does not specify that no one is to have "other gods," but that *Israel* is to have no other gods. It is connected with Yahweh's "jealousy" or "zeal" (cf. W. H. Schmidt, *Das erste Gebot*, 18–21, 30–33; Brongers, *VT* 13 [1963] 269–70, 279–84), described more fully in the expansion of the second commandment.

This first of the commandments, in sum, is the essential foundation for the building of the covenant community. Yahweh had opened himself to a special relationship with Israel, but that relationship could develop only if Israel committed themselves to Yahweh alone. Yahweh had rescued them and freed them, delivered them and guided them, then come to them. The next step, if there was to be a next step, belonged to them. If they were to remain in his Presence, they were not to have other gods.

4   As the first commandment forbids any association with other gods to those who would be Yahweh's, the second commandment and the two that follow it set special dimensions of their relationship with him. The people of Israel are not to worship other gods at all. Following this most fundamental of requirements are three specifications of how Yahweh *is* to be worshiped. The first of these specifications is a prohibition of the use of images in the worship of Yahweh. פֶּסֶל means to "cut or shape" something, stone in particular, and the noun פֶּסֶל refers to an image, of whatever likeness and involving a variety of materials, made for use in the worship of diety. As Bernhardt (*Gott und Bild*, 17–68) has shown, such images were used throughout the ANE as a means of suggesting the presence of deity, not as objects of worship: the image "was much more something corporeal that the divine influence (*das göttliche Fluidum*) possessed" (67).

Gutmann (*HUCA* 32 [1961] 161–68) has laid to rest the false notion that the second commandment forbade visual art of any sort to the ancient Israelites and their Jewish descendants. He reckons the second commandment their "earliest pronouncement about art," the purpose of which "seems to have been to assure loyalty to the invisible Yahweh," who "probably remained" even with the construction of Solomon's lavishly symbolic temple "the unseen God of the desert experience." The question is, whose image is being forbidden to Israel, Yahweh's, or those of the gods rival to Yahweh? Obbink (*ZAW* 47 [1929] 264–74) has suggested that the second commandment forbade the making of images of any kind, that it meant that Yahweh's worship was to kept pure of defacement with "all kinds of heathen material," that it referred specifically to images of Anu, Enlil, Ea, etc. and so is a kind of elaboration of the first commandment. Von Rad (*Theology*, I, 216), similarly, has noted: "Here the commandment is drafted wholly with reference to the commandment forbidding the worship of other gods," and he describes it as a late and specialized prohibition against representing Yahweh by "an image belonging to another deity."

These theories do not, however, allow for the difference between the first and the second commandments (indeed, Obbink, Dutch Reformed, and von Rad, Lutheran, may reflect the confessional traditions that treat vv 3–6 as a single commandment; see Reicke, *Die Zehn Worte*), or for the differences between the essential statement of the second commandment (v 4a) and the lengthy and layered expansion of it (vv 4b–6; cf. Zimmerli, *Gottes Offenbarung*, 236–42). The first commandment states definitively that each individual who would enter the covenant with Yahweh is to have no other gods. Only disobedience of that command would allow the use of images of foreign gods, a point von Rad recognizes in his connection of the two commandments. Further, the emphatic לְךָ "for yourself," surely unnecessary if v 4a is only an extension of v 3, may be a clue to the direction the second commandment is taking: the worshiper who has made a commitment to worship only Yahweh must not compromise that worship by making it easy, that is, by adopting for his own use shaped images to provide a concrete center for worship, a practice common to all of Israel's neighbors. The personal reference of this and indeed all the commandments must be kept clearly in mind. A paraphrase of the commandment might even be, "Not a one of you is to have a shaped image for the worship of Yahweh."

The amount of attention given to the second commandment in the layered expansion following it shows that it, like commandments four and ten, was a difficult one for the people of Israel to keep. And the nature of the expansion shows that what is really at stake is not the worship of other gods by the use of idols and images connected with them, though that may often have been a result of the violation of this prohibition. The second commandment has to do with Yahweh himself and his gift of his Presence to Israel. Israelites are forbidden to make images for the worship of Yahweh because he is Yahweh, as Lev 19:4 says. Nothing created can serve to represent him, not even in the whole range of the created order, from top to bottom, and even in the realms of the mythopoeic creatures, in the heavens above and in the waters below the earth, because Yahweh has made every thing and every being. He is in a way in them all, but, what is more important, he is beyond them all. He is "The One Who Always Is" (see *Comment* on 3:13–15), Yahweh, the "I AM" who is present with them. No image conceivable to them could serve to represent him. They must worship him as he is, not as they can envision him or would like him to be.

5 The plural pronoun "them" brings together the range of possibilities suggested by v 4b and may well refer also, as Zimmerli (*Gottes Offenbarung*, 235, n. 3, 236–38) has proposed, to the "other gods" of v 3. If so, it is because of what Childs (405) has aptly called an interpretation "in the later redaction" which puts the second commandment "within the shadow of the first." To shaped images representing Yahweh (at least), Israel is not to bow down or to succumb before them to any enticement to service. A still fuller redactional explanation of the second commandment is given, however, in the appositional phrase in which Yahweh describes himself as אֵל קַנָּא "a jealous God." קַנָּא refers here and five other times in the OT to a justi-fied jealousy of Israel's God. The adjective קַנּוֹא is used twice, the noun קִנְאָה is used twenty-four times, and the verb קָנָא six times in reference to this jealousy (cf. Sauer, *THAT* 2:647–50), always in contexts where the promised loyalty of Yahweh's (= Elohim's) people is in question. The phrases אֵל קַנָּא\קַנּוֹא and יהוה קַנָּא (both of which occur in Exod 34:14) are used only in passages in which other gods are mentioned.

The basis for this jealousy of Yahweh is the expectation of undiluted loyalty specified by the first commandment (cf. Brongers, *VT* 13 [1963] 280–84). This reference to it in the explanatory expansion of the second commandment underscores both Yahweh's demand to be worshiped as he is and also the insight that any compromise of such worship leads inevitably to a divided or even a redirected loyalty that Yahweh has every right, even every obligation, to punish. Yahweh's jealousy is a part of his holiness (Exod 34:14) and is demanded by what he *is*. It is justified by the fact that it comes only upon those who, having promised to have no God but him, have gone back on that promise. Those who do so show that they "hate" him, that they hold him in contempt: upon them in result must come a deserved judgment, across four generations. The language of the covenantal threat may be present in these words; but even more, the insight that indifference to commitment is contagious, in a family or in a society.

6 In vivid contrast to this specific limitation of judgment is the unlimited response of Yahweh to those who love him, who keep their promise to set him in first place, and so keep his commands. "Thousands" might better be read "an innumerable descendancy," as the emphasis is upon the progeny of faithfulness and Yahweh's unending goodness to them all.

7 The third commandment must be read against the background of the extended meaning of "name" in the OT (see van der Woude, "שֵׁם Name," *THAT* 2:935–63; Pedersen, *Israel* 1–II, 245–59), and in particular, in the light of the importance of the extensive theology of the "name" and the "names" of God (Grether, *Name und Wort Gottes*, esp. 1–58, 159–85). Such texts as Exod 20:24, 33:18—34:8; Num 6:27; Deut 6:13; 10:8; 12:5, 11; 16:2, 6, 11; 2 Sam 6:18; Pss 69:31 [30]; 72:19, 105:3, and Isa 50:10, out of a long and intriguing list, only begin to suggest the considerable extent of the rhetoric and the theology connected with Yahweh's name and the other names that are related to it. The name "Yahweh" occurs some 6828 times in the OT (by the count of Jenni, "יהוה Jahwe," *THAT* 1:704; BDB, 217, has "c. 6823"); "Elohim" occurs 2600 times (W. H. Schmidt, "אלהים Gott," *THAT* 1:154). "Yahweh" is used exclusively in reference to Israel's God in the OT, and most of the occurrences of "Elohim" refer to Israel's God. When the variety of other names, titles, and epithets and the usages of שֵׁם "name" in reference to Yahweh/Elohim are added to the occurrences of Yahweh and Elohim, an impressive total suggests how important the use of the divine names in the confession and worship of ancient Israel actually was, and how necessary therefore was some instruction regarding their use, in particular the use of "Yahweh."

Yet far more than the utterance of the divine name is intended in the third commandment. נשׂא means "lift up, raise, carry, even wear." שָׂא suggests "nothingness, insubstantial thing," even "lie." In general terms, this commandment prohibits a lack of seriousness about Yahweh's Presence in Israel, demonstrated through a pointless, misleading, or even false use of his name. שׁוא has been assigned a wide and somewhat ambiguous range of meaning (cf. Klopfenstein, *Die Lüge*, 315–20), and has also been taken quite specifically (1) to be equivalent to שֶׁקֶר "lie," and so equivalent here to false swearing or witness-giving (see the summaries of Klopfenstein, *Die Lüge*, 18–21, and Childs, 410–11); and (2) as "a noun for an idol," to form with נשׁא + לְ an idiom meaning "give to an idol." On this view, the third commandment becomes a prohibition against giving Yahweh's name to a "non-god," a temptation of syncretism (Staples, *JBL* 58 [1939] 327–29).

The meaning of the third commandment probably lies beyond these opinions, though its range is broad enough to cover even the magical usage argued by Mowinckel (*Psalmenstudien I* [Amsterdam: Schippers, 1961] 50–58) and adopted more tentatively by Klopfenstein (*Die Lüge*, 316–21). This commandment is couched in language deliberately chosen to permit a wide range of application, covering every dimension of the misuse of Yahweh's name. Yahweh had not withheld his name but had freely given it to Moses and so to Israel as both a summary and an extension of the revelation of his Presence. His sovereignty is such that he was not subject to the manipulation of his worshipers, and thus he opened himself to his people with as much fullness as they could stand. Not surprisingly, there are no incantation texts in the OT. Yahweh could not be controlled, or even altered in his set purpose, by men.

The third commandment is directed not toward Yahweh's protection, but toward Israel's. Yahweh's name, specifically the tetragrammaton but in principle *all* Yahweh's names and titles, must be honored, blessed, praised, celebrated, invoked, pronounced, and so shared. To treat Yahweh's name with disrespect is to treat his gift lightly, to underestimate his power, to scorn his Presence, and to misrepresent to the family of humankind his very nature as "The One Who Always Is." So serious was such an abuse, and apparently also so widespread, that the third commandment was expanded at some point in its history by a warning. Any member of the covenant community who dishonors Yahweh's name, and so Yahweh's Presence, will not be left unpunished by Yahweh. What this punishment is to be is not specified. That it will be is stated as a solemn certainty.

8–10 The fourth commandment is the longest in the Decalogue, because it is the most expanded of all the commandments. No other commandment has received as much reapplication and as many defining and justifying clauses as this one. The probable reason for its expansion is the difficulty the people of Israel had keeping it, a difficulty attested by the attack of Amos (8:4–8) on the greedy merchants fidgeting for the sabbath to pass. Much work has been done toward the recovery of the original, or beginning, form of the fourth commandment, both by deleting what may be supposed to be additions (Stamm, *TRu* 27 [1961] 200–1; Harrelson, *Ten Commandments*, 41–42, 207) and also by the conversion of the positive form of MT to an assumed negative form (Rabast, *Das apodiktische Recht*, 35–38; Nielsen, *Ten Commandments*, 84, 88–89). Any such reconstruction is of course hypothetical, though the proposal of a shortened form of the commandment has far more to commend it than does conversion to a negative form.

זְכוֹר, a qal infinitive absolute, is the equivalent of an emphatic imperative. It means "remember," as always in contexts of covenantal obligation, in the sense of "observe without lapse" or "hold as a present and continuing priority." SamPent reads שְׁמוֹר "keep," as does the parallel version of the commandment in Deut 5:12; Nash Papyrus (Burkitt, *JQR* 15 [1903] 395), however, has זְכוֹר, and LXX also reads "remember" (μνήσθητι). Some scholars (Keszler, *VT* 7 [1957] 9–10; Childs, *Memory*, 52–55) argue the priority of זְכוֹר; others (Köhler, *TRu* 1 [1929] 180–81; Hulst, *Studia*, 153–59) contend for שְׁמוֹר. Noth (164) and Andreasen (*OT Sabbath*, 83) argue that both verbs, in this usage, come to mean about the same thing; Childs (*Memory*, 55) has suggested that the Deuteronomist "substituted" שָׁמוֹר for זָכוֹר "because of a particular theology of remembrance." This distinction, if it is present, is a very precise one.

Considerable attention has been given to the word שַׁבָּת "Sabbath," particularly as regards its etymology and its possible cultic and calendrical associations. This work, which is helpfully reviewed by de Vaux (*Ancient Israel* 2:475–80; cf. also Meek, *JBL* 33 [1914] 201–12) and Andreasen (*OT Sabbath*, 94–121), has produced no firm conclusions. There is a wide agreement that the institution of the sabbath is an ancient one in Israel, and that the noun שַׁבָּת belongs to the semantic field of שׁבת "rest, cease." The OT clearly uses שַׁבָּת as a term denoting a day of cessation, for religious reasons, from the normal daily routine. שַׁבָּת is a day of "stopping," a day designed to interrupt the normal activity of work, and a definite and fixed day. Robinson has argued that both נוח and שׁבת have nothing to do with "rest" as relaxation, but refer instead to "stopping for settlement" and "coming to an end" of something (*ZAW* 92 [1980] 33–42). The theory that שַׁבָּת originally occurred once a month rather than weekly (Meinhold, *ZAW* 48 [1930] 122–28) or on some other nonweekly schedule (see Andreasen, *OT Sabbath*, 96–100) simply does not fit the OT usage (cf. Cannon, *ZAW* 49 [1931] 325–27; North, *Bib* 36 [1955] 187–89, 193–96).

Quite apart from the set days of religious festivity or solemn assembly, none of which is referred to in the Decalogue, the sabbath day is to be thought of as extraordinary in the week instead of in the year. It is to be remembered without exception, set apart from all other days as a day for holy purposes, and kept free of the customary labor of sustenance of the other six days, precisely because it belongs to Yahweh. The six days alloted for the "business as usual" (מלאכה) of life must be made to suffice. On the sabbath day, nobody is to undertake such "usual work." The singular pronoun "you" is supplemented by a list of six potential sources of labor, taking in the family, the employees, the work-animals and even the visitor stopping temporarily with the Israelite. The detailed specification of this expansion is sometimes attributed to humanitarian concern (so Menes, *Vorexilischen Gesetze*, 37–40; Rodorf, *Sunday*, 12–17; cf. Mathys, *TZ* 28 [1972] 242–55). More likely, it is an attempt to plug obvious loopholes: not only is the Israelite not to work on the sabbath, neither is anyone else, or even any animal, that might conceivably be doing his work for him.

11 A still further justification of this requirement, beyond the assertion that the sabbath day belongs to Yahweh, is added. Yahweh himself respects this day as a day of surcease from the labor of the other six days: his work of creation was accomplished in six days, and then he rested. This justification of the sabbath-rest by reference to the P account of creation in Gen 1:1–2:4a may be less "an etiology for the sanctification of the sabbath" by tying it to the "very structure of the universe" (Childs, 416) than another attempt to persuade the sons of Israel to keep the fourth commandment. Yahweh himself kept the sabbath, and blessed it: Israel therefore could hardly do otherwise.

The Deuteronomists make still another (and no doubt still needed) attempt; adding "as Yahweh your God commanded you" (Deut 5:12) to what is the end of Exod 20:8, they give as a reason not Yahweh's rest after his work of creation, but the exodus from the slavery of Egypt (Deut 5:15, which begins with וזכרת "and remember," the verb of Exod 20:8). Keeping the sabbath, for them, is a testimony of Israel's election and deliverance: in Egypt there was no day of interruption of the unending round of forced labor; Moses' requests for time to worship were met by Pharaoh with scorn; but Yahweh "brought them out from there" and so commands them to celebrate the sabbath day as a "stopping day" proclaiming not only their dependence upon Yahweh but also their independence of all other peoples and powers.

12 With the fifth commandment, the second basic direction of the commandments as the fundamental principles of life in covenant with Yahweh is taken. The first four commandments set forth the principles guiding Israel's relationship to Yahweh; the last six commandments set forth the principles guiding Israel's relationship with the covenant community, and more broadly, with the human family. As the second, third, and fourth commandments are in many ways extensions of the first commandment, the first four commandments are the foundation for the final six commandments. And *all* of the commandments, as principles governing covenant relationships, are founded on the ultimate OT statement of relationship, which stands as prologue to the ten commandments: "I am Yahweh, your God" (see above, on v 2). Because Yahweh is, and is *Israel's* God, Israel both *is* and *must become* a certain and special people. What Israel is and is to be is determined by Yahweh's gift of himself to them first, and second, by their gift of themselves to him in response. That response involves Yahweh first (commandments one through four) and all humankind second (commandments five through six).

The transition from Yahweh's expectation of his people in relation to himself to his expectation of his people in relation to the human family is this commandment establishing a norm for the relationship with father and mother. Just as the relationship with Yahweh is the beginning of the covenant, so this relationship is the beginning of society, the inevitable point of departure for every human relationship. The first relationship beyond the relationship with Yahweh, who according to the OT is the giver of life, is the relationship to father and to mother, who together are the channel of Yahweh's gift of life. No other human relationship is so fundamental, and none is more important. The fifth commandment is thus both as foundational to commandments six through ten as the first commandment is to commandments two through four, and also is the logical link from the relationship of Israel to Yahweh to the relationship of Israel to humankind.

This commandment, like the one preceding it, is stated positively, and like that one, has been "returned" by some commentators (Nielsen, *Ten Commandments*, 115–18; Harrelson, *Ten Commandments*, 92–105; cf. H. Schmidt, *Eucharisterion*, 78–82, who omitted the fourth and fifth commandments altogether) to a supposed negative original form. To date, no convincing evidence for such an alteration has been put forward (see Gerstenberger, *Wesen*, 43–50; A. Phillips, *Criminal Law*, 66, 80), or for the suggestion of Andrew (Stamm & Andrew, *Ten Commandments*, 96) that the fourth and fifth commandments were handed down in both positive and negative forms.

The piel imperative singular כבד means "honor, give weight to, glorify, esteem," in the sense of giving a place of precedence, of taking someone seriously. This verb is so used both of human beings, as here, and of Yahweh, as in 1 Sam 2:30, Isa 24:15, Ps 22:24 [23], or Prov 3:9 (cf. also Gamberoni, *BZ* 8 [1964] 169–72). To "give honor" to father and mother means more than to be subject to them, or respectful of their wishes: they are to be given precedence by the recognition of the importance which is theirs by right, esteemed for their priority, and loved for it as well. As Yahweh is honored for his priority to all life, so father and mother must be honored for their priority, as Yahweh's instruments, to the lives of their children. Lev 19:3, in the chapter of the Holiness Code that gives special application of the Decalogue, even uses ירא "have reverence for, stand in awe of," instead of כבד in the repetition of the fifth commandment.

As Gamberoni (*BZ* 8 [1964] 175–84) has demonstrated, the fifth commandment is foundational to a considerable body of parent and progeny material in the OT in both legal and wisdom collections, and Harrelson (*Ten Commandments*, 92–95) is correct in his insistence that adults are the ones to whom the commandment is primarily directed. Certainly, the whole range of filial relationship is generally involved, but the focus is upon those who are responsible and "in charge," those who follow their parents and precede their children in shaping Israel's responsibility in covenant. There is no reason to argue, as Kremers (*EvT* 21 [1961] 156–61) does, that the parents here are the "representatives (*Stellvertreter*) of God," on a par with preacher, teacher and priest. In a sense, they are more than that, representing only themselves. The parents represent Yahweh no more nor less than does any other member of the covenant community, and Israel is commanded to honor them not to provide social security or because they are proxy to Yahweh, but because Yahweh requires it of those who would enter into covenant with him.

The equal status of the mother in this and other versions of the fifth commandment (MT of Lev 19:3 even puts "mother" before "father") is significant. The OT world was predominantly a male world, yet here as at other points in the OT (e.g., the Deuteronomists' introductions of the kings of Israel and Judah), the woman is given appropriate recognition. Nearly always, it is the woman in her all-important role as mother who is accorded such recognition (cf. Boecker, *Redeformen*, 75–76, esp. n. 5) but even so, such an emphasis is exceptional in the ANE.

The promise and the implied warning that follow the fifth commandment are unique in the Decalogue. The Deuteronomistic tone of the language of this addition has often been noted and has been cited as evidence for dating the promise in the exilic or the postexilic periods (cf. Lohfink, *BZ* 9 [1965]

25–32). These words must be read in the light of such texts as Exod 21:15, 17; Lev 20:9; and Deut 21:18–21; 27:16. Disrespect for one's parents was a serious offense in the covenant community, and rebellion against them was punishable by death, precisely because such disrespect and rebellion constituted disobedience of Yahweh. The addition to the fifth commandment thus has a double meaning: while appropriate honor accorded father and mother could contribute for a number of reasons to the length of one's days in Yahweh's promised land, a lack of respect for them could just as certainly mean an abrupt end to those days.

13 The sixth commandment and the two commandments following it are recorded in MT with just six consonants each (the negative particle לא plus a four-letter verb form). These three commandments may well give us our best idea of the original form of each of the "ten words." They are also the three that have been transmitted in a different order in the Masoretic and the Old Greek traditions (see above, n. 20:13.a). While it is not possible to determine with certainty which order is precedent, the Masoretic order appears to have been the more influential (Flusser, *Textus* 4: 223–24). It is at least possible that the brief form of these commandments had some bearing on the shifts in their sequence.

The precise meaning of the sixth commandment depends on the definition of רצח. This verb occurs just over forty times in the OT, far less frequently than the more general terms הרג "kill, slay, destroy," (more than 160 times) and the hiphil of מות "cause to die, kill" (more than 200 times). Stamm (*TZ* 1 [1945] 81–90) has made a thorough study of the usage of רצח in the OT, and A. Phillips (*Criminal Law* 83–109) has considered the sixth commandment against its ANE context. רצח plainly refers to killing that can be understood to be murder (so Ps 94:6b or 1 Kgs 21:19), and some translators so render it (see NEB, for example); but רצח can also refer to unintentional killing, "manslaughter," as in Deut 19:3, 4, 6, and Josh 20:3, and to the legal execution of a convicted killer, as in Num 35:30. Stamm (*TZ* 1 [1945] 87–90) concluded that רצח is a verb of specialized application, referring to killing that brought illegal violence into the covenant community. Reventlow (*Gebot und Predigt,* 71–77) refined Stamm's theory, arguing that the Decalogue emerged from concrete situations and that the concrete situation of the sixth commandment involved the killing of the blood-feud (*Blutrache*).

Neither of these specialized definitions, however, is borne out fully by the usage of רצח in the OT, a difficulty Childs (420–21) attempts to solve by proposing a continuing shift in the meaning of רצח from its earlier technical sense ("a type of slaying which called forth blood vengeance") to later and broader applications ("acts of violence against a person which arose from personal feelings of hatred and malice"). The problem posed by such a solution is that it presents a degree of ambiguity to the understanding of a commandment which cannot, for obvious reasons, be dated with any certainty: is רצח here to be understood in its earlier, "technical" sense or in its later, "broad" sense? Schulz, commenting that Reventlow's "supposition" is based on false assumptions (*Das Todesrecht* 9–15, esp. 11, n. 20; note also his remark about Stamm's "risking"), connects the sixth commandment to Exod 21:12:

"The one who strikes a man, killing him (וָמֵת), will certainly be put to death." This connection has the advantage, if it can be sustained, of giving a firm point of reference for the sixth commandment. Whatever broadening of application it may have had in later years, its basic prohibition was against killing, for whatever cause, under whatever circumstances, and by whatever method, a fellow-member of the covenant community.

Such a general understanding of רצח fits its pattern of usage in the OT: the verb refers only to the killing of persons, never to animals; it can refer to capital punishment (once in the OT, Num 35:30: . . . כל־מכה־נפשׁ יִרְצַח אֶת־הָרֹצֵחַ "anyone striking dead a person . . . the killer shall be killed") but not to killing in war; and it describes no specific means of killing. Both Hosea (4:2) and Jeremiah (7:9) use רצח in lists of abuses of covenant commitment obviously based on the Decalogue. And it is important to understand this commandment, along with all the rest, as one in a series of *Yahweh's* expectations of those who would enter into covenant with him. רצח is an act of killing, premeditated or not, related to vengeance or not, that violates the standard of living Yahweh expects of those who have given themselves to him. The primary reference of the commandment is religious, not social. Stamm's emphasis (see also Stamm and Andrew, *Ten Commandments,* 99) on רצח as a verb describing killing that occurs primarily within the covenant community may be a correct one. What is certain is that רצח describes a killing of human beings forbidden by Yahweh to those who are in covenant with him. The use of such a specialized term in the specific context of the Decalogue leaves the way open for the killing of the Yahweh-war or capital punishment, both of which are of course permitted by the OT, and also sets apart other uses of רצח by relating them inevitably to the obligations of the covenant with Yahweh.

14 The ANE attitude toward adultery has been surveyed by Kornfeld (*RB* 57 [1950] 92–109). Rabinowitz (*JNES* 18 [1959] 73) and Moran (*JNES* 18 [1959] 280–81) have commented, respectively, on texts from Egypt and Ugarit in which, as in the OT (Gen 20:9; cf. Exod 32:21,30,31; 2 Kings 17:21), adultery is referred to by the discreet euphemism, "the great sin." Moran describes texts published by Nougayrol (*Palais Royal* 4:125–48) involving what appears to be an adulterous liaison by the foreign wife of Ammištamru, a king of Ugarit, which led to the lady's flight to her father Benteŝina, extradition from her country, Amurru, and eventual execution. In each case, the lady's crime against Ammištamru is called a "great sin."

The Hebrew verb for this "great sin," and the verb of the seventh commandment, is נאף "commit adultery." It is used in the OT with both men and women as subject, though far more frequently of men, and, by analogy, as a designation of idol worship, the violation of the bond of covenant relationship with Yahweh. "Great sin" is used in the OT of both these betrayals.

The literal reference of the seventh commandment is shown by such passages as (1) Lev 18:20; 20:10; and Deut 22:22 to have been sexual intercourse of a man with the wife of another man; (2) Deut 22:23–27, sexual intercourse of a man with the fiancée of another man; and (3) Hos 4:13; Ezek 16:32, sexual intercourse of a wife with a man, probably a married man (cf. זָרִים "strangers" of Ezek 16:32; and Humbert, *RÉtSém* 27 [1937] 49–64), other than her husband. That the fiancée of a man was considered and treated insofar as sexual fidelity was concerned just as she would be when she became the man's wife is made clear by Deut 22:23–29.

That adultery was considered a serious breech of the covenant relationship with Yahweh is shown both by the bluntness of the references to it and by the severity of the penalties inflicted for it. Jeremiah (5:7) includes adultery along with the worship of "no-gods" and "bunching up at the whore house" among sins that make Yahweh's forgiveness difficult. Hosea (4:2) includes adultery with swearing a curse falsely, deceitful lying, killing (רצח, as in v 13), stealing (גנב, as in v 15), destruction and piling one bloody deed onto another as a part of an inclusive charge against Israel (Hos 4–8). Job (24:13–17) lists the adulterer along with the murderous thief as a creature of the dark. The penalty for adultery was death, by stoning (usually, Deut 22:24) or by burning (Gen 38:24; Lev 20:14, 21:9), depending apparently upon the specific circumstances. Though a milder punishment was specified for other sexual offenses, as for example the seduction (Exod 22:16–17) or rape of a virgin (Deut 22:28–29), adultery, in any of the liaisons by which it was possible, was punishable by death.

This attitude toward adultery is fully understandable only in view of the fact that more than the integrity of marriage and the home and more than the integrity of personal honor were at stake in the covenantal setting of Yahweh's "ten words." The integrity of the Israelite's relationship with Yahweh himself was at stake. Everywhere in the ANE, Israel concluded, adultery was a crime against persons; but in Israel it was first of all and even more a crime against Yahweh (Gen 20:9; 39:9; Jer 3:1, and cf. Kornfeld, *RB* 57 [1950] 100–109, A. Phillips, *Criminal Law*, 117–18). Most telling of all in this connection is the use of adultery as a description of Israel's obsession with idolatry (Isa 57:1–13; Jer 3:6–9; Ezek 23:36–49, and all the references to Israel's "great sin," predominant among them Exod 32:21–34, which may involve, in the light of לצחק "to play" of 32:6, a *double entendre*). Adultery with the husband or the wife or the betrothed of another was, like idol worship, a turning away from commitment to Yahweh.

15 Critical analysis of the Decalogue has tended generally to suggest a shortening of the longer commandments to a form more like the terse expression of the sixth, seventh, and eighth commandments in the order of MT. A number of scholars, however, have favored lengthening the eighth commandment by the addition of a direct object believed to have been omitted from the original form of the commandment in the interest of giving it a broader application. The scholar generally credited with this suggestion is Albrecht Alt (*Kleine Schriften*, 333–40), though this interpretation appears to have been anticipated by rabbinic expositors, in both the Tannaitic midrash on Exodus (Petuchowski, *VT* 7 [1957] 397–98) and also the Babylonian Talmud (Gottstein, *TZ* 9 [1953] 394–95).

Alt's concern was to establish a clear difference between the eighth and the tenth commandments, to justify the inclusion of a commandment against stealing with commandments against such more serious offenses as killing and adultery by demonstrating a reference to stealing of a very special kind, and to establish a sequence of commands "protecting the God-given basic rights of each individual Israelite"—life (v 13), marriage (v 14), liberty (v

15), and reputation (v 16); in whatever order they were handed down, these "Grundrechte" were each of equal importance (Alt, *Kleine, Schriften* 338). To achieve these purposes, Alt proposed that the eighth commandment originally had an object, as does its verb גנב "steal" in Exod 21:16 and Deut 24:7, and that it therefore prohibited, though not stealing in general, the kidnapping of a free Israelite man (on Alt's interpretation, 339, only the man was a nondependent, and so free; everyone else is provided for, in a list excluding the free man, by the tenth commandment).

A number of scholars have followed Alt's suggestion (for example, Nielsen, *Ten Commandments*, 85, 91; Stamm, *TRu* 27 [1961] 298–99; Keszler, *VT* 7 [1957] 11–12; A. Phillips, *Criminal Law*, 130–32); others, for a variety of reasons, have found it unconvincing (so Andrew, Stamm and Andrew, *Ten Commandments*, 106; Hyatt, 215; Gerstenberger, *Wesen*, 63–64, 77–81; Harrelson, *Ten Commandments* 135–36). גנב means "steal"; if the verb has any special connotation beyond this fundamental idea, it would be "surreptitious stealing" (Judg 17:2–5; Prov 29:24), stealing under cover of darkness (Job 27:20) or confusion (2 Kgs 11:2) or even trust (Gen 31:19,32). Such a sense of duplicity and of stealthiness cannot be said to fit the majority of the OT usages of גנב, however, and so גנב is best defined as a verb depicting stealing of any kind to which the meaning "stealing in secret or by duplicity" can also sometimes apply.

Horst (*Gottes Recht*, 173–75) referred to the inclusion of stealing in a list of three or four OT "deeds of jealousy" (*Neidingswerke*): "murder, stealing, adultery and perjury." While it is clear that each of the commandments five through ten describes deeds breeching human relationship and therefore compromising the relationship with Yahweh that is the purpose of the entire Decalogue, perhaps too much has been made of the interconnectedness of the commandments themselves. What binds them together is not their supposed comprehensiveness or their listing of social problems of equal weight with equal penalties or their progressive development of the essential problems of organized society, but the fact that they are commanded by Yahweh as his ten principles for those who would live their lives in relationship, first of all, with him. These are the commands, according to Exodus, that Yahweh himself made "in person" to Israel at Sinai. That is what gives the commandments their special place, and not the seriousness of the penalties inflicted when they were broken, or their place in a comprehensive legal system. Too much has been made of the relation of the ten commandments to other laws in the OT and beyond it. Not enough has been made of the way in which virtually all of the OT legal system is rooted in the ten commandments.

The eighth commandment is best understood perhaps as a prohibition of stealing of any kind under any circumstances. We need look no further than our own experience of life to know how disruptive of relationships stealing can be. But we must keep firmly in mind that *Yahweh* is represented as requiring that those in covenant relationship with him are not to steal. As with each of the commandments, the ultimate penalty for stealing is not the penalty of the community but the penalty of Yahweh. What Israel faces for breaking the commandments, as chaps. 32–34 so dramatically show, is not the loss of life, but the far worse loss of Yahweh's Presence.

16 The language of the ninth commandment connects it to the judicial process in the covenant community, a process described in broad terms by Köhler (*Hebrew Man,* 127–50). ענה means "answer, give reply, testify," especially when, as here, it is followed by בְּ "for, against, in the case of." The noun רֵעַ "companion, neighbor, friend, fellow-citizen" refers always in the OT to a person with whom one stands in a reciprocal relationship, and in legal contexts, to a fellow member of the covenant community (cf. Fichtner *Wort und Dienst* 4:23–31). עֵד "testimony, evidence" appears to be derived from עוד "do again, repeat," and refers to what amounts to a repeated account, an answer given as evidence.

שֶׁקֶר, which qualifies the עֵד, means "lying, deceiving, false, fraudulent." עֵד שֶׁקֶר occurs in the OT in reference to a lying testimony in a judicial context in Deut 19:18; Ps 27:12; and Prov 6:19; 12:17(שְׁקָרִים); 14:5; 19:5, 9 (שְׁקָרִים); and 25:18 (cf. also, variously, שׁבע "swear" plus שֶׁקֶר, Lev 5:22 [6:3]; Jer 5:2; Zech 8:17). In Deut 5:20, שֶׁקֶר is replaced by שָׁוְא "nothingness, emptiness, worthlessness, something vain," to form a phrase found only there and intended apparently to broaden the application of the ninth commandment to include any evasive or worthless testimony. Klopfenstein (*Die Lüge,* 21) has suggested that the Exodus version of this commandment refers more to the relationship of the witness towards a neighbor against whom he has given a perfidious report, while the version in Deuteronomy tends more to describe the malicious character of the witness himself. This distinction however is more precise than the evidence in the OT will allow.

That the whole matter of the responsibility of the individual Israelite for the integrity of the legal process was taken quite seriously in the covenant community of Israel is shown by a number of OT texts (e.g., Exod 23:1; Num 35:30; Jer 7:8; Ps 24:4; Prov 25:18; and Job 31:30). The testimony of at least two witnesses was required to sustain a charge (Deut 19:15; Num 35:30), and the penalty for false accusation was severe (Deut 19:16–21). In fact, there was even provision for punishing those who frustrated or defeated justice by refusing to come forward to give needed testimony. The ninth commandment provided an obvious and no doubt needed protection of the legal process at the crucial point where the evidence of wrongdoing within the covenant community was given.

In addition to the obvious application of this commandment to the maintenance of justice in the covenant community, however, there is also a wider implication of the requirement of truthfulness, reflected not only in the broader statement of Deut 5:20 but also in the fact that the truthfulness in legal testimony is presented not as a requirement of a system of jurisprudence but as a requirement of Yahweh. This commandment, like all the others, describes what the life of the Israelite obedient to Yahweh's expectation is to be like. That he is not to give a lying testimony in a legal proceeding is at the root of the ninth commandment, but the testimony the Israelite gives before the elders in the gate is not to be considered something separate from his witness under less formal circumstances.

Andrew (*Int* 17 [1963] 427–33), in his helpful review of the broader implications of the ninth commandment, has stressed the "emphasis on persons" ("*you* . . . your *neighbor*"; even "witness of falsehood" instead of "false witness") by linking the commandment to a series of OT passages dealing with lying and deception and by stressing the "emptiness of falsehood" and the "positive, even violent and vindictive harm" it does, bringing "pointlessness and harm into . . . relationships with God and people. . . ." The false witness was inimical to the relationship with Yahweh, upon which everything, including the very being of the Israelite, was dependent. The reputation of the neighbor was important, just as the Israelite's own reputation was important, of course. But however important these reputations were within the community, they were important to Yahweh most of all, for these people, as his people, were to be *his* witness to the world.

17 The tenth commandment, like commandments two, three, four and five, has been expanded in the definition and application of the principle it sets forth. As suggested already, such expansion was probably the result of need: these five commandments were the ones with which the covenant community had the greatest difficulty. Like the ninth commandment, this one too is directed specifically to relationship within the covenant community. Like each of the commandments, this one too is addressed to each individual member of the covenant community, and like the second, third, fifth and ninth commandments, it includes also a singular possessive personal pronoun, "*your* neighbor."

The application of the tenth commandment is determined by the exact meaning of the verb חמד. At base חמד means "desire, yearn for, covet, lust after" someone or something, specifically for one's own use or gratification. The question whether the verb may also suggest action as well as desire, particularly since the other nine commandments appear to command specific actions, has complicated the understanding of the tenth commandment. Herrmann (*Beiträge*, 69–72) and Nielsen (*Ten Commandments*, 101–5), for example, have taken the view that חמד means both the desire and the scheming and actions impelled by it, an argument they sustain by reference to such passages as Exod 34:24; Deut 7:25; Josh 7:21; Mic 2:2; and Ps 68:17. Coates (*ZAW* 52 [1934] 238–39), Stoebe (*Wort und Dienst* 3:108–15), and Moran (*CBQ* 29 [1967) 543–48), on the other hand, argue for the more subjective basic definition, on the grounds that there are ample examples of the prohibition in the ANE of such subjective longings and that such a definition better fits *all* the OT occurrences of חמד and its derivatives, including the texts cited in support of the "desire and take" definition.

Hyatt (*Encounter* 26 [1965] 204–6), listing parallels in Egyptian literature, suggested an "original form" of the tenth commandment that was an injunction against someone "in a position of authority" opening himself to bribery through "inordinate desire"; so this commandment was connected with the ninth commandment and "the integrity of the judicial system of the desert period." A. Phillips (*Criminal Law*, 149–52) goes much farther in the same general direction with his argument that חמד "desire" is a replacement for an original verb that referred to the seizure of the house (taken in its literal meaning) of the local elder, who would then, by the loss of his status as a property-owner, lose also his authority as a judge. Such a theory is made necessary by Phillips's assumption (1–2 and *passim*) that "the Decalogue constituted ancient Israel's preexilic criminal law code given to her at Sinai."

Both sides in this debate have taken the use in Deut 5:21 of אוה "desire, incline towards, long for, lust over" instead of the second חמד "desire" of Exod 20:17 as support for their respective cases. The two verbs are however very close in meaning, so close that A. Phillips (*Criminal Law*, 150) and Childs (426–27) can say that the Deuteronomists used אוה to emphasize the subjective nature of חמד, while Stamm (Stamm and Andrew, *Ten Commandments*, 104) and Nielsen (*Ten Commandments*, 43) propose that the Deuteronomists were attempting with this change to tone down the objective action implied by חמד, and move the commandment towards what Stamm calls "mental coveting." The two verbs are much too nearly synonymous, however, to justify the distinctions these scholars have proposed, and in any case, the expansion of the commandment in Exodus repeats חמד instead of using אוה or any other verb meaning "covet." In every OT passage in which חמד leads to actual possession, a second verb is supplied to make that additional meaning clear. If חמד had meant "covet and seize," such a second verb would have been unnecessary.

Another possibility is that חמד, as a verb meaning "desire obsessively, covet or lust after for oneself" and describing a mental and emotional process interior to a person's being, was the deliberate and careful choice of a verb for the commandment that ends the ten words. Just as the first commandment, "You are not to have other gods," provides the foundation for covenantal relationship, so this tenth commandment, "You are not to desire for yourself . . . ," describes the foundation for the severance of covenantal relationship. חמד is by choice a reference to an obsessive covetousness that could be the gateway to the violation of every other principle in the Decalogue. Thus coveting for oneself the gold and silver with which idols are decorated leads to idolatry, the violation of the first commandment. Desiring the "free love" of the fertility cults leads both to the worship of other gods and to sexual irresponsibility, the violation of the first and the seventh commandments (Isa 1:29). Yearning after the possessions of others may lead to stealing, a violation of the eighth commandment (Mic 2:2; Josh 7:21–26, which includes also a violation of the third commandment, since Achan had apparently sworn the oath of Yahweh-war loyalty).

Before Ahab's obsessive desire for Naboth's vineyard was satisfied, the ninth and sixth commandments had been broken (1 Kgs 21). Before David's lust for Bathsheba was sated, the seventh, eight, and sixth commandments were broken (2 Sam 11–12). The coveting merchants of Amos's day broke the fourth and the eighth commandments in their fever to possess (Amos 8:4–6). The citizens of Judah in Jeremiah's time, deifying their desires and longing after a material and local security, violated the first, third, sixth, seventh, and ninth commandments, and above all, by making Yahweh's temple into a fetish, the second commandment as well (Jer 7:1–15). And the son whose determined desire for his own way led him to strike (Exod 21:15) or abuse (Exod 21:17) his father or his mother was guilty of breaking the fifth commandment.

The tenth commandment thus functions as a kind of summary commandment, the violation of which is a first step that can lead to the violation of any one or all the rest of the commandments. As such, it is necessarily all-embracing and descriptive of an attitude rather than a deed. It was perhaps set last in the Decalogue precisely because of this uniquely comprehensive application.

בית "house," in accord with this broad application, is used in its collective sense, in reference to the "neighbor's" entire family and his entire property, as for example in Gen 7:1 or Deut 11:6. LXX reverses the sequence of "house" and "wife" in the text of Exod 20:17, as also does MT in the parallel version of this commandment in Deut 5:21, thus making "house" a more specific term and setting up a descending sequence from a man's most valuable possession in the OT view, his wife (Prov 31:10–31), to his least valuable ones. This change may be regarded as a later shifting of emphasis within the form of the expanded tenth commandment. In its original form, the commandment must have been deliberately comprehensive, with the reference to the neighbor's house taking in all that belonged to any fellow member of the covenant community.

The basic form of the tenth commandment thus prohibits an obsessive desire for any property belonging to any other person bound to the covenant with Yahweh. The expansion of the basic form specifies five categories of the most valuable possessions the neighbor could have: wife, male slave, female slave, ox, and ass. Moran (*CBQ* 29 [1967] 548–52) has reviewed an extensive series of similar lists from Ugaritic legal texts and established a fairly consistent formula for the listing of an owner's total property (" 'house and field' + specifications [buildings, various forms of cultivation, personnel, livestock] + generic formula, 'everything else belonging to him' "). One of the texts Moran lists (550–51) is an almost word-for-word parallel (cf. Nougayrol, *Palais Royal* 3:111, 115–16) to Exod 20:17.

As the apparent function of such lists is to set forth a comprehensive statement of the ownership of property, this expansion of the tenth commandment gives support to the view that it is a summary commandment prohibiting the kind of thinking and feeling that might lead, in turn, to the violation of the other commandments of Yahweh. In the list of Exod 20:17, only the living resources are actually named. The rest of the neighbor's possessions, his material goods, are provided for both by the collective term "house" and by the catch-all phrase at the end of the addition to the commandment, "anything that belongs to your neighbor." Whoever expanded the tenth commandment may thus be said not only to have sought to make specific what covetousness meant in the context of covenant community; he also reinforces the comprehensive summary nature of the commandment itself.

Explanation

Whatever the time origin of the Decalogue, and whatever the *Ur*-form of the individual commandments that make it up, whatever the provenance of the "ten words" in Israel's worship and in Israel's legal practice, this most influential of all law codes must be seen in Exodus as the center of the narrative that is at the very heart of the OT. By location as by content, the Decalogue is set forth in Exodus as the single address of Yahweh himself directly to his people, stating the fundamental principles for living in relationship with him. It is possible that the Exodus setting of the Decalogue may give us information not only about the covenant community's belief concerning the origin and the authority of the commandments, but also about the biblical interrelation of revelation and law and the biblical view of law as liberation. If this is even partially true, we should take the Exodus location of the commandments far more seriously than we have done.

Yahweh's Advent to the people of Israel at Sinai amounts to the primal experience of Israel's faith. Throughout the narrative of Exodus, from the revelation to Moses forward, Yahweh has demonstrated, by one mighty deed after another, the reality of the claim made in his special name, "the One Who Always Is." Unlike other gods, for whom claims were made, Yahweh is represented over and over again making his claims for himself; through deeds and through interpreting words, Yahweh has presented himself to the people of Israel, establishing a relationship between himself and the descendants of Abraham, Isaac, and Jacob.

Then at last Yahweh comes to these people at Sinai, in an awesome experience for which they were carefully prepared, and defining his relationship with them ("I am Yahweh, your God, who brought you forth from the land of Egypt"), he then gives them the basic outline of their response to what he had become to them, his directions for what might be called their covenant of being, his definition of the standards of *their* relationship to *him*. The first four commandments set forth the principles guiding Israel's relationship to Yahweh. The last six commandments set forth the principles guiding Israel's relationship to the covenant community and, both indirectly and directly, to the whole family of humankind *because* of the prior relationship with Yahweh. The order of these principles of relationship is significant, because it moves from Israel's first priority, Yahweh, to Israel's second priority, family and neighbor, all of course in the larger context set by the introduction to the Sinai narrative sequence (summed up especially in Exod 19:4–6; see *Comment* above) which has in view Israel's relationship, as Yahweh's witness, to all men and women everywhere.

The Decalogue begins with Yahweh's all-embracing statement that he has made himself Israel's God. The autokerygmatic "I am Yahweh, your God, who brought you forth from the land of Egypt" describes Yahweh's relationship with Israel as a gift of grace. The first commandment follows this statement, requesting of those who will make a response to Yahweh's gift an undivided loyalty. This undivided loyalty is the foundation for the nine commandments that follow. The tenth commandment, then, with its emphasis on the attitude of mind and heart that opens the way to compromise, is a summary commandment, a prohibition of an attitude that precedes the violation of any or all of the other commandments.

The ten commandments thus present the foundational layer of Yahweh's expectation of those who, in response to his gift of himself, desire to give themselves to him. This foundational layer, in turn, is woven carefully into the primary OT account of Yahweh's giving of himself, the Advent at Mount Sinai. And in some ways most important of all, this foundational layer describing what Israel was to become and how, is set forth not as the expectation of Moses or Aaron or any collection of leaders, but as the expectation of Yahweh, delivered to the people in person when he came to them at Sinai.

Israel's Response to Yahweh's Coming (20:18-21)

Bibliography

Becker, J. *Gottesfurcht im Alten Testament.* AnBib 25. Rome: Päpstliches Bibelinstitut, 1965. **Greenberg, M.** "נסה in Exodus 20:20 and the Purpose of the Sinaitic Theophany." *JBL* 79 (1960) 273–76. **Roberts, B. J.** *The Old Testament Text and Versions.* Cardiff: University of Wales Press, 1951. **Wolff, H. W.** "The Elohistic Fragments in the Pentateuch." *Int* 26 (1972) 158–73.

Translation

[18] *And all the people were experiencing* [a] *the rumblings of thunder and the bolts of lightning* [b] *and the sound of the ram's horn and the mountain smoking: and as the people* [c] *took it in,* [d] *they trembled and drew some distance back.* [e] [19] *Then they said to Moses, "You* [a] *speak with us, and we promise we'll hear* [b]*—but don't let God keep speaking* [c] *with us, lest we die!"* [20] *But Moses replied to the people, "Don't be afraid, for it is with the purpose* [a] *of giving you the experience* [b] *that God has come, so that* [a] *reverence for him might grip you* [c] *and prevent* [d] *you from sinning."* [21] *So the people took a position at a distance, while Moses approached the thick cloud where God was.*

Notes

18.a. רֹאִים, masc pl qal act ptcp ראה; lit., "seeing," but given the succession of obj, the verb is taken above in BDB's (907) sense of "5. *see* = perceive" and "7. of mental observation." The ptcp indicates the action of the people during Yahweh's theophany, from the moment the people took their place at the foot of Sinai through the speaking of the "ten words." Cf. Cassuto, 252.

18.b. לפידם "torches," i.e., "flames, flashes," in this context, of lightning. SamPent has "And all the people heard (שמע) the rumblings . . . and the sound . . . and were seeing (וראים) the bolts . . . and the mountain smoking, and all the people were afraid. . . ."

18.c. SamPent, LXX, Tg Ps-J have "all the people."

18.d. וַיַּרְא "and so, as they saw." ראה taken here also as in n. 18.a. SamPent, LXX, Syr, Vg, other versions read instead וַיִּרְאוּ "and so they were afraid." MT makes perfect sense if ראה is not read literally. Cf. Barthélemy, *Preliminary and Interim Report*, 115–16.

18.e. ויעמדו מרחק "and they took up a position from a distance."

19.a. The impv דַּבֵּר "speak" is made emphatic by the addition of the pers pronoun אתה "you." SamPent begins at this point the much more elaborate version of the people's plea recorded also in Deut 5:24–27. The sequence from Deuteronomy is inserted verbatim into SamPent's version of Exod 20:19, between ויאמרו אל משה "then they said to Moses" and ואל ידבר עמנו אלהים פן נמות "but don't let God keep speaking with us, lest we die," an addition dictated apparently by the other additions following the Decalogue and designed to legitimize Mount Gerizim as a place where Yahweh was to be worshiped. Cf. Roberts, *Text and Versions*, 189.

19.b. וְנִשְׁמָעָה. The addition of the "cohortative ה" to שמע gives the sense of "self-encouragement . . . a resolution or a wish" (GKC, ¶ 48*e*), rendered above "we promise we'll hear."

19.c. יְדַבֵּר, the piel impf דבר "speak," taken in this context in its "iterative" sense (GKC ¶ 52*f*).

20.a. בעבור "on account of, for the sake of, in the interest of, in order that."

20.b. נַסּוֹת, piel inf constr נסה "test, try, attempt, even get accustomed to"; see BDB, 650, and esp. Greenberg (*JBL* 79 [1960] 274–76), who argues from the "expanded version of the Sinai story in Deut 4–5" that the purpose of the Sinai theophany, according to both Exod

20:20 and Deut 4:10, was "to give Israel a direct, palpable experience of God," and that piel of נסה in this verse has the "factitive" meaning "give X experience of."

20.c. תהיה . . . על פניכם "be upon your faces," i.e., "be always before you, on your mind."

20.d. לבלתי תחטאו "in order that you might not sin." Cf. BDB, 116 § 4.

Form/Structure/Setting

These verses, as noted already (*Form/Structure/Setting* on 19:1–15 and 19:16–25), are the closing bracket of the central narrative of the Sinai narrative sequence. The account of the preparation of the people of Israel for Yahweh's Advent is given in Exod 19:9–15, the opening bracket of the central narrative. That central narrative is given in 19:16–19a and 20:1–17, the account of Yahweh's Advent and Yahweh's ten words, best understood as a unit disrupted in the composite of Exodus by the insertion of material dealing with the sacerdotal/prophetic intermediacy of Moses (19:19b–25; cf. above). This account of the people's reaction to the awesome theophany and its pointed revelation thus serves as the conclusion, or closing bracket, to a central narrative sequence moving from 19:9–15 to 19:16–19a and 20:1–17 to 20:18–21. The larger Sinai narrative sequence to which these verses are central includes a general introduction, 19:1–8, and an account of the solemnization of the covenant, 24:1–18; it is concluded by an account of covenant breaking, redefinition of the relationship with Yahweh's Presence, and the renewal of the covenant, in 32:1–34:35.

The connection of 20:18–21 with the account of Yahweh's theophany must not be made exluding the Decalogue (as for example Noth, 168, or Hyatt, 217, do). The reaction of the people is presented in the composite of Exodus as reaction not only to the phenomena surrounding the theophany and to the theophany itself but also to the revelation of the Decalogue, presented as an integral part of the theophany. The usual source-assignment of these verses has been to E (so Beer, 104, E¹; Noth, 168; Hyatt, 217), but the reasons given are not determinative and the composite Sinai narrative sequence has been too many times expanded and reworked to make precise source-analysis either possible or much of a help to an understanding of the passages constituting it. The form of the composite of which these verses are an integral part is determined not by the influence of sources but by the governing theme, the Advent of Yahweh.

Comment

18–19 The experience of the people through the whole of the theophany of Yahweh, from the first sounds and sights presaging it through the intensification of those phenomena with Yahweh's arrival and even through the giving of the "ten words," is summed up in the ראים "experiencing" and the וירא "they took it in" of this verse. רֹאִים, a qal active participle, summarizes the continuity of the people's experience, along with a list of the phenomena accompanying the theophany in precisely the same order in which they occur in 19:16–18: thunder, lightning, the sounding of the ram's horn, and the mountain smoking. This summation is then confirmed by the qal imperfect of ראה with special *waw*, a verb form suggesting narrative continuity and the next step in the people's experience: having experienced the phenomena of Yahweh's Advent and then Yahweh's own voice, the people became more and more frightened. As they "saw" what was happening to them, "realized, took in" the experience of which they were a part, the people trembled, and drew back even from the perimeter of safety set about Sinai for their protection.

Such an interpretation of רֹאִים and וַיִּרְא is confirmed, both by the people's panic-stricken request of Moses and also by the statement by Moses of the purpose of the theophany. The people plead with Moses, "*You* speak with us." The imperative is made doubly emphatic by the addition of the personal pronoun, as it is by the "promise" that they will "hear, listen attentively" to whatever Moses has to say to them (see nn. 19.a, b). "*You* speak" implies by its emphasis as by its context the awesome speaking of Yahweh which the people want now to avoid, as their further plea says: "Don't let God keep speaking (piel imperfect of דבר) with us, lest we die!"

20 Moses' comforting reply further encompasses the whole experience the people have had, particularly in the use of נסה "experience." The people must have no fear, he says, because God had come for the purpose of giving them the experience of his Presence. נַסּוֹת, the piel infinitive construct of נסה, has generally been translated "test, prove," with varying implications: a test of faith (Rylaarsdam, *IB* 1:990), a test of obedience (Cassuto, 253; Hyatt, 217), a test of proper respect (Beer, 105), even a test of whether they would disregard the boundaries of holiness around Sinai (Noth, 168). Previously in the narrative of Exodus, at 15:25 (see *Comment* above); 16:4; 17:2, נסה is used in exactly such a manner, in the first two instances in reference to Yahweh putting the people to a test of their trust in him to provide for their physical needs, in the third in reference to the people putting Yahweh to a test of patience with their complaint against Moses (and so against Yahweh) about the provision of water.

Here, however, נסה has a meaning consonant with the two usages of ראה "see, experience" in v 18. As Greenberg (*JBL* 79 [1960] 274–75) has shown, נסה also means "test, prove" in the sense of trying something on (1 Sam 17:39), of getting used to something (Deut 28:56), of experiencing something or someone in depth and at first hand (2 Chr 32:31). And though his theory of a piel factitive meaning for נסה and certain other verbs is not entirely convincing (cf. Childs, 344), Greenberg makes a convincing case, with his comparison of the Exodus sequence with its interpretative parallel in Deut 4 and 5, for נסה having the sense "give . . . a direct, palpable experience of," in this verse as in Eccl 2:1 and Judg 3:1–3. The Samaritan Pentateuch's expansion of Exod 20:19 by the insertion of Deut 5:24–27 (see n. 19.a.) lends at least general support to Greenberg's proposal, in that it underscores Israel's experience of the Advent of Yahweh with the verbs ראה (hiphil, "cause to see"), שמע ("hear") and ראה (qal, "see," followed by "that God speaks") in sequence.

This awesome firsthand experience of the Presence of Yahweh and the speaking of Yahweh, Moses continues, is for the further purpose that Israel might have reverence (יראה) for Yahweh always before them as a constant preoccupation of mind and so might not sin. Having reverence for Yahweh is a basic emphasis of Israel's teaching tradition (Becker, *Gottesfurcht,* 125–209; Stähli, ירא "fürchten," *THAT* 1:774–78); Wolff (*Int* 26 [1972] 158–73) has claimed this "Fear of God" as "the most prominent theme of the Elohist." What is meant by such "reverence" or "fear" is a respect for Yahweh/Elohim that will give a constant emphasis to his way for living and relationship, and so avoid the missing of the way (חטא) that is sin. The use of אל־תיראו "you must not be afraid" followed by ובעבור תהיה יראתו על־פניכם "in order that there might be reverence (fear) of him before your face" is a deft touch of didactic narrative. Yahweh/Elohim comes to Israel at Sinai to give them so vivid and unforgettable an experience of himself, including his own statement of his principles for life in relationship with him, that they will not only not forget but will follow his way as a first priority of life. Such, at any rate, is the emphasis of the composite that is Exodus and the memory of Sinai that permeates much of the teaching of the OT.

21 The people, still frightened, make no response to Moses. How consoling they found Moses' words, we are not told. They remain in a position removed from the perimeter to which Moses led them for the experience of the theophany, and Moses, crossing that boundary, moves toward the thick cloud that protects the people and Moses as well from the mysterious and powerful Presence of Elohim (= Yahweh).

Explanation

The essential point of this brief conclusion to the central theophany narrative of the Sinai narrative sequence is Israel's experience of the Advent of Yahweh on Sinai. The compilers of Exodus have gone to great lengths to make unmistakably clear that Israel experienced at Sinai what Moses had experienced there, and what he had brought Israel there to experience. "All the people" heard the thunder and saw the lightning, heard the ram's horn and saw the mountain smoking. All the people, nearly overwhelmed by their unique and awesome experience, shook with fear, drew back from the foot of the mountain, and pled with Moses to take their place in proximity to the Presence of Elohim (= Yahweh), hear by himself the fearsome voice of God, and then report the words to them. This request, to which Moses does not accede either here or elsewhere in Exodus or the OT, may well be the beginning of what developed into a tradition of Mosaic intermediacy.

Moses' attempt to allay the fear of the people is a pointed repetition of the emphasis of this brief section. The people did hear and see all that had them so scared, but they have been given the experience deliberately, as a gift, not that they might be afraid of Elohim (= Yahweh), but that they might have reverence for him, and so take seriously his way of living in relationship both to him and with one another.

That all the people took seriously what they had experienced at the boundary of the mountain of the Presence, this passage leaves no doubt. How seriously they took Moses' interpretation of what they had experienced is made clear first by the account of the making of the covenant, which must originally have followed this passage immediately, but second, by the account of the breaking of the covenant, which must originally have followed immediately the account of its making. Thus the compilation of Exodus becomes not only a theological history but a theological biography—an account of faith, but an account also of the compromise of faith, the neglect of faith, the loss of faith and the renewal of faith.

Yahweh's Application of His Principles: "The Book of the Covenant" (20:22–23:33)

Bibliography

Allegro, John M. *Qumran Cave 4: I (4Q158–4Q186).* DJD V. Oxford: At the Clarendon Press, 1968. **Alt, A.** "Das Verbot des Diebstahls im Dekalog." *Kleine Schriften* I. Munich: C. H. Beck'sche Verlagsbuchhandlung, 1953. 333–40. ———. "The Origins of Israelite Law." *Essays on Old Testament History and Religion.* Oxford: Basil Blackwell, 1966. 81–132. **Auerbach, E.** "Das Zehngebot—Allgemeine Gesetzes-Form in der Bibel." *VT* 16 (1966) 255–76. **Batto, B. F.** "The Reed Sea: *Resquiescat in Pace.*" *JBL* 102 (1983) 27–35. **Baumgartner, W.** "Zum Problem des Jahwe-Engels." *Zum Alten Testament und Seiner Umwelt.* Leiden: E. J. Brill, 1959. 240–46. **Beyerlin, W.** "Die Paränese im Bundesbuch und ihre Herkunft." *Gottes Wort und Gottes Land.* Göttingen: Vandenhoeck & Ruprecht, 1965. 9–29. **Boer, P. A. H. de.** "Some Remarks on Exodus xxi. 7–11." *Orientalia Neerlandica.* Leiden: E. J. Brill, 1948. 162–66. **Brichto, H. C.** *The Problem of "Curse" in the Hebrew Bible.* JBLMS 13. Philadelphia: Society of Biblical Literature and Exegesis, 1963. **Brockington, L. H.** *The Hebrew Text of the Old Testament: The Readings Adopted by the Translators of the New English Bible.* Oxford and Cambridge: Oxford and Cambridge University Presses, 1973. **Carmichael, C. M.** "A Singular Method of Codification of Law in the *Mishpatim.*" *ZAW* 84 (1972) 19–25. **Cazelles, H.** *Études sur le code de l'alliance.* Paris: Letouzey et Ané, 1946. **Conrad, D.** *Studien zum Altargesetz: Ex 20:24–26.* Marburg Dissertation, 1968. **Daube, D.** *Studies in Biblical Law.* New York: KTAV Publishing House, 1969. **David, M.** "The Codex Hammurabi and Its Relation to the Provisions of Law in Exodus." *OTS* 7 (1950) 149–78. **Déaut, R. le.** "Critique textuelle et exégèse—*Exode XXII 12 dans la Septante et le Targum.*" *VT* 22 (1972) 164–75. **Diamond, A. S.** "An Eye for an Eye." *Iraq* 19 (1957) 151–55. **Driver, G. R.** *Canaanite Myths and Legends.* Edinburgh: T. & T. Clark, 1956. ———. "Linguistic and Textual Problems: Jeremiah." *JQR* 28 (1937–1938) 97–129. **Driver, G. R.** and **J. C. Miles.** *The Babylonian Laws.* 2 vols. Oxford: Clarendon Press, 1952. **Falk, Z. W.** "Exodus xxi 6." *VT* 9 (1959) 86–88. ———. *Hebrew Law in Biblical Times.* Jerusalem: Wahrmann Books, 1964. **Fensham, F. C.** "Clauses of Protection in Hittite Vassal-Treaties and the Old Testament." *VT* 13 (1963) 133–43. ———. "Exodus xxi 18–19 in the Light of Hittite Law ¶ 10." *VT* (1960) 333–35. ———. "New Light on Exodus 21:6 and 22:7 from the Laws of Eshnunna." *JBL* 78 (1959) 160–61. ———. "'D in Exodus 22:12.'" *VT* 12 (1962) 337–39. ———. "The Rôle of the Lord in the Legal Sections of the Covenant Code." *VT* 26 (1976) 262–74. **Finkelstein, J. J.** "Ammi-ṣaduga's Edict and the Babylonian 'Law Codes.'" *JCS* 15 (1961) 91–104. ———. "Sex Offences in Sumerian Laws." *JAOS* 86 (1966) 355–72. **Frey, H.** "Das Ineinander von Kirche und Welt im Licht der Komposition des Bundesbuchs." *Wort und Dienst* 1 (1948) 13–35. **Friedrich, J.** *Die hethitischen Gesetze.* Leiden: E. J. Brill, 1959. **Gaster, T. H.** *Myth, Legend, and Custom in the Old Testament.* New York: Harper & Row, 1969.

Gilmer, H. W. *The If-You Form in Israelite Law.* SBLDS 15. Missoula, MT: Scholars Press, 1975. **Gordon, C. H.** "אלהים in Its Reputed Meaning of 'Rulers, Judges.'" *JBL* 54 (1935) 139–44. **Greenberg, M.** "Some Postulates of Biblical Law." *Yehezkel Kaufmann Jubilee Volume.* M. Haran, ed. Jerusalem: Magnes Press, 1960. 5–28. ———. "The Biblical Conception of Asylum." *JBL* 78 (1959) 125–32. **Halbe, J.** *Das Privilegrecht Jahwes, Ex 34, 10–26. Gestalt und Wesen, Herkunft und Wirken in vordeuteronomischer Zeit.* FRLANT 114. Göttingen: Vandenhoeck and Ruprecht, 1975. **Henrey, K. H.** "Land Tenure in the Old Testament." *PEQ* 86 (1954) 5–15. **Hoftijzer, J.** "Ex. xii 8." *VT* 7 (1957) 388–91. **Horst, F.** "Der Eid im Alten Testament." *Gottes Recht.* TBü 12. Munich: Chr. Kaiser Verlag, 1961. 292–324. Also in *EvT* 17 (1957) 366–84. **Humbert, P.** "Les adjectifs 'zâr' et 'nôkri' et la 'femme étrangère' des proverbes bibliques." *Mélanges Syriens offerts à Monsieur René Dussaud,* vol. 1. Paris: Librairie Orientaliste Paul Geuthner, 1939. 259–66. **Jackson, B. S.** "The Problem of Ex. xxi 22–25 (*Ius Talionis*)." *VT* 23 (1973) 273–304. **Jepsen, A.** *Untersuchungen zum Bundesbuch.* BWANT 41. Stuttgart: W. Kohlhammer Verlag, 1927. **Kapelrud, A. S.** *Baal in the Ras Shamra Texts.* Copenhagen: G. E. C. Gad-Publisher, 1952. **Köhler, L.** "Hebräische Vocabeln I." *ZAW* 54 (1936) 287–93. ———. *Hebrew Man.* New York: Abingdon Press, 1946. **König, E.** "Stimmen Ex 20:24 und Dtn 12:13f. zusammen?" *ZAW* 42 (1924) 337–46. **Kosmala, H.** "The So-Called Ritual Decalogue." *ASTI* 1 (1962) 31–61. **Kraus, H.-J.** *Worship in Israel.* Richmond: John Knox Press, 1966. **Lehmann, M. R.** "Biblical Oaths." *ZAW* 81 (1969) 74–92. **Lewy, I.** "Dating of Covenant Code Sections on Humaneness and Righteousness." *VT* 7 (1959) 322–26. **Lewy, J.** "Origin and Significance of the Biblical Term 'Hebrew.'" *HUCA* 28 (1957) 1–13. **Loewenstamm, S. E.** "Exodus xxi 22–25." *VT* 27 (1977) 352–60. **Loretz, O.** "Ex 21,6; 22,8 und angebliche Nuzi-Parallelen." *Bib* 41 (1960) 167–75. **McKay, J. W.** "Exodus xxiii 1–3, 6–8: A Decalogue for the Administration of Justice in the City Gate." *VT* 21 (1971) 311–25. **Mendelsohn, I.** "The Conditional Sale into Slavery of Freeborn Daughters in Nuzi and the Law of Ex 21:7–11." *JAOS* 55 (1935) 190–95. **Morgenstern, J.** "The Book of the Covenant." *HUCA* 5 (1928): 1–151 (pt. 1); 7 (1930): 19–258 (pt. 2); 8–9 (1931–1932): 1–150 (pt. 3); 33 (1962) 59–105 (pt. 4). **Neufeld, E.** "The Prohibitions Against Loans at Interest in Ancient Hebrew Laws." *HUCA* 26 (1955) 355–412. **North, R.** "Flesh, Covering, and Response, Ex. xxi 10." *VT* 5 (1955) 204–6. ———. "Separated Spiritual Substances in the Old Testament." *CBQ* 29 (1967) 419–49. ———. "The Derivation of Sabbath." *Bib* 36 (1955) 182–201. **Noth, M.** *The Old Testament World.* London: Adam and Charles Black, 1966. **Patrick, D.** "The Covenant Code Source." *VT* 27 (1977) 145–57. **Paul, S. M.** *Studies in the Book of the Covenant in the Light of Cuneiform and Biblical Law.* VTSup 18. Leiden: E. J. Brill, 1970. **Pfeiffer, R. H.** "The Transmission of the Book of the Covenant." *HTR* 24 (1931) 99–109. **Ploeg, J. van der.** "Šāpaṭ et Mišpāt." *OTS* 2 (1943) 144–55. **Rabinowitz, J. J.** "Exodus xxii 4 and the Septuagint Version Thereof." *VT* 9 (1959) 40–46. **Radin, M.** "The Kid and Its Mother's Milk." *AJSL* 40 (1923–1924) 209–18. **Rendtorff, R.** *Studien zur Geschichte des Opfers im Alten Israel.* WMANT 24. Neukirchen-Vluyn: Neukirchener Verlag, 1967. **Robertson, E.** "The Altar of Earth (Exodus XX, 24–26)." *JSS* 1 (1948–1949) 12–21. **Robinson, G.** "The Idea of Rest in the Old Testament and the Search for the Basic Character of Sabbath." *ZAW* 92 (1980) 32–42. **Scharbert, J.** " 'Fluchen' und 'Segnen' im Alten Testament." *Bib* 39 (1958) 1–26. **Snijders, L. A.** "The Meaning of זר in the Old Testament." *OTS* 10 (1954) 1–154. **Speiser, E. A.** "Background and Function of the Biblical Nāśī'." *CBQ* 25 (1963) 111–17. ———. "The Stem PLL in Hebrew." *JBL* 82 (1963) 301–6. **Talmon, S.** "The Gezer Calendar and the Seasonal Cycle of Ancient Canaan." *JAOS* 83 (1963) 177–87. **Wagner, V.** "Zur Systematik in dem Codex Ex 21:2—22:16." *ZAW* 81 (1969) 178–82.

Translation

²² *So Yahweh said to Moses, "Here is what you are to say to the sons of Israel: 'You yourselves* ª *have seen that from the heavens I have spoken with you.* ²³ *You must* ª *not make rivals* ᵇ *with me: gods of silver and gods of gold you are not to make for yourselves.* ²⁴ *An altar of earth you are to make for me, and you are to offer* ª *upon it your wholly-burned offerings, your completion-offerings,* ᵇ *your flock-animals and your herd-animals. In every place* ᶜ *in which I cause my name to be remembered, I will come to you, and I will bless you.* ²⁵ *If you make me an altar of stones, you are not to build it of cut stone; when you dress the stone* ª *with your cutting-tool, you render it unfit for holy use.* ²⁶ *And you are not to go up stairs against my altar, so that you will not expose your genitals upon it.'* ª*

²¹:¹ *"These are the guiding decisions* ª *that you are to establish in their presence:* ² *'When you acquire a Hebrew slave, six years he is to serve;* ª *in the seventh, he is to go out a free man, without payment to you.* ³ *If he comes by himself, he is to go out by himself; if he is husband of a wife, his wife shall go out with him.* ⁴ *If his owner* ª *gives him a wife, and she presents him sons or daughters, the wife and her children belong to her* ᵇ *owner, and the slave* ᶜ *is to go out by himself.* ⁵ *If, however, the slave says earnestly, "I love my owner, my wife, and my sons* ª*—I will not go out free,"* ⁶ *his owner is to bring him near to God,* ª *and bring him near to the door or to the door-post; there his owner is to pierce his ear with the piercing-tool: then he shall serve him without release.* ᵇ*

⁷ *" 'When a man sells his daughter into slavery, she is not to go out as the male slaves go out.* ⁸ *If she is unsatisfactory in the opinion of her owner, who has set her apart for himself,* ª *he is to permit her to be bought free. He has no right to sell her to a strange family,* ᵇ *because he has severed his relationship with her.* ⁹ *If he sets her apart for his son, he is to treat her as he would treat daughters.* ª ¹⁰ *If he takes for himself another woman,* ª *he is not to cut back on her right to food, her right to clothes, or her right to intercourse.* ᵇ ¹¹ *If he does not provide for her these three rights, she is to go out a free woman, without any payment of money.*

¹² *" 'One who strikes a man a fatal blow is certainly to be put to death,* ¹³ *unless he did not pre-plan the blow,* ª *and God allowed him into his power: then I will establish for you a place to which he may escape.* ¹⁴ *But when a man has seethed with contempt* ª *against his neighbor, to kill him by crafty plotting, you are to take him from the place of my altar, for execution.*

¹⁵ *" 'One who strikes his father or his mother is certainly to be put to death.* ¹⁶ *One who abducts a man and sells him or is found confining him* ª *is certainly to be put to death.* ¹⁷ *One who curses his father or his mother is certainly to be put to death.*

¹⁸ *" 'When men are struggling furiously,* ª *and one of them strikes his fellow with a stone or a tool,* ᵇ *so that he does not die but is confined to his bed,* ¹⁹ *if he can rise and walk about outside leaning on his staff, the one who struck is to be exempt from punishment, except that he is to take responsibility for his victim's incapacity* ª *and for his complete recovery.* ²⁰ *When a man strikes his male slave or his female slave with a stick* ª *and the slave dies from the beating,* ᵇ *he is certainly to suffer the punishment for it,* ᶜ ²¹ *though if for a day or two days the slave lives, he is not to suffer punishment,* ª *because the slave is his capital investment.* ᵇ*

²² " 'When men are scuffling with each other, and they hit a pregnant woman, resulting in the premature birth of her children, ª but without harm, ᵇ the man who struck the blow ᶜ is certainly to pay damages in the amount fixed against him by the husband of the woman: he is to give in accord with an objective evaluation. ᵈ ²³ If, however, there is harm, he is to give life in place of life, ²⁴ eye in place of eye, tooth in place of tooth, hand in place of hand, foot in place of foot, ²⁵ burning in place of burning, ª bruise in place of bruise, wale in place of wale. ²⁶ When a man strikes the eye of his male slave or the eye of his female slave and blinds it, he shall send out the slave free, in place of his eye. ²⁷ If he knocks out the tooth of his male slave or the tooth of his female slave, he shall send out that slave free in place of his tooth.

²⁸ " 'When a bull ª gores ᵇ a man or a woman fatally the bull is certainly to be stoned to death, and his flesh is not to be eaten; the bull's owner is exempt from punishment. ²⁹ If, however, the bull is habitually belligerent, ª and its owner has been plainly warned and yet has not confined ᵇ it and it kills a man or a woman, the bull is to be stoned to death, and its owner also is to be put to death. ³⁰ If an indemnity has been set for him, he is to give the indemnity-payment for his life, in the full amount set for him. ³¹ Even if a bull ª gores a son or gores a daughter, this same guiding decision is applied to him. ³² If the bull gores a male slave or a female slave, he is to give the slave-owner thirty shekels of silver, and the bull is to be stoned.

³³ " 'When a man opens a pit, or digs a pit and does not cover it over, and a bull or an ass ª falls into it, ³⁴ the owner of the pit is to give compensation: he is to give money in payment to the animal's owner, and the dead animal is to be his. ³⁵ When a man's bull ª attacks his neighbor's bull ª and it dies, they are to sell the surviving bull and halve the money; they are also to halve ᵇ the dead animal. ³⁶ If, however, the bull is known from experience to be habitually belligerent, and its owner has not confined ª it, he is certainly to give compensation: a bull for the bull killed; the dead animal is to belong to him. ³⁷ [22:1] When a man steals a bull or a flock-animal and butchers· it or sells it, he is to give the compensation of five herd-animals in place of the bull, and four flock-animals in place of the one flock-animal. ª

22:1 [2] " 'If the thief is discovered in the act of breaking and entering and is struck a fatal blow, there is no guilt of bloodshed for him ² [3] unless the sun has risen upon him: then there is guilt of bloodshed for him.

" 'He is certainly to give compensation: if he has nothing, he is to be sold to compensate for what he has stolen. ³ [4] If the stolen animal is actually found in his possession alive, whether it is a bull, an ass, or a flock-animal, he is to give double compensation.

⁴ [5] " 'When a man allows a field or a vineyard to be eaten over, ª or lets his cattle out and they eat over the field of another, ᵇ he is to give compensation from the best crop of his own field and from the best fruit of his own vineyard. ⁵ [6] When a fire gets out and sets aflame the stubble of a mown field ª and destroys stacked sheaves or the standing grain or the entire crop, ᵇ the one who caused the burning is certainly to give compensation.

⁶ [7] " 'When a man gives his neighbor money or anything valuable for safekeeping and it is stolen from the man's house, if the thief is caught, he shall give double compensation. ⁷ [8] If the thief is not caught, the owner of the house is to be brought into the Presence of God, ª to determine whether he has reached out his own hand to

his neighbor's property. [8] [9] *For every report of transgression, whether it involves a bull, an ass, a flock-animal, a garment, or any missing thing about which someone says, "This is it," the report of both parties involved is to come to God.* [a] *The one whom* [b] *God blames as guilty is to give double compensation to his neighbor.*

[9] [10] " *'When a man gives his neighbor an ass or a bull or a flock-animal or* [a] *any animal for safekeeping and it dies or is maimed or is carried away, and there is no witness,* [10] [11] *an oath in Yahweh's Presence* [a] *is to be between the two of them whether either reached out his hand to his neighbor's property: and the owner of the animal* [b] *is to be content with the oath* [c] *and the man* [b] *is to give no compensation.* [11] [12] *If the animal* [a] *has certainly been stolen from him, he is to give compensation to its owner.* [12] [13] *If it has plainly been mauled by predators,* [a] *he is to bring it as evidence:* [b] *for the mauled animal, he is not to give compensation.* [13] [14] *When a man asks a loan from his neighbor, and the borrowed animal* [a] *is maimed or dies* [b] *in the absence of his neighbor, he is certainly to give compensation,* [14] [15] *though if its owner was with it, he is not to give compensation. If it was hired, the loss is the owner's risk.* [a]

[15] [16] " *'When a man seduces a virgin maid who is not engaged to be married and has intercourse with her, he is to pay the marriage price for her and take her for himself as a wife.* [16] [17] *If her father is adamant in his refusal to give her to him, he is to pay a sum equal to the marriage price of virgin maidens.*

[17] [18] " *'A sorceress is not to be allowed to live.* [18] [19] *Anyone who couples with an animal is certainly to be put to death.* [19] [20] *One who sacrifices to the gods* [a] *is to be destroyed under ban (except to Yahweh by himself alone).* [b]

[20] [21] " *'You are not to maltreat a newcomer, nor are you to oppress him, because you were newcomers in the land of Egypt.* [21] [22] *You must not take advantage of* [a] *any widow, or an orphan.* [22] [23] *If you do take advantage of such a person,* [a] *if he cries out in distress to me, I will certainly hear his cry to me,* [23] [24] *and I will be furious,* [a] *and I will kill you with a sword, so that your wives will be widows and your sons will be orphans.*

[24] [25] " *'If you cause my people* [a] *to borrow money, the poor among you, you are not to relate to them as a money-lender; you* [b] *must not set interest for them to pay.* [c] [25] [26] *If you actually take as collateral your neighbor's coat until the sun goes down, you must return it to him then,* [26] [27] *because it is his sole covering—it is his coat for his bare skin: in what else is he to sleep? So it will be when he cries out to me that I will pay attention, for I am compassionate.*

[27] [28] " *'You are not to show disrespect for* [a] *God, and you are not to curse a leader of your people.* [28] [29] *You are not to hold back your bumper crop and your vintage wine and richest oil.* [a] *You are to give me the firstborn of your sons.* [29] [30] *You are to do the same with your bull and your flock-animal:* [a] *seven days it is to remain with its mother; on the eighth day you are to give it to me.* [30] [31] *You must be men set apart for me; so you are not to eat meat torn by predators in the field. You are to throw it out to the dog.* [a]

23:1 " *'You are not to pass on* [a] *a report without foundation. You are not to lend your influence to a wicked man, to sustain a wrong testimony.* [b] [2] *You are not to follow the crowd into wickedness. You are not to give testimony in a contested matter that confirms a distorted account of the crowd.* [a] [3] *You are not to give an unfair advantage* [a] *to the poor in a contested matter.*

[4] " *'When you chance to meet the bull of your enemy, or his ass* [a] *wandering loose, you must* [b] *return it to him.* [5] *When you see the ass of one who hates you lying*

down under its load, you are by no means to leave it there: you must^a *help him rearrange the load.* ^b

6 " 'You are not to manipulate the case-decision given to your needy in his contested matter. ⁷ Have nothing to do with ^a a lying complaint. Do not ruin ^b the innocent and the righteous, because I ^c will not let the wicked off. ⁸ You are not to accept a bribe, because the bribe blinds ^a people with perfect vision and turns the case of the ones who are actually right upside down. ⁹ You are not to oppress a newcomer. You ^a know by experience the life of the newcomer, because you were newcomers in the land of Egypt.*

10 " 'Six years you are to sow your land, and gather in its harvest; ¹¹ the seventh year, you are to rest the land and leave it undisturbed. The needy of your people are to eat its volunteer crop, ^a and their leftovers, the wild animals are to eat. So you are to do also with your vineyard and your olive orchard. ¹² Six days you are to do your work, and on the seventh day you are to rest, in order that your bull ^a and your ass may be at rest, and that the son of your female slave and the newcomer may catch their breath. ^b*

13 " 'With regard to everything I have said to you, you are to be on your guard. You are not to bring to mind the name of any other gods; such is not to be heard from your mouth.*

14 " 'Three times in the year, you are to keep a sacred feast to me. ¹⁵ You are to keep the sacred feast of unleavened bread cakes: for seven days you are to eat unleavened bread cakes, just as I instructed you, at the set time in the month of the green grain; because in that month, you went out from Egypt. You are not to appear in my Presence without an offering. ¹⁶ You are to keep the sacred feast of the early crop-harvest, the firstfruits of your work, that you have sown in the field. You are to keep the sacred feast of the ingathering harvest at the end of the year when you gather in your work from the field. ¹⁷ Three times in the year all your males are to appear in the Presence of the Lord, ^a Yahweh.*

18 " 'You are not to combine with anything leavened ^a the blood of my sacrifice. The fat of my sacred feast is not to be kept through the night until morning. ¹⁹ The very first of the first-fruits of your ground you are to bring to the house of Yahweh your God. You are not to cook a kid in the milk of its mother. ^a*

20 " 'See, I am sending out a messenger ^a in front of you to look after you on the way and to bring you to the place ^b which I have made ready. ²¹ Pay close attention in his Presence ^a and listen to his voice. You are not to resent ^b him, because he will not let your transgressions pass—for my Presence ^c is with him. ²² If you pay careful attention to his ^a voice and do everything I say, then I will treat your enemies as my enemies and I will show hostility toward those who are hostile to you. ²³ When my messenger goes in front of you and brings you to the Amorites and the Hittites and the Perizzites and the Canaanites ^a and the Hivites and the Jebusites and I destroy them utterly, ²⁴ you are not to worship their gods, you are not to serve them, and you are not to do their will: instead you are to throw them down completely, and you are to shatter into bits their sacred pillars.*

25 " 'You are to serve Yahweh your God, and he ^a will bless your bread ^b and your water. I will remove sickness from your midst. ^c ²⁶ No woman ^a will miscarry ^b or be barren in your land, and I will guarantee the full measure of your days. ²⁷ I will send out in front of you my dreading-fear, and I will plunge into disarray all the people you come up against and present you with the back of all your enemies'*

necks [28] *and send out in front of you the panic-terror so it will drive headlong before you the Hivites,* [a] *the Canaanites, and the Hittites.* [29] *I will not drive them headlong before you in a single year, lest the land become a wasteland and the wild animals outnumber you.* [30] *Gradually I will drive them headlong before you, until you shall have become numerous and occupy the land as your possession.* [31] *I will fix your borders, from the "sea of rushes" to the "sea of the Philistines," and from the wilderness to the River, when I give into your power those* [a] *who dwell in the land and you drive them headlong before you.* [32] *You are not to covenant with them or with their gods.* [33] *They are not to dwell in your land, else they may cause you to sin against me: when you serve their gods, that* [a] *will entrap you.'* "

Notes

22.a. The phrase is identical to the beginning of 19:4; see n. 19:4.a.

23.a. תַּעֲשׂוּן "you must make" with "paragogic *nun*"; see GKC ¶ 47*m*, and n. 4:15.b. above.

23.b. The lit. reading לֹא תַעֲשׂוּן אִתִּי is "you must not make with/beside me." MT marks the major pause in the sentence with אִתִּי "with me," a division ignored by some translators (e.g., RSV, NEB), who move forward an object from the second half of the sentence. As Davies (173) says, however, אִתִּי is parallel to the עַל־פָּנַי "in my presence" of 20:3, and the division of MT (followed also by SamPent) is better taken at face value. The meaning clearly is that Israel is not to set up rivals to Yahweh, making him by forbidden iconography something he is not. For clarity, the word "rivals" is added above. Cf. Barthélemy, *Preliminary and Interim Report*, 116–17, and, *contra*, Childs, 446–47; Cazelles (*Code de l'alliance*, 39–40), after a careful review of alternatives, concludes that אִתִּי is the key to a correct reading of the verse, and notes, "Elle désigne alors une simple relation. Il faut donc traduire: 'En ce qui me concerne, à mon sujet,' autrement dit: 'Dans mon culte.' " ["It thus designates a simple correction. It is necessary therefore to translate: 'In that which concerns me, in my sphere,' or in other words: 'in my cult.' "]

24.a. זֶבַח, lit., "slaughter for sacrifice," comes to mean "sacrifice," and more generally still, as here, "offer."

24.b. שְׁלָמִים were "promised offerings," made in fulfillment of a vow to Yahweh; see Rendtorff (*Geschichte des Opfers*, 123–33), " 'Schlussopfer' oder 'Abschlussopfer'."

24.c. SamPent has במקום "in the place" instead of בכל המקום "in every place."

25.a. נוּף "move to and fro," here of the motion of a chisel over native stone; "the stone" is added above for clarity. Cf. BDB, 631–32.

26.a. SamPent reads אליו "to it."

21:1.a. הַמִּשְׁפָּטִים "guiding decisions"; see van der Ploeg, *OTS* 2 [1943] 151–55, who describes the range of meaning of מִשְׁפָּט as extending from "judgment" to "custom" to "right" and even to "religion."

2.a. SamPent, LXX, Vg add "you."

4.a. אֲדֹנָיו "his lord, master"; see BDB, 10–11.

4.b. SamPent, LXX, Vg read "his."

4.c. וְהוּא "and he," of which the slave is the clear antecedent.

5.a. בָּנַי here is generally read "children" (see BDB, 121 § 2), but there is no clear reason it should be; v 4, which mentions "sons and daughters," uses the more appropriate יְלָדִים for "children"; the same term might be expected here if "children" were intended.

6.a. LXX reads πρὸς τὸ κριτήριον τοῦ θεοῦ "to the place of God's decision."

6.b. לְעֹלָם "forever," i.e., as long as the slave lives.

8.a. L notes a Q here, לֹו "to him" for the לֹא "not" of the text; that reading is followed above. If K is taken, the owner does *not* designate the girl for himself because she has proven unsatisfactory. The difficulty of that reading led NEB to emend יְעָדָהּ "to set apart" to יְדָעָהּ "know" following the reading of the Peshiṭta (Brockington, *Hebrew Text*, 11), and thus to the translation "If her master has not had intercourse with her. . . ." Hoftijzer *VT* 7 [1957] 388–91) has suggested that the text be taken as it stands and translated "who is not taking the decision about her to let her be redeemed," i.e., by her own family. Hoftijzer has not, however, demonstrated his case, particularly in the light of the provisions that follow. The L text with its Masoretic Q correction of לא to לו makes better sense. Cf. LXX, Vg.

8.b. עם נכרי, lit., "a foreign people," indicates here a family outside the circle of the girl's biological family, outside the circle of her family by purchase, and perhaps even outside the covenant community of Israel. Cf. Humbert, *Mélanges* 1: 262–63; de Boer, *Orientalia*, 162; Snijders, *OTS* 10 (1954) 66; Hoftijzer, *VT* 7 (1957) 390–91; Cazelles, *Code de l'alliance*, 48–49.

9.a. כמשפט הבנות, lit., "according to the right of the daughters."

10.a. אֲחֶרֶת "another" (fem).

10.b. North (*VT* 5 [1955] 204–6) has suggested that each of the three rights, expressed by "the unusual words" שאר "flesh," כסות "covering, clothing," and ענה "cohabitation," refers to the wife's marital rights: "her physical satisfaction, her honorable standing in the harem [harem—'protection' or 'accommodation' from כסות as 'covering'] or her right of parenthood." The first two terms are probably more generally intended, but the third does appear to refer to the woman's right to have her sexual needs met; cf. BDB, 773, and KB, 720. LXX has τὴν ὁμιλίαν, a term used in classical Greek of sexual intercourse (LSJ, 1222).

13.a. לא צדה "he did not lie in ambush."

14.a. זיד "boil up, seethe, act presumptuously" is used also of the Egyptian gods, acting with insolent attitude toward Israel, and so toward Yahweh; see n. 18:11.a; BDB, 267.

16.a. ונמצא בידו "or he is found in his power."

18.a. ריב "struggle" plus paragogic *nun;* see n. 20:23.a.

18.b. אגרף is apparently from גרף "sweep, scoop away" (BDB, 175). The term occurs only here and in Isa 58:4, and though it is generally read "fist" (cf. Cassuto, 272), there is no good reason why some kind of tool may not be intended. Such a reading fits both the context and the apparent etymology better: see KB, 10. Cazelles (*Code de l'alliance,* 53) favors a more general sense, *poing:* "force." SamPent omits "with a stone or a tool."

19.a. שבתו יתן "his time off he is to give." "Victims" is added for clarity. Fensham (*VT* 10 [1960] 333–35), following Hittite parallels, proposes by some reconstruction "but he shall provide someone in his place." The effect being the same, the reconstruction is neither necessary nor justified.

20.a. SamPent omits "with a stick."

20.b. תחת ידו "under his power," i.e., under the owner's abuse while remaining a responsibility of the owner.

20.c. SamPent has מות יומת "he is certainly to be put to death."

21.a. SamPent reads יומת "to be put to death."

21.b. כספו "his money."

22.a. ויצאו ילדיה "and her children go out, are born"; see BDB, 423. Premature labor and birth as a result of accidental blow are clearly the point here; the question of the survival of the child or children is ambiguous, though the context, which makes allowance even for bruises and wales, must surely imply penalty also for the loss of, or injury to, the child or children being carried by the woman (cf. Jackson, *VT* 23 [1973] 291–93; Cassuto, 275). Cf. LXX, SamPent.

22.b. אסון occurs only 5x in the OT: here and in the next verse and 3x in reference to the "harm" Jacob fears may befall his youngest son, Benjamin. The term thus seems to imply either death or serious injury. BDB (61–62) derive it from אסה, having to do with sorrow, and Jackson (*VT* 23 [1973] 274–77, 290–93, 302) argues that the term means "calamity" to "some person other than the direct victim" and therefore refers in this verse to the fetus.

22.c. MT has simply ענוש יענש "he is certainly to pay damages," but the reference is clearly to the one who inflicted the blow.

22.d. ונתן בפללים "he is to give in accord with an objective evaluation." Speiser (*JBL* 82 [1963] 301–6) has suggested the meaning "to assess, reckon," for פלל, and "estimate, assessment, calculation" for פללים, in part on the basis of a Hittite parallel fixing sums of money and the attachment of property as restitution in such cases. Cf. ANET, 190 § 17.

25.a. SamPent has מכוה "burn-mark, blister" instead of כויה "burning."

28.a. SamPent adds או כל בהמה "or any animal."

28.b. SamPent has יכה "strikes."

29.a. נגח הוא מתמל שלשם "he is a gorer for some time back."

29.b. LXX has ἀφανίσῃ "destroyed."

31.a. MT has only "he"; the antecedent is clear, however, and so has been added above.

33.a. See n. 28.a above.

35.a. See n. 28.a above.

35.b. The emphasis is indicated by *nun paragogicum*, perhaps because inequity in the division of the bull's carcass was a common abuse.

36.a. See n. 29.b above.

37.a. The instruction of this verse is continued by 22:2b–3 [3b–4]; 22:1–2a [2a–3] appears to have been inserted into the sequence at an inappropriate place. Some translators (so RSV, NEB) rearrange the text, to present a more logical sequence. Cassuto (281–83) suggests that the order of MT is intentional, with vv 1–2a [2–3a] serving as "directives" called for by the beginning of the laws dealing with theft. (Cf. also Cazelles, *Code de l'alliance*, 63).

22:4 [5].a. בער means "burn, consume" so as to devastate, even to destroy (BDB, 128–29). The problem addressed here is not a simple grazing of a planted crop or a vineyard, but the destruction of a crop or a season's grape harvest through the negligence of allowing animals to roam freely.

4 [5].b. LXX expands the verse considerably, as does SamPent (see also 4Q158: 10–12, DJD V), but without changing its basic meaning.

5 [6].a. ומצאה קצים "and finds thorns." קוֹץ is probably from a root that means "cut off" (BDB, 881) and so "sharp, spikey." In this verse the reference is to the sharp stubble left in the field after the ripe grain has been cut. It is, along with the weeds and dry grass surrounding it, highly inflammable.

5 [6].b. השׂדה "the field."

7 [8].a. קרב + אל־האלהים "come near to God" always suggests in the OT coming near to a place of God's Presence, usually, as here, for some cultic purpose. Cf. Durham, *Touch, Taste and Smell*, 111–13, and Fensham, *VT* 26 (1976) 263–66, 271. LXX adds "and is to affirm by oath."

8 [9].a. SamPent has "Yahweh."

8 [9].b. MT has יַרְשִׁיעֻן "they must blame as guilty," a 3d masc pl hiph impf with *nun paragogicum*. SamPent has ירשיענו "he blames him as guilty," a 3d masc sg hiph impf plus the 3d masc sg pronom suff. MT's form is noted as *hapax legomenon* by the *Masora parva*, and LXX also reads the verb as a sg.

9 [10].a. SamPent has או כל "or any" instead of MT's וכל "and any"; cf. LXX.

10 [11].a. שבעת יהוה "the oath of Yahweh" refers to the solemn oath, sometimes involving a self-curse, sworn in Yahweh's Presence. No more serious and consequential an oath was possible. Cf. Horst, *Gottes Recht*, 294–97; Lehman, *ZAW* 81 (1969) 86–91.

10 [11].b. MT has only the pronoun; the antecedent is supplied for clarity.

10 [11].c. ולקח "and he is to take"; BDB (543 § 4.f) translates "*receive, accept* . . . shall accept the oath as satisfactory."

11 [12].a. See n. 10.b above.

12 [13].a. טרף יטרף "plainly been mauled."

12 [13].b. LXX (cf. Tg Ps-J, Vg) reads, instead of MT עֵד "witness," the prep עַד "to," implying the bringing of the owner to the mauled animal, rather than *vice versa*. See the detailed discussions of Fensham, *VT* 12 (1962) 337–39, and Le Déaut, *VT* 22 (1972) 164–75.

13 [14].a. See n. 10.b. above.

13 [14].b. LXX adds ἢ αἰχμάλωτον "or is taken away."

14 [15].a. בא בשכרו "it comes in his rental fee."

19 [20].a. לאלהים "to the gods," to which SamPent adds אחרים "other"; so also LXXᴬ. See Cassuto (*Genesis I* [Jerusalem: Magnes Press, 1961] 166–67) for a detailed discussion of the pointing of the preps before אלהים.

19 [20].b. This final phrase, awkwardly placed in MT and absent altogether from SamPent, appears to be a qualifying addition. See Cazelles, *Code de l'alliance*, 76–77, and *Comment* below.

21 [22].a. Piel of ענה "afflict, humble, bow down, weaken" + *nun paragogicum*.

22 [23].a. MT has אתו "him"; the Versions generally have a pl, in agreement with the apparent double antecedent.

23 [24].a. חרה אפי "and it will kindle my anger," an OT idiom for intense divine anger.

24 [25].a. LXX has τῷ ἀδελφῷ "the brother."

24 [25].b. MT has תשימון "you (pl) must set"; LXX, Syr, Vg have a sg verb.

24 [25].c. עליו נשׁך "upon him interest." "People" and "poor" are taken here as collective terms, and so the sg pronom suffs (לו and עליו) are read as pls, "them."

27 [28].a. Brichto (*Problem of "Curse,"* 150–65, 176–77) has demonstrated that piel of קלל in reference to אלהים "God" refers not to blasphemy, but to "the lack of fear or respect for the ethical standards which the Deity expects of man."

28 [29].a. מלאה and דמע are, lit., the "fullness" and the "dripping" of the crops of field, vineyard, and olive grove.

29 [30].a. LXX adds καὶ τὸ ὑποζύγιόν σου "and your beast of burden."

30 [31].a. SamPent has השלך, hiph inf abs of שלך "throw" instead of לכלב "to the dog" and omits paragogic *nun* from the verb.

23:1.a. The idiom, נשא "lift up" plus שוא "vain nothingness" is the one employed in the third commandment, Exod 20:7. See nn. 20:7.a,b, and *Comment* above.

1.b. Lit., "You are not to set your hand with a wicked man to be a witness to wrong." יד "hand" is read above in its connotation of "power" = "influence."

2.a. There is a play on the verb נטה "stretch out, bend, incline, even accommodate to" (cf. BDB, 639–41). לנטת אחרי רבים להטת is "to bend after many to cause bending."

3.a. הדר is "swell up, adorn, honor," even by exaggeration, and hence in this case to give an unjust edge to a poor man in a legal proceeding. This instruction calls for an impartiality so remarkable that some critics (*BHS*) propose an emendation of MT's ודל "and poor" to גדל "great" or even (*HALAT*, 213) to דל וגדול "poor and great" with reference to Lev 19:15. There is no satisfactory justification for such alteration of this text.

4.a. See n. 21:28.a.

4.b. This special emphasis is indicated by the inf abs preceding the verb.

5.a. See n. 4.b.

5.b. There appears to be a play on two roots עזב, one meaning "leave off, abandon," used first in the verse, and one meaning "restore, repair," used 2× here for emphasis. See BDB, 736–38; Cassuto, 297–98; and cf. Driver, *JQR* 28 (1937–38) 126. LXX has συνεγερεῖς αὐτὸ "help him lift it"; Vg *sublevabis* "you will lift up."

7.a. מדברשקר תרחק "from a word of lying you are to be distant."

7.b. הרג "kill," used here in its figurative sense, in reference to the conviction through false evidence of the innocent.

7.c. LXX has "and you . . ." and adds ἕνεκεν δώρων "for bribes."

8.a. SamPent, LXX, Tg Ps-J, Tg Onk add "eyes of."

9.a. ואתם ידעתם "and *you* know by experience."

11.a. MT has no object; "its volunteer crop" is clearly implied, however, by שמט "drop, let fall = rest, leave fallow" and נטש "leave alone, forsake = leave uncultivated." The land is to be permitted to produce what it will, without attention, and the poor are to be free to harvest such a "volunteer" crop.

12.a. SamPent reads this sequence differently: עבדך ואמתך כמוך וכל בהמתך "your male slave and your female slave like yourself, along with all your animals."

12.b. Niphal נפש "breathe for oneself = take a break, be refreshed." See BDB, 659, 661.

17.a. SamPent has ארון "ark" instead of MT's האדן "the Lord," both here and at 34:23. LXX reads here κυρίου τοῦ θεοῦ σου "the Lord your God." See Fensham, *VT* 26 (1976) 267.

18.a. לא־תזבח על־חמץ "you are not to combine with anything leavened." LXX has these also the additional words found in MT only in 34:24. On חמץ "that which is leavened" see BDB, 329.

19.a. SamPent adds כי עשה זאת כזבח שכח ועברה היא לאלהי יעקב "for it would make a sacrifice of forgetfulness and would pass along to the God of Jacob."

20.a. SamPent, LXX and Vg have "my messenger."

20.b. LXX reads γῆν "land."

21.a. השמר מפניו "guard yourself or be guarded from his presence." The messenger comes with divine authority, and so is an extension of the Divine Presence. The command has about it a sense of urgent tension, as the end of the verse shows.

21.b. אל־תמר בו, lit., "do not be bitter against him." LXX has μὴ ἀπείθει αὐτῷ "do not disobey him."

21.c. כי שמי בקרבו "for my name is with him"; see *Comment* on 3:13.

22.a. SamPent and LXX have "my voice" (בקולי, ἐμῆς φωνῆς).

23.a. LXX adds here "the Girgashites." SamPent has a different order and also adds "the Girgashites."

25.a. LXX and Vg read "I will bless" (εὐλογήσω, *benedicam*).

25.b. LXX adds καὶ τὸν οἶνόν σου "and your wine."

25.c. LXX has ἀφ᾽ ὑμῶν "from you."

26.a. The subj is indicated by the 3d fem sg form of the verb.

26.b. מְשַׁכֵּלָה, the fem sg piel ptcp of שׁכל "be bereaved," suggests bereavement because of the loss of a child; so "miscarry," a tragedy in some ways even more frustrating than barrenness, listed next in this verse.

28.a. LXX lists first τοὺς Ἀμορραίους "the Amorites" and then follows the same list and sequence as MT.

31.a. Cairo Geniza fragment adds "all" before "those."

33.a. SamPent has יהיו "they will" instead of MT's יהיה "he will." Cf. LXX, Tg Onk.

Form/Structure/Setting

The lengthy collection of laws extending from Exod 20:22 through 23:33, varied in form and reflecting an array of contexts, presents a unity only as a composite made necessary by the setting into which it has been placed. The title ספר הברית "The Book of the Covenant" occurs outside the collection itself, at 24:7, and though that title, along with "all Yahweh's words and all the guiding decisions" in 24:3, is commonly applied to Exod 20:22–23:33, there is no way to determine exactly how much of this collection was suggested by the title at any given point in Israel's history. That the collection expanded with the passage of time and with the emergence of new contexts of need is suggested by the range of application of the laws contained in it, as also by its somewhat layered and often arbitrary organization. The many attempts to find unifying motifs in it, or a logical or a theological sequence, have been generally unconvincing.

Form-critical analysis of the laws in this collection has produced an array of helpful studies which have described both the OT legal forms and the ANE forms to which in many cases the OT laws are quite similar (see Cazelles, *Code de l'alliance*, 147–68). Here again, however, there has been sometimes a tendency to press both the patterns and the contexts from which they are held to have emerged somewhat farther than the OT evidence will justify. With regard to such collections as the one at hand, or the "Holiness Code" of Lev 17–26 or the broad range of laws in Deut 12–26, the search for a single pattern of organization, or for the uniform linking of several patterns, is futile. The success of an array of scholars in pointing out different patterns within the same collections should have shown us long ago that what we have in the legal collections of the OT are compendia, legal anthologies, lists of precedents, the application to every dimension of living of the principles of the covenant with Yahweh. As noted above, (*Form/Structure/Setting* on 20:1–17), the first such applications of the principles of living in covenant with Yahweh may well have been made by Moses and by the "men of ability" appointed by him to aid him in such a task. This is exactly the picture presented by Exod 18:13–26 (see above) and no telling reason has yet been presented why it should not be taken seriously.

The results of form-critical study can thus be taken as illuminative of recurring patterns, wherever they may occur, both within and beyond the OT, but not as necessarily determinative of either context of application or context of origin. A "casuistic" or "apodictic" law, a "when" form or a participial form (Cazelles, *Code de l'alliance*, 103–29, presents a detailed survey) are not in themselves sufficient evidence to fix the situation of a given law or sequence of laws, insofar as application, provenance, development, or origin are concerned. Alt's (*Essays*, 123–32) famous oversimplification of the origin and application of the apodictic form should alone be enough to have convinced us of this fact.

What we must keep in mind as we consider the law-collections of the OT is that they are cumulative in their organization. Their uniformity consists in their single purpose, the explanation and the application to life of the principles laid down by Yahweh for life in covenant with him. The subject of the origin and original provenance of the individual laws and the forms in which they are expressed does not of necessity have a primary bearing on the use of a given law and law-form in a given collection. The laws and the forms in which they are set forth are as varied as the problems that arise whenever life is attempted according to a specific set of standards. With each new problem, a new application of the standards must be made, and that gives rise to another interpretation that can be added, no doubt in successively revised statement, to a steadily growing accumulation of such applications. It may be misleading to think of such a cumulative body of precedent decisions as a "code" of laws, particularly in the somewhat formal and official sense that term implies.

The insights of form-critical study of the "Covenant Code" are best utilized therefore in a nonformal and so nonrestrictive manner, and attempts to subdivide this collection into a series of source codes, each set forth in a single pattern (as Jirku did, *Weltliche Recht*, 32–42), or into a series of five "ten commandment" collections pieced together (so Auerbach, *VT* 16 [1966] 255–65), must be seen as both highly speculative and in any case largely beside the point. What is important about these laws in their present setting is their meaning for Israel in attempting to live in covenant with Yahweh. The characterization of these laws as מִשְׁפָּטִים "judgments" of various kinds (Jepsen, *Bundesbuch*, 55–56, 82–96), as דברים "words," משפטים "judgments," חקים "statutes," and מצות "commandments" (Morgenstern, *HUCA* 7 [1930] 20–34, 56–63; 8–9 [1931–32] 1–150, esp. 140–50), as casuistic and apodictic (Alt, *Essays*, 91–103, 125–32, with a considerable following), as casuistic, participial, unconditional, and conditional specifications, "you will" and "if you" (Cazelles, *Code de l'alliance*, 109–14), as casuistic and "prohibitive" (Gerstenberger, *"Apodiktischen Rechts"* 23–30, 42–54), or as commands, prohibitions, and "If-You formulations" (Gilmer, *If-You Form*, 25–26, 113–15) is instructive as a means of understanding the possible types of OT legal formulary; but these characterizations, all dealing with the same basic material and yet presenting vastly differing possibilities, must not be taken as determinative in the establishment of the meaning and application of the laws preserved in the OT. These laws, whatever their point of origin and their form, must be seen first in the context of their present setting, as specific attempts to focus Yahweh's principles for those who are struggling to bring their living into conformity with Yahweh's covenant.

The same, of course, can be said of the relation of the laws of the OT to their ANE parallels. As instructive as these comparisons inevitably must be (see ANET, 159–223; Cazelles, *Code de l'alliance,* 147–68; Paul, *Book of the Covenant,* 43–105; Boecker, *Law,* 135–75; David, *OTS* 7 [1950] 149–78; Falk, *Hebrew Law,* 73–151; Driver and Miles, *Babylonian Laws, passim,* see references, 2:516), they cannot be permitted to displace the OT laws as uniquely important in their own setting. The very fact that these laws are *in* the OT, and in contexts that link them to Yahweh's expectation of his people, should suffice to make clear their uniqueness in an OT setting, whatever importance they may have elsewhere as well. The chief value of the ANE parallels for the study of the OT laws is the light they may shed upon meaning. The establishment of the dependence of "Mosaic law" upon the laws of Hammurapi, a popular exercise in the first quarter of the twentieth century, is now recognized for the misleading oversimplification it always was and should warn us against an overzealous pressing of ANE collections as source and parallel versions of such OT collections as the "Covenant Code." The theory that some of the laws in the "Covenant Code" were taken by the Israelites from their Canaanite neighbors (Alt, *Essays,* 97–103; Jepsen, *Bundesbuch,* 101; Hyatt, 220–24) remains unsubstantiated (cf. Cazelles, 166–68) because no Canaanite collection of laws has yet been uncovered, though such borrowing is certainly probable. S. M. Paul (esp. 99–105) has plausibly suggested that we should think of the legal material of the Book of Exodus as "an eclectic adaptation of native and fringe Mesopotamian legal traditions" gathered by the Israelites in Canaan, "which probably served as a 'melting pot for cuneiform law.' "

A great deal has been made of the marked difference in form between the first part of the "Covenant Code," with its predominantly casuistic form, and the second part, with its predominantly apodictic form (Beyerlin, *Gottes Wort,* 19–29; Boecker, *Law,* 138–41; Halbe, *Das Privilegrecht Jahwes,* 391–413; Paul, *Book of the Covenant,* 34–45; Wagner, *ZAW* 81 [1969] 176–82). The division between the two halves is usually made between 22:16 [17] and 17 [18], though this division is not universally accepted (Halbe, 418, makes the separation between vv 19 [20] and 20 [21]). 23:20–33 is clearly not a part of the legal collection, and it is often regarded as a kind of "coda" (Paul, 34–36), "epilogue" (Childs, 486–87), collection of "Closing Promises and Exhortations" (Hyatt, 250–52), or "peroration in the manner of Deut 17f. and Lev. 26" (Beyerlin, *Sinaitic Traditions,* 5). Some scholars (e.g., Noth, 192–94; Beyerlin, *Sinaitic Traditions,* 4–5) consider 23:20–33 a Deuteronomistic composite, perhaps based on material from an earlier source or sources (cf. Wellhausen, *Prolegomena,* 28–38; S. R. Driver, xxvii, 247–51; R. H. Pfeiffer, *HTR* 24 [1931] 100–101). Paul (27–42, 101–2) argues that the Decalogue serves as a prologue to the "Covenant Code," 23:20–33 as an epilogue and an integral part of a structure analogous to early Mesopotamian legal compilations. Intriguing though this theory is, it presses the ANE material a bit hard. General correspondence is clear; precise patterns are too much in the eyes of the beholder.

What the "Book of the Covenant" does present is a wide-ranging collection of laws, drawn no doubt from Canaanite-Mesopotamian and perhaps also Egyptian and Hittite and any other available reservoirs, set deliberately into the narrative of Yahweh's Advent and Israel's response at Sinai. Whatever the respective origins of the individual laws, whatever the history of the subcollections and layers that lie behind the collection in its present form, the "Book of the Covenant" must be understood primarily as an integral part of the Sinai narrative of the coming of Yahweh and the birth of Israel (cf. Patrick, *VT* 27 [1977] 145–57). Wherever these laws originated, and whenever, they stand now as an exposition and an application of life lived in relationship with Yahweh. The composite presented by Exodus thus makes an essential point, one that must not be overlooked in the separation of these laws from their setting, either individually or as a collection: these laws are Yahweh's requirements for those who would be his special people. As Paul (*Book of the Covenant*, 36–42; cf. Greenberg, *Y. Kaufmann Jubilee*, 11–12) has correctly pointed out, "the ultimate source and sanction" of this law is Yahweh, and its purpose, as Exod 19:4–6 makes clear, is the formation of "a holy nation."

It is therefore a mistake to consider the "Covenant Code" wholly apart from its setting; or to juggle and relocate the verses reporting Israel's response to Yahweh's theophany (20:18–20) or the verses that close and apply the collection (23:20–33); or to apply the verses that open the account of the solemnization of the covenant with Yahweh (24:1–8) to the Decalogue alone. The "Covenant Code" is Yahweh's application to the context of daily living of the fundamental requirements of those in covenant with him. The range of context to which those requirements obviously apply makes clear the cumulative nature of the collection, as does the hodge-podge arrangement of the individual laws and their expansion into paragraphs. The "Covenant Code" is held together not by a consistent literary form or style, not by the organization of a single compiler or a single historical setting, but by the theological assertion that these laws, as different as they are in form and application and origin, are all Yahweh's, and so are all expected of the people who reckon themselves to be his.

Comment

22   The instruction of Yahweh to Moses, clearly set in place as a means of connecting the "guiding decisions" of the "Book of the Covenant" to the Sinai theophany and hence of course to divine authority, is linked by its opening phrase to the beginning of the "Eagle's Wings" address in 19:4. This emphasis on the theophany as *experienced* by Israel is an important authentication of the instructions as given by Yahweh, in contrast to any that might originate with men. These are not Moses' "guiding decisions," but *Yahweh's*, just as the commandments are the ten words of *Yahweh's* expectation, not Moses' expectation. This attempt to authenticate the laws that interpret and apply the ten commandments is far more important than the reference to Yahweh speaking מִן־הַשָּׁמַיִם "from the heavens," though this phrase has attracted more attention because of the references in chaps. 19 and 20 to Yahweh/Elohim speaking in the vicinity of Mount Sinai. The contrast is more supposed than real, however. Yahweh/Elohim is not said to speak *from* the mountain, and Deut 4, which makes repeated reference (Deut 4:12, 15, 33; cf. also 5:4, 22, 24, 26) to Yahweh speaking מִתּוֹךְ הָאֵשׁ "from the middle of the fire," refers in a single verse (4:36) to Yahweh causing Israel to hear his voice מִן־הַשָּׁמַיִם "from the heavens" and to Israel seeing "his great fire upon the earth" and hearing his words הָאֵשׁ מִתּוֹךְ "from the middle of the fire." The point of Exod 20:22 is not where Yahweh was when he spoke his instructions, but that the instructions are unequivocally *his*.

23 The opening verse of the law-collection proper is appropriately a variation on the first two of the ten commandments. Whether this verse originally began the Book of the Covenant is a matter of some speculation, since 21:1 has the appearance of a superscription. If 21:1 is a superscription, the questions of how much of what follows is introduced by it and of why it does not follow 20:22 are raised (see Childs, 464–67; Boecker, *Law*, 144–46). What is certain, once again, is the order of the received text, and that order is begun with an emphatic command against setting idol-gods in rivalry with Yahweh. Such a command is in logical sequence to the authentication of the instructions that follow as Yahweh's instructions: these are *his* guiding principles for Israel, and *he* is to be Israel's only God. So obvious a summary of the first two commandments may have been placed at the beginning of the Book of the Covenant precisely because it was such a loosely organized miscellany.

24–26 The three verses setting forth an ancient instruction about the building and use of altars are not so appropriately a beginning to the Book of the Covenant. These verses, along with vv 22–23, are sometimes referred to as a "prologue" (Boecker, *Law*, 144–50) or an "introduction" (Noth, 175–77) to the Book of the Covenant, but these altar instructions are not appropriate prologue to what follows them, nor is there any reason why they should be linked to the two verses preceding them (so Childs, 465–66) any more than any other group of verses in the collection of laws in 20:24–23:19 should be so linked. The attempt to find a logical sequence in such covenantal-legal collections is at best frustrating, and at worst misleading. The location of these verses having to do with the altar preceding the sequences of "guiding decisions" (מִשְׁפָּטִים) in 21:1–23:19 is probably to be understood on two bases: (1) the altar instructions are *not* מִשְׁפָּטִים, but commands similar to the commands concerning the media of worship in chaps. 25–31, and (2) the emphasis here, as in that sequence, is on the Presence of Yahweh in the midst of his people, Israel; so there, the sequence on the media of worship is begun with a reference to a מִקְדָּשׁ "holy place" where Yahweh is to "dwell, settle down" in their midst (25:8), and here, the sequence of the "guiding decisions" is begun with a reference to the altar, the place where Israel came into closest contact with Yahweh, the source of the guiding decisions.

The specifications of an earthen altar and an altar of undressed stones has generally been taken as an indication of the antiquity of these instructions (Wellhausen, *Prolegomena*, 29–30; Noth, 176–77). What is more important, even if these instructions are quite old, is the statement that Yahweh himself will choose the place where such altars are to be built and that he will come in person to his people assembled at these places and there bless them. The discussion as to whether the earthen altar (אֲדָמָה מִזְבַּח) was simply soil carefully piled (and specially absorbent of the blood of the sacrifice, Cazelles, *Code de l'alliance*, 40–41) or clay brick (Conrad, *Altargesetz*, 21–24), or a combination of field soil and field stones and even boulders (in which case a single altar, rather than two, is intended by vv 24 and 25; see Robertson, *JSS* 1

[1948–49] 18–21) is also secondary to the main point of the instruction of v 24 that has served as a lodestone for several commands involving altars and has drawn the collection of them to the beginning of the Book of the Covenant. That main point, of course, is linked to the Presence of Yahweh, established as a given in the places of his choice, many places, all places (cf. König, *ZAW* 42 [1924] 337–40) where his blessing is given, and in the midst of his special people.

The command against the carving or sculpting of stones used in the construction of an altar is not to be taken as a primitive or anti-iconic instruction. The older view, that undressed stone possessed a "special numinous quality" (Galling, "Altar," *IDB* 1:97) is also probably a false trail; Conrad (*Altargesetz* 43–50) has argued persuasively that the restriction is anti-Canaanite. The command against mounting steps by an altar may also be directed against Canaanite practice (so Conrad, 123–24), despite the stated reason, though the exposure of the nakedness of the priest leading worship is reflected at other places in the OT (cf. Lev. 6:10 and Exod 28:42–43).

21:1 The "guiding decisions" (מְשָׁפְּטִים) that Moses is to "establish" (שׂוּם) to the people of Israel as authoritative are, in the broadest application of the term, all the case-decisions or precedent-decisions within the composite we now call the Book of the Covenant. The longest sequence of these, of course, is to be found in 21:2–22:16. Additional "guiding decisions" are found in the Book of the Covenant, however, at 22:24–26 and 23:4–5, and these too may be understood as included in the reference of 21:1. Beyond these "guiding decisions" of 21:2—22:16, and alongside those in chaps. 22 and 23, there are commands like those in 20:23–26: they represent, as do the ten commandments, the stated principles of life in relationship with Yahweh. The "guiding decisions" are the application of those stated principles, themselves an expansion of the still more generally stated principles set forth by the ten commandments (see *Form/Structure/Setting* on 20:1–17).

2 The first extended section of "guiding decisions" has to do with the ownership of slaves. Vv 2–11 are a kind of miscellany under the general topic "the treatment of one's slaves," with guidance concerning the treatment of both male (vv 2–6) and female (vv 7–11) slaves. The reference to a "Hebrew slave" (עֶבֶד עִבְרִי) has been taken both as a designation of a "native" slave, an Israelite slave (Hyatt, 228), and also as indicating an underprivileged social group, disadvantaged persons who might easily fall into the oppression of slavery (Cazelles, *Code de l'alliance*, 44–45). The term "Hebrew" is used in Exodus as the kind of word the Egyptians employ in reference to the Israelites, but not as a name the Israelites apply to themselves (so also is the term used in 1 Samuel by the Philistines: 4:6, 9; 14:11, 21; 29:3). De Vaux (*Early History*, 212) has described the עִבְרִי slave of Exod 21:2 as a temporary slave who might or might not have been an Israelite. In Deut 15:12–18 and Jer 34:8–22, the same phrase clearly does apply to an Israelite, and the paraphrase of Exod 21:2 in Jer 34:14 at least suggests the possibility that the deliberate use of עִבְרִי may be a more specific designation than some commentators have been willing to accept, though the argument of Lewy (*HUCA* 28 [1957] 2–8) that the term means "resident alien" and is a "derogatory appellation" cannot be sustained.

Whatever such a slave's nationality, he was clearly a slave with a certain hope of freedom after a set term of servitude. It may be appropriate to think of such an עבד עברי "Hebrew slave" as less than a full citizen but as more than a full slave. At the end of six years, whatever the cause of his servitude, he was to go free without cost to himself, presumably with the status of full and unencumbered citizenship. That the fulfillment of this hope of the seventh year was dependent upon the religious integrity of the slavemaster is shown by Jer 34:14–18, as is the seriousness with which Yahweh was believed to take the slavemaster's covenantal responsibility.

3–5 Nor do the "Hebrew" slave's rights end with his right of release; if his wife has accompanied him into servitude, she is to accompany him into freedom. If, however, his wife has married him during his servitude, obviously by the permission and through the provision of his owner, both the wife and any children born to such a union must remain with the owner when the "temporary" slave claims his freedom of the seventh year. They are obviously the owner's property. This provision raises the need for recourse for the temporary slave who does not want to be separated from his wife and any children his union in servitude may have produced. Thus is a further provision made: he may swear an oath of loyalty to his owner and to his family, and so forgo, presumably forever (so לעלם "without release, forever," in v 6), his right of seventh-year release.

6 The formal ceremony for such a disavowal of his return to a status of freedom requires that the owner bring the man into the Presence of God, that is, to the sanctuary (cf. Falk, *VT* 9 [1959] 86–88) and perhaps even to the altar there, no doubt to repeat in that place his formal renunciation of freedom. האלהים has sometimes been taken as implying "judges" or "rulers" representing divine authority (so BDB, 43; Tg Onk: דיניא; LXX has πρὸς τὸ κριτήριον τοῦ θεοῦ "before the court of God"), but as Gordon (*JBL* 54 [1935] 139–44) has demonstrated, such a translation is both unnecessary and incorrect. The "door or the doorpost" where the slave's ear is pierced is probably the door of the sanctuary (cf. Fensham, *JBL* 78 [1959] 160–61; Loretz, *Bib* 41 [1960] 167–70); it may have been the door of the owner's house, but in either case, more than merely a suitable "wooden support" for the ear-piercing (Cassuto, 267) is in view. The piercing of the ear, perhaps for the insertion of a ring or tag of some kind (Mendelsohn, "Slavery in the OT," *IDB* 4: 385), was a public indication of a permanent slavery, and had therefore to be carried out in a public place. By this ceremony, the "temporary" slave became a "permanent" slave, through devotion to his family.

7–11 The expectation of seventh-year release was denied to women (note however the later provision of Deut 15:12, where the man and the woman are both accorded the right of freedom in the seventh year). Though an owner may be unhappy with a female slave he has bought for himself (on the uses to which such female slaves were put, see Mendelsohn, *IDB* 4:385–86), he is to permit her to be freed by the payment of a price, apparently by her family, or he is to make provision for her to remain within his own family, perhaps as a daughter-in-law. Despite his own dissatisfaction with her, he has no right to sell her to "a strange family" (עם נכרי), a family unknown to her, perhaps even one outside the covenant community of Israel (cf. Hoftijzer, *VT* 7 [1957] 390–91). If he keeps her within his own family, yet takes another woman as his own wife or concubine, he is not to deny her the basic rights which his purchase of her for himself guaranteed in the first place. North (*VT* 5 [1955] 204–6) has proposed that שְׁאֵר may here refer not to food, but to the full range of physical satisfaction, that כְּסוּת implies "harem-protection," and not merely clothing, and that עֹנָה describes the right to bear children, and not just the right of sexual intercourse. As intriguing as his interpretation is, it yet implies more than the OT usage of these terms will sustain. If the owner refuses to provide the female slave with these fundamental rights, he waives his claim of possession, and she is free to go her own way. The provisions here stipulated for such a woman make it very likely that she was not sold into slavery for general purposes, but only as a bride, and therefore with provisions restricting her owner-husband concerning her welfare if he should become dissatisfied with the union. Mendelsohn (*JAOS* 55 [1935] 190–95; cf. Henrey, *PEQ* 86 [1954] 5–8) has cited Nuzian sale contracts which almost exactly parallel the Exodus provisions. Such an interpretation makes clear why the provisions for such a slave-bride are given in sequence to the "guiding principles" for the protection of the male temporary slave: the slave-bride had special rights, too, and if they were violated, she too could go free.

12–36 Next in sequence are two collections of "guiding principles" dealing with harm, chiefly physical harm, inflicted willfully or through negligence. Cases carrying the death penalty are appropriately set first (vv 12–17), and these are followed by cases calling for a less severe penalty (vv 18–36). The loose arrangement of such sequences has been explained by Daube (*Biblical Law*, 74–77, 85–89) as the result of "laziness, undeveloped legal technique, writing on stone or the like, oral transmission of the law, and regard for tradition," and the tacking of supplementary laws onto the end of extant collections, rather than the insertion of them into their logical place in a given sequence.

12–17 The death penalty is specified for one who strikes a premeditated fatal blow against a man, for one who strikes either of his parents, for one who is guilty of kidnapping for the commerce of slave-trading, and for the one who curses (קלל) either of his parents. These capital-penalty "guiding principles" are stated in the direct apodictic form of the "stated principles" of the sequences of the Book of the Covenant of 22:17–23:19. This form is no doubt a reflection of the seriousness of the offense. 22:17–18 are provisions of identical type and form; their location at a separate place in the Book of the Covenant is a reflection of the cumulative arrangement of the collection.

13–14 In a case where a blow resulting in death was not preplanned, and God permitted the enemy to come into the hand of one who struck the blow as *un crime de passion,* a place of sanctuary from the death penalty is to be provided. Just where this place is, we are not told, but the following statement (v 14) that the person guilty of murder cunningly planned can be taken even from Yahweh's own altar implies, at least, that the place of temporary sanctuary was the altar of Yahweh, *any* altar of Yahweh, wherever located (cf. de Vaux, *Ancient Israel* 1:160–61; *contra* Greenberg, *JBL* 78 [1959] 125–27, 132). Sanctuary at the altar was a temporary measure (and in one exceptional instance, it was not respected: 1 Kgs 2:28–35), until the innocence or guilt of the fugitive could be demonstrated. When the fugitive's claims of innocence were vindicated, he was free to go (1 Kgs 1:50–53). When he was found guilty, as here, he was dragged from the altar and executed.

15, 17 The two capital offences against parents (vv 15 and 17, presented in direct sequence in LXX) both involve the violation of the fifth commandment. Striking (נכה) either parent is a reversal of the respect they are due. Cursing them is taken equally seriously because, as Brichto (*Problem of "Curse,"* 132–35) has suggested, קלל here apparently means something like "repudiation," and may not involve a spoken "curse" at all. Deut 27:16, the second curse of the "Schechemite Dodecalog," reads "Cursed (ארור) is the one who dishonors (מַקְלֶה, a hiphil participle of קלה, read by some versions מְקַלֵּל, a piel participle of קלל) his father or his mother." Brichto (134, n. 41) even speculates that the Deuteronomic law dealing with the rebellious and contentious son (Deut 21:18–21) who must be stoned to death is "an expansion" of the "terse statement of Exod 21:17."

16 Kidnapping a free man for sale into slavery, whether he has actually been sold or is being confined for sale later, is also a capital crime. Some scholars (so Alt, *Kleine Schriften* 1:333–40; Phillips, *Criminal Law*, 130–32) have connected this crime with the eighth commandment, in part because גנב "steal" is used in Exod 20:15 as well as in the verse at hand. While Exod 20:15 is certainly inclusive of "man-stealing," however, its application must be made much broader (see *Comment* above). Daube (*Biblical Law*, 95) has plausibly explained the awkward phrase ונמצא בידו, which is translated here "or is found confining him" (see n. 21:16.a), as an interpolation designed to remove a loophole that might enable a slave dealer who had not actually sold his victim to escape the penalty of death.

18–21 Actions involving less serious harm to the integrity of the covenant community than murder, homicide, abduction for purpose of slavery, and the repudiation of parents were more frequent, no doubt, and are so accorded a much longer list of "guiding principles." A man who strikes another with a stone or a tool in a fight, thus taking an unfair advantage in the struggle, must be held responsible for the work the injured man cannot do and for his victim's recovery as well, while the wounded man is to be free of any punishment beyond the suffering his injury causes. A slave owner who strikes his slave a fatal blow with a stick or a club (שבט) is to be punished unless the slave survives the blow for a day or so. In that case, he is to suffer no punishment beyond his financial loss in the death of his slave.

22–25 If two men in a scuffle inadvertently strike a pregnant woman, causing by the trauma of the blow the premature birth of her children (so MT; SamPent and LXX read "child"), if there is no harm, presumably either to the mother or the newborn child or children, the man who actually inflicted the blow is to pay compensation, fixed by the woman's husband on the basis of an assessment agreed upon by an objective third party (cf. Speiser, *JBL* 82 [1963] 301–6). If, however, there is a permanent injury, either to the woman or, presumably, to the child or the children she was carrying, equal injury is to be inflicted upon the one who caused it. Jackson (*VT* 23 [1973] 290–97) argues that v 22 sets the payment for the loss of the fetus, v 23

the bodily harm done to the mother: "the remedy for a lost foetus is substitution, but that for the mother is talionic" (cf. *contra,* Loewenstamm, *VT* 27
[1977] 352–60). The Code of Hammurapi, *ANET* 175:209, provides a payment
of ten shekels of silver for the loss of a fetus in a similar instance; the Middle
Assyrian Laws, *ANET* 184:50 specify a life as payment for the loss of a fetus.
Paul (*Book of the Covenant,* 70–73) assumes the loss of the fetus also in Exod
21:22, translating ויצאו ילדיה "and a miscarriage results"; the text, however,
is not that specific, referring as it does to "her children going out" (cf. BDB,
423h).

This law of the talion, for a long time thought to be a more primitive
kind of penalty, the reflection of a barbaric law form, has been shown by
more recent comparative studies to be a later development, designed to remedy the inevitable abuses made possible by monetary payment for physical
injury. See, for example, the comments of Diamond (*Iraq* 19 [1957] 151–
55), Finkelstein (*JCS* 15 [1961] 98–104), or Paul (*Book of the Covenant,* 70–
79), who calls "the principle of *lex talionis* . . . an important advance in the
history of jurisprudence."

26–27   In the case of bodily injury to slaves, whose status does not qualify
them for equal compensation, the owner whose abuse results in the loss of
an eye or a tooth is to free that slave, a remarkably humanitarian provision
directed at cruelty and sadism in a slave-owner.

28–32   Harm done by animals carelessly managed is also regarded as the
responsibility of the owner, and appropriate restitution is to be made. If a
bull not known to be dangerous suddenly gores someone fatally, the bull is
to be killed, but the owner is to suffer no punishment beyond this quite
considerable financial loss. If, however, the bull is known to be dangerous
and its owner warned of the consequences of his negligence, a fatal attack
is to be compensated by the death of both the bull and its owner. An indemnity
payment is permitted in such a case, but it is an indemnity not for the life
of the bull's victim, but for the life of the owner, put into jeopardy not by
malicious intent but by negligence. This payment was to be of an amount
apparently set by the victim's family, thus that varied from case to case. The
same "guiding principle" is applied to the death of a son or a daughter: no
less penalty is to be exacted if the bull's victim is a child, but in the case of
a slave, a monetary compensation of thirty silver shekels is set, along with
the death of the bull.

33–36   The further collection of "guiding principles" on harm relates
to the losses sustained by the owner whose livestock is injured through negligence or theft leading to butchery or resale. Thus the man who leaves an
open pit is to pay compensation to the owner of any animal that falls into
it, apparently in the amount of the animal's value uninjured, and to keep
the carcass of the dead animal. If a bull unexpectedly attacks and kills a
neighbor's bull, the aggressive animal is to be sold and the two parties are
to halve the proceeds of this sale *and* the dead animal. If, on the other hand,
the attacking animal was known to be belligerent and its owner has taken
no precautions, he must replace the dead animal, which he is then permitted
to keep.

37, 22:2b–3 [22:1, 3b–4]   The thief who steals a bull or a flock animal either to butcher for his own use or to sell for money must pay the compensation of five herd-animals for the bull, four flock-animals for one flock-animal stolen; if he is unable to pay such compensation, he is himself to be sold to raise the money needed for the compensation payment. If an animal that has been stolen is found alive in his possession, the thief is required to pay double compensation. Whether this involves double the price of the stolen animal in addition to the return of the animal to its owner (Friedrich, *Hethitischen Gesetze*, 41, n. 3) or the return of the animal plus a single compensation payment (Goetze, *ANET*, 192:70) is unclear.

22:1–2a[22:2–3] The "guiding principle" concerning the death of a thief killed in the course of his crime is obviously not in logical sequence with the livestock laws that precede and follow it. Attempts to rearrange the text (Beer, 112–13; RSV) and attempts to suggest a purpose for the arrangement as it stands (Cassuto, 282; Childs, 474) are unconvincing, however. The order may best be accounted for by Daube's theory (see above, p. 322). The thief who is discovered at his work and struck fatally brings no guilt of bloodshed upon the one who has struck him unless the attack and the death resulting from it occur during the daylight hours when the person being burglarized can see the thief and so allow justice to follow its normal course.

4–5 [5–6] The sequence of "guiding principles" dealing with harm through negligence and theft is followed by a miscellany concerned with property loss ranging from the potential of a crop (vv 4–5) to a marriage price (vv 15–16). First in the sequence is the loss of the potential of a field or a vineyard through negligence involving livestock or fire. In the first instance, the potential crop is destroyed by the grazing and trampling of the stock; in the second, a fire allowed to burn out of control destroys the harvested grain or the standing grain or even the entire crop. In the case of the loose animals, the negligent owner must give up the best of his own crop as compensation. In the case of the uncontrolled fire, the terms of the compensation are not specified. The expanded version of v 4 in LXX has been explained by Rabinowitz (*VT* 9 [1959] 40–44), probably correctly, as "doctoring the text" by the "Alexandrian translators" to reflect the laws affecting agricultural economy in Egypt under Ptolemy II.

6–8 [7–9] The "guiding principles" designed to protect property put into the care of, or loaned to, another member of the covenant community deal primarily with loss by theft, but include also liability of other kinds. A primary concern of these provisions is a kind of "bonding" of the person to whom the possessions are entrusted, not least by reminding him in advance of his own liability. Thus when something of value is put into a neighbor's care and is missing when the owner comes to claim it, a thief must first of all be sought. If one is found, he is required in penalty of his crime to compensate the owner of the property double the amount of the property's value. The "neighbor," רֵעַ, is here as at other places in Exodus (cf. 2:13; 20:16–17; 21:14) a fellow Israelite, one bound by the same covenant to Yahweh; the thief, of course, might belong to any group. "Neighbor" must not therefore be understood here in its contemporary sense; possessions would not be entrusted for safekeeping to someone who lived nearby, or who was a friend only. The additional covenantal bond is precisely what makes the situation here described so serious. If no thief is found, the suspicion of theft falls upon the person to whom the property has been entrusted, and he must be brought into the Presence of God so that his own innocence or culpability may be established.

7 [8] LXX includes here the additional idea of the taking of an oath (καὶ ὀμεῖται) of innocence before God, and many commentators have followed this line (so Noth, 184; Cassuto, 286; Hyatt, 238; Childs, 475–76), assuming that the willingness or unwillingness of the property holder to swear in God's Presence would establish his guilt or his innocence. This is not, however, what MT says. קרב אל־האלהים refers here as at many other places in the OT to a drawing near to the Presence of God to receive a *divine* opinion, not merely the testimony, albeit under special circumstances, of the accused and accusing parties. קרב "draw near" in the hiphil stem is a special cultic term for bringing a sacrifice or an offering into God's Presence; it is so used eighty-nine times in Leviticus and forty-nine times in Numbers. קרב is also used in a variety of passages (cf. Exod 16:9–10; 1 Sam 14:36–37; Deut 5:27), as here, to describe drawing near to a place of theophany. The property owner and the person to whom he has entrusted his possessions are thus to be understood as coming into the Presence of God, no doubt at the local sanctuary or holy place, to seek an oracle of God (cf. Beer, 114).

8 [9] Whatever the loss, whether of livestock, clothing, or any other object of value, if it is found among the property of the trusted neighbor and the owner claims it ("This is it," i.e., the animal or article entrusted and "lost"), the two parties with their disputant claims are to come to God to seek in his Presence the oracle of divine pronouncement. The procedure for this step is left unspecified, no doubt because it was well known. Perhaps it involved the sacred lot, *urim* and *thummim.* Whatever the means of designation, the property owner or the trustee would be declared guilty of deception, and that declaration, which as a divine word was the final word, required the payment of a double compensation to the injured party.

9–10 [10–11] In a case in which only livestock is involved, and the animal left for safekeeping suffers death or injury or disappears and there is no witness to the loss, the owner *and* the trustee, either of whom might be making a false claim, are to swear שבעת יהוה "Yahweh's oath," or an oath in Yahweh's Presence that each is telling the truth. Lehmann (*ZAW* 81 [1969] 78–82) has proposed that such an oath carried with it a curse against the one who played it false; Horst (*Gottes Recht,* 306–8) notes that this oath was taken in Yahweh's name and that Yahweh as witness to the oath was also its guard and guarantor. Such an oath would of course be the final and highest protestation of innocence, and the procedure here differs from the approach to the divine Presence for an oracle (vv 6–8 [7–9]) because both parties are open to suspicion. The owner is to accept such an oath of the innocence of the trustee in harm to or the loss of his animal, and, presumably, the trustee would similarly accept the oath with regard to the owner. The trustee would not need to pay any compensation.

11–14 [12–15] If, however, the loss of the animal through theft shall have occurred because of the negligence of the trustee, the trustee must pay compensation. If predators have mauled the animal and he can produce the maimed animal or its carcass in evidence, he need pay no compensation. In the event that the animal is in the trustee's keeping at his own request, as a loan, he is to pay compensation if it is injured or dies unless (1) the owner was with it at the time of its injury or death, and so could have looked after his own interests, or (2) the owner had rented it for a fee and so had already calculated the risk he was taking and provided for compensation in the fees he charged.

15–16 [16–17] The man who seduced an unbetrothed virgin and so compromised her father's opportunity to arrange a marriage for her was required to pay her marriage price and marry her himself (cf. Finkelstein, *JAOS* 86 [1966] 362–68). The terms of this "guiding principle" indicate that its primary focus is financial, both with regard to the father of the unattached girl and also with regard to the young woman herself. The marriage money (מֹהַר) was in the way of compensation to a young woman's family for her loss into another family, and it may have reverted to the bride herself upon the occasion of the death of her father or her husband (de Vaux, *Ancient Israel* 1:26–29). In case the girl's father considered the match unsuitable for his daughter, as well he might under the circumstance, the man involved was still to pay as a penalty a sum equivalent to the marriage price for young women eligible to be married.

22:17–23:19 [22:18–23:19] The reappearance in v 17 [18] of the apodictic form in the statement of the "guiding principles" of the Book of the Covenant and the recurrence of that form through most of the remainder of the collection has led many commentators to the view that 22:17 [22:18]–23:19 and 21:2–22:16 [22:17], characterized more by the casuistic form, are separate collections. The dividing point is variously set (see above, *Form/Structure/Setting*), and some scholars argue for the precedence of the "casuistic" section (so Paul, *Book of the Covenant*, 43–45, who regards 21:2–22:16 [22:17] "the formal legal corpus"), some for the precedence of the "apodictic" section (so Beyerlin, *Gottes Wort*, 19–29, who argues for a parenetic collection of "commandment- and prohibition-sequences" prior to the incorporation of the collection of the case laws; cf. also, and more fully, Halbe, *Privilegrecht Jahwes*, 413–23). As interesting as these suggestions are, they tend by their subjectivity to be mutually canceling. What remains certain, of course, is the present form of the Book of the Covenant, and that form presents a variety of legal formulary given unity by its theological purpose, the exposition and application of the principles of life in covenant with Yahweh. It should come as no surprise that the two major halves of the Book of the Covenant each contain laws in "when . . . you" form, commandment form, and prohibition form. Whatever prior organization the Book of the Covenant may have had, in any of its parts or as an expanding whole, it stands now as a "new" collection, to a "new" purpose, with its own unique form.

17–19 [18–20] Three offenses for which the death penalty is commanded are listed together, perhaps by reason of their seriousness. The sorceress (sorcerers, the masculine plural form of the same Hebrew participle, are mentioned in Mal 3:5) is not to be permitted to live because her craft was an attempt to escape or to alter the will and the work of Yahweh. The OT uniformly opposes sorcery (cf. Deut 18:9–14; 2 Kgs 9:21–26; Mic 5:10–15;

Jer 27:8–11; Nah 3:1–4), without ever specifying exactly what it is (Cazelles, *Code de l'alliance*, 75, refers to "dark and noxious practices"). Copulation with any animal also is to be punished by death, not only because it was a sexual deviation (cf. Lev 18:23; 20:16; Deut 27:21), but even more because of its associations with animal cults and fertility worship among Israel's neighbors (cf. Cazelles, 76). The third offense punishable by death involves the violation of the first commandment, and is therefore, like the two offenses that precede it, an attack upon Yahweh himself. V 19 [20] is awkwardly stated, and its final phrase appears to be an addition called for by the lack of any modifier for אלהים "gods, God." SamPent adds a modifier, אחרים "strange, other," and is missing the additional phrase; LXX^A has both. Alt (*Essays*, 112, n. 73) thought אחרים the original reading, followed by מות יומת "he is certainly to be put to death"; by error, the יחרם "he is to be destroyed under ban" of MT replaced אחרים rendering מות יומת "he is certainly to be put to death" redundant, but necessitating the tack-on phrase to avoid ambiguity. The verb חרם means to devote to sacred use, or if that is impossible, as here, to destroy under the ban of what is to be used for Yahweh's purpose alone.

20–26 [21–27]   V 20 [21] begins a sequence of prohibitions and commands that are in one way or another protective of defenseless and disadvantaged persons, and the similar concerns of 23:1–9, which take up the situation of the innocent, among men and animals, the needy, and again the newcomer, have prompted the suggestion that these verses may originally have been a part of an "ethical" code interpolated into the Book of the Covenant. I. Lewy (*VT* 7 [1959] 322–26), for example, has suggested a "Torah of humaneness, justice, and righteousness" in addition to the ten commandments, known throughout Israel, predating the prophets of the ninth and eighth centuries and reflected in "the Deuteronomic Code." He even suggests that Exod 22:20–26 [21–27] and 23:1–9 are from the hand of "the Yahwist master narrator," "the first prophet of ethico-centered religion." While this latter suggestion amounts to a speculation founded on a row of speculations, the presence in the Book of the Covenant of these provisions for the defenseless and the innocent certainly need not be taken, as they often have been, as indications of the influence of prophetic teaching. Concern for the disprivileged and humanitarian sensitivity are reflected throughout the OT, in every major dimension of its teaching.

The "newcomer," גר, as a temporary dweller, a "tourist" for a short or an extended time, was without familial and professional and sometimes national connections and so was open to abuse. The people of Israel knew the plight, for they had suffered it in Egypt, and they were not to maltreat or oppress those in a similar situation in the land over which they themselves ruled (cf. 23:9). Nor were they to "humiliate," to "weaken" still further any widow or orphan: though their means of redress among men were limited, Yahweh himself was to be their protector. A cry of distress from such a defenseless person would certainly be heard by Yahweh and just as certainly provoke his furious anger, in result of which the offending Israelite would himself be slain, leaving his own wife and children in the same defenseless position as those whom he had maltreated.

24–26 [25–27] The poor are similarly to be looked after as the special concern of Yahweh. If the exigencies of existence force them to borrow money, the Israelite must keep in mind that these people are Yahweh's people too, despite their poverty. Thus the arrangement with them must be a special one, the arrangement of the family: the one who advances the money is not to do so as a businessman but as a fellow member of Yahweh's family (cf. Neufeld, *HUCA* 26 [1955] 357–59, 365–66, 375–76, 394–99). No interest is to be charged, and if collateral is held, it must be returned before its absence causes hardship. It is collateral more for the benefit of the feelings of the borrower than for the security of the lender. If these covenantal family ties are not respected and there is a cry of distress to Yahweh, he will hear it, because they are "family" and because he is compassionate: חַנּוּן "compassionate" is used only of Yahweh (thirteen times), and usually in tandem with רַחוּם "caring." The confession of Yahweh חַנּוּן אָנִי "I am compassionate," may be understood as the foundational explanation of all the commands and "guiding principles" having to do with the defenseless members of the covenant community.

27–30 [28–31] Members of the covenant community are to show no disrespect for (they are not to "make light of," קלל) God. As Brichto (*Problem of "Curse,"* 150–65) has shown, blasphemy or the cursing of God is not at issue here, despite the assertion of some commentators (so Cassuto, 293–94; Hyatt, 244) that it is. To show disrespect for God is to act in any manner inimical to the relationship in covenant with him, indeed to ignore or to refuse to obey any of his commands or "guiding principles." One such act would be to curse (ארר) a leader (נשיא) of the covenant community; a second would be to hold back that to which Yahweh is entitled, whether from the produce of field, vineyard, and orchard or the womb or the herd or the flock. It is necessary, indeed, that the members of the covenant community be קדש "holy," set apart for Yahweh: to the extent and in any way in which they are not so set apart, they are showing disrespect for the one to whom they have claimed special relationship.

The נשיא was not the king, but an administrative leader elected by the assembly of the people and believed therein to have been elected also by Yahweh (Speiser, *CBQ* 25 [1963] 111–17). With regard to him the stronger word ארר "curse" is used, a choice that is quite deliberate. As Scharbert (*Bib* 39 [1958] 5–14, esp. 9) has noted, the piel of קלל "show disrespect" and qal of ארר are by no means synonymous, though many commentators have made them so, and more is intended even than Brichto's (*Problem of "Curse"* 158–59) idea of bringing a leader into disfavor with God by the irresponsibility of the people for whom he has special responsibility. ארר "curse" here should be taken literally, to signify the reversal of the שלום "health, wholeness" of the leader elected by the people because he was elected by God. As such, to curse a leader is to attempt the negation of a blessing of Yahweh, thus an act of disrespect for the divine authority by which the covenant came to be.

28–29 [29–30] An appropriate respect for Yahweh also requires priority for him in the matter of offerings. מלאתך ודמעך, literally, "your fullness and your dripping," refer to the bounty of the harvest. "Fullness" is translated above by "bumper crop" and "dripping" ("squeezings") by "vintage wine and richest oil" (cf. Cazelles, *Code de l'alliance*, 82). The prohibition is against a token offering from a bounteous crop, a legalistic expression of the obligation as opposed to a joyous offering in thanksgiving. Firstborn sons are Yahweh's, as also are the firstborn animals of herd and flock: to hold any of these back is to show disrespect for Yahweh similar to that revealed by a token offering from bountiful crops. Israel's gifts must demonstrate an appropriate acknowledgement of the gifts of Yahweh that make their gifts possible. First-born sons were dedicated in Israel to Yahweh both actually and vicariously, but in service, not by sacrifice (cf. de Vaux, *Early History*, 443–44, and see *Comment* on 13:11–12); the firstborn animals of herd and flock were to be given on the eighth day, that is, only when the animal could safely be taken from its mother.

30 [31]   Respect for Yahweh means, therefore, that those in relationship with him must be set apart for him. An example of such set-apartness is abstinence from food improperly gained: the people of Israel are not to eat the meat of animals killed by wild beasts. In time, such a requirement had to do at least in part with restrictions related to blood (כי הדם הוא הנפש "for the blood is the life," Deut 12:23); earlier, it may also have been linked both to the practices of Israel's neighbors and a fear of the contamination, either physical, or ritual, of an animal killed by unknown predators. The plural verbs of this verse, often taken as an indication that it was an insertion from another law code, may better be understood in relation to the plural אנשי־קדש "men set apart" as a concluding and summary statement addressed to Israel as a whole following a series of commands and guiding principles addressed to each individual member of the covenant community.

23:1–3   With the first nine verses of chap. 23, we come once again to a list of provisions concerned with ethical and humane behavior, verses some-times linked with 22:20–26 [21–27]; see above. The first three verses deal with reputations both good and bad and have a primary connection with legal procedures in the covenant community. Passing along a groundless report is forbidden, as is the support of a false testimony by shoring up a bad reputation with a good one. Going the wrong way because the majority is headed there is forbidden, as is the testimony sympathetic to that given by a majority but distorted report. And giving an unfair advantage in a legal proceeding to the poor, who had no advantage at all, is forbidden, an insight into human temptation so perceptive that some commentators (so Noth, 189, and *BHS*) albeit wrongly, have felt compelled to emend דל "and poor, weak," to גדל "great, important."

4–5   The reappearance in these two verses of the "when . . . you," "guid-ing principle" form and the difference in subject matter in these two verses with what precedes and follows them have led some interpreters to consider them dislocated. Driver (237), for example, would relocate them after 22:24 or 27. Other commentators (cf. Noth, 188–89; Childs, 480–81) have sought a connection of context that might justify the apparent *non sequitur*. As Daube (*Biblical Law*, 74–101) has shown, however, ancient law codes are not always arranged and transmitted in logical and consistent sequence, and Carmichael (*ZAW* 84 [1972] 19–25), following Daube, has made the additional point that the "guiding principles" are not "in the strict, practical sense" legislation, but "laws . . . basically addressed to the conscience" and sometimes parallel in arrangement "to the moral precepts in the Book of Proverbs."

The point at issue in these two verses is not so much a humane attitude toward a lost or improperly laden animal as it is a refusal to take advantage of another's misfortunes because he happens to be an enemy. The loose animal is usually enjoying himself, and the animal that lies down under a poorly arranged load is protecting himself. The one at risk here is the owner, who may lose a valuable animal altogether or have to unload and reload an animal in an insecure spot and without help. Under normal circumstances, there would be no question about catching a stray animal or helping even a stranger rearrange a load. But if the animal should belong to an enemy, to one who hates (and is perhaps therefore hated), there is a temptation to permit and to hope for the worst to happen, and to take satisfaction from its occurrence. A member of the covenant community is forbidden to do so; instead, he should catch and return the straying animal, or assist in the arrangement of a poorly placed load.

6–8 The instructions related to legal proceedings are taken up again in these verses. The view of Frey (*Wort und Dienst* 1 [1948] 22–29) that these verses are addressed to the judge in a case at law and that vv 1–3 are addressed to the witnesses, and the view of McKay (*VT* 21 [1971] 321–25) that vv 1–3 plus vv 6–8 formed a decalogue of instructions for judges and elders administering justice in the city gate are too restrictive. There is no reason why these commands cannot be applied to anyone involved in a determinative role in a legal proceeding. There is to be no "bending," no "watering down" of a case-decision affecting a needy, disadvantaged person, and no entertainment of any complaint that has no foundation in truth. The innocent righteous person is not to be ruined (literally, "killed," הרג) by unjust legal procedure. Yahweh "will not make the wicked righteous" (לא־אצדיק רשע), and so let them off at the expense of an innocent person wrongly convicted, no matter what the law court may do (cf. Fensham, *VT* 26 [1976] 299–70, who emphasizes the first-person address of Yahweh in v 7). No bribe is to be accepted, because a bribe changes what people see and upends justice.

9 The repetition of the command against maltreating a "newcomer" (see *Comment* on 22:20), set at this point perhaps because of the context of injustice in the instructions regarding legal proceedings, is followed here as earlier by a summary statement with second person plural verbs. Each member of the covenant community is to have compassion for such a disadvantaged person because all of them together have known the experience of his plight.

10–12 The concept of a seventh-year release, whether of land or of a "temporary" slave (see *Comment* on 21:2–11) is probably patterned on the much older practice of a seventh-day release, the sabbath day of rest. Both practices are commended in these verses, which are no doubt linked because of their parallel six-plus-one pattern. After six years of cultivation and harvest, land is to be left alone for a year. Whatever the land produces on its own, the "volunteer crop" which comes through no effort of cultivation, the poor of the land are to have, and anything they leave, the wild animals are not to be deterred from eating. Vineyards and olive orchards are to be left alone in the seventh year, unpruned, unguarded, and unharvested. As the owner will not have worked for their produce, so he is not to take it or to be concerned with it. As de Vaux (*Early History*, 173–75) has noted, there is here no indication of whether a general or a staggered sabbatical year is meant, insofar as all Israel is concerned. Lev 25:1–7, which refers to a sabbath rest for the land, clearly implies a general sabbath year every seventh year following entry into the promised land. The sabbath day is of course a rest day commanded generally, here with no justifying reasons as in 20:8–11 apart from the statement that rest for the Israelite means rest also for the animals and the people under his authority. North (*Bib* 36 [1955] 185–201) has argued that שַׁבָּת "sabbath" is derived from the root שׁבת "cease, stop," that the sabbath has connections with the lunar month and the Babylonian *šapattum* as a day of penance, and that sabbath observance may be linked, in its earliest OT form, to "the Mosaic revelation" (cf. Cazelles, *Code de l'alliance*, 92–95, and note Robinson's proposal, *ZAW* 92 [1980] 37–42, that שׁבת has no connection with "rest").

13 The summary nature of Yahweh's statement concerning all that he has said, the use in it of inclusive plural verb forms, and the recurrence of the theme of the first commandment of the Decalogue, which also begins the Book of the Covenant (see *Comment* on 20:23), gives v 13 the appearance of a conclusion to the collection of commands and guiding principles. It is after all a caution to guard or keep the instructions Yahweh has given, to avoid even thinking of the name (or "presence," שֵׁם) of any god other than Yahweh, and a command against speaking the name of any such "strange" deity. Further, the commands that now follow this summary statement with its recurring prohibition of worship directed toward any save Yahweh could be supplementary, post-collection addenda of the kind Daube (*Biblical Law*, 74–101) calls "codas" to the "codes." They deal with (1) the sacred festivals of the year (vv 14–17) and (2) a miscellany of instructions connected mostly with sacrifices and offerings (vv 18–19); a large part of these addenda reappear, partially in verbatim form, in 34:18–26 (see *Comment* below).

Carmichael (*ZAW* 84·[1972] 19–21) sees 23:9–19 as a sequence of laws patterned after the sequence of 22:20–30, made by a scribe influenced by the compilations of the Book of Proverbs (23–25), and demonstrating a loose correspondence of individual laws. 23:13, on this view, is held to correspond to 22:27 [28]. Hyatt (247) thinks 23:13 "a summary addition," and wonders whether it may originally have come following 23:19, at what is now the end of the law collections of the Book of the Covenant. Intriguing though these and other speculations like them are, we must not fail to take seriously the text as it stands. For some compiler(s), the present order of Exod 23 was the one to be transmitted, and v 13 may best be seen in its present sequence not as dislocated or the parallel of some other sequence, but as the conclusion of at least a subsection within the larger compilation that is the Book of the Covenant.

14–17 The three sacred feasts commanded in the instructions of vv 14–17 comprise the three principal events of Israel's religious calendar, perhaps because of their significant connection with the three principal events of Israel's ongoing physical life—the first harvest of grain, the early barley; the harvest of the other cereal crops seven weeks later; and the final harvest of all the crops in the autumn. Of the several OT listings of these three sacred feasts (see also Exod 34:18–23; Deut 16:1–17; and Lev 23:1–44), the one at hand appears to be the oldest (see de Vaux, *Early History,* 470–74, 484–506; Kraus, *Worship in Israel,* 26–70). These agricultural festivals were probably taken into Israelite life from the Canaanites, early in the period of Israel's settlement in Canaan (cf. Talmon, *JAOS* 83 [1963] 177–87), but as the OT calendars show, they were made into festive celebrations of thanks to Yahweh, no doubt as an attempted safeguard against syncretistic influence.

15 The first of the three festivals commanded of Israel by Yahweh, the feast of unleavened bread cakes, was set "in the month of the green grain" (חדש האביב), the time of the earliest harvest, the harvest of barley planted in winter (Zohary, "Flora," *IDB* 2:286). "Green grain" may refer either to the barley itself or to the growing wheat and spelt, to be harvested seven weeks later, or to both (cf. Talmon, *JAOS* 83 [1963] 182–86). Unleavened bread cakes were made from the new barley, and enjoyed as the first bounty of the crops of another year. The association of this festival with the remembrance of exodus deliverance, as also the association of a spring lambing festival with that same deliverance by means of the Passover, was a remarkable contribution of Israel's religious leaders (see *Comment* on 12:14–20). The absence of any mention in this verse of Passover is entirely logical, since the point of reference here is the agricultural festival from which the feast of unleavened bread cakes was taken. The offering Yahweh expects is the acknowledgment of his gift of the first grain harvest and thanksgiving for the beginning of another crop year.

16–17 The second of the appointed festivals was in a way a continuation of the first, as it too celebrated the harvest of grain, the wheat and spelt that ripened later. This "early crop-harvest" was a further harbinger of the fuller harvest to follow at the end of the agricultural year. It is called the "sacred feast of sevens (weeks)" (חג שבעת) in Exod 34:22, because it came by prescription seven weeks after the harvest of the early grain (Deut 16:9–12). This harvest was the "first fruits" of the autumnal harvest, which was in turn the occasion of the third and largest of the three festivals of thanksgiving, the sacred festival of the ingathering harvest. This festival came at the end of the year, from an agricultural standpoint, and celebrated all of Yahweh's bounty, of field and orchard and vineyard alike.

The section on the three sacred feasts is ended with a repetition of the statement of requirement with which it began, this time specifying that every male is to appear three times annually in the Presence, that is, in a place set aside for the worship of Yahweh, here called "the Lord, Yahweh" (האדון יהוה), Cassuto (303) says "in antithesis" to the Canaanite address of Baal as "Lord," a point that might make more sense if the contrast were with a double name such as "Aliyn Baal" ("The One Who Prevails: Baal," Kapelrud, *Baal* 47–50).

18–19 The commands and "guiding principles" of the Book of Covenant are closed with four miscellaneous instructions. The first two of these instructions have sometimes been connected with Passover (cf. Tg Onk, Sperber, 1:128; Gispen, 232), but there is no justification in the text for doing so, and the instructions are better taken more generally. The prohibition of any combination of leaven with the blood of a sacrifice offered to Yahweh and of the keeping of the fat from such a sacrifice beyond the time prescribed for its disposal are both linked to the association of blood and visceral fat with the very essence of the life that is Yahweh's gift to all his creatures. The OT exclusion of the blood and the visceral fat of any sacrificial animal to the use of Yahweh alone is without exception (see Exod 29:12–13; Lev 3:16–17; 7:22–27; 8:14–30; Num 18:17; cf. Rendtorff, *Geschichte des Opfers*, 145–48). Leaven would be considered an impurity in combination with the blood of the sacrifice to Yahweh; the fat was Yahweh's alone and was to be offered to him promptly. The very first of the harvest was to be given to Yahweh, both as an indication that the crops came as his bounty to Israel and also to prevent a waiting for Yahweh's part that might eliminate it altogether. The prohibition of cooking a kid in the milk of its own mother has been variously explained on magical grounds (Gaster, *Myth, Legend, and Custom*, 250–63, following Frazer) or as a reaction against Dionysian (Radin, *AJSL* 40 [1923–24] 213–18) or Canaanite (G. R. Driver, *Canaanite Myths*, 121:6–14; Kosmala, *ASTI* 1 [1962] 50–56) religious practices. The use of this verse to explain Jewish dietary restrictions is far less obscure than its origin, about which we remain unsure.

20–33 The conclusion or epilogue to the Book of the Covenant is a kind of parallel to the beginning of the collection of "guiding principles" and commands and instructions (20:22–23; see *Comment* above), and similarly has as a foundational motif absolute loyalty to Yahweh and complete rejection of all other deities. Commentators have often remarked on the different style of these verses and their similarity to Deuteronomistic language and theology (cf. Noth, 192–94: "a generally deuteronomistic stamp in style and content"; or Hyatt, 250: "the Deuteronomistic redactor . . . has built upon E tradition"), as on the fact that law-collections generally are ended with adjurations and promises (Cassuto, 305; Paul, *Book of the Covenant*, 35–42). A general assumption has arisen, to the effect that Exod 23:20–33 has been lifted from another context and set somewhat awkwardly into its present location as a typical concluding section to a long and complicated sequence of laws of mixed form and type.

Strangely missing from Exod 23:20–33, however, is the insistence on obedience to the laws just listed, an insistence repetitively and pointedly called for at the end of the Holiness Code (Lev 26:3–46) or following the "Schechemite Dodecalogue" of Deut 27:15–26 (so Deut 28) or even the Code of Lipit-Ishtar (*ANET*, 161) or the Code of Hammurapi (*ANET*, 177–80). In fact, insofar as the specific laws of the Book of the Covenant are concerned, this conclusion seems almost to be a conclusion to something else entirely; with its reference to the Presence of Yahweh and the promised land to be entered and settled and the temptations to be faced there, it might appear more at home in the narrative of the departure from Sinai in the Book of Numbers. The plain fact is, of course, that the editors of the tetrateuchal narrative did *not* set this passage there, though they might have done. Wherever they found it, and however they emended it, they put it here, and as Childs (486) has wisely insisted, it must be seen in its present role if it is to be properly understood.

The primary reference of Exod 23:20–33 is not the collection of laws preceding it, but the broader frame into which those laws too are set, a frame suggested also by the verses (20:22–23) that have been placed immediately before the laws themselves. Here, as there, the emphasis is upon Yahweh, whose commands and guiding instruction the laws are: Yahweh, who is and will be present with the people who enter covenant with him; Yahweh, who will guide his people and provide for them and protect them; Yahweh, who will expect, because he has every right to do so, the undiluted loyalty of the people he has "brought out," the people who are, in response, about to commit themselves to his service. It is hardly a coincidence that virtually the first (20:23) and last (23:32–33) words of the present sequence of the Book of the Covenant are Yahweh's insistence upon the absolute loyalty of his own people, in content and effect summary restatements of the first two of the ten commandments.

20–24 Thus the reference to the messenger whom Yahweh is to send out, here as everywhere in the OT a reference to an extension of Yahweh's own person and Presence, is in fact a restatement of the promise and proof of Presence motif that dominates the narrative of Exod 1–20. The "attendant" or "messenger" (מלאך) will perform the guiding, protecting, instructing, interposing functions that Yahweh's pillars of cloud and fire and Yahweh's attendant and providing Presence have performed earlier in the exodus narrative. Von Rad ("מַלְאָך in the OT," *TDNT* 1:77–78) referred to the מלאך יהוה as "the personification of Yahweh's assistance to Israel," and noted that Yahweh and his מלאך are "obviously one and the same," the מלאך being "an important literary theologization" introduced to soften "primitive tradition" regarding Yahweh's theophanic Presence. This is of course one possibility (see Ficker, "מַלְאָך" *THAT* 1: 906–8, for a summary review of the five major theories), but however the combination Yahweh/Yahweh's messenger came about, the "messenger" here is the equivalent of Yahweh himself, thus another way of indicating Yahweh's Presence. Indeed, North (*CBQ* 29 [1967] 429–32) has proposed, following an extensive review of the OT, that "the basic sense" of מלאך is "Presence," or, with regard to God's appearance to men, "manifestation," and that מלאך יהוה is at least "in some cases an expression for God himself" (cf. Baumgartner, *Zum Alten Testament*, 244–46).

This is why the messenger's guidance can be trusted: his guidance is Yahweh's guidance into the land "made ready," the gift of which will fulfill the second half of the covenant promise of progeny and land. Exodus begins with an account of the first half of this promise, and ends, at least in its narrative sequence, with the anticipation of the fulfillment of its second half. Paying close attention to the Presence of Yahweh's messenger and listening to his voice is equal to paying close attention to Yahweh's Presence and listening to Yahweh's voice. They must not "resent" or "be bitter against" (מרה) the "messenger's" guidance and counsel, because to do so will bring punishment authorized by Yahweh, whose "name" (שם = "Presence") is "within him" (בקרבו). This latter statement is virtually an assertion of equivalence: the "messenger" = Yahweh.

Paying careful attention to the messenger, Israel will hear what Yahweh himself is saying. If they are obedient to do what Yahweh says, Israel's enemies will become his enemies (cf. Gen 12:3, 27:28–29; Deut 28:1–7; Josh 1:1–9), and he will destroy those who would contest Israel's occupation of the land. Fensham (*VT* 13 [1963] 138–42) has linked this verse to the "clauses of protection" in the vassal treaties of the Hittites and has noted that Yahweh's protection came only to "an obedient nation." As they settle in this new

land, Israel is to take care to maintain the integrity of the covenantal relationship with Yahweh: they must not worship the gods of the peoples of the
land of Canaan. They must rather oppose them passionately, overturning
their images and destroying the sacred pillars of their gathering places, the
מצבות which may themselves have been iconic symbols of deity (cf. Noth,
OT World, 178).

25–33 Israel's service, rather, is to be given to Yahweh alone, who blesses
the people who are committed to him in a variety of ways. The blessing-list
of vv 25–28 is but a sample of such longer lists of Yahweh's benefits as the
one given in Deut 28:1–14, and is rooted in the blessing-cursing rhetoric
of OT covenantal theology. Staff of life, bread and water, basic health, the
healthy birth of healthy children, and length of life will all receive Yahweh's
own attention. He will send his "dreading-fear" (אימה) and his "panic-terror"
(צרעה), the confusing and dispiriting depression that comes upon those
against whom war is divinely waged (Köhler, *ZAW* 54 [1936] 291 and *Hebrew
Man*, 98–99); in result, Israel's enemies will be in total disarray when they
arrive. Israel will not have to face armed and dangerous resistance; the enemies
that remain will be presented to them in complete vulnerability (so "back
of all your enemies' necks"), and most of them will already have been driven
out headlong.

29–30 This reference to so complete and sweeping a conquest presents
an idealized prospect that never came to pass and so is followed immediately
by a qualification: the headlong displacement of Israel's enemies is to be a
managed rout, to take place across a number of years so that Israel will not
be faced with the keeping and defense of the land until they shall be numerous
and experienced enough to cope. Whether this qualification was original to
this narrative of promise or was a later addition made necessary by history
is impossible to say. The fact that even the qualified ideal was never achieved,
even in the most general sense, may favor the first of the two possibilities.

31 Yahweh's delimitation of the borders of Israel's possession of land
from the border of Egypt ("the sea of rushes," ים־סוף, has also been connected with the Gulf of Aqabah, Hyatt, 156–62, 252 and the Red Sea, Batto,
JBL 102 [1983] 27–35) to the Mediterranean (ים פלשתים), and from the
southern desert (מדבר) to the river Euphrates (הנהר) in the north is a description of the territorial limits of Israel in the days of Davidic-Solomonic glory.
This specification may provide a hint about the time of the reference in vv
29–30 to a "managed" displacement.

32–33 Once again, the singularity of the devotion expected by Yahweh
is stressed. Israel is not to covenant with the people of the land or their
gods. These peoples must be displaced, to prevent their influencing Israel
against Yahweh, primarily by the advocacy of their gods: service of these
gods, in any manner whatever, would constitute an entrapment of Israel.
Israel is to have no other gods, not in any form, not for any reason.

Explanation

The conclusion to the Book of the Covenant, like its beginning, summarizes
its point and its emphasis and links it unmistakably to the Decalogue that is

its root. Like the Decalogue, the Book of the Covenant is presented as *Yahweh's* expectation of Israel (see *Explanation* on 20:1–17). The "guiding principles," the commands, the prohibitions that make up the collection that is Exod 20:23–23:19 are all to the end that the integrity of Israel's relationship to Yahweh be guaranteed. The Decalogue begins with the command that Israel have no god other than Yahweh. The Book of the Covenant begins (20:23) and ends (23:32–33) with that same command, and all that lies between that beginning and that ending is designed to assure its obedience.

The obvious fact that the Book of the Covenant is a compilation, and presents laws in a mixture of forms and reflecting a variety of backgrounds in no way detracts from such a purpose. If anything, so multiform a collection drawn into a single focus enhances it. Any such collection invites attention to the parts that make it up, and is usually treated in its component parts far more fully than in its sum. That is certainly the case with the Book of the Covenant, which has attracted more proposed organizational patterns and subpatterns and interlocking and independent internal divisions than any other sequence or narrative, cultic or legal, in Exodus.

We cannot afford to overlook, however, even though we have often done so, that the Book of the Covenant is presented in Exodus as a unit, a whole, and that it has been located by a tradition and by editors (who might have put it elsewhere) immediately after the narrative of Yahweh's Advent before Israel at Sinai and immediately before the account of the solemnization of the covenantal relationship. What makes so obviously diverse a collection a unit? And why was it inserted into so dramatic a narrative at so climactic a point in what seems at a first look so distracting a manner?

All these questions and others they suggest may be answered by the recognition of the Book of the Covenant as the primary guide, applying the ten commandments, to the conduct of life in relationship with Yahweh, the God who has delivered Israel and who is now present with Israel. The Book of the Covenant is a kind of theological rule for life in the Presence of Yahweh. It is an exposition, an application of his ten words. Whatever its sources, wherever and whenever their "original" provenance, the collection that is now the Book of the Covenant has a single focus: its concern is how to serve Yahweh who is present, and him alone.

This is the reason why the collection is begun and ended as it is, with the essential emphasis of the first two of the ten commandments. This is the binding theme that makes so diverse a collection a single code. This is the key to an understanding of "laws" that are basically religious in their motivation, and designed to cement, cultivate and display a divine-human relationship. This is the explanation for the location of the collection at so crucial a point in the narrative of Yahweh and Israel. And this is why the Book of the Covenant is in a way not an interruption of that narrative at all: it is a rule for life in Yahweh's Presence that links the narrative of Yahweh come to Israel with the narrative of Israel's approach to Yahweh by providing the rule by which such an approach can be made by such a people to such a God.

The Making of the Covenant: The People and Their Leaders (24:1–18)

Bibliography

Allegro, John M. *Qumran Cave 4: I (4Q158–4Q186)*. DJD V. Oxford: At the Clarendon Press, 1968. **Gordon, C. H.** *Ugaritic Literature.* Rome: Pontifical Biblical Institute, 1949. **Graesser, C. F.** "Standing Stones in Ancient Palestine." *BA* 35 (1972) 34–63. **Humbert, P.** "Etendre la main." *VT* 12 (1962) 383–95. **Jenni, E.** " 'Kommen' im theologischen Sprachgebrauch des Alten Testaments." *Wort-Gebot-Glaube. Beiträge zur Theologie des Alten Testaments.* ATANT 59. Zurich: Zwingli Verlag, 1970. 251–61. **Mann, T. W.** *Divine Presence and Guidance in Israelite Traditions: The Typology of Exaltation.* Baltimore: Johns Hopkins University Press, 1977. **McKenzie, J. L.** "The Elders in the Old Testament." *Bib* 48 (1959) 522–40. **Möhlenbrink, K.** "Josua im Pentateuch." *ZAW* 59 (1942–1943) 14–58. **Nicholson, E. W.** "The Antiquity of the Tradition in Exodus XXIV 9–11." *VT* 25 (1975) 69–79. ———. "The Covenant Ritual in Exodus XXIV 3–8." *VT* 32 (1982) 74–86. ———. "The Interpretation of Exodus XXIV 9–11." *VT* 24 (1974) 77–97. **Patrick, D.** "The Covenant Code Source." *VT* 27 (1977) 145–57. **Perlitt, L.** *Bundestheologie im Alten Testament.* WMANT 36. Neukirchen-Vluyn: Neukirchener Verlag, 1969. **Rendtorff, R.** *Studien zur Geschichte des Opfers im Alten Israel.* WMANT 24. Neukirchen-Vluyn: Neukirchener Verlag, 1967. **Roberts, J. J. M.** "The Hand of Yahweh." *VT* 21 (1971) 244–51. **Schmid, H.** *Mose. Überlieferung und Geschichte.* BZAW 110. Berlin: Verlag Alfred Töpelmann, 1968. **Schmid, R.** *Das Bundesopfer in Israel.* SANT 9. Munich: Kösel Verlag, 1964. **Schnutenhaus, F.** "Das Kommen und Erscheinen Gottes im Alten Testament." *ZAW* 76 (1964) 1–22. **Taylor, J.** "Sapphire." *A Dictionary of the Bible.* Ed. J. Hastings. New York: Charles Scribner's Sons, 1902. 4:403. **Westermann, C.** "Die Herrlichkeit Gottes in der Priesterschrift." *Wort-Gebot-Glaube. Beiträge zur Theologie des Alten Testaments.* ATANT 59. Zurich: Zwingli Verlag, 1970. 227–49. **Zenger, E.** *Die Sinaitheophanie.* Forschung zur Bibel 3. Würzburg: Echter Verlag Katholisches Bibelwerk, 1971.

Translation

[1] *Then to Moses he said, "Climb up toward Yahweh: you, and Aaron, Nadab ("Willing One") and Abihu ("My Father is He"),[a] and seventy of the elders of Israel, and bow down in worship at a respectful distance.[b]* [2] *Moses by himself is to come close to Yahweh[a]—the others[b] are not to come close, nor are the people to climb up with him."[c]*

[3] *Next,[a] Moses came and recounted to the people all Yahweh's[b] words, all the guiding principles. All the people responded as with a single voice, and said, "All the words that Yahweh has spoken, we will do."[c]* [4] *So Moses wrote down all Yahweh's words. Then, rising early in the morning, he built at the base of the mountain an altar and twelve pillars,[a] one for each[b] of the twelve tribes of Israel.*

[5] *Next, he sent out young men of the sons of Israel to offer up whole burnt offerings and sacrifice completion-sacrifices[a] of young bulls[b] to Yahweh.[c]* [6] *Moses took half of the blood and put it into open basins;[a] the other half of the blood he dashed upon the altar.* [7] *Then he took the book of the covenant and read it aloud[a] in the hearing of the people. Thus they said, "All that the Yahweh has spoken, we will do, and we will pay attention."[b]*

[8] *So Moses took the remaining[a] blood and dashed it upon the people, saying,*

"See now the blood of the covenant that Yahweh has contracted [b] *with you, a covenant made specific by all these words."* [c]

[9] *At long last Moses and Aaron, Nadab and Abihu* [a] *and seventy of the elders of Israel climbed up.* [10] *And then they saw* [a] *the God of Israel!* [b] *Beneath his feet was something like a mosaic pavement of lapis lazuli,* [c] *like the span* [d] *of the heavens in depth.* [e] [11] *Yet toward the leaders* [a] *of the sons of Israel, he did not stretch out his hand: thus they had a vision* [b] *of God, and there they ate and drank.*

[12] *Yahweh then said to Moses, "Climb on up toward me at the summit of the mountain,* [a] *and be there; I will give you the tablets of stone on which are* [b] *the instruction* [c] *and the commandment I have written to direct the people.* [d] [13] *Thus did Moses rise, along with Joshua his assistant, and Moses* [a] *climbed up higher on the mountain of God.* [14] *To the elders, he said, "Wait for us in this place until we return to you. Look, Aaron and Hur are with you—whoever has a lot to say* [a] *can approach them."* [15] *So Moses* [a] *climbed up higher on the mountain, and the cloud concealed the mountain.* [16] *Thus the glory of Yahweh* [a] *settled onto Mount Sinai, and the cloud concealed it six days; then on the seventh day Yahweh* [b] *called out to Moses from the midst of the cloud.* [17] *The spectacle of the glory of Yahweh, to the eyes of the sons of Israel, was like a consuming fire at the mountain's peak.* [18] *Then Moses went into the midst of the cloud, climbing up higher on the mountain. In fact, Moses was* [a] *on the mountain forty days and forty nights.*

Notes

1.a. הוא "he" in אביהוא "Abihu" probably refers to Yahweh, as in Isa 43:25, אנכי אנכי הוא "I, I am he." SamPent adds here two other sons of Aaron, Eleazar ("God has helped") and Ithamar ("Date-palm region").

1.b. מרחק "from far" in this context indicates that the movement up toward Yahweh is to be kept under careful limitations. LXX has "they" rather than "you" (pl) as subj of the verb שחה "bow down in worship," and adds τῷ κυρίῳ (= "Yahweh") as direct object.

2.a. LXX has τὸν θεόν "to God."

2.b. והם "and they," i.e., those who have accompanied Moses.

2.c. MT עמו "with him" is read μετ᾽ αὐτῶν "with them" by LXX, but the change is unnecessary. Moses has been told to "climb up" and whom to bring with him. The final clause of v 2 is a further specification: the people are not to be included in the ascending group.

3.a. The special *waw* beginning this verse links it with some part of the narrative prior to the instructions given to Moses in vv 1–2, instructions carried out in vv 9–11. The thematic connection is with the Book of the Covenant, given the present form of the text.

3.b. LXX reads τοῦ θεοῦ "God's."

3.c. LXX has here the same statement made by the people in v 7.

4.a. SamPent and LXX read אבנים "stones," instead of the sg מצבה "pillar" of MT.

4.b. לשנים עשר "to the twelve . . ."; 4Q158:4, DJD V, has למספר "for the counting" before this phrase.

5.a. זבחים שלמים "offerings of wholeness" signify the "conclusion" or "fulfillment" of something, in this case the sealing of covenantal relationship. See Rendtorff, *Geschichte des Opfers*, 132–33; Schmid, *Bundesopfer*, 103–26.

5.b. SamPent adds בני בקר "sons of a herd animal."

5.c. See n. 2.a above.

6.a. אגן "basins," apparently some kind of rounded vessel. Cf. the מזרק "dashing-basin" of Exod 27:3 and 38:3, a container apparently designed with such "dashing" or "tossing" in mind (זרק).

7.a. קרא: the Arabic cognate means "read aloud, recite (the Ḳorʾān)," according to BDB (894).

7.b. ונשמע "and we will hear," indicating in this context hearing with attention, interest; cf. BDB, 1033 § 1.f.

8.a. "Remaining" is added for clarity.

8.b. כרת "cut." See BDB, 137 § III.1. and 503 § 4.

8.c. על "concerning, according to," read in this context "made specific by." The Cairo Geniza fragment has "guiding decisions" (see n. 21:1.a) instead of "words."

9.a. SamPent also adds Eleazar and Ithamar here.

10.a. ראה "see."

10.b. LXX has τὸν τόπον οὗ εἱστήκει ἐκεῖ ὁ θεὸς τοῦ Ισραηλ "the place where the God of Israel had stood."

10.c. כמעשה לבנת הספיר "like the working of a pavement of lapis lazuli."

10.d. וכעצם "and like the bone, substance, self" (BDB, 782–83), taken here as the frame or scope of the heavens: what is most apparent about the heavens is their vastness.

10.e. לטהר "with reference to purity," read above as "depth," the depth of the sky suggested by the deep blue of lapis lazuli.

11.a. אציל "corner, side, support." The אצילים are lit. the "pillars" of the people of Israel.

11.b. חזה "see." LXX has the very different reading, καὶ τῶν ἐπιλέκτων τοῦ Ισραηλ οὐ διεφώνησεν οὐδὲ εἷς· καὶ ὤφθησαν ἐν τῷ τόπῳ τοῦ θεοῦ "And from the elect of Israel, not one failed to answer the roll-call; and they were seen in the Presence of God. . . ."

12.a. ההרה "mountainward," here in reference to the higher part of the mountain where Yahweh is.

12.b. MT has simply . . . את־לחת האבן והתורה "the tablets of stone *and* the instruction. . . ." Cf. Childs, 499.

12.c. התורה "the instruction."

12.d. MT has "them," of which the obvious antecedent, the people, is added above for clarity.

13.a. LXX lacks "Moses" here, and has a pl instead of the sg "climbed" of the MT.

14.a. מי־בעל דברים "whoever is a lord of words," i.e., anybody who is impatient with the long wait, and talks about it a great deal.

15.a. LXX adds καὶ Ἰησοῦς "and Joshua."

16.a. LXX has τοῦ θεοῦ "God."

16.b. MT has simply "he called," but the obvious subject of קרא is Yahweh; LXX indeed reads κύριος. "Yahweh" is added above for clarity.

18.a. LXX adds ἐκεῖ "there."

Form/Structure/Setting

The jigsaw puzzle appearance of the narrative of Exod 24, even to an untrained eye, has been the subject of extensive and often conflicting commentary. Vv 1–2 contain instructions that make them seem less in sequence to what has preceded them than the verses that follow, 3–8. Vv 9–11 recount the fulfillment of the instructions given in vv 1–2, and vv 12–18 set forth a narrative that has links to both the preceding narratives, but leave dangling the question of the whereabouts and the activity of the group that accompanied Moses onto the mountain during his long stay by himself nearer to the Presence of Yahweh. For example, compare v 14 with the continuation of the narrative in chap. 32, where Aaron is once again with the people and where Moses descends the mountain in the company of Joshua, who is not mentioned as in the ascending group in chap. 24 before v 13.

Most source-critics have assigned the bulk of Exod 24 to E, though they sometimes speculate the presence also of J tradition and various redactorial hands. Beer (125–27) for example, assigns the entire chapter to E¹ and redactorial material, with the exception of vv 15b–18a, which he gives to P. Hyatt (253–54) gives vv 3, 4b–6, 8, 12–14, and 18b to E; 1–2, 9–11 to J; 15–18a to P; and 4ᵃ, 7 to a deuteronomistic redactor. Beyerlin (*Sinaitic Traditions,* 14–18, 30) proposes that 1a, 3–8, 9–11, 12, 13b, (15a), 18b belong to E, and regards 1b–2 "a theological correction," 13a, 14 "E probably" (48), and 15b–18a to P. Noth (194–201, 243) attributes vv 1–2 to E as reworked by a redactor, 9–11 to E, 3–8 to an "independent" Book of the Covenant source (cf. Patrick, *VT* 27 [1977] 145–57, who proposes that vv 3–8, along with Exod 19:3b–8 and 20:22 are a "narrative framework for the Covenant Code," written after the compilation of the Code itself, in the northern kingdom and prior to 721 B.C.), 12–15a to J, and 15b–18 to P. And Childs (499–502) assigns vv 3–8 to E and 15b–18a to P, but considers the remainder of the chapter too difficult to assign with objectivity.

As such a sampling reveals, Exod 24 is too complicated a composite, with too few characteristic signature-phrases, to permit anything more than a general speculation about its sources. The chapter is presented to us as a whole however, and it has a function in the narrative of Exodus which too much atomization has tended to obscure. The compilers who gave the chapter its present sequence were apparently intent on what the various pieces of their finished jigsaw would suggest. They were not as bothered by internal consistency and logical sequence as we seem to be. Not only is their combination of the materials they had available important; so also is their finished product.

Nicholson (*VT* 32 [1982] 74–86, and *VT* 24 [1974] 77–97) has treated Exod 24 in relation to the larger narrative sequence in Exod 19–24; Perlitt (*Bundestheologie,* 156–238) has seen it in the even larger frame of a Sinaipericope setting forth a covenant-theology; and Beyerlin (*Sinaitic Traditions,* 1–26, 167–68) has linked all the Sinai traditions to a cultic re-presentation in Canaan of Yahweh's Presence revealed and Yahweh's covenant promulgated. While the literary analysis of each of these scholars again reflects the problematical nature of chap. 24, the attempt to see the composite as a whole, with a specific purpose and in relation to a larger narrative context, is certainly a move in the right direction. Exod 24, with all of its inconsistencies, provides an obvious conclusion to the events set in motion in Exod 19, though in somewhat more general terms than Nicholson (*VT* 32 [1982] 83–85) suggests. Indeed, the awkwardness of the Exod 24 composite may be accounted for by the need of the editors who created it to bring to conclusion a series of strands, each of them anticipated by the narrative of chaps. 19–23, most of them summarized in the "eagle's wings" speech of 19:4–6, and all of them together creating an ideal "end" to the exodus narrative—an "end" dramatically highlighted in Exodus by the placement immediately following chap. 24 of the lengthy section of cultic instructions for the media of worship in Yahweh's Presence.

The fact that such an ideal "end" is not the true end of the exodus narrative is made clear by the tension-filled narrative of Exod 32–34, which also concludes with the making (or remaking) of the covenant, and also is followed by a very similar lengthy section of cultic instructions. As noted already (*Form/Structure/Setting* on 19:1–15), we have in Exodus at least the major parts of a Sinai narrative sequence, the form of which is determined by a theological purpose. That purpose is the presentation, using every available tradition, of the primary theme of Exodus, the gift of Yahweh's Presence to Israel at

Sinai. There is little wonder that this narrative as it is preserved in Exodus
is complex, forced apart at a number of points by related material of both
a primary and a secondary nature. Given the importance of the subject and
its centrality not only to Exodus but to the OT and even to the entire Bible,
such expansion and accretion are inevitable and a pointed testament to the
subject they extend and distort. Our chief difficulty in understanding these
narratives with all their excess baggage has been our susceptibility to distraction, by the parts and the seams, from the whole, the sum of admittedly
mismatched blocks of material. Having examined the parts, and needfully
so, we have somehow become unable, or at least too reluctant, to see them
together as those who put them together saw them, and with important intentions.

Certainly the narrative of the "real" end of Exodus makes better sense
immediately following the narrative of the "ideal" end. Such may have been
the original sequence of the Sinai narrative. But it is not so in the Exodus
presented us by the Bible. Similarly, the rearrangement of Exod 24 may help
us in the important task of reconstructing the separate traditions and interests
that are commingled in the received text. We must not neglect the most
painstaking research along these lines. But there is also a great deal to be
learned by reflection on the one chapter of that story about which we have
greatest certainty, the text as it is.

Considered as a whole rather than a patchwork of fragments, Exod 24
may be seen as an attempt, following the decalogue and the Book of the
Covenant expanding it, to provide (1) an account of the solemnization of
the covenant by the people of Israel; (2) an account of an additional preparation and authorization of Israel's leaders; (3) an anticipation of a continuing
revelation of Presence and Guidance; and (4) the beginnings (along with
20:19, 21) of the elevation of Moses as Yahweh's special representative and
as Israel's special advocate. Undergirding all this is the "constant" of the
Sinai narrative sequence, indeed of the entire Book of Exodus—the Presence
of Yahweh among his people. This "constant" and these themes are what
give Exod 24 its form, and as uneasy as that form may seem on logical or
source-critical grounds, quite dramatically it presents the summary for which
the "ideal" end of Exodus calls.

Comment

1-2 Despite the obvious connection of these two verses to vv 9-11, where
the instructions given in them are carried out, they serve also as a transition
from the warning at the end of the Book of the Covenant (23:32-33) to the
account of the actual commitment of Israel to the special relationship with
Yahweh. Yahweh addresses Moses, here assumed still to be in the position
in which he has received the commands and "guiding principles" of the Book
of the Covenant (cf. 20:21-22), and gives him further instructions applying
only to himself and Israel's leaders. Aaron, two of his sons, and seventy
elders of Israel are to accompany Moses up the mountain, after Moses has
delivered Yahweh's instructions to Israel and received their response. These
instructions are posed by the composite narrative as given to Moses while

he is still on Sinai, near the thick cloud surrounding Yahweh's Presence, and to be followed after he has carried out the prior responsibility of passing Yahweh's application of his "ten words" along to Israel. Indeed v 2 makes clear both the exclusion of the people from these instructions and also the subsidiary if special position of those who are to accompany Moses: Moses himself is to "come close" (niphal of נגשׁ) to Yahweh, the elders are to worship "at a respectful distance," and the people are not to climb up the mountain at all. The seventy elders mentioned here may be taken as a reference to "all the elders" of Exod 18:12, or to the "men of ability" described in 18:21–26, though other "seventy elder" traditions (cf. Num 11:16–17, 24–25; Deut 1:9–18) may also be reflected (cf. H. Schmid, *Mose,* 67–69; McKenzie, *Bib* 48 [1959] 522–28).

3–4 Following Yahweh's delivery to Moses of these additional instructions regarding himself and the leaders who assist him, Moses "came," בא, a verb that in this sequence can be taken to mean Moses' return to the people to give them the instructions of Yahweh applying the principles laid down in the ten commandments, the instructions that became in time our Book of the Covenant. Moses reviewed for the people this further revelation of Yahweh, as he had been bidden (in the present composite, at 21:1), and they responded with the set phrase of commitment, "Everything Yahweh has spoken, we will do" (19:8; 24:3, 7). Then Moses set down in writing Yahweh's words of command and guiding principle, and early the next morning he made preparation for the ceremony of Israel's formal entry into covenant with Yahweh. This preparation involved the construction of an altar and twelve pillars at the foot of Mount Sinai, the altar representing the Presence of Yahweh (see *Comment* on 20:24–26) and the twelve pillars, each of the twelve tribes of Israel. Graesser (*BA* 35 [1972] 34–39) has maintained that the מצבה "pillar" was a "thing set up" נצב which called attention to itself as something placed, and served among other functions a "legal" purpose, "to mark a legal relationship between two or more individuals," here between each tribe and Yahweh and so between tribe and tribe.

5–8 These preparations made, Moses delegated young men to offer both wholly burned offerings and also "completion-sacrifices," sacrifices closely linked with covenant-making and covenant relationships (cf. R. Schmid, *Bundesopfer,* 118–25). Moses' use of the blood of these sacrificial animals is a further confirmation of the relational nature of the "completion-sacrifices" and the ceremonial of Exod 24:3–8 (so R. Schmid, 30–33, 75–80): one half of it he dashed upon the altar, the symbol of Yahweh's Presence; the other half, he dashed upon the people. In between these two acts, Moses read the newly written Book of the Covenant to the people, and they responded with the set phrase of commitment, to which is added here the additional assurance that they will pay attention and take seriously the words of Yahweh, all of which they have previously promised to do. This assertion Moses then confirms, for as he dashes the remaining blood upon the people, he reminds them that the covenant, contracted with Yahweh, has been solemnized in blood, having been made clear to the people by the words that Yahweh has spoken. Zenger's (*Sinaitheophanie,* 74–76, 216) view, that the ceremony involving the dashing of the blood is a deuteronomistic addition to the narrative, is questionable; much more appropriate is Nicholson's (*VT* 32 [1982] 80–83) idea, that the blood ceremonial is a means of consecrating Israel as Yahweh's holy people.

9–11 With his primary task completed, Moses can now turn to the additional instructions Yahweh has given him, instructions applying only to himself and a select group of leaders singled out earlier on Jethro's advice (18:13–26). The apparent purpose of the climb up onto Sinai of this special group is that they shall have the experience, as Moses has had already, of a still more intimate contact with the Presence of Yahweh. In such a manner are they uniquely equipped for their service of guidance and teaching, of leadership through interpretation. The narrative is forthright in its statement of what happened on the mountain: the special group actually saw the God of Israel. Despite attempts by ancient translators and modern commentators to qualify this blunt statement and make it more consistent with the bulk of OT tradition, it must be taken seriously as it stands. ראה primarily means see with one's eyes, and the account goes on to describe, at least in part, what the group saw and to state that (somewhat surprisingly?) no harm came to them. The first qualification of the experience may be the use in v 11 of the verb חזה, which can mean to see with one's eyes *or* in a visionary experience, but even that usage may be no more than a simple parallel.

10 Despite the assertion that Moses and his special companions saw God, however, the description of what they saw concentrates not on the appearance of God but on the appearance of what lay at his feet. This can be taken to imply that a description of God original to this passage has been respectfully deleted, or, as is more likely, that the group was not given permission to lift their faces toward God and so could describe only what they actually did see, the "pavement" beneath him, before which they were prostrate in reverential awe. Later in the Exodus narrative (33:18), a confident Moses asks permission to be shown (hiphil imperative of ראה) Yahweh's glory (כבוד) and is refused because, Yahweh tells him (33:20), a man cannot see (ראה) Yahweh's face (פנים) and live. Here, no such permission is asked and none of course is granted. Thus what Moses and his companions experience is a theophany of the Presence of God, not a vision of his person, and what they see, bowed before even that awesome reality, is what could be seen from a position of obeisant prostration, the surface on which his Presence offered itself. That surface is described as "like a working (a pattern) of bricks of lapis lazuli, and like the very essence of the heavens as regards purity." Taylor (*Dictionary* 4:403) has noted that lapis lazuli was available in the biblical period in both a natural (from Cyprus and Scythia) and an artificial (from Egypt) form, and that it fits the eleven OT references to ספיר. According to some translators (Gordon, *Ugaritic Literature*, 33: text 51: V: 96–97; Clifford, *Cosmic Mountain*, 112; cf. Driver, *Canaanite Myths*, 97: Baal II: V 18–19), the description of Baal's palace sometimes includes lapis lazuli. The reference in v 10 may therefore be a double one, calling up the deep dark blue of an endless sky and the building materials of legendary divine dwelling-places.

11 The uniqueness of the experience of Moses and those who were with him is underlined by the statement that they were not harmed by God: God "did not stretch out his hand" toward Israel's leaders. Here, as in Exod

20:18–20, those who experienced God's special nearness may have feared harm. No harm befell them, however, for they were where they were by divine permission. Humbert (*VT* 12 [1962] 387–89) has pointed out that שׁלח יד "he stretched out a hand" is in the OT a human gesture for the most part, but is used of God himself in five texts (here; at Exod 3:20; 9:15; Ezek 8:3; Ps 138:7), and refers in its three uses in Exodus to a "hostile or punitive action." Roberts (*VT* 21 [1971] 246–49) has set forth a series of extrabiblical parallels indicating that the primary meaning of such "hand of God" expressions was the depiction of a "disastrous manifestation of the supernatural power." This power was not used against Moses and his companions, because they were present by divine invitation. Thus they had a vision (חזה) of God and ate and drank in his Presence.

This meal has often been taken as a covenant meal (so Hyatt, 257–58; Childs, 507), a position vigorously opposed by Nicholson (*VT* 24 [1974] 84–94), who proposes that 24:9–11 records only a tradition of theophany at the mountain of God, *sans* Moses and *sans* covenant, and that the meal of v 11 is a means "of worshipping and rejoicing in God's Presence" (see also Nicholson, *VT* 25 [1975] 69–79). While Nicholson is surely right in his emphasis upon the theophany as the essential point of these verses, his interpretation of the meal may go a bit too far, especially when vv 9–11 are considered in their present setting. The covenant has been solemnized already, in a ceremony that surely included the leaders who accompany Moses, a bit later, onto the mountain of Yahweh's Presence. These leaders are then given their own unique experience of Yahweh, certainly as a means of reinforcing their self-confidence and undergirding their authority in the tasks of leadership before them. The meal they eat in Yahweh's Presence may therefore have special connections both with what they have experienced and with what they are to do (cf. von Rad, *OT Theology* 1:254). The strongest impression left by this quite remarkable theophany account, an impression given above all by its unusual description of God's Presence and the group's response, is that it may be from a different, and perhaps also an ancient, strand of tradition, one reflected only rarely in the OT.

12 The further instruction of Yahweh to Moses, that he alone should climb still higher up the mountain to receive the tablets of stone containing Yahweh's instruction and commandment, are a part of the tradition glorifying Moses as Yahweh's chosen intermediary (see *Comment* on 17:1–15; cf. Mann, *Divine Presence*, 144–49, 154). The tablets of stone Yahweh promises to give to Moses are the tablets written on both sides (Exod 32:15), the tablets Moses is subsequently to break in his anger at the people's idolatry (32:19). Precisely what was written on them is nowhere said in the OT, not even here where Yahweh owns having done the writing. Tradition has assumed that the original stone tablets bore the ten commandments largely because of Exod 34:1, in which Yahweh proposes to write on the second pair of tablets "the words that were on the first tablets," and because of 34:27–28, in which Yahweh dictates to Moses, who writes on the tablets "the words of the covenant, the ten words" (דברי הברית עשׂרת הדברים). The OT references, however, are not consistent, as even these passages in Exod 24 and 34 show, and the phrase in v 12, "the tablets of stone and the instruction and the commandment I have written to direct the people," does not clear up the difficulty. While the tradition that the tablets contained the ten commandments may be seen to have been started very early and must for that reason alone be taken seriously, this first and possibly earliest reference to the contents of the tablets is ambiguous.

13–14 Joshua is four times (here; 33:11; Num 11:28; Josh 1:1) mentioned in the OT as the "assistant" or "minister" (מְשָׁרֵת שֵׁרֶת) to Moses, and the narrative of 32:17–18 makes it plain that we are to assume that he alone accompanied Moses during at least some of the additional climb up Sinai (cf. Mölenbrink, *ZAW* 59 [1942–43] 24–28, who considers the reference to Joshua here and in 32:17 later additions to the narrative). The instruction Moses gives to the elders, taken in the context of Exod 24 as a whole and as a part of the entire Sinai narrative sequence, shows that we are to think of the elders, along with Aaron and Hur (cf. Exod 17:10, 12), as remaining on the mountain in the place of their special experience of God's Presence until Moses and Joshua return to them. That the account of that return is missing from Exodus may be inferred from the fact that Aaron, and presumably also Hur and the (other?) elders, are in the camp with the people at the foot of the mountain when the idolatry of the golden calf takes place, as also when Moses returns to the camp with the tablets of stone (Exod 32). The designation of Aaron and Hur as "in charge" in Moses' absence may also be assumed to have carried over when the special group returned to the camp below, where Aaron became the focus of the people's complaints in Moses' absence (32:1–6).

15–18 These matters attended to, Moses climbed higher onto Sinai, apparently accompanied at first by Joshua and then moving on by himself, there to receive the promised tablets containing Yahweh's "instruction and commandment." The cloud (עָנָן) that concealed the mountain, from the midst of which Yahweh called out to Moses, and into the midst of which Moses went is, as Mann (*Divine Presence,* 256–57) has shown, a special symbol in Exodus of divine guidance, divine communication, and divine Presence. The settling glory (כָּבוֹד) of Yahweh, similarly a symbol of the divine Presence, is an extension of the theophanic experience of chaps. 19 and 20 and 24:9–11. Both the cloud and the glory in these verses are paralleled in 40:34–38, the paragraph that concludes the Book of Exodus.

Westermann (*Wort-Gebot-Glaube,* 230–40) has shown how carefully P has combined the coming and staying and speaking of Yahweh on the mountain with the coming and staying and Word-receiving of Moses, and has called attention to the assertion that the sight of this glory was visible to the sons of Israel on the plain below the mountain, in a special authentication of all that Yahweh was saying and giving in that special place, at that special time, to, and so through, his special intermediary, Moses.

Thus the "spectacle of the glory of Yahweh, like a consuming fire at the mountain's peak," is *not* to be taken as a memory of a volcanic eruption: this language, once again, is the language of theophany, the description in graphic symbols of Yahweh's advent (cf. Schnutenhaus, *ZAW* 76 [1964] 1–21; Jenni, *Wort-Gebot-Glaube,* 251–61). Israel is shown here to have experienced a continuation of the awesome events narrated in chaps. 19 and 20, at the beginning of a long period in which Moses is to receive the further "instruction and commandment" of Yahweh. Whatever this teaching may originally have been, the placement at the end of chap. 24 of what amounts to the Priestly prologue to the lengthy section on the media of worship in Yahweh's Presence gives the impression that the revelation following the ceremony of Israel's entry into covenant with Yahweh was a revelation guiding the first obligation of a people so committed, their worship of the God who had bound himself to them.

Explanation

As obvious and as complex as the composite form of Exod 24 is, it is the finished form of the chapter, viewed in relation to the still larger whole of the Sinai narrative sequence, that presents the chapter's essential point. Exod 24 presents what may be called the "ideal end" to a narrative sequence begun in chap. 19, the narrative of the Advent of Yahweh to his people at Sinai. In chap. 19, after a careful preparation of the people of Israel over a three-day period and amidst an awesome array of phenomena symbolizing his Presence, Yahweh comes. In chap. 20, to an Israel waiting thunderstruck he speaks the basic principles of life in relationship with him, and following their fearful response and at their request, he then reveals to Moses the particularities of applying these principles to everyday life, 20:22–23:33. Then, in chap. 24, all this revelation is brought to a happy response as the teaching is shared with Israel. Israel makes a positive response; a covenant of relationship is joined and solemnized with appropriate ceremony; the leaders of Israel are given a preparatory and authenticating experience of Yahweh's still more intimate Presence; and Moses is commanded still higher onto the mountain to receive the tablets containing instruction and commandment, and further guidance still for Israel's life of response.

A more appropriate conclusion to the Sinai narrative sequence could hardly be imagined. Indeed, the only flaw apart from some ambiguity in detail is that this "conclusion" is *not* the conclusion of the Sinai narrative sequence. This is why it can be called the "ideal end," the conclusion we all may have hoped for, Yahweh himself above all. There is another end to the Sinai narrative sequence, a "real" conclusion, and chap. 24 must be seen as continued by that "real end," which is located in Exodus as chaps. 32–34. Just as chap. 24 is a culmination of chap. 19–23, so chaps. 32–34 are a culmination of the high prospects of chap. 24. Indeed, chap. 24 may be said to face four directions at once: its narrative directions are up the mountain toward Yahweh, and down the mountain, toward Israel; and its thematic directions are backward, toward Yahweh's great advent to Israel, and forward, toward Israel's great departure from Yahweh, a departure that results in the possibility of Yahweh's departing from Israel.

Now what can be said to bind all this together? What makes a unity of a sequence of chapters so strung out through Exodus, themselves the result of an often loose arrangement of varied tradition, presented in various forms and styles? Just as there is in this sequence no chapter that is any more obvious a composite than chap. 24, so also there is no chapter that provides a better paradigm of the whole. Exod 24 is bound together by the theme of divine Presence: the chapter begins with a special call to a special group to come closer to the Presence that has come close to them; proceeds to narratives of covenant-making with the Presence, an intimate experience of the Presence, and a summons of Moses yet more closely to the Presence; then ends with the anticipation of a special revelation about response to the Presence. The narrative sequence of Exod 19–24, 32–34 begins with the advent of the Presence to Israel and ends with a qualification of the relation of Israel to that Presence, including in between a loyal response negated by a disloyal betrayal, the threat of withdrawal of the Presence, and a first great outpouring of forgiving mercy. Everywhere the preoccupation is with Yahweh in Israel's midst and what that means for Israel and Yahweh alike, and nowhere is that preoccupation stated more intensely or more hopefully than in chap. 24, the "ideal end" of Exodus that Israel did not conserve.

II. Yahweh's Instructions for the Media of Worship (25:1—31:18)

The Call for Materials (25:1–9)

PARALLEL VERSES:
35:4–9

Bibliography

Brenner, A. *Colour Terms in the Old Testament.* JSOT 21. Sheffield: JSOT Press, 1982. **Cross, F. M., Jr.** "The Priestly Tabernacle." *BAR* 1. Garden City: Doubleday, 1961. 201–28. Also *BA* 10 (1947) 45–68. ———. "The Priestly Work." *Canaanite Myth and Hebrew Epic.* Cambridge: Harvard University Press, 1973. 293–325. **Gradwohl, R.** *Die Farben im Alten Testament.* BZAW 83. Berlin: Verlag Alfred Töpelmann, 1963. **Haran, M.** *Temples and Temple-Service in Ancient Israel.* Oxford: Clarendon Press, 1978. **Hurvitz, A.** "The Usage of שׁשׁ and בוץ in the Bible and Its Implication for the Date of P." *HTR* 60 (1967) 117–21. **Jensen, L. B.** "Royal Purple of Tyre." *JNES* 22 (1963) 104–18. **Jepsen, A.** "Zur Chronologie des Priesterkodex." *ZAW* 47 (1929) 251–55. **Johnson, A. R.** *The Vitality of the Individual in the Thought of Ancient Israel.* Cardiff: University of Wales Press, 1964. **Kaiser, O.** *Introduction to the Old Testament.* Minneapolis: Augsburg, 1975. **Kaufmann, J.** "Probleme der israelitisch-jüdischen Religionsgeschichte," *ZAW* 48 (1930) 23–43. **Keel, O.** *The Symbolism of the Biblical World.* New York: Seabury Press, 1978. **Koch, K.** *Die Priesterschrift von Exodus 25 bis Leviticus 16.* FRLANT 53 (N.F.). Göttingen: Vandenhoeck & Ruprecht, 1959. **Rad, G. von.** *Die Priesterschrift im Hexateuch.* BWANT 13. Stuttgart: W. Kohlhammer, 1934. **Vink, J. G.** "The Date and Origin of the Priestly Code in the Old Testament." *OTS* 15 (1969) 1–144.

Translation

¹ *During that time,* [a] *Yahweh spoke thus to Moses:* ² *"Speak to the sons of Israel, so that they will take for me an offering: from every man whose mind* [a] *urges him, they are to take my offering.* ³ *This is the offering they are to take from such men:* [a] *gold, silver, copper,* ⁴ *violet yarn, purple yarn, scarlet yarn,* [a] *fine linen, goats' hair,* ⁵ *red-dyed* [a] *rams' hides, sea-cows'* [b] *hides, acacia lumber,* [c] ⁶ *oil for light, balsam spices for the Oil of Anointment and for the special-formula incense,* [a] ⁷ *gemstones and stones to be set on the ephod and the breastpiece.*

⁸ *"They* [a] *are to make me a holy place, and I will dwell in their midst.* [b] ⁹ᵃ *In accord with everything I will show you,* [b] *the plan for the Tabernacle* [c] *and the plan for all its equipment, precisely so* [d] *you* [e] *are to make it."*

Notes

1.a. Special *waw*, so translated in the context of the sequence of chap. 24 to chap. 25.
2.a. לב "heart" = "mind" in such a context; see BDB, 523–25; Johnson, *Vitality,* 77–79.

3.a. מֵאִתָּם "from them"; the antecedent rather than the pronoun is used above for clarity.

4.a. תּוֹלַעַת שָׁנִי is, lit., "worm of scarlet," the *coccus ilicis* which produces when correctly processed a scarlet dye; see BDB, 1040, 1069; Brenner, *Colour Terms*, 143–44.

5.a. מְאָדָּמִים a masc pl pual ptcp from אָדַם, "be red."

5.b. תְּחָשִׁים "sea cows" were apparently sea creatures whose skin produced a leather favored for sandals (Cassuto, 326; BDB, 1065); the dugong, the dolphin, and the porpoise have all been suggested. For an alternate view, see Cross, *BAR* 1:220, n. 21, who proposes "an imported (?) specially finished leather."

5.c. "Trees of acacias."

6.a. סַמִּים is used in the OT only in connection with קְטֹרֶת "incense." It appears to be a collective term for various aromatic ingredients, other than לְבֹנָה "frankincense," used in incense. Cf. Durham, *Touch, Taste and Smell*, 339–40.

8.a. LXX reads "you."

8.b. LXX has καὶ ὀφθήσομαι ἐν ὑμῖν "and I will be seen among you."

9.a. LXX begins this verse καὶ ποιήσεις μοι "and you are to make for me."

9.b. SamPent and LXX add "on the mountain" (בָּהָר, ἐν τῷ ὄρει).

9.c. מִשְׁכָּן, lit., "dwelling-place," has so special a significance in the Priestly sections of the OT that it and its various equipment will be capitalized in the translation.

9.d. וְכֵן "and yes (indeed)."

9.e. This "you" is pl, in reference to Moses *and* Israel; the "you" following "show" in this verse is sg, referring to Moses alone. LXX and SamPent read both as singular.

Form/Structure/Setting

The lengthy section of material recording Yahweh's instructions for the media of worship in his Presence, Exod 25–31, has for a long time been recognized as a unity in orientation if not also a unity in its organization by a single source. Virtually from the beginning of a comprehensive source-analysis of the Pentateuch, that single source has been held of course to be P, and no recent commentator has made any alternate suggestion that has gained acceptance. While the dates for a Priestly source and its possible growth from an early to a late and increasingly complicated form have been fairly often debated, no one can have serious reservations about the cultic and sacerdotal nature of this material or its somewhat shuffled and considerably altered repetition in chaps. 35–40.

The form of this Priestly material is dictated above all by the subject matter it treats, and that subject matter is founded on an essential theological assumption, that with the making of the covenant, Yahweh has in fact come to take up residence among his people. Such a residence demands response and provision of very special kinds, and that is what these chapters are intended to guide. They are begun, in fact, with a reference to a "holy place" (מִקְדָּשׁ) in which Yahweh can "settle down" (שָׁכַן) in their midst, and they are moved through a detailed specification of the primary symbols of his settlement, each a graphic representation of some aspect of the theological narrative of the deliverance, provision, guidance, and coming of Yahweh's Presence in Exodus.

There is indeed a progression in the sequence of the instructions of chaps. 25–31. Appropriately first are the specifications for the Ark (25:10–22), the supreme post-Sinai symbol of the Presence of Yahweh, and for the implements of the Presence related to and so kept near to the Ark: the Table for the Presence-bread (25:23–30), and the Seven-branched Lampstand of pure gold (25:31–40). These instructions are followed immediately by the plan for the

Tabernacle (26:1–37), the sanctuary and most holy shelter of Yahweh's Presence, to which are linked the instructions for the Altar of Burnt Offerings (27:1–8) and the Forecourt to the Tabernacle (27:9–19), both adjunctive in function as in location to the Tabernacle itself. Next are given the descriptions of the priestly vestments (28:1–43) and the directions for the authority-giving preparation of the priestly ministers themselves (29:1–46). These chapters of the Priestly instructions thus have the appearance, at least, of organization in three interlocked circles of symbol and function: outward from the presence of Yahweh (the Ark and the symbols of his provision and light) to the sheltering sanctuary of that Presence (the Tabernacle) and thence to the areas of preparation (the Altar and the Forecourt to the Tabernacle in which it was placed) for entry into that most intimate arena of the Presence. The three circles were perpetually joined by the movement through them of the priests, clad in the vestments of memory and ministry, and so the directions concerning priestly equipment and ordination are set last.

Following these chapters of instruction are three series of appendices: one dealing with four additional symbolic accessories to worship in the Presence (the Golden Altar of the Special Formula Incense, 30:1–10; the Bronze Laver for Ceremonial Ablutions, 30:17–21; the Special Formula Anointing Oil, 30:22–33; and the Special Formula Incense, 30:34–38), into which has been worked the instructions for Atonement (a further preparation of the people, 30:11–16); one dealing with the designation of the Artisans (31:1–11) who are to carry out the preparation of the symbolic implements of worship in the Presence; and one dealing with the sabbath (31:12–18) in which the reality and the deeds of the Presence were specially to be remembered.

The comparison of this carefully arranged order with the sequence of the account of the implementation of the instructions in chaps. 35–40 is instructive. There, the sabbath is mentioned first (35:1–3) instead of last; the artisans are logically mentioned at the beginning (35:30–36:1) of the narrative of manufacture and construction; the Tabernacle is listed before (36:8–38) the Ark (37:1–9); the Golden Altar of the Special Formula Incense is treated before (37:25–28) the Altar (38:1–7); the Bronze Laver for Ceremonial Ablutions is given a single verse (38:8); the preparation of the priests, the daily offering, the Atonement offering, and the Special Formula Incense and Anointing Oil are not mentioned at all, and there is a great deal of very repetitive summary (35:10–19; 36:2–7 following upon 35:20–29; 38:21–31; and 39:32–43). The two sequences, when compared even in a general way, give the impression that a sequence of instructions carefully framed in a pattern theologically oriented (chaps. 25–31) have been in hand for a somewhat later, far more loosely framed account of implementation (chaps. 35–40), one with a somewhat altered interest. There can be little doubt that the two sections are from the same circle, or that they reflect the same general theological assumptions. The differences of order and inclusion between them may be accounted for as differences in emphasis, particularly since chaps. 35–40 may be understood as taking the theological assertions of chaps. 25–31 as granted.

A frequent assertion of the source critics is that the material of these chapters is like other cultic and legal material in P inserted into a somewhat thin narrative, one freely pulled apart to admit the material that is P's major concern (cf. Eissfeldt, *Introduction*, 204–8). A further assumption is that P is the latest of the tetrateuchal/pentateuchal sources, and that much of the material it sets forth is far later than its context suggests, belonging as it does to the exilic periods. This oversimplification was popularized first by Wellhausen and has been followed, often with only cosmetic modification, by far the majority of scholars since (cf. Wellhausen, *Prolegomena*, 17–167; McNeile, i–v, 155–56; Driver, xv–xvii, 257–63; Fohrer, *Introduction*, 178–86; Vink, *OTS* 15 [1969] 8–63). This opinion, which itself had dramatically overturned the earlier and widespread view that P was the earliest and basic pentateuchal source (Eissfeldt, 164–65; Bentzen, *Introduction* 1:32–37, 63–70) eventually set P into last place in the chronological sequence of the sources, and left room for doubt only about the sources or subdivisions of P itself.

For most of the twentieth century, that is the direction that discussion of the P material has taken; following form-critical and traditio-analytic procedures, P, regarded as a late source in its canonical appearance, has been subdivided into early and later layers of material, often expanded by supplementary additions. Von Rad (*Priesterschrift*, 1–89), for example, proposed a division into three subsources: a basic and older source, P^A, a later source, P^B, and a "Book of Descendencies" (תולדות), a suggestion followed in part by Galling's (in Beer, 13, 128–29) P^A, P^B and P^S. These divisions, however, did not gain extensive support. They gave way, in part because of the complexity into which they led, to a simpler source-division of P material into P^G (for *Grundschrift*) and P^S (for material supplementing the foundational source), with the addition by some source critics of still other supplemental layers (see Bentzen, *Introduction*, 32–39; Kaiser, *Introduction*, 102–15, Soggin, *Introduction*, 134–46) such as P^H (the Holiness Code of Lev 17–26) or P^O (the sacrificial instructions of Lev 1–8, "O" for *Opfer*).

This kind of source-critical analysis has led to very subjective and often conflicting results, and increasingly scholars have turned to a much broader analysis of the P material, one informed more by tradition-history techniques than by source-criticism. This change, in turn, has had the effect of broadening considerably the time-span of the P material and has tended to give P a somewhat wider sphere of influence in the creation of both OT theology and the OT itself. As early as 1929 and 1930, Jepsen (*ZAW* 47 [1929] 251–55) and then Kaufmann (*ZAW* 48 [1930] 27–37) contended that the point of departure of P was the Solomonic Temple in Jerusalem. More recently, Cross (*Canaanite Myth*, 323–25) has proposed a date in the sixth century B.C., "late in the Exile," for the composition by "a narrow school or single tradent" of a work made up of written and oral documents and designed to reconstruct "the covenant of Sinai and its associated institutions" with Israel's restoration in mind (cf. also Rendtorff, *Überlieferungsgeschichtliche Problem*, 130–46). Far more persuasive is the suggestion of Haran (*Temples*, 1–12) that "P is the literary product of circles of the Jerusalemite priesthood of the First Temple," "remarkably utopian" in its content and so given circulation only in the Priestly inner circle until the time of Ezra, who included the P material in his program of guidance for the postexilic community.

What makes the theory of Haran so attractive is that, unlike the somewhat tenuous and highly theoretical approach to Exod 25–31 and 35–40 of Koch

(*Priesterschrift*, 5–40, 96–104), who has sought by form-literary techniques to isolate a series of ritual *Vorlage* underlying the P material from Exod 25 through Lev 16, it is founded on the institution of temples and temple service as they can be known in both Priestly and non-Priestly texts in the OT. Haran, arguing that P was concerned with real institutions, however idealized in projection, notes that those institutions were pre-exilic in origin. P's point of departure is thus real and not imaginary, and the Priestly work may be said to move forward from historical institutions and problems toward utopian projections rather than backward from flights of sacerdotal fancy to largely fictional supposition.

Haran has pointed us in a right direction. There simply must be at the base of the Priestly material of Exodus something more than an imaginary blueprint for institutions and implements that never existed. A shift to a different center, however, may be suggested not only by the P material but also by the context into which it has been set in the composite Book of Exodus. It is not the Tabernacle or the institution of Priestly service that is at the root of Exod 25–31 and 35–40, nor is it an array of ancient rituals or some attempt to reconstruct the past and encourage Israel in exile. What these chapters make plain, by their content as by their placement, is that the theme at their center is Yahweh's Presence in the midst of his people. Like the narrative into which they are set, these chapters are theological in their origin, theological in their statement, and theological even in their arrangement; that is indeed one important reason why they are placed where they are, in a manner so obviously disruptive of the narrative preceding and following them. As Exodus through chap. 24 is shaped by the promise of Presence, the proof of Presence, and the coming of Presence, so these chapters are shaped by the need to keep current and extend that same Presence through a carefully presented and interlocked sequence of symbols.

Exod 25–31 must thus be seen primarily as a whole, just as the received text presents these chapters. As important as the seams of growth within these chapters may be, as for example between the primary material of chaps. 25–29 and the supplemental material of chaps. 30–31, the impact of these seven chapters taken together must not be lost. The same can be said of chaps. 35–40, though the point made in the first sequence by a very tight organization is made there by what is emphasized, both by inclusion and by repetition. That there are subsidiary points to be made, both about the origin of the material and its relevance to changing OT contexts, is not to be doubted; these subsidiary points, however, must not be permitted to become a distraction. First and foremost, these chapters, clearly the product over a lengthy period of time of the Priestly circle, are about the Presence of Yahweh in the midst of a people who have covenanted with him to serve him.

Comment

1–2 The placement of these verses in sequence to the narrative of Moses' climb still further up Sinai toward Yahweh's Presence and their introduction with the narrative special *waw* shows that, in the Exodus composite, they are to be understood as the content of the still further revelation Moses received from Yahweh on Israel's behalf. The people themselves received the "ten words"; Moses then received and communicated to them the "guiding principles" and further commands applying the "ten words" to their daily living: with this information before them, the people entered into covenant with Yahweh. Then and only then was Moses called still further up into Yahweh's Presence to be given by Yahweh himself the directions for and, as regards the Tabernacle, a vision of (25:40) the media of worship that were to call to mind the fact of Yahweh's Presence.

The call for materials is prefaced by the instruction that the materials be given first as an offering (תרומה), that is, as an act of worship, and second, as a joyous expression to be made only by those "compelled" by their own desire to do so. Just how excessively successful this call was is shown by the sequel narrative, which dwells repetitively on the abundance of the fine materials given (35:20–29; 36:2–7; cf. 38:21–31; 39:32–43).

3–7 The materials themselves represent a catalog of opulence: the finest metals, the finest fabrics, the finest leathers, the finest wood, the finest oil and incense and semiprecious stones. The metals are obviously listed in a descending sequence of value, and Haran (*Temples*, 160) maintains that the colored yarns are as well, with violet (Brenner, *Colour Terms* 146, "blue purple") the most costly dyed material, purple a bit less so and scarlet less so still, though all dyed materials were precious because of the expense of the dye. Gradwohl (*Farben*, 66–78), discussing the organic dyes among which are the ones listed in v 4, notes that twelve thousand murex snails were required to yield 1.4 grams of pure dye (cf. Jensen, *JNES* 22 [1963] 108–9) of the variety I have translated "violet" above (תכלת).

Fine linen (שׁשׁ) was probably Egyptian, an imported fabric (Hurvitz, *HTR* 60 [1967] 119–21); goats' hair (עזים) referred to natural, undyed wool, the least expensive of the fabric materials mentioned. The ram-skin leather was tanned, or dyed red (or both). The sea-cow leather may have been cured only; in this case, there may be here a descending value in these materials as well (cf. Haran, *Temples*, 162–63). Acacia is a hard and long-lasting wood (Trever, "Acacia," *IDB* 1:23), apparently well suited for both carving and overlay work. Balsam spices were a mixture of three ingredients (the formula is given in Exod 30:34–36) added to pure frankincense (לבנה זכה) along with salt to create a Special Formula Incense used only on the Golden Altar (cf. Haran, 241–43). אבני־שׁהם "gemstones" is by itself an indeterminate phrase, but if these are the stones of the two shoulderpieces of the ephod, as seems probable, since the same phrase is used in the descriptions of the ephod (28:9–12; 39:6–7; cf. Haran, 168 n. 43), they were of an engravable substance, such as cornelian or onyx or even lapis lazuli. The אבני מלאים "stones to be set" might then refer either to the semiprecious stones to be set onto the breastpiece (28:17–21; 39:10–14) or to all the stones to be set on both ephod and breast-piece.

8–9 The "holy place" (מִקְדָּשׁ) which Israel is to make has a wider reference than just the Tabernacle (מִשְׁכָּן), mentioned specifically in v 9. מקדשׁ includes the Tabernacle, of course, but its broader reference is to any and every place of Yahweh's theophany (cf. Josh 24:26; Exod 15:17; Amos 7:9; Ezek 11:16).

Any place where Yahweh comes to dwell is in that coming and residence a holy place, and any place so designated is to be respected as such by the people in covenant with Yahweh. As for the Tabernacle as a pattern of and for such holy places, Yahweh will make it the authoritative ideal by prescribing its plan and the plan for all its furnishings and equipment to Moses on Sinai. This prescription, which may have involved a vision (אני מראה אותך "I will show to you") as well as instructions, was to be followed to the letter. Goppelt ("τύπος," *TDNT* 8:256–57) has suggested that תבנית, as Yahweh's "plan" or "pattern," may reflect a concept of a heavenly temple as the macrocosm to which the Tabernacle is the microcosmic parallel, an idea of which Keel (*Symbolism,* 171–76) has found reflections in the Psalms.

Explanation

The essential points made by this brief introduction to the lengthy collection of priestly materials on the media of worship in Yahweh's Presence are several in number. To begin with, all that is to follow in chaps. 25–31 is connected with Moses' solitary climb farther up the mountain to receive Yahweh's special instructions. Second, all that is to be brought in the way of materials is requested not as an obligation, but as a free and joyous offering—an emphasis that has important implications also for what is to be made of these materials and the use to which those media of worship are to be put. Third, the materials that are specified are the finest and rarest available. However much some of them may reflect an Israelite affluence later than the Sinai-wilderness period of Exodus, we must not miss the theological point the listing makes: nothing short of the finest and best is to be associated with the response to Yahweh. Fourth, Israel's construction of a holy place is a means of their acceptance and realization of his Presence in residence among them. He will reveal to them the plan for their worshipful response, they will follow that plan precisely, and doing so will teach them many things about his Presence and about their lives in response to his residence in their midst. The call for materials for the media of worship is thus a call for a joyous response to the Presence of Yahweh, a response guided by Yahweh as it is occasioned by Yahweh. Above all, the call for materials, issued by Yahweh and guided by Yahweh, makes clear that what is at the center of the priestly preoccupation is not a sanctuary nor the institution of sacerdotal order, but Yahweh alone, present as a gift.

The Instructions for the Ark   (25:10–22)

PARALLEL VERSES:
37:1–9

Bibliography

Danthine, H. "L'imagerie des trones vides et des trones porteurs de symboles dans le proche orient ancien." *Mélanges Syriens,* vol. 2. Paris: Librairie Orientaliste Paul

Geuthner, 1939. 857–66. **Davies, G. H.** "The Ark of the Covenant." *ASTI* 5 (1967) 30–47. **Dibelius, M.** *Die Lade Jahves.* FRLANT 7. Göttingen: Vandenhoeck & Ruprecht, 1906. **Hartmann, R.** "Zelt und Lade." *ZAW* 37 (1917–18) 209–44. **Maier, J.** *Das Altisraelitische Ladeheiligtum.* BZAW 93. Berlin: Verlag Alfred Töpelmann, 1965. **May, H. G.** "The Ark—A Miniature Temple." *AJSL* 52 (1935–36) 215–34. **Morgenstern, J.** "The Ark, the Ephod and the 'Tent of Meeting.'" *HUCA* 17 (1942–43) 153–266 and 18 (1944) 1–52. **Rad, G. von.** "The Tent and the Ark." *The Problem of the Hexateuch and Other Essays.* Edinburgh: Oliver and Boyd, 1966. 103–24. **Reimpell, W.** "Der Ursprung der Lade Jahwes." *OLZ* 19 (1916) 326–31. **Rost, L.** "Die Wohnstätte des Zeugnisses." *Festschrift Friedrich Baumgärtel.* Erlangen: Verlag Universitätsbund Erlangen, 1959. 158–65. **Schmidt, H.** "Kerubenthron und Lade." *EYXAPIΣTHPION.* FRLANT 19. Göttingen: Vandenhoeck & Ruprecht, 1923. 120–44. **Schmitt, R.** *Zelt und Lade als Thema alttestamentlicher Wissenschaft.* Gütersloh: Gütersloher Verlagshaus Gerd Mohn, 1972. **Schrade, H.** *Der Verborgene Gott.* Stuttgart: W. Kohlhammer Verlag, 1949. **Vaux, R. de.** "Ark of the Covenant and Tent of Reunion." *The Bible and the Ancient Near East.* Garden City, NY: Doubleday, 1971. 136–51. ———. "Les chérubins et l'arche d'alliance, les sphinx gardiens et les trônes divins dans l'ancien orient." *Bible et Orient.* Paris: Les Éditions du Cerf, 1967. 231–59.

Translation

[10] "*They* [a] *are to make an Ark of acacia lumber, two and a half cubits in length, one and a half cubits wide, and one and a half cubits tall.* [11] *You are to overlay it with pure gold: inside and outside you are to overlay it, and you are to make upon* [a] *it an encircling golden beading.* [b] [12] *You are also to cast for it four golden rings and place them upon its four corners,* [a] *two rings upon one side and two rings upon the other side.* [13] *You are to make carrying-poles of acacia lumber, and overlay them with gold.* [14] *You are to thrust the carrying-poles into the rings upon the sides of the Ark, to lift the Ark by them.* [15] *In the rings of the Ark, the poles are to remain:* [a] *they are not to be withdrawn from it.* [b]

[16] "*You are to place into the Ark the Testimony* [a] *that I am giving to you.* [17] *You are to make an Ark-Cover* [a] *of pure gold, two and a half cubits in length and one and a half cubits wide.* [18] *You are to make two golden cherubs (you are to make them in hammered metal* [a]*) for the two ends of the Ark-Cover.* [19] *Make* [a] *one cherub for one end and the other cherub for the opposite end; a part of the Ark-Cover* [b] *you are to make the cherubs, upon the two ends of it.* [20] *They are to be cherubs with spreading wings uplifted, protecting with their wings the Ark-Cover, and each is to be turned towards the other, while the faces of the cherubs are to be towards the Ark-Cover.* [21] *You are to place the Ark-Cover upon the top of the Ark, and into the Ark you are to put the Testimony* [a] *that I am giving to you.* [22] *I will meet you* [a] *there by appointment,* [b] *and I will speak with you, from above the Ark-Cover, from between the two cherubs upon the Ark of the Testimony, everything that I will give into your charge concerning the sons of Israel.*"

Notes

10.a. LXX and SamPent have "you," sg.

11.a. SamPent has ל "for."

11.b. זר is a "circlet, band, border," apparently a kind of decorative bead-molding around the side or upper edges of the Ark.

12.a. פַעֲמֹת are, lit., "thrustings, strikings" (פעם), and so can refer to foot-steps or anvil-blows or that which thrusts out, as here, the sides or corners of the Ark. LXX has κλίτη "sides"; Vg has *angulos* "corners."

15.a. MT has יִהְיוּ "they are to be."

15.b. The masc sg suff refers to the Ark.

16.a. See n. 16:34.b.

17.a. כַּפֹּרֶת is derived from כפר "cover over" but must be understood in the context of meaning of the piel כִּפֶּר "make atonement for." Cf. BDB, 498.

18.a. מִקְשָׁה from קשׁה "be hard, severe" appears to refer to hammered rather than poured metalwork.

19.a. SamPent reads יעשׁו and puts this verb at the end of v 18. LXX has ποιηθήσονται "they are to be made."

19.b. מִן־הכפרת תעשׁו "a part of the Ark-Cover you are to make." מן "from," read above "a part of," is used here in what BDB (579–81) describe as a "partitive" sense.

21.a. SamPent ends the verse here, omitting what follows in MT.

22.a. "You" is singular in this verse in reference to Moses.

22.b. יעד, here in niphal and with לְ following, to give the reflexive sense described by BDB (416–17): Yahweh "appoints himself" to meet Moses at the prearranged place and perhaps at a prearranged time. LXX misses this sense by taking the verb as the niph rather of ידע to give γνωσθήσομαι "I will make myself known." SamPent reads as does MT: Vg has *inde praecipiam* "I will anticipate from there."

Form/Structure/Setting

See *Form/Structure/Setting* on 25:1–9.

Comment

Scholarly discussion of the Ark is extensive, not only as regards the varied appearances and functions of the Ark in the OT, but also as regards the age and authenticity of the descriptions of the Ark and the meaning of its symbolism. Helpful surveys have been made by Dibelius, Maier, and Schmitt, the latter of whom has provided (*Zelt und Lade*, 316–36) an extensive bibliography on the Ark (see also Zobel, "אֲרוֹן" *TDOT* 1:363–64) and the tent, to which the Ark is sometimes related. The passage at hand, wholly from P, has often been regarded a late and idealized description, entirely untrustworthy as a guide to the when, how and why of the Ark (cf. Noth, 203; Hyatt, 265–66).

While the theological-liturgical bias of the Priestly interest in the Ark is as obvious as it is logical, the description in these verses should not be regarded as just so much dreamy fiction. There is no reason that every reference to the Ark in the OT must mesh with every other one, any more than there is justification for disregarding the information suggested in a passage because that passage is assigned to a "late" source. The theological symbolism of the Priestly description of the Ark may well be the most important suggestion of its function available to us, and we must not lose sight of the fact that the Priestly concepts were drawn not as esoteric self-preoccupation but as a means of demonstrating confession and eliciting response connected with the fundamental claims of belief in the Present Yahweh. However much the Priestly descriptions may elaborate the earlier traditions, they are carefully assembled and deliberately located in the text, and the elaboration should be taken as an expansion, rather than as a cancellation, of the roots from which it has grown.

Thus the first point to be made about the instructions of Yahweh concerning the Ark is made by the placement of those instructions. The Ark is the foremost symbol of Yahweh's Presence beyond Sinai, and so its design and specifications are given first after the call for materials for the media of worship. Beyond this information, the function of the Ark is suggested with graphic symbols that quite probably draw on traditions far older than the final opulent form of the Ark may suggest. There has been too much of a tendency to interpret the symbolism and use of the Ark in exclusive and either/or terms, either as a box containing holy objects (so Hartmann, ZAW 37 [1917–18] 225–44; von Rad, Problem of the Hexateuch, 112–114; Zobel, TDOT 1:370–71) or as an empty symbol of Yahweh's residence (so Morgenstern, a tent-symbol, HUCA 17 [1942–43] 229–65, 18 [1944] 47–52; or May, a "miniature temple," AJSL 52 [1935–36] 221–34) or as a throne on which Yahweh was invisibly seated (so Dibelius, Lade Jahves, 59–71; Maier, Ladeheiligtum, 54–60, 64–74) or as a footstool upon which Yahweh was thought to stand (so Schrade, Verborgene Gott, 46–51; Keel, Symbolism, 166–67; cf. Reimpell's suggestion of a "stage," OLZ 19 [1916] 326–31). As the OT references to the Ark (cf. de Vaux's summary, Ancient Israel, 297–302) show, it had more than a single use, and so also it must have more than a single symbolic meaning.

Haran (Temples, 246–59) has argued quite plausibly that the Ark served as both container and throne; de Vaux (The Bible 136–40) has suggested that the second function amounted to an extension of the first and has listed parallels (Bible et Orient, 231–59, with plates I–VII) from ANE literature and art suggesting a throne containing law codes that were binding upon those who worshiped the king or the deity present or believed to be present above the throne-footstool. What is perhaps most important about the symbolism of the Ark, in whatever period of its existence, is its intimate connection with the Presence of Yahweh (cf. von Rad, Problem of the Hexateuch, 108–10; Davies, ASTI 5 [1967] 42–45) and that connection is precisely the concern of the Priestly description set forth in the verses at hand, as well as in the parallel to them in Exod 37:1–9. Whatever other roles the Ark may have had, its chief role, for P, was the suggestion of Yahweh's Presence at hand.

10–15 Thus must the Ark be constructed of the same wood to be used throughout the Tabernacle, and thus must it be adorned with pure gold. Its size, by P's specifications, was unimposing: 2½ x 1½ x 1½ cubits would be roughly equivalent (see Sellers, "Weights and Measures," IDB 4:836–38) to 3′ 6½″ long by 2′ 2¼″ wide and high. Its appearance, on the other hand, would have been striking according to P's pattern, given its lining and covering of pure gold, decorated by a further beading of gold all around it, as by the four golden rings by which the Ark could be lifted and carried, and by gold-covered carrying poles inserted through them at all times. The purpose of such an arrangement, of course, was that the Ark might be moved without contact by human hands, an emphasis upon both its portability and the holiness of Yahweh's Presence. The sight of such a box so prepared for movement and so lavishly decorated would have made the Priestly message unmistakable.

16 The Testimony (העדת) Moses was to place into the Ark is probably to be understood as the tablets of stone on which were written the ten commandments setting forth the principles of life in relationship with Yahweh (cf. Deut 10:1–5). Rost (*Festschrift P. Baumgärtel*, 163–65) expands still further the application of the term "Testimony" on the basis of the phrase מִשְׁכַּן הָעֵדֻת "Tabernacle of the Testimony" (Exod 38:21; Num 1:50, 10:11) to include the range of Yahweh's testimony to his Presence, in "eine Wohnstätte des Zeugnises." In this verse, as in v 21, however, the reference is to something Yahweh is giving to Moses for Israel, something that can be put into the container formed by the Ark. As de Vaux (*Bible et Orient*, 256, and n. 1) has suggested, "the Ark contained the 'testimony,' עֵדֻת, which is synonymous with בְּרִית 'covenant,' and which designates the solemn law given by God to Israel. The Ten Words are, in effect, the provisions of the pact of Sinai . . ." (see also the survey of Schmitt, *Zelt und Lade*, 98–106, 110–28).

17–22 The Ark-Cover כפרת, to be made of pure gold, was to be of the same length and width as the Ark, and was to be placed on top of it. Onto this Cover, indeed made as a part of it at each end, were to be placed two cherubs made of hammer-worked gold. These cherubs were to be made with their wings spread and stretched out over the Ark-Cover, their bodies turned toward each other, their faces bowed towards the Ark-Cover. The cherubs have usually been connected with Yahweh's throne, both as guardians and as bearers (see Danthine, *Mélanges syriens* 2:857–66; Schmidt, *EYXAPIΣ-THPION*, 120–44; de Vaux, *Bible et Orient* 231–59, with plates I–VII; Keel, *Symbolism*, 166–71). The statement that Yahweh will speak with Moses "from above the Ark-Cover and from between the two cherubs," along with the phrase ישב הכרבים "the One sitting upon the cherubs" (1 Sam 4:4; 2 Sam 6:2; 2 Kgs 19:15; Pss 80:2; 99:1; Isa 37:16), give the impression that the cherubs of the Ark-Cover were associated in some way with Yahweh's Presence above the Ark. Whether they were a part of, or were bearers of, an invisible throne remains indeterminate (cf. Schmitt, *Zelt und Lade*, 128–31, 173–174).

The Ark-Cover has sometimes been called the "propitiatory" (BDB, 498; Childs, 513, 524), in connection with the ritual of atonement that took place before it (Lev 16) and the obvious derivation of its name from כפר, which in the piel form is a primary OT term for propitiation, atonement, and sacral cleansing. This definition of כפרת is obviously derived from the later function of the Ark-Cover and may indeed describe one way in which the Ark-Cover was thought of in later priestly ritual. Given P's description of the Ark in Exodus, however, the fullest description anywhere in the OT, it is just as appropriate, and perhaps even more so, to assume that the כפרת takes its name from its placement, "covering" the Ark. "Cover" after all appears to have been the original meaning of כפר.

Even so, the Ark-Cover must be thought of as more than simply a part of the Ark; as Haran (*Temples*, 247–53) has shown, the two are frequently mentioned separately in the OT and are in fact placed in physical contact only by P. This juxtaposition may be a reflection of the fact that these two objects were exactly the two most intimately associated with Yahweh's immanent Presence. The Ark contained his ten words, the symbol of "everything I will give into your charge concerning the sons of Israel," and was placed as a footstool beneath the Ark-Cover, the symbol of his throne protected by guardian cherubs (so Schmidt, *EYXAPIΣTHPION*, 132–44). Above these two objects, in the priestly symbolism, Yahweh's Presence was most powerfully concentrated. Thus the Ark and the Ark-Cover were overlaid with a sheath of pure gold and their location was the location to which Moses and his priestly descendants would come to meet Yahweh and to ask and receive his instructions. There, Yahweh promised to meet Moses by appointment and to speak to him "from above the Ark-Cover, from between the two cherubs upon the Ark of the Testimony." It is this statement, an obvious summary combination of the Ark and the Ark-Cover, that makes clear P's linking of the two most intimate symbols of Yahweh's Presence. Exod 25:10–22 must therefore be seen, as Schmidt (*EYXAPIΣTHPION*, 141) has said, as the principal passage in the OT for P's view of the Ark.

Explanation

The location of the instructions for the Ark and the Ark-Cover first in the sequence of Yahweh's instructions for the media of worship in itself suggests the special significance of these two objects. They are in effect the foci of Yahweh's revelation to Israel, the place of his special instruction in person. The opulence of the two objects suggests their unique nature also, as does the special arrangement for their transportation, the inclusion of and attention given to the cherubs, and above all the summary connection of the two as the place *par excellence* of the Presence of Yahweh in the context of Israel's worship. Here at the first of the instructions for the media of worship there are given the instructions for the center of that worship, the two symbols of the innermost circle of Yahweh's Presence in the midst of his people.

The Instructions for the Table   (25:23–30)

PARALLEL VERSES:
37:10–16

Bibliography

Josephus. *Jewish Antiquities, Books I-IV.* LCL. Cambridge: Harvard University Press, 1957. **Kelso, J. L.** *The Ceramic Vocabulary of the Old Testament.* BASOR Supplementary Studies Nos. 5–6. New Haven: 1948. **Kennedy, A. R. S.** "Shewbread." *A Dictionary of the Bible.* J. Hastings, ed. New York: Charles Scribner's Sons, 1902. 495–97.

Translation

²³ "You are to make a Table of acacia lumber,ᵃ two cubits in length, one cubit wide, and one and a half cubits tall. ²⁴ You are to overlay it with pure gold,ᵃ and you are to make for it an encircling golden beading. ᵇ ²⁵ You are also to make for it an encircling border a handbreadth wide, and you are to make an encircling golden

beading for this border. ª ²⁶ *You are to make for the Table* ª *four golden rings and fix the rings to the four corners where its feet are.* ᵇ ²⁷ *The rings are to hang* ª *against the border, as attachments* ᵇ *for the carrying-poles for lifting the Table.* ²⁸ *You are to make the carrying-poles of acacia lumber, and overlay them with gold; with them, the Table is to be lifted.* ²⁹ *You are to make for the Table* ª *dishes and pans, and pitchers and bowls for the pouring of libations.* ᵇ *You are to make them of pure gold.* ³⁰ *And you are to place upon the Table before me the Bread of the Presence* ª *continuously."*

Notes

23.a. LXX reads χρυσίου καθαροῦ "of pure gold."

24.a. This clause is logically missing from LXX.

24.b. As on the Ark; see n. 25:11.b.

25.a. MT has למסגרתו "for its border."

26.a. MT has לו "for it"; "Table," the clear antecedent, is used above for clarity. LXX and Vg omit the prep phrase.

26.b. Lit., "at four of its feet."

27.a. תֶּהְיֶיןָ "they are to be," apocopated qal impf of היה.

27.b. לבתים "for houses," i.e., the rings were for the carrying-poles, which remained, "lived" in them at all times. See BDB, 108–9.

29.a. MT has קערתיו וכפתיו וקשותיו ומנקיתיו "its dishes and its pans, and its jars and its bowls. . . ." The clear antecedent is Table, so "for the Table" is substituted above for the four pronouns.

29.b. אשר יסך בהן "which it is poured out with them." נסך "pour" most frequently refers in the OT to the pouring of drink offerings. BDB, 650–51; cf. Haran, *Temples*, 216.

30.a. לחם פנים "Bread of the Presence."

Form/Structure/Setting

See *Form/Structure/Setting* on 25:1–9.

Comment

The Table described in these verses is variously designated in the OT as שלחן הפנים "the Table of the Presence" (Num 4:7), שלחן הטהר "the Pure Table" (Lev 24:6, 2 Chr 13:11), שלחן המערכת "the Table of the Row-arrangement" (2 Chr 29:18), and even השלחן אשר עליו לחם הפנים זהב "the golden Table, upon which is the Bread of the Presence" (1 Kgs 7:48). In each instance, the same piece of furniture is intended. The Table described here as made of acacia, is roughly 3' long by 1'6" wide by 2'3" high (see Sellers, "Weights and Measures," *IDB* 4:836–38), and overlaid with gold. This Table, like the Ark, was decorated by a golden beading all around and had in addition a golden border approximately 3" wide (Sellers, 838) encircling it, similarly decorated. Like the Ark, this Table too was to be moved without the direct contact of human hands, by the use of gold-plated acacia poles inserted through golden rings attached to the Table for that purpose.

29 The Table was to be equipped with containers of four kinds, all of them of pure gold. The first of these, the קערה, appears to have been a dish or plate onto which the Bread of the Presence was placed (Kelso, *Ceramic Vocabulary*, 31, no. 77); the second, the כף, was a small pan (Kelso, 22, no. 47), onto which לבנה זכה "pure frankincense" was placed as an accompani-

ment offering to the Bread of the Presence (Lev 24:7); the third, the קשׂוה,
was a pitcher for the wine of the libation, or drink-offering (Kelso, 31, no.
78); the fourth, the מנקיה, was a bowl (cf. Kelso, 24, no. 54) into which
the libation was poured.

30 These four containers were kept upon the Table along with the לחם
פנים "Bread of the Presence," for which, apparently, the Table was primarily
constructed. This special Bread was placed on the Table each Sabbath, along
with a "reminder-offering" (אזכרה) of frankincense (Durham, *Touch, Taste
and Smell*, 347–55); The Bread of the previous week was eaten by the priests
(though cf. 1 Sam 21:1–6) and the frankincense was burned (Lev 24:7). The
Bread was arranged in two rows of six loaves each (Lev 24:5–6), the frankincense alongside it (or, according to Josephus, *Antiquities*, III, ll. 143–44, on
top of the loaves), the loaves on the קערת "dishes," the frankincense in
the כפות "pans." The origin and the exact significance of this Presence-
Bread are not clear. The offering of frankincense as an אזכרה suggests that
the Bread came to be considered a grain-offering of a very special kind (cf.
Haran, *Temples*, 209–10), but the careful placement of the Bread on so lavish
a Table and the inclusion of the Table in the list of the instructions for the
media of worship in Yahweh's Presence show that it was in some way a special
symbol of Yahweh present with his people. It is at least possible that the
Bread and the wine of the libation suggested his nearness in the availability
of food provided and blessed by him and so kept continuously before him
in acknowledgment of his giving nearness. Any idea of food being provided
for Yahweh (cf. Kennedy, *Dictionary*, 497; Hyatt, 268–69) is surely as removed
from this provision as from the offering of sacrifices; whatever primitive peoples may think about food for their gods, the people of Israel cannot by
any stretch of the socio-theological imagination be put into such a category.

Explanation

The Table of the Bread of the Presence is another symbol by which Yahweh's nearness was suggested. By its opulence as by the containers and the
food and drink placed continuously upon it and periodically renewed, this
Table announced: "He is here," and here as one who gives sustenance.

The Instructions for the Lampstand   (25:31–40)

PARALLEL VERSES:
37:17–24

Bibliography

Cook, S. A. "Candlestick." *Encyclopedia Biblica.* New York: Macmillan, 1899. 1:644–
47. ———. "Notes and Queries: Hebrew Inscription at Fik." *PEQ* 35 (1903) 185–
86. **Goodenough, E. R.** "The Menorah among Jews of the Roman World." *HUCA*

23 (1950–51) 449–92. **Kennedy, A. R. S.** "Snuffers, Snuffdish." *A Dictionary of the Bible.* J. Hastings, ed. New York: Charles Scribner's Sons, 1902. 4:557. ———. "Tabernacle." *A Dictionary of the Bible.* J. Hastings, ed. New York: Charles Scribner's Sons, 1902. 4:653–68.

Translation

[31] "*You are to make a Lampstand of pure gold. The pedestal and the branching* [a] *of the Lampstand are to be made* [b] *of hammered metal:* [c] *its lampcups,* [d] *its bud-husks* [e] *and its flowers are to be an integral part of it.* [f] [32] *Six branches* [a] *are to extend* [b] *from its sides, three branches for lamps* [c] *on one side and three branches for lamps* [c] *on the other side,* [33] *with three lampcups like almond blooms with bud-husks and flowers on one branch and three lampcups like almond blooms with bud-husks and flowers on the matching branch,* [a] *and so on* [b] *for all six of the branches extending from the Lampstand.* [34] *On the Lampstand itself* [a] *there are to be* [b] *four lampcups like almond blooms, each with their bud-husks and their flowers,* [35] *and a bud-husk underneath each pair of branches where the six branches extend from the Lampstand.* [a] [36] *These* [a] *bud-husks and branches are to be an integral part of the Lampstand;* [b] *the whole of it is to be* [c] *a single implement of hammer-worked pure gold.*

[37] "*You are to make it seven lamps; these lamps* [a] *are to be elevated* [b] *in order to give light upon the area in front of the Lampstand.* [c] [38] *The wick-removers and wick-trays* [a] *for the Lampstand* [b] *are to be* [c] *pure gold.* [39] *One talent of pure gold is to be used for the Lampstand* [a] *in all these accessories.* [40] *See that you make them in accord with the plan that you are being shown on the mountain.*"

Notes

31.a. The קנה "stalk or stem or shaft or column" of the Lampstand, the design of which imitates a plant or tree. Cf. BDB, 889; Kennedy, *Dictionary*, 663–64.

31.b. LXX, SamPent, Syr have "you are to make."

31.c. See n. 25:18.a.

31.d. The גביע "lampcup" was a lampholder in the shape of a flower. Surrounding it at its base was the כפתור "bud-husk" (see n. 31.e.).

31.e. כפתור "bud-husk," the bud or flower base of leaves and stem, the calyx, out of which grew the פרח, the flower itself.

31.f. ממנה יהיו "from, a part of it they are to be." The whole Lampstand assembly was to be of one piece, and in imitation of a branching almond tree in bloom. Cf. Cassuto, 342–44; Kennedy, *Dictionary*, 663–64.

32.a. See n. 31.a.

32.b. יצאים "are going out," as if they were growing out of the trunk of a tree.

32.c. Lit., "three branches of a Lampstand."

33.a. MT has בקנה האחד . . . בקנה האחד "on the one branch . . . on the other branch."

33.b. SamPent adds תעשה "you are to make."

34.a. ובמנרה "Lampstand" is definite here, indicating an emphasis on the central stalk or trunk of the Lampstand as opposed to the branches that extend from it and that have already been described.

34.b. "There are to be" is added for clarity.

35.a. MT repeats 3× the phrase וכפתר תחת שני הקנים ממנה "and a bud-base underneath two of the branches from it." לששת הקנים "at, toward, near the six branches" locates the bud-bases along the main trunk of the Lampstand.

36.a. MT has כפתריהם וקנתם "their bud-husks and their branches," in obvious reference to the stem and six branches of the Lampstand: thus the translation "these," in the context of vv 34–35.

36.b. MT has ה "it"; the antecedent is added above for clarity.

36.c. MT כלה "the whole"; "is to be" is added for clarity. This final clause of v 36 is a summary description of the Lampstand as one implement, despite its various parts, before its detachable equipment is described.

37.a. MT has נרתיה "its lamps."

37.b. והעלה "and are to be elevated"; read "and you are to elevate" by LXX, SamPent, Vg.

37.c. על־עבר פניה "upon the side of its face."

38.a. מלקחים, from לקח "take, seize," describes a tool like pliers or tweezers, used for removing spent wicks from lamps; מחתה, from חתה, "snatch up, usu. fire, coals" (BDB, 367), describes the pan or dish onto which such wicks were placed. Cf. Cassuto, 345, and Kennedy, *Dictionary*, 557.

38.b. מלקחיה ומחתתיה "its wick-removers and its wick-trays"; the antecedent of these poss pronouns is the Lampstand, supplied above for clarity.

38.c. LXX adds ποιήσεις "you are to make" at the end of v 38.

39.a. MT has "it."

Form/Structure/Setting

See *Form/Structure/Setting* on 25:1–19.

Comment

The Lampstand, like the Table and the Ark, was a symbol of the immediate Presence of Yahweh and so was constructed with pure gold. The Ark and the Table, had they been made solely of gold, would have been extremely heavy; thus they were made of acacia and overlaid with pure gold. Of smaller bulk, the Lampstand could be made entirely of pure gold, and thus for the first time an exact amount of gold for the construction is mentioned (v 39): a ככר "talent," approximately sixty-six to seventy pounds (Sellers, "Weights and Measures," *IDB* 4:831) of gold.

31–36 This Lampstand was to be made of hammered rather than cast gold and was by its pattern to suggest a growing tree, apparently an almond tree, the life-promising "awakening" tree of Jeremiah's call (Jer 1:11–12). The pedestal and main upright of the lamp were the "tree's" trunk, and "growing" out from this trunk on either side were three "branches." Each of these branches ended in the leafy base of a bud, from which opened the petals of an almond flower, and into this receptacle was fixed a lampholder or cup. This bud-and-bloom motif was repeated along both the trunk or shaft of the Lampstand and also along the six branches extending from it, four times on the trunk (v 34) and three times on each branch (v 33). The bud-and-flower design was located at the top of the central trunk, apparently where each pair of branches left the trunk; its location on the branches is not specified (for a different interpretation see Kennedy, *Dictionary*, 664, and cf. Cassuto, 342–43).

As Goodenough (*HUCA* 23 [1950–51] 450–52) has indicated, the original significance of this Lampstand is obscure, though connections with the tree of life, the burning bush, and even the planets have all been suggested (cf. also Cook, *Encyclopedia*, 646–47, and *PEQ* 35 [1903] 185–86). The OT gives no direct clue as to the symbolism of the Lampstand, though the description of it given by P and the location of that description with the descriptions of the Ark and the Table make plain the connection of the Lampstand with Yahweh's Presence. The light and the fire of the lamps themselves must have been linked also to Yahweh's theophany, of which brightness and fire were primary symbols.

37–40 Seven lamps were placed on the Lampstand, one for each of the seven lampcups at the end of the trunk and the six branches. They were located at the tops of these extensions so as to give their light to a wider area, and they were so arranged that their light shone in front of the Lampstand, that is, with their burning wicks all in one direction, toward the area in front of the Lampstand (cf. Num 8:1–3). Special tools (מַלְקָחַיִם) were to be made for the adjustment and removal of the wicks, along with special containers for receiving the spent wicks for disposal. The Lampstand and most of its accessories were to be made from a talent of pure gold; there is some ambiguity about the lamps, the material for which is not specified (in the Temple of Solomon, they were made of gold as well, according to 1 Kgs 7:49). Of the three Presence-symbols of chap. 26, it is only the Lampstand and its equipment about which the further caution of v 40 is given, though this verse can also be taken to apply to the Ark and the Table as well.

Explanation

By its light as by its reminder of the "awakening tree," the Lampstand attested Yahweh at hand, present and active among his people. The repeated bud-and-flower motif suggested the almond tree bursting with bloom. The fire and light of the seven lamps were reminders of Yahweh's coming in brightness. In company with the Table attesting Yahweh's Presence in bounty and the Ark attesting Yahweh's Presence in mercy and revelation, the Lampstand symbolized Yahweh's Presence in perpetual wakefulness, through the reminder of the almond tree and the continual brightness of the living fire (cf. Num 17:16–26 [17:1–11]). The watcher over Israel never nodded, much less slept (Ps 121:4).

The Instructions for the Tabernacle (26:1–37)

PARALLEL VERSES:
36:8–38

Bibliography

Benzinger, I. "Tabernacle." *Encyclopedia Biblica.* New York: Macmillan, 1903. 4:4861–75. **Clements, R. E.** *God and Temple.* Philadelphia: Fortress Press, 1965. **Cross, F. M., Jr.** "The Priestly Tabernacle." *BA* 10 (1947) 45–68. Also in *BAR* 1 (Garden City: Doubleday & Company, 1961): 201–28. **Fretheim, T. E.** "The Priestly Document: Anti-Temple?" *VT* 18 (1968) 313–29. **Gooding, D. W.** *The Account of the Tabernacle.* TextsS 6. Cambridge: At the University Press, 1959. **Haran, M.** "The Divine Presence in the Israelite Cult and the Cultic Institutions." *Bib* 50 (1969) 251–67. ———. "Shiloh and Jerusalem: The Origin of the Priestly Tradition in the Pentateuch." *JBL* 81 (1962)

14–24. _____. *Temples and Temple-Service in Ancient Israel.* Oxford: Clarendon Press, 1978. **Kennedy, A. R. S.** "Tabernacle." *A Dictionary of the Bible.* J. Hastings, ed. New York: Charles Scribner's Sons, 1902. 4:653–68. **Rabe, V. W.** "The Identity of the Priestly Tabernacle." *JNES* 25 (1966) 132–34.

Translation

¹ *"The Tabernacle you are to make of ten curtains of woven fine linen and violet yarn, purple yarn, and scarlet yarn;* [a] *with cherubs artistically embroidered* [b] *you are to make them.* ² *The length of each curtain is to be twenty-eight cubits, and the width of each curtain, four cubits; all the curtains are to have an identical measurement.* ³ *Five of the curtains are to be joined one to another, and the remaining five are to be joined one to another.* ⁴ *You are to make violet loops along the edge of the curtain at the end of the first set, and you are also to make them on the edge of the end-curtain of the second set.* ⁵ *You are to make fifty loops on the first end* [a]*-curtain, and you are to make fifty loops on the end-curtain in the second set: the curtains with* [b] *loops are to be opposite one another.* ⁶ *You are to make fifty fasteners of gold and you are to join the curtain-sets one to another with the fasteners; thus the Tabernacle will be in one piece.* [a]

⁷ *"You are to make curtains of goats' hair, for a tent to go over* [a] *the Tabernacle; you are to make eleven of these curtains.* ⁸ *The length of each curtain is to be thirty cubits, and the width of each curtain, four cubits; the eleven curtains are to have an identical measurement.* ⁹ *You are to join five of these curtains in a unit, then the remaining six in a unit. You are to fold the sixth curtain over toward the front of the tent.* ¹⁰ *You are to make fifty loops along the edge of the curtain at the end of the first set, and fifty loops along the edge of the curtain at the end* [a] *of the second set.* ¹¹ *You are to make fifty fasteners of copper, and attach the fasteners to the loops, and so you are to join the tent* [a] *so that it will be in one piece.* ¹² *The additional area, the remaining part of the curtains of the tent, the half-curtain remaining, is to hang down the rear of the Tabernacle.* ¹³ *The cubit on either side, in the remaining part of the length of the curtains of the tent, is to be allowed to hang free upon the sides of the Tabernacle, on both sides, to cover it.* ¹⁴ *You are also to make a cover for the tent of red-dyed* [a] *rams' hides and a cover of sea-cows' hides* [b] *to protect it.* [c]

¹⁵ *"You are to make the standing supports* [a] *for the Tabernacle of acacia lumber.* ¹⁶ *The length of each* [a] *support* [b] *is to be ten cubits, and the width of each support, a cubit and a half,* ¹⁷ *with two upright braces* [a] *to each support, each joined to the one next to it:* [b] *thus you are to make all the supports of the Tabernacle.* ¹⁸ *You are to make the supports for the Tabernacle so: twenty supports for the Negev side, facing south,* [a] ¹⁹ *and you are to make forty pedestals of silver to hold up* [a] *the twenty supports, two pedestals underneath one support, for its two braces, and two pedestals underneath the next support for its two braces;* ²⁰ *and for the second side of the Tabernacle, facing north,* [a] *twenty supports,* ²¹ *along with forty pedestals of silver for them, two pedestals underneath one support and two pedestals underneath the next support.* ²² *For the deep* [a] *side of the Tabernacle, westward, you are to make six supports,* ²³ *and you are to make two supports* [a] *for the corners of the Tabernacle on the deep side:* ²⁴ *they are to be doubled at the bottom, and they are to be joined, to form a unit;* [a] *at the top where there is a single ring.* [b] *That is the pattern for both of them:* [c] *they are to be the corners.* ²⁵ *In all* [a] *there are to be eight supports, along with their sixteen pedestals of silver, two pedestals underneath one support,* [b] *and two pedestals underneath the next support.*

²⁶ *"You are to make cross-members of acacia lumber, five for the supports of one side of the Tabernacle,* ²⁷ *and five cross-members for the supports of the other side of the Tabernacle, and five cross-members for the supports of the side of the Tabernacle on the deep side, westward.* ²⁸ *The middle cross-member, at the midpoint of the supports, is to pass along from end to end.* ²⁹ *You are to overlay the supports with gold, and you are to make rings of gold for them* ᵃ *as attachments to secure* ᵇ *the cross-members. You are to overlay the cross-members with gold.* ³⁰ *Thus you are to raise the Tabernacle, in accord with its specifications, which you have been shown on the mountain.*

³¹ *"You are to make a Veil of violet yarn and purple yarn and scarlet yarn and woven fine linen: with cherubs artistically embroidered* ᵃ *he* ᵇ *is to make it.* ³² *You are to suspend it with hooks of gold from* ᵃ *four columns of acacia overlaid with gold and set in four pedestals of silver.* ³³ *You are to suspend the Veil beneath the fasteners,* ᵃ *and you are to bring into the space made separate by the Veil* ᵇ *the Ark of the Testimony. The Veil is to divide for you the Holy Space from the Holiest Space.* ³⁴ *You are to place the Ark-Cover* ᵃ *upon the Ark of the Testimony in the Holiest Space.* ³⁵ *You are to place the Table outside the space made separate by the Veil, and the Lampstand on the side of the Tabernacle towards the south, opposite the Table: you are to put the Table on the north side.* ᵃ

³⁶ *"You are to make a Screen for the opening of the tent, of violet yarn and purple yarn and scarlet yarn and woven fine linen, embroidered in variegated patterns.* ᵃ ³⁷ *You are to make five columns of acacia for the Screen, and overlay them with gold;* ᵃ *their hooks are also to be of gold, but you are to cast five pedestals of copper for them."*

Notes

1.a. See above, *Comment* on 25:3–7.

1.b. מעשה חשב is, lit., "work of reflection"; the cherubs are to be worked into the fabric of the curtains with great care and skill.

5.a. MT has simply היריעה האחת "the one curtain" here, but has "end-curtain" in reference to the second set. "End" is added here for clarity.

5.b. MT has only ללאת "loops," but the sense of the verse indicates that the end-curtains with the loops added are to be opposite each other.

6.a. אחד "one, a whole," here indicating a self-contained space.

7.a. על "upon" the Tabernacle.

10.a. "At the end" added here for clarity; it is in the text in reference to the first set.

11.a. LXX has τὰς δέρρεις "leather screens," in reference to the goats' hides with the hair still on them; cf. v 7 in LXX.

14.a. See n. 25:5.a.

14.b. See n. 25:5.b.

14.c. MT has "above," designating this covering as "above" the first cover; see Kennedy, *Dictionary*, 659, and for an opposing view, Cassuto, 353–54.

15.a. הקרשים . . . עמדים "standing supports." The exact nature of the קרשים "supports" has been much debated, as interpreters have proposed either solid boards (Haran, *Temples*, 150–51) or rectangular frames (Kennedy, *Dictionary*, 659–60). Quite clearly the framework supporting the Tabernacle is being described; it is the nature of that framework that remains obscure.

16.a. "Each" is added here for clarity. אחד "each" modifies קרש "support" at the end of the verse and so can be understood here as well. SamPent, LXX have it in both places.

16.b. LXX adds ποιήσεις "you are to make."

17.a. ידות "braces," taken here in the sense of "hand" connoting strength, power. Note also BDB, 390, "side, stay, support, tenon." Tenon may be too technical a term since it refers only to what would be the end of one of the upright ידות, the smaller part that would fit into a mortise. יד "brace" appears to refer to the entire upright, each of which is one side-piece of a standing support. Cf. Kennedy, *Dictionary* 660 and Hyatt, 274. LXX reads ἀγκωνίσκους "small angles."

17.b. The ידות "braces" are joined (משלבת), each to its "sister," a technical impossibility if "tenons" are lit. intended.

18.a. לפאת נגבה תימנה, lit., "to the side Negevward, toward the south," or "to the south side, southward." LXX curiously reverses the direction: πρὸς βορρᾶν "facing north."

19.a. תחת, lit., as translated farther on in the verse, "underneath."

20.a. LXX here has πρὸς νότον "facing south."

22.a. ירכתי המשכן is, lit., "the recesses of the Tabernacle." The reference here is to the closed end opposite the entrance, the short side terminating the two long sides.

23.a. The Cairo Geniza fragment has אדנים "pedestals."

24.a. תמים "perfection, wholeness," signifying the joining or dovetailing of the two frames at each corner for added strength. SamPent here has תאמים "doubled" again; cf. LXX, Tg Onk. Cassuto, 356, thinks the two terms are an intentional word-play.

24.b. MT אל־הטבעת האחת "toward the one ring," apparently a means of binding the supports together (though cf. Kennedy, *Dictionary,* 661, with an illustration).

24.c. MT כן יהיה לשניהם "thus it is for the two of them." LXX οὕτως ποιήσεις "thus you are to make."

25.a. והיו "and they are," i.e., the sum total of the six supports of the end wall plus the two bracing corner supports.

25.b. This phrase "two . . . support" is absent from SamPent.

29.a. MT has ואת־טבעתיהם תעשה זהב "and their rings you are to make gold."

29.b. See n. 25:27.b.

31.a. See n. 1.b.

31.b. יעשה "he is to make," apparently in reference to the artisan who will do the work, Bezalel or Oholiab or those working under their supervision (Exod 31:1–11; 35:30–36:1). LXX has the usual "you," as do Syr, Cairo Geniza fragment.

32.a. MT ונתתה אתה על "You are to give it upon. . . ."

33.a. הקרסים are the golden fasteners of v 6, by which the two sets of curtains are joined to make the long rectangle of the Tabernacle. LXX reads ἐπὶ τοὺς στύλους "onto the pillars," the "supports" of the translation above.

33.b. שמה מבית לפרכת "therewards within as regards the Veil."

34.a. LXX has Veil instead of Ark-Cover here, and reads κατακαλύψεις τῷ καταπετάσματι "You are to cover up (veil) with the Veil. . . ."

35.a. Following this verse, SamPent locates MT's section on the altar of the special-formula incense, Exod 30:1–10.

36.a. מעשה רקם refers to artistic variegation of colors, probably into specific patterns.

37.a. SamPent has זהב טהור "pure gold."

Form/Structure/Setting

See *Form/Structure/Setting* on 25:1–9. Gooding (*Tabernacle* 3–4, 19–28) has made a study of the LXX translation of Exodus and has given a detailed analysis of the P sections in particular. He has concluded that LXX has followed MT "fairly closely" in rendering chaps. 25–31, apart from some inconsistency and ambiguity in the translation of technical terms. In chaps. 35–40, by contrast, LXX presents a sequence widely divergent from that of MT, a fact that Gooding (78–101) attributes not to a different translation or to a different *Urtext,* but to the translator's attempt "to improve and complete the original translation." Gooding (52–59) holds chap. 38 to be an exception to his assessment and proposes that it is either a translation from a separate hand or has been extensively reworked by an editor.

Comment

The study of the P account of the Tabernacle in Exod 26 and 36 and in related references has frequently been preoccuppied with an insoluble question: whether the Tabernacle, which is described in quite specific but still sometimes obscure detail, is in any sense an historical or "real" object. The single most influential answer to this question to date has been that of Wellhausen (*Prolegomena*, 38–51), who for a whole array of reasons, chief among them the OT silence about the Tabernacle outside P and the implausibility of the construction and use of so ornate and elaborate a cultic sanctuary in the wilderness, argued that the Tabernacle never existed, and that what the Priestly writers have given us in Exodus is a retrogression, perhaps even with some idealization, of the Solomonic Temple. This view was taken up and echoed by so large and continuing an array of scholars that it took on, for many years, the aura of a regnant hypothesis (cf., e.g., Kennedy, *Dictionary*, 666; Benzinger, *Encyclopedia*, 1474; Driver, 430–32; Noth, 201, 211–14; Clements, *God and Temple*, 114–16).

Increasingly, however, this view has been qualified, as earlier dates have been proposed for P (see *Form/Structure/Setting* on 25:1–9) and as the other OT "tents" associated with Yahweh's Presence have been studied with greater care, both in the light of revised opinions about the provenance and the sources of P and also following traditio-historical rather than literary-critical techniques. In 1947, Cross (*BAR* 1:209–28) proposed an evolving tent tradition, extending from a desert tent through "David's 'Tent of Yahweh' " to a "schematic and ideal" culmination in the Priestly Tabernacle. In 1962, Haran (*JBL* 81 [1962] 17–24) suggested that P's presentation of the Tabernacle is "*a pre-Jerusalemite shrine legend now extant only in its Jerusalemite dress.*" This "shrine legend," in Haran's (20–22) view, is to be linked to Shiloh, to which P thought the Sinai Tabernacle, constructed on Yahweh's instructions, had been brought at the time of the conquest of Canaan. Also in 1962, Davies ("Tabernacle," *IDB* 4:502–6) suggested that the E tradition of a wilderness tent of meeting became the basis for P's elaborate conception, with augmentation en route by Shiloh and Davidic traditions (cf. Rabe, *JNES* 25 [1966] 132–33). In 1968, Fretheim (*VT* 18 [1968] 313–29) argued that P was opposed to any such permanent and royally sponsored structure as the Temple built by Solomon and thus proposed the elaborate and portable Tabernacle, more befitting "true Yahwism," and in reflection of a lengthy pro-tent tradition, as an argument against the rebuilding of a fixed structure in the postexilic period.

The proposal of some historical base or bases for the Tabernacle continues, and no one has taken up the cause more often or more thoroughly than Haran, who brought together in 1978 in revised form many of his earlier articles, reasserting (*Temples*, 197–98) that the Priestly writers, while projecting "utopian views," "undoubtedly believed in the reality of the subject-matter transmitted through them" and forwarded a "temple legend" whose "absolute authenticity" they took for granted. For Haran, this "legend" remains Shiloh (*Temples*, 198–204), a connection for which hard evidence is very scarce. Such detailed linkages apart, however, the connection of P's Tabernacle with early and historical rootage has now been solidly established. While few scholars would suggest, as Knight (161) does, that the Tabernacle as P describes it actually existed in the wilderness, there is an increasing affirmation of the antiquity of a tent symbolizing the Presence of Yahweh among his covenant people.

It is precisely at this point—the meaning of the Tabernacle and the various OT tents of Yahweh—that the work most valuable for understanding the OT is to be done. The historicity of the Tabernacle that P describes, or the design of the tent of Moses' day, if there was one, or the permanence of the structure at Shiloh, or the decoration of David's tent for the Ark, or even an exact reconstruction of the P Tabernacle and how it worked are not the central issue of the OT presentation of the Tabernacle. However much these considerations may be of help in illumining that presentation, they yet remain secondary to its essential point, an essential point made unmistakably clear by Exod 25–31 and 35–40 considered as a kind of parallel and complementary whole and by the location of these units in the larger Exodus narrative, the major purpose of which both focuses and is enhanced by the essential point of the two P sections. Haran's (*Bib* 50 [1969] 251–67) trenchant criticism of Clements's *God and Temple* has made the point that the Temple built by Solomon in Jerusalem was a continuation of longstanding tradition, not a departure from it, as also were the interpretations of both P and D regarding the reality of Yahweh's Presence in the midst of Israel. This tradition, in its fundamental assertion, had to do with just that reality which was continually being depicted and symbolized in narrative as in royal and priestly and prophetic and sapiential material. Haran is entirely correct in his insistence that the varying expressions of the theology of Yahweh's Presence, from period to period, as from circle to circle within the given periods, were inter-complementary and not inter-conflictory.

This point may be pressed still further, to suggest that the P descriptions of the Tabernacle in Exodus, along with all the descriptions that accompany them, are a kind of gathering and culmination of symbolic expressions of Yahweh's Presence, drawing on a theological assertion identified especially with Sinai, but clearly present also in the stories of the fathers. The symbols so glorified and elaborated by P, from the Ark to the priestly vestments, and above all the Tabernacle, are not to be understood as P's own invention, whether real objects or fantastic ones are supposed, but as an actual part of a continuing and ever-evolving confession, at every level of Israel's theological life and in every period of Israel's existence, of the reality of Yahweh's Presence.

This is made clear not only by the description of the objects themselves, and by their function as suggested by such description, but also by the insertion of this description into the Exodus narrative, and at the particular points at which the insertion has been made. That narrative is above all a narrative of Yahweh's Presence, a coming and calling Presence that proves himself repeatedly in mighty deed, in rescue, in guidance, in provision, and comes climactically at Sinai to invite a response from Israel to all that he is and all that he does. Such a narrative could hardly incorporate so extensive a sequence of materials as that presented by Exod 25–31 and 35–40 if they dealt with themes contrary to its fundamental emphasis. The inclusion of this P material is another demonstration of the thematic continuity manifested to a lesser degree by the application and expansion of the ten commandments by the Book of the Covenant.

Even the placement of the P material is a guide to its application: the

instructions for the media of worship come immediately after Israel responds
to the invitation to covenant relationship in Yahweh's Presence; and they
are carried out immediately after an unthinkable threat of the withdrawal
of the gift of Yahweh's Presence is averted by the renewal of the covenant
relationship in his Presence. No other location, in Exodus or in the OT,
would provide a more intimate connection with the very theme which is the
preoccupation also of the P material.

Thus once again it is Exodus as a whole, Exodus in the form in which
we have received it, that provides the important key by which one part of
the book, the Priestly material of chaps. 25–31, and in particular the description of the Tabernacle in chap. 26, is to be understood. Whatever its origins,
how much of it ever existed and when, however it actually may have looked
and worked if it did exist, the primary significance of the Tabernacle is what
it suggests to us about the theology of Yahweh's Presence. For that theology,
P's Tabernacle description is nothing less than a cumulative archive.

1–6 The Tabernacle was to be made of ten curtains woven of the expensive
fabric and yarns specified in 25:4 (see above) and joined together to form
two sets of five curtains each. These two sets were then to be connected by
means of fifty loops on each end-curtain and fifty golden fasteners to form
a continuous length approximately sixty feet long (end to end) and forty-
two feet high (top to bottom). Onto each of these curtains cherubs were to
be embroidered, with great care and artistic skill.

7–14 To protect this first expensive and beautifully fashioned set of curtains, an additional set of curtains and two covers were to be made. The
curtains were to be made of cured but untanned goatskins, with the hair
still in place (so עזים), and were to consist of two sets of curtains, one made
of five curtains joined together and one made of six curtains joined together,
the two sets connected by means of one hundred loops and fifty copper
fasteners to form a continuous length approximately sixty-six feet long (end
to end) and forty-five feet high (top to bottom). This length of curtains was
large enough to shelter the Tabernacle proper from top to bottom with
enough additional height to extend beyond the Tabernacle curtains and
enough additional length to provide protective material at both the front
and the back of the Tabernacle.

Two further covers were to be fashioned to protect the two sets of curtains:
a cover of tanned rams' hides and a cover of sea-cows' hides, apparently
arranged in that sequence. The fabric of the finished Tabernacle was thus
to consist of four layers: an inner set of tent-curtains of fine cloth; an outer
set of tent-curtains of cured goatskins with the hair still in place, six feet
longer and three feet higher than the first set, to afford a protective overlap;
an inner cover of tanned rams' hides; and an outer cover of sea-cows' hides.

15–25 These curtains and covers, which enclosed the Holy Space and
the Holiest Space and protected the special objects within that space, were
to be held in place by a series of upright supports anchored in pedestals of
silver and bound together by a series of cross-members and two special corner
supports. The supports and the cross-members were to be made of acacia,
and overlaid with gold; the pedestals were to be made of silver. The standing
supports were to be 15′ high and 2¼′ wide, and each was to be supported

by two silver pedestals, one for each of its יָדוֹת, the side-braces that formed the length of the upright support, which were inserted into the silver pedestals, and were arranged touching, each one, the side-brace of the next upright frame. These supports, forty-eight in number, were arranged twenty plus eight plus twenty, to give a frame-work of three sides, 45' × 18' × 45', oriented with the "open" or supportless side towards the east. The two corner frames were doubled at the bottom but joined at the top, to form a kind of brace at the points where the strain would be greatest.

26–30 These upright supports were to be held in place by a series of fifteen cross-members, five for each of the three "closed" sides of the Tabernacle. These cross-members were attached to the upright supports by rings of gold, though at just what points, apart from a "middle cross-member, at the mid-point of the supports," the text does not specify. This arrangement of course was to facilitate portability: the upright supports were light but strong and created a framework over which the curtains embroidered with cherubim could be hung and through which they could be seen, as in a sequence of frames of gold. The supports, in turn, were held rigid by the series of silver pedestals double their number, by the fifteen cross-members attached to them by golden rings, and by the two specially constructed corner supports. The entire structure could thus be struck and packed for transportation or reassembled at a new location in a relatively short period of time.

This summary of details, though based on the text, is still theoretical, not only because some details of the construction of the Tabernacle are left unmentioned, but also because our understanding of such technical terms as קְרָשִׁים "supports," יָדוֹת "braces," וָוִים "hooks," and בְּרִיחִם "cross-members" is limited at best (cf. the discussions of Kennedy, *Dictionary*, 658–62; Davies, "Tabernacle," *IDB* 4:498–502; Haran, *Temples*, 149–74; and the confusion of LXX concerning the translation of such terms, Gooding, *Tabernacle* 20–28). No proposed reconstruction or artist's sketch or model of the Tabernacle to date can be accepted fully, simply because the information available is too incomplete and ambiguous, in spite of its extent. We cannot even be sure whether this inexactitude is owing to a lack of familiarity, to overfamiliarity, or to the fantastic projection of a final form that never really existed.

31–35 The space formed by the Tabernacle, approximately 810 square feet, 34,020 cubic feet, was to be further subdivided by a veil matching the inner curtains in material and pattern, and apparently at a point 30', or twenty cubits, from the opening of the Tabernacle, a location determined by the specification that the veil be hung beneath the fasteners that joined together the two sets of five curtains that formed the inner "tent" of the Tabernacle (cf. v 6). This created a smaller space 10 × 10 × 10 cubits, approximately 15' × 15' × 15', and a larger space 20 × 10 × 10 cubits, approximately 30' × 15' × 15'. The smaller space was to be designated the Holiest Space (קֹדֶשׁ הַקֳּדָשִׁים "the Holy of Holies"), and the Ark with its special Cover (see *Comment* on 25:10–22) was to be placed there. The larger space was to be designated the Holy Space, and there the Table and the Lampstand were to be placed, on the south and north sides of the Tabernacle respectively, and opposite each other.

36–37 The open east end of the Tabernacle was to be closed by a Screen, to be made of the same material as the inner curtains and the Veil, but embroidered in multicolored patterns rather than with cherubs. This Screen was to be hung by golden hooks onto five columns of acacia overlaid with gold, but since these columns were apparently open to the outer court, which is not shielded from view by the rams' hide and sea-cows' hide covers, their five pedestals were to be made of copper, like the various implements of the outer court (cf. 27:1–8, 10; 30:17–18). As Haran has shown (*Temples*, 158–65), there is a "material gradation" from more to less precious materials the greater the distance from the Holiest Space and the Holy Space.

Explanation

The Tabernacle is at the center of the instructions concerning the media of worship in Yahweh's Presence, precisely because it houses the Ark and the Ark-Cover, which are *the* symbol par excellence of Yahweh's Presence in Israel's midst and so, logically, *the* center and the beginning point of the instructions. This connection is made unmistakably clear not only by the provision of the Holiest Space for the Ark and the Ark-Cover alone, but also by the repetition on the veil and the inner curtains of the Tabernacle of the cherub motif (see *Comment* on 25:17–22) and the use only of gold and the richest of the decorative fabrics within the Tabernacle itself.

Paralleling this lavish designation of the center of Yahweh's Presence, however, there is a complementary, almost contradictory emphasis upon the temporary nature of Yahweh's settlement. Just as the Ark and the Ark-Cover are made and kept portable by the presence of lifting/carrying poles kept permanently in place, so the Tabernacle is made up of smaller parts designed for ready disassembly and reassembly. Its supporting framework is made up of twenty-eight upright frames, set up in fifty-six pedestals, and made rigid by fifteen cross-members inserted through rings. Its two layers of curtains are held together by fifty fasteners each, its protective covers are readily removable, and its Veil and its Screen are suspended by hooks from columns mounted in detachable pedestals. The emphasis in every case is on portability, and the point, in sum and repeatedly, is that Yahweh's Presence, so precisely symbolized by gradations of ever more opulent materials, is a Presence on the move, a Presence that cannot be suggested by a stationary location, a Presence that Israel's worship and so also Israel must be prepared to follow to a new place at a moment's notice.

The Instructions for the Altar (27:1–8)

PARALLEL VERSES
38:1–7

Bibliography

Aharoni, Y. "Arad: Its Inscriptions and Temple." *BA* 31 (1968) 2–32. ———. "The Horned Altar of Beer-sheba." *BA* (1974) 2–6. **Amiran, R.** and **Y. Aharoni.** *Ancient*

Arad. Jerusalem: The Israel Museum, catalogue no. 32, 1967. **Gressmann, H.** *Die Ausgrabungen in Palästina und das Alte Testament.* Tübingen: J. C. B. Mohr, 1908. **Kennedy, A. R. S.** "Tabernacle." *A Dictionary of the Bible.* J. Hastings, ed. New York: Charles Scribner's Sons, 1902. 4:653–68. **Lucas, A.** *Ancient Egyptian Materials and Industries.* 3d ed. rev. London: Edward Arnold & Co., 1948.

Translation

¹ *"You are to make the* ᵃ *Altar of acacia lumber, five cubits in length and five cubits in width: the Altar is to be square, and three cubits in height.* ² *You are to make horns for it, one on each of its corners: its horns are to be an integral part of it, and you are to overlay it* ᵃ *with copper.* ³ *You are to make pots for its ashes,* ᵃ *and cleaning shovels,* ᵇ *and dashing-basins,* ᶜ *and pronged-forks,* ᵈ *and fire-holders for it. You are to make all of its equipment of copper.* ⁴ *You are to make for it a grate, a strainer* ᵃ *made of copper, and you are to make the strainer* ᵃ *with four rings of copper, one upon each of its four corners,* ᶜ ⁵ *and to place it* ᵃ *below the rim of the Altar downwards: the strainer is to extend half the height* ᵇ *of the altar.* ⁶ *You are to make carrying-poles for the Altar, carrying-poles of acacia lumber, and you are to overlay them with copper.* ⁷ *These carrying-poles are to be thrust* ᵃ *through the rings, to be the carrying-poles on the two sides of the Altar when it is lifted.* ⁸ *You are to make the Altar* ᵃ *hollow, of planks; exactly as he has shown you on the mountain, so they are to make it."* ᵇ

Notes

1.a. SamPent and LXX have "an altar."

2.a. LXX reads αὐτά "them."

3.a. לְדַשְׁנוֹ, a piel inf constr from דשׁן "be fat," is apparently a reference to the greasy ash deposited from burning fat on the altar. LXX has στεφάνην τῷ θυσιαστηρίῳ "a brim, edging for the altar" instead of "pots for its ashes." Cf. BDB, 206.

3.b. יע is from יעה "to sweep up to take away," hence "cleaning-shovel." Cf. BDB, 418.

3.c. A מזרק is a bowl or basin designed specifically for the dashing or throwing of liquids. BDB, 284.

3.d. מזלגת were apparently long probe-forks used to move meat-sacrifices on the Altar. Cf. מזלג, 1 Sam 2:13–14.

4.a. רשׁת "net," here a kind of sieve or strainer, from ירשׁ "take possession of, inherit." Its function was to catch and hold the coals of fire and any unconsumed pieces of the sacrificial offerings, but to allow ashes and grease to fall through and air to enter from the bottom.

4.b. LXX reads τῇ ἐσχάρα "the grate" here.

4.c. "Corner" is used to translate קצה here and פנה in v 2. The difference between the two terms, in this context, is slight: קצה lit. means "extremity," as the border of a territory or the end of a staff (BDB, 892); פנה means "corner" of something squared or presenting angles (BDB, 819).

5.a. LXX has αὐτούς "them" in apparent reference to the rings—cf. Vg. MT refers to the feminine singular רשׁת "strainer."

5.b. והיתה הרשׁת עד חצי המזבח, lit., "and the strainer is to be to a point half of the Altar."

7.a. וְהוּבָא is 3d masc sg hoph pf; SamPent, LXX, Vg, Syr, Tg Onk have the equivalent of 2d masc sg hiph pf, "and you are to thrust."

8.a. MT has "it." Altar, the clear antecedent, is used above.

8.b. This verse has the appearance of an explanatory addition, one prompted perhaps by the ambiguity of the description of the Altar.

Form/Structure/Setting

See *Form/Structure/Setting* on 25:1–9

Comment

The instructions for the construction of the Altar are in some ways the most ambiguous of all the instructions of the P sections. While the size of the Altar is given precisely and its accessories are carefully listed (our limitation here is understanding technical terminology), the exact construction of the Altar itself is far from clear. As a result, a number of interpretations of these verses have been given, and the most that can be said of them, the one below included, is that they are reflective guesses.

1–3 The Altar was to be made of acacia wood overlaid with copper, an instruction that is clear enough, but still a bit of a puzzle both because of the conflicting directions given in Exod 20:24–26 and also because of the practical difficulty of burning sacrifices on a wooden Altar, even one sheathed in copper. The size of the Altar is unambiguous: it was to be approximately 7½′ square and 4½′ tall. The Altar was to have קרנות "horns," one at each of its four corners. Speculation about the exact significance of these horns continues, since the OT nowhere makes any statement about their meaning, but their appearance has been clarified by the discovery of a horned altar (disassembled) at Beersheba (Aharoni, *BA* 37 [1974] 2–6). The Beersheba altar, like the one described in these verses, violates the prohibition of Exod 20:24–26 not only in the use of dressed stone but also in the incision into one of its stones of "a twisting snake." An altar made of undressed stones and earth, though covered with plaster, was discovered at Arad; its dimensions are exactly those of v 1, and Aharoni has speculated that original horns, made of clay and plaster, may have been broken off (*BA* 37 [1974] 2; see also *BA* 31 [1968] 19, 21, and Amiran and Aharoni, *Ancient Arad*, 25). The earlier view that these horns represented the horns of animals sacrificed (Driver, 292) has been supplemented by the suggestion (Gressmann, *Ausgrabungen*, 27–28) that they represented מצבות "pillars" (see *Comment* on 24:3–4). Whatever the case, they were the holiest part of the Altar (Exod 29:10–12; Lev 4:18–21; 1 Kgs 2:28–34). The accessories for the Altar, all to be made of copper, included a pot or pail for ash removal, along with a special shovel for that purpose, basins for dashing liquids, pronged forks for the manipulation of the meat and fat being burned, and special pans to hold and transfer coals of fire.

4–8 The most obscure detail of the Altar's structure and function is the grate, which has been understood as a kind of trellis-work base (so Kennedy, *Dictionary*, 657–58) that served in part as a step (McNeile, 174) or formed a kind of "Collar" (Good, "Grating," *IDB* 2:470) with only an ornamental purpose (Cassuto, 363–64). Since the altar was only 4½′ high, however, and since the grate extended downward for half of this height, such a step would have been both unnecessary and a cumbrance, as it would have meant that the top of the Altar would have been below the waist of even a short priest standing on the step. The description of the grate as רשת a "strainer" or "network" of copper may just as easily be taken as suggesting that the grate was inside the Altar, not outside of it, and that it functioned as both a holder for the Altar fire (the melting-point of copper is 1,083° C.; cf. Lucas, *Egyptian Materials*, 243–44) and a kind of strainer that would permit ashes and grease to fall to the bottom of the Altar, while holding both the fire and anything placed upon it in the top half of the Altar. This would create the draft necessary for a hot fire, yet protect the wooden Altar and its copper overlay from a direct exposure to the fire itself.

The grate/strainer is to be placed under the rim (presumably at the top of the Altar) downwards half the height of the Altar, and thus the four rings by which the Altar was to be lifted and carried are attached to the four corners of the grate/strainer, which could more easily bear the Altar's weight than could its plank sides. Indeed, this structure may have necessitated the assurance of the summary statement of v 8 that the Altar was hollow, a 7½′ square of copper-sheathed planking. No bottom is mentioned, and the bottom of the Altar was probably left open to facilitate the cleaning, for which the tools of v 3 are specified. The pronouns of v 8b refer, in order, to Yahweh ("he"), Moses ("you"), and Israel or Israel's artisans ("they"); this stylistic shift further suggests that this verse may be an addition.

Explanation

The Altar is a testimony of the attention to detail given worship in Yahweh's Presence. That worship was to be carefully planned and deliberately managed, precisely arranged and properly carried out. Once again, the movement of Yahweh's Presence is stressed: the altar is to be made portable. To such extent is this so that some interpreters have questioned whether an altar would even be usable unless filled with dirt or stones. The materials to be used in the altar and its accessories, finally, reflect the distance at which it is to be placed from the central symbol and the holiest space of Yahweh's Presence.

The Instructions for the Tabernacle Court (27:9–19)

PARALLEL VERSES:
38:9–20

Bibliography

Kennedy, A. R. S. "Tabernacle. *A Dictionary of the Bible*. J. Hastings, ed. New York: Charles Scribner's Sons. 4:653–68.

Translation

⁹ *"You are to make the Courtyard of the Tabernacle: for the Negev side, facing south, there are to be draperies of woven fine linen for the Courtyard, one hundred*

cubits in length for that one side. [10] *They are to have twenty columns and twenty pedestals of copper; the hooks of the columns and their rings are to be silver.* [a] [11] *So also for the length* [a] *of the north side, draperies a hundred cubits* [b] *long, and twenty columns and twenty pedestals of copper, with the hooks of the columns and their rings of silver.* [12] *The width of the Courtyard on the west side is to be fifty cubits' length of draperies, with ten columns and ten pedestals,* [13] *and the width of the Courtyard on the east side, toward the sunrise, is to be fifty cubits.* [14] *There are to be fifteen cubits' length* [a] *of draperies on one side of the entrance,* [b] *with three columns and three pedestals,* [15] *and fifteen cubits' length of draperies on the other side of the entrance, with three columns and three pedestals.* [16] *For the entrance* [a] *of the Courtyard there is to be a screen twenty cubits across, of violet yarn and purple yarn and scarlet yarn and woven fine linen, embroidered in variegated patterns, with four columns and four pedestals for it.* [b]

[17] *"All the columns all around the Courtyard are to have silver rings and silver hooks; their pedestals are to be of copper.* [18] *The Courtyard is to be a hundred cubits long, fifty cubits wide at each end,* [a] *and five cubits high, bordered* [b] *by woven fine linen and copper pedestals.* [19] *All* [a] *the tools* [b] *of the Tabernacle, whatever the job,* [c] *and also its anchor-pegs* [d] *and all the anchor-pegs of the Courtyard, are to be of copper.* [e]

Notes

10.a. According to Exod 38:19, these rings are silver overlay, not solid silver.

11.a. LXX omits "the length of."

11.b. MT has simply קלעים מאה ארך "draperies a hundred long." SamPent has באמה "in the cubit" instead of ארך "long." LXX has πηχῶν μῆκος "a hundred cubits long." "Cubit" is added above for clarity.

14.a. MT has simply וחמש עשרה אמה קלעים "fifteen cubits of draperies"; LXX adds ὕψος "height."

14.b. לכתף "for the shoulder" is a reference to the draperies extending from the corner to the opening on the east side of the Courtyard; v 15 refers to the other "shoulder" of this entrance. לכתף . . . ולכתף is thus translated "on the one side of the entrance . . . on the other side of the entrance.

16.a. לשער "gate, entryway," translated "entrance" in sequence to vv 14–15.

16.b. MT has put the pl pronom suff, עמדיהם ארבעה ואדניהם ארבעה "their four columns and their four pillars." Cassuto (366) thinks the first "their" refers to the twenty cubits (an unlikely explanation) or is a slip (a better explanation), and the second "their" to the four columns.

18.a. MT has חמשים בחמשים "fifty with, alongside fifty." SamPent has "cubits" instead of the second "fifty."

18.b. MT has simply משזר . . . ואדניהם woven . . . pedestals"; "bordered by" is added above for clarity.

19.a. SamPent has ועשית את כל "And you are to make all" at the beginning of this verse.

19.b. כלי is rendered "tools" here (as in 1 Kgs 6:7), since the "vessels" or "equipment" (cf. 25:9, 29) of the inner service of the Tabernacle were to be made of pure gold.

19.c. עבדתו "its labor" (Cairo Geniza: "their labor"), taken here to mean need of whatever kind in the placement, assembly, disassembly and transportation of the Tabernacle and its Courtyard.

19.d. A יתד was a pin or peg used to anchor or secure anything, here the tent or its cover. Exod 35:18 and 39:40 refer also to the "ropes, cords" used with these pegs. This phrase is missing from LXX.

19.e. SamPent adds here ועשית בגדי תכלת וארגמן ותולעת שני לשרת בהם בקדש "and you are to make vestments (or coverings) of violet yarn and purple yarn and scarlet yarn for ministry in worship with them in the Holy Space."

Form/Structure/Setting

See *Form/Structure/Setting* on 25:1–9.

Comment

9–16   The Courtyard that was to surround the Tabernacle and to separate
it and the activities before it from the world outside was to be designated
by draperies of woven fine linen suspended by hooks and rings of silver
from columns of unspecified material (presumably acacia) set in pedestals
of copper. This Courtyard was to be approximately 150′ across the south
and north sides and 75′ across the west and east sides, thus comprising a
total area of some 11,250 square feet. The entrance to the Courtyard was of
course on the east side, paralleling the opening of the Tabernacle itself,
and on that side, the draperies were to extend 22½′ in from the southeast
and northeast corners respectively, with the resulting 30′ opening to be covered by a 30′ Screen made of the same material and apparently in the same
pattern as the Screen covering the opening to the Tabernacle (Exod 26:36;
see n. 26:36.a, and *Comment* above).

Altogether, fifty-six columns were to suspend the draperies, and four columns were to suspend the Screen. The arrangement of these sixty columns
is not specified, nor is the placement of the Tabernacle within the Courtyard
made clear. Cassuto (366–68) proposes that each corner had a post, which
must be counted only once to give the specified number. Haran (*Temples*,
154–55; fig. 1, 152) suggests that the columns were placed every 2½ cubits,
"in the *middle* of each imaginary space of five cubits." Haran also suggests
(155), following rabbinic commentators, that the Tabernacle was located approximately 30′ from the western perimeter of the Courtyard, and 30′ from
each of the two side perimeters to their respective sides of the Tabernacle
(cf. Kennedy, *Dictionary*, 656–57). In the absence of any specification in the
OT, any certainty is of course impossible.

17–19   The linen draperies that enclosed the Courtyard constituted an
effective but entirely portable barrier to interference or distraction from outside the space set aside for special worship in Yahweh's Presence. Since the
height of the Courtyard draperies was 7½′ and the height of the Tabernacle's
upright supports was 15′, the draperies' purpose was not to block any view
of the Tabernacle, or the view of anything outside the Courtyard taller than
the draperies and their supporting columns, but to shut off the view at ground
level. Indeed, a view from outside the Courtyard of the Tabernacle standing
within the Courtyard, given what and whom it symbolized, was entirely desirable.

The use of copper for the pedestals supporting the draperies and the
Screen covering the entrance of the Courtyard is indicative, again, of the
decreasing gradation of the special materials with an increasing distance from
the Holy Space and the Holiest Space of Yahweh's Presence. This is the
reason, also, for the use of copper for the anchor-pegs and the tools employed
in the tasks of preparation, assembly and disassembly, packing and unpacking.
These were all used outside the Tabernacle itself, and so were seen outside

it; thus they did not need to be made of the gold reserved for every nonfabric object within the Tabernacle. The silver hooks and rings for the columns holding up the draperies and the Screen also belong, apparently, to what Haran (*Temples*, 164–65) has called the "concentric circles" of diminishing holiness.

Explanation

Once again, the Courtyard symbolizes both the movement of Yahweh's Presence and the uniqueness of the place where (as also of the people among whom) he chooses to settle, however temporarily. A deliberate tension is presented by these accounts, a tension between a Yahweh who may move at a moment's notice and a Yahweh whose Presence demands a sequence of special spaces set off by carefully prescribed patterns designated by a specific order of materials. All these materials are precious, but they suggest by their decreasing value the fact that anything (or anyone) must be better with increasing nearness to Yahweh's Presence. This lesson is not merely a lesson for worship: as the narrative of Exodus makes clear, it is what every lesson in worship is supposed to be, a lesson for the living of life.

The Command for the Keeping of the Light (27:20–21)

PARALLEL VERSES:
Lev 24:1–3

Bibliography

Levine, B. A. "The Descriptive Tabernacle Texts of the Pentateuch." *JAOS* 85 (1965) 307–18.

Translation

20 "*You are to command the sons of Israel to obtain for you pure olive oil, pounded, not pressed,* [a] *for the light, so that a lamp may be lit* [b] *regularly.* [c] 21 *In the Tent of Appointed Meeting, outside the Veil before the Testimony, Aaron is to see to it,* [a] *along with his sons, from evening until morning in Yahweh's Presence. This is a perpetual requirement for all the generations of the sons of Israel.*"

Notes

20.a. כתית "beaten," refers to olive oil extracted by pounding the olives by hand as opposed to the much quicker and less thorough method of crushing them in an olive press.

20.b. להעלת, lit., "to raise, lift up" the lamp, and so to cause it to give light. BDB, 749.

20.c. תמיד "continually" here means on a regular basis, each night, as v 21 shows.

21.a. יערך refers to Aaron "setting in order, arranging" the fueling, the trimming, and the lighting of the lamp.

Form/Structure/Setting

See *Form/Structure/Setting* on 25:1–9. These two verses, which are paralleled in Lev 24:1–3 but nowhere in Exodus, appear to be a bit out of place here, and some commentators have considered them an addition (so Galling, in Beer, 139; Noth, 217). Haran (*Temples*, 209, n. 6) considers these verses "in about the right place," though he objects to the inclusion of Aaron's sons as "an erroneous insertion," a conclusion disputed in turn by Levine (JAOS 85 [1965] 311–12). If the verses are secondary to the Exodus narrative, they may have been attracted to their present location by the instructions that follow, dealing with the sacral vestments of Aaron and his sons. Cassuto (369–72) treats the two verses as the first of three commands to Moses introductory to the instructions for the sacral vestments, but 27:20–21 do not fit readily with 28:1–5, which are concerned with the sacral vestments as symbols of priestly authority and hence of Yahweh's Presence. The most logical explanation of the verses is that they are indeed additional to the original sequence of the P composite but are attracted there by their reference to a perpetual duty of Aaron and his sons. What this explanation does *not* tell us is why the verses were set here instead of farther along, after the instructions for the priests' ordination.

Comment

20 The command for pure olive oil extracted by hand-pounding with a pestle in a mortar is consonant with the specification of only the best for use in Yahweh's Presence. Such oil gives off a bright light and almost no smoke, by contrast with pressed oil (cf. Gispen, 261–62). The reference to "the light" (מאור) is apparently here a general one, even though מנרת המאור in Exod 35:14 is a clear reference to the Lampstand; נר may mean a (cf. Haran's view, *Temples*, 208, n. 4, that נר is used here "in a collective sense") lamp on the Lampstand or even somewhere else in the Holy Space.

21 Aaron is to attend to this light, and in due course his sons are also, and he is to "arrange" or place it in the Holy Space, outside the Veil, in the Tabernacle, referred to here as elsewhere in P (according to BDB, 14, some 131 times) as אהל מועד, the "Tent of Appointed Meeting" or the "Tent of Promised Presence." In Exod 39:32; 40:2, 6, 29, indeed, P uses the phrase משכן אהל מועד "Tabernacle of the Tent of Appointed Meeting," a composite phrase that may reflect an attempt at consolidation (see below, on 33:7–11). The light is to be kept burning in Yahweh's Presence through the night, from evening until morning (cf. 1 Sam 3:3) and the command that it be so provided is a command in perpetuity, throughout Israel's generations.

Explanation

The light burning through the night in Yahweh's Presence was to be only the best light that could be provided, because of its location. As such, it attested the importance of that location, even as it symbolized the Presence that made the location significant. The mention of Aaron and his sons as responsible for this light is a statement in support of Priestly authority.

The Instructions for the Priests' Vestments (28:1–43)

PARALLEL VERSES: 39:1–31

Bibliography

Arnold, W. R. *Ephod and Ark.* HTS 3. Cambridge: Harvard University Press, 1917. **Buck, A. De.** "La Fleur au Front du Grand-Prêtre." *OTS* 9 (1951) 18–29. **Chagall, M.** and **J. Leymarie.** *The Jerusalem Windows.* New York: George Braziller, 1967. **Elliger, K.** "Ephod und Chosen." *Festschrift Friedrich Baumgärtel.* EF 10. Erlangen: Universitätsbund, 1959. 9–23. Also in *VT* 8 (1958) 19–35. **Farrer, A.** *A Rebirth of Images.* Boston: Beacon Press, 1963. **Goodenough, E. R.** *By Light, Light.* New Haven: Yale University Press, 1935. **Haran, M.** "The Form of the Ephod in the Biblical Sources," *Tarbiz* 24 (1955) 380–91. **Lipiński, E.** " ʾŪrīm and Tummīm." *VT* 20 (1970) 495–96. **May, H. G.** "Ephod and Ariel." *AJSL* 56 (1939) 44–69. **Noth, M.** "The Background of Judges 17–18." *Israel's Prophetic Heritage.* B. W. Anderson and W. Harrelson, eds. New York: Harper & Brothers, 1962. 68–85. **Reiner, E.** "Fortune-Telling in Mesopotamia." *JNES* 19 (1960) 22–35. **Robertson, E.** "The ʾŪrīm and Tummīm; What Were They?" *VT* 14 (1964) 67–74. **Rowley, H. H.** *Worship in Ancient Israel.* London: S.P.C.K., 1967.

Translation

¹ *"You are to bring near to yourself, from the midst of the sons of Israel, Aaron your brother, and his sons with him, to give priestly ministry* ᵃ *to me: Aaron, and Nadab and Abihu, Eleazar ("God has helped") and Ithamar ("Date-palm region"), Aaron's sons.* ² *You are to make sacral vestments for Aaron your brother, for splendor and for beauty.* ³ *You are to instruct* ᵃ *all who have wise minds, whom I have filled with creative artistry,* ᵇ *that they are to make Aaron's vestments, to set him apart to give priestly ministry to me.* ⁴ *These are the vestments they are to make: a Breastpiece, an Ephod, a Robe, a Tunic with a checked pattern, a Turban, and a Sash. So they are to make sacral vestments for Aaron your brother and for his sons who are to give priestly ministry to me:* ⁵ *they are to use* ᵃ *gold, and violet yarn and purple yarn and scarlet yarn and fine linen.*

⁶ *"They are to make the Ephod of gold, violet yarn, purple yarn, scarlet yarn, and woven fine linen artistically embroidered.* ⁷ *It is to have two shoulder-pieces joined to its two sides, thus making one garment.* ᵃ ⁸ *The elaborate belt of the Ephod, made as a part of it,* ᵃ *is to be of identical workmanship, in gold, violet yarn, purple yarn, scarlet yarn, and woven fine linen.* ⁹ *You are to take two* ᵃ *onyx-stones and engrave*

upon them the names of the sons of Israel, ¹⁰ six of their names on one stone and the six names remaining on the other stone, following the order in which they were born. ¹¹ After the art of an engraver of gemstones, an inscriber of seals, you are to engrave the stones with the names of the sons of Israel; you are to mount them in a setting of gold filigree. ¹² You are to place the two stones onto the shoulder-pieces of the Ephod as stones to call to mind ᵃ the sons of Israel. Aaron is to carry their ᵇ names into Yahweh's Presence on his two shoulders as a reminder. ¹³ You are to make gold filigree, ¹⁴ and two ropes ᵃ of pure gold (you are to make these like tightly-twisted cordage) and you are to place the ropes of twisted cordage onto the filigree. ᵇ

¹⁵ "You are to make a Breastpiece of Judgment; you are to make it artistically embroidered as the Ephod is: you are to make it of gold, violet yarn, purple yarn, scarlet yarn, and woven fine linen. ¹⁶ It is to be a square folded double, a span in length and a span in width. ¹⁷ You are to set in it an arrangement of gemstones, four rows of gemstones: the first row is to be a row of sardius, peridot, and emerald; ¹⁸ the second row, turquoise, lapis lazuli, and jasper; ¹⁹ the third row, jacinth, agate, and amethyst; ²⁰ and the fourth row, green feldspar, sardonyx, and green jasper; ᵃ filigrees of gold are to be their setting. ²¹ The stones are to be as the names of the sons of Israel, twelve in number, each with one name engraved as on a seal: they are to represent the twelve tribes.

²² "You are to make for the Breastpiece tightly twisted ropes, made like cordage of pure gold. ᵃ ²³ You are to make for the Breastpiece two rings upon the two edges ᵃ of the Breastpiece. ²⁴ You are to put the two twisted cords of gold into the two rings at the edges of the Breastpiece, ²⁵ and the two ends of the two twisted cords you are to put onto the two filigrees ᵃ and thus fasten them ᵇ onto the shoulderpieces of the Ephod on its front.

²⁶ "You are to make two rings of gold and place them onto the two edges of the Breastpiece, upon its inner side next to the Ephod. ᵃ ²⁷ You are to make two rings of gold and put them onto the two shoulderpieces of the Ephod at a lower point on its front, at a point just above where the elaborate belt of the Ephod is fastened. ²⁸ Then they are to bind the Breastpiece by its rings to the rings of the Ephod with a twisted cord of violet yarn, so that the Breastpiece may hang snugly ᵃ above the elaborate belt of the Ephod, and not fall forward from the Ephod.

²⁹ "Thus is Aaron to carry the names of the sons of Israel on the Breastpiece of Judgment upon his heart whenever he enters the Holy Space, as a perpetual reminder in the Presence of Yahweh. ³⁰ You are to put ᵃ into ᵇ the Breastpiece of Judgment the Urim and the Thummin, and they are to be upon Aaron's heart ᶜ whenever he enters Yahweh's Presence. Thus is Aaron to carry the Judgment of the Sons of Israel upon his heart perpetually in the Presence of Yahweh.

³¹ "You are to make the Robe of the Ephod wholly of violet yarn. ³² In its center there is to be an opening for his head, and all around the opening there is to be woven reinforcement: ᵃ this is to give it sturdiness, ᵇ so that it cannot be ripped. ³³ You are to make on its skirts pomegranates of violet yarn and purple yarn and scarlet yarn; ᵃ these are to be all around its skirts, with bells of gold among them all around: ³⁴ a golden bell and a pomegranate, a golden bell and a pomegranate, interspersed upon the skirts of the Robe, all around. ³⁵ This robe is to be worn by ᵃ Aaron when he ministers in worship, ᵇ so that its sound can be heard when he enters and leaves the Holy Space in the Presence of Yahweh, so that he will not die.

³⁶ "You are to make a Flower ᵃ of pure gold, and you are to engrave upon it,

like a seal-engraving, 'Set Apart for Yahweh.' [37] *You are to place it upon the Turban with a twisted cord of violet yarn: locate it* [a] *on the front side of the Turban.* [38] *It is to be on the forehead of Aaron, and so Aaron is to carry the guilt of iniquity for the acts and implements set apart,* [a] *that the sons of Israel have set apart as the free gifts of their set-apartness. It is to be upon his forehead perpetually to gain acceptance for them in Yahweh's Presence.*

[39] *"You are to pattern-weave the Tunic with fine linen, and you are to make a Turban with fine linen, and you are to make a Sash, embroidered in variegated patterns.* [a] [40] *For the sons of Aaron, you are to make tunics and you are to make for them sashes and high hats;* [a] *you are to make them for splendor and for beauty.* [41] *You are to vest* [a] *them, Aaron your brother and his sons along with him, and you are to anoint them and you are to ordain them,* [b] *and you are to set them apart, so that they may give priestly ministry to me.* [42] *You are to make for them undergarments of plain linen to clothe naked genital areas; these undergarments* [a] *are to extend from the waist to the thighs,* [43] *and they are to be on Aaron and on his sons when they enter the Tent of Appointed Meeting or when they approach the Altar to minister in worship in the Holy Space, that they may not carry guilt of iniquity and in consequence die. This is a requirement forever, for him and for his descendants after him."*

Notes

1.a. לְכַהֲנוֹ, used also in vv 3 and 4, is a piel inf constr with a 3d masc sing pronom suff, lit., "to minister him as priest." SamPent and LXX omit the suff. The usage is curious (cf. Cassuto, 371) but apparently deliberate, and the following "to me" makes its meaning quite clear.

3.a. תדבר "you are to speak," in this context "instruct, explain."

3.b. רוח חכמה "a spirit of wisdom."

5.a. לקח, lit., "take," here in reference perhaps to receiving the offering brought by the people; translated "use" in view of the larger context.

7.a. וחבר "and so it is joined united" (SamPent has יחבר). The "two sides" or "two edges" of the Ephod are apparently its front and its back, described here as united by the two shoulder-straps, shown by v 12 to have a double purpose. Cf. Josephus, *Antiq.* III. 11.165–66.

8.a. אשר עליו "that is upon it." This "belt" or "band" is used in the OT only in reference to the Ephod, and always in one of two phrases: חשב האפוד or, as here, חשב אפדתו.

9.a. LXX here adds λίθους "stones," reading "two stones, onyx-stones."

12.a. אבני זכרן, lit., "stones of remembrance." SamPent has אבני זכרן הנה "they are stones of remembrance for"; cf. LXX.

12.b. LXX has τὰ ὀνόματα τῶν υἱῶν Ισραηλ "the names of the sons of Israel."

14.a. These שרשרת are not link-chains, as the clause of instruction immediately following shows.

14.b. LXX adds a note on the attachment of these ropes to the front of the shoulderpieces.

20.a. The gemstones listed for the four rows of the Ephod are impossible to identify with certainty. The translation above generally follows the proposals of Garber and Funk, "Jewels and Precious Stones," *IDB* 2:900–902. Each stone must have been clearly differentiated in its setting; clearly, no two mountings employed the same stone.

22.a. LXX has what is substantially MT's v 30 at this point, and the correspondence in versification through the rest of the chapter is varied accordingly. Indeed LXX follows a somewhat different sequence through its v 29.

23.a. That these would have to be the front edges of the folded square, at the top, is made likely by the continuation of the description, esp. vv 26–28.

25.a. The filigrees mounting the onyx stones onto the shoulderpieces of the Ephod.

25.b. MT has simply "and so you are to give upon the shoulderpieces of the Ephod toward the front of its face"—"them" is added in the parallel to this verse in 39:18 (see below) and so is included above for clarity.

26.a. Lit., "upon its edge which is towards the side of the Ephod, inside."

28.a. MT has להיות "to be," here translated "hang snugly," given the context.

30.a. SamPent begins this verse with ועשית את האורים ואת התמים "You are to make the Urim and the Thummim," then continues with the verse as MT has it.

30.b. Both SamPent על and LXX ἐπὶ (v 26) read "upon."

30.c. Both here and in v 29, לב is translated "heart," because of the obvious physical sense of the text. It is important that the function of לב as "mind" in the OT context be remembered (cf. Johnson, *Vitality*, 75–87).

32.a. מעשה ארג "woven reinforcement."

32.b. "Like the opening of a תחרא it is to be for it." תחרא is used only here and in 39:23, and its meaning is obscure. The proposals include "prob. (linen) corselet" (BDB, 1065), "coat of mail" (Tg Onk), and "an oversewn edge: *lit.*, like the opening of a womb" (NEB). These are all guesses, and since the point is clear despite the lack of a definition for the term, it may be better to make the point without inventing a simile."

33.a. SamPent, LXX add "and woven fine linen."

35.a. MT has simply והיה על "and it is to be on. . . ." The meaning is unmistakable, and "This Robe" and "worn by" are added above for clarity.

35.b. לשרת "for service in worship."

36.a. ציץ is a flower or a blossom of some kind, however stylized. DeBuck, *OTS* 9 [1951] 18–29, who proposes on the basis of Egyptian art that the flower, predominantly the lotus, is a symbol of "the vital impetus, a manifestation of the creative power of nature" (19). The popular translation "plate" is an attempt to suggest an engravable surface, but it may go too far in that direction.

37.a. והיה, lit., "and it is to be."

38.a. את־עון הקדשים, lit., "the guilt of the set-apart things," in the broadest reference inclusive of all that the Israelites bring and do in worship, and so translated above.

39.a. See n. 26:36.a.

40.a. מגבעות, from גבע, a root with which "hill, elevation" are connected. Some kind of tall headdress, different from Aaron's Turban, perhaps is meant, though a different turban is also a possibility; cf. 29:9.

41.a. Hiph of לבש, here indicating a clothing or dressing in holy array, a vesting with authority suggested by the symbols of the office, an investiture. See also Pss 29:2 and 96:9.

41.b. מלא יד "fill the hand," is an idiom for "ordain" in the OT.

42.a. MT has simply "they." The antecedent is added above for clarity.

Form/Structure/Setting

See *Form/Structure/Setting* on 25:1–9.

Comment

These elaborate instructions for the sacral vestments of "Aaron and his sons," that is, for the head priest and those who served under his direction, are a strange mixture of clarity and obscurity. On the one hand, they are redundant in their specificity, as for example in the directions for the shoulder-pieces of the ephod; on the other hand, they do not supply enough data to give a clear idea of what is intended, as for example on how and in precisely what order the vestments were put on, or on the exact description of the lesser priests' clothing. Part of this obscurity is certainly the result of our ignorance of some of the terms used in the instructions, as for example the names of the semiprecious stones of the Breastpiece of Judgment, or the design of the collar of the Robe, or the headdress of the lesser priests. Another barrier to our understanding is the context in and for which these instructions were prepared. Their curious mingling of repetition and terseness suggests that these instructions were set down for people who knew what was being described, who had seen the vestments, in various combinations, in use; thus the instructions omit what would have been, for such persons, too obvious to require statement, but would have made the descriptions clearer to us.

Just how much of the wardrobe described here was worn, for just how long, and by exactly whom, is similarly impossible for us to say. The composite set forth in this chapter no doubt reflects an evolution of vestments, and perhaps also an adaptation of royal sacral vestments to priestly sacral use following the demise of Israel's sacral monarchy with and beyond the Babylonian exile. There can be little doubt that in pre-exilic Israel, certainly in the united monarchy of David and Solomon, and probably in the monarchies of Judah and Israel, the ruling king was always in title and frequently in practice the head or chief priest, in the terminology of this chapter, "Aaron." Thus at least some of the ornate vestments described here probably began as vestments for the sacral king, performing his duties as Yahweh's own anointed one. As time passed, the kings turned over some of these duties to the priests; then with the successive Assyrian and Babylonian destructions of the two monarchies, the priests took over the royal vestments, and by the postexilic period, many of the royal functions as well.

1–5 The designation of Aaron and his sons to give priestly ministry to Yahweh may thus be understood as a legitimation of priestly service at a royal level, much as Aaron himself has been legitimized in the Priestly source in Exodus by making him Moses' "brother" (see *Comment* on 4:14–17). The chief symbols of that legitimation, according to this chapter, are the sacral vestments, the very robes of office that may once have been the exclusive property of the kings. It is for this reason, indeed, that despite the inclusion of Aaron's sons in vv 1, 4, 40–43, the clear preoccupation of the instructions for the priests' vestments is what "Aaron," the head priest, is to wear. Thus are the vestments to be made "for splendor and for beauty," of the same expensive materials as the Tabernacle, by artisans specially endowed by Yahweh, and for the express purpose of setting "Aaron" apart to give priestly ministry to Yahweh. The sacral vestments described in this chapter are eight in number, though v 4 lists only six, omitting the engraved flower worn at the front of the Turban (vv 36–38) and the undergarments of plain linen (vv 42–43). The six that are listed are not listed in the order in which they are discussed or in any order of vesting.

6–14 First to be described is the Ephod, which is in Exod 28 plainly a garment, though one made of precious material. In 1 Sam 2:18; 22:18 and 2 Sam 6:14, a linen ephod is mentioned, apparently as a simple, and brief, shiftlike garment, perhaps covering the body only from the waist to the mid-thighs. In Judg 17:5; 18:14–20, an ephod is mentioned in connection with what appears to be an idol (Noth, *Prophetic Heritage,* 72–73). In Judg 8:24–27, an ephod made of captured Midianite gold is mentioned as a cause of idolatry in Israel. In 1 Sam 23:10 [9], an ephod at Nob is apparently a free-standing object behind which Goliath's sword, "wrapped in the mantle," is stored. In 1 Sam 23:9–11; 30:7–8 an ephod is connected with the consultation of Yahweh. And in the present chapter, as in Exod 39:2–7, an ephod of elaborate workmanship is one of the sacral vestments reserved for the head priest. So many contrasting references have led to a variety of interpretations (see Arnold, *Ephod and Ark, passim;* May, *AJSL* 56 [1939] 44–69; Elliger, *Festschrift F. Baumgärtel,* 19–35; Haran, *Tarbiz* 24 [1955] 380–91; Davies, "Ephod (Object)," *IDB* 2:118–19; de Vaux, *Ancient Israel,* 349–52), no one of which successfully explains the connection between the different ephods or the differing uses of one ephod. Haran's view (*Temples,* 167–68) that a single golden ephod is meant is stretched too far by the references; de Vaux's (351–52) suggestion that the ephod was somehow a receptacle for sacred lots is also an imposition upon some of the references. It is better to think of a garment that evolved from a simple shift or skirt to the elaborate vestment of P, and perhaps also of a devolution from a garment for deity (de Vaux, 350) to a garment for a human serving deity and, on occasion, speaking for deity.

6–8 Whatever the origin and the other roles of an ephod, in Exod 28 the Ephod is clearly a garment, and an elaborate one, though for all the details given concerning its materials and its decoration, we are left in the dark about just how and where it fitted the head priest's body. The Ephod described here had at least four parts: the main part of the garment, two shoulderpieces, and an elaborate belt. The fabric for these parts was to be identical to that to be used in making the Tabernacle, though in addition, the shoulderpieces were each to be decorated with an onyx-stone in a setting of gold filigree. Just how the shoulderpieces fitted the body of the Ephod, and exactly how the elaborate belt was fitted, and what was its function, is not clear, any more than are the length and construction of the body of the Ephod. We are not told whether the shoulderpieces functioned as suspenders to hold the Ephod in place, only that they were joined to the "two sides" of the Ephod, apparently its front and back, to make "one garment."

9–14 The chief function of the shoulderpieces was apparently to provide a mounting place for the two onyx stones into which were incised, in their genealogical order (see Gen 46:8–27; Exod 1:1–5), the names of the twelve sons of Israel. The stones, mounted in settings of gold filigree, were thus borne on "Aaron's" shoulders into Yahweh's Presence. Their function was to serve as reminders, calling to mind the twelve sons of Jacob, the theoretical progenitors of all Israel. For whom this reminder was intended is not said; it is very likely that both "Aaron" and Yahweh are in view. Also to be attached to the filigree settings of the shoulderpieces were two ropes made of pure gold thread twisted tightly together; these were for the attachment of the Breastpiece, which is described next.

15–21 The Breastpiece of Judgment, so named because it too incorporated gemstones bearing the names of the twelve sons of Israel and because it contained the Urim and the Thummim, the media of Yahweh's oracle, was also made of the special Tabernacle fabric. As in the manufacture of the Ephod, this material was here too to be artistically embroidered, though the design is not specified in either case as it is for the Tabernacle ("with cherubs," Exod 26:1). The Breastpiece was to consist of a single piece of this fabric, folded over to form a square approximately nine inches by nine inches (Sellers, "Weights and Measures," *IDB* 4:837–38). Onto this square, by settings of gold filigree, twelve different gemstones were to be mounted, each of them engraved with the name of one of the twelve sons of Jacob.

The specific varieties of gemstones employed can only be surmised, as we cannot translate the terms employed for them with any certainty. Garber and Funk (*IDB* 2:900–904) have a thorough treatment of gemstones known to be available in the OT period (cf. also Frerichs, "Edelsteine," *BHH* 1, cols. 362–64), and Lucas (*Egyptian Materials,* 442–61) presents a detailed account of the precious and semiprecious stones used in ancient Egypt from the First Dynasty forward. The difficulty is that we cannot with any accuracy translate the Hebrew terms for the stones used in the Breastpiece; thus we cannot establish the color patterns, and indeed we can only guess that each stone was a different color since each one has a different name. The rabbinic commentators worked out elaborate symbolic color schemes, sometimes linked to the signs of the Zodiac (Goodenough, *By Light*, 99–100; Garber and Funk, 904–5), and it is upon this tradition that the colors of Chagall's magnificent *Jerusalem Windows* for the Hadassah Hospital synagogue are based (Chagall and Leymarie, xiv–xvi).

The stones would have been finished *"en cabachon,* i.e., in rounded, convex forms with smooth or polished sides" (Garber and Funk, *IDB* 2:899), and then engraved with the names of the twelve sons of Jacob. They were set onto the Breastpiece in three horizontal rows of four stones each. The connection of gemstones with theophany is both widespread and ancient (cf. Garber and Funk, 904–5; Farrer, *Rebirth*, 216–44), and may be reflected in the placement of the Urim and the Thummim (v 30) *behind* the gemstones of the Breastpiece and the engraving of the names of the twelve sons of Israel *onto* the gemstones, facing the implements with which the Presence was intimately associated within the Holy Space and the Holiest Space.

22–29 For the Breastpiece, as for the Ephod, ropes of pure gold thread twisted tightly together were to be made, then passed through gold rings attached to the top corners of the Breastpiece, and attached to the filigree mountings on the two shoulderpieces. (Cassuto, 377, thinks the gold ropes of v 22 are the same ropes mentioned in v 14; the text is not clear about the use of that first pair of ropes.) Another pair of gold rings at the bottom corners of the Breastpiece was to be attached by means of a rope made of violet yarn to two gold rings attached to the Ephod. In this manner, the Breastpiece was held firmly against the top of the Ephod, from the elaborate belt up towards the two shoulderpieces. Just how these various ropes were to be tied, and by whom, is not said. With the Breastpiece and the Ephod thus in place, "Aaron" would enter the Holy Space of the Tabernacle with a double reminder of Israel, one on his two shoulders and one on his chest, over his heart.

30 Into the Breastpiece, by what means we are not told, the Urim and the Thummim were to be placed. That the Urim and the Thummim were an oracular device of some sort is established by the few OT references to their function (cf. Num 27:21; Deut 33:8; 1 Sam 28:6; Ezra 2:63; Neh 7:65; and LXX 1 Sam 14:41). What sort of device they were, and how the message of Yahweh contained in them was understood, we have no hint in the OT. A variety of suggestions has been made, all of them largely guesswork: two

stones, each of a different color (Lipiński, *VT* 20 [1970] 495–96); small objects
made of metal or gemstones, engraved with symbols (Mendelsohn, "Urim
and Thummim," *IDB* 4:740); small pebbles or dice or "little sticks" (de Vaux,
Ancient Israel, 352); flat stones, each with an "auspicious" and an "inauspi-
cious" side (Rowley, *Worship*, 67). Robertson (*VT* 14 [1964] 71–72) has even
suggested the twenty-two letters of the alphabet "inscribed or engraved"
on "discs or tablets of wood or metal," serving both as symbols of writing,
a gift of God, and as arithmetical, odd-even symbols, א equalling "one" and
suggesting אור "light," and ת equalling "twenty-two" and suggesting תם
"end"; אורים "Urim" would thus represent the odd-number letters, תמים
"Thummim" the even-number letters, and any three letters might suggest
a verb root. The practice of oracle-seeking by a variety of means, including
the use of positive and negative stones, is widely attested in the ANE (cf.
Reiner, *JNES* 19 [1960] 24–31), and the Urim and Thummim are without
doubt an Israelite version of such practices. Just what they were and how
they worked, however, we cannot say without more data.

31–35 The next vestment to be described is the Robe of the head priest,
called the Robe of the Ephod because it was to be worn under the Ephod,
and therefore under the Breastpiece as well. This Robe was to be made of
a less opulent material, though still of one of the special yarns employed in
the Tabernacle, the Ephod, and the Breastpiece, the violet yarn always mentioned first in the listing of the three colored yarns. The Robe was apparently
to be without fastenings of any kind, and was to have an opening only for
the head and arms, since it was to be pulled on over the head like a sweater
or a nightshirt. There is no mention of sleeves; the attention given to reinforcing the opening for the head and neck suggests that that area of the garment
was expected to have continual wear and stress. The skirts of this "wholly
violet" Robe were to be decorated with pomegranates (embroidered, apparently, with the usual three colored yarns, including the violet yarn of which
the Robe itself was made; though cf. Haran, *Temples*, 168–69, 171, who thinks
of the pomegranates as "suspended") interspersed with bells made of gold,
a pattern to be continued all around the skirt.

The pomegranates appear to have suggested the fruitfulness of Yahweh's
provision (cf. Deut 8:8; Num 13:23; Feliks, "Granatapfel, Granatbaum," *BHH*
1:607). The bells are explained as a necessary accompaniment to "Aaron's"
movements into and out of the Holy Space, required by Yahweh. As Haran
(*Temples*, 214–18, 223–24) has suggested, these bells must be understood
as an integral part of a total ritual involving all of man's senses; but this
ritual had a double application: Yahweh's "needs" also were symbolized by
the sounds, the sights, the provisions, and the smells of the Tabernacle and
its Court.

36–38 The Flower of pure gold to be worn like a medallion or a brooch
on the front of the head priest's Turban may in its floral design have suggested
Yahweh's provision in nature; the primary function of this decoration, however, is made clear by the inscription it bore. "Set apart for Yahweh" refers
not alone, indeed not even primarily to "Aaron" and his successors, as v
38 makes plain. It is Israel that is "set apart for Yahweh," "Aaron" of course
among Israel and representing Israel (as the king had done from David for-

ward), and the Flower with its inscription serving as a perpetual reminder that "Aaron" in Yahweh's Presence was as Israel in Yahweh's Presence. Any "guilt of iniquity" associated with Israel's worship would be made more obvious by this constant reminder, which would also symbolize Yahweh's acceptance of a people forgiven by his grace.

39 The Tunic and the Turban of the head priest were both to be woven of fine linen (שׁשׁ), the Tunic in a checked pattern. This Tunic was apparently a long, shirtlike garment worn under the Robe (Meyers, "Dress and Ornaments," *IDB* 1:869), though the text names it only. The Sash was to be embroidered apparently in the variegated pattern of the Screen for the tent (cf. 26:36). Its material is not specified; presumably it was the mixture of colored yarns and fine linen used for the Screen.

40–41 Following this almost cursory description of no less than three of "Aaron's" sacral vestments, there is an even briefer listing of the clothing of "Aaron's sons," the assisting priests, and a description of the undergarment all priests were to wear whenever they ministered in the places of Yahweh's Presence. The ordinary priests were to have tunics, but apparently not with the checked pattern of "Aaron's" Tunic. They were also to have sashes, again apparently of less opulent material, and high hats or turbans, again different from that of the head priest. The vesting of the priests is specified as the first part of a three-part procedure establishing priestly authority: the other two steps are anointing and ordination, and such texts as Ps 133:2 and Lev 8:12 imply that the ritual of authorization may have been carried out in just such a sequence.

42–43 The instructions for the priests' vestments close with what has the appearance of an addendum dealing with the single garment that was to be a common requirement for both the head priest and those who ministered under his supervision. It is an undergarment of plain linen, required in perpetuity of all priests, that they may not violate the prohibition reflected also in Exod 20:26, a prohibition of the exposure of genitalia in the areas of Yahweh's Presence.

Explanation

The essential point of the priestly vestments is the central point of all the instructions concerning the media of worship: Yahweh is present, and Israel must respond to that Presence, be guided in that response, and be reminded constantly in worship as in life of the reality of the Presence and of the need for response. The vestments are double symbols: they signify priestly authority, and they signify the priestly confession of the source of that authority. Exod 28 begins with a reference to the singling out and bringing near (to Moses, Yahweh's representative and messenger) of "Aaron" and his assisting "sons" (v 1). It closes, apart from the addendum about the priests' undergarment, with a reference to the ceremony of setting apart, in which each priest was vested, anointed, and ordained to the service of ministry in Yahweh's Presence (v 41).

In between such an opening and closing, the sacral vestments are listed and described, and each of them reflects, in one way or another, the double

symbolism they carry. The Ephod of gold, the material used most often for
the objects closest to Yahweh's Presence, includes also the engraved onyx-
stones through which Israel was to be brought to mind in Yahweh's Presence.
The Breastpiece of Judgment, attached to the Ephod, was through its twelve
engraved gemstones to keep Israel before Yahweh and to signify the glow
of the Presence through Israel. The Urim and the Thummim placed inside
this Breastpiece were to suggest Yahweh's judgment and specific direction
of his people. The Robe of the Ephod was a reminder of Yahweh's plenty
and nearness, and the engraved Flower on the Turban was a reminder that
Israel and all that Israel undertook were set apart to Yahweh—made what
they were by him and in need of becoming what they were called to be in
his Presence. In sum, every article of the sacral vestments made the same
point, each with its own specific accent: Yahweh is here, we are his, and we
must both know this and show this.

The Instructions for the Priests' Ordination
(29:1–46)

PARALLEL VERSES:
Lev 8:1–33

Bibliography

Gray, G. B. *Sacrifice in the Old Testament.* New York: KTAV, 1971. **Kutsch, E.** *Salbung als Rechtsakt.* BZAW 87. Berlin: Verlag Alfred Töpelmann, 1963. **Levine, B. A.** "The Descriptive Tabernacle Texts of the Pentateuch." *JAOS* 85 (1965) 307–18. ———. "Ugaritic Descriptive Rituals." *JCS* 17 (1963) 105–12. **Noth, M.** "Office and Vocation in the Old Testament." *The Laws in the Pentateuch and Other Studies.* Edinburgh: Oliver and Boyd, 1966. 228–49. **Schmid, R.** *Das Bundesopfer in Israel.* SANT 9. Munich: Kösel-Verlag, 1964. **Vriezen, T. C.** "The Term *Hizza:* Lustration and Consecration." *OTS* 7 (1950) 201–35. **Walkenhorst, K.-H.** *Der Sinai: im liturgischen Verständnis der deuterono-mistischen und priesterlichen Tradition.* BBB 33. Bonn: Peter Hanstein Verlag, 1969.

Translation

[1] *"Now this is what you are to do for them to set them apart to give priestly ministry to me: take one bull-calf and two perfect rams,* [2] *unleavened bread, unleavened cakes soaked* [a] *in oil, and thin unleavened wafers smeared with oil.* [b] *(You are to make these* [c] *of the finest wheat-flour.)* [3] *Put the cakes* [a] *into one basket and bring them near,* [b] *in the basket, along with the bull and the two rams.* [4] *You are to bring Aaron and his sons near to the opening of the Tent of Appointed Meeting, and you are to wash them with water.*

[5] *"You are to take the vestments, and you are to clothe Aaron in the Tunic and* [a] *in the Robe of the Ephod, and in the Ephod and in the Breastpiece, and you are to wrap around him the elaborate belt of the Ephod.* [6] *You are to place the Turban*

upon his head, and place the Emblem of Set-Apartness ª upon the Turban. ⁷ You
are to take the Oil of Anointment and you are to pour it upon his head and so
anoint him. ⁸ You are to bring his sons near ⁹ and clothe them in Tunics and bind
around them sashes, ª Aaron and his sons, ᵇ and bind on them high hats, ᶜ and priestly
service will be theirs as a requirement in perpetuity.

¹⁰ "So you are to ordain Aaron and his sons: you are to bring the bull near to
the opening ª of the Tent of Appointed Meeting, and Aaron and his sons are to lay
their hands upon the head of the bull. ¹¹ Then you are to slaughter the bull in the
Presence of Yahweh at the opening of the Tent of Appointed Meeting, ¹² and you
are to take some of the blood of the bull and put it upon the horns of the Altar
with your finger; all the remaining ª blood, you are to pour out at the bottom of the
Altar. ¹³ You are to take all the fat that surrounds the entrails and the appendage
on the liver and the two kidneys along with the fat that is on them, and you are to
offer it as smoke ª on the Altar. ¹⁴ The meat of the bull, and his hide and his offal,
you are to burn in the fire outside the camp—it is an offering for sin.

¹⁵ "You are to take one of the rams, and Aaron and his sons are to lay their
hands upon the head of the ram; ¹⁶ then slaughter the ram, and take his blood and
dash it upon the Altar, all around. ¹⁷ You are to cut the ram into pieces, wash his
entrails and his legs, and put them on his pieces and upon his head. ¹⁸ Then you
are to offer as smoke on the Altar the entire ram. It is a wholly burned offering to
Yahweh, an appeasing smell, ª a gift by fire to Yahweh.

¹⁹ "You are to take the second ram, and Aaron and his sons are to lay their
hands upon the head of the ram. ²⁰ You are to slaughter the ram, and take some of
his blood and put it on the lobe of Aaron's right ear and on the lobe of his sons'
right ears, on the thumb of their right hands, and on the big toe of their right feet.
Then you are to dash the remaining blood upon the Altar, all around. ²¹ You are to
take some of the blood that is on the Altar and some of the Oil of Anointment and
sprinkle it upon Aaron and upon his vestments and upon his sons along with him,
and upon their vestments; thus he is to be set apart, and his vestments, and his
sons and their vestments, his sons along with him.

²² "You are to take from the ram the fat and the fat tail, the fat that surrounds
the entrails and the appendage on the liver and the two kidneys along with the fat
that is on them, and the right leg (since this is a ram of ordination), ²³ and one
round loaf of bread and one cake of bread with oil, ª and one thin wafer from the
basket of unleavened bread that is in Yahweh's Presence. ²⁴ You are to place all this
upon the palm of Aaron and upon the palms of his sons, and you are to present
them as a symbolic offering ª in Yahweh's Presence. ²⁵ You are then to take these
gifts ª from their hands, and you are to offer them as smoke upon the Altar, in addition
to the wholly burned offering as an appeasing smell in Yahweh's Presence, a gift by
fire to Yahweh.

²⁶ "You are to take the breast of the ram of Aaron's ordination and present it as
a symbolic offering in Yahweh's Presence; it will then be your part. ²⁷ You are to set
aside the breast of the symbolic offering and the leg of the gift held aloft, ª that which
is presented ᵇ and that which is raised in presentation, ᶜ a part of the ram of ordination
that belongs to Aaron and that belongs to his sons: ²⁸ it is for Aaron and for his
sons, a share in perpetuity from the sons of Israel, because it is a gift held aloft,
and a gift held aloft by the sons of Israel from their completion offerings, their gift
held aloft to Yahweh. ª

²⁹ *"The sacral vestments that are for Aaron are to be for his sons after him, to be worn for anointing and ordination ceremonies.* ª ³⁰ *The priest from among his sons who succeeds him is to wear them for seven days when he enters the Tent of Appointed Meeting to minister in the Holy Space.*

³¹ *"You are to take the ram of ordination, and you are to boil his meat in a place set apart;* ³² *and Aaron and his sons are to eat the flesh of the ram, and the bread that is in the basket, at the opening of the Tent of Appointed Meeting.* ³³ *They are to eat these gifts* ª *by which atonement was made for their ordination and their setting-apart. No outsider is to eat them* ᵇ *because they are holy.* ³⁴ *If any of the meat of ordination or any of the bread is left over until the morning, you are to burn the remainder with fire—it is not to be eaten, because it is holy.*

³⁵ *"So you are to do, for Aaron and for his sons, in strict accord* ª *with everything I have commanded you: you are to ordain them seven days.* ³⁶ *You are to make a sin offering of a bull every day, for the atonement, and you are to make a sin offering for the Altar as your atonement for it, and you are to anoint it for its setting apart.* ³⁷ *You are to make atonement for the Altar for seven days, and so you are to set it apart, and so the Altar is to be most holy: anything touching the Altar will become sacred.*

³⁸ *"This is what you are to offer upon the Altar—two year-old lambs per day, regularly:* ª ³⁹ *you are to offer one lamb in the morning and you are to offer the second lamb between sundown and nightfall.* ª ⁴⁰ *Along with the first lamb, offer* ª *a tenth of an ephah of fine flour mingled with a fourth of a hin of oil (pounded, not pressed)* ᵇ *and a fourth of a hin of wine as a drink offering;* ⁴¹ *the second lamb you are to offer between sundown and nightfall, accompanied by a cereal offering and by a drink offering, as in the morning. You are to offer it by fire for an appeasing smell to Yahweh.* ⁴² *It is to be a continual wholly burned offering, down through your generations, at the opening of the Tent of Appointed Meeting in the Presence of Yahweh: I will meet you* ª *there by appointment, to speak to you there.* ⁴³ *I will meet* ª *the sons of Israel there by appointment; it* ᵇ *will be made sacred by my glory:* ⁴⁴ *I will set apart as sacred the Tent of Appointed Meeting and the Altar, and I will set apart Aaron and his sons, to give priestly ministry to me.*

⁴⁵ *"So I will dwell in the midst of the sons of Israel, and I will be their God,* ⁴⁶ *and they will know that I am Yahweh their God who brought them forth from the land of Egypt on account* ª *of my dwelling in their midst. I am Yahweh their God."*

Notes

2.a. בלל "mingle, mix." The reference could be either to mixing the flour with the oil or to soaking, moistening the bread cake already prepared with oil.

2.b. SamPent omits "smeared with oil."

2.c. MT has "them"; "these" is used above in reference to the three forms of bread, treating this instruction as secondary and so parenthetic to the list of things to be included in the offering.

3.a. MT has "them"; the antecedent is supplied above for clarity.

3.b. Hiph of קרב is a technical term in P for bringing something near to Yahweh's Presence. It is so used 89× in Leviticus, 49× in Numbers.

5.a. SamPent reads the remainder of this verse so: "and you are to bind around him a sash and clothe him in the Robe and put upon him the Ephod and the Breastpiece and wrap around him the elaborate belt of the Ephod."

6.a. נזר הקדש "the Emblem of Set-Apartness"; the reference is to the ציץ זהב "golden flower" of 28:36–38, here described as the "crown" or "designation" of the "apartness" or "sacredness." Cf. BDB, 634.

9.a. MT has אבנט "a sash"; SamPent has אבנטים "sashes."

9.b. This phrase is absent from LXX, and the inclusion of Aaron does make it seem a bit out of place.

9.c. See n. 28:40.a.

10.a. SamPent reads לפני יהוה פתח "into the Presence of Yahweh at the opening."

12.a. MT has simply כל-הדם "all the blood." LXX has τὸ δὲ λοιπὸν πᾶν αἷμα "all the remaining blood."

13.a. Hiph of קטר lit. means "to cause a smoke"; "burning" is not the point of the verb, even though fire or hot coals were necessary to create the smoke. Both the hiph and piel forms of קטר depict a making of smoke as an act of worship. Cf. Durham, *Touch, Taste and Smell*, 309–11, 316–26.

18.a. ריח ניחוח "an appeasing smell" occurs 43× in the OT, in every case in reference to deity, and in 40 instances that deity is Yahweh. Of its occurrences, 38 are in P passages, 4 in Ezekiel, and one in J (Gen 8:21), and the phrase describes an odor of gratification or appeasement of God. Cf. Durham, *Touch, Taste and Smell*, 286–98.

23.a. The reference here is to the three kinds of bread, listed and described more fully in v 2.

24.a. והנפת אתם תנופה lit. is "and you are to wave them, a wave offering." The תנופה was itself a symbolic offering of something presented by a ritual manipulation, or waving, in Yahweh's Presence. "Aaron" and his "sons," their hands "filled" with the symbols of their ordination, are here described as such a symbolic offering, given to Yahweh, yet kept for his service. LXX reads here καὶ ἀφοριεῖς αὐτοὺς ἀφόρισμα "and you are to set them apart, a special designation."

25.a. MT has אתם "them"; the antecedent is added for clarity.

27.a. התרומה "the gift held aloft."

27.b. הונף "presented."

27.c. הורם "raised in presentation."

28.a. SamPent has what is substantially v 21 of MT at this point.

29.a. MT has למשחה בהם ולמלא-בם את-ידם "to anoint in them and to fill in them their hand."

33.a. MT has "them."

33.b. LXX has ἀπ' αὐτῶν "from them"; MT leaves the object to be understood.

35.a. ככה "thus." Cf. BDB, 462.

38.a. See n. 27:20.c. ליום תמיד here means "daily, on a regular basis." SamPent adds עלת תמיד "a continual offering." Cf. LXX.

39.a. בין הערבים, lit., "between the pair of evenings."

40.a. "Offer" is supplied from the context, for clarity.

40.b. See n. 27:20.a.

42.a. This "you" is pl in MT (sg in LXX and at MT 30:6, 36); the second "you" is singular.

43.a. SamPent reads "I will present myself to be sought . . ."; LXX has "I will command. . . ."

43.b. So MT, ונקדש. LXX, Syr, Tg Ps-J read a 1st pers sg verb here.

46.a. לשכני. Cf. GKC ¶114*f,o*.

Form/Structure/Setting

See *Form/Structure/Setting* on 25:1–9.

Comment

The instructions for the priests' ordination specify a ritual of vesting, a ritual of anointing, and the climactic ritual of ordination, along with their accompanying symbolic and wholly consumed offerings. These instructions, reported as carried out by Moses in Lev 8, have the appearance of having evolved over a long period of time, and they may reflect both royal and priestly ceremonies of investiture. Walkenhorst (*Der Sinai*, 33–115) has analyzed Exod 29 with Lev 8–9 at some length, comparing the treatments of the rituals of washing, vesting, anointing, sin offering, and the wholly-burned and the partly-consumed offerings, and has concluded that the question of the relationship of sequence between the two chapters and a possible older core of liturgical material remains in question (see esp. 37–44). Levine (*JAOS* 85 [1965] 310–14), after a much briefer analysis, has come to the conclusion that Exod 29 is not the source of Lev 8, and that the reverse may be true, with Exod 29:1–37 being "probably based" on Lev 8:13–36.

Without additional information, the question remains insoluble, and what is most significant about both sequences is what they suggest about the priestly concept of liturgical authority. Whatever the origin of the ideas and symbols set forth in these chapters, and whatever the sequence of their development, the presentation of them in the composites that are Exodus and Leviticus has an implication all its own.

1–4 The sacrificial animals and the cereal offerings that are to accompany the ordination rituals are listed first. As befits the solemnity of the occasion and the location of the ceremony, only the best is to be "brought near" (hiphil of קרב) for use in the ordination. Then Aaron and his sons are to be "brought near" to the opening of the Tabernacle ("Tent of Appointed Meeting"; see *Comment* on 27:21) and washed in preparation for the rituals to come. As de Vaux (*Ancient Israel*, 460–61) correctly points out, such washing was necessary both *before* contact with holy things, and sometimes *after* such contact (cf. Levine, *JCS* 17 [1963] 105, on parallels in the Ugaritic texts).

5–9 Thus prepared, "Aaron" (representative of each head priest) was to be vested with the sacral garments symbolizing his office; of the vestments described in chap. 28, only the undergarment of plain linen is unmentioned in this vesting, though the Sash is apparently deemphasized. Thus vested, Aaron was to be anointed; the special Oil of Anointment to be used for this purpose is described in Exod 30:22–33. Aaron's "sons" (representative of the assisting priests) are to be vested in the garments appropriate to them, though there is no mention here, as there is in Exod 28:41, 30:30, and 40:15, of an anointing of these assistants. It is generally argued that the exclusive designation of the anointing as Aaron's alone is indicative of an earlier form of the tradition (so Hyatt, 295), though Levine (*JAOS* 85 [1965] 312) argues a somewhat opposite view. The purpose of this vesting and anointing, the text makes quite clear, is the establishment in perpetuity of the right and obligation of priestly service (v 9). For a full survey of anointing and its OT significance, see Kutsch (*Salbung*, 1–27).

9 The next step in the ceremony of ordination was to be a complex ritual of sacrificial and symbolic offering by which (1) atonement was to be made for Aaron, thus "purifying" him for the service of ministry to Yahweh, and (2) the commitment of Aaron to this service was symbolized. This sequence was to be the climax of the ceremony, and above all constituted the ordination itself; thus it is introduced by the statement at the end of v 9: "So you are to ordain Aaron and his sons." The idiom for ordain, מלא יד "to fill the hand," has been much discussed (see Noth, *Laws* 231–33), in particular as to whether a literal or a figurative sense is implied. No definitive answer can be supplied, but in the context of Exod 29, both senses are probably intended: vv 23–24 describe the gifts that are to be placed on the palm of Aaron and the palms of his sons before they are burned on the Altar; vv 27–28 describe the symbolic offering that is to be the share in perpetuity of Aaron and his sons; and v 34 refers to "the meat of ordination" (בְּשַׂר הַמִּלֻּאִים "the flesh of the fillings").

10–14 The ritual in which the priests to be ordained laid their hands upon the head of the bull-calf to be sacrificed was preparatory to the atonement for their sins. The place in which this ritual and the entire ceremony of atonement was carried out, the opening of the Tabernacle, is significant. Here, where Yahweh's Presence met them by appointment, Yahweh would come to grant them authority. Without that authority, they could go no further and do nothing more. The bull-calf was to be wholly disposed of: its blood was to be used to anoint the Altar-horns, which symbolized especially the Presence of Yahweh at the Altar (see *Comment* on 27:2), then poured out at the bottom of the Altar (Gray, *Sacrifice*, 365–66, has noted that only the blood of sin-offerings was so disposed of); its entrail fat, liver-appendage, and kidneys were to be "offered as smoke" on the Altar; and its meat, its hide, and its offal were to be burned *outside* the camp: the bull-calf had become polluted, an offering for sins (on חַטָּאת see Rendtorff, *Geschichte des Opfers,* 199–234).

15–25 The first of the two perfect rams was to be slaughtered after the laying-on of hands; its blood was to be dashed upon the Altar all around, then the ram, properly dismembered and washed, was to be offered as a gift to Yahweh wholly burned, and on the Altar. The meat of this sin offering was to be burned *outside* the camp, and it is not referred to as a gift to Yahweh. The second ram, however, also after Aaron and his sons had laid their hands upon its head, was to be slaughtered, then treated in the following manner: its blood was to be smeared on the right ear lobe, the right thumb, and the right big toe of the priests being ordained, actions whose significance remains a puzzle (cf. Lev 14:14), then dashed upon the Altar. Some of this scattered blood was then to be collected, along with some Oil of Anointment, and then sprinkled (נָזָה) upon Aaron, his sons, and their sacral vestments. And it is *this* act, v 21 notes precisely, that sets Aaron and his sons *and* their vestments apart for ministry to Yahweh.

Vriezen (*OTS* 7 [1950] 205, 207–19, 233–35) has suggested that the rituals involving this special sprinkling are rites of lustration and consecration of the most elevated kind, rites that can be performed only on the authority of God. Following this lustration, specified parts of the second ram, along with samples of each of the three kinds of unleavened bread (v 2) were to be placed in the hands of the priests being ordained, and they were then to be presented as a symbolic offering (literally, "waved as a wave-offering," נוּף תְּנוּפָה) in Yahweh's Presence. The gifts in the priests' hands were then, following this symbolic offering of the priests themselves, to be burned on the Altar as a gift by fire to Yahweh.

26–34 The remaining parts of this second ram, called "the ram of ordination," the breast and the leg, were to be presented, as Aaron and his sons

had been, as a symbolic offering in Yahweh's Presence; then they were to
become the share of the priests from the "completion offerings" (זבחי שלמים;
cf. Schmid, *Bundesopfer,* 27–39) of Israel. This meat was to be boiled in a
special place; then Aaron and his sons were to eat it, along with the bread
remaining from the ordination ritual, at the opening of the Tabernacle. These
gifts, the remaining tokens of their purification for Yahweh's service and
their setting apart for it, were to be eaten only by the priests. As foodstuff
that had become holy, any leftovers were to be burned with fire.

35–37 The instructions for the ordination of Aaron and his sons are
brought to a close by a brief summary statement, but this statement and
the instructions preceding it have attracted (1) a brief notice about Aaron's
sacral vestments: they are to be worn by Aaron and his successors for anointing
and ordination ceremonies and for the seven-day period of ministry in the
Holy Space; (2) an instruction for the atonement and setting-apart of the
Altar, which is so important an implement in the ceremonies of ordination;
(3) the designation of the offering to be made routinely on this Altar twice
a day; and (4) a summary of the theology of Yahweh's Presence in relation
to the Tabernacle, one that serves both to underscore the authority of the
ordination of the priests and also as a conclusion to the main chapters of
priestly instructions, the ones dealing with the symbols of Yahweh's intimate
Presence (chap. 25), the Tabernacle that houses them (chap. 26), the Altar
and the Tabernacle Court (chap. 27), the Priests' Vestments (chap. 28) and
the Priests' ordination (chap. 29). The two chapters that follow these five,
30 and 31, are also closely connected by their subject matter to the Tabernacle
and the service of Yahweh's Presence there, as noted above (see *Form/Struc-
ture/Setting* on 25:1–9), but they have the appearance of supplementary appendices, related thematically and not organically.

38–44 The offering to be made twice daily on the Altar on a regular
basis, that is, apart from sin offerings or such special ceremony offerings as
those involved in ordination, was to consist of a lamb accompanied by approximately 1.6 quarts of fine flour, and a quart each of fine oil and wine (cf.
Sellers, "Weights and Measures," *IDB* 4:834–35). It was offered in the morning, probably at the beginning of the day's activity, and in the evening just
before nightfall; thus the day was opened and closed with gifts to Yahweh,
from whom all gifts were believed to come. These offerings were to be made,
again, at the opening of the Tabernacle, the place where Yahweh had promised
to meet his people. How literally this location is meant to be taken, in view
of the position, in the Courtyard of the Tabernacle, of the Altar on which
the offerings were "turned into smoke," is not clear; perhaps the offerings
were actually presented at the opening of the Tabernacle, at some stage in
Israel's liturgical history, before they were taken to the Altar to be burned.

Far more important than the movement of the giver and the gift in this
summary statement is the movement of Yahweh's Presence, as the expansion
of the statement in the conclusion to the five main chapters of priestly instructions shows. Yahweh's promise to be present is referred to four times in vv
42–44; the place of Israel's meeting with the Presence, the opening to the
Tabernacle, is referred to three times in vv 42–43, and is said to be made
sacred, specially set apart, by Yahweh's glory (כבוד = Presence). Yahweh

will also set apart by his Presence the Tabernacle itself, the Altar, and Aaron and his sons, to give priestly ministry. With this summation in v 44, the whole of chaps. 25–29 are brought to conclusion, with the subject matter of chap. 29, the priestly ordination, appropriately set last.

45–46 The closing verses of chap. 29 are a broader and more revealing summary still. They reiterate the promise of Presence that is the constant of the first nineteen chapters of Exodus, repeat twice the autokerygmatic statement of 6:2 and 20:2 (see above), and declare Yahweh's coming to dwell in Israel's midst as the demonstration of his assertion that he is Israel's God. This latter statement is as remarkable and sensitive a summary as is to be found in Exodus, for it handily reverses the "proof of the Presence" sequence (alluded to in v 46 by the reference to the "bringing forth" from Egypt) of the first nineteen chapters of Exodus into a "Presence giving proof" interpretation of the chapters following the Book of the Covenant. Thus as the chapters leading up to Yahweh's Advent on Mount Sinai demonstrate Yahweh's Presence by what *Yahweh* does, the chapters that follow that Advent are here interpreted as chapters that demonstrate that Yahweh is present by what *Israel* does, first of all in the way they are to live, and second, in the places, the symbols, and the acts of their worship.

Explanation

The authority for the ordination of Aaron and his sons, declared in one way or another in nearly every verse of chap. 29, is Yahweh at hand. In the place appointed for the ceremony, in the rituals of vesting, anointing, atonement, and offering in ordination of Aaron and his sons, in the Altar and its horns that receive the wholly-burned offerings and the blood, in the gifts of the herd, the flock and the grain and grape and olive harvests, in all the movements of these rituals and certainly in any words spoken with those movements, Yahweh's Presence was celebrated and confessed. With the sprinkling upon Aaron and his vestments and his sons of the Oil of Anointment and the blood of the ram of ordination, a rite that could only be authorized by Yahweh and the consummating rite of the ordination, Yahweh's Presence was asserted. With the presentation of Aaron and his sons as an offering symbolically given, Yahweh, the recipient of the gift and the object of the priestly ministry, was known to be near. In the holiness of the remaining foodstuffs, of the vestments, and of the Altar, Yahweh's Presence was declared. And so that this point might be unmistakable, the summary of chap. 29 and of all the chapters of instruction preceding it states clearly that through the knowledge of Israel that he is present, Israel is to know that Yahweh is their God.

The Instructions for the Altar of Incense (30:1–10)

PARALLEL VERSES:
37:25–28

Bibliography

Albright, W. F. *The Archaeology of Palestine and the Bible.* New York: Fleming H. Revell Co., 1933. **Beek, G. W. van.** "Frankincense and Myrrh in Ancient South Arabia." *JAOS* 78 (1958) 141–52. **Glueck, N.** "Incense Altars." *Translating and Understanding the Old Testament.* Nashville: Abingdon Press, 1970. 335–41. **Hoonacker, M. van.** "La date de l'introduction de l'encens dans le culte de Jahve." *RB* 11 (1914) 161–87. **Langhe, R. de.** "L'autel d'or du temple de Jerusalem." *Bib* 40 (1959) 476–94. **Löhr, M.** *Das Raucheropfer im Alten Testament.* Halle (Saale): Max Niemeyer Verlag, 1927. **Weiner, H. M.** *The Altars of the Old Testament.* Leipzig: J. C. Hinrichs'sche Buchhandlung, 1927. **Wright, G. E.** *Biblical Archaeology.* Rev. ed. Philadelphia: Westminster Press, 1962.

Translation

[1a] "You are to make an Altar to make incense smoke.[b] You are to make it of acacia lumber, [2] a cubit in length and a cubit wide. It is to be square, and two cubits tall. Its horns are to be an integral part of it. [3] You are to overlay it with pure gold: its top, its sides all around, and its horns. You are to make for it an encircling golden beading.[a] [4] You are to make for it two rings of gold, and you are to attach[a] them beneath its beading on two sides, two opposing sides, as attachments for carrying-poles with which to lift it. [5] You are to make the carrying-poles of acacia lumber, and you are to overlay them with gold.

[6] "You are to put it in front of the Veil that is before the Ark of the Testimony, before the Ark-Cover which is over the Testimony;[a] there I will meet you[b] by appointment. [7] Aaron is to make Special-Formula[a] Incense smoke upon it; morning by morning when he trims[b] the lamps, he is to make it smoke, [8] and when Aaron sets the lamps alight[a] between sundown and nightfall, he is to make it smoke, a continuing incense in Yahweh's Presence, down through your generations. [9] You are not to offer up upon it profane incense,[a] or a wholly-burned offering or a cereal-offering, nor are you to pour out upon it a drink-offering. [10] Aaron is to make atonement upon its horns one time a year: with the blood of the sin offering for atonement he is to make atonement for it one time a year, down through your generations. It is to be most holy."

Notes

1.a. See n. 26:35.a.

1.b. קטר. מִקְטַר קְטֹרֶת. קטר in the hiph and piel stems can refer to making fat or meat or incense smoke, but the emphasis is on the smoke, not the burning; see n. 29:13.a. קטרת may signify "sacrifice-smoke" as well as "incense-smoke," though in this context, it clearly refers to the latter. Cf. Löhr, *Raucheropfer,* 168–70; Durham, *Touch, Taste and Smell,* 308–26.

3.a. See n. 25:11.b.

4.a. תעשה "make."

6.a. "Before . . . Testimony" is missing in SamPent and LXX.

6.b. See above, n. 29:42.a.

7.a. סמים קטרת means "aromatic incense-smoke." As סמים is always used in the OT (16×) in connection with קטרת, and always to refer to the special ingredients added to frankincense to make the "most holy" incense (Exod 30:34–38), סמים קטרת is here translated "Special Formula Incense." Cf. Haran, *Temples*, 241–43.

7.b. בהיטיבו "in his making good."

8.a. בהעלת "in causing to go up," i.e., in placing the lighted lamps up on the lampstand, whence they can give light.

9.a. זרה קטרת "strange incense," i.e., incense made and used for ordinary purposes.

Form/Structure/Setting

See *Form/Structure/Setting* on 25:1–9.

Comment

1–5 The Altar of Incense was to be a small altar, approximately a foot and a half square and three feet tall (Sellers, "Weights and Measures," *IDB* 4:836–38). It was to be made of acacia, and entirely overlaid with gold, for which reason it is sometimes called הזהב מזבח "the Altar of Gold" (cf. Exod 39:38; 40:5, 26; Num 4:11; 2 Chr 4:19). De Langhe (*Bib* 40 [1959] 489–94) has argued, incidentally, that "gold" may be a mistranslation of זהב in reference to the Altar of Incense; basing his theory on such texts as Isa 60:6; Ps 141:2; and Jer 4:30, he suggests that this Altar was originally called הַזָּהָב מִקְטַר, lit., "the place-of-burning of the yellow aromatic material," and that when מקטר was replaced by מזבח, the use of זהב to refer to a yellow aromatic substance was forgotten. Given the extensive use of gold for the other furnishings of the Holy Space and the Holiest Space, however, de Langhe's theory becomes less plausible. This Altar of Incense was to be decorated with an encircling beading of gold similar to that of the Ark (25:11) and the Table (25:24) and equipped with rings and carrying-poles for moving it, as were the Ark, the Table, and the Altar for burned offerings.

6–10 The location of the Altar of Incense was inside the Holy Space of the Tabernacle, before the Veil that closed off the Holiest Space, and behind which was the Ark, the Testimony in the Ark, and the Ark-Cover above them both. Just how the Altar of Incense was positioned in relation to the Table and the Lampstand (cf. 26:35), we are not told, though v 6 implies that it was set in a central position before the Veil, at the point at which Yahweh proposed to meet Moses by appointment. On this Altar, "Aaron" was to offer only the Special Formula Incense described in 30:34–38; all other incense and all other offerings that were burned were to be excluded from it. On a routine basis, at the times of the trimming of the lamps in the morning and the lighting and placing of the lamps in the evening, Aaron was to make incense smoke on this Altar daily. This schedule is very close to the schedule set for daily offerings on the Altar of burned offerings in the Tabernacle Courtyard, and both sets of daily rituals must have had special significance for the acknowledgement and worship of Yahweh present. On the annual Day of Atonement (see Lev 16), atonement was to be made for the Altar of Incense by the application to its horns of blood from the sin-offering for atonement.

For some years following Wellhausen's (*Prolegomena*, 64–65) assertion that the use of incense came late in Israel, as a postexilic "innovation from a more luxuriously-developed foreign cultus," most commentators suggested that the references to incense and incense-altars were later additions to the text of the OT. As early as 1914, however, van Hoonacker (*RB* 11 [1914] 161–87) challenged the Wellhausenist position at length and point by point and concluded that incense was used in Israel's worship long before the seventh century B.C. and that there was an altar of incense in the Temple of Solomon, just as P maintains. In 1927, Max Löhr (*Raucheropfer*, 164–89) and H. M. Weiner (*Altars* 16–17, 23–31) criticized the view of the Wellhausenists as one with no basis. Albright (*Archaeology*, 108–9), Wright (*Biblical Archaeology*, 114–15), Galling ("Incense Altar," *IDB* 2:699), van Beek (*JAOS* 78 [1958] 141–52) and Glueck (*Translating*, 325–41), among others (cf. Durham, *Touch, Taste and Smell*, 373–77), have reviewed the archeological evidence for incense altars and incense use in the OT period and have found more than enough data to make the early use of incense plausible, though as Haran (*Temples*, 235–38) has noted, the discovery of an incense altar *in situ* in an Israelite sanctuary has yet to be made. More important still is Haran's (230–45) correct distinction between the incense of the Tabernacle Court, the frankincense used variously with burned offerings, and the Special-Formula Incense used inside the Tabernacle itself, on the Golden Altar of Incense, though Haran's insistence on a distinction between the piel and hiphil usages of קטר is not sustained by the 112 OT occurrences (42 piel and 70 hiphil; see, for a detailed discussion, Durham, 316–25).

In sum, there is little reason why the use of incense and incense altars cannot be as early in Israel's worship as the OT suggests. And though the Altar of Gold may be a later elaboration of a somewhat plainer altar—and a reflection of the stone incense altars that were a commonplace in Canaan—there is little reason to suggest that it is any later than other elaborate furnishings of the Tabernacle.

Explanation

The Golden Altar of Incense, by its expensive construction as by its placement and the special incense offered upon it, is established as yet another symbol of Yahweh at hand. Whatever the period in which such an Altar came into use, and indeed whether it ever even existed, the theological declaration of the Priestly description remains the same. Of all the purposes that have been proposed for the burning of incense, none is given in the OT and none provides a satisfactory explanation for the OT practice. The most that can be said with assurance is that making incense smoke was a further attestation of the belief in Yahweh's Presence.

The Instructions for the Atonement Money
(30:11–16)

Bibliography

Scott, R. B. Y. "Weights, Measures, Money and Time." *Peake's Commentary on the Bible.* New York: Thomas Nelson and Sons, 1962. 37–41. **Speiser, E. A.** "Census and Ritual Expiation in Mari and Israel." *Oriental and Biblical Studies.* Philadelphia: University of Pennsylvania Press, 1967. 171–86.

Translation

[11] *Then Yahweh spoke to Moses to say:* [12] *"When you count the heads of the sons of Israel for the purpose of assembling them, each man is to give atonement money* [a] *for himself to Yahweh, as they are counted,* [b] *that there may be no smiting* [c] *against them because of their being counted.* [b] [13] *Everyone who moves over into the counted group* [a] *is to give a half-shekel (by the measure of the set-apart shekel; there are twenty gerahs to a shekel), a half-shekel as a contribution to Yahweh.* [14] *Everyone who moves over to the counted group who is twenty years old or more is to give this contribution for Yahweh.* [15] *The rich are to give no more and the poor are to give no less than the half-shekel in making this contribution for Yahweh in atonement for themselves.* [16] *You are to take the money of atonement* [a] *from the sons of Israel, and you are to give it for the expense* [b] *of the Tent of Appointed Meeting, that it may be a reminder in the Presence of Yahweh for the atonement of yourselves."*

Notes

12.a. כפר, lit., "life-price, ransom, atoning payment." Note כסף הכפרים "money of atoning payments" in v 16.

12.b. בפקד אתם "in numbering them." The first occurrence of this phrase is lacking in LXX; it is translated above in two different ways, given the context of the verse.

12.c. נגף refers always in the OT to Yahweh's disastrous blow; see n. 12:13.b.

13.a. Cf. Speiser, *Oriental*, 182: עבד על-הפקדים "emerges as 'one who is entered among the enrolled.' "

16.a. LXX has τῆς εἰσφορᾶς "of the contribution."

16.b. עבדה, lit., "labor, service," here referring to upkeep and day-to-day expenses.

Form/Structure/Setting

See *Form/Structure/Setting* on 25:1–9.

The interruption of the lengthy sequence of Yahweh's instructions by the introductory sentence of v 11 has frequently been taken as an indication that this section is an addition to the instructions (so Noth, 236, and even Cassuto, 393) that have preceded it, as also, and for the same reason, are the five sections that follow: 30:17–21; 30:22–33; 30:34–38; 31:1–11; and 31:12–18. Galling (in Beer, 147–53) refers to this section and the three that follow it as "supplements from various hands," and to 31:12–18 as a "conclusion to the announcement of the requirements."

The miscellaneous nature of these sections can hardly be doubted, any more than can their semiarbitrary sequence. They have, however, been put into Exodus because they were considered significant by those responsible for the traditions connected in one way or another with Israel's worship in Yahweh's Presence, and there may well be more of a design in their arrangement than seems apparent to us. The section at hand, for example, amounts to the endowment of the upkeep of the place and equipment for worship in Yahweh's Presence. It is located where it is, no doubt, because of the references to atonement in the instructions for the Altar of Incense, though its real purpose was to ensure the financing of the Tabernacle and the worship carried on there.

Comment

11-12 The provision for the payment of a set sum of money contains two assumptions that cannot be satisfactorily explained, given only the information available in the OT. The first of these assumptions is that a head count of males aged twenty or more was to be made. Though Num 1 reports Yahweh commanding such a census, the connection of that command to the counting referred to in Exod 30:11-16, generally made by commentators (so Noth, 236; Hyatt, 293), is by no means assured. Another counting, and quite possibly a periodic counting given the continuing needs of the Tabernacle, may be in view. The second assumption is that such a head count might result in harm, and harm brought by Yahweh unless the atonement sum was paid. Given such a possibility, why would the count be made in the first place? And how would the payment of a half-shekel a head, a payment that sounds very much like a bribe, avert Yahweh's anger?

A variety of speculations has been made, most of them linked in one way or another to the idea of a military census because of the narrative of 2 Sam 24. So Gispen (283), for example, refers to the soldier who was regarded as "a potential taker of human life" and to the pride in the count that might provoke divine jealousy, and Knight (180) speaks of the danger of gathering information that might be useful to an enemy, thus constituting an act of disloyalty toward one's own deity. A more reasonable, if still partial explanation has been given by Speiser (*Oriental,* 171–86), on the basis of a comparison of biblical passages with texts from Mari. Speiser connects the counting with "new land grants" and political structures, notes that it is far more than "a routine mustering process," and though he still relates the procedure to an "underlying" military purpose, he maintains that a kind of purification was in view vis-à-vis "the cosmic 'books' of life and death." By the time of the requirement set forth in the passage at hand, the older and more ominous implications of such a life-and-death "calling to account" had been weakened. The atonement-money, a remnant of the earlier concept, thus became the reason for preserving the practice, and its proceeds were turned in a new direction—the support of the Tabernacle and its services of worship.

13-14 Whatever the reasons for the counting, and whatever there was about such a numbering that was originally believed to displease Yahweh, the count and the atonement payment it required became somehow a source of support for the Tabernacle. Just how early such a procedure was practiced is impossible to say. The frequent assumption that this passage is a late justification of a postexilic poll tax (so McNeile, 196–97; Noth, 236) cannot be fully sustained. What seems clear is that the support of the Tabernacle is the primary reason for the inclusion of this instruction in its present form and location. There may be a memory of the procedure employed in counting and collecting in the language of vv 13–14. The males twenty years old and older were allowed as they were counted to move from the uncounted to the counted group, and as each man "passed over" (עבר), he paid the half-shekel atonement money for himself. This half-shekel is certainly to be regarded as money, but probably as a weight of precious metal rather than as coinage (cf. Hamburger, "Money, Coins," *IDB* 3:423–24). The metal was quite possibly silver, and a half-shekel, ten gerahs, would weigh approximately 5.7 grams, 0.2 of an ounce (Sellers, "Weights and Measures," *IDB* 4:832–33). The phrase שקל הקדש "the set-apart shekel" has not been clearly understood; it may mean only the measure of the sanctuary, or it may refer to a different weight (cf. Sellers, 833; Scott, *Peake's Commentary*, 38).

15–16 The sum thus fixed was not by any standard a large amount, but the instruction that rich and poor alike were to give precisely this payment is an important indication of the equality with which all men were received in Yahweh's Presence. They were all to give equally because they were all to be received and remembered equally; the money was to be used for the expense of the Tent where Yahweh by appointment came to meet them. Thus it would be a זכרון "reminder" of each of them on an equal basis in the place before which they were to gather in his Presence. זכרון is the term used of the ambiguous "reminder" for Israel in Exod 13:9, as also of the gemstones on the shoulderpieces of the Ephod and on the Breastpiece of Judgment that were to be a "reminder" for Yahweh.

Explanation

Thus even so pragmatic and routine a necessity as the financial support of the Tabernacle and its ministry of worship is turned into an expression of the central confession of Israel's faith. An existing procedure of counting and taxation was apparently turned from a census with an element of fear (of military service and of divine punishment) to a passing into the ranks of those who would be remembered, each one equally, in the place where Yahweh came by promise. Here, then, as elsewhere, atonement comes to mean blessing, the blessing of being in Yahweh's Presence, rather than escape, a flight from that same Presence. By the payment of the atonement money, Israel is to be remembered, not forgotten.

The Instructions for the Laver for Washing
(30:17–21)

PARALLEL VERSE:
38:8

Translation

¹⁷ Then Yahweh spoke to Moses to say: ¹⁸ "You are to make a Laver of copper with its pedestal of copper, for washing, and you are to put it between the Tent of Appointed Meeting and the Altar and you are to put water into it. ¹⁹ Aaron and his sons are to wash their hands and their feet in this water. ᵃ ²⁰ Whenever they enter the Tent of Appointed Meeting, they are to wash in this water, so that they will not die. Also whenever they approach the Altar to minister in worship to make an offering by fire ᵃ into smoke for Yahweh, ²¹ they are to wash their hands and their feet, ᵃ so that they will not die. This is to be for them a requirement forever, for Aaron ᵇ and for his sons down through their generations."

Notes

19.a. ממנו "from it."
20.a. אִשֶּׁה; cf. Gray, *Sacrifice*, 9–13.
21.a. LXX adds ὕδατι ὅταν εἰσπορεύωνται εἰς τὴν σκηνὴν τοῦ μαρτυρίου νίψονται ὕδατι "with water whenever they enter the Tent of Appointed Meeting; they are to wash with water."
21.b. MT לו "for him," but Aaron is the obvious antecedent.

Form/Structure/Setting

See *Form/Structure/Setting* on 25:1–9 and 30:11–16.

Comment

17–19 The Laver of copper was for the ceremonial cleansing of the priests' hands and feet when they entered the Tabernacle or approached the Altar for ministry there. The washing of hands and feet is clearly related to the priests' approach to the places of Yahweh's Presence and their handling of the implements of his Presence; but a broader symbolism of purity may also be intended. No dimensions are given for this Laver, either here or in the parallel reference in Exod 38:8, but it is not to be regarded as of anything like the size of the ten massive Lavers of Solomon's Temple (1 Kgs 7:27–39), which with their stands were more than eight feet tall and held two hundred and forty-three gallons each (Garber, "Laver," *IDB* 3:76–77).

20–21 The requirement that the priests should wash before carrying out their duties in Yahweh's Presence is specified as a permanent one, to be kept on pain of death. There was to be no carelessness in the matter of respect for Yahweh's nearness. The duties before which the priests were so to cleanse themselves are listed as (1) entry into Tabernacle, apparently for any purpose whatever, and (2) coming to the Altar to minister there. The general designation for this latter ministry is causing an offering to smoke by fire, לְהַקְטִיר אִשֶּׁה, a phrase that is intended to describe all the offerings made on the Altar, herd offerings, flock offerings or field offerings. אִשֶּׁה is a general term for any offering made by fire, either in part or wholly (cf. Gray, *Sacrifice* 9–10; de Vaux, *Ancient Israel*, 417).

Explanation

Not alone the Laver and the permanent requirement that the priests should wash in its water before attending duty near Yahweh's Presence, but even more the specification that neglect of the requirement may lead to death, all attest with unmistakable clarity the belief in Yahweh's Presence. Performing the obligations of ministry in the Presence was not enough; preparation and fitness for the performance of those obligations were equally important.

The Instructions for the Anointing Oil and the Special-Formula Incense (30:22–38)

Bibliography

Beek, G. van. "Frankincense and Myrrh in Ancient South Arabia." *JAOS* 78 (1958) 141–52. **Noth, M.** "Office and Vocation in the Old Testament." *The Laws in the Pentateuch and Other Studies.* Edinburgh: Oliver and Boyd, 1966. 228–49.

Translation

²² Then Yahweh spoke to Moses to say: ²³ "You yourself take the best aromatic spices: ᵃ five hundred shekels ᵇ of powdered ᶜ myrrh, half that much cinnamon spice (two hundred and fifty shekels), two hundred and fifty shekels of cane spice, ²⁴ five hundred shekels of cassia, by the measure of the set-apart shekel, ᵃ and a hin of olive oil. ²⁵ You are to blend these ᵃ into a sacred Oil of Anointment, compounded in a spice-mixer's mortar, ᵇ as a spice-mixer's blend. This is to be the sacred Oil of Anointment.

²⁶ "You are to anoint with it the Tent of Appointed Meeting and the Ark of the Testimony, ²⁷ the Table and all its containers, the Lampstand and its ᵃ accessories, the Altar of Incense, ²⁸ the Altar of wholly-burned offerings and all its accessories, and the Laver and its pedestal. ²⁹ You are thus to set them apart, and they are to be most holy: anything touching them must similarly be set apart. ᵃ

³⁰ "You are to anoint Aaron and his sons, and so you are to set them apart to give priestly ministry to me. ³¹ To the sons of Israel you are to say, 'This is to be my sacred Oil of Anointment down through your generations. ³² It is not to be poured upon the flesh of laymen, ᵃ nor are you to blend any like it, by its formula. It is set apart, and it must be set apart as regards you. ³³ A man who mixes any like it, or

*who puts any of it upon someone inappropriate,*ᵃ *is to be ostracized from his people.'"*
   ³⁴ *Then Yahweh said to Moses, "Take for yourself aromatic spices: resin droplets,*ᵃ
*mollusk scent,*ᵇ *and galbanum gum,*ᶜ *aromatic spices along with pure frankincense,*
one part frankincense to an equal part of the aromatic spice mixture; ³⁵ *you are to*
blend these into an incense of mixed aromatics, a spice-mixer's blend, salted, pure,
set apart. ³⁶ *You are to pound some of this into a fine powder, and you are to put*
it in front of the Testimony in the Tent of Appointed Meeting, there where I will
*meet you*ᵃ *by appointment. It is to be most holy to you.* ³⁷ *The incense that you are*
*to blend by this*ᵃ *formula, you are not to blend for yourselves; as far as you are*
concerned, it is set apart for Yahweh. ³⁸ *A man who blends any like it, to smell it*
himself, is to be ostracized from his people."

Notes

23.a. ראש בשמים "the chief, superior, head aromatic spices."
23.b. "Shekels" is added here and 3× more in vv 23 and 24 on the basis of the statement
in v 24 of the standard of measurement for the shekel intended.
23.c. מר־דרור, lit., "free-running" or "flowing myrrh." "Liquid myrrh" (RSV) is a possibility,
but as myrrh was collected as a gum resin by cutting the bark of *Balsamodendron Myrrh* (van
Beek, *JAOS* 78 [1958] 141–43), the hardened globules of the gum appear also to have been
ground into a powder that would have been easy to store and would have been poured from
a container.
24.a. See *Comment* on v 14.
25.a. עשית אתו "you are to make it."
25.b. רקח מרקחת "a spice-mixture of an ointment-pot"; cf. BDB, 955.
27.a. SamPent, LXX read "all its."
29.a. יקדש "it will be set apart, holy." Holiness, like uncleanness, is considered infectious
by touch-contact in the OT. Thus anyone or anything touching these most holy implements
of the worship of Yahweh's Presence became holy upon contacting them, a situation that necessitated precaution. See more fully Durham, *Touch, Taste and Smell*, 108–45; cf. NEB's reading, "shall
be forfeit as sacred."
32.a. אדם "mankind," used here as a general term in reference to all humankind except
those being ordained as priests to Yahweh.
33.a. זר "inappropriate" here designates anyone outside the circle of those set apart by
ordination, as "foreign, strange," so far as this special Oil of Anointing is concerned.
34.a. נטף "resin droplets" refers to an aromatic substance we can no longer identify. Its
name suggests that it was harvested in droplets, but so were nearly all aromatic gum resins.
Cf. Durham, *Touch, Taste and Smell*, 334–35.
34.b. שחלת "mollusk scent" refers to the "cover" or "shell" of a mollusk common along
the coast of the Red Sea, which produced a pungent, musky odor when it was burned. Cf.
Durham, *Touch, Taste and Smell*, 335–36.
34.c. חלבנה refers to another gum resin, frequently connected with the *Ferula Galbanifera*,
and so often called "galbanum." Cf. Durham, *Touch, Taste and Smell*, 336–37.
36.a. See n. 29:42.a.
37.a. Lit., "by its formula."

Form/Structure/Setting

See *Form/Structure/Setting* on 25:1–9 and 30:11–16.
   There are two appendix sections in this sequence, one dealing with the
recipe for the special Oil of Anointment, and one with the recipe for the
Special Formula Incense for use on the "Golden Altar" described in 30:1–
10. Each of the two sections begins with an introductory phrase ascribing
authority for the formulas to Yahweh, and they probably come together because of the similarity of their content.

Comment

22–25 The formula for the sacred Oil of Anointment is reasonably clear, both as regards the ingredients of the special mixture and the relative proportions in which they were to be added. Only the form in which the aromatic ingredients were to be used remains ambiguous, whether liquid or dry. On the whole, a dry, powdered form is the preferable guess, in part because a weight measure as opposed to a liquid measure is used to describe their proportions. Thus approximately 16 lbs. 10 oz. (5.7 kilos) each of cinnamon and cane spice were added to approximately one gallon of olive oil (Sellers, 832, 835). Cassuto (397–98), depending largely upon rabbinic commentary, explains the relatively small amount of oil to be mixed with approximately 33½ lbs. of aromatic spices by suggesting that the spices were "cooked" with water in a lengthy process of distillation. If such a process *was* employed, the OT gives no hint of it. Lucas (*Egyptian Materials*, 104–10) describes the Egyptian process of pressing gum resins with oil, then removing the oil by squeezing the resultant paste in a cloth to extract the oil. The oil thus became the base, one that absorbed and then retained the fragrance of a variety of flowers or aromatic substances. This seems a far likelier possibility for the production of the Oil of Anointment, which was after all not needed in large quantities but was required to be specially fragrant, and no doubt expensive. The fact that it is described as blended in a "spice-mixer's mortar," manufactured by what amounted to a professional process, lends support to such a suggestion.

26–33 This special-formula oil was to be used to anoint the symbols of Yahweh's nearness already identified as sacred by their close association with his Presence, the Tabernacle itself, and the furnishings of the Tabernacle and its Courtyard. This anointing amounted to a formal declaration that these implements were all in the category of "most holy," and thus that anyone or anything coming into physical contact with them would become infectiously holy and so must be either (1) appointed to such contact, through ordination (cf. Num 4:15–20), or (2) appropriately isolated and dealt with (so Uzzah is stricken dead for touching the Ark [2 Sam 6:6–8], albeit with an apparently good intention; those who misuse the special oil or incense were to be ostracized [Exod 30:33, 38]).

This is the oil to be used, of course, in the anointing ceremony that was a part of Aaron's ordination (29:7), as in the sprinkling of the sacral vestments (29:21) of the priests. As Noth (*Laws*, 238–40) has pointed out, anointment in the ANE not only symbolized the special authority conferred on the king or the priest being anointed, it also bestowed, through the " 'life-giving oil,' " what Noth calls "permanent additional vital energy." Under no circumstances, therefore, was the Oil of Anointment to be used on any person other than a priest being ordained, and employing its special formula to blend any of the oil for any personal use is strictly forbidden, upon pain of being "cut off" from one's own people, a penalty whose awful consequences are dramatized by the story of Cain (Gen 4:11–16).

34–35 The Special Formula Incense is similarly unique, and similarly restricted to use only in worship in Yahweh's Presence. The formula for this incense is given just as specifically as the formula for the Oil of Anointment, though without the mention of exact quantities. Three aromatic spices mixed together were to be matched by an equal amount of frankincense. The aromatic spices can no longer be identified with certainty, though two of them, the first and the third in the sequence of v 34, appear to have been produced by shrubs or trees; the middle one was produced by a shellfish. Frankincense (לבנה) was also a gum-resin incense, though more common and less expensive than the other fragrant substances of the Special Formula Incense, thus more widely used (cf. Lucas, *Egyptian Materials*, 111–13). לבנה is used twenty-one times in the OT, seventeen times in connection with worship (always as an accompaniment to cereal offerings); נטף "resin droplets," שחלת "mollusk scent," and חלבנה "galbanum gum" are used only here, in the special incense formula. Like the Oil of Anointment, this incense mixture was to be blended by professional methods, apparently with a small amount of salt, for a reason now unknown (Cassuto, 400, takes ממלח to mean "pure," not as a reference to salt at all).

36–38 The proper blend having been achieved, a portion of this Special Formula Incense was to be pulverized into a very fine powder to prepare it for use. Apparently the blend was stored in its coarse, resin-grain form. The reference to the placement of the powdered form of the incense "in front of the Testimony in the Tent of Appointed Meeting" seems strangely ambiguous and has led some commentators (for example, Noth, 239) to suggest that censers rather than the Altar of Incense may be in view. The text is no more amenable to that view, however, than it is to the view that the "Golden Altar" is implied here. The location specified in v 36 is near enough to the location of that Altar in 30:6 to give weight to the opinion that the Altar of Incense, not a censer or censers, is the place where the Special-Formula Incense in powdered form was to be placed. Like the Oil of Anointment, this incense too was to be reserved for the exclusive use of worship in Yahweh's Presence, with the same penalty assessed against anyone who should make any for any other use.

Explanation

The Oil of Anointment and the Special Formula Incense are additional symbols of the Priestly belief in and confession of the Presence of Yahweh in the midst of Israel. Like the materials of the Tabernacle and its furnishings, or the sacral vestments, the ingredients of this oil and this incense are rare and expensive: the best is to be employed in the worship of Yahweh. Like everything else connected with the Tabernacle, the Oil of Anointment and the Special Formula Incense are to be painstakingly prepared by the most professional methods. And like the Holy Space and the Holiest Space, and all the implements of worship within those areas and before them in the Courtyard, the Oil and the Incense are reserved for use only in the worship of Yahweh. In every possible way, Yahweh's Presence in Israel was to be conveyed as both real and unique. And Israel's response, designed to be a part of that message, had also to be both real and unique, costly and reserved for Yahweh alone.

The Designation of the Artisans   (31:1–11)

PARALLEL VERSES:
35:10–19; 35:30–36:1

Translation

¹ *Then Yahweh spoke to Moses to say:* ² *"Take note—I have called out by name Bezalel ("In El's protecting shadow"), son of Uri ("My flame"), son of Hur,* ᵃ *of the tribe of Judah;* ³ *I have filled him with the spirit of God, in wisdom and in discernment and in skill* ᵃ *and in workmanship of every kind,* ⁴ *to design intricate patterns for work in gold, in silver, and in copper,* ⁵ *in engraving gemstones for setting,* ᵃ *and in carving wood, to make workmanship of every kind.*

⁶ *"Note also that I have myself put alongside him* ᵃ *Oholiab ("Tent of father"),* ᵇ *son of Ahisamach ("My brother has sustained"), of the tribe of Dan, and that I have put wisdom into the mind of all those already skilled,* ᶜ *so that they may make everything I have commanded you—* ⁷ *the Tent of Appointed Meeting, the Ark of the Testimony, the Ark-Cover over it, and all the equipment of the Tent,* ⁸ *the Table and* ᵃ *its equipment, the pure Lampstand and all its equipment, the Altar of Incense,* ⁹ *the Altar of wholly-burned offerings and all its equipment, the Laver and its pedestal,* ¹⁰ *the elaborately sewn* ᵃ *vestments, the sacred vestments of Aaron the priest and the vestments of his sons, for their priestly ministry,* ᵇ ¹¹ *and the Oil of Anointment and the Special Formula Incense for the Holy Space.* ᵃ *In accord with everything I have commanded you they are to work."*

Notes

2.a. "Child" or "White One" or even "of Hurrian descent"; see n. 17:10.a.

3.a. ובדעת "and in skill"; דעת refers to knowledge gained by experience, so is taken to refer to "skill" in the sequence above, which attempts to describe the artisan divinely endowed.

5.a. LXX omits "for setting."

6.a. LXX reads αὐτὸν "him" as a dir obj, followed by καὶ "and."

6.b. LXX has Ελιαβ = אֱלִיאָב "God of father."

6.c. ובלב כל־חכם־לב "and into the heart (= mind) of everyone wise of heart (= mind)."

8.a. SamPent, LXX, Syr, Cairo Geniza have "all."

10.a. שׂרד "elaborately sewn" describes braid-work, stitched and over-stitched; cf. BDB, 975, and Haran, *Temples*, 172–73.

10.b. לכהן; lit., "to give priestly ministry," to which LXX adds the usual μοι "to me."

11.a. לקדשׁ "for the Holy Space," here a reference to the Tabernacle generally and the space before the Veil in particular. Cf. Haran, *Temples*, 172, n. 50.

Form/Structure/Setting

See *Form/Structure/Setting* on 25:1–9 and 30:11–16.

This appendix section and the one following it serve, in the composite Exodus, as a logical conclusion to Yahweh's instructions concerning the media of worship in Yahweh's Presence. These verses note the designation of the artisans in charge of the work of making the Tabernacle and the furnishings, equipment, vestments, and supplies, so they afford an opportunity for a summary listing of them all. Vv 12–17 review the command of the sabbath as the day above all days for reflection on the reality and the meaning of Yahweh present in Israel's midst, the day when the significance of the symbols of Yahweh's Presence could be pondered and treasured. The summary nature of these two sections is further suggested by v 18, which recounts the conclusion of Yahweh's speaking to Moses and mentions the gift to him of the two tablets of the Testimony containing the ten words that began the entire sequence of Yahweh's revelation on the mountain.

Comment

1–5 The designation and special endowment by Yahweh of Bezalel as the supervising artisan for the manufacture of the various media of worship is a logical conclusion to the sequence of instructions Yahweh has given to guide this process. Just as logically, Bezalel is mentioned at the beginning of the narrative of the implementation of these instructions, in 35:30–36:1, immediately after the account of the offering of the requisite materials (35:4–29). Bezalel, appropriately enough from the tribe of Judah, is described as specially endowed for his assignment by an infilling of the divine spirit, which adds to his native ability three qualities that suit him ideally for the task at hand: wisdom (חכמה), the gift to understand what is needed to fulfill Yahweh's instructions; discernment (תבונה), the talent for solving the inevitable problems involved in the creation of so complex a series of objects and materials; and skill (דעת), the experienced hand needed to guide and accomplish the labor itself. Bezalel, so gifted, is the ideal combination of theoretical knowledge, problem-solving practicality, and planning capability who can bring artistic ideals to life with his own hands. That such a comprehensive equipping is intended here is suggested also by the summary listing of what Bezalel is to accomplish: he is to design intricate patterns in three metals, gold, silver and copper; to engrave gemstones; and to carve wood; all these talents are required for "workmanship of every kind." In sum, Bezalel is made expert by Yahweh himself for every kind of work necessary for fulfilling the instructions given to Moses on Sinai.

6–11 Bezalel is also to have an assistant, Oholiab, and the additional advantage of workmen who will, like himself, be divinely augmented to the work at hand. The summary list of all that is to be made by Bezalel and Oholiab and their helpers is a review of everything described in chaps. 25–30. The introduction in v 10 of בגדי השרד "elaborately sewn vestments" is not a reference to some new vestment not mentioned before (Cassuto, 403, suggests that optional winter garments might be meant), but simply the use of a general term to describe all the elaborately made and decorated sacral vestments (cf. Haran, *Temples*, 172–73). All the work to be undertaken by these divinely equipped artisans and craftsmen has been described to Moses by Yahweh himself. Yahweh had chosen to have the media of his worship made by men (and women, according to 35:25–29), albeit persons specially equipped for their tasks by him, but the works they were to produce had been described in detail already to Moses. No room is left for creative variations on the plans Yahweh had given.

Explanation

As the materials for the symbols of Yahweh's Presence had to be only the best, so also the workmanship by which they were created had to be the finest. To this end, artisans already both skilled and gifted had their abilities enhanced and were to be guided by an ideal artist, one made wise and practical and facile by Yahweh himself. The resulting Tabernacle and equipment were thus to be the undoubted result of a divine-human partnership, but one which left by divine intention no possibility of a human error or willful aberration. Bezalel, filled with Yahweh's spirit, was to be as one divinely possessed, and Israel, looking at anything made under his direction, was to think not of Bezalel and his helpers, but only of Yahweh present.

The Instructions for Keeping the Sabbath (31:12–18)

PARALLEL VERSES:
35:1–3

Bibliography

Thomas, D. W. "Some Further Remarks on Unusual Ways of Expressing the Superlative in Hebrew." *VT* 18 (1968) 120–24. **Weingreen, J.** "The Case of the Woodgatherer (Numbers XV 32–36)." *VT* 16 (1966) 361–64. ———. "The Deuteronomic Legislator— a Proto-Rabbinic Type." *Proclamation and Presence.* New corr. ed. Ed. John I Durham and J. R. Porter. Macon: Mercer University Press, 1983. 76–89.

Translation

¹²*Then Yahweh said this* ᵃ *to Moses:* ¹³*"You speak to the sons of Israel, and say, 'Be sure* ᵃ *that you keep my sabbath, because that is a sign between me and you down through your generations, that you may know by experience that I am Yahweh, the one who sets you apart.* ¹⁴*You are to keep the sabbath because it is set apart for you: anyone who desecrates it is strictly* ᵃ *to be put to death; when anyone does customary labor* ᵇ *on it, that person is to be ostracized from among his people.* ¹⁵*Six days is customary labor to be done. On the seventh day, there is to be a sabbath of sabbath-rest, set apart for Yahweh: anyone doing customary labor on the day of the sabbath is strictly to be put to death.* ¹⁶*The sons of Israel are to keep the sabbath,* ᵃ *to respect* ᵇ *the sabbath down through their generations as a perpetual covenant.* ¹⁷*Between me and the sons of Israel it is to be a sign in perpetuity—because in six days Yahweh made the heavens and the earth, then on the seventh day he rested and so caught his breath.' "*
¹⁸*Finally Yahweh* ᵃ *gave to Moses, when he had completed speaking with him on Mount Sinai, the two tables of the Testimony, tables of stone written by God's own hand.* ᵇ

Notes

12.a. לאמר . . . יאמר "he said to say."
13.a. אך "surely."
14.a. מות יומת "is strictly to be put to death."
14.b. מלאכה "customary labor"; see *Comment* on 20:9–10.
16.a. LXX has σάββατα "sabbaths" here, and αὐτά "them" instead of the second "sabbath" of this verse.
16.b. לעשות "to do."
18.a. MT has simply "he"; the antecedent is added above for clarity.
18.b. באצבע אלהים "by the finger of God," which Thomas (120–21) suggests may be here, as in 32:16, an attempt to indicate a superior kind of writing.

Form/Structure/Setting

See *Form/Structure/Setting* on 25:1–9, 30:11–16, and 31:1–11.

Comment

12–17 Yahweh's strict instructions regarding the keeping of the sabbath provide an appropriate conclusion to the extended instructions to Moses begun specifically at 25:2, and in broader terms, with the revelation to the people of Israel in 20:2–17. Indeed, the fourth of the commandments is recorded in language (20:8–11) closely parallel to the instructions set forth here, at several points. These instructions are somewhat wider in their application than the ban of working on the Tabernacle and its various equipment on the sabbath day (so Noth, 240–41, and Cassuto, 403–5), however. They are intended as a conclusion to the whole series of instructions concerning the media of worship, a conclusion designed to call attention to the importance of stopping to reflect on the reality of the Presence of Yahweh, of providing a regular time for honoring that Presence in worship. It is precisely this conclusion to the instructions for the media of worship that provides the introduction to the narrative of the implementation of those instructions, in 35:2–3. In fact, if the account of Israel's first disobedience and its aftermath were to be removed from the sequence of the Book of Exodus and these two collections of Priestly material were brought together, the two sets of instructions regarding the sabbath day would become a repetitive bridge connecting command to obedience, blueprint to construction. Further, the sole specific concern of the instruction of 35:2–3 has nothing to do with the building of the Tabernacle or its equipment but sets forth a ban against kindling a fire on the sabbath day.

13 Keeping the sabbath is set forth here with the broad significance of a general sign (אוֹת), throughout Israel's generations, that Yahweh is the one who has made them special. Keeping his sabbath is one way of realizing that specialness, of keeping keen the sense of it, just as the Tabernacle and the various symbols contained within it were a continuing way of representing the Presence at hand that made that specialness a reality. The intention of this sign and the reason it must be kept so regularly and so conscientiously is that Israel might know Yahweh's Presence by experience, in every generation, and be reminded constantly that only by that Presence are they a people set apart. It is for this reason that the sabbath command is to be kept so strictly. Disregard for the sabbath, either by neglect or by a violation of the strictures concerning it, is disregard for Yahweh: and disregard for Yahweh is disregard for the reason and the possibility of Israel's existence as a people.

14–15 Israel was thus to keep every seventh day as a sabbath-rest, set apart for Yahweh. Any desecration of the sabbath (no specific example is given) was to result in death. The performance of customary labor on the sabbath is accorded the penalty of exclusion from the community in v 14 and the penalty of death in v 15, a discrepancy Noth (241) attributes both to emphasis and "secondary addition," but one that has more to do with the kind of labor, its intention and its result. Num 15:32–36, the case of the man found gathering wood on the sabbath may be, as Weingreen (*VT* 16 [1966] 361–64) has suggested, a violation of the specific ban against kindling a fire on the sabbath (Exod 35:3; cf. also Weingreen's later reversal, *Proclamation*, 87–89). Exod 34:21 warns against sabbath labor during the busy agricultural seasons, and Jer 17:21 forbids lifting a burden on the sabbath to those who would "guard their lives." No further specific examples are cited in the OT, but these are enough to suggest that every case of supposed sabbath violation was reviewed as individual unless there was a very close precedent.

16–17 The fact that the sabbath commandment is called a perpetual covenant between Yahweh and Israel, and "a sign in perpetuity," is an additional reason to extend the application of these verses to a frame far broader than the prohibition of work on the Tabernacle on the sabbath. The reason the sabbath is to be kept is that Yahweh has commanded it as a sign of the covenant in perpetuity between himself and Israel, the covenant by which Israel had made a response to the gift of Yahweh's Presence. The precedent for the sabbath is stated as Yahweh's own rest after the six days of creation. The result of the keeping of the sabbath is that Israel will know, generation after generation, the experience of Yahweh's nearness.

18 The words of Yahweh's concluding instruction are followed by a reference to the ten commandments, with which the teaching on Mount Sinai was begun. Yahweh completed his revelation of himself and his way by giving to Moses the two stone tables of the Testimony, that is, the ten words, described as written by his own hand. It is this tradition, along with the unique contents of the tables, that gave them the name Testimony and a special place in the Ark, which came thereby to be called the Ark of the Testimony (cf. 25:16–22).

Explanation

The repetition of the sabbath-commandment as the conclusion to the long sequence of Yahweh's instructions for the media of Israel's worship provides a bracket from the beginning of Yahweh's teaching on the mountain to its end. A restrictive sabbath observance also provides a continuing means of Israel's reflection upon the Presence of Yahweh, and so a continuing means of sensitizing Israel to the reality of that Presence, as communicated by the symbolism of the Tabernacle and its equipment. Because of this, the sabbath-commandment is referred to as a sign in perpetuity of the covenant with Yahweh, and a means of helping Israel to know by experience that it is Yahweh at hand who makes them a unique people. If even Yahweh stopped to catch his breath after six days of customary labor, so also should Israel. And in that stopping, as Israel came to know Yahweh, Israel would come also to know themselves.

III. Israel's First Disobedience and Its Aftermath (32:1–34:35)

Israel's Sin with the Golden Calf (32:1–6)

Bibliography

Aberbach, M., and **L. Smolar.** "Aaron, Jeroboam, and the Golden Calves." *JBL* 86 (1967) 129–40. **Bailey, L. R.** "The Golden Calf." *HUCA* 42 (1971) 97–115. **Brichto, H. C.** "The Worship of the Golden Calf: a Literary Analysis of a Fable on Idolatry." *HUCA* 54 (1983) 1–44. **Coats, G. W.** *Rebellion in the Wilderness.* Nashville: Abingdon Press, 1968. **Davis, D. R.** "Rebellion, Presence, and Covenant: A Study in Exodus 32–34." *WTJ* 44 (1982) 71–87. **Eissfeldt, O.** "Lade und Stierbild." *ZAW* 58 (1940–41) 190–215. **Faur, J.** "The Biblical Idea of Idolatry." *JQR* 69 (1978) 1–15. **Gevirtz, S.** "חֶרֶט in the Manufacture of the Golden Calf." *Bib* 65 (1984) 377–81. **Key, A. F.** "Traces of the Worship of the Moon God Sin among the Early Israelites." *JBL* 84 (1965) 20–26. **Lehming, S.** "Versuch zu Ex. XXXII." *VT* 10 (1960) 16–50. **Lewy, I.** "The Story of the Golden Calf Reanalysed." *VT* 9 (1959) 318–22. **Lewy, J.** "The Assyro-Babylonian Cult of the Moon and Its Culmination in the Time of Nabonidus." *HUCA* 19 (1945–46) 405–89. **Loewenstamm, S. E.** "The Making and Destruction of the Golden Calf." *Bib* 48 (1967) 481–90. **Loza, J.** "Exode XXXII et la redaction JE." *VT* 23 (1973) 31–55. **Moberly, R. W. L.** *At the Mountain of God: Story and Theology in Exodus 32–34.* JSOTSup 22. Sheffield: JSOT Press, 1983. **Noth, M.** "The Background of Judges 17–18." *Israel's Prophetic Heritage.* Ed. B. W. Anderson and W. Harrelson. New York: Harper & Brothers, 1962. 68–85. ———. "Zur Anfertigung des Goldenen Kalbes." *VT* 9 (1959) 419–22. **Ostwalt, J. N.** "The Golden Calves and the Egyptian Concept of Deity." *EvQ* 45 (1973) 13–20. **Petuchowski, J. J.** "Nochmals 'Zur Anfertigung des "Goldenen Kalbes." ' " *VT* 10 (1960) 74. **Sasson, J. M.** "Bovine Symbolism in the Exodus Narrative." *VT* 18 (1968) 380–87. **Vermeylen, J.** "L'affaire du veau d'or (Ex 32–34). Une clé pour la 'question deutéronomiste'?" *ZAW* 97 (1985) 1–23. **Wainwright, G. A.** "The Bull Standards of Egypt." *JEA* 19 (1933) 42–52. **Zenger, E.** *Die Sinaitheophanie.* Forschung zur Bibel 3. Würzburg: Echter Verlag Katholisches Bibelwerk, 1971.

Translation

[1] *Then the people realized that Moses was long overdue* [a] *coming down from the mountain, and so they came together against* [b] *Aaron, and they said to him, "Get busy!* [c] *Make gods for us who can lead us,* [d] *because this Moses, the man who brought us up from the land of Egypt, we have no idea what has become of him."* [2] *So Aaron said to them, "Snatch the rings of gold from the ears of your wives, your sons, and your daughters and bring them to me."* [3] *All the people snatched from themselves the rings of gold that were in their ears, and they brought them to Aaron,* [4] *who took them from their hands and immediately began to press the gold* [a] *with a metalworking tool.* [b] *Thus he made a calf with a shaped sheathing.* [c] *Then they* [d] *said, "These are your gods, Israel, who brought you up from the land of Egypt."*

⁵ *When Aaron saw their reaction,* ᵃ *he built an altar in front of it, and then Aaron made an announcement: he said, "Tomorrow is to be a sacred day for Yahweh!"*

⁶ *So they* ᵃ *got up early the next day, and they offered wholly-burned offerings, and they brought completion-offerings. And then the people sat down to eat and to drink, after which they rose to frivolity.*

Notes

1.a. בֹּשֵׁשׁ is a *polel* from בוֹשׁ, "be ashamed, dismayed." The sense here reflects the people's fright and indignation; given their feeling of need in the isolation of Sinai, Moses' long delay is in their opinion either irresponsible or tragic: "a shame," we might say.

1.b. קהל + על "come together upon, to, against."

1.c. קוּם "rise up" for action. See BDB, 878, 6.

1.d. Lit., "who can go in front of us."

4.a. אתו "it" clearly refers to the metal made available in the rings; thus the antecedent is used above. יָצַר can be either a 3d masc sg hiph impf of צרר "tie up, press," as above, or a 3d masc sg qal impf of צוּר "confine, bind." The meaning in either case is that the gold is being stressed, pressed into sheets. Such a working of small and relatively thin pieces of gold would have been easier than melting the gold down, since the melting point of gold is 1,063° C. (cf. Lucas, *Egyptian Materials,* 263–65).

4.b. חרט "metalworking tool," a kind of shaping or engraving tool with which Aaron apparently was thought to have shaped a covering of gold around a solid core, probably of wood; see Judg 17:4, and cf. von Rad, *OT Theology* 1:216, n. 61 with Noth, *Prophetic Heritage,* 72, n. 12. Cf. also Smolar and Aberbach, "Calf, Golden," *IDBSup* 123; and note the alternative of Gevirtz, *Bib* 65 (1984) 378–79, who proposes that חרט was a "bag" or "purse," by analogy with חרטים in 2 Kgs 5:23.

4.c. מסכה from נסך "weave," BDB, 651, II. The alternate possibility, מסכה from נסך "pour out," BDB, 650, I, may be either "molten metal" or perhaps "molded metal," a rubbed gold overlay. Note also the theory of Faur (*JQR* 69 [1978] 10–12), who connects מסכה with anointment and perhaps libation by which the calf-image was consecrated and so became "a living idol."

4.d. So MT, apparently in reference to the people's reception of the calf Aaron had produced. LXX has "he said," making the statement an announcement of Aaron.

5.a. MT has simply וירא "and he saw, perceived"; ראה is used here as in v 1 above, where it is translated "realized." Cf. BDB, 970, 5. "Their reaction," the obvious sense of the statement, is added above for clarity. Syr reads "he feared" instead of "he saw."

6.a. LXX reads this verb and the two that follow it as sgs, thus connecting the early rising and the sacrifices and offerings with Aaron's activity, rather than the people's.

Form/Structure/Setting

Any consideration of the literary form of the narrative of the making of the golden calf in Exod 32:1–6 must take into consideration the relation of this brief but crucial narrative to the larger literary complex of which it is a part, Exod 32–34. And that linkage necessarily raises the question of the still larger Sinai narrative sequence of Exod 19:1–20:21; 24; and even chaps. 25–31, 35–40, which leads in turn eventually to some review of the entire composite that is Exodus, both as we know it and in its various component parts. Reference has been made already (see *Form/Structure/Setting* on 24:1–18) to chaps. 32–34 as the "real end" of Exodus, a narrative conclusion to the "ideal end" presented by chap. 24, and perhaps even the original conclusion to the Sinai narrative sequence. But note has been taken also of how irretrievable such underlying sequences are and how necessary to an understanding of Exodus (or any other biblical text) is a careful reading of the composite form of the text in the whole with which the canonical book presents us (see *Form/Structure/Setting* on 19:1–15).

Even a cursory reading of Exod 32–34 reveals to the reader a labyrinth of seams and separate paths, a labyrinth explored and reviewed at length and in sometimes mutually contradictory detail by a variety of commentators (see, e.g., Beer, 153–65; Noth, 243–46; Beyerlin, *Sinaitic Traditions*, 18–26; Zenger, *Sinaitheophanie*, 77–108). Attempts to consider Exod 32–34 as a whole, however, have sometimes led to assertions of a fundamental unity, transcending a patchwork that is ultimately irrecoverable and in some cases purely imaginary (see, e.g., Childs, 557–64, 610; Davis, *WTJ* 44 [1982] 71–87; Brichto, *HUCA* 54 [1983] 4–40; and above all Moberly, *Mountain of God*, 11–14, 38–189).

The source critics have assigned most of Exod 32–34 to J and E, though they have disagreed somewhat broadly on which source is responsible for what passage—Beyerlin (*Sinaitic Traditions*, 18–22) and Hyatt (300–304) give most of chap. 32 to E, while Noth (243–46) and Clements (204–6) assign the same material to J. Loza (*VT* 23 [1973] 50–55), after a careful analysis of what he calls "the JE redaction" of Exod 32, comes to the conclusion that the chapter contains passages in which the redactor of JE is "un vrai auteur," as Wellhausen (*Prolegomena*, 83–98) suggested might sometimes be the case. And Moberly (*Mountain of God*, 43), after a detailed and intensive analysis, has referred to the "impenetrability" of Exod 32–34. Vermeylen (*ZAW* 97 [1985] 3–23) has argued that the text of chaps. 32–34 is the result of a series of no less than five redactions, the first four of them deuteronomistic, the last of them showing the provenance of P.

In the sections that follow, the conclusions of source and form criticism and tradition-historical study will be reviewed, as they have been throughout this commentary. Beyond the valuable data provided by such studies, however, there remains the need to consider the text of each pericope of the biblical text as a whole and in the light of the theological purpose binding the pericopae into larger sequences, entire books, and even whole sections of the Bible. Of all the shorter composites that make up the composite Exodus, none is more uniformly and dramatically presented than Exod 32–34, and none provides a more singular and sustained emphasis upon the undergirding theological motif of the entire Book of Exodus. Brichto has referred to "an exemplary rhetorical achievement" in which even "every discrepancy is deliberate," "a tapestry-like presentation of a theological principle" (*HUCA* 54 [1983] 1, 4). Here, the theological yearning of the narrative of Exod 1–17 (on chap. 18 as dislocated, see *Form/Structure/Setting* on 18:1–12), which has finally been satisfied in Exod 19–20, provided a guidance for response in Exod 20:22–23:33, guaranteed by covenant and the authorization of leadership in Exod 24, and repeatedly suggested in the symbolism of the media of worship in chaps. 25–31 (and even chaps. 35–40), is thrown into terrifying jeopardy by a shattering act of disobedience that threatens to plunge Israel into a situation far deadlier and more ignominious than Egyptian bondage at its worst. The special treasure-people whose identity has been established by the arrival in their midst of the Presence of Yahweh himself are suddenly in danger of becoming a people with no identity at all, a non-people and a non-group fragmented by the centrifugal forces of their own selfish rebellion and left without hope in a land the more empty because it has been so full of Yahweh's own Presence.

A powerful tension is thus set up, one far more powerful, even, than the tension of expectation in Egypt, at the sea, and in the wilderness. All that has been received is about to be lost, and the loss is the greater because it is Israel's own fault. An Israel from whom Yahweh's Presence has departed is far worse than an Israel that had not known that Presence. The drama of the situation is multiplied by a layering of traditions about Yahweh's punishment and Moses' intercession—but at last it is resolved by Yahweh's mercy. Yahweh will not withdraw his Presence. Though things cannot be the same, because Israel's innocence as the people of Yahweh's Presence has been lost, Yahweh will remain with them still. The shattered covenant is renewed, and the shattered tablets of the ten words are replaced, and Moses' authority, compromised by the surly rebellion of the golden calf, is reestablished by the shining of his face, the result of his time on Sinai and in the Holiest Space in the Presence of Yahweh.

It is a tight narrative, despite the separate layers so obvious in it, and it is so permeated by the central theological concern of Exodus that a coincidental assembly of such parts in such a sequence and across a wide span of time is just not a possibility. If a narrative paradigmatic of what Exodus is really about were to be sought, Exod 32–34 would be the obvious first choice.

That these chapters are paradigmatic of Israel's relationship with Yahweh throughout the OT is also obvious, and the farthest thing from coincidence. However many layers of tradition make up Exod 32–34, whatever their time and context of origin, and whatever the inconsistencies in their juxtaposition, these three chapters constitute a marvelous literary unity, bound together as is the entire book of Exodus by theological emphasis. This is why the consideration of any of the individual parts of this narrative of disobedience and mercy, even one so apparently intrusive to it as the narrative of the Tent of Appointed Meeting (33:7–11) or the narrative of Moses' shining face (34:29–35) must be considered in the context of the entire sequence. The seams and discrepancies of Exod 32–34 are far more obvious and bothersome to us than they were to those who compiled the sequence. Whenever these seams and discrepancies are permitted to obscure the continuity and singleness of this powerful sequence, they have become too obvious, as the tail that wags the dog.

Exod 32:1–6 has generally been considered a unity, belonging to the "basic source" that provided the nucleus for the narrative of chap. 32 (so Driver, 347–50; Beer, 13, 153; Beyerlin, *Sinaitic Traditions,* 18–22; Hyatt, 301–4; Childs, 558–62). Attempts to subdivide it into variant (Gressmann, *Mose und seine Zeit,* 199; Lehming, *VT* 10 [1960] 21–24, 50) or even differing accounts (so Noth, 244–45) have properly gained no following. Not only are vv 1–6 a unit, they are the unit that sets up the tension of the entire narrative sequence of Exod 32–34. In one way or another, virtually everything in the sequence of punishment, mercy, covenant renewal, and reconciliation is set in motion by this terse narrative of disobedience. This is only one of the telling reasons why the golden calf episode cannot be the propagandistic plant from the Rehoboam-Jeroboam era it has sometimes been made out to be (cf. Noth, *Pentateuchal Traditions,* 142–45; Aberbach and Smolar, *JBL* 86 [1967] 135–40).

Comment

1 The impression given by the report of Israel's reaction to Moses' lengthy absence on Mount Sinai (set by the verse immediately preceding in the Sinai narrative sequence, 24:18, as "forty days and forty nights," the standard phrase for a long period of time) is one of frightened impatience. Any absence of their leader, the one person who has been their representative to Yahweh from the moment of his return to them in Egypt, would have been unsettling. His absence in such a place, with so much yet to be done by way of provision and guidance, would have been problematic if even only a few days were involved. With the passage of a long period of time, the people are represented as nearly in a frenzy, some perhaps assuming Moses had deserted them, others more charitably fearing some tragedy had befallen their leader.

This is the context within which the impulsive surge of the people against Aaron is to be understood, rather than as a continuation of the rebellion/ murmuring tradition; as Coats (*Rebellion,* 188–89) points out, Israel's problem is not here with Moses' leadership, but with Moses' absence. The people assemble themselves, gather as a group (niphal קהל) against (על) Aaron and command him, with two terse imperatives, to make them gods to lead them (literally, "go in front of" them), that is, to take the place of Moses, who is given credit for leading them up from Egypt, and whose protracted absence is stated as the justification of their demand. The request of the people for "gods" (אלהים) is taken by some commentators as a cry for *a* god as opposed to an array of gods (so Hyatt, 304; Moberly, *Mountain of God,* 46–48; Bailey, *HUCA* 42 [1971] 99–100), not because Moses was viewed as a god, but because with Moses gone, access to Yahweh is cut off, and another deity is needed. There is, however, no reason to read אלהים here as anything but a plural, the more so since it is followed by a plural verb. The people may well be asking for "gods" because their neighbors had gods, and because their one God seemed gone with the absence of Moses.

2–4 Aaron's response to the threatening approach of the assembled people may be intended to indicate his own agitation under their pressure. He tells them, also by the use of two imperatives, the first a piel imperative, to "snatch off, tear away" their earrings of gold, and to bring them (hiphil) to him. When they do so, Aaron begins immediately (special *waw* in context) to make a calf (עגל). The exact nature of this calf and Aaron's work in making it have been the subject of considerable discussion and conjecture, in part because of the ambiguity of the text and in part because of our uncertainty about the proper translation of the terms חרט and מסכה. To begin with, Aaron is said to start "pressing or causing to be narrow" (hiphil צרר) "it" (אתו); this is taken here, given the sequence of vv 2–4, to mean the gold, and this antecedent is used instead of the pronoun of MT in the *Translation* above. Some commentators, however, believe "calf" to be the antecedent of "it," because of the reference farther along in v 4 and the statement of

Aaron in v 24 (so Loewenstamm, *Bib* 48 [1967] 481, 487–90). This is unlikely.

Such a translation of יָצַר better fits the little we know about the noun חֶרֶט, which refers to a tool used as a stylus and apparently for stripping or peeling (cf. BDB, 354–55; note LXX, ἐν τῇ γραφίδι "with a stylus"). Attempts to make חֶרֶט a device for molding or casting metal, one of the earliest of them the paraphrase of Targum Onkelos (cf. Loewenstamm, *Bib* 48 [1967] 486), have taken the word to refer to a die or mold of some kind (Hyatt, 304). Noth (*VT* 9 [1959] 419–22), by the emendation of חֶרֶט to חָרִט, has proposed that Aaron collected the gold in a bag or purse preparatory to melting it down, an interpretation given also and much earlier by rabbinic exegetes (Petuchowski, *VT* 10 [1960] 74; cf. Loewenstamm, 487 and Gevirtz, *Bib* 65 [1984] 377–81). Such emendation is unnecessary, however, if יָצַר is taken to mean "press, bend," and מַסֵּכָה gives additional support for such an interpretation if it is taken from II נסך "weave" (BDB, 651), as it means "woven stuff, covering," or as proposed above, "shaped sheathing." Faur (*JQR* 69 [1978] 11–12), following a suggestion of the nineteenth century scholar Elie Benamozegh, has suggested that מַסֵּכָה may be derived from סכך "cover, screen," and mean the "anointment" of an idol as an "act of consecration."

4 The words with which Israel greeted the product of Aaron's labor have often been connected with the very similar announcement of Jeroboam in 1 Kgs 12:28, and the obvious thematic connections between the two narratives have given rise to an elaborate array of speculation about which of the two passages is earlier and about the way in which each of the two accounts has influenced the other. Scholars have suggested that the entire golden calf episode was (1) created by the deuteronomists to discredit the northern cultus of Jeroboam, which placed one calf of gold at Bethel in the south and another at Dan in the north (Noth, *Pentateuchal Traditions*, 142–45, among many); (2) an ancient story of idolatry in the wilderness in Moses' time recalled and used to condemn Jeroboam (Cassuto, 407–10, among others); and (3) an ancient story of an entirely acceptable cultic practice begun by Aaron and utilizing a bull image in the worship of Yahweh, taken by Jeroboam as an entirely legitimate precedent for the cultus which he claimed, after all, to be Yahweh's, then later reworked by the Zadokite priesthood to attack both Jeroboam *and* Aaron (Aberbach and Smolar, *JBL,* 86 [1967] 129–40, among others).

As Childs (559–61) has noted, the thematic links between Exod 32:1–6 and 1 Kings 12:25–33 are altogether too apparent to be doubted, but the existence of an idolatrous calf tradition prior to the time of Jeroboam can be denied on no convincing argument. Among other things, the denial to the narrative of Exod 32–34 of the calf episode, or at least something very like it, removes the reason for the remainder of that narrative. Far too much that is an integral part of Exodus is lost thereby, and for no telling reasons. The integrity of the composite narrative of Exod 32–34 simply demands the reliability of the calf story in some form.

The widespread presence of bull images in ANE worship has been thoroughly confirmed by Eissfeldt (*ZAW* 58 [1940–41] 199–215; cf. also Wainwright, *JEA* 19 [1933] 42–52), and attempts have been made to connect the golden calf with the lunar cult of the god Sîn, brought by the patriarchal fathers from Haran and possibly even reflected in the name "Sinai" (Bailey, *HUCA* 42 [1971] 103–15; cf. also J. Lewy, *HUCA* 19 [1945–46] 405–89, and Key, *JBL* 84 [1965] 20–26), and also with the Egyptian representation of Amon-Re as a bull, "the 'Bull, chief of all the gods' " (Ostwalt, *EvQ* 45 [1973] 17–19). One scholar (Sasson, *VT* 18 [1968] 383–87) has even made an imaginative though implausible suggestion that the golden calf is to be understood as a symbol of the "continued, reassuring presence" of the absent Moses (cf. also the proposal of Brichto, *HUCA* 54 [1983] 41–44). These theories go beyond what the text will allow, not least because the entire composite of Exod 32–34 turns on the fact that the making and worship of the golden calf are an unacceptable idolatry that threatens the destruction of the relationship between Yahweh and Israel. The probability that the calf was a symbol of divinity widely used among Israel's neighbors of course makes Israel's idolatry even worse.

The apparent acceptance of the golden calf by Israel as their gods "who brought them up from the land of Egypt," is taken by Faur (*JQR* 69 [1978] 11–12) as a part of a ritual of consecration by which the people hoped to have God "identify with" the calf and "make his glory dwell among them." The evidence for such a ritual in the OT is very skimpy (Faur builds his case, for the most part, on Egyptian and Babylonian texts—9–10, nn. 51–54).

5 It is within some such framework, however, that the response of Aaron to the people's acceptance of the calf is best to be understood. He built an altar, a standard OT reaction to the manifestation of deity, and then announced a חג "sacred feast" (the same term is used in reference to the Passover in 12:14 and to the three principal events of Israel's religious calendar, in 23:14–17), for the next day. What is more striking about this sacred feast is that Aaron designates it a חג ליהוה "sacred feast for Yahweh" (the very phrase used in 10:9; 12:14; 13:6; Lev 23:6, 34, 31, 39 and Hos 9:5). This pronouncement has been taken both as an indication of an original acceptability of the calf cult (cf. Newman, *People of the Covenant,* 179–87) and also as an attempt to "rehabilitate" Aaron after his lapse under pressure (cf. Hyatt, 302; Aberbach and Smolar, *JBL* 86 [1967] 135–40; I. Lewy, *HUCA* 19 [1945–46] 319), but whatever overtones may have emanated from it or attached themselves to it, Aaron's deliberate announcement, made in response to the people's declaration about the calf, must be taken in the composite of Exod 32–34 at face value.

It is precisely the attempt to worship *Yahweh* by means he has already declared totally unacceptable that makes the sin of the golden calf so destructive, far more so than a simple shift of allegiance to "other" or "foreign" gods. The people receive the calf with the confession "These are your gods, Israel, who brought you up from the land of Egypt," an act they had attributed to Moses, albeit certainly as Yahweh's representative, in v 1. And Aaron, in obvious and specific response, declares a sacred day to *Yahweh,* not to the calf, or to any other god or gods. The composite of Exod 32:1–6 is not an account of the abandonment of Yahweh for other gods; it is an account of the transfer of the center of authority of faith in Yahweh from Moses and the laws and symbols he has announced to a golden calf without laws and without any symbols beyond itself. Moses is the representative of a God invisible in mystery. The calf is to be the representative of that same God, whose invisibility and mystery is compromised by an image he has forbidden. The terrible irony of the foolish, impulsive action of Israel is incisively summed up in the trenchant summary of Ps 106:19–20:

> They made a calf at Horeb,
> They bowed themselves down to an overlaid image (מַסֵּכָה)
> They swapped their Presence (כְּבוֹדָם)
>   for a likeness of a grass-eating bull.

כבוד here as in P describes the invisible immanent Presence of Yahweh, given to Israel at Sinai, symbolized by the cloud and by the Tabernacle and all its furnishings.

6 In demanding such an image, the people have violated, first of all, the second commandment. This is made clear in the composite by the identification of the calf with the rescue from Egypt, by Aaron's construction of an altar for sacrifices, by his declaration of a חג "sacred feast" for Yahweh, and by the people's worship the next morning by the very offerings Yahweh has specified for himself. Whatever additional commandments came to be thought of as compromised in the development of the traditions that grew up around the calf episode, and no doubt they were several, the first, third, and seven commandments among them, the emphasis in 32:1–6 is primarily on the second commandment. Israel has violated Yahweh's own unambiguous requirement about how he is to be worshiped. There can be little surprise, therefore, that they rise from their communion meal to frivolity. לצחק "to laugh, make fun" has a connotation also of sexual play (Gen 26:6–11; 39:6c–20). The contrast with the ritual and the communion meal of chap. 24, which may originally have immediately preceded the narrative of 32:1–6, is devastating and must not be lost with the insertion of the instruction narratives of chaps. 25–31. The celebration of an obligating relationship in Exod 24 becomes in Exod 32 an orgy of the desertion of responsibility.

Explanation

Exod 32:1–6 thus sets the stage for an additional revelation at Sinai. In the absence of Moses, the people ask for a new point of focus for their worship of Yahweh, and when Aaron provides it, they both acclaim it and begin the abandonment of the commitments they had made when Moses provided the point of focus. The calf represented Yahweh on *their* terms. Yahweh had made clear repeatedly that he would be received and worshiped only on *his* terms.

Thus the sin of the golden calf sets in motion several motifs: the judgment of the covenant, the blessings of which Israel had only just begun to enjoy; the tension between the Absence and the Presence of Yahweh; the further definition of the nature of the present Yahweh; the exercise of Yahweh's mercy; and the reassertion of Moses' authority as Yahweh's representative. Because of Israel's embrace of an idol in the worship of Yahweh, Israel comes to a new understanding of themselves, of Moses, and above all, of Yahweh himself.

Moses' Anger and Yahweh's Judgment (32:7–35)

Bibliography

Aberbach, M., and **L. Smolar.** "Aaron, Jeroboam, and the Golden Calves." *JBL* 86 (1967) 129–40. **Andersen, F. I.** "A Lexicographical Note on Exodus XXXII 18." *VT* 16 (1966) 108–12. **Brichto, H. C.** "The Worship of the Golden Calf: A Literary Analysis of a Fable on Idolatry." *HUCA* 54 (1983) 1–44. **Burrows, M.** *The Dead Sea Scrolls of St. Mark's Monastery.* Vol. 2. New Haven: ASOR, 1951. **Cassuto, U.** "Baal and Mot in the Ugaritic Texts." *IEJ* 12 (1962) 77–86. **Coats, G. W.** "The King's Loyal Opposition: Obedience and Authority in Exodus 32–34." *Canon and Authority.* Ed. G. W. Coats and B. O. Long. Philadelphia: Fortress Press, 1977. 91–109. **Driver, G. R.** *Semitic Writing.* Rev. ed. London: Published for the British Academy, 1954. **Edelmann, R.** "To עֲנוֹת Exodus XXXII 18." *VT* 16 (1966) 355–58. **Fensham, F. C.** "The Burning of the Golden Calf and Ugarit." *IEJ* 16 (1966) 191–93. **Gradwohl, R.** "Die Verbrennung des Jungstiers, Ex 32, 20." *TZ* 19 (1963) 50–53. **Gunneweg, A. H. J.** *Leviten und Priester.* FRLANT 89. Göttingen: Vanderhoeck & Ruprecht, 1965. **Kuschke, A.** "Die Menschenwege und der Weg Gottes im AT." *ST* 5 (1952) 106–18. **Lehming, S.** "Versuch zu Ex XXXII." *VT* 10 (1960) 16–50. **Loewenstamm, S. E.** "The Making and Destruction of the Golden Calf." *Bib* 48 (1967) 481–90. ———. "The Making and Destruction of the Golden Calf—a Rejoinder." *Bib* 56 (1975) 330–43. **Loza, J.** "Exode XXXII et la redaction JE." *VT* 23 (1973) 31–55. **Perdue, L. G.** "The Making and Destruction of the Golden Calf—A Reply." *Bib* 54 (1973) 237–46. **Thomas, D. W.** "Some Further Remarks on Unusual Ways of Expressing the Superlative in Hebrew." *VT* 18 (1968) 120–24. **Valentin, H.** *Aaron: Eine Studie zur vor-priesterschriftlichen Aaron-Überlieferung.* OBO 18. Göttingen. Vandenhoeck & Ruprecht, 1978. **Whybray, R. N.** "עֲנוֹת in Exodus XXXII 18." *VT* 17 (1967) 122.

Translation

[7] *Then Yahweh spoke to Moses: "Go! Descend!* [a] *Your people, whom you brought up from the land of Egypt, have gone to ruin!* [8] *They have already* [a] *turned away from the life* [b] *to which I have commanded them! They have made for themselves a calf with shaped sheathing, and they have bowed themselves down to it, they have made sacrifices to it, and they have said, 'These are your gods, Israel, who brought you up from the land of Egypt.' "* [9] *Yahweh* [a] *said further to Moses, "I have seen this people, and I know them* [b] *to be obstinate:* [c] [10] *now do not interfere with me,* [a] *and my anger will burn hot against them. I will destroy them,* [b] *and I will make you alone* [c] *into a great nation."* [d]

[11] *But Moses attempted to calm* [a] *Yahweh his God: he said, "Why, Yahweh, does your anger burn hot against your people, whom you brought up from the land of Egypt with great strength and with a forceful hand?* [b] [12] *Why give the Egyptians an excuse to say,* [a] *'For an evil purpose he brought them out, to slaughter them in the*

*mountains, and to obliterate them from the face of the land?' Turn from the heat of
your anger, and be moved to pity concerning such injury to your people.* ¹³ *Remember
Abraham, Isaac, and Israel* ª *your servants, to whom you bound yourself by oath,* ᵇ
*to whom you spoke so: 'I will make your descendants as many as the stars of the
heavens, and this whole land of which I spoke I will give to your descendants,* ᶜ *and
they will take possession of it* ᵈ *in perpetuity.'* "

¹⁴ *Thus was Yahweh moved to pity concerning the injury that he had spoken of
doing to his people.*

¹⁵ *So Moses turned and began to descend from the mountain, with the two tablets
of the Testimony in his hand, tablets with writing on both sides: on the front side
and on the back side,* ª *they had writing.* ¹⁶ *The tablets were the work of God, and
the writing was the writing of God engraved* ª *on the tablets.*

¹⁷ *Then Joshua heard the racket of the people celebrating, and he said to Moses,
"A noise of battle in the camp!"* ¹⁸ *But Moses answered,* ª

*"Not the sound of heroes exulting,
Not the sound of losers lamenting,
the sound of random singing* ᵇ
is what I hear!"

¹⁹ *And sure enough, when he came near to the camp, he saw the calf and the
frenzied dancing. Then Moses' anger burned hot, and he threw down out of his
hand the tablets and he broke them to bits at the bottom of the mountain.* ²⁰ *He
took the calf that they had made, he burned it in the fire, then he ground it until it
was a fine powder, he sifted it onto the surface of the water, and he made the sons
of Israel drink.*

²¹ *Next, Moses said to Aaron, "What did this people do to you that you should
have brought down on them so great a sin?"* ²² *Aaron replied, "May the anger of
my lord not burn hot—you know from experience* ª *the people, that they are evil by
nature.* ᵇ ²³ *Thus it was they said to me, 'Make gods for us who can lead us, because
this Moses, the man who brought us up from the land of Egypt, we have no idea
what has become of him.'* ª ²⁴ *So I said to them, 'Whoever has gold, let them snatch
it from themselves!' They then gave it to me, I threw it into the fire, and this calf
came right out!"*

²⁵ *Thus Moses saw the people, that they were out of control, because Aaron had
let them get out of control, fair game for the whispered slander* ª *of those who are
set against them.* ᵇ ²⁶ *So Moses took a position in the entrance to the camp, and he
said, "Who is Yahweh's? To me!" Thus he gathered to himself all the sons of Levi.*
²⁷ *Then he said to them, "Thus says Yahweh, God of Israel, 'Each of you put his
sword at his side. Pass through the camp and come back, from the entrance and
back again,* ª *and kill, each of you his brother, and each of you his neighbor, and
each of you his friend.'* " ²⁸ *The sons of Levi did what Moses ordered,* ª *and on that
day nearly three thousand men from the people fell.* ²⁹ *Then Moses said, "Ordain
yourselves* ª *today for Yahweh, for each of you against his own son and against his
own brother has put upon himself* ᵇ *this day a blessing."*

³⁰ *On the next day Moses said to the people, "You have yourselves sinned a great
sin. I will now go up toward Yahweh.* ª *I may possibly be able to make atonement
for your sin."* ³¹ *Thus Moses went back towards Yahweh and said, "I beg you:* ª
This people have sinned a great sin, they have made for themselves gods of gold.
³² *Now, if you will, forgive their sin* ª—*if not, pray* ᵇ *erase me from your book that*

you have written." ³³ *Yahweh replied to Moses, "Whoever sins against me, I will blot him from my book.* ³⁴ *Now go. Guide the people toward the destination of which I have spoken to you.* ᵃ *Look—my messenger will go in front of you. Yet on the day of my taking account, I will take account upon them for their sin."*

³⁵ *Thus did Yahweh level a blow* ᵃ *upon the people because they demanded* ᵇ *the calf that Aaron made.*

Notes

7.a. The two impvs are set in rapid sequence by *maqqeph;* the effect is almost "Go-descend!" Cf. LXX, βάδιζε τὸ τάχος ἐντεῦθεν κατάβηθι "Walk hastily, descend from here!"

8.a. סרו מהר "they have turned away in a hurry."

8.b. הדרך "the way, path," indicating here as at so many points in the OT the manner or style of living directed by the covenant relationship. Cf. Kuschke, *ST* 5 (1952) 106–18.

9.a. This entire verse is absent from LXX. Cf. Deut 9:13 in MT, LXX.

9.b. והנה "and just look."

9.c. קשה־ערף "stiff-necked," i.e., difficult to yoke, unruly. An equivalent contemporary idiom is "hard-headed."

10.a. הַנִּיחָה לִּי: this hiphil impv of נוח commands Moses to leave Yahweh alone, to refrain from bothering him.

10.b. וַאֲכַלֵּם piel of כלה, "bring to an end, finish."

10.c. אותך "you"; "alone" is added above to make clear that the pron is sg, referring only to Moses.

10.d. SamPent adds here what is substantially Deut 9:20.

11.a. חלה + פני lit. means "make sweet or pleasant the face of."

11.b. SamPent reads ובזרוע נטויה "and with an arm stretched out"; cf. LXX, and see 6:1 above.

12.a. "Why will the Egyptians say to say . . . ?"

13.a. SamPent and LXX have "Jacob" here.

13.b. אשר נשבעת להם בך, lit., "whom you swore yourself to them by yourself."

13.c. LXX has εἶπας δοῦναι τῷ σπέρματι αὐτῶν "which you spoke to give to them."

13.d. This pronoun is absent from MT, present in SamPent, LXX, Syr.

15.a. מזה ומזה "from this and from that."

16.a. חרות "engrave" occurs only here; BDB (362) think it is a misspelling of חרוש "cut" on the basis of Jer 17:1; חרות occurs three times in the Qumran Cave I *Manual of Discipline* (10:6, 8, 11; cf. Burrows II, *loc. cit.*)

18.a. אמר with special *waw;* MT has "he": "Moses," the obvious antecedent, is added for clarity.

18.b. ענות is 3× repeated in Moses' poetic response to Joshua, the first 2× as a qal inf constr of ענה "sing," this 3d time as a piel inf constr. In each instance, singing is referred to: in the 1st case the singing of the strong (גבורה), in the 2d, the singing of the weak (חלושה); in the 3d case, there is no word to qualify the singing, but the inf constr has been pointed an intensive by the Masoretes, an indication perhaps of yet a 3d kind of singing. Thus ענות is translated above "random singing," the disorganized, haphazard singing of a wild debauch. In the consonantal text, of course, all three words are the same. Thus *BHS* suggests the loss of a word in the 3d line of Moses' answer (Andersen, *VT* 16 [1966] 111, suggests צחוקה "scornful laughter" and sets אנכי שמע "what I hear" outside the poem proper). As it stands, however, the poem consists of three balanced 2 + 2 lines. LXX is a muddle, suggesting apparently that the revelers' wine was beginning to work.

22.a. The subj is made emphatic by the use of the independent pers pronoun אתה "you" along with the 2d pers masc sg form of the verb. LXX adds τὸ ὅρμημα τοῦ λαοῦ τούτου "the impulsiveness of this people" following "know."

22.b. כי ברע הוא "because on evil they (are set)." SamPent has כי פרוע הוא "because they are out of control."

23.a. Aaron's report here of what the people said to him is a verbatim duplication of 32:1, excepting only the beginning impv, קום "rise up."

25.a. MT has simply לשמצה "to a whispering," but in this context it refers to the exposure of the people to the criticism of their enemies.

25.b. בקמיהם "by the ones who rise up against them."

27.a. משער לשער "from an entrance to the entrance." A single, main entrance is implied by ושובו "and come back."

28.a. כדבר משה "according to the word of Moses."

29.a. מלאו ידכם "ordain yourselves"; LXX has "you have ordained yourselves," and rsv, neb follow such a reading. Barthélemy *et al.* (*Preliminary and Interim Report,* 145) take the verb to be a 3d com pl qal pf and read "they have filled your hand," understanding Yahweh to be "the author of the ordination." These readings are all attempts to avoid the difficult sense of the passage, which apparently suggests that the Levites have, by their uncompromising loyalty, earned a unique ordination to the service of Yahweh.

29.b. עליכם "upon yourselves."

30.a. LXX has τὸν Θεόν "God."

31.a. SamPent reads הנה "look here" instead of אָנָּה; BDB 58: "a strong particle of entreaty." LXX follows MT but adds "Yahweh" after "I beg you."

32.a. SamPent has שא . . . תשא "if you will forgive . . . forgive," followed by LXX and Tg Ps-J.

32.b. נא "pray" is omitted by SamPent. Cf. LXX, Syr, Vg.

34.a. MT has simply אל אשר־דברתי לך "toward which I have spoken to you," but the intention of the statement is clear. LXX adds τὸν τόπον "the place"; cf. Tg Onk, Tg Ps-J.

35.a. נגף; see n. 7:27.b.

35.b. MT has עשו, lit., "they did, made". The sense appears to be that the people are held primarily responsible, though Aaron actually made the calf from their earrings. Vg reads *pro reatu vituli* "for the guilt of the calf." Tg Ps-J "because they prostrated themselves before the calf" (Le Déaut, 259).

Form/Structure/Setting

The section at hand continues the narrative of Israel's first disobedience following the solemnization of the covenant by depicting, with a dramatic layering of separate traditions, the immediate aftermath of the sin with the golden calf, from the deliberately contrasted perspectives of both Moses and Yahweh. As noted already (see *Form/Structure/Setting* on 32:1–6), any part of Exod 32–34 must be understood within and in specific connection with the entire composite, which presents a dramatic and tight-knit narrative, filled with tension and striking contrasts, and moved skillfully forward in the service of the basic theological goal of the entire Book of Exodus.

What holds Exod 32:7–35 together, despite its obvious component parts with their equally obvious logical *non sequiturs,* is its focus on the response of both Yahweh and Moses to Israel's sin with the golden calf. This focus is actually continued into chap. 33, where it is brought to conclusion in a verse (17) that provides also the modulation of the narrative into what amounts to a new revelation of Yahweh on Mount Sinai (33:18–34:9), a renewal of the relationship between Yahweh and his people and a consequent remaking of the covenant (34:10–28), and a reestablishment of the authority of Moses as Yahweh's proper representative (34:29–35).

There appear to be at least three narratives of the response of Yahweh to Israel's sin of the calf, into which has been worked also the related account of Moses' response. These three narratives probably represent three separate contexts of interest, each of them nearer to us from the events at Sinai, though of course no one of them may give as accurate an impression of the *meaning* of what happened there as all of them do together, in the narrative of Exod 32–34. The most important of the three narratives, at least from the perspective of the theological emphasis of Exodus, may (only *may*) also be the oldest of them. It is the narrative of Yahweh's response by the removal from Israel altogether of his Presence, given to them after so much careful preparation at Sinai. This narrative appears primarily in 33:1–6, 12–17, though it is reflected at other points in the composite of 32–34 (e.g., at 32:9–10, 33–34, 34:10, 29–35), and it has attracted to it the important section about the Tent of Appointed Meeting that is *not* the Tabernacle (33:7–11). The second of the narratives, in importance and perhaps in sequence of origin, is the narrative of Yahweh's response by the affliction upon Israel of a powerful blow, very much like his blow against the Egyptians in the death of their firstborn (12:23, 27). This narrative appears only briefly in Exodus, chiefly in 32:35, though there may be reflections of it in 32:9–10, 20, 34; Num 11:1–12:16; chap. 14; 21:4–9; and Deut 9:6–24. The third of the narratives, in importance and almost certainly in sequence of origin, is the narrative of Yahweh's response through his command of the Levites in 32:25–34. There is nothing quite like this account anywhere else in the OT, and it appears to be a justification of the Levites as deserving ordination by virtue of their uncompromising loyalty. It may well come from a context in which the Levites were for some reason under attack, a context we are now unable to reconstruct with any certainty.

In the composite that is Exod 32–34, all three of these narratives (at least) have been molded into one, and have drawn to themselves in that process (and perhaps also on the way to it) such additional traditions as those concerned with Yahweh's advocacy of Moses, Moses' advocacy of Israel, the description of the tablets containing the commandments of Yahweh, the Tent of Promised Meeting *outside* the camp, and the additional revelation of Yahweh concerning himself and his ways. The employment of so many separate layers in the composite of a single continuous narrative has inevitably meant some logical inconsistency, and unfortunately these inconsistencies have attracted far more attention than has the narrative as a whole, as regards both the source criticism and the traditio-historical analysis of these chapters.

Beer (13, 152–155), for example, assigns 32:7–14 to his E supplement, vv 15–16 to E and E[1], vv 17–18 to J[1], vv 19–24 to E and E[1], vv 25–29 to J[1], vv 30–34 to E supplement, and v 35 to E and E[1]. Lehming's (*VT* 10 [1960] 25–50) *"Versuch"* presents an even more fragmented Exod 32, involving twelve sources and twenty-seven bits and pieces for 32:7–35. Noth (243–46, 248–52) gives most of this sequence to J, except for vv 9–14, which he calls "a deuteronomistic addition." Loza (*VT* 23 [1973] 38–45, 50–55) attributes most of Exod 32:7–34 to R[JE]. Hyatt (300) gives 32:7–14 to "a Deuteronomic Redactor," vv 15–20 and v 35 to E, vv 21–34 to "a Supplementer of E."

The layers of tradition of Exod 32:7–35 quite similarly are distributed into smaller sections and even fragments dealing with such subjects as Moses as a royal intercessor (cf. Coats, *Canon and Authority* 94–100, 105–9), Jeroboam's calf symbols at Bethel and Dan (cf. Aberbach and Smolar, *JBL* 86 [1967] 129–40), the intrusion of Deuteronomistic special interests (cf. Loza's comparative analysis, *VT* 23 [1973] 32–38, of Exod 32:7–14 and Deut 9),

Aaron *pro* and *con* (cf. Valentin, *Aaron,* 206–303), Levitical origins and cultic roles (Gunneweg, *Leviten,* 29–37, 88–95), and even an Aaron-cultus at Bethel, based on a positive etiology connected with Sinai (Beyerlin, *Sinaitic Traditions,* 126–33).

As fascinating and helpful as these considerations of source and traditio-history are, however, they must be taken as contributory (or not contributory) to Exod 32–34 as a whole, and they must not be allowed to leave the impression of a jumble of pieces haphazardly assembled. The narrative of Exod 32–34, like the narrative of the other pericopae and larger sequences in Exodus, and for that matter the canonical book of Exodus as a whole, has an important purpose and impression of its own, and simply must be taken seriously in its canonical form (cf. Brichto, *HUCA* 54 [1983] 1–4, 41–44).

Comment

7–8   The announcement to Moses by Yahweh that Israel has turned away from the path to which their covenant relationship with Yahweh had committed them is sometimes linked with the move of Moses described in v 15 (so Noth, 244–45, 248–49), in which case vv 9–14 become an interpolation, usually from a Deuteronomistic context. This has been the approach in part because of a supposed logical inconsistency betwen Yahweh's announcement of what Israel has done and Moses' own later discovery (vv 18–19) and in part because there are two accounts of Moses' intercession and Yahweh's change of approach, one in 32:11–14 and a second in 32:30–34. In fact, there is a third account of Moses' intercession and Yahweh's mercy, in 33:12–17, and a fourth account in 34:9–10 which becomes the basis for the renewal that comes by virtue of Yahweh's forgiveness. And each of these accounts is a valuable contribution to the impact of the narrative as a whole. As Childs (567–68) has pointed out, the narrative of vv 7–14 must not be taken out of the larger sequence of Exod 32, which he sees as presented in a dramatic contrasting of what is going on at the top of Sinai with what is going on below, in the plain.

More important still is the even larger narrative: (1) Yahweh tells Moses to descend the mountain, and why; he announces his intention to destroy the people and continue his plan with Moses alone; Moses pleads against this, stating four reasons; Yahweh pulls back from obliterating Israel (vv 7–14); (2) Moses descends with the tablets, discovers the sin of the calf at first hand, and grows angry himself, breaking the tablets, destroying the calf, and making Israel drink the detritus of their own image (vv 15–20); (3) Moses confronts Aaron, receives a report that what has happened is as bad as he feared, and calls upon those truly loyal to Yahweh to aid in the punishment of those who apparently are the leading and worst offenders (vv 21–29); (4) Moses again intercedes for the people, identifying himself with them if Yahweh will not forgive them, but Yahweh promises punishment for the guilty in due course and then proceeds to level a blow of unspecified nature upon the people in punishment for their affair with the calf (vv 30–35). The larger narrative is not complete at this point, of course; indeed all this is in a way a preparation for what is still to come.

Exod 32 thus presents a deliberately repetitive mosaic of reaction to the sin of the calf; a didactic dramatization of the seriousness of Israel's sin, alternating the anger of Yahweh with the anger of Moses; and the pleading of Moses with the tempering of Yahweh's intended punishment. Even so, chap. 32 leaves an impression of incompleteness, of exploration, of movement toward some punishment to be decided upon that will be more fitting for a sin as monstrous as Israel's. This impression is quite intentional: the sequence of Exod 32 is a brilliant coaxing of disparate parts into a narrative of movement toward something, a something revealed with all the more impact because of such a preparation.

7–10 The terse imperatives of Yahweh's command to Moses provide a dramatic continuation of the narrative of the calf that ends with the words, "they rose to frivolity." A momentum of haste is built by a chain reaction of verbs: "Go! Descend! . . . you brought . . . have gone to ruin . . . have turned away quickly . . . have made a calf . . . have bowed themselves down . . . have made sacrifices . . . have said . . . ," and that sequence is matched by an intermeshed sequence describing Yahweh's prior action and present response: "I have commanded . . . I have seen . . . I know . . . my anger will burn hot . . . I will destroy . . . I will make you alone . . . ." Following such an outburst, it is not surprising that Moses "attempted to calm Yahweh his God."

11–14 Moses' whole concern is with the people: he seems not to have realized the gravity of their actions, that they have themselves negated their privileged relationship with Yahweh. Thus he gives a series of reasons why Yahweh should not carry through his intended destruction of Israel: (1) Yahweh has gone to great trouble to free them from the Egyptians and bring them this far; (2) the Egyptians will interpret such an action wrongly, as a slander of Yahweh's intention and ability; (3) Yahweh should have pity on his own people, faced with such harm; and (4) there is the important matter of the promise to the fathers, to whom Yahweh had bound himself by oath, to give them both a numberless progeny and a wide land. At the end of these logical arguments of Moses (paralleled in part by Num 14:13–19 and Deut 9:25–29), Yahweh is not reported to have said anything (though cf. Num 14:20–23), but is said to have been moved with pity for Israel under such a threat as he had made. The implication of this statement is of course that he tempered but did not altogether waive his judgment, and this implication is confirmed in the continuation of the narrative, at both 32:34 and 35 and also at 33:17 and 34:6–7.

15–16 The report of Moses' descent of the mountain is begun with two verbs with special *waw* that match Yahweh's two imperative commands in v 7: Moses "turned" from his work of receiving Yahweh's instructions for living and worshiping and "began to descend" Sinai with the tablets containing the Testimony (see *Comment* on 31:18) in his hand. This report has attracted a unique description of the tablets as having writing on both sides and as being themselves the work of God. The writing on them is once again said to have been God's (as in 31:18). G. R. Driver's (*Semitic Writing*, 78–80) comment about early writing in stone, and Thomas's (*VT* 18 [1968] 120–21) note that this is a way of expressing the superlative nature of the writing on the tablets miss the point of this statement, the intention of which is to confirm God as the source of the commandments and therefore the authority behind them.

17 The trip down the mountain is presented with skillful brevity, the level of suspense being raised by what is *not* said, and by what we must therefore supply. In 24:13 (in the narrative that may originally have immediately preceded this one), we were told that Joshua accompanied Moses for a part of his further climb up the mountain. In the narrative of chap. 32, Moses has rejoined Joshua, and when they are within earshot of the camp below, Joshua catches the sound of Israel's wild celebration and blurts out the breathless phrase, "A noise of battle in the camp!"

18 Moses' reply, a short but graphic poem that has the texture of an ancient and well-worn report of a momentous event, belongs to the same genre as the song of Miriam/Moses (Exod 15:1 and 21). The poem turns on the threefold use, once in each of its three four-beat lines, of the word עַנּוֹת, pointed by the Masoretes עֲנוֹת in the first two lines and עַנּוֹת in the third line. The root of this form, ענה, can have to do with "answering, responding, being busy with, being bowed down by, singing" (cf. BDB, 772–77). Here it is apparently intended to describe a kind of responsorial or answering recitation or traditional expression. In response to Joshua's fear that he has caught the sounds of a battle, Moses rules out the two options that would mean the exultant victory-cry of triumph or the keening lamentation of defeat, then goes on to state what *he* hears—the disorganized, conflicting answering of random singing. Andersen (*VT* 16 [1966] 110–12) has made two proposals: (1) the loss of a word in the third line, for which he suggests a form of צחק "laugh;" (2) an original עֲנוֹת עֲנוֹת, to give "a sound of antiphonal singing" = a sound of worship; Edelmann (*VT* 16 [1966] 355, supported by Whybray, *VT* 17 [1967] 122) has made the unlikely proposal that עַנּוֹת in the third line of the poem should be read עֲנָת in reference to the Canaanite goddess Anat, without suggesting why.

19–20 When Moses arrived in the camp, he saw that he was right, and *his* anger then "burned hot." When this account has been taken as a separate narrative tradition, considered in isolation from its context, this reaction is usually explained as Moses' initial reaction when he first discovered the people's sin (see Hyatt, 301–4). In the composite narrative of Exod 32, however, Moses' reaction upon *seeing* the people's frenzied idolatry is contrasted with his earlier reaction upon *being told* about Israel and the calf by Yahweh, and his anger is thus paralleled with the anger of Yahweh's response. The seriousness of Israel's lapse is thus doubly and very effectively emphasized.

Moses' shattering of the tablets may be taken more as a symbol of the shattered relationship between Yahweh and Israel than as an expression of Moses' fury, and the total destruction of the calf is a further indication of the dreadful nature of Israel's sin. There is no basis for drawing a connection between Moses' requiring Israel to drink the remains of the burned and ground-up calf and the oracle-ritual of jealousy in Num 5:11–15, though such a connection has sometimes been made (so S. R. Driver, 353; Noth, 249–50; Gradwohl, *TZ* 19 [1963] 50–53; cf. *contra*, Moberly, *Mountain of God*, 199, n. 46). The more probable link may be with the "blow" of Yahweh referred to in v 35 (cf. Num 21:4–9, where the people are punished for speaking against Yahweh by the often fatal bites of serpents).

The destruction of the golden calf by burning and by grinding has been variously explained, sometimes as an evidence of a two-layered calf, wooden core and gold overlay (cf. Loewenstamm, *Bib* 48 [1967] 481–82; Fensham, *IEJ* 16 [1966] 191). While this may indeed be the case, the sequence "burning . . . grinding . . . scattering" occurs also in a Ugaritic text describing the destruction of the Canaanite god Mot by the goddess Anat (cf. Cassuto, *IEJ* 12 [1962] 77–86; ANET, 140:ii), and this has led to the view that the account of Moses' destruction of the calf is related to a set idiom describing the destruction of a god or an idol (Loewenstamm, *Bib* 56 [1975] 338–41, and, *contra,* Perdue, *Bib* 54 [1973] 237–46), perhaps even an idiom describing "ritual acts in a fixed form" (Fensham, 192–93).

21–24 The account of Moses' inquiry of Aaron concerning the calf can hardly be the attempt to exonerate Aaron it has sometimes been made out to be (cf. Cassuto, *Exodus,* 419–21; Hyatt, 309), at least not in the form in which it occurs here. The answer of Aaron to Moses' attempt to find some excuse for his capitulation only makes Aaron's guilt worse by showing that he *has* no excuse, beyond expediency under pressure and his own weakness. Aaron's response is begun in a manner quite similar to the beginning of Moses' response to Yahweh in v 11, but there the parallel ends. Moses uses a list of logical reasons that shift attention away from the people to the work, the reputation, the character, and the promises of Yahweh (vv 11–13); Aaron attempts to call attention away from his own involvement by putting the blame for what has happened on the people. He succeeds thereby only in appearing absurd: his accurate quotation of nearly the whole of what the people said to him (v 23 vis-à-vis v 32) loses its impact because he is not strong enough to let it speak for itself, and the line about the calf emerging by itself from the fire is not a myth of divine autogeneration (so Loewenstamm, *Bib* 48 [1967] 487–90), but the dazzling insight of a master narrator designed to show the hopelessness of Aaron's leadership and perhaps the contrasting magnificence of the leadership of Moses (cf. Childs's list of comparisons, 570).

25–29 The motif of Aaron's lack of control of Israel provides the transition to the next section of the composite narrative. After his interview with Aaron, Moses saw that the people were "out of control" because Aaron had allowed them to go out of control, and indeed that Aaron had thereby left them vulnerable to the slander of their enemies, a theme taken up with repeated dismay in the laments of the Psalter (see, for example, Pss 4, 5, 7, 22, 25, 26, 31, 35, 39, 41, 52, 55, 59, 64, 69, 70). Thus the narrative of the loyal Levites is introduced: whatever else it may have been as a separate narrative, this account does not function in the composite as a means of discrediting Aaron (who has already discredited himself) or primarily as an etiology of Levitical ordination (a matter dealt with in other texts) but as the report of how the out-of-control Israelites were brought under control once again.

The invitation Moses gives is to those who are "Yahweh's," that is, Yahweh's on Yahweh's terms, not *via* a calf or any other substitute devised by humans. Whether those who rallied to Moses' side had remained aloof from the calf-business or were, in the earliest form of the tradition, all Levites is of course impossible to say. The text says nothing on the former point, and its reference to the gathering and obedience of an all-Levite group of unbending loyalists is of course very suspicious, as Gunneweg (*Leviten*, 29–37; cf. Lehming, *VT* 10 [1960] 40–45), among many others, has pointed out. What is at the base of this account is in all likelihood an ancient story of those who remained loyal to Yahweh against all pressure to do otherwise, whether from the majority or family or neighbor or friend. The loyalty of such men (cf. also the loyalty of Aaron's grandson Phinehas, Num 25:6–12) provided in itself a kind of ordination to Yahweh's service that resulted in a blessing, but it is not likely that this "ordination," despite the use of the יד + מלא "fill + hand" idiom to describe it, was regarded as ordination to the ministry of worship in Yahweh's Presence described, for example, in Exod 29. Gunneweg, indeed, has described (14–81) the Levites to begin with as a kind of non-Priestly teaching order.

30–35 The further intercession of Moses for the people, presented in the composite as occurring on the day following the slaughter by the loyalists, though it presents Moses in a splendid light, is still quite inconclusive so far as Israel's situation is concerned. This is so for two reasons: (1) this narrative is designed to depict a Moses willing to suffer the plight of his people, over against an Aaron looking out only for himself, and (2) the movement of the composite is still forward, both in terms of the punishment of Israel, here predicted as certain but left undefined, and also in terms of Israel's continuation as Yahweh's people, if there is to be any, beyond the sin of the golden calf. Once more, whatever place this narrative had as a separate tradition, it has here been woven with consummate skill into a sequence rising toward the summit and conclusion of the book of Exodus.

Thus Moses, reminding the people once more of the gravity of their sin, announces to them that he will reascend the mountain toward Yahweh to seek atonement for them. He pleads with Yahweh, this time stating with candor the sin and its critical seriousness. In a phrase that seems awkwardly incomplete in Hebrew (either a word has dropped out or the narrator is attempting to represent Moses having difficulty saying what he wants to say), Moses asks Yahweh to forgive Israel or to erase his own name from the book Yahweh has written, a reference apparently to a register of those loyal to Yahweh and thereby deserving his special blessing (cf. Ps 69:28; Isa 4:3; Ezek 13:9; Durham, "Psalms," *BBC* [Nashville: Broadman, 1970] 4:310–12). It is a magnificent petition, but one that dramatizes both the seriousness of Israel's sin and the impossibility of the healing of relationship by anyone save the persons who have compromised it. Yahweh cannot overlook what Israel has done, for their sin has destroyed the basis of his interchange with them. Moses cannot atone by the sacrifice of himself for a disobedience of which he is not guilty. Yahweh's response to Moses makes this abundantly clear. No one save Yahweh himself can undertake to do what Moses here wants to do, and even he cannot accomplish it for those unwilling to open themselves.

Thus Yahweh's answer is no surprise: the one who sins must be blotted from the book; Moses is to go and to guide the people toward a prearranged destination. Then suddenly, there is a flashing reflection of what is to come, of what Yahweh has in mind: his messenger will go before Moses. It is a hint only, and the suspense is maintained by an immediate shift back to the reality of Israel's most terrible moment: there is to be a day of taking account, and Yahweh will take account (פָקַד) upon Israel for their sin. This sobering announcement, the only possible answer to Moses' prayer, has attracted the brief notice of a blow leveled by Yahweh at Israel because of their sin with the calf. As noted above (on v 20), this verse is probably a remnant of a tradition describing an epidemic of some kind as Yahweh's punishment of Israel because of the calf. It serves now as an emphatic underscoring of Yahweh's response to Moses and adds to the suspense to be resolved only in chap. 33.

Explanation

The tight composite narrative of Exod 32–34 is brought tumbling toward its climax by the accounts of Moses' anger and Yahweh's judgment in 32:7–35. The monstrous and unthinkable sin of Israel with the golden calf, described in 32:1–6, calls for an immediate and drastic response, and these remaining verses of chap. 32 provide a mosaic of response traditions, all of which *might* have been Yahweh's response but none of which really and finally was. Thus these traditions have been molded into a suspenseful narrative pulling us toward what amounts to the only possible response of Yahweh, given the framework of theological emphasis that supports the Book of Exodus as a whole. The series of Moses' reactions has been interwoven with traditions about Yahweh's response in so skillful a manner that we are caught up in an ascending sequence of possibilities, each of which seems *the* response until the next one comes along. Moses' reactions, each one of which seems so natural and so entirely appropriate, are crystal-clear to us, in part because they are either of us or of us as we would like to be, and so we are drawn into the serious drama that is really our own story anyway. Yahweh's response seems clear at first and then ambiguous as he draws back from his first intention, then refuses to forgive, then announces darkly an account-taking to come. At the end of chap. 32, we have no answers, only questions: what *will* Yahweh do? what is to become of Israel? Moses? the Covenant-Promises? the Revelation, the Guiding Principles, the Instructions?

All this is quite deliberate. Moses' first response, upon hearing what Israel has done, is to plead with Yahweh to spare the lives of Israel; his second response, upon seeing what Israel is doing, is outraged anger; his third response is to assess the situation at hand, probing for the reasons for it; his fourth response is to bring Israel under control by the slaughter of a large number of them, apparently their leaders in the matter of the calf; his fifth response is to plead with Yahweh for mercy for Israel, even at the cost of the loss of his own special relationship with Yahweh. The range of this response includes survival, anger, reason, an end to the sinning, and merciful forgiveness. Yahweh's first response is anger, his second response pity. Though he does not follow through with his threat to destroy Israel, he also does not forgive them their sin. In fact, his anger does not pass. Moses changes from section to section of the narrative of Exod 32:7–35, but Yahweh does not, really. And we are brought up to Exod 33 with all questions, one small hint in the command to Moses and the promise of the messenger (v 34), but no answers. It is a brilliant, symphonic preparation for the climax of the Book of Exodus.

The Command to Leave Sinai   (33:1–6)

Bibliography

Baumgartner, W. "Zum Problem des 'Jahwe-Engels.' " *Zum Alten Testament und Seiner Unwelt.* Leiden: E. J. Brill, 1959. 240–46. **Coats, G. W.** "The King's Loyal Opposition: Obedience and Authority in Exodus 32–34." *Canon and Authority.* Ed. G. W. Coats and B. O. Long. Philadelphia: Fortress Press, 1977. 91–109. **Rudolph, W.** "Der Aufbau von Exodus 19–34." *Werden und Wesen des Alten Testaments.* BZAW 66. Berlin: Verlag von Alfred Töpelmann, 1936. 41–48. **Vermeylen, J.** "L'affaire du veau d'or (Ex 32–34). Une clé pour la 'question deuteronomiste'?" *ZAW* 97 (1985) 1–23.

Translation

¹ *Then Yahweh spoke to Moses: "Go! Ascend from this place, you and the people whom you have brought up from the land of Egypt* ᵃ *to the land I swore to cede to Abraham, to Isaac, and to Jacob, saying, 'to your descendants I will give it.'* ² *I will send out in front of you a messenger,* ᵃ *and I will drive out headlong the Canaanites, the Amorites, the Hittites,* ᵇ *the Perizzites, the Hivites, and the Jebusites.* ³ *To a land gushing with milk and honey you are to go;* ᵃ *however, I am not going up in your midst lest I destroy you en route, because you are an obstinate people."*

⁴ *When the people heard this dreadful news,* ᵃ *they plunged themselves into deep mourning.* ᵇ *Not one of them wore* ᶜ *his festive dress.* ᵈ ⁵ *Indeed, Yahweh had said to Moses, "Say to the sons of Israel, 'you* ᵃ *are an obstinate people: I go up in your midst for one moment, and I will finish you off! Now put off from yourselves your festive dress. I will decide* ᵇ *what I am to do with you.' "* ⁶ *Thus the sons of Israel divested themselves of their festive dress from Mount Horeb on.*

Notes

1.a. The statement of Yahweh to Moses to this point is very close to his statement in 32:7. There the message was for Moses; here it is for Israel as well.

2.a. LXX has τὸν ἀγγελόν μου "my messenger," and this messenger, rather than Yahweh, expels the peoples of the land.

2.b. SamPent includes at this point the Girgashites to give the list of seven peoples recorded in Deut 7:1. LXX also includes the Girgashites but omits the Canaanites, who are nevertheless added in some LXX texts (see Rahlfs's note on Exod 33:2).

3.a. MT has no verb in the opening clause of this verse, which may be understood as governed by the impvs that begin Yahweh's statement in v 1. LXX adds καὶ εἰσάξω σε "and I will lead you in"; Vg has *et intres* "and you will enter." The attempt above is to keep the sense of the governing impv.

4.a. הדבר הרע הזה "this evil word."

4.b. Hithp אבל "mourn, lament," generally for the dead (cf. BDB, 5); the most abject remorse and grief are intended here.

4.c. שׁית "put on, donned."

4.d. עדי refers to ornamental or fancy dress, any attire that might suggest not just joyful life, but even life as normal; cf. BDB, 725–26.

5.a. אתם "you" pl here; אתה "you" sg in the similar statement of v 3.

5.b. LXX reads δείξω σοι "I will show you" instead of "I will decide."

Form/Structure/Setting

See above, *Form/Structure/Setting* on 32:1–6 and 32:7–35. The shifting pronouns (v 3 vis-à-vis v 5) and awkward syntax (v 3, following upon v 1, with the parenthetic v 2) and unusual sequencing (v 5, with its command regarding festive dress, preceded [v 4] by the report that the people did not put it on, then followed [v 6] by the report that they took it off) have led to a frequent assessment of this section as a composite of material from several sources. Rudolph (*Werden und Wesen*, 45–46, 48), for example, considered it a mixture of J (v 1a), non-J polemical material (vv 3b–6) and secondary, interpolative material (vv 1b–3a); Beer (13, 156–57) divided it among his J² (vv 1, 3, 4), the JE redaction (v 2), and E, to which he attributed vv 5–11 as a unit (vv 5–6, E²; vv 7–11, E); Noth (253–54) regarded it "of Deuteronomic origin" but nevertheless a patchwork held together with the rest of the "very varied pieces of Ex. 33" "by the theme of the presence of God in the midst of his people;" Hyatt (312–15) thought it a Deuteronomic redaction using material from J (vv 1, 3a) and E (vv 3b–6); Beyerlin (*Sinaitic Traditions*, 22–24) has allocated vv 1–3a to J and vv 3b–4 and 5–6 to two variants of E connected with 32:34; Vermeylen (*ZAW* 97 [1985] 8–15 has assigned vv 2–4 to the second of his "redactions by the Deuteronomistic school" and vv 1, 5–6 to the third of them.

In fact, the variety of these opinions and others like them suggest (1) that any precise divisions of Exod 33:1–6 into component sources is, without more information than we have, impossible; (2) that the differences within these verses that have been taken as indications of separate sources and variants may in some instances have been deliberately kept or even introduced by the compiler of this sequence; and (3) that these verses are best understood as a whole and within the larger whole, Exod 32–34, of which they are a part. The use of a variety of materials here, as throughout the Exod 32–34 composite, is clear; but these verses cannot be subdivided with any certainty, and the attempts to do so have tended to obscure the very deliberate momentum the narrative is intended to present.

Exod 33:1–6 continues the preparatory composite of 32:7–34, at the end of which 32:35 has been placed, a fragment of a tradition of Yahweh's punishment by epidemic (see above), attracted by Yahweh's assertion (v 34) of a day of accounting to come. Yahweh has already commanded Moses to "go, guide," and has promised that his divine messenger will go in front of Moses. The command is now taken up again, and the hint of the messenger and his work is given explication, but the real result of the sin of Israel with the calf is mentioned for the first time: because of what Israel has turned out to be, Yahweh's Presence will go with them no longer. The most they can expect is a divine messenger to guide them. Yahweh's presence in their midst, in the aftermath of what has happened, is too dangerous.

Thus all the questions piled up at the end of chap. 32 are answered, and the answer is so incredible and so unexpected by Israel that it is given twice (vv 3 and 5). It plunges Israel into the grief that death alone can bring and poses in a new and more terrible way the awful question of their own fate. That question is still left deliberately unresolved; Yahweh has yet to decide on its solution (v 5). And so Israel falls into an attitude of abject gloom. This terrible statement of Yahweh and the resultant devastating grief, the first twice stated, the second three times emphasized in the sequence of only four verses (3–6), are the center of Exod 33:1–6 and the expression of the purpose that gives this section its form. The compiler has deliberately piled up repetitions of his theme to create a powerful and dramatic preparation for what is to come, the single answer to the one question uppermost in both Yahweh's mind ("I will decide what I am to do with you," v 5) and Israel's mind ("they plunged themselves into deep mourning," v 4).

Comment

1   There is a rhetorical connection between this verse and 32:7. There, Yahweh says to Moses alone: "Go! Descend!" Here, he gives Moses a command that includes Israel also: "Go! Ascend. . . ." Here and there, Israel is called the people whom *Moses* brought up from the land of Egypt. It is almost as if Yahweh cannot bear to take any responsibility for a people who have behaved as Israel has. In view of their disregard for their covenant relationship, he has no obligation to take any further responsibility. Yet he does. It is a motif that comes to an apex in 34:6–10, and is focused with searing sharpness by Num 11:10–23. The reference to the covenant promise to the fathers is connected of course with 32:13, and the expansion of the hint of the divine messenger given in 32:34 also underscores the continuity between 33:1–6 and the sequence that precedes it.

2–3   The sending of this divine מלאך "messenger" has generally been taken as a positive move on Yahweh's part, against which the statement immediately following, that Yahweh himself will not go up among them, becomes a *non sequitur* and for some scholars an indication therefore of another source or of a layer within a source (cf. Rudolph, *Werden und Wesen*, 45–46; Beyerlin, *Sinaitic Traditions*, 22–24; Hyatt, 313; Childs, 585–86). Another view is possible, however. Yahweh's command of Moses and Israel to leave Sinai, the mountain of his Presence, must be read as more than a mere transition to the next part of the narrative. Israel has by the sin with the calf destroyed both their right to remain near a place of Yahweh's Presence and also Yahweh's desire to be present in their midst. His command that they leave Sinai must be seen in this light. It is like Yahweh's expulsion of the man and the woman from the Garden of Delight (Gen 3:14–24) or even Yahweh's separation of Cain from his family and from the soil (Gen 4:10–16). It is the first hint, indeed, of the punishment Yahweh had decided to bring upon Israel.

The interpolation of the tradition of the promise of land to the fathers, made necessary by the need to state a destination for Moses and Israel, if they are to leave Sinai, suggests the inclusion also of the tradition concerning the displacement of hostile peoples from the land, and that in turn calls for a repetition of the tradition of the richness and desirability of the land. These traditions, in turn, require the inclusion of a means of guidance, hinted at in 32:34 and promised still farther back in the Exodus composite, at 23:20–24 (see above), but the nature of the guidance this messenger is to give is immediately qualified by the stark announcement of the punishment Yahweh will mete out to Israel for their sin with the calf. It is not to be a plague, and it is not to be death by some other means. Indeed, it is to be the most appropriate response possible to Israel's compromise of their relationship with him, and a punishment worse than death.

They are to go up, guided by his messenger, to the place he had chosen and in which he had intended to live in their midst, but without him. In the place of his Presence, there was to be only Absence. It is a punishment, announced at this point in the sequence of the Book of Exodus, that negates every announcement, every expectation, every instruction except those now being given. There will be no special treasure, no kingdom of priests, no holy nation, no Yahweh being their God, no covenant, no Ark, no Tabernacle, no Altar, no cloud of Glory. The messenger promised in 23:20–24 was, as is so often the case in the OT, a close equivalent, at the very least, of Yahweh's Presence (see esp. 23:21, "my Presence is with him"—cf. above; Baumgartner, *Zum Alten Testament*, 244), but the messenger mentioned here is quickly and very specifically qualified: (1) his function is guidance only, and (2) Yahweh plainly states that he himself will *not* go up with them. Israel must leave Sinai, the place where they have known Yahweh's Presence, and they must journey forth in a way to have been graced by his Presence to a place to have been filled with his Presence with no hope of his Presence ever again (cf. Coats, *Canon and Authority*, 100–101).

4–6 In the light of such an interpretation, the account of the people's reaction makes sense both as a continuation of the narrative of vv 1–3 and also as an expression of bitter and hopeless grief. The people could hardly be expected to be plunged into such abysmal grief by an announcement of a tempered judgment. What they are told by Yahweh amounts to the worst of all possible outcomes from their point of view, but the only one we could logically expect, given the theological framework of Exodus. Yahweh's word is thus quite appropriately called "dreadful news," and the people thus "plunge themselves into deep mourning."

As an expression of their grief, the people do not wear any "ornamentation" or "festive dress" (עֶדְיוֹ), and by this inclusion of yet another tradition of Yahweh's terrible announcement and the people's abject grief, the compiler of this sequence provides an explanation of this symbol of the people's mourning and effectively doubles the impact of his narrative. Yahweh had told Moses to say to Israel, "You are an obstinate people" (this time with a plural "you," by contrast to the collective singular "you" of the similar statement of v 3), and to explain to them the awesome danger involved in his continued Presence with them, even "for a single moment." He had also instructed that they should divest themselves of any festive dress. In the context of the composite narrative, this latter instruction may be taken as an indication that an immediate expression of the people's grief was to become a permanent one, not least because their grief was to be a permanent one.

There is no reason to assume that the festive dress the people here put off was what they had put on for festivities at Sinai (so Beer, 156), nor is there any basis for the assumption that the ornamentation the people set aside here was used to make the Tent of Appointed Meeting mentioned in the verses that follow (7–11; cf. Driver, 358), or the Ark (Dibelius, *Lade Jahves*, 45–47; Davies, 238; cf. Haran, 262–65), and it is, of course, useless to see any discrepancy between this setting aside of festive dress and the call for special materials for the construction of the Tabernacle and its equipment and the sacral vestments of chaps. 25 and 35. The present text is concerned only with depicting Israel's profound mourning of the threatened loss of Yahweh's Presence and to express that grief has utilized a tradition, no doubt quite ancient, of mourning dress.

The punishment of Yahweh having been announced and the people having been plunged into deep grief, there remains still the question of Israel's fate. The people are to be guided to the land promised them and prepared for them by Yahweh, who is represented as determined to keep his word on that score. But without Yahweh's Presence, what is to become of Israel? At the end of this section, that matter remains unresolved: Yahweh says, "I will decide what I am to do with you." Thus the dramatic narrative of Exod 32–34 is opened to its next and climactic stage by a tiny glimmer of light across the black darkness cast by the announcement of Yahweh's Absence. Yahweh must yet decide what he is to do with his ex-people.

Explanation

The terrible announcement of Yahweh's punishment, anticipated with rising suspense throughout Exod 32:7–34, is made in 33:1–6 in two stages: Israel is to leave Sinai, where Yahweh gave his Presence to them, and even worse, they are to make their way without his Presence. Their sin with the golden calf, a rejection of their relationship with Yahweh, is to end in the removal of any possibility of further relationship. Yahweh will leave them, and even with Moses and the divine messenger to guide them, they will be alone, all alone. The great narrative of promised Presence and the great narrative of the Advent of Presence are thus to be brought to an abrupt and empty conclusion by a narrative of Absence.

Little wonder that the people plunge themselves into deepest mourning and remove all suggestions of joy from themselves. They have lost their very identity, as Moses is later to say (33:16). All that Yahweh had planned has come to a bitter end by their irresponsible behavior. All that they already were stands canceled.

And in such a manner the narrative of Exod 32–34, and also of Exodus as a whole, is brought to the threshold of its own Holiest Space.

The Tent of Appointed Meeting   (33:7–11)

Bibliography

Dumermuth, F. "Josua in Ex. 33, 7–11." *TZ* 19 (1963) 161–68. **Rad, G. von.** "The Tent and the Ark." *The Problem of the Hexateuch and Other Essays.* Edinburgh: Oliver & Boyd, 1966. 103–24. **Rost, L.** "Die Wohnstätte des Zeugnisses." *Festschrift Friedrich Baumgärtel.* Erlangen: Verlag, Universitätsbund Erlangen, 1959. 158–65. **Sellin, E.** "Das Zelt Jahwes." *Alttestamentliche Studien R. Kittel.* BWANT 13. Leipzig: J. C. Hinrichs, 1913. 168–92. **Vaux, R. de.** "Ark of the Covenant and Tent of Reunion." *The Bible and the Ancient Near East.* Garden City, NY: Doubleday & Company, 1971. 136–51.

Translation

> [7a] *And Moses was accustomed to take [b] the Tent and he would set it up outside the camp, at some distance from the camp, and he would call it a "Tent of Appointed Meeting." Everyone seeking the will of Yahweh [c] was accustomed to go out to this [d] Tent of Appointed Meeting, which was outside the camp.* [8] *When Moses would go out to the Tent, all the people were accustomed to stand up, and each man would take a position [a] at the opening of his own tent. They would gaze at Moses until he entered the Tent.* [9] *When Moses went into the Tent, the column of cloud was accustomed to come down and would station itself at the opening of the Tent, and Yahweh [a] would speak with Moses.* [10] *When all the people would see the column of cloud standing at the opening of the Tent, all the people would stand up: then each man would prostrate himself in worship at the opening of his own tent.* [11] *So Yahweh would speak to Moses face to face, just as a man speaks to his neighbor. Moses [a] would return to the camp, but his helper Joshua, son of Nun ("One Who Increases"),[b] a young man, was not accustomed to leave the interior of the Tent.*

Notes

7–11.a. This entire section appears to be a unit inserted into an otherwise dramatic and forward-moving composite narrative and so is marked by a vertical line in the left margin. See below, *Form/Structure/Setting.*

7.b. The verbs in this sequence of five verses appear to present a sequence of customary actions, which are indicated above by the use of "was accustomed to" with the governing impf verbs, followed by the use of "would" with the series of pf verbs with special *waw.* Cf. GKC, ¶ 112e. It is possible, since this section seems to be a part of a larger sequence dealing with a wilderness tent, that the beginning and perhaps also the end of the sequence lie outside the verses we have.

7.c. בקש "seek" (cf. also דרש "seek") with Yahweh as dir obj has the near-technical meaning of seeking an oracle from Yahweh. See Gerleman, "בקש *suchen,*" *THAT* 1:335.

7.d. MT leaves אל־אהל מועד "to a tent of appointed meeting" indefinite, but the context makes clear that the same tent is intended.

8.a. LXX has σκοπεύοντες "stand looking" instead of "take a position."

9.a. MT has simply ודבר "and he spoke." Yahweh, clearly the subj of the verb, is added above to avoid an ambiguous translation.

11.a. MT has simply ושב "and he returned"; "Moses" is added above for clarity.

11.b. נון "propagate, increase," BDB, 630. Noth (*Personennamen,* 229–30) includes נון in his list of names taken from "animal names" and makes it equivalent, though with no explanation, to "fish."

Form/Structure/Setting

See *Form/Structure/Setting* on 32:1–6 and 32:7–35.

These verses are so strikingly different in both content and style from the dramatically arranged narrative composite that precedes and follows them that they have given rise to a wide variety of explanations concerning their origin, and above all their purpose in relation to their present setting. They have been attributed to both J (Newman, *People of the Covenant*, 63–71; possibly, says Noth, 254–55, though he favors a "special tradition" taken up by J) and also (more generally) to E (Beer, 156–59; Hyatt, 314–15), though not universally as a unity (cf. Beyerlin, *Sinaitic Traditions* 112–26, who thinks E took over an old tradition and then reworked it). In fact, there is not enough clear evidence in Exod 33:7–11 to make a firm source assignment.

The location of these verses here has likewise stimulated considerable discussion. A conjecture of some years' standing (going back at least to Wellhausen, *Composition des Hexateuchs*, 93) that Exod 33:7–11 continues an account (generally assigned to E) of the making (from the Israelites' cast-off "ornaments" of 33:4–6) of the Ark, for which in turn the Tent described here was to provide the shelter, is an argument without evidence. Despite frequent attempts to connect the Ark and this Tent of Appointed Meeting (see esp. Beyerlin, *Sinaitic Traditions*, 112–26; de Vaux, *The Bible* 136–51; and also, by a somewhat different theory, von Rad, *Problem of the Hexateuch*, 102–24) no strong and convincing argument for doing so has yet been presented, a fact which has led Haran (*Temples*, 267–69; for an earlier version of the discussion of the "*ʾohel moʿedh*," see *JSS* 5 [1960] 50–65), among others, to propose *two* tents in pre-Priestly tradition, one within the camp of Israel, to house the Ark between journeys (cf. also de Vaux, 141–42), and one outside the camp, entirely empty, that provided a place of meeting with Yahweh. The former of these two tents is of course a speculation, though a reasonable one. The OT refers to two tents that function in such a manner, one of them the Tent outside the camp, described in the verses at hand; but the other one is the Tabernacle of P, described in Exod 26:1–37 and 36:8–38.

The tradition of a Tent outside the camp, set up specifically as a meeting place appointed by Yahweh, a place where he made his Presence available on a periodic basis, to Moses primarily, but through Moses to any honest suppliant, is best regarded as an ancient tradition. This ancient tradition is reflected in Num 11:16–30; 12:4–16; Deut 31:14–15; and 1 Sam 2:22, and recalled, perhaps, in 1 Chr 16:39–40; 21:29–30; and 2 Chr 1:3, 13, albeit in a somewhat garbled fashion (cf. Haran, *Temples*, 199–200), but the primary description of its purpose is in the section at hand, Exod 33:7–11. This Tent for trysting, pointedly remembered as the אֹהֶל מוֹעֵד "Tent of Appointed Meeting," literally, a "tent of assembly by appointment," had no connections with the Ark, or with any other palpable symbol of Yahweh's Presence, nor with any rituals of sacrifice or offering. It was exclusively and solely a place where Yahweh's Presence could be met, as Haran (265–69) has described it, a kind of post-Sinai point of theophany (though Haran's insistence, 265–67, that Moses met Yahweh only *outside* the Tent, at its entrance, seems a bit forced).

When this Tent originated, of course, we have no way of knowing, but there is no good reason to deny it to the wilderness period. How long it was in use in its original and "pure" form is equally impossible to say. By the time of the P concept of the Tabernacle, the tradition of a Tent of Appointed Meeting had become amalgamated with the concept of Yahweh's Presence in his people's midst (cf. Rost, *Festschrift F. Baumgärtel,* 158–65; Childs, 530–37; Haran, *Temples,* 271–75), and thus capital letters are used in the translation of P's usages of אהל מועד, to give "Tent of Appointed Meeting." About the significance of the Tent of Appointed Meeting however there can be little question: its name, the OT references to it, and even its integration into the P tradition of the Tabernacle all make clear that this Tent was a primary symbol of Yahweh's Presence, and especially of the accessibility of that Presence to those in need of guidance, represented primarily by Moses.

This significance of the Tent of Appointed Meeting, even more than the style of 33:7–11 or its discontinuity with the narrative surrounding it, makes clear the complete dislocation of these verses in their present setting. The whole point of the composite narrative of 32:1–33:6 is that Yahweh, because of the sin of Israel with the calf, is *not* accessible to his people, and indeed intends fully that they should henceforth know only Absence. 33:12–17 continues that narrative and resolves its terrible tension at last with Yahweh's decision *not* to withdraw his Presence. An account of an appointed place in which Yahweh is accustomed to make himself available to his people simply does not fit into such a narrative. Attempts to make it fit, whether by the supposition of original information now missing (Dibelius, *Lade Jahves,* 45–47; Sellin, *Alttestamentliche Studien* 168–72; de Vaux, *The Bible,* 140–42; Clements, *God and Temple,* 36–38) or by the theory that the Tent of Appointed Meeting provided access to Yahweh in spite of his judgment (Cassuto, 429–32; Moberly, *Mountain of God,* 63–64) serve only to call further attention to the obvious inconsistencies presented by these verses. Childs (591–93) suggests that vv 7–11 either have found their way into chap. 33 "by sheer accident" or that these verses, though originally independent of the narrative of Exod 33, have been deliberately located where they now are because of the topical connection (Moses as intercessor) and as a means of showing "a transformed people" and "an indirect" accompaniment of Israel by Yahweh. Childs's theory is imaginative, but perhaps too much so; though it is an admirable attempt to take seriously the text in its canonical form, it might work better if vv 7–11 had been located at the end of the dramatic Presence-Absence narrative, following 33:17 or 34:9 or even 34:35. As it stands, this brief notice about the Tent of Appointed Meeting simply cannot be made to fit its present location in the received text.

How, then, did these verses come to their canonical place? Childs's (591) suggestion of a "sheer accident" is nearer the truth than his other theory, but it too may be a bit excessive. The old tradition of a trysting Tent may have been considered by the compilers of Exodus too important to omit, and thus they may well have tried several locations for it. They could not locate it before the narrative of the revelation by Yahweh of his Presence at Sinai, nor in too close a proximity to the P accounts of the Tabernacle, with which it could (and has) so easily become confused. Thus finally, they placed it in the account of the aftermath of Israel's sin with the calf (1) because it dealt with the subject of access to Yahweh's Presence, about to be denied because of that sin, and (2) because of the practical problem created by Yahweh's order to Moses and Israel to leave Sinai. There is no hint, anywhere in the OT, that access to Yahweh's presence at the Tent of Appointed Meeting was in any way a weakened or more aloof kind of access; the problem is that until the decision of Yahweh is revealed in 33:17, Israel has *no* access, of any kind. Indeed, Moses' own authority as Yahweh's representative to Israel, compromised by Israel's request for the calf in 32:1, is not fully reestablished in the narrative before 34:27–35.

The location of Exod 33:7–11 may thus be seen to have a logical basis, in some ways more of one than Exod 18, which also appears to be dislocated (see above). But it is nevertheless an unfortunate placement, because it is one that interrupts the single most powerful compiled narrative in the entire Book of Exodus. For that reason alone the movement of Exod 32:7–11 into its present location can be fixed in a period later than the compilation of the narrative sequence preserved in 32:1–34, 33:1–6, 12–34:9.

Comment

7–9 The action of Moses in setting up *the* Tent (הָאֹהֶל) has been variously taken as an action for himself (Cassuto, 430; Haran, *Temples*, 264, n. 6; cf. LXX, which even calls the Tent "his Tent") or for the ark (Beyerlin, *Sinaitic Traditions*, 114; de Vaux, *The Bible*, 141). וּנְטָה־לֹו is better read either "he would set it up for him (= Yahweh)" (so Beer, 156, n. 7ᵈ) or, as translated above, "he would set up לֹו," i.e., "he would perform the setting-up operation with reference to it (= the Tent)," taking "it" here as a dative of specification, or reference (as in 2 Sam 6:17, where the same phrase occurs, interestingly enough in reference to the Ark). This verse appears to be a part of a sequence, the loss of whose first part makes the statement about Moses' action more ambiguous than it would otherwise be. The essential point of v 7, in any case, is the placement well outside the camp (a point triply emphasized) of a tent aptly named by Moses "the Tent of Appointed Meeting."

This Tent was deliberately located outside the normal patterns of traffic and provided a place of access to the Presence of Yahweh for those seeking to know his will, whether by oracle or in some other manner. When Moses left the camp on his way to the Tent, Israel knew that an appointed meeting with Yahweh was at least possible. Therefore they gazed after Moses, not out of any respect or deference to him (so Childs, 592–93), but because of the unique experience of communion with Yahweh about to take place. The people's gaze was on Moses until he entered the Tent; then they had something else as the focus of the experience, for when Moses had entered the Tent, the column of cloud both symbolizing and concealing Yahweh's Presence would descend and take up a position at the opening of the Tent. From this cloud, Yahweh would speak to Moses, and presumably (v 7) through Moses to anyone else who might come out to the Tent with a petition.

10 At their first sight of the column of cloud at the entrance of the Tent, the people knew that the appointed meeting had passed from possibility to reality, and they would respectfully and appropriately stand and then prostrate themselves in worship before the opening of their own tents. Though so much is not said, we may assume that the people remained in a position of adoration and obeisance as long as the cloud was in place, indicating the continuation of Yahweh's conversation with Moses. Whatever historical memory may or may not be reflected here, the theological point, awe in the Presence of Yahweh, is presented with telling impact.

11   The reference to the intimacy of Yahweh's communion with Moses is almost certainly to be considered a reflection of the traditions represented by the narratives of 33:12–17 and 33:18–34:9. As the second of these narratives makes clear, "face to face" is here to be understood as an idiom of intimacy, not as a reference to theophany. Following the conversation with Yahweh, presumably indicated by the ascension or disappearance of the cloud, Moses returned to the camp, a move that apparently would mean a return to normal activity in the camp. The continued presence in the Tent of Joshua is not to be taken as an indication of some continuing cultic activity there, whether of priestly service (cf. Beyerlin, *Sinaitic Traditions*, 114–16) or by a continuation in Moses' absence of an intermediary function before Yahweh (cf. Dumermuth, *TZ* 19 [1963] 161–68). Joshua here or elsewhere in Exodus is Moses' assistant, and his role in the Tent is probably that of a guard.

Explanation

The five verses of Exod 33:7–11, therefore, as important as they are, are nonetheless completely out of place in the taut narrative of Exod 32:1–34:9. They have been attracted to their present location by logical associations of both topic and overall sequence in the Book of Exodus. Even so, they now disrupt an otherwise carefully directed narrative mosaic.

The verses themselves are concerned with the continuation of access to Yahweh's decision-giving Presence after the departure from Sinai, with the symbolism of his Presence in that role, with the role of Moses in continuing communion with Yahweh, and with the response of Israel, as typified by the men of Israel, during the times of that communion.

Moses' Plea for Mercy and Yahweh's Answer (33:12–17)

Bibliography

Baumann, E. "ידע und seine Derivate im Hebräischen." *ZAW* 28 (1908) 22–41, 110–43. **Eissfeldt, O.** *Die Komposition der Sinai-Erzählung Exodus 19–34.* Berlin: Akademie Verlag, 1966. **Labuschagne, C. J.** "The Emphasizing Particle *Gam* and Its Connotations." *Studia Biblica et Semitica.* Wageningen: H. Veenman & Sons, 1966. 193–203. **Muilenburg, J.** "The Intercession of the Covenant Mediator (Exodus 33:1a,12–17)." *Words and Meanings.* Ed. P. R. Ackroyd and B. Lindars. Cambridge: University Press, 1968. 159–81. **Rudolph, W.** "Der Aufbau von Exodus 19–34." *Werden und Wesen des Alten Testaments.* BZAW 66. Berlin: Verlag von Alfred Töpelmann, 1936. 41–48.

Translation

¹² So Moses replied ᵃ to Yahweh, "Consider! ᵇ You have said to me, 'Ascend with ᶜ this people!' Yet you ᵈ have not let me know ᵉ whom you will send forth with me. You have said, 'I know you by name, ᶠ and you have indeed ᵍ found favor in my estimation.' ¹³ Now, please, if I really have found favor in your estimation, please let me know your intention, ᵃ in order that I may keep on finding ᵇ favor in your estimation. And consider: that this people is your very own people." ᶜ

¹⁴ Then Yahweh ᵃ said, "My Presence will go. ᵇ Thus will I dispel your anxiety." ᶜ ¹⁵ Moses ᵃ replied to him, "If your Presence does not go, do not bring us ᵇ up from this place. ¹⁶ How indeed is it to become known as a fact ᵃ that I have found favor in your estimation, I myself and your people, except in your going with us? In that are we separated, ᵇ I myself and your people, from all the people who are upon the surface of the earth."

¹⁷ Thus Yahweh said to Moses, "Indeed the very thing ᵃ you have spoken, I will do: because you really have found favor in my estimation, and I know you by name." ᵇ

Notes

12.a. ויאמר "and he said," continuing the narrative of 33:1–5, to which 33:6 is an explanatory note, following which 33:7–11 is a disrupting insertion; see *Form/Structure/Setting* on 33:7–11.

12.b. ראה; "consider" cf. BDB, 907 § 7.

12.c. העל את־העם הזה is, lit., "Cause to go up this people." The hiphil impv הַעַל is, however, a rhetorical link to the qal impv עֲלֵה of v 1. Both these occurrences of impv עלה thus are translated above by "ascend."

12.d. The emphasis is shown by the use of אתה "you" in addition to the 2d masc sg hiph of ידע "know."

12.e. לא הודעתני "you have not caused me to know, revealed to me."

12.f. LXX has παρὰ πάντας "beyond, above all."

12.g. גם "indeed," a particle of emphasis, as Labuschagne (*Studia*, 193–203) has shown.

13.a. דרכך "your way," taken here in the sense of "purpose, direction, intention," and as a specific reference to Yahweh's statement in v 6, "I will decide what I am to do with you (לך = Israel)." LXX has a different reading altogether: ἐμφάνισόν μοι σεαυτόν· γνωστῶς ἴδω σε "show me yourself, so that I may see you clearly."

13.b. אֶמְצָא, impf, continuing action, following the pf מָצָאתִי earlier in the verse.

13.c. The emphasis, indicated above by "very own," is suggested by the order of the words עמך הגוי הזה, lit., "*your people* (is) this people." There is here also a clever play on the words גוי "people, nation" and עם "people," with גוי as a more general term and עם a more intimate term in this context.

14.a. MT has only ויאמר "and he said," but Yahweh is the clear subject so is added above to avoid ambiguity.

14.b. יֵלֵכוּ "they will go." This 3d masc pl qal impf הלך is a rhetorical link with the 2d masc sg qal impv of הלך in v 1, so both occurrences are translated "go." Cf. LXX Αὐτὸς προπορεύσομαί σου "I myself will go before you."

14.c. והנחתי לך "thus I will give rest, quiet to you." See BDB, 628 § 1.

15.a. MT has only ויאמר "and he said," but the subj of·the verb is clearly Moses.

15.b. LXX reads "me."

16.a. יִוָּדַע "known as a fact," 3d masc sg niph impf of ידע; read here as sure knowing, the knowing of experience as opposed to hearsay or mere rumor. Cf. Muilenburg, *Words and Meanings*, 179.

16.b. Niph פלה "be separated, distinguished from." LXX has καὶ ἐνδοξασθήσομαι ἐγώ τε καὶ ὁ λαός σου παρὰ πάντα τὰ ἔθνη "and I and your people shall be glorified, held in high honor . . . beyond all the nations."

17.a. גם את־הדבר הזה "indeed the very thing"; cf. Labuschagne, *Studia* 200.

17.b. See n. 12.f.

Form/Structure/Setting

See *Form/Structure/Setting* on 32:1–6 and 32:7–35.

With these verses, we are returned to the sequence of the composite narrative begun at Exod 32:1 and interrupted at 33:6 by the insertion of the account of the Tent of Appointed Meeting. Like most of the component sequences of the larger narrative sequence of which they are a part, these verses too must be understood primarily not in terms of any original source or sources from which they may have come, but as carefully integrated into a meaningful narrative sequence. The usual source assignment of Exod 33:12–17 is to J (so Driver, 360–62; Beyerlin, *Sinaitic Traditions*, 98–107; Hyatt, 316), with a frequent linking of this sequence to 24:3–11 (so Rudolph, *Werden und Wesen*, 46–48) as an "original locus" (Muilenburg, *Words and Meanings*, 162, n. 1). This assignment cannot, however, be maintained as anything more than general conjecture, as the divergent opinions indicate (Beer, 13, 158–59, e.g., considers 33:12–17 from the hand of J^s; Eissfeldt, *Composition*, 11, 31, largely a secondary addition to E; Zenger, *Sinaitheophanie*, 194–97, an amalgam of his "jehovistisches Geschichtswerk" [different from his "jahwistisches Geschichtswerk"], vv 12–14 and his "deuteronomistic revision," vv 15–17).

Muilenburg (*Words and Meanings*, 162–81), applying his rhetorical-critical technique, has proposed that Exod 33:12–17, along with its "introduction" in 33:1a, has preserved an ancient cultic liturgy presenting the plea of "the mediator of the covenant" to "Israel's Lord and Suzerain," Yahweh, reflecting ANE covenant-treaty formulary, and emphasizing, by the fivefold use of ידע, a special "covenantal knowing" "between Suzerain and vassal." Terrien (*Elusive Presence*, 138–52) considers these verses a part of his third collection of Sinai theophany traditions (108–9): 33:1a, 12–23, in his view, present in response to Yahweh's command to depart Sinai (33:1a) three pleas of Moses and three responses from Yahweh. These suggestions, interesting attempts to take seriously both the form and the language of Exod 33:12–17 in the context of the larger narrative with which it is contiguous, are to be commended. Both of them catch and communicate the excitement and tension of this powerful narrative as no source-analytical treatment has ever done, and Muilenburg's essay presents a stimulating array of rhetorical suggestions.

Even so, both Muilenburg and Terrien impose upon the text of Exod 33:12–17 patterns that are too much in the eye of the interpreter, patterns that do not connect these verses sufficiently with the larger narrative sequence of which they are the theological, and therefore by design, the literary high point. Everything in this tautly drawn narrative has moved toward and anticipated this climactic pleading of Moses, with its account of Yahweh's withdrawing his threat of Absence and beginning the restoration of the gift of his Presence. This narrative is indeed the centerpiece of a carefully arranged sequence of pieces of tradition from a wide variety of sources, and it can be appropriately understood only in its setting, just as the narratives that provide that setting can best be understood only in view of the dramatic center these verses provide.

The narrative of the calf (32:1–6) sets up the crisis, Israel's disobedience

of Yahweh and its rejection of Moses. The narrative of Moses' anger and
Yahweh's judgment (32:7–34) defines the crisis as a serious one with serious
consequences. The narrative of the command to leave Sinai (33:1–6), with
its devastating announcement of those consequences and its foreboding anticipation of a decision yet to come concerning Israel's fate, raises the tension
to an unbearable intensity. The narrative at hand, of Moses' plea for mercy
and Yahweh's anger (33:12–17), resolves that tension, though in a manner
that in no way lessens the seriousness of Israel's responsibility. And the three
narratives that follow renew (1) the understanding of Yahweh's Presence and
nature (33:18–34:9), (2) the covenant of relationship (34:10–28), and (3) the
authority of Moses (34:29–35), all of which were both misunderstood and
rejected by the sin with the calf. Exod 33:12–17 is at the very center of the
composite narrative of Presence-Absence-Presence which provides the theological center of Israel's struggle to belong to Yahweh.

Comment

12 Moses' reply to Yahweh is a response not to 32:34 (so Noth, 256;
Hyatt, 316), but to Yahweh's speech of command in 33:1–3. Yahweh had
ordered Moses to "ascend from this place," along with the people (עָם; 33:1).
Moses now repeats that order, quoting Yahweh's verb "ascend." He then
proceeds to raise with Yahweh the question "How?" Yahweh has not revealed
to Moses what only he (note *you*, emphasized) can reveal: who is to go with
Moses to make possible the departure of such a people as Israel under the
promise of Yahweh's Absence from such a place as Sinai, the one place where
Yahweh's Presence has been most real? This is not, as it is sometimes understood to be, a request for guidance: guidance has been promised already in
33:2, a verse with which this verse, were it such a request, would be in conflict.
What Moses is asking here is an echo of what he has asked before: " 'Who
am I, that *I* am to go, that I am to bring?' " (3:11). " 'Suppose I come and
say and they ask שְׁמוֹ מַה?' " "what is his name?" (3:13, see above).
As Terrien (*Elusive Presence,* 139–40) has correctly pointed out, Moses really
wants (and needs) to know something about Yahweh himself, and Moses
presses his question on the strength of the favor he has won with Yahweh.
There is no narrative earlier in Exodus in which Yahweh has made the statement
Moses attributes to him here, though 32:10 reflects a similar theme. Muilenburg (*Words and Meanings,* 177–81) has commented on the importance of
Moses' statement that Yahweh knows him by name (the statement is actually
made by Yahweh in v 17), following Baumann's (*ZAW* 28 [1908] 22–41) understanding of יָדַע as indicating in such usages "a personal association," noting
that Yahweh's knowing Moses by name is a singling out that demonstrates
Yahweh's favor upon him.

13 Thus Moses presses his request, which is somewhat more specific than
Terrien proposes. Moses wants and needs to know Yahweh's "intention,"
his "way," specifically, his decision where Israel's fate is concerned. The reference is to 33:6, where Yahweh, having announced (v 3) the withdrawal of
his Presence, had said, "I will decide what I am to do with you." In the

dialogue between Yahweh and Moses in Exod 3, Yahweh had tied his Presence to Moses' request for authority in Egypt: " 'The point is, I AM with you.' " (3:12). " 'I AM has sent me forth' " (3:14). Now Moses, with his insistence on knowing who is to go with him as he leaves Sinai and with his urgent plea (נא "please" occurs twice in v 13) that Yahweh reveal to him his intention concerning Israel, is just as clearly tying Presence to his willingness to obey Yahweh's command. Only if Yahweh's Presence accompanies him and Israel as they depart Sinai can Moses keep on finding favor in Yahweh's estimation. The implication is clear: without Yahweh's Presence, Moses will soon incur Yahweh's disfavor. As a closing plea, Moses ends his speech with the imperative with which he began it: "consider" (ראה); he began by asking Yahweh to consider what he was commanding, and he ends by asking him to consider that Israel, deftly referred to as הגוי הזה "this people," a designation with overtones of generality, is עמך "your people," which is placed first in the clause, for emphasis, and gives the intimate phrase "your very own people."

14–15 It is a masterpiece of a speech, the intention and effect of which are confirmed by Yahweh's immediate response, powerfully expressed by two simple sentences that contain, in Hebrew, only two words each. "My Presence will go" is linked by its verb (ילכו) to the first of Yahweh's imperative commands to Moses in 33:1: "Go!" (לך). "Thus will I dispel your anxiety" is the confirmation of Moses' intent in his plea. Nothing else, indeed, will give Moses rest from the fear gripping him, as his relief-laden reply further indicates: if Yahweh's Presence is not to go, Moses does not want either Israel or himself (MT "us"; LXX's "me" is an alteration of the text probably based on a misunderstanding of it) brought up from Sinai. The reason for this is quite clear: without Yahweh's Presence, Israel and Moses are not just certain to fail the destiny set before them; they cannot even begin it, because they will have lost their identity as "a special treasure," Yahweh's "own kingdom of priests and holy people" (19:5–6; see above).

16 All this is made doubly clear by Moses' summary confession of what Yahweh's Presence means to Israel, the final part of his plea, and the statement of the reason for Israel's abject grief and for his own urgent anxiety. Only Yahweh's Presence with Israel and with Moses will give credence to the assertion that Moses, and Israel along with him (and because of him), have found favor with Yahweh. Only Yahweh's Presence with Moses and Israel separates them from all other people throughout the world. It is the lesson Moses learned on Sinai at the time of his call: he alone was not equal to the task of challenging Pharaoh, but he was not to be alone. It is the lesson Israel learned, by the mighty acts in Egypt, by the deliverance at the sea, by the guidance and provision in the wilderness, and above all by the theophany and the revelation at Sinai: what they had seen, what they had been given, what they had the chance of becoming, all were the direct result of the Presence in their midst of Yahweh.

Incredibly enough, the people had somehow not realized this until they were under the prospect of Yahweh's Absence; then it became all too terribly clear, and they were overwhelmed by bitter grief. Moses had known it all along, and so his reaction was the quickest and most passionate, and his need to reverse the terrible prospect of Absence was the most urgent. The matter had come down finally to whether Israel as a special people would continue to exist or not, and Moses' own fate is bound up with his people's fate. His plea for them is not merely the reflex of a sense of responsibility. Moses' own real existence is caught up in Israel's real existence.

Whatever historical memory may or may not be preserved in this marvelous narrative is really beside the point. Its theological insight is universal, equally applicable to divine-human relationship and ministry in any age. No people, no matter how religious they are and for whatever reasons, can be a people of God without the Presence of God. Moses has posed the ultimate either/ or: Yahweh's decision to withdraw his presence from Israel *is* the decision of Israel's fate. Without Yahweh's presence, in the dark and chaotic umbra of his Absence, Israel will cease to exist.

17 Thus comes Yahweh's answer a second time, so anxiously anticipated, so carefully prepared for. The answer remains direct and simple, an eloquent affirmation of the clear either/or Moses has posed: "Indeed (גַּם) the very thing you have spoken, I will do." Moses' has focused the issue in terms of Israel's existence or nonexistence as a special people. This brilliant narrative presents Yahweh "seeing the point," and affirming without argument and without repetition (in itself a remarkable rhetorical surprise) that Moses is right, that he must not withdraw his Presence from Israel. And so Yahweh says simply, "Indeed the very thing you have spoken I will do." It is a brilliantly arresting conclusion to a magnificent narrative sequence, dazzlingly effective in its brevity, masterfully bold in its presentation of a Yahweh who is so secure that he does not mind being upstaged by his own servant Moses. This answer is the most convincing possible testimony of the favor in which Yahweh holds Moses, as Yahweh proceeds immediately to say. And this answer, in turn, sets the stage for the next component of the narrative sequence, in which, in a passage unique in the OT, Yahweh describes himself and Moses falls prostrate in worship.

Explanation

In a brief passage, displaying profound insight and presented with the consummate skill of a literary genius, the composite narrative of Exod 32– 34 is brought to its zenith. Moses focuses the real issue of the aftermath of Israel's sin with the calf. Though Israel has cancelled any possible claim to a continuation of the gift of Yahweh's Presence, deserving only the Absence Yahweh has promised, Israel cannot continue to exist without that Presence. The entire great undertaking, made possible from beginning to end by Yahweh's Presence, is about to come to a humiliating and complete finish because of Yahweh's Absence.

Moses is represented raising the question by asking who is to go with him and with Israel, by asking what is Yahweh's intention, by insisting, in a reflection of the "eagle's wings" speech (19:4–6), that Israel remains Yahweh's own people. The real question, of course, is the continuation of Yahweh's Presence with Israel, and when Yahweh, reversing his earlier threat, promises after all that he *will* go, Moses blurts out in a flood of relief, this real concern.

commanded him, ^c *and he* ^d *took in his hand two tablets of stone.* ⁵ *Then Yahweh came down in the cloud. He took his place beside him there, and he called out the name, Yahweh.* ⁶ *Next Yahweh passed in front of him and called out:* ^a

"Yahweh! Yahweh! ^b
—a God compassionate and favorably disposed:
—reluctant to grow angry,
    and full of unchanging love and reliableness;
⁷—keeping unchanging love for the thousands;
—taking away guilt and transgression and sin;
—certainly not neglecting just punishment,
    holding responsible for the guilt of the fathers
      both sons and grandsons,
        to the third and the fourth generations."

⁸ *Immediately, Moses hurriedly bowed down toward the earth and prostrated himself in worship.* ⁹ *Then he said, "Please, if I have found favor in your estimation, Lord, please go, Lord, in our midst. Though this is a stubborn people, you forgive our guilt and our sin, and you take us for your own possessions."*

Notes

18.a. MT has ויאמר "and he said." "Moses" is added above for clarity.
18.b. LXX^B has here as in v 13 ἐμφάνισόν μοι σεαυτόν "show me yourself."
19.a. "Yahweh," the obvious subj, is added to MT's ויאמר "and he said" for clarity.
19.b. LXX appears to be following a different text: "I will pass in front of you my glory (δόξα) and I will call in (ἐπί) my name, Κύριος (= Yahweh), across from you."
20.a. האדם "man" used here in its generic sense, to refer to any human being.
21.a. MT has מקום אתי "a place with me."
21.b. על־הצור "on the rocky cliff." Cf. BDB, 849.
22.a. כפי "my cupped hand, my palm"; cf. BDB, 496–97.
34:1.a. LXX adds καὶ ἀνάβηθι πρός με εἰς τὸ ὄρος "and climb up to me up on the mountain."
2.a. Niph of נצב "station, position oneself for a specific purpose or duty." Cf. BDB, 662.
4.a. MT has only ויפסל "and he chiseled out"; Moses is clearly the subj, so is added for clarity; SamPent has Moses, as does the Ethiopic version.
4.b. "Moses" is lacking in SamPent, Vg.
4.c. כאשר צוה יהוה אתו "exactly as Yahweh commanded him" is the phrase used repeatedly in the narrative of the fulfillment of Yahweh's instructions in Exod 39–40 (see for example 39:1, 5, 21, 26). "All this he did" is supplied above on the basis of the sequence of verbs ("chiseled . . . set off early . . . ascended") with special *waw*.
4.d. LXX adds Μωυσῆς "Moses" here, and LXX^A adds μεθ' ἑαυτοῦ "with him" to "took."
6.a. Yahweh's self-description is arranged as a sequence of defining phrases following the double pronunciation of the tetragrammaton, not to indicate any poetic form, but to give this recital something of the sonorous impact it has in Hebrew.
6.b. LXX has Κύριος ὁ θεὸς "Lord God."

Form/Structure/Setting

See *Form/Structure/Setting* on 32:1–6; 32:7–35; and 33:12–17.

This continuation of the composite narrative of Exod 32–34 has been broadly assigned by source critics to J (Davies, 237, 242–45; Hyatt, 312, 318–19); to J, J compilation, and supplements (Rudolph, *Werden und Wesen*, 46–48; Beer, 13, 158–61; McNeile, 215–18); to a combination of J and E material (Driver, 362–67; Beyerlin, *Sinaitic Traditions*, 24–26); or even to a combination of J, E, Deuteronomistic, and P traditions (Zenger, *Sinaitheophanie,* 93–96, 196–200). This very variety affirms the difficulty if not the impossibility of any detailed allocation of 33:18–34:9 to the sources that have contributed its layers, and with this sequence as with the remainder of the narrative of chaps. 32–34, we are on far surer ground if we consider the sequence a layered composite, carefully integrated into the larger whole of which it is now a part and understandable only in the context of that whole. The clues to the theological themes being emphasized are far clearer than the clues to the sources from which these verses may have been drawn.

The central theme of this sequence is, once again, Yahweh's Presence (cf. Brichto, *HUCA* 54 [1983] 27–29). Yahweh has withdrawn the threat of his Absence and promised Moses that he will, after all, go with him and with Israel as they leave Sinai. Thus Moses asks that he might see Yahweh's glory (= Presence), following which request there comes a theophany, the declaration by Yahweh of his name, and a further revelation of Yahweh's nature. This experience is remarkably parallel to Moses' first experience on Sinai as he asked, in effect (and in result) for the proof of Yahweh's Presence when Yahweh commissioned him to go to Pharaoh's Egypt and bring Israel forth (cf. Exod 3:7–4:23). In 33:14 and 17, when Yahweh promises that he *will* go, Moses wants to *see* that Yahweh is present. As before, Moses, like the people he is to lead, wants proof. Thus the request of Moses in 33:18 leads naturally from Yahweh's promise to go, affirmed by his agreement to "do the very thing" Moses has spoken, to Yahweh's proof, in yet another unique theophany, that he is present. And that in turn leads to a preparation for the renewal of the shattered covenant relationship by (1) a preparation of new tablets of stone to replace the broken pair and (2) a reassertion of Yahweh's nature, this time in relation not to what Yahweh *does,* but to what Yahweh *is.* All this provokes Moses once more to obeisant and awed worship and to a repetition, by way of reaffirmation, of his plea for Yahweh's Presence.

Several points are suggested by such a consideration of Exod 33:18–34:9 as a composite unit within the setting of Exod 32–34 and against the still larger Exodus narrative as a whole. The first is that the blending of earlier traditions dealing with separate themes has here been accomplished deliberately and with a masterful style. The second is that the thematic connections of this sequence with Exod 3–4 are by no means merely coincidental: one of the two narratives, probably this one, has been shaped under the influence of the other one. The third is that this composite is a carefully planned anticipation of the remainder of the taut narrative of Exod 32–34. And fourth is that even the repetitious lines (such as the supplementary account of Yahweh's instructions to Moses, in 34:2–3 vis-à-vis 33:21–23 and 34:4–5, or 34:9 vis-à-vis 33:12, 13, and 17) or the paralleling of the conditions laid down in 19:12–13, 23 by 34:3 are entirely deliberate. While it is possible to take these parallels as indications of separate traditions reporting the same events (so Wellhausen, *Composition,* 329–35, who considered Exod 34 "the Decalog narrative of J") it is far more important to recognize the effect of the whole into which narrative components now no longer traceable have been assembled. The theory of parallel sources, once they are taken beyond broad generality,

becomes very tenuous. They have tended, furthermore, to draw needed attention away from the composite whole, which has both a purpose and a canonical
life of its own.

Comment

18 The request of Moses to see the glory of Yahweh is effectively a request
that Yahweh demonstrate the reality of his promise to be present, indeed
that he prove his Presence once again, as he did before the solemnization
of the covenant that has since been shattered. כבוד "glory" in this context
is very close to a synonym for פנים "face, Presence," as the ensuing narrative
shows. Neither term is intended to suggest "human features," as Eichrodt
(*Theology of the OT* 2:29–40; cf. also Davies, "Glory," *IDB* 2:401–2; Westermann, *Wort-Gebot-Glaube*, 227–49 and "כבד," *THAT* 1:801–12) has shown.

19–23 What Moses asks, however, is more than Yahweh is willing to grant,
for Moses' own good. Yahweh's response to Moses' request stresses first
what Yahweh will do: he will cause all his טוב "goodness" to pass in front
of Moses, and he will call out in his hearing (literally, "in his presence")
the name "Yahweh." טוב here is sometimes taken (cf. Mannati, *VT* 19 [1969]
488–90) to imply the "beauty" of Yahweh and so to suggest a theophany,
as it appears to do in Psalm 27:13 (note, however, the argument of Mannati,
490–93). But though Yahweh does indeed come to Moses in theophany, what
he gives to Moses is quite specifically *not* the *sight* of his beauty, his glory,
his Presence—that, indeed, he pointedly denies. What he gives rather is a
description, and at that, a description not of how he *looks* but of how he *is*.

The calling out of the name "Yahweh" as an accompaniment or perhaps
even a conclusion to the passing of Yahweh's טוב is an important clue to
what Yahweh promised Moses. טוב refers not to an appearance of beauty
but to a recital of character. Exod 33:19a is yet another parallel to Exod
3:14. To the question מַה־שְּׁמוֹ, "What is his name?" or, better, "What is he
really like?" Yahweh replied, "I really *AM*" (cf. *Comment* on 3:13–14). To
Moses' request for a look at his Presence, Yahweh replied, "I will reveal to
you what I *am*, not how I look." And in both instances, Yahweh followed
his revelation with the calling out of his special name, "Yahweh."

Yahweh follows this promise with a statement of his sovereignty. His favor
and his compassion are given only on his terms (Childs, 596, helpfully links
this tautology to אהיה אשר אהיה "I AM the One Who Always Is" in 3:14;
cf. also Cross, *Canaanite Myth*, 153–54, and Walker, *JBL* 79 [1960] 277). Then
he explains why Moses cannot see his Presence. The human family cannot
look upon Yahweh and survive: the gap between the finite and the infinite
is too great; it is an experience of which man is incapable. Yahweh thus
makes provision for the experience Moses is to have by designating a place
on Sinai in the fissure of a rocky cliff. There Moses can stand as Yahweh's
glory (= Presence) comes near and passes by.

An ancient tradition that Yahweh's Presence came near Moses in spatial
terms is clearly reflected here, not least in the additional report that Yahweh
would protect Moses from any accidental (and fatal) sight of that which he
could not endure to see by the placement over him of his palm until his

Presence shall have passed by. These provisions transmit an air of frightening expectation.

34:1–3 The further instructions to Moses involve more practical matters— the preparations Moses can himself make. He is to prepare two tablets to replace the two he shattered, on which Yahweh will write the words that he wrote (cf. 31:18; 32:16) on the first ones. Moses is to be ready by morning, to ascend Sinai alone, to station himself at the designated spot at the summit of the mountain, after having insured, as he had once before (19:12–13, 23), that neither human nor animal is to come anywhere near the mountain. This repetition by Yahweh of his instructions, with expansions, is not a doublet, but a dramatic heightening of the tension already set up so skillfully by 33:20–23.

4–5 The tension is then wound tighter still by the narrative of Moses' obedience of Yahweh's instructions, moved forward by a sequence of imperfect verbs connected by special *waw,* verbs translated above as a tightly connected staccato sequence. When all Moses' preparations were made, Yahweh descended in the cloud that both hid and symbolized his Presence, came to a position near the spot to which he had directed Moses, and called out his name, "Yahweh." (For a review of the position that these last two verbs have Moses, rather than Yahweh, as subject, see Childs, 603; as he concludes, Yahweh is far the better choice in the composite narrative, despite the ambiguity of v 5b.)

6 In accord with his promise, Yahweh passed by Moses, apparently with the various precautionary measures in place, and twice more (according to the composite narrative) called out his name: "Yahweh! Yahweh!" This double pronounciation of the tetragrammaton must not be taken as an appositional expansion (so Cassuto, 439) or as a redundant statement to be reduced by the deletion of the second "Yahweh" (so LXX; though note that LXX[A] has a second Κύριος "Lord"). It is a deliberate repetition of the confessional use of the tetragrammaton (see *Comment* and *Explanation* on 3:11–12, 14–22), emphasizing the reality of Yahweh present in his very being, linking this proof to Moses to the earlier proof-of-Presence narratives that are begun in Exod 3, and providing an anchor line for the list of five descriptive phrases to follow, phrases that define how Yahweh, "The One Who Always Is," really is.

In Exod 3, Yahweh declares, "I really AM," and then proceeds to prove that confession by the mighty acts in Egypt, by the deliverance at the sea, by the guidance and provision in the wilderness, and above all by his Advent at Sinai. Here, in response to Moses' request that he demonstrate that he really is present to go with Israel despite his earlier threat that he would *not* do so, Yahweh once again says, in effect, the same thing: "Yahweh! Yahweh!" As he said in 3:16, "This is my name from now on: and this is to bring me to mind generation after generation." Now, in response to Moses asking yet the same question over again, Yahweh calls out his name over again, twice this time, and then he proceeds to describe himself, to say, "I AM, and this is how I AM."

6–7 The confession that follows the double calling of Yahweh's name is clearly reflected in eight OT passages, three of them in the Psalms (86:15;

103:8; 145:8) and one each in Num 14:18; Joel 2:13; Nah 1:3; Neh 9:17; and Jonah 4:2. Possible allusions to it can be discovered at additional places in the OT, Exod 20:5 among them (cf. also Scharbert, *Bib* 38 [1957] 132–37, and Dentan, *VT* 13 [1963] 34, n. 4). Dentan (34–51; cf. also Scharbert, 130–50) has made a careful analysis of these passages and Exod 34:6–7, and has reached the conclusion that this "entire formula" was produced by the circle of Israel's Wise Men and set into the Exodus narrative by them in their "ultimate redaction of the Pentateuch."

A variety of commentators (cf. the summary of Dentan, *VT* 13 [1963] 36–37, and note also Beyerlin, *Sinaitic Traditions,* 137–38, and Hyatt, 322–23) have assumed such a cultic origin and a liturgical use for this summary of Yahweh's characteristics. Moberly (*Mountain of God,* 128–31), however, has argued for the reverse of such a proposal, suggesting that the "formula" of Exod 34:6–7 is so apt a development of its context that one must assume a narrative origin for these verses and a borrowing of them for cultic usage, rather than the other way around. In fact, we have no basis for certainty regarding the origin of these verses; they are certainly a part of a confession of faith about Yahweh (as Dentan, 37, suggests), but probably of a very ancient one, far older than the Wisdom movement in any formal sense and connected with Israel's oldest perceptions of Yahweh and his relationship to those he claimed as "his own people." This confession may have been refined, and even expanded, by the addition of supplementary phrases in the use of it in both narrative summary and liturgy; but its beginning may be assumed to be quite old, at least as old as the early development of the use of the name "Yahweh" for confessional purposes.

The description of Yahweh set forth here is an apt one for the narrative of Israel's first disobedience and Yahweh's judgment. Yahweh's compassion had just been demonstrated (32:14), and his tendency to be favorable was in the process of exercise (33:12–17). His slowness to grow angry had been attested from the moment of Israel's complaint at the sea (14:11–12), and his unchanging love and reliableness were the reason Moses had still been able to plead after the terrible cancellation made by the people's disobedience with the calf. His keeping of unchanging love to the thousands and the removal of their guilt, their transgression and their sin (the multiplication of terms is a deliberate attempt at comprehensive statement) were in process. And his serious view of obligation and commitment was the very basis of the crisis provoked by the worship of the calf and the reason that Israel's fate had hung so precariously in the balance.

Yahweh's confession of his nature is a powerful exegesis of the meaning of "Yahweh! Yahweh!," one brilliantly matched to (or by) the narrative of which it is a part and one that summarizes dramatically that Yahweh will not accommodate his nature to the vagaries of his people's commitment. He is willing to give himself to them, but they must take him as he is, exactly as he is. He will not compromise, and therefore *they* must not. Such a confession not only makes all the more clear what a rebellion the disobedience with the calf was, it also anticipates what the next step simply *must* be: the people must renew their commitment, both by reviewing what it is and also by making it all over again. Thus the next sequence in the narrative of Exod

32–34 is introduced: once more the people must hear what they are to obey; once more Yahweh, favorably disposed and full of unchanging love, is opening himself to them.

8–9 Following such a powerful recital, the revelation not of what Moses asked for but of what he needed, Moses hastily prostrated himself in worship. No other response was appropriate. Then, when Moses did speak, he could only plead repetitiously for what Yahweh had already granted, acknowledging the people's guilt and sin, including himself with them, and ask for what Israel had not deserved and could never earn—that they should be Yahweh's own, his inheritance, his possession (נחל). The rhetorical link of this response of Moses with Yahweh's invitation to Israel in 19:5 is staggering.

Explanation

Moses' second request of Yahweh for a proof of his Presence ends as did the first such request, with a declaration, by Yahweh, of his confessional name. The first request was made in the context of Moses' concern both that Israel would believe him and also that Yahweh could indeed free them from the Pharaoh's bondage. This second request is made in the context of Moses' concern that Yahweh really will be present and really will go up from Sinai with Israel, in spite of what has happened. Yahweh has promised, but Moses wants assurance.

As the first request became the question that led to the revelation of Yahweh's name, so the second request becomes the plea that leads to the revelation of Yahweh's character. The parallel can hardly be fortuitous.

Yahweh's response to this second request becomes in turn not only the exegesis of the revelation of his name, given in response to the first request, but also the preparation for the renewal of the shattered relationship by the instructions given Moses concerning (1) the provision of two new stone tablets and (2) the separation and reascension of Mount Sinai, and by (1) the new descent of Yahweh onto the mountain, and (2) the new revelation of his name and his nature there. With the conclusion of this sequence, all is in readiness for the renewal of the covenant between Yahweh and Israel.

The Renewal of the Covenant Relationship
(34:10–28)

Bibliography

Brongers, H. A. "Der Eifer des Herrn Zebaoth." *VT* 13 (1963) 269–84. **Davis, D. R.** "Rebellion, Presence, and Covenant: A Study in Exodus 32–34." *WTJ* 44 (1982) 71–87. **Horn, H.** "Traditionsschichten in Ex 23, 10–33 und Ex 34, 10–26." *BZ* 15 (1971) 205–22. **Kosmala, H.** "The So-Called Ritual Decalogue." *ASTI* 1 (1962) 31–61. **Langlamet, F.** "Israël et 'l'habitant du pays': Vocabulaire et formules d'Ex XXXIV, 11–16." *RB* 76 (1969) 321–50. **Morgenstern, J.** "The Oldest Document of the Hexateuch." *HUCA* 4 (1927) 1–138. **Pfeiffer, R. H.** "The Oldest Decalogue." *JBL* 43 (1924) 294–310. **Rowley, H. H.** "Moses and the Decalogue." *Men of God.* London: Thomas Nelson and Sons, 1963. 1–36. Also *BJRL* 34 (1951–52) 81–118. **Scharbert, J.** "Formgeschichte und Exegese von Ex 34, 6f und Seiner Parallelen." *Bib* 38 (1957) 130–50. **Wilms, F. E.** "Das jahwistische Bundesbuch in Ex 34." *BZ* 16 (1972) 24–53. ———. *Das jahwistische Bundesbuch in Exodus 34.* SANT 32. Munich: Kösel Verlag, 1973. **Winnett, F. V.** *The Mosaic Tradition.* Toronto: TUP, 1949.

Translation

¹⁰ Thus Yahweh ᵃ said, "Look: I am making a covenant. ᵇ In the sight of all your people I will do extraordinary deeds as yet unimagined ᶜ in all the earth and among all the nations, and all the people among whom you now are will see the doing of Yahweh, that what I am doing with you is awesome. ¹¹ You yourself ᵃ keep that which I am commanding you today. Watch me driving out headlong before you the Amorites, the Canaanites, the Hittites, the Perizzites, the Hivites, and the Jebusites. ᵇ ¹² Guard yourself against making a covenant with those who live in the land into which you are going, that they not become a trap in your very midst. ¹³ Rather are you to pull down their altars completely, ᵃ and shatter their sacred pillars utterly, and cut down their holy poles to the ground. ᵇ

¹⁴ "Indeed you are not to bow down in worship to another god, ᵃ because Yahweh's very name is 'Jealous': he is a jealous God, ¹⁵ and does not want you ᵃ making a covenant with those who live in the land. ᵇ When they prostitute themselves after their gods, and offer sacrifices to their gods, and call out to you, you might eat of their sacrifice, ¹⁶ and even take their daughters for your sons, ᵃ with the result that when their daughters prostitute themselves after their gods, your sons will prostitute themselves after their gods.

¹⁷ "You are not to make for yourselves gods of shaped metal. ᵃ

¹⁸ "You are to keep the sacred feast of unleavened bread cakes: for seven days you are to eat unleavened bread cakes, as I instructed you, at the set time in the month of the green grain, because in the month of the green grain, you went out from Egypt. ᵃ

¹⁹ "Every creature that opens the womb is mine—all your male ᵃ livestock, the firstborn of cattle and of sheep. ²⁰ You are to replace ᵃ the firstborn ass with a sheep: if you do not replace it, then you are to break its neck. ᵇ Every child ᶜ firstborn of your sons you are to replace. ᵈ You are not to appear in my Presence without an offering. ᵉ

²¹ "Six days you are to work, and on the seventh day you are to rest. ᵃ Even in ploughing time ᵇ and in crop harvest, you are to rest.

²² "You are to celebrate ᵃ the sacred feast of weeks, the firstfruits of the wheat harvest, and the sacred feast of the ingathering harvest at the completion of the year. ²³ Three times in the year all your males are to appear in the Presence of the Lord, Yahweh the God of Israel. ᵃ ²⁴ Indeed I will disinherit nations ᵃ there ahead of you, ᵇ and I will make your borders far apart. No man shall desire for himself your land when you go up to present yourself in the Presence of Yahweh your God three times in the year.

²⁵ "You are not to combine with anything leavened ᵃ the blood of my sacrifice, and the sacrifice of the sacred feast of the Passover is not to be kept through the night until morning. ᵇ

²⁶ *"You are to bring the very first of the firstfruits of your ground to the house of Yahweh your God.*

"You are not to cook a kid in the milk of its mother." ^a

²⁷ *Then Yahweh said to Moses, "You yourself write these words, for on the basis* ^a *of these words I have made a covenant with you and with Israel."* ²⁸ *So he* ^a *was there with* ^b *Yahweh forty days and forty nights: bread he did not eat and water he did not drink.*

He wrote upon the tablets the words of the covenant, the Ten Words. ^c

Notes

10.a. MT has only ויאמר "and he said," but Yahweh is clearly the speaker. LXX adds Yahweh as subj and Moses as indir obj; Vg adds *Dominus* "Lord" (= Yahweh) as subj.

10.b. LXX adds σοι "(with) you," though LXX^A does not.

10.c. אשר לא־נבראו "that are not yet created." Note BDB, 135: "of something new, astonishing."

11.a. שמר־לך, lit., "keep (impv) with regard to yourself." Langlamet (*RB* 76 [1969] 329) suggests that the addition here of לך "to you" modifies the sense of שמר to "prends garde," "fais attention," giving an emphatic tone to the review of commandments about to follow. The sg "you" here and throughout this passage before v 27 is to be taken as referring to Israel and esp. to each individual Israelite.

11.b. SamPent adds והגרגשי "and the Girgashites" to this list, and follows a different order. LXX also includes the Girgashites, also giving a total of seven peoples. See n. 33:2.b.

13.a. The three impf verbs of this verse have the added emphasis of "paragogic *nun*"; cf. GKC, ¶ 47m.

13.b. Following this verb (the third one with the emphatic *nun*) LXX adds καὶ τὰ γλυπτὰ τῶν θεῶν αὐτῶν κατακαύσετε ἐν πυρί "and the carved images of their gods you are to burn in fire." Cf. Deut 7:5, 25.

14.a. LXX reads θεῷ ἑτέρῳ "other gods."

15.a. פן־תכרת, lit., "lest you cut (= make)." On פן as an "averting, or deprecating" conj, cf. BDB, 814.

15.b. LXX adds ἐγκαθημένοις πρὸς ἀλλοφύλους "to embrace ways foreign" to their covenant promises.

16.a. LXX adds here καὶ τῶν θυγατέρων σου δῷς τοῖς υἱοῖς αὐτῶν "and give your daughters to their sons."

17.a. אלהי מסכה "gods of shaped metal"—see n. 32:4.c.

18.a. This verse is nearly a verbatim parallel of Exod 23:15. The primary differences are the repetition here of the phrase בחדש האביב "in the month of the green grain" (SamPent reads בו "in it") and the concluding sentence of 23:15, which reappears in this sequence as the final sentence of v 20.

19.a. MT has תזכר "she is remembered," though cf. Barthélemy, 150: "The verb form תזכר has an active meaning 'to put asunder the male beasts,'" and Cassuto's proposal, 445, that תזכר refers to cattle dropping, i.e., giving birth to, a male. Another possibility, more frequently followed (LXX; Vg; BDB, 270 § II 4; Childs, 604), is the emendation הזכר, "the male." The meaning is substantially the same, by any of these alternatives. LXX omits "all your livestock."

20.a. See n. 13:13.b.

20.b. LXX has τιμὴν δώσεις "you are to give compensation-money" instead of MT's וערפתו "break its neck,"

20.c. כל בכור "every firstborn one." The parallel verse, Exod 13:13, has וכל בכור אדם "every firstborn human," a reading which SamPent has here as well.

20.d. This verse, to this point, is closely parallel to Exod 13:13.

20.e. This sentence is paralleled verbatim by the last sentence of Exod 23:15.

21.a. This sentence is very similar to the first part of Exod 23:12; the verb here is עבד "work"; there it is עשה "do, make," and followed by מעשיך "from your doing."

21.b. LXX has τῷ σπόρῳ "seed-sowing time" instead of MT's "plowing time."

22.a. תעשה, lit., "you are to do." LXX adds μοι "to me." Cf. BDB, 794–95, II.6.

23.a. This verse is a close parallel of 23:17. The difference is the addition at the end of this verse of אלהי ישראל "God of Israel."

24.a. SamPent adds רבים "many."

24.b. מפניך "from in front of you."

25.a. לא־תשחט על־חמץ; cf. n. 23:18.a.

25.b. This verse parallels in part Exod 23:18.

26.a. This verse is a verbatim parallel of Exod 23:19.

27.a. על־פי הדברים האלה "upon the mouth of (= speaking of) these words." Cf. BDB, 805 § 6.d.

28.a. LXX adds Μωυσῆς "Moses."

28.b. SamPent adds לפני "in the Presence of," a reading followed also by LXX.

28.c. עשרת הדברים "the Ten Words," in reference to the ten commandments, occurs also in the OT in Deut 4:13 and 10:4.

Form/Structure/Setting

See *Form/Structure/Setting* on 32:1–6, 32:7–35, 33:12–17, and 33:18–34:9.

The analysis of the form of this section has been dictated, in the main, by two considerations: (1) that these verses represent a parallel account of the initial making of the covenant on Sinai, relocated at this point in the Exodus narrative and minimally redacted to give a narrative of covenant renewal, and (2) that we are here presented with an alternative list of commandments, a so-called "ritual decalogue" in contrast to the "ethical decalogue" of Exod 20:2–17. Linked to these two proposals, of course, are various theories about which tetrateuchal sources are contributory to the compilation of Exod 34:10–28 as this section stands in the sequence of the received text.

The most frequent source assignment of this sequence is to J (Wellhausen, *Composition*, 83–98, 334–35; Noth, 260–67; Childs, 607–9), though virtually all commentators posit also at least some redactional supplementation. Beer (13, 159–62), for example, proposes this complex analysis: vv 10a, 14a, 17, 19a, 20d, 21ab, 23, 25–26, 27–28 to J²; 10b–d, Rᴾ; 11–13, 15–16, 24, Rᴰ; 14b, 18, 22, Rᴶᴱ; 19b–20, 21b, R. Driver (368–74) somewhat more simply assigns vv 10a, 14, 17–18ab, 19–23, 25–28abc to J; 10b–13, 15–16, 18cd, 24 to Rᴶᴱ; and 28d ("the ten commandments") he calls "a gloss." Hyatt (318–19, 323–26), more simply still, gives vv 10, 17–23, 25–28 to J; 11–16, 24 to Rᴰ; noting that "the ten commandments" of 28d is *not* a gloss, but "part of the J tradition." As this representative sampling shows (cf. also the comparative chart of Zenger, *Sinaitheophanie*, 228–30), however, the source criticism of Exod 34:10–28, beyond quite broad designations, is very subjective and therefore productive of somewhat arbitrary conclusions.

Attempts to discover here a separate and culturally oriented decalogue have resulted in equally complex and diverse results, as the studies of Halbe (*Das Privilegrecht*, 13–255) and Wilms (*BZ* 16 [1957] 24–53; *Das jahwistische*, 15–135) in particular have shown. Though many scholars have followed Wellhausen's (*Composition*, 333–34) suggestion along these lines and have argued that the "decalogue" of Exod 34 is far earlier than the decalogue of Exod 20 (so for example Morgenstern, *HUCA* 4 [1927] 54–98; Mowinckel, *Le Décalogue*, 19–30, 43–55; Rowley, *Men of God*, 7–36), or far later than the decalogue of Exod 20 (Pfeiffer, *JBL* 43 [1924] 294–310; Winnett, *Mosaic Tradition*, 30–56, 155–71), the difficulties involved in these proposals raise more problems than they solve.

These complications have led to the suggestions of Rudolph (*"Elohist,"* 59–60), considerably extended by Beyerlin (*Sinaitic Traditions,* 81–88), that the decalogue now in Exod 20:2–17, though in an earlier form, was the decalogue referred to in Exod 34:27–28, and that "the kernel" of 34:10–26, a variant of the ancient covenantal requirements reflected also in Exod 23:12–19, replaced "the original Decalogue" in the J "account of the making of the covenant" because of the pressures of syncretism following the settlement in Canaan. Related traditio-historical approaches have been taken by Horn (*BZ* 15 [1971] 206–22), who compares Exod 34:10–26 with 23:10–33 and proposes parallel older and later traditions dealing with the calendar of the sacred festivals and with the occupation of the promised land; by Wilms (*BZ* 16 [1972] 25–26, 51–53; cf. also *Das jahwistische,* passim), who argues that Exod 34 contains neither a decalogue nor an account of covenant renewal (which he terms "eine literarische Fiktion"), but a "Landgabebundestext" (vv 11–17), a "Festkalendar" (vv 18–24) and "Ergänzungstoroth" (vv 25–26) all of which together constitute a "small lawbook" made up of five prohibitions and twelve commandments and belonging to the J source-stratum; by Kosmala (*ASTI* 1 [1962] 38–57), who denies that Exod 34:14–26 has anything to do with a "decalogue" and argues instead, by a comparison of Exod 34:14–26 with 23:14–19 and Deut 16:1–17, that Exod 34:18–24 preserves "an ancient feast-calendar," to which 34:25–26 adds four stipulations related to the Passover; or even, concerning only 34:11–16, by Langlamet, who, after a detailed rhetorical analysis of these six verses (*RB* 76 [1969] 327–50, 481–503), concludes (503–7) that they are pre-deuteronomic, intermediary between J and Deuteronomy, and that they preserve a passionate attack on cooperation with Canaan that appears to predate Solomon.

These theories too, despite their presentation of some thought-provoking analysis and fecund suggestion of detail, remain altogether too subjective, however, and altogether too fragmentary in their approach to Exod 34:10–28 as a part of the narrative of chaps. 32–34. Whatever may be the past history of these verses, whatever other literary complexes they may once have belonged to, and by whatever routes they may have come to their present location, it is precisely that location in which their purpose and meaning is first of all to be found. Too much attention has been given to the seams and inconcinnities of Exod 34:10–28, both real and imaginary. Far too little attention has been given to the function of these verses as a part of the larger Presence-Absence-Presence narrative in which they stand (though cf. Davis, *WTJ* 44 [1982] 81–84; and Moberly, *Mountain of God* 95–106, 131–40, 157–61).

Exod 34:10–28 has been woven with some care into the larger narrative whole that is now Exod 32–34, with the express purpose of suggesting the renewal of the covenant relationship between Yahweh and Israel. This section has been pieced together from material taken from several areas of interest (e.g., covenant renewal, the avoidance of syncretistic influence, Yahweh the "jealous God," gifts and sacred festivals due to Yahweh) to present an overall impression of covenant renewal (1) emphasizing complete loyalty to Yahweh (a deliberate contrast to the terrible sin with the calf) whose justified jealousy (see *Comment* on 20:5) is stressed as a warning against the temptation of a

divided loyalty, and (2) summarizing, in a deliberate mingling of themes from
the ten commandments and what is now called the Book of the Covenant,
an array of requirements directed against exactly the kind of disobedience
the sin with the golden calf presented. That there are inconsistencies and
some ambiguity in such a compilation goes without saying: they are at least
as inevitable here as they are in literary compilations throughout the OT.
The people who originally compiled this sequence, however, and those for
whom their compilation was made would not only have been less concerned
about such matters than we have been; they would have been far less likely
to have been sidetracked by them from the movement and the message of
the sequence as a whole.

Comment

10   The tone of the renewal sequence of 34:10–28 is set in its beginning
verse by Yahweh's double announcement that he is in the process of making
a covenant (אָנֹכִי כֹרֵת בְּרִית) and that Israel with whom he makes it is to
be both the subject and the medium of נִפְלָאֹת "extraordinary deeds" that
will command the attention of the peoples all about them. נִפְלָאֹת provides
a rhetorical link with Exod 3:20, where Yahweh promises his נִפְלָאֹת in the
Egypt of Pharaoh, there too as a proof of his Presence (see above). The
deeds yet to be done are, however, to be more remarkable still: they have
not before been created (בָּרָא), and thus nobody will have conceived in advance of them that such things could be.

11–13   One of the first of those deeds (but certainly not the compass of
them) is the displacement from the promised land into which Israel is to
go of the hostile peoples (note also v 24, below), a motive stressed earlier
in the composite narrative of Exod 32–34 (33:1–2; see above), and mentioned
also with exactly the purpose and implication it has here in the conclusion
to the Book of the Covenant, at Exod 23:23–33 (see above). Israel must
guard against (cf. the detailed study of שָׁמַר by Langlamet, *RB* 76 [1968]
327–29) any covenantal alliance with these peoples as a dangerous means
of entrapment. They must extirpate from the land the altars, sacred pillars,
and sacred poles of these peoples, thus removing even the possibility of
any compromise in their worship of and loyalty to Yahweh. This theme is a
frequent one throughout the OT, especially as the pressures of syncretism
became more and more intense. Its employment here is in direct and specific
reaction to Israel's sin with the golden calf.

14–16   The sequence is thus continued with a reference to the first and
second commandments (Exod 20:3–6), in particular by a reference to Yahweh
as a jealous God, expanded here by the unique assertion, "Yahweh's very
name is 'Jealous'" (though cf. Deut 4:24; 5:9; 6:15; Sauer, "קָנְאָה Eifer,"
THAT 2:647–50; and Brongers, *VT* 13 [1963] 269–84). Loyalty to Yahweh
must be absolutely undiluted. There is to be no worship of any other god
of any kind, and Israel simply must avoid any covenant with the inhabitants
of the land into which they are going; such alliances may lead to a fraternization
that could begin with the eating of sacrifices made to other gods and end
with intermarriage and the embrace of other gods by Israel's children. Of

course vv 11–16 are repetitive, perhaps intentionally so, in their passionate introduction to the renewal of the covenant that (1) is cautionary at exactly the point of Israel's covenant-shattering sin with the calf, (2) begins at precisely the same point as does the decalogue of 20:2–17, and (3) starts out just as does the collection of requirements and guiding decisions in the Book of the Covenant (cf. 20:22–23).

17 This introductory sequence is appropriately brought to a climax by the first of a series of Yahweh's requirements designed to present a broad summary of covenant obligation with a particular bearing on the necessity of maintaining undiluted loyalty to Yahweh in the setting of the new land to which Israel is going. This requirement is linked specifically to the sin with the golden calf by the use of the word מסכה "shaped metal," the term used to describe the calf in 32:4 and 8 (see also Deut 9:16; 2 Kgs 17:16; cf. Lev 19:4; and Davis, *WTJ* 44 [1982] 82, and Moberly, *Mountain of God,* 99–100). As noted above (n. 32:4.b,c and *Comment* on 32:2–4), מסכה appears to refer to a metal sheathing molded around a solid core of wood. In the context of this renewal narrative, the use of so specific a term must be a deliberate rhetorical connection. The application of vv 11–16 is thus made crystal clear and given the authority of a requirement for the future heavily emphasized because of the disobedience of the past.

18–26 The summary series is continued by a list that parallels (cf. the detailed list of parallels drawn by Scharbert, *Bib* 38 [1957] 132–37, Horn, *BZ* 15 [1971] 206–12, and Kosmala, *ASTI* 1 [1962] 38–44) laws in the Book of the Covenant (esp. 23:12–19) and in Exod 13:11–16 that set Israel apart from all other peoples as Yahweh's own unique and loyal people, following the note struck by the first of them, in v 17. Thus are mentioned (1) Passover (v 18), in a nearly verbatim parallel of 23:15 (see above); (2) the offering, in actuality or by replacement, of the firstborn (vv 19–20), in a parallel in part of substance, in part verbatim, of 13:12–13 (see above; Moberly, *Mountain of God,* 100, considers this an attempt to mark Israel as different from Canaan at the point of redemption rather than sacrifice of the firstborn son: "an example of the distinction . . . even when there are similarities"); (3) the rhythm of worship and rest following six days of work (v 21), in a close parallel to 23:12 (see above), with the addition of a statement not found elsewhere in the OT, that the rhythm of seventh-day rest is not to be interrupted even by the busiest work-seasons, plowing time and harvest time— this requirement, which would certainly have set Israel apart, has the sound of a negative experience about it; (4) the calendar of the three principal sacred feasts (vv 22–23), a parallel in general content to 23:14–16, with a very close parallel to 23:17 (see above)—this feast, called "the sacred feast of the early crop-harvest" in 23:16, is called "the sacred feast of weeks" here (cf. Deut 16:9–10), and there is added here both a reference to the motif of widely spaced borders (= a large and secure land) and also an intriguing assurance that Yahweh will prevent the covetous desire (חמד is the verb of the tenth commandment, 20:17) of anyone for the land of the Israelite who is away observing one of the three great feasts (thus removing another excuse against obedience); (5) respect for the unique sanctity of Passover, by keeping all leaven separate from it (see *Comment* on 12:15, 19–20) and by consuming or burning any remaining parts of the sacrificial animal before morning (see 12:8–10), a general parallel of 23:18 (see above); (6) the command that the firstfruits of the ground be offered to Yahweh (v 26a), a verbatim parallel of 23:19a (see above); and (7) the command against cooking a kid in its mother's milk (v 26b), a verbatim parallel of 23:19b (see above), connected by Kosmala (50–56) with Canaanite fertility worship mainly on the basis of a reconstructed text from Ugarit. While Kosmala's suggestion cannot be proven, the inclusion of this command in the summary list of 34:17–26 almost certainly implies that it has something to do with a practice that had the potential of drawing Israel into a compromise of loyalty to Yahweh.

27–28 The final verses of the renewal narrative, clearly placed to provide a conclusion, nevertheless leave an impression of ambiguity because of Yahweh's command to Moses to write "these words," because of the question of the subject of "wrote" in v 28, and because of the inclusion at the end of that verse of the phrase עשרת הדברים "the Ten Words," a phrase that occurs elsewhere only in Deuteronomy. "These words" in v 27 are usually assumed to be the ten commandments elsewhere said to have been written by Yahweh himself. The ten commandments are simply not present in the summary series immediately preceding, however, despite numerous and very imaginative efforts to find them there. The first "he" of v 28 clearly refers to Moses, as does the second, but the third "he" has been taken to refer both to Moses (so Driver, 374; Hyatt, 326) and also to Yahweh (so Beer, 162; Childs, 604). And "the Ten Words" at the end of v 28 has fueled the speculation that Exod 34 was originally J's account of the making of the covenant, or that this chapter originally contained an early version of the decalogue of 20:7–17 (see *Form/Structure/Setting* above), or that a later editor added this last phrase and imposed on the chapter an impression it was never intended to present (cf. esp. Childs, 607–9, 615–17).

None of these theories does justice to Exod 34:27–28 viewed strictly in its present location and as a conclusion to a deliberately arranged covenant renewal narrative. While there is always the possibility that such a deliberate arrangement has been compromised by yet another well-meaning redactor's addition or rearrangement, it is nevertheless possible to interpret these verses as they stand as an apt final paragraph to the renewal narrative. What Moses is commanded to write in v 27 is exactly what he has been held responsible for in the revelation of Yahweh's requirements and guiding principles and, for that matter, given the full composite narrative of Exodus, in the instructions for the media of worship in Yahweh's Presence as well. "These words" may be taken as a reference to the whole of Yahweh's explanatory revelation regarding the application of the principles set forth in his own "Ten Words." It is on the basis of this entire range of revelation that Yahweh "has made" a covenant with Moses and with Israel (cf. this pairing in 32:30–32; 33:12–17; 34:9; note Davis, *WTJ* 44 [1982] 83). We are indeed told, immediately following this command of Yahweh, that Moses was a very long time carrying it out; the usual designation of a considerable period of time, "forty days and forty nights," is given, with the added note that Moses neither ate nor drank during this time with Yahweh.

The final sentence of the renewal narrative should then be read as a new paragraph, in sequence both to 34:10 and 34:1, setting forth in specific clarification of the statement of Yahweh's command to Moses to write (v 27) that what *Yahweh* wrote, by way of contrast, was what he had written before and what he had promised to write again, namely, "the words of the covenant, the Ten Words." The awkwardness of the final sentence of v 28 may well suggest that it was appended to the end of the renewal narrative to resolve the very confusion it has increased. In any case the sentence can be taken as a reference to the writing Yahweh did, just as he had promised, immediately following the different (though unfortunately ambiguous) designation of the writing Moses was to do.

Certainty is of course impossible in the interpretation of these verses. The suggestion above, like the other approaches to these verses, amounts finally to a guess. Its merit, if it has any merit, lies in its attempt to see the composite narrative as making sense in its canonical form. Moberly (*Mountain of God,* 101–6, 209–10, nn. 197–99) makes a similar proposal, though his suggestion of the "independence" of v 28b and his assumptions that "the writer" of Exod 34 "assumes the tradition made explicit in Deut 10:1–4" and "takes for granted that the reader . . . will naturally read v 28b . . . with Yahweh as subject" seem to me to go a bit far, even as guesswork. Very few people have after all read these verses in such a manner.

Explanation

The genius of this composite reporting the renewal of the covenant relationship between Yahweh and Israel is that it does not make any attempt to replicate the dramatic narrative of the first solemnization of the covenant in Exod 24. Instead, it appropriately stresses the Achilles' heel of the first covenant relationship—Israel's willingness to compromise the promise of undiluted loyalty to Yahweh—by reviewing the requirements whose obedience would make defection far less likely.

The narrative of renewal is thus introduced, following Yahweh's statement that he is again "making a covenant," by a repetitive emphasis upon his active Presence among them, upon his demand for absolute singleness in his people's loyalty to him, and upon the relationships they simply *must* avoid if they are not to compromise their loyalty to Yahweh yet again. Following this introduction, a summary series of Yahweh's requirements, each of them addressing some aspect of the compromise of a single loyalty, is listed. The people are not to make gods of shaped metal for themselves, no matter whom they may represent—a direct allusion to their sin with the calf. They are to keep Passover, and to keep it as directed, and also the Sabbath and the three great yearly sacred feasts. They are to consider every firstborn creature Yahweh's, some to be given, some, including their own sons, to be redeemed; they are to give firstfruits to Yahweh. They are not to boil a kid in the milk of its mother.

In such a manner, with a deliberate and repeated emphasis upon Yahweh's absolute requirement of an undivided loyalty, with a multiplication of the caveats against compromise, and with a summary review of commandments designed to emphasize the people's uniqueness, to themselves as well as to others, the composite narrative of covenant renewal is presented. It is a brilliantly apt sequence, carefully linked to both the decalogue and the Book of the Covenant, and consciously drawn with the composite narrative of 32:1–33:18 in view. The very disloyalty that led to the shattering of the first covenant thus becomes the focus of the summary stipulations that introduce the second covenant. And the continuity between the two covenants is shown by the continuing active Presence of Yahweh, who writes once more the principles of life in covenant with Yahweh, and by the continued application of those principles in the requirements and guiding principles Moses is required to receive and to transmit to Israel.

Moses' Shining Face   (34:29–35)

Bibliography

Coats, G. W. "The King's Loyal Opposition: Obedience and Authority in Exodus 32–34." *Canon and Authority.* Ed. G. W. Coats and B. O. Long. Philadelphia: Fortress Press, 1977. 91–109. **Cross, F. M., Jr.** "The Priestly Work." *Canaanite Myth and Hebrew Epic.* Cambridge: Harvard University Press, 1973. 293–325. **Davis, D. R.** "Rebellion, Presence, and Covenant: A Study in Exodus 32–34." *WTJ* 44 (1982) 71–87. **Dhorme, E.** *L'emploi métaphorique des noms de parties du corps en hébreu et en akkadien.* Paris: Librairie Orientaliste Paul Geuthner, 1963. **Dumermuth, F.** "Moses strahlendes Gesicht." *TZ* 17 (1961) 241–48. **Jaroš, K.** "Der Mose 'strahlende Haut.'" *ZAW* 88 (1976) 275–80. **Jirku, A.** "Die Gesichtsmaske des Mose." *ZDPV* 67 (1944–1945) 43–45. **Morgenstern, J.** "Moses with the Shining Face." *HUCA* 2 (1925) 1–27. **Reindl, J.** *Das Angesicht Gottes im Sprachgebrauch des Alten Testaments.* 1st ser. TS 25. Leipzig: St. Benno-Verlag, 1970. **Sasson, J. M.** "Bovine Symbolism in the Exodus Narrative." *VT* 18 (1968) 380–87. **Seebass, H.** *Mose und Aaron Sinai und Gottesberg.* EvT 2. Bonn: H. Bouvier Verlag, 1962.

Translation

    [29] *When at long last Moses descended[a] Mount Sinai with the two tablets of the Testimony in hand,[b] Moses was not aware as he descended the mountain that the skin of his face shone[c] because of Yahweh's speaking with him.* [30] *Then Aaron and all the sons of Israel[a] saw Moses, and indeed[b] the skin of his face shone! Thus were they afraid to come close to him.* [31] *So Moses called out to them, and Aaron and all the chief men of the congregation came back to him.* [32] *Next Moses spoke to them, and after that,[a] all the sons of Israel came close.[b] Then he made them responsible[c] for everything Yahweh had spoken to him on Mount Sinai.*

    [33] *When Moses had finished speaking with them, he put a veil over his face.* [34] *Then whenever Moses came into the Presence of Yahweh to speak with him, he took off the veil until he went out; and whenever he went out and spoke to the sons of Israel what he had been commanded,[a]* [35] *the sons of Israel saw Moses' face, that the skin of Moses' face shone. Then Moses[a] would put the veil back on his face until he went in to speak again with Yahweh.[b]*

Notes

29.a. מֹשֶׁה בְּרֶדֶת וַיְהִי "when at long last Moses descended"; special *waw* with היה plus inf constr of ירד in the context of chaps. 33–34.

29.b. MT has מֹשֶׁה בִּיד "in the hand of Moses," the 2d of 3 occurrences of the name מֹשה in this verse. SamPent has בידו "in his hand."

29.c. קרן, lit., "sent out horns of light, glowed."

30.a. LXX reads πάντες οἱ πρεσβύτεροι "all the elders" instead of "all the sons of Israel."

30.b. והנה "and behold." Cairo Geniza fragment has כי "for."

32.a. ואחרי־כן "and after that"—cf. BDB, 486.3.

32.b. SamPent, LXX, Syr, Vg add "to him."

32.c. ויצום "Then he ordered them, put into their charge."

34.a. SamPent has יצוהו "he commanded him"; LXX reads ὅσα ἐνετείλατο αὐτῷ κύριος "what Yahweh commanded him."

35.a. SamPent omits the 3d occurrence of "Moses."

35.b. MT has simply אתו "him." The clear antecedent, Yahweh, is added above for clarity.

Form/Structure/Setting

See *Form/Structure/Setting* on 32:1–6, 7–35; 33:12–17; 33:18–34:9, 10–28.

This brief conclusion to the Presence-Absence-Presence narrative of Israel's first disobedience and its aftermath handily deals with the single theme left hanging after the sin with the calf—the question of Moses' authority as Yahweh's representative. Israel had not intended to reject Yahweh, though their action, a terrible disobedience of their covenantal promises, was in effect a rejection. Moses, however, they dismissed during his absence with the sarcastic words of anxiety, "because this Moses . . . we have no idea what has become of him" (32:1). Following that rejection, Moses is represented in the composite narrative of Exod 32–34 as both angry toward and solicitous of Israel, as pleading with Yahweh on their behalf, as persuading Yahweh to show forgiving mercy, as receiving the favor of an additional special theophany on Sinai, and as the intermediary once again of Yahweh's covenant instructions in the summary of those instructions relating particularly to the disobedience into which Israel had fallen—an appropriate review to accompany the renewal of the covenant. One matter still remains unresolved: Israel has not reaffirmed Moses as Yahweh's authoritative representative, the transmitter of Yahweh's own revelation and instructions, so quickly disregarded during his absence on Sinai and in spite of that rejection so active, even at terrible risk to himself (cf. 32:31–33 and 33:12–16), on Israel's behalf. The purpose of these seven verses that conclude the Presence-Absence-Presence narrative is to provide a resolution to this one remaining question posed by Israel's disobedience.

Source criticism has frequently assigned these verses to P, and linked them to the narrative of the giving (at 24:15–18) or the narrative of the completion (at 31:18) of Yahweh's instructions to Moses on Mount Sinai (cf. Beer, 162–65; Beyerlin, *Sinaitic Traditions*, 3–4; Hyatt, 318, 326; Cross, *Canaanite Myth*, 314: "a Priestly postscript to the JE section," 32:1–34:28b). Some scholars have suggested, however, that the P characteristics of Exod 34:29–35 are additions to a narrative belonging originally to some other source: Morgenstern (*HUCA* 2 [1925] 1–12), for example, suggested J, specifically his J2, the combination of J and Kenite narrative material (cf. Seebass, *Mose und Aaron*

32, 50–60); Noth (260 & 267) proposed that these verses were from "a special tradition comparable with 33:7–11," into which have been inserted "a few observations by J" (vv "29aa, 32b") and "some elements of P language" (" 'Aaron,' 'all the leaders of the congregation,' 'the tables of the testimony' ").

Once again, evidence for any precise assignment to underlying sources is indeterminate, and reference to such traditio-historical motifs as cultic horned masks designed to signify the divinely affirmed authority of priestly figures (Gressmann, *Mose und seine Zeit*, 246–51; Jirku, *ZDPV* 67 [1944–45] 43–45; Jaroš, *ZAW* 88 [1976] 275–80; cf. Bailey, "Horns of Moses," *IDBSup*, 419–20) and a glowing face as a sign of Moses' elevation to a semidivine state (Morgenstern, *HUCA* 2 [1925] 8–27; cf. Coats, *Canon and Authority*, 104–5, and Dumermuth, *TZ* 17 [1961] 243–48) are similarly far too speculative to be sustained by the scanty OT evidence. Whatever ANE ideas and practices may lie behind these verses in their present form remains a puzzle of which we have far too few pieces for even a tentative reconstruction (cf. Moberly, *Mountain of God*, 179–80). Until further information is available, the most we can reasonably attempt is some understanding of why this narrative of a shining face, which had consequently to be veiled to avoid frightening people, became the conclusion to a brilliantly arranged composite narrative of Israel's shattering of the covenant relationship with Yahweh and of the renewal of that relationship after the entirely justified threat of the withdrawal of Israel's *raison d'être*, the Presence of Yahweh.

The answer to that inquiry can be seen with any clarity only when Exod 34:29–35 is viewed as an integral part of the larger narrative sequence of Exod 32–34, and specifically as the concluding section of that sequence, which began, in its very first verse, with a rejection by Israel of the human intermediary through whom Yahweh had chosen to give the application of his ten commandments, his guiding principles, and his instruction for the media, the times, and the ways of worship in his Presence. If Moses should remain discredited, both the repetition of Yahweh's revelation and instruction given already and also the continuing revelation and instruction to be given through him would be compromised. Moses' authority must therefore be reestablished in the eyes of the very people who have rejected him, and by none other than Yahweh himself. That is undertaken in these verses and in a manner that keeps Yahweh and Yahweh's Presence central, just as it is throughout all the rest of the Exodus narrative.

Comment

29 Moses' descent from Sinai a second time with the two tablets, pointedly called here as in 32:15 שְׁנֵי לֻחֹת הָעֵדֻת "the two tablets of the Testimony" (see *Comment* on 16:32–34), is a deliberate contrast to his first descent in 32:7–35. There, he came down to rejection and chaos; here, he comes down to awe and acceptance. What makes the difference is obviously the reestablishment of Moses as Yahweh's own messenger. And what symbolizes that difference is Moses' shining face. While there can be no doubt concerning *what* was shining or glowing, since the text quite unambiguously specifies that it was עוֹר פָּנָיו "the skin of his face," just what the skin of Moses' face was doing remains the subject of continuing discussion. The verb קָרַן occurs only in this passage, three times (vv 29, 30, 35). Its connection with horns, קְרָנַיִם, is far more defensible than its connection with light (cf. Jaroš, *ZAW* 88 [1976] 276–79), and the hiphil of אוֹר would far more clearly have suggested "shining" than does קָרַן—unless the author of this narrative had some specific and different kind of shining in mind.

Moberly (*Mountain of God*, 108–9) suggests that the use of קֶרֶן was a deliberate attempt to link Moses, as Yahweh's choice of a representative, with the calf, the people's choice of a representative of Yahweh, "a daring parallelism" (cf. a similar connection, for very different reasons, by Sasson, *VT* 18 [1968] 384–87). The fatal flaw in this theory, however, lies in the fact that the word for "horn," קֶרֶן, is nowhere used in the composite narrative of Exod 32–34. Dumermuth (*TZ* 17 [1961] 243–48), on the basis of a comparison of similar phenomena from other religious traditions (Gautama Buddha, Ramakrishna, and Swiss mysticism) proposes a mystical inner transformation somewhat inadequately described as a glowing face.

In fact, we simply do not have enough information to enable us to form any clear understanding of what is meant by the use of קֶרֶן to describe what happened to the skin of Moses' face as a result of his close communion with Yahweh, but the key must certainly lie in Yahweh and not in Moses, as the use of this narrative to reassert Moses' rejected authority shows. It is at least possible that קֶרֶן was deliberately used rather than הֵאִיר "shine, give light," for example, because the narrator intended to suggest a light or a shining that was separate from Moses' own person, an appendage-light, an exterior light, a light that was a gift to Moses from Yahweh, a sign precisely of an authority that was his by virtue of his special fellowship with Yahweh, an authority of which Moses himself was unaware, as the text plainly says.

30–32 The reaction of Aaron and Israel to Moses' shining face was fear. The transformation of his appearance was striking, and apparently it suggested to them the fearful circumstances of the Sinai theophany of Exod 19–20 and 24 (cf. the comparison of Childs, 617–18), which was, of course, exactly what it was supposed to do. Only when Moses called out to Aaron and the leaders who represented the people, and only when they drew near and conversed with Moses without harm, did the people themselves feel that it was safe to come close to Moses. And then it was that Moses began the process of reviewing for them the revelation he had received on Sinai. The specific reference of v 32b, in the context of Exod 34, is the review of the commandments and instructions connected especially with disloyalty and the conditions that lead to disloyalty (34:10–27). The larger reference, however, in the context of the composite narrative of Exod 32–34 and the still broader composite frame of Exod 19–31, is the full extent of Yahweh's covenantal due. The verb that describes this review of Moses is revealing: וַיְצַוֵּם, piel imperfect of צוה, "Then he made them responsible for, gave into their charge," in effect turned over to them the commandments and instructions given to him by Yahweh for their guidance in living the life in relationship to Yahweh's Presence. This amounts, given the context, to Israel's recommitment to the requirements of covenant relationship.

33 When Moses had completed this review and recommitment of Israel, he put a veil, מסוה, over his face. Just why Moses did this we are not told, though the assumptions generally are that he did so (1) to avoid frightening the people and (2) to indicate the end of his "official" communication of Yahweh's revelation. With the veil in place, Moses would be speaking once again for himself. The word מסוה is used in the OT only in this passage (in vv 33, 34, 35), and its exact meaning is impossible to discover without further information. The term appears to have been derived from a root (סוה) that has to do with covering (cf. BDB, 691, and סותה "his mantle, cloak" in Gen 49:11). This ambiguity has given rise to the widespread theory that the מסוה was a cultic mask of some sort (so Gressmann, *Mose und seine Zeit*, 249–51; Jirku, *ZDPV* 67 [1944–45] 43–45; Hyatt, 327; Jaroš, *ZAW* 88 [1976] 278–80), but such a notion cannot be supported by the text in its present form, not least, as has often been pointed out, because the function of the מסוה is exactly the reverse of the function of a cultic mask (cf. Morgenstern, *HUCA* 2 [1925] 4, n. 9; Dumermuth, *TZ* 17 [1961] 241–43; Childs, 609–10, though note also 618–19; Davis, *WTJ* 44 [1982] 84–85, esp. n. 29). The מסוה must rather be regarded as a covering of some sort, a veil or cloth through which Moses could see but which would obscure from the view of those around Moses the glowing skin of his face.

What is far more significant than the appearance of Moses' face, or the means by which he obscured that appearance, is what this unusual sight, which may after all be largely a theological metaphor, implies in the context of Exod 32–34. Davis (*WTJ* 44 [1982] 84–85) has suggested a dual meaning: the unveiled face symbolizing "renewed acceptance," the shining face of Yahweh "reflected from Moses' face," the veiled face symbolizing "the catastrophe of rebellion." Only the first of these two suggestions has any biblical basis, and that in the light of the OT theology of Yahweh's "shining face" (cf. Num 6:25; Ps 80; Dhorme, *L'emploi métaphorique*, 51–56; Reindl, *Angesicht Gottes*, 137–45). Moberly (*Mountain of God*, 108) proposes that the shining face of Moses *without* any covering was a deliberate putdown of the use of cultic masks to represent deity: "It is a man and not an object who has the role of mediating Yahweh." This view seems to impose on the text more than is there and more than we know, as Moberly (179) himself later admits, of what may or may not have been a practice in the *Sitz im Leben* from which this tradition comes.

34–35 Nothing more than a guess can be attempted, but it is possible that both the shining skin of Moses' face and also the veil which hides that shining from view are to be understood as symbols of Moses' reaffirmed authority, and nothing more. The text itself seems to suggest as much by its shift, following the narrative reference to the veil, to the statement of the continuing and habitual practice of Moses with the veil. *Whenever* Moses came into Yahweh's Presence (wherever this was, the Tabernacle, the Tent of Meeting of Exod 33:7–11, or even Sinai or some other place of theophany, is deliberately left unspecified thus making the statement inclusive), he removed the veil and so spoke with Yahweh "face to Presence" (cf. Exod 33:11), in intimate communion. Having absorbed the brightness of Yahweh's Presence, Moses' glowing face as he departed from Yahweh's Presence to communicate Yahweh's Word to Israel, left no doubt about the authority of the words he spoke. Then, when the divine message had been delivered, Moses would always put the veil once again over his face. This hiding of the glow was the symbol that Moses' further words were his own, not to be confused with what Yahweh had said. One might well imagine, in such a case, that the veil was at least as much for Moses' benefit as for Israel's.

Explanation

The concluding section of the narrative sequence of Exod 32–34 reverses the last of the dire effects of Israel's sin with the golden calf. The rejection of Moses, made so impulsively and in selfish and thoughtless panic while he was away with Yahweh on Sinai, is negated by Yahweh himself, who once more does for Moses what Moses cannot do for himself. As a result of his work of receiving Yahweh's instructions in the brightness of Yahweh's Presence, Moses' face glows with a supernatural light. This light leaves no doubt about Yahweh's favor toward Moses and no doubt about the source of the requirements and guiding principles Moses announces to Israel. As if to underline the uniqueness of that symbolism, Moses exposes his face when he is in Yahweh's Presence and also as he passes along to Israel what Yahweh has revealed to him for them. Then Moses covers his face—until the next time.

Thus at the end of the Presence-Absence-Presence narrative Moses' credibility is restored. Israel can no longer doubt what he says when he reports Yahweh's Word to them, and Israel can no longer wonder where he is and what he is doing and whether he will return when he is beyond their sight. The way is thus cleared for the continuation of Yahweh's revelation, particularly in the fulfillment of the instructions he has already given.

IV. Israel's Obedience of Yahweh's Instructions   (35:1–40:38)

The Offering of the Materials and the Recognition of the Artisans   (35:1–36:7)

PARALLELS, IN SEQUENCE:
31:12–18 = 35:1–3; 25:1–7 = 35:4–9;
31:6–10 = 35:10–19; 31:1–6 = 35:30–36:1

Bibliography

Alter, R. *The Art of Biblical Narrative.* New York: Basic Books, 1981. **Cross, F. M.** "The Priestly Work." *Canaanite Myth and Hebrew Epic.* Cambridge: Harvard University Press, 1973. 293–325. **Elliger, K.** "Sinn und Ursprung der priesterlichen Geschictser-zählung." *Kleine Schriften zum Alten Testament.* TBü 32. Munich: Chr. Kaiser Verlag, 1966. 174–98. **Gray, J.** *The KRT Text in the Literature of Ras Shamra.* 2d ed. Leiden: E. J. Brill, 1964. **Kearney, P. J.** "Creation and Liturgy: The P Redaction of Ex 25–40." *ZAW* 89 (1977) 375–86. **Koch, K.** *Die Priesterschrift von Exodus 25 bis Leviticus 16.* Göttingen: Vanderhoeck & Ruprecht, 1959. **McEvenue, S. E.** *The Narrative Style of the Priestly Writer.* AnBib 50. Rome: Biblical Institute Press, 1971. **Muilenburg, J.** "A Study in Hebrew Rhetoric: Repetition and Style," *Congress Volume: Copenhagen, 1953.* VTSup 1. Leiden: E. J. Brill, 1953. 97–111. **Vink, J. G.** "The Date and Origin of the Priestly Code in the Old Testament." *OTS* 15 (1969) 1–144.

Translation

¹ Then Moses called to assembly the whole congregation of the sons of Israel, and he said to them, "These are the words that Yahweh has commanded to be obeyed: ᵃ ² 'Six days is customary labor to be done. ᵃ The seventh day, you are to keep sacred, ᵇ a sabbath of sabbath-rest belonging to Yahweh: anyone who does customary labor during it is to die. ³ You are not to build a fire in any of your dwelling places on the sabbath day.' "

⁴ Next Moses said this to the whole congregation of the sons of Israel: "This is the word that Yahweh has commanded; he said, ᵃ ⁵ 'Take from your own possessions ᵃ an offering for Yahweh: everyone whose mind urges him is to bring it, ᵇ Yahweh's offering of gold, silver, copper, ⁶ violet yarn, purple yarn, scarlet yarn, fine linen, goats' hair, ⁷ red-dyed rams' hides, sea-cows' hides, acacia ᵃ lumber, ⁸ oil for light, aromatic spices for the Oil of Anointment and for the Special Formula Incense, ⁹ and gemstones and stones to be set on the Ephod and the Breastpiece.

¹⁰ " 'All who are wise in mind among you are to come and to make all that Yahweh has commanded: ¹¹ the Tabernacle, its tent, its cover, its fasteners, its supports, its crossmembers, its columns, and its pedestals; ¹² the Ark, its carrying-poles, the Ark-Cover, and the Veil separating the Holiest Space; ᵃ ¹³ the Table, its carrying-

poles, all its equipment, and the Bread of the Presence; ᵃ ¹⁴ the Lampstand for the light, its equipment, its lamps, ᵃ and oil for the light; ¹⁵ the Altar of Incense and its poles, the Oil of Anointment, the Special Formula Incense, and the Veil for the opening at the opening of the Tabernacle; ¹⁶ the Altar of wholly-burned offerings, the copper grate belonging to it, its carrying-poles, all its equipment, and the Laver and its pedestal; ¹⁷ the draperies of the Courtyard, its columns and its pedestals, and the Screen for the entrance of the Courtyard; ¹⁸ the anchor-pegs of the Tabernacle, the anchor-pegs of the Courtyard, and their ropes; ¹⁹ the elaborately sewn vestments for ministry in worship in the Holy Space, the sacral vestments for Aaron the priest and the vestments of his sons for priestly ministry.' "

²⁰ Thus the whole congregation of the sons of Israel went out of Moses' presence; ²¹ then they came, every man whose mind prompted ᵃ him, everyone whose spirit urged him, bringing an offering for Yahweh for the manufacture of the Tent of Appointed Meeting and for all its work, and for the sacral vestments. ²² They came, the men and the women as well, everyone whose mind urged it: they brought nose-rings and earrings and finger-rings ᵃ and bangles, ᵇ all of them articles of gold, every person ᶜ presenting by gesture ᵈ an offering ᵉ of gold to Yahweh. ²³ Every person who owned ᵃ violet yarn, purple yarn, scarlet yarn, fine linen, goats' hair, red-dyed rams' hides, and sea-cows' hides brought them. ²⁴ Everyone who could contribute a present of silver or copper brought it as Yahweh's present, and everyone who owned acacia lumber useful to the workmanship ᵃ of construction brought it. ²⁵ Every woman who knew how ᵃ set her hands to making yarn; then they brought yarn: violet yarn, purple yarn, scarlet yarn, and fine linen. ²⁶ All the women whose minds prompted them with skill ᵃ spun the goat's hair. ²⁷ The leaders brought gemstones and stones to be set on the Ephod and the Breastpiece, ²⁸ aromatic spices, and oil for light, for the Oil of Anointment, and for the Special Formula Incense. ²⁹ All the men and the women whose minds urged them to bring anything for the workmanship that Yahweh had commanded through Moses to be done did so as Israelites, making a voluntary offering to Yahweh.

³⁰ Next Moses said to the sons of Israel, "Take note—Yahweh has called out by name Bezalel, son of Uri, son of Hur, of the tribe of Judah, ³¹ then filled him with the spirit of God, in wisdom, in discernment, and in skill and in workmanship of every kind, ³² to design intricate patterns for work in gold, in silver and in copper, ³³ in engraving gemstones for setting, and in carving wood to make elaborate workmanship of every kind. ³⁴ And he has put it into his mind to teach, both him and Oholiab, ᵃ son of Ahisamach, of the tribe of Dan, ³⁵ filling them with wisdom of mind to do every kind of workmanship, whether of a metal-worker, ᵃ a designer, ᵇ an embroiderer in violet yarn, purple yarn, scarlet yarn and fine linen, or a weaver: they are able to do ᶜ any kind of workmanship and work out complex plans. ³⁶:¹ Bezalel and Oholiab and every person wise of mind to whom Yahweh has given ᵃ wisdom and discernment to be skilled and to accomplish all the workmanship of the construction of the Holy Space are to make all that Yahweh has commanded."

² So Moses called out Bezalel and Oholiab and every person wise of mind to whom Yahweh had given wisdom of mind, all those whose mind prompted them to take on the work ᵃ and do it. ³ Then they had from Moses the whole of the contribution that the sons of Israel had brought to make possible ᵃ the workmanship of the construction of the Holy Space. Yet they brought the voluntary offering to Moses ᵇ still, morning after morning, ⁴ so that all expert craftsmen busy with ᵃ all the workmanship of the

*Holy Space came, man after man leaving his specialized task, the work they all were
doing,* [5] *and they said to Moses this: "The people are bringing far more than is
required for the construction of the workmanship Yahweh has commanded to be done."* [a]
[6] *Thus Moses gave an order, and an announcement was passed along through the
camp to the effect that neither any man nor any woman was to produce anything
more for the contribution for the Holy Space: then the people restrained their giving.*
[7] *What they had given* [a] *was sufficient for the accomplishment of the workmanship,
with some left over.*

Notes

1.a. אתם לעשת "to do them."

2.a. LXX and Syr read "you are to do." SamPent has יעשה "it (masc) is to be done."

2.b. קדש לכם יהיה "it is to be for you set apart."

4.a. לאמר.

5.a. מאתכם "from with yourselves"; the offering is to be specifically Israel's, taken from
what is theirs, as opposed to any other possible sources.

5.b. This obj suff is absent from SamPent, Syr, Tg Onk, Tg Ps-J.

7.a. L unaccountably has שִׂטִים שָׁטִים instead of שָׁטִים "acacia," but the parallel in 25:5 makes
plain that שִׂטִים is correct.

12.a. MT has המסך פרכת "the Veil of the covering." מָסָך is the term for the Screen covering
the opening of the Tabernacle (26:36–37), but the word is used also to designate the Screen
covering the opening of the Courtyard of the Tabernacle (27:16). In sum, all three coverings
connected with the Tabernacle and its Courtyard are referred to by the noun מָסָך.

13.a. This last phrase, "and . . . Presence," is not in LXX.

14.a. SamPent and LXX add "all" before "its equipment" and do not have "its lamps."

21.a. Lit., "whom it lifted him, his heart."

22.a. SamPent reads עגיל "hoop, ring" of some sort.

22.b. כומז "bangles": an article of jewelry no longer known to us, though it appears to be
derived from a root that means "bunch, heap" (BDB, 484; cf. KB, 443, 458). None of the
articles of jewelry in this list can be translated with complete assurance, though the first three
appear to be rings of some kind.

22.c. איש "man" in its distributive, inclusive sense; see BDB, 36. SamPent omits this איש;
cf. LXX.

22.d. זהב תנופת הניף "he waved a wave-offering of gold": the waving of an offering was
a gesture of dedication to Yahweh in Yahweh's Presence.

22.e. Cairo Geniza fragment has תרומת, a "raising, contribution" of gold.

23.a. "Whom it was found with him."

24.a. SamPent reads simply העבדה למלאכת "for the workmanship of construction."

25.a. חכמת־לב "wise of heart (= mind)": the woman skilled at spinning and weaving is
intended.

26.a. Lit., "all the women whose hearts lifted them with wisdom."

34.a. See n. 31:6.b.

35.a. חָרָשׁ "engraver, skilled craftsman" in 1 Sam 13:19; Jer 10:9; and Deut 27:15 clearly
refers to a worker in metal, and in the latter two examples (cf. also Isa 44:9–11), to the specialized
metal-worker who does the refined work of idol-making and decoration.

35.b. חֹשֵׁב a "thinking, inventing, devising one." Cf. BDB, 362–63.

35.c. עשׂי "doers of."

36:1.a. LXX has ᾧ ἐδόθη "to whom was given."

36:2.a. לקרבה "to draw near, approach" the work.

3.a. אתה לעשׂת "to do it."

3.b. MT "to him"; antecedent added for clarity.

4.a. העשׂים "the ones doing."

·5.a. See n. 3.a.

7.a. והמלאכה "and the work, workmanship."

Form/Structure/Setting

See *Form/Structure/Setting* on 25:1–9 and 26:1–37.

The repetition in Exod 35–39 of information already given in chaps. 25–31 has frequently been pointed out and quite often attributed to a later and secondary layer of the P material. So Galling (Beer, 13, 165), e.g., attributed most of chaps. 25–29 to his P^A and P^B, all of chap. 30 and the first eleven verses of chap. 31 to his P^S (the latest layer of P), and most of chaps. 35–40 to P^S. So also for Elliger (*Kleine Schriften*, 174–75), very little of 35–40 belongs to the earlier layer of P (Elliger's P^g). Koch's (*Priesterschrift*, 7–48) theory of ritual *Vorlage* underlying P^g and providing for it both authority and agenda leads to a three-layered concept: the first layer consisted of an array of compact ritual *Sätze* orally transmitted and connected with a pre-Jerusalemite cultus. To this layer Koch (42–45) assigned only 40:1–15 of chaps. 35–40; the second layer, P^g, a written tradition connected with Jerusalem, included only 35:20–29 (Koch, 39–40) from chaps. 35–40; the third layer, made up of additional material connected with the fulfillment of divine commands, Koch (38–48) held to include the bulk of chaps. 35–40.

Vink, who connects the "Priestly Code" to Ezra's mission (*OTS* 15 [1969] 18–63), takes the somewhat different view that chaps. 35–40 are linked closely to chaps. 30–31 and that these chapters together are to be termed "P-*Grundschrift*," while 25:1–29:42 are "closer to the *Vorlage*" (102–8). According to Vink's theory, chaps. 35–40 are much nearer to the mainstream of P than chaps. 25–29, but that mainstream is post-exilic and so somewhat later than many literary critics would maintain. Cross (*Canaanite Myth*, 323–25) has recently argued for a sixth-century date for P and has suggested that the tetrateuchal P strata "never existed as an independent narrative document." Kearney (*ZAW* 89 [1977] 375–86), following Cross, has proposed that "a P editor," following the ANE linking of Temple building with divine creation, presented in Exod 25–40 a unity based on Gen 1:1–2:3: "creation (ch. 25–31), fall (ch. 32–33) and restoration (ch. 34–40)." According to Kearney's theory, chaps. 25–31 present seven speeches of Yahweh to Moses, based on the seven days of creation; chaps. 35–40 echo this structure faintly in speeches made by Moses, and chaps. 32–34 are JE material edited by P "to effect a balance" between what amounts to Yahweh's revelation to Moses (25–31) and Moses' revelation to Israel (35–40).

None of these varied theories gives any satisfactory answer to the question of the similarities and differences of Exod 25–31 and 35–40, however, despite their helpful illumination of a number of detailed points. They tend toward too late a dating for the underlying concerns of P, primarily because they identify these concerns too much in terms of the context in which they believe P to have come to its final form. It is all over again far too much a case of dating the whole of P, this time in terms of its conceptual rather than its literary *Sitz,* in or too near the period of its end form. As noted above (*Form/ Structure/Setting* on 25:1–9), the nucleus of the P material in Exodus may best be seen not by isolating the P material but by viewing it as an integral part of the composite Exodus. What links Exod 25–31 and 35–40 is not primarily a series of literary connections, but a series of theological ones; and at

the heart of the theological connections is the ever-present irreducible minimum of the Book of Exodus, the immanent Presence of Yahweh.

The similarities of Exod 25–31 and 35–40 may all be accounted for on
the basis of their rootage in this all-encompassing theme: both sections, each
in its own way, are preoccupied with Israel's need to experience the reality
of Yahweh's Presence. The differences between Exod 25–31 and 35–40 may
all be accounted for if four probabilities are kept in mind: (1) Exod 35–40
is based on the same theme as Exod 25–31 but follows a different order;
(2) Exod 35–40 omits or adds material in comparison with Exod 25–31 in
relation to its own separate purpose and was not intended simply to duplicate
chaps. 25–31; (3) the obvious repetition of parts of Exod 25–31 in Exod
35–40, sometimes even a verbatim repetition, is for didactic and liturgical
reasons, and perhaps also by reason of genre; and (4) the two sections are
seen as having developed along with both the Exodus composite and, to a
degree, alongside each other, and are viewed in the context of Exodus as a
whole rather than as parts in isolation.

The theme "Yahweh's Presence in Israel's Midst" is presented in Exod
25–31 by extending a call for the offering of materials worthy of symbolizing
and remaining near Yahweh's Presence, then following that call with a series
of instructions for the preparation of such media, listed in a sequence moving
from the most intimate of those symbols (the Ark) to the symbol farthest
from it (the Tabernacle Court). This order provides for the linking of the
three circles of nearness to Yahweh's Presence (see *Form/Structure/Setting* on
25:1–9), is expanded by various appendices, and is closed by the establishment
of the command to keep the sabbath as a sign of the uniqueness of a people
among whom Yahweh is resident.

The theme "Yahweh's Presence in Israel's Midst" is presented in Exod
35–40 in an order that begins with this sabbath-emphasis, then moves logically
to the gathering of materials and the recognition of the artisans, to the actual
construction of the Tabernacle and its equipment and its Court, to the preparation of the sacral vestments of those who will minister in and join the
three circles of nearness, to the erection of the Tabernacle and the climactic
arrival onto it and in it of Yahweh's Presence. Into this sequence have been
inserted two summary sections, one dealing with the precious metals used
in the fulfillment of Yahweh's instructions and one dealing with the fulfillment
of all those instructions.

Some matters dealt with in chaps. 25–31, as for example the ordination
of the priests or the collection of the atonement money, are not included
in this sequence because they would be both inappropriate and irrelevant,
perhaps even impossible, before the arrival of Yahweh's Presence. So also
the account of the coming of that Presence could hardly be given before
the Tabernacle had actually been constructed and set up.

The repetitious style of the Priestly source is well known (cf. McEvenue,
Narrative Style, 10–21, 49–50, 167–71), though far too little attention has been
given to the reasons for such repetition, either in the Priestly material or in
the OT as a whole (cf. Muilenburg, *Congress Volume*, 97–111; Alter, *The Art*,
88–113). The repetition in Exod 35–40 of material in chaps. 25–31 is probably
quite deliberate and should not therefore be regarded as merely the insignifi-

cant duplication of a later and supplementary source. The redactor who brought Exodus into the form in which we know it must certainly have been aware of the similarities between the two sections, including the numerous points where the parallels are verbatim. The fact that the repetition remains suggests some purpose for it, and given the essential nature of the theme underlying the two sections, that purpose may be understood as both didactic—the instruction of Israel and Israel's priests concerning fundamental symbols and practices that were all too frequently either corrupted or abandoned—and liturgical—the ordering of movement and perhaps also word in the round of worship by which Israel both asserted and reinforced faith. Cassuto (453) has suggested also the influence of the ANE genre of the giving of divine instructions which are then reported as carried out by a detailed repetition of the instructions. Cassuto's example is the Ugaritic account of King Keret's dream (Gray, *KRT Text,* 12–14) in which El gives instructions subsequently followed by Keret and repeated nearly verbatim in the account (15–18) of his accomplishments.

Finally, chaps. 25–31 and 35–40 need to be seen as complementary of one another. The questions of which section is nearer a supposed *Vorlage* and of how one section can be seen to presuppose or to supplement the other tend to draw attention away from the manner in which the two sections complete each other as instruction and obedience, as promise and fulfillment. Yahweh instructs Moses and gives him the visionary pattern of his intentions in chaps. 25–31; Moses passes along the instructions and his understanding of them as they are carried out in chaps. 35–40. The first sequence begins with the call for materials; the second section begins with the offering of these materials. The first section ends with instructions for the priests' ordination, then is followed by a sequence of supplemental material which ends with an emphasis on keeping the sabbath as a sign of the special relationship founded on Yahweh's Presence. The second sequence ends with the advent of Yahweh's Presence onto and into the newly built and erected Tabernacle, an authentication of the symbols and an authorization of the beginning of worship with them. In sum, there is an intercomplementary relationship between Exod 25–31 and Exod 35–40 throughout, one that links these sections far more closely and far more consequentially than has generally been assumed.

Comment

1–3 The second sequence dealing with the symbols of worship in Yahweh's Presence begins where the first sequence left off, with the reminder of Israel's special identity as the people among whom Yahweh dwells—the sabbath day. As noted above (*Comment* on 31:12), this strict command of a day set apart serves as a bridge, binding Exod 25–31 and Exod 35–40 together. This reference does not call the sabbath a sign (אוֹת) as 31:12–18 does, and there is added here a prohibition against building a fire on the sabbath, one definition of what is meant by customary work on the sabbath, quite possibly one having to do with the preparation of food (cf. Exod 16:22–30, and see above).

4–9 Moses' call for the offering of materials for the construction of the Tabernacle and its equipment is a review of the materials listed earlier in 25:3–7, but particular and repeated emphasis is laid on the fact that it is to be (1) an offering of the people's own possessions and (2) entirely a voluntary offering. This point, hinted in 25:2, is stressed here at the beginning of this sequence (v 4), at its end in the report of the over-lavish gift (36:5–7), and also *within* the sequence, at vv 21–22, 29.

10–19 The listing of what Yahweh has commanded to be made is similarly a review of objects listed earlier, but again with a special emphasis, one also hinted at earlier (31:6): the artisans and their assistants are persons already gifted whose minds and hands Yahweh will now endow even more lavishly. There is to be a partnership of human genius and dexterity with divine direction, the whole enhanced by a further divine outpouring: 35:10, 25–26, 30–35; 36:1–3.

20–29 The account of the bringing of the offering for the media of worship is both an additional review of materials listed previously (with some supplemental additions) and a description of skilled labor that preceded the work of Bezalel and Oholiab and the expert craftsmen who assisted them. For the first time, women are specifically mentioned as participants in both the giving and the preparation of materials for giving. A series of articles of gold jewelry, some if not all of it to be understood as belonging exclusively to women, is listed, and women skilled at spinning are said to have made yarn of the colored fibers, the fine linen and the goat's hair. That this and other labor of preparation of the materials to be brought are to be considered a part of the voluntary gifts is suggested by 36:5–6.

30–36:2 The recognition of Bezalel and Oholiab is a repetition of the account of Yahweh's call of them in 31:2–11, with the additional report that they are able themselves to *do* any kind of specialized workmanship, have been given the ability to unravel the most complex plans, and have also been inspired by Yahweh to teach those who are to assist them in what they must know to fulfill the tasks necessary to the completion of Yahweh's instructions concerning the media of worship. Two of the colored yarns mentioned here and throughout the instruction connected with the Tabernacle and the sacral vestments, violet yarn (תכלת) and purple yarn (ארגמן), are mentioned also in Jer 10:9 as clothing for idols, מַעֲשֵׂה חֲכָמִים "work of skilled craftsmen." The parallel to the instructions in Exodus is striking.

3–7 The account of the offering of the materials for the Tabernacle, its equipment, and its supplies as a willing offering of labor and possessions, placed into the skilled hands of expert craftsmen with thinking and dexterity divinely enhanced, is brought to a confirming conclusion by a report of the superabundance of preparing and giving. So many materials came to be brought day after day, beyond the point of obvious sufficiency, that the craftsmen under the supervision of Bezalel and Oholiab had to stop their labor and inform Moses. Moses then sends word through the camp not only that both men and women are to stop giving, but also that they are to stop producing things for contribution—a deft hint that the joy of the response to Yahweh's call for voluntary gifts was so great as to obscure the fact that the gifts were impeding progress on the Tabernacle, rather than making it possible. And even after Moses by command persuaded the people to restrain themselves from giving, there was still well more than enough for the task at hand.

Explanation

The complementary relationship of Exod 35–40 to Exod 25–31 is made plain by this beginning sequence, which starts where the earlier section left off—with an emphasis on the importance of the sabbath—and which reviews the instructions given earlier as it starts the narrative of their fulfillment. Everything to be made and everything to be used in that process, the artisans who are to direct and supervise the work and the manner of their enablement— all are reviewed, with important supplementary information, as for example, the source of the gold to be used (it came from the women's financial security, their dowry-jewelry), the involvement of women in the preparation of materials, and the full endowment of Bezalel and Oholiab to understand, to do, and to teach how to do.

Yet something more is stressed in this sequence also: the fulfillment of Yahweh's instructions was not merely dutiful, it was exuberant. The voluntary nature of the offering that is being called for is stressed throughout this beginning, as is the involvement of all the people, both men and women, in a giving, a preparation for giving, and more giving still—all of which leads, as the actual work of the craftsmen gets under way, to an embarrassment of riches and an order by Moses that the giving and the preparation for giving cease. The point is thus established before Israel's formal worship can even be begun that Israel's response to Yahweh present in their midst is to be in no way routine, in no way a reluctant meeting of requirement. For Yahweh who has come to them, they can give only their best, and they can never give what they consider enough. That we generally consider this the unrealistic ideal of priestly euphoria may well be more a commentary on us than on this ecstatic narrative.

The Construction of the Tabernacle (36:8–38)

PARALLEL VERSES:
26:1–37

Bibliography

Gooding, D. W. *The Account of the Tabernacle.* Texts S 6. Cambridge: University Press, 1959. **Jellicoe, S.** *The Septuagint and Modern Study.* Oxford: Clarendon Press, 1968. **Katz, P.** Review of D. W. Gooding, *The Account of the Tabernacle. TLZ* 85 (1960) 350–55. **Roberts, B. J.** *SOTS Book List* 16 (1961) 25. **Robinson, H. W.** *Corporate Personality in Ancient Israel.* Rev. ed. Philadelphia: Fortress Press, 1980. **Rogerson, J. W.** "The Hebrew Conception of Corporate Personality." *JTS* 21 (1970) 1–16. **Vaux, R. de.** "Bulletin." *RB* 68 (1961) 291–92.

Translation

⁸ *So all those wise of mind for the accomplishment of the workmanship made the Tabernacle* ª *of ten curtains of woven fine linen and violet yarn, purple yarn, and scarlet yarn; with cherubs artistically embroidered Bezalel* ᵇ *made them.* ⁹ *The length of each curtain was twenty-eight cubits, and the width of each curtain, four cubits; all the curtains had an identical measurement.* ¹⁰ *He joined five curtains one to another, then the remaining five curtains one to another.* ª ¹¹ *Next he made violet loops along the edge of the curtain at the end of the first set, and he also made them along the edge of the end-curtain of the second set;* ¹² *he made fifty loops on the first end* ª*-curtain, and he made fifty loops on the end-curtain in the second set: the curtains with* ᵇ *loops were to be opposite, one to the other.* ¹³ *He made fifty fasteners of gold, then he joined the curtain-sets one to the other with the fasteners: thus the Tabernacle was in one piece.*

¹⁴ *He next made curtains of goats' hair, for a tent to go over the Tabernacle; he made eleven of these curtains.* ¹⁵ *The length of each curtain was thirty cubits, the width of each curtain, four cubits; the eleven curtains had an identical measurement.* ¹⁶ *Then he joined five of these curtains in a unit, and the remaining six in a unit.* ª ¹⁷ *He made fifty loops along the edge of the curtain at the end of one set, and he made fifty loops along the edge of the curtain at the end* ª *of the second set.* ¹⁸ *Then he made fifty fasteners of copper* ª *to join the tent, so that it would be in one piece.* ᵇ ¹⁹ *Next he made a cover for the tent of red-dyed rams' hides and a cover of sea-cows' hides to protect it.* ª

²⁰ *He proceeded to make the standing supports for the Tabernacle of acacia lumber.* ²¹ *The length of each support was ten cubits, and the width of each support, a cubit and a half,* ²² *with two upright braces to each support, one joined to the other: thus he made all the supports of the Tabernacle.* ²³ *He made the supports for the Tabernacle so: twenty supports for the Negev side, facing south,* ²⁴ *and he made forty pedestals of silver to hold up the twenty supports, two pedestals underneath one support, for its two braces, and two pedestals underneath the next support for its two braces;* ²⁵ *and for the second side of the Tabernacle, facing north, he made twenty supports,* ²⁶ *along with forty pedestals of silver for them, two pedestals underneath one support, and two pedestals underneath the next support;* ²⁷ *for the deep* ª *side of the Tabernacle, westward, he made six supports,* ²⁸ *and he made two supports for the corners of the Tabernacle on the deep side:* ²⁹ *they were doubled at the bottom, and they were joined; they made a unit at the top where there was a single ring: thus he made two of them, for the two corners.* ³⁰ *In all, there were eight supports, along with their sixteen pedestals of silver, two pedestals underneath each support.*

³¹ *Next he made cross-members of acacia lumber, five for the supports of one side of the Tabernacle,* ³² *and five cross-members for the supports of the other side of the Tabernacle, and five cross-members for the supports* ª *of the Tabernacle on the deep side, westward.* ³³ *He made the middle cross-member to pass through the midpoint of the supports from end to end.* ³⁴ *He overlaid the supports with gold, and he made rings of gold as attachments for the cross-members, then he overlaid the cross-members with gold.* ª

³⁵ *Then he made a Veil of violet yarn and purple yarn and scarlet yarn and woven fine linen: he made it with cherubs artistically embroidered.* ³⁶ *He made for it four columns of acacia, and he overlaid them with gold; their hooks were gold, and he cast for them four pedestals of silver.* ª ³⁷ *Next he made a Screen for the opening*

*of the Tent, of violet yarn and purple yarn and scarlet yarn and woven fine linen,
embroidered in variegated patterns,* ³⁸ *along with its five columns and their hooks.
He overlaid the tops of the columns* ᵃ *and their rings with gold. Their five pedestals
were copper.*

Notes

8.a. LXX has τὰς στολὰς τῶν ἁγίων "the robes of the holy spaces" here, and from this point
forward follows a sequence very different from that of MT. *BHS* (148, n. 36:8b) gives a handy
equivalence summary.

8.b. MT has "he" here and throughout the remainder of chap. 36. That Bezalel is the subj
of this sequence of verbs, and the antecedent of these pronouns, is made clear by the similar
sequence of chap. 37, in whose first verse, however, Bezalel is named, but in the verses following,
right through 38:9, referred to simply as "he." Bezalel is of course referred to clearly as the
one in charge of the entire process and all the craftsmen.

10.a. The content of that part of the description of the making of the Tabernacle recorded
in vv 10–34 of this chapter is missing altogether from LXX, a fact that Gooding (*Tabernacle,*
66–77) attributes to the translator's intentional abbreviation of the text he was putting into
Greek.

12.a. See n. 26:5.a.

12.b. See n. 26:7.a.

16.a. An additional sentence about the position of the sixth curtain (26:9b) is omitted by
MT here.

17.a. See n. 26:10.a.

18.a. MT omits here the phrase about attaching the fasteners to the loops; cf. 26:11.

18.b. MT omits from the sequence at this point the explanation of what is to be done with
the extra length of the curtains making up the protective tent. Cf. 26:12–13.

19.a. See n. 26:14.c.

27.a. See n. 26:22.a.

32.a. SamPent, Tg Ps-J, Cairo Geniza add צלע "side" here, as in 26:27.

34.a. The instruction about raising the Tabernacle, included by MT at 26:30, is appropriately
omitted here.

36.a. Three verses about the arrangement of the furniture of the Tabernacle, included at
this point in the instructions (see 26:33–35), are appropriately omitted here, where the *construction*
of the Tabernacle is the subject.

38.a. MT has ראשיהם "their tops"; the antecedent is substituted for clarity.

Form/Structure/Setting

See *Form/Structure/Setting* on 25:1–9 and 35:1–36:7.

The differences between this account of the making of the Tabernacle
and the instructions for this work in 26:1–37 involve either the omission of
material appropriate to the earlier sequence and not so here, or such quite
minor matters as changes in spelling (from *plene* to defective, for example)
and the use of parallel idioms, or the logical change from action commanded
to action performed. For far the majority of this section, this second sequence
is a verbatim parallel of the first.

While this is so for MT, however, and the Samaritan Pentateuch, and in
general for the Targumic paraphrases, it is not so for LXX, which from this
chapter right through to the end of Exodus follows an order and in many
cases an inclusion of content very different from that of MT. D. W. Gooding
has given a brief review of previous attention to this question (*Tabernacle,*
1–7, 29–39) with considerable appraisal of the consequential nineteenth-cen-
tury work of Popper and a careful survey of the LXX Exodus, with special

attention to both the order and the content of chaps. 25–31 (19–28) and
35–40 (40–59, 64–77) and an analysis of technical terminology relating especially to ritual and to the Tabernacle (8–18). Gooding (99–101) reached the
conclusion that the same translator translated both chaps. 25–31 and chaps.
35–40 (excluding chap. 38, the work "in its present form" of a later editor),
that he followed a Hebrew text substantially the same as our MT, abbreviating
and omitting material at will, and that the original order of chaps. 35–40 in
the translation of LXX "in all major respects" preserved the order of MT
(78–98). Indeed, Gooding presents (102–4) a fascinating reconstruction of
the original order of chaps. 35–40, which in his view were rearranged somewhat later than they were translated, and by another hand.

On the whole, Gooding's careful argument is convincing. It has been received with enthusiasm by some scholars (e.g., Katz, *TLZ* 85 [1960] 350–
55; Jellicoe, *Septuagint*, 272–76) and with qualification by others (for example
Roberts, *Book List* 25; de Vaux, *RB* 68 [1961] 291–92), and it remains the
most thorough treatment in the twentieth century of the LXX version of
Exodus.

The account of the construction of the Tabernacle is set at the beginning
of the narrative of Israel's obedience of Yahweh's instructions to Moses on
Sinai, not out of a desire to present a chiastic parallel to those instructions
(so Cassuto, 461–62), since a real chiastic order is not presented in the narrative of Exod 35–40, but, more probably, for two reasons: (1) the making of
the Tabernacle presents the longest and most complex of the various construction narratives; and (2) more important still, the editor(s) who arranged 35–
40 wanted to bracket the construction narratives with the accounts of the
construction (36:8–38) and the erection (40:1–33) of the Tabernacle, before
which and after which is the further bracket of (1) Israel's response to the
call for materials (35:4–36:7) and (2) Yahweh's response to the completion
of all his instructions (40:34–38).

Comment

8–38 The account of the construction of the Tabernacle by Bezalel and
his assistants contains no new information and no surprising changes or omissions. It is a more compact account than the account setting forth the instructions for the Tabernacle, thirty-one verses as opposed to the thirty-seven
verses of chap. 26. The six verses in Chap. 26 that are omitted from the
parallel account here are 26:12–13, the somewhat ambiguous explanation
of the placement of the remaining half-curtain of the protective tent of goats'
hair curtains; 26:30, the instruction that the Tabernacle, completed in full
accord with what Moses was shown on Sinai, is to be raised (cf. 40:16–33);
and 26:33–35, the directions for the arrangement of the symbolic furniture
of the Tabernacle.

Each of these omissions is entirely logical, given the purpose of the narrative
of Exod 36:8–38, and not one of them offers therefore any justification for
attributing this account of the Tabernacle to a tradition separate from the
one that produced Exod 26:1–37. The other differences between the two
accounts are all quite minor, the most notable of them being the omission
of an additional sentence about the folding of the "sixth curtain" of the

protective goats' hair tent (26:9b, see 36:16) and the phrase "and attach the fasteners to the loops" in the account of the copper fasteners connecting the two sets of curtains comprising this protective tent (26:11; see 36:18).

8 The construction of the entire Tabernacle is attributed to Bezalel (see n. 8.b), following the reference in 36:8 to "all those wise of mind for the accomplishment of the workmanship." This is not by way of suggesting that Bezalel worked alone, as v 8 and the narrative of 35:30–36:7 alone make clear. Nor is the plural verb of v 8, followed by the singular verbs in the remainder of the narrative to be considered a "discrepancy" that "escaped the notice of the author" (Noth, 276). Bezalel is Yahweh's called-out and inspired "artistic director," responsible for supervising the work and assuring that it is carried out in strict accord with Yahweh's instructions delivered to Moses on the mountain. Bezalel represents the group working under his direction, and their work is in a real sense Bezalel's work, just as a king's messenger represents the king who sent him, and in a sense therefore *is* the king (cf. Robinson, *Corporate Personality*, 34–37 and Rogerson, *JTS* 21 [1970] 7–16).

Explanation

The lengthy repetition of the often abstruse details of the Tabernacle in this account of its construction is further evidence of the preoccupation of the Priestly theologians with the representation of Yahweh as a Presence on the move. Not one of the omissions of material present in Exod 26 has to do with this image of portability, and the repetition in chap. 36 in such full measure of the details given in chap. 26 provides a didactic reinforcement of the impression made there. See *Explanation* on 26:1–37.

The Construction of the Ark, the Table, the Lampstand, and the Altar of Incense (37:1–29)

PARALLELS IN SEQUENCE:
25:10–22 = 37:1–9; 25:23–30 = 37:10–16;
25:31–40 = 37:17–24; 30:1–10 = 37:25–28;
30:22–25 and 34–36 = 37:29

Bibliography

Rad, G. von. *Die Priesterschrift im Hexateuch.* BWANT 13. Stuttgart: W. Kohlhammer, 1934.

Translation

¹ *Next, Bezalel made the Ark of acacia lumber, two and a half cubits in length, one and a half cubits wide, and one and a half cubits tall.* ² *He overlaid it with*

pure gold, inside and outside; then he made for it an encircling golden beading.
³ *He cast for it four golden rings to go on* ª *its four corners, two rings upon one side and two rings upon the other side.* ⁴ *He made carrying-poles of acacia lumber, and he overlaid them with gold,* ⁵ *then thrust the carrying-poles into the rings upon the sides of the Ark, to lift the Ark.* ª

⁶ *He made an Ark-Cover of pure gold, two and a half cubits in length and one and a half cubits wide.* ⁷ *He made two golden cherubs (he made them of hammered metal) for the two ends of the Ark-Cover,* ⁸ *one cherub for one end and the other cherub for the opposite end; he made the cherubs a part of the Ark-Cover,* ª *a part of its two ends.* ⁹ *They were cherubs with spreading wings uplifted, protecting with their wings the Ark-Cover, and each was turned toward the other,* ª *while the faces of the cherubs were toward the Ark-Cover.* ᵇ

¹⁰ *He made the Table of acacia lumber, two cubits in length, one cubit wide, and one and a half cubits tall.* ¹¹ *He overlaid it with pure gold, and he made for it an encircling golden beading.* ¹² *He also made for it an encircling border a handbreadth wide, and he made an encircling golden beading for this border.* ¹³ *Then he cast for the Table* ª *four golden rings, and he fixed the rings to the four corners where its feet are.* ¹⁴ *The rings hung against the border, attachments for the carrying-poles for lifting the Table.* ¹⁵ *He made the carrying-poles of acacia lumber to lift the Table,* ª *and he overlaid them with gold.* ¹⁶ *He also made the containers that go on* ª *the Table:* ᵇ *its dishes and its pans and its bowls and pitchers for the pouring of libations,* ᶜ *of pure gold.* ᵈ

¹⁷ *He made the Lampstand of pure gold. He made the pedestal and the branching of the Lampstand of hammered metal: its lampcups, its bud-husks and its flowers were an integral part of it.* ª ¹⁸ *Six branches extended from its sides, three branches for lamps on one side and three branches for lamps on the other side,* ¹⁹ *with three lampcups like almond-blooms with bud-husks and flowers on one branch and three lampcups like almond-blooms with bud-husks and flowers on the matching branch,* ª *and so on for all six of the branches extending from the Lampstand.* ²⁰ *On the Lampstand itself there were four lampcups like almond blooms, each with their bud-husks and their flowers,* ²¹ *and a bud-husk underneath each pair of branches where the six branches extend from it.* ª ²² *These* ª *bud-husks and branches were an integral part of the Lampstand;* ᵇ *the whole of it was a single implement of hammer-worked pure gold.* ²³ *He made seven lamps;* ª *and the Lampstand's* ᵇ *wick-removers and wick-trays were pure gold.* ²⁴ *He used one talent of pure gold in making the Lampstand* ª *and all its accessories.* ᵇ

²⁵ *He made the Altar of Incense of acacia lumber, a cubit in length and a cubit wide, square, and two cubits tall; its horns were an integral part of it.* ª ²⁶ *He overlaid it with pure gold: its top, its sides all around, and its horns; and he made for it an encircling golden beading.* ²⁷ *He made for it two rings of gold, beneath its beading on two sides, two opposing sides, as attachments for carrying-poles with which to lift it.* ²⁸ *Then he made carrying-poles of acacia lumber and he overlaid them with gold.* ª

²⁹ *He also made the sacred Oil of Anointment and Special Formula Incense, pure, a spice-mixer's blend.* ª

Notes

3.a. MT here has simply עַל "on, upon"; in 25:12 נָתַתָּ "you are to place" is included.

5.a. The instruction that the carrying-poles are to remain in the rings, 25:15, and the instruction that the Testimony is to be placed into the Ark, 25:16, are omitted from this construction narrative. SamPent adds בהם "with them" to the end of this verse; cf. LXX 38:4.

8.a. See n. 25:19.b.

9.a. SamPent reads אחד אל אחד "one toward one."

9.b. The verse about the location of the Ark-Cover and the Testimony (25:21) and the verse about speaking "from between the two cherubs" (25:22) are omitted here, though 40:20 summarizes the first of the two.

13.a. "Table" is added here for clarity, as at 25:26, where the verb "make" is used, rather than the verb "cast," as here. MT has לו "for it"; SamPent omits the indir obj.

15.a. This phrase comes in MT at the end of the verse.

16.a. על, as in n. 3.a.

16.b. The parallel to this verse, 25:29, omits "the containers . . . the Table."

16.c. See n. 25:29.b.

16.d. 25:29 has "you are to make" before "pure gold"; the expected "he made" has been omitted here, as also is the instruction regarding the placement on the Table of the Bread of the Presence, 25:30. That parallel is in 40:23.

17.a. On the translation of this verse, see nn. 25:31.a-f.

19.a. MT has בקנה אחד . . . בקנה האחד "on the one branch . . . on another branch," unlike 25:33 (and SamPent here), omitting the article with the second "one branch."

21.a. See n. 25:35.a. This verse ends with "from it;" 25:35 ends with "from the Lampstand," as do some Syr texts here.

22.a. See n. 25:36.a.

22.b. See n. 25:36.b.

23.a. The specification of the placement of these lamps and the reason for that placement, included at this point in 25:37, is omitted here, and the conclusion to this verse is parallel to 25:38.

23.b. See n. 25:38.b.

24.a. MT "it."

24.b. The summary instruction concerning strict adherence to the plan revealed on Sinai, included at 25:40, is omitted here.

25.a. This verse is a compression of 30:1-2.

28.a. Five verses dealing with the location, use, restrictions and atonement of the Altar of Incense, 30:6-10, have been omitted here.

29.a. This verse is a compact summary of 30:22-38.

Form/Structure/Setting

See *Form/Structure/Setting* on 25:1-9 and 35:1-36:7.

Comment

1-28 There is no additional information in this narrative of the construction of the Ark, the Table, the Lampstand, and the Altar of Incense. Too much has been made of the fact that the Altar of Incense is *not* included in the list of instructions in chap. 25, but is described separately in 30:1-4, and yet *is* included with the other furnishings mentioned in chap. 25 in the construction narrative here (cf. Driver, 328-29; von Rad, *Priesterschrift*, 75-77; Noth, 277-78). There is not sufficient evidence in the separation of the instructions for the Altar of Incense from the instructions for the Ark, the Table, and the Lampstand in Exod 25-31 to sustain the view that the Altar of Incense was not a part of P's earlier list of the media of worship (note Haran, *Temples*, 227-29). Why these articles are separated in chaps. 25-31 is not clear. The reason for treating them together in the narrative of construction of chap. 37 is a logical one: they are all articles that belong to the Holy Space and the Holiest Space of the Tabernacle. The construction narratives, though they are quite detailed, are summary narratives, and the inclusion of the account of the construction of the Altar of Incense with the accounts of the construction of the Ark, the Table, and the Lampstand simply confirms the assertion of 30:34–38 that this Altar, like the Special Formula Incense blended for exclusive use on it, belongs to the very special worship of the Holy Spaces of the Tabernacle.

The omissions from these construction narratives are entirely logical and have to do for the most part with those parts of the instruction narratives that have no bearing on construction: thus the instructions about (1) the position of the carrying-poles for the Ark (25:15); (2) the placement of the Testimony into the Ark (25:16); (3) the location of the Ark-Cover and the Testimony (25:21); (4) Yahweh's promise to speak from between the two cherubs (25:22); (5) the placement of the Bread of the Presence on the Table (25:30); (6) the placement of the lamps and the reason for it (25:37); (7) the strict adherence to the plan for the Lampstand revealed to Moses on Sinai (25:40); (8) the location, use, restrictions, and atonement for the Altar of Incense (30:6–10); and (9) the formulae for the sacred Oil of Anointment and the Special Formula Incense (30:22–38).

In sum, the construction narratives of chap. 37 are approximately twenty-nine verses shorter than their parallel instruction narratives in chaps. 25 and 30 without the loss of a single detail affecting the actual construction of the Ark, the Table, the Lampstand, and the Altar of Incense. The editor of these narratives of construction has clearly had in hand, in a form very close to their present form, the narratives of instruction, and has excerpted from them only what was deemed necessary for the account of the actual building of the media of worship, rearranging the sequence of the narratives of instruction as he thought appropriate.

29 The inclusion of the brief notice about the Special Formula Incense was no doubt suggested by the account of the construction of the Altar of Incense on which that incense was used. The equally brief notice about the Oil of Anointment was also included, in part because of the similarity of the formulae for these two special substances, but perhaps more because they are treated together in the narrative of instruction, as is suggested by the order in which the two substances are mentioned in this one verse summary: it is the reverse of a logical order, and the order of 30:22–28.

Explanation

See *Explanation* on 25:10–22, 23–30, 31–40; 30:1–10, and 22–38.

The Construction of the Altar of Wholly-Burned Offerings, the Laver, and the Tabernacle Court (38:1-20)

PARALLELS IN SEQUENCE:
27:1-8 = 38:1-7; 30:17-21 = 38:8;
27:9-19 = 38:9-20

Bibliography

Cross, F. M. "The Priestly Houses of Early Israel." *Canaanite Myth and Hebrew Epic*. Cambridge: Harvard University Press, 1973. 195-215.

Translation

[1] *He made the Altar of wholly-burned offerings of acacia lumber, five cubits in length and five cubits in width, square,* [a] *and three cubits tall.* [2] *He made horns for it, one on each of its four corners: its horns were an integral part of it, and he overlaid it with copper.* [3] *He made all the equipment of the Altar: the pots, the cleaning-shovels, the dashing-basins, the pronged forks* [a] *and the fire-holders. He made all of its equipment of copper.* [4] *He made for the Altar a grate, a strainer* [a] *made of copper* [b] *underneath its rim downwards for half its height.* [5] *He cast four rings on the four corners to the copper grate as attachments for the carrying-poles.* [6] *He made the carrying-poles of acacia wood, and he overlaid them with copper;* [7] *then he thrust the carrying-poles through the rings upon the sides of the Altar, to lift it with them. He made the Altar* [a] *hollow, of planks.* [b]

[8] *He made the Laver of copper and its pedestal of copper* [a] *of the mirrors of the women arrayed for ministry who ministered in turn* [b] *at the opening of the Tent of Appointed Meeting.*

[9] *He made the Courtyard: for the Negev side, facing south, the draperies of the Courtyard were of woven fine linen, a hundred cubits of them,* [a] [10] *with twenty columns and twenty pedestals of copper;* [a] *the hooks and rings of the columns were silver.* [11] *Facing the north side were a hundred cubits* [a] *with twenty columns and twenty pedestals of copper, with the hooks and the rings of the columns of silver,* [12] *and facing the west side were fifty cubits of draperies with ten columns and ten pedestals, with the hooks and the rings of the columns of silver,* [a] [13] *and facing the east side, toward the sunrise, were fifty cubits.* [14] *Fifteen cubits of draperies were on one side of the entrance,* [a] *with three columns and three pedestals,* [15] *and so also on the other side of the entrance. On either side of the entrance* [a] *of the Courtyard were fifteen cubits of draperies, with three columns and three pedestals.* [b] [16] *All the draperies, all around the Courtyard, were of woven fine linen,* [a] [17] *and the pedestals for the columns were of copper, with the hooks and the rings of the columns of silver,* [a] *and their tops overlaid with silver; the rings of all the columns of the Courtyard were of silver.* [b]

[18] *The Screen of the entrance to the Courtyard was embroidered in variegated patterns of violet yarn, purple yarn, scarlet yarn, and woven fine linen, twenty cubits long and five cubits high, corresponding in measurement to the draperies of the Courtyard,*

[19] *with four columns and four pedestals of copper, with silver hooks; their tops were overlaid, and their rings were made of silver.* [a] [20] *All the anchor-pegs, for the Tabernacle and* [a] *for the Courtyard all around, were of copper.* [b]

Notes

1.a. This word is omitted by SamPent.

3.a. On this instrument and the two preceding it, see nn. 27:3.b,c,d.

4.a. See n. 27:4.a.

4.b. From this point forward through the end of v 5, there is a compression of the text of 27:4b–5, which is more detailed.

7.a. See n. 27:8.a.

7.b. Vv 6 and 7 are a compression of 27:6–8, with one significant omission: the final clause of 27:8, which urges that the Altar be made precisely in accord with the revelation to Moses on Sinai. See n. 27:8.b.

8.a. The continuation of this verse in 30:18 specifies the use of the laver and its location, and 30:19–21 expands on the requirement that Aaron and his sons wash their hands and their feet before they minister in worship. All this has been replaced here by an obscure note about the source of the copper used in making the laver and its pedestal.

8.b. צבא הצבאת אשׁר צבאו refers to the regimented service of soldiers and Levites, to Yahweh's "angelic" armies, to the array of the heavenly bodies (cf. BDB, 838–39). This final clause of v 8 occurs nowhere else in the OT, and is obscure, especially in the light of 1 Sam 2:22, where צבא appears to refer to cultic prostitution (cf. Cross, *Canaanite Myth,* 201–3; McCarter, *I Samuel,* AB 8 [Garden City, NY: Doubleday, 1980] 81, 91–93).

9.a. MT has simply מאה באמה. LXX (37:7) reads ἑκατὸν ἐφ᾽ ἑκατόν "a hundred by a hundred."

10.a. SamPent omits "of copper."

11.a. See n. 9.a.

12.a. Though the narratives of construction are generally more compact than the narratives of instruction, the repetition of this closing phrase, "with the . . . of silver" is additional; cf. 27:12.

14.a. See n. 27:14.b.

15.a. מזה ומזה לשׁער "from this (side) and from that (side) with regard to the entry-way."

15.b. This verse too is an expansion of the narrative of instruction, 27:15, though it simply adds words, not information.

16.a. This verse is not in the narrative of instruction, though its information is at least implied by 27:18b.

17.a. SamPent has "with their hooks of silver," omitting "and the rings of the columns."

17.b. This verse is an expanded statement of the content of 27:17.

18–19.a. Vv 18 and 19 are an expanded statement of the content of 27:16, with additional information about the size of the Screen and the ornamentation and fittings of the columns.

20.a. LXX (37:18) has just τῆς αὐλῆς "for the Courtyard."

20.b. This verse is a compression of 27:19, omitting the reference to the tools of the Tabernacle; see n. 27:19.b.

Form/Structure/Setting

See *Form/Structure/Setting* on 25:1–9 and 35:1–36:7.

Comment

1–7 There is no information in this account of the construction of the Altar beyond that given already in the instruction narrative in 27:1–8. Indeed, that narrative has been shortened here by the reduction of the content of 27:4b–5 (cf. 38:4–5) and 27:6–8 (cf. 38:6–7).

8 While the five verses of instructions regarding the Laver (30:17–21) have been reduced appropriately to a brief notice that Bezalel made the Laver and its pedestal of copper, there has been added a brief and mystifying note concerning the source of that copper. The fact that the Laver and its pedestal are not listed among the items made from the more than three and a half tons of copper (38:29–31) given in response to Yahweh's call for the voluntary offering of materials has led to the view that the Laver and its pedestal were less important than the other furnishings of the Courtyard of the Tabernacle, intended for a purpose preliminary to the actual ministry of worship (Haran, *Temples,* 159), and had therefore to be made of material not included in the offering designated as Yahweh's (Cassuto, 466–67). This seems to be an explanation contrived to fit a scanty argument from silence, as there are too many other reasons why the Laver and its pedestal may have been omitted from Exod 38:29–31 (as also were "all the tools of the Tabernacle," 27:19, the copper for which appears to have come from the voluntary offering).

Even more of a puzzle is just who the "women arrayed for ministry" were, what their ministry was, and why they had mirrors of copper they had not already contributed, following Moses' delivery of Yahweh's invitation. These women have been called every fanciful thing from cleaning women (Driver, 391; Hertzberg, *I Samuel,* OTL [Philadelphia: Westminster, 1964] 36) to dancing girls and musicians (Hyatt, 330; Davies, 251), and their service has been connected with the Tabernacle (Hyatt, 330), the separate Tent of Appointed Meeting *outside* the camp (cf. 33:7–11; Gispen, 325), and even Moses' own tent, set up "as a place of meeting between himself and the Lord" (Cassuto, 429–32, 467). In the context of Exod 38, however, it is difficult to imagine that the reference to the Tent of Appointed Meeting can mean anything but what it means everywhere else in the P composite, the Tabernacle. And yet, as a variety of commentators have pointed out (so Driver, 391), the Tabernacle, not yet erected, can hardly have had a ministry of women arrayed at its opening.

This puzzle is further complicated by the use of צבא "minister" to refer to a special regimented service of Levites in connection with the Tent of Appointed Meeting (Num 4:23: כל־הבא לצבא צבא לעבד עבדה באהל מועד "all who can enter for ministry to do the work in the Tent of Appointed Meeting"; cf. Num 8:24) and even more by the reference in 1 Sam 2:22 to the sons of Eli sinning against Yahweh by copulating with "the women who ministered in turn at the opening of the Tent of Appointed Meeting" (הנשים הצבאות פתח אהל מועד), a phrase almost identical to the one used in Exodus (הצבאת אשר צבאו פתח אחל מועד "the women arrayed for ministry who ministered in turn at the opening of the Tent of Appointed Meeting"). This reference in 1 Sam 2:22 seems certainly to refer to cultic prostitution of some kind (note Galling's reference in Beer, 172, to " 'Aphrodite'-Spiegeln" and 2 Kgs 23:7, and Cross's connection, *Canaanite Myth,* 201–3, of the incident in 1 Sam 2:22 with the account in Num 25:1–15 of the sin of Israel with the Baal of Peor), but any such connection would be so totally out of place in Exod 38 as to make its inclusion there unthinkable.

The obvious reason for the inclusion of the information of Exod 38:8 is that it specifies the source of the copper used in the manufacture of the

Laver and its pedestal. Undoubtedly, this information was not only clear but considered necessary by the P redactor of Exod 38, and it is not likely that a reference associating the Laver with anything so antithetical to the P concept of cultic acceptability as cultic prostitution would have been included without some such explanation as that given in Num 17:1–5 [16:36–40], regarding the use upon the Altar of the copper of the censers of Korah's company of rebels. The best we can do with Exod 38:8 is to note its obvious purpose and then to confess ignorance, until some further information is available, as to who the women at the opening of the Tent of Appointed Meeting were, why they were there, what they were doing, and whether their mirrors were for personal or ritual use. We know for certain only that these mirrors were regarded by P as the source of the copper for the Laver and its Pedestal, and that that information was for some reason considered significant.

9–20 The account of the construction of the Courtyard includes no such entirely new additional information; it has been reworked more thoroughly than most of the parallel P material, including as it does only a little compression (cf. 38:20 vis-à-vis 27:19), and uncharacteristically, considerable expansion (38:12 vis-à-vis 27:12; 38:15 vis-à-vis 27:15; 38:16 vis-à-vis 27:18b; 38:17 vis-à-vis 27:17; 38:18–19 vis-à-vis 27:16) of the account of instruction. This expansion involves, for the most part, repetition and rearrangement, though vv 18 and 19 include a comparative statement about the size of the Screen and the report that the columns supporting it had tops overlaid with silver (cf. 36:38).

Explanation

See *Explanation* on 27:1–8, 9–19.

Once again, the attention given to the details in the construction narratives, details even expanded in the case of the Courtyard, attest the importance of the symbols of Yahweh's Presence in the priestly view of worship.

A Summary of the Metals Used in the Tabernacle and Its Courtyard   (38:21–31)

Bibliography

Scott, R. B. Y. "Weights, Measures, Money and Time." *Peake's Commentary on the Bible.* New York: Thomas Nelson and Sons, 1962. 37–41.

Translation

²¹ *These are the inventories of the Tabernacle, the Tabernacle of the Testimony, as recorded* ᵃ *upon the command of Moses by the work of the Levites under the authority* ᵇ *of Ithamar, son of Aaron the priest.* ²² *Bezalel, son of Uri, son of Hur, of the tribe*

of Judah, made everything Yahweh had commanded Moses, [23] *with the help of* [a] *Oholiab, son of Ahisamach, of the tribe of Dan, a metalworker, a designer,* [b] *an embroiderer
in violet yarn, purple yarn, scarlet yarn, and fine linen.*
[24] *All the gold used for the workmanship in all the workmanship of the Holy
Space, was gold of the symbolic offering,* [a] *twenty-nine talents, seven hundred and
thirty shekels (by the measure of the set-apart shekel).* [b] [25] *Silver from the inventories
of the congregation was a hundred talents, a thousand seven hundred and seventy-
five shekels (by the measure of the set-apart shekel).* [a] [26] *This comes to a beka per
person, half a shekel (by the measure of the set-apart shekel) for each one who moved
over into the counted group* [a] *who was twenty years old or more, six hundred and
three thousand, five hundred and fifty of them.* [27] *A hundred talents of the silver
were for casting the pedestals of the Holy Space, the pedestals of the Veil: a hundred
pedestals for a hundred talents, a talent per pedestal,* [28] *and of the thousand seven
hundred and seventy-five shekels* [a] *he made the hooks for the columns and he overlaid
their tops and made rings for them.* [29] *Copper from the symbolic offering was seventy
talents, two thousand, four hundred shekels,* [30] *with which he made the pedestals for
the opening of the Tent of Appointed Meeting, the copper Altar and its copper grate,
and all the equipment of the Altar,* [31] *the pedestals of the Courtyard all around, the
pedestals for the opening of the Courtyard, all the anchor-pegs for the Tabernacle,
and all the anchor-pegs for the Courtyard all around.*

Notes

21.a. Pual of פקד "be attended to, mustered, reviewed, looked after carefully." Cf. BDB,
823–24; פְּקֻדָה, a noun derived from פקד, is the word translated "inventories" earlier in the
verse (where it occurs in a pl constr form).
21.b. ביד "in, by the hand of."
23.a. MT has ואתו "and with him," though the sense throughout is that Oholiab serves as
an assistant.
23.b. On these terms, which occur also in 35:35, see nn. 35:35.a,b.
24.a. תנופה "symbolic offering"; see nn. 29:24.a, 35:22.d.
24.b. See *Comment* on 30:14.
25.a. The parenthetic note is absent from SamPent and LXX (39:2).
26.a. See n. 30:13.a.
28.a. "Shekels" supplied from the context; cf. v 25.

Form/Structure/Setting

See *Form/Structure/Setting* on 25:1–9 and 35:1–36:7.

Comment

21–31 This summary of the metals used in the construction of the Tabernacle, its Courtyard, and their furnishings has no parallel in the narratives
of instruction, for the obvious reason that it is an account of the results of
the voluntary offering requested by Yahweh at the beginning of the narratives
of instruction (25:1–3). Even so, there is no new information here, apart
from the summary amounts of the three metals, the explanation of the amount
of silver as largest by virtue of its connection with the head-count of Israelite
males twenty and above, and the note that Ithamar, mentioned two other

times in Exodus (6:23 and 28:1), was in charge of the inventory-taking (on the further supervisory work of Ithamar, see Num 4:21–33; 7:1–8).

24 The amounts of metal given in the voluntary offering and so recorded in the inventories are remarkable, and the inclusion of this information appears to serve two purposes: (1) a further testimony of the joyous generosity of Israel, and (2) an additional evidence of the magnificence of the spaces and the furnishings devoted to Yahweh's Presence. The total amount of the gold brought was approximately 2,210 pounds; of silver, approximately 7,601 pounds; of copper, approximately 5,350 pounds (cf. Sellers, "Weights and Measures," *IDB* 4:832–33; by the different equivalences of Scott, *Peake's Commentary* 38–39, these amounts are somewhat lighter: approximately 1,828 pounds of gold; 6,286 pounds of silver; and 4,425 pounds of copper, by the " 'sacred' shekel," which Scott reckons as lighter than the "common shekel," .3333 ounce as opposed to .4 ounce; Sellers' equivalence is .403 ounce for both shekels).

The availability of gold, silver, and copper in the ANE, even in such large amounts, is by no means unrealistic, as the extensive research of Lucas (*Egyptian Materials*, 222–91) on the use of metals in Egypt has shown. Though the perspective of P tends, as Haran (*Temples*, 10–12, 122–31, 194–204) has maintained, to be somewhat "utopian," the reference to such considerable quantities of precious and semiprecious metals is not to be taken as discrediting the Priestly narrative, the primary purpose of which, after all, is theological, not statistical. It is probably not unrealistic to speak of such quantities of these metals in the service of Yahweh in the Solomonic temple, and in any case, P's intention, the dramatic presentation of a theology of Yahweh's Presence in Israel's midst, is the constant in the light of which all these texts must be read.

25–28 The size of the voluntary offering of silver, some eighty pounds more than the combined offerings of gold and copper, is linked to the fulfillment of Yahweh's instruction that a half-shekel of silver be taken from each male twenty years of age or older, a gift for atonement and for the expense of the Tabernacle (cf. 30:11–16, and above). The actual amount of silver is thus linked to the narrative of the census commanded by Yahweh in Num 1, where the total number of Israelite males, excluding the Levites, is given (Num 1:46) as 603,550, the total given in Exod 38:26, for each one of whom a beka, or half-shekel of silver, was paid, giving a total of 301,775 shekels, or 100 talents, 1,775 shekels. The tradition of an offering received for the support of the Tabernacle may well be older than the organization of the kind of census described in Numbers, however, and it is clear here as in 30:11–16 that the real point of this narrative is not the counting of Israel but the huge offering of costly materials for the media of worship in Yahweh's Presence.

The use to which the silver and the copper were put is specified in summary terms in vv 27–28 and vv 30–31. The gold is said, in an even more terse summation, to have been used for all the workmanship of the Tabernacle. The gradation of these metals vis-à-vis closeness to Yahweh's Presence (cf. Haran, *Temples*, 158–65) as well as the three interlocked circles of symbol and function outward from Yahweh's Presence (see *Form/Structure/Setting* on 25:1–9) are implicit in this summary.

Explanation

See *Explanation* on 25:1–9.

The impression left by this summary of the inventories of gold, silver, and copper received in the voluntary offering (even the silver atonement-money is referred to three times [30:13, 14, 15] in the brief narrative calling for it as a "contribution for Yahweh") is one of generosity and opulence. The Priestly writers, far from being daunted by the thought of such large quantities of precious metals, were concerned rather to dramatize it by way of exemplifying the appropriate response to Yahweh's Presence. The metals were singled out as the most costly of the materials employed in the construction of the Tabernacle and its furnishings, as the three materials that most clearly designated the three successive circles of nearness to Yahweh's immanent Presence, and as the materials that most readily suggested by both their cost and quantity the abundance of Israel's generosity. Then this summary of the inventories of the metals was set here in the Exodus composite as a kind of conclusion to the narrative of the construction of the Tabernacle and its equipment.

The Making of the Sacral Vestments (39:1–31)

PARALLEL VERSES:
28:1–43

Translation

¹ *From the violet yarn, the purple yarn, and the scarlet yarn they* ᵃ *made elaborately sewn vestments for ministry in worship in the Holy Space, and they made the sacral vestments for Aaron, exactly as Yahweh had commanded Moses.* ᵇ

² *Thus Bezalel* ᵃ *made the Ephod of gold, violet yarn, purple yarn, scarlet yarn, and woven fine linen.* ³ *They hammered the gold into thin sheets; then he* ᵃ *cut it into twisted strands to interweave* ᵇ *with the violet yarn, the purple yarn, the scarlet yarn, and the fine linen, an artistic embroidery.* ᶜ ⁴ *They made shoulderpieces for it, joined to its two sides, thus making one garment;* ⁵ *its elaborate belt, made as a part of it, was of identical workmanship, in gold, violet yarn, purple yarn, scarlet yarn, and woven fine linen, exactly as Yahweh had commanded Moses.* ᵃ

⁶ *Then they* ᵃ *took* ᵇ *the onyx-stones, mounted in a setting of gold filigree, engraved as a seal is engraved with the names of the sons of Israel,* ⁷ *and he* ᵃ *placed them onto the shoulderpieces of the Ephod as stones to call to mind the sons of Israel, exactly as Yahweh commanded Moses.* ᵇ ⁸ *He* ᵃ *made the Breastpiece, artistically embroidered as the Ephod is, of gold and violet yarn, purple yarn, scarlet yarn, and woven fine linen;* ⁹ *it was a square folded double. They* ᵃ *made the Breastpiece a span in length and a span in width, folded double.* ᵇ ¹⁰ *They set in it four rows of gemstones: the first row was a row of sardius, peridot, and emerald;* ¹¹ *the second row, turquoise, lapis lazuli, and jasper;* ¹² *the third row, jacinth, agate, and amethyst;* ¹³ *and the fourth row, green feldspar, sardonyx, and green jasper;* ᵃ *all were mounted in a setting*

of gold filigree, in their arrangements. [b] [14] *The stones were as the names of the sons of Israel; they were twelve in number, each with one name engraved as on a seal: they represented the twelve tribes.*
[15] *They made upon the Breastpiece tightly twisted ropes, made like cordage of pure gold;* [16] *then they made two filigrees of gold* [a] *and two rings of gold, and they put the two rings upon the two edges of the Breastpiece.* [17] *They put the two twisted cords of gold into the two rings at the edges of the Breastpiece,* [18] *and the two ends of the two twisted cords they put onto the two filigrees, and thus they fastened them* [a] *upon the shoulderpieces of the Ephod on its front.*
[19] *Next they made two rings of gold, and they placed them* [a] *onto the two edges of the Breastpiece, upon its inner side next to the Ephod.* [20] *They made two rings of gold, and they put them onto the two shoulderpieces of the Ephod at a lower point on its front, at a point just above where the elaborate belt of the Ephod is fastened.* [21] *Then they bound the Breastpiece by its rings to the rings of the Ephod with a twisted cord of violet yarn, so that the Breastpiece hung snugly* [a] *above the elaborate belt of the Ephod, and did not fall forward from the Ephod, exactly as Yahweh had commanded Moses.* [b]
[22] *They* [a] *made the Robe of the Ephod, a work woven* [b] *wholly of violet yarn.* [23] *The opening of the Robe, in its center, was like the opening of a sturdily reinforced garment yoke,* [a] *so that it could not be ripped.* [24] *They made on the skirts of the Robe pomegranates of violet yarn, purple yarn, and scarlet yarn woven,* [a] [25] *and they made bells of pure gold, and then they put the bells among the pomegranates on the skirt of the Robe, all around among the pomegranates,* [26] *a bell* [a] *and a pomegranate, a bell* [a] *and a pomegranate, interspersed upon the skirts of the Robe all around, for ministry in worship, exactly as Yahweh had commanded Moses.* [b]
[27] *They made the Tunic of fine linen, a woven work for Aaron and his sons,* [28] *the Turban of fine linen, the high-hat headwear* [a] *of fine linen, and the linen undergarments of woven fine linen,* [29] *the Sash of woven fine linen and violet yarn, purple yarn, and scarlet yarn, embroidered in variegated patterns, exactly as Yahweh had commanded Moses.* [a]
[30] *They made a Flower, the Emblem of Set-Apartness, of pure gold, and they engraved upon it an inscription, like a seal-engraving, "Set Apart for Yahweh,"* [31] *and they fixed upon it a twisted cord of violet yarn, to attach it to the Turban at the top, exactly as Yahweh had commanded Moses.* [a]

Notes

1.a. "They" refers to the artisans working under the supervision of Bezalel and Oholiab; cf. 36:8.
1.b. This verse is a compression of the content of 28:1–5.
2.a. MT has "he," which is undoubtedly the intended reading, despite the "they" of SamPent and Syr; as noted above, n. 36:8.b, this "he" refers to Bezalel. Throughout the remainder of chap. 39, "he" in reference to Bezalel and "they" in reference to the artisans working under his guidance are intermingled.
3.a. SamPent, Tg Onk, Tg Ps-J, Syr have "they."
3.b. לעשות בתוך "to work into the midst of," a graphic description of weaving and embroidery with such different and different-colored materials.
3.c. This verse, apart from its last two words, is an addition to the instructions of 28:6.
5.a. This final clause, "exactly . . ." is additional to a slightly rearranged 28:8.
6.a. Vg has "he."

6.b. MT has ויעשו "then they made," i.e., "made ready."

7.a. SamPent and Syr have "they."

7.b. Vv 6–7 are a compression of the detailed instructions of 28:9–14.

8.a. See n. 7.a.

9.a. SamPent has "he."

9.b. This verse is an expansion, by repetition, of 28:16. SamPent omits "folded double."

13.a. See n. 28:20.a.

13.b. This final clause is a slight expansion of 28:20.

16.a. This phrase is additional to the instruction of 28:23.

18.a. This pl pronoun is absent from the instruction of 28:25; its presence here may clarify the description there.

19.a. "Them" is not in MT here, but it is included at this point in 28:26, and is thus added above for clarity.

21.a. See n. 28:28.a.

21.b. This final clause is additional to 28:28, and SamPent adds still more: ויעשו את־האורים ואת־התמים כאשר צוה יהוה את־משהו "and then they made the Urim and the Thummim, exactly as Yahweh had commanded Moses." 28:29–30, the explanation of the significance of the Breastpiece and the instruction that "Aaron" is to wear it "upon his heart" whenever he enters Yahweh's Presence are appropriately omitted from the narrative of construction at this point.

22.a. See n. 7.a.

22.b. This phrase is an expansion of the instruction of 28:31.

23.a. MT is a compressed and rearranged version of 28:32, also employing the difficult term תחרא in its only other OT occurrence (see n. 28:32.b). A literal translation is all but impossible ("like the opening of a תחרא, an edge for its opening all around"), but the intention of the description is clear.

24.a. SamPent, LXX (36:32), Syr, Vg all include the equivalent of the usual שׁשׁ here, to give the reading "and woven fine linen."

26.a. SamPent has פעמון זהב "a golden bell."

26.b. Vv 24–26 are a rearrangement of 28:33–35, with some additions (the bells here are of *pure* gold; and the recurrent clause about Moses' command is included) and some deletions, the most significant of which is the instruction about the purpose of the Robe and when it was to be worn.

28.a. פארי המגבעת "high-hat headwear"; פאר, a term for a headdress of some kind, occurs in Exodus only here (cf. Ezek 24:17, 44:18); on מגבעות, see n. 28:40.a.

29.a. Vv 27–29 are a considerably abbreviated summary of 28:39–43, omitting especially the instructions of purpose and function of 28:40b, 41, 42b, c, and 43, and adding the concluding clause about Yahweh's command to Moses.

31.a. Vv 30–31 are a slight compression of 28:36–37. 28:38, the instruction about the meaning of the inscribed Flower on the Turban and when it is to be worn, has been omitted altogether. The concluding "exactly . . ." is additional.

Form/Structure/Setting

See *Form/Structure/Setting* on 25:1–9 and 35:1–36:7.

Comment

1–31 The narrative of the making of the sacral vestments is, like the major part of the construction narratives, a compressed parallel of its comparable instruction narrative and one from which any reference to purpose and function and also some descriptive details have been omitted. Even with the addition of information about the manufacture of gold thread for the Ephod (v 3), the sevenfold repetition of the quality-control clause "exactly as Yahweh had commanded Moses," the inclusion of supplementary details (vv 16, 18,

22, 25, 28) and some repetition (vv 9, 13), this account of the fulfillment of Yahweh's instructions is still eleven verses shorter than the instructions themselves.

3 The description of the manufacture of gold thread by hammering gold into gold leaf, then cutting the gold leaf into thin strands which could be used as decorative thread, conforms to Egyptian methods of gold-working (Lucas, *Egyptian Materials,* 263–65; cf. also 284). The description of the manufacture of the sacral vestments themselves appears to have in view the fuller details of the narratives of instruction in chap. 28, though enough detail— sometimes more than enough detail—is included here to give a reasonably clear impression of how the vestments looked and how they were worn. The intermixture of "he" (referring to Bezalel) and "they" (referring to the artisans working under Bezalel's supervision), sometimes taken as an indication of the mingling of primary and secondary sources (so Driver, 394–95; Noth, 279), may just as readily be seen as a deliberate interplay, in the composite Exodus, attributing the work on the sacral vestments both to the guidance of Bezalel and to the craftsmanship of those who assisted him.

1, 5, 7, 21, 26, 27, 31 The sevenfold repetition of the phrase that concludes the major sections of this narrative of the making of the sacral vestments is an attempt to connect the completion of Yahweh's instructions with their revelation, while underscoring again the origin and authority of the concept of the vestments, their initial connection with Moses (and not Aaron, significantly), and the literal precision with which any instruction of Yahweh should always be carried out.

Finally, the omission from this narrative of manufacture of any mention of the Urim and Thummim, a point often discussed (Noth, 279; Hyatt, 331–32; Clements, 239; Childs, 637), is entirely in accord with the deletion from all of the narratives of construction of most of the references to purpose, function, placement, and the like, and the omission of the title "Breastpiece of Judgment," used in chap. 28 only in the paragraph dealing with the Urim and Thummim, is only to be expected.

Explanation

See *Explanation* on 28:1–43.

The significant additional emphasis of this narrative of the making of the sacral vestments is that the conception of the vestments is from Yahweh, has been commanded through Moses, and has been realized without divergence from Yahweh's instructions.

A Summary of the Fulfillment of Yahweh's Instructions (39:32–43)

PARALLEL VERSES:
31:7–11; 35:11–19

Bibliography

Westermann, C. *Blessing.* Philadelphia: Fortress Press, 1978.

Translation

³²*And so all the labor of the Tabernacle of the Tent of Appointed Meeting was accomplished: the sons of Israel had made everything that Yahweh had commanded of Moses, just so had they done it.* ᵃ ³³*Thus they brought the Tabernacle* ᵃ *to Moses, the Tent and all its parts: its fasteners, its supports, its cross-members, its columns, its pedestals,* ³⁴*the cover of red-dyed rams' hides and the cover of sea-cows' hides, the Veil of the Screen,* ³⁵*the Ark of the Testimony, its carrying-poles and its Ark-Cover,* ³⁶*the Table and all its equipment, and the Bread of the Presence,* ³⁷*the pure Lampstand and its lamps all arranged,* ᵃ *all its equipment, and the oil for the light,* ³⁸*the Altar of Gold, the Oil of Anointment, the Special Formula Incense, the Screen for the opening of the Tent,* ³⁹*the Altar of Copper, the grate of copper for it, its carrying-poles and all its equipment, the Laver and its pedestal,* ⁴⁰*the draperies of the Courtyard, its columns and its pedestals, the Screen for the entrance to the Courtyard, its anchor-ropes and its anchor-pegs, and all the tools* ᵃ *for the labor of the Tabernacle, for the Tent of Appointed Meeting,* ⁴¹*the elaborately sewn vestments for ministry in worship in the Holy Space, the sacral garments for Aaron the priest and the vestments of his sons for priestly ministry.* ᵃ

⁴²*In accord with everything Yahweh had commanded Moses, just so had the sons of Israel done all the labor.* ⁴³*Then Moses looked at all the workmanship, and in fact* ᵃ *they had done it exactly as Yahweh had commanded: just so had they done it. So it was that Moses blessed them.*

Notes

32.a. כן עשו "just so had they done it."

33.a. LXX (39:13) has τὰς στολὰς "the vestments."

37.a. Lit., "its lamps, the lamps of the row." The reference is to the arrangement of the lamps on the branches of the Lampstand, facing the area in front of the Lampstand. See *Comment* on 25:37–40.

40.a. See n. 27:19.b.

41.a. This verse is a verbatim repetition of 35:19.

43.a. והנה "and behold, just look."

Form/Structure/Setting

See *Form/Structure/Setting* on 25:1–9 and 35:1–36:7.

Comment

32, 43   In due course—no reference is made to a specific period of time—Yahweh's instructions for the preparation of the media of worship were all carried out. An essential point of this report of the completion of that work, made at both the beginning (v 32) and the end (v 43) of the sequence, is that everything had been done in precise conformity to Yahweh's directions. It is a point made repeatedly through the entire narrative of construction. Inspired and specially gifted by God, Bezalel, Oholiab, and their helpers nevertheless stay strictly with the plans laid down by Yahweh through Moses. The media of worship in Yahweh's Presence, though made by the hands of men and women, are Yahweh's conception, not theirs, and even their special talents are harnessed, augmented and guided by his Presence.

33–41   Israel thus is reported to have brought to Moses the completed components of the Tabernacle, its Courtyard, and all their furnishings and equipment. Only Moses received Yahweh's instructions on Sinai at first hand, and only Moses was shown by Yahweh the vision of how things were to be, so only Moses can determine whether what Bezalel and his helpers have made is in keeping with Yahweh's intention. The inventory of what has been made, and is therefore brought to Moses for his inspection, is a considerable expansion of the summary list of 31:7–11 and a parallel with some variation and minor expansion of the summary list of 35:11–19. No new information is given in the list, which is virtually an index list drawn from the separate narratives of construction.

42–43   When Israel had brought to Moses all that they had made, pointedly referred to once again as "everything Yahweh had commanded Moses," Moses looked at (ראה) the workmanship, המלאכה: not just the objects made, but specifically at how they had been made by those entrusted with and guided in the task. The term is a derivative of לאך, a verb having to do with sending an appointed messenger (cf. BDB, 523), and it refers to the specialized workmanship of professionals in a variety of OT texts (cf. Jer 18:3; Ps 107:23; Prov 24:27; Lev 13:48), and frequently in P it refers to workmanship in the construction of the Tabernacle and the Temple. When his inspection had been completed, Moses was satisfied that Yahweh's intention had been followed exactly.

And so it was that Moses "blessed them," that is, all who were a part of the preparation of the media of worship in Yahweh's Presence—those who gave, those who directed, those who labored with their hands, those who brought the completed work for him to see, in effect, the collective whole, all Israel. Cassuto (477) connects this blessing with the blessing of God upon humankind and upon the sabbath in the Priestly narrative of creation, and Westermann (*Blessing*, 42–45) relates the structure of P from Exod 19:1 to Lev 9:23 to a theology of blessing and coming. This latter motif is reflected in this account of Moses' reaction to Israel's giving and workmanship, when paired with Yahweh's own reaction after the Tabernacle and its Courtyard have been set up and their furnishings put in place: Yahweh's glory (= his Presence) comes upon and into the Tabernacle (40:34–35). This sequence is stated in the single verse cited by Westermann, Lev 9:23.

Explanation

The work thus having been done in accord with Yahweh's instructions and confirmed by Moses, who alone has seen the vision on Sinai, all is in readiness for the building of the Tabernacle and its Courtyard, for the arrangement of the equipment of both, and for the beginning of worship in the Presence of Yahweh. One gift yet remains to be given, the gift to which all that has been made is a perpetual testimony. That gift, Yahweh alone can give. And Moses prepares the people to receive it by blessing them.

The Tabernacle Set Up, the Priests Cleansed, Yahweh's Glory Comes (40:1–38)

Translation

¹ *Then Yahweh spoke to Moses to say:* ² *"On the first day of the first month, you are to set up the Tabernacle of* ᵃ *the Tent of Appointed Meeting.* ³ *You are to place therein the Ark of the Testimony, and you are to screen the Ark with the Veil.* ᵃ ⁴ *You are to bring the Table in, and you are to see to* ᵃ *arranging it; you are to bring the Lampstand in, and you are to set in place* ᵇ *its lamps.* ⁵ *You are to put the Altar of Gold for incense in front of the Ark of the Testimony, and you are to place the Screen at the opening of the Tabernacle.*

⁶ *"You are to put the Altar of the wholly-burned offerings in front of the opening of the Tabernacle of* ᵃ *the Tent of Appointed Meeting,* ⁷ *and you are to put the Laver between the Tent of Appointed Meeting and the Altar, and you are to put water therein.* ⁸ *You are to place the Courtyard on all four sides,* ᵃ *and you are to put the Screen at the entrance of the Courtyard.*

⁹ *"Then you are to take the Oil of Anointing, and you are to anoint the Tabernacle and everything in it, and you are to set it apart, and all its equipment, and it is to be holy.* ¹⁰ *You are to anoint the Altar of the wholly-burned offerings and all its equipment, and you are to set apart the Altar, and the Altar is to be utterly holy.* ᵃ ¹¹ *You are to anoint the Laver and its pedestal, and so you are to set it apart.*

¹² *"You are to bring Aaron and his sons near* ᵃ *to the opening of the Tent of Appointed Meeting, and you are to wash them with water.* ¹³ *You are to clothe Aaron in the sacral vestments, and you are to anoint him and set him apart, that he may give priestly ministry to me.* ¹⁴ *You are to bring his sons near and clothe them in Tunics,* ¹⁵ *and you are to anoint them as you shall have anointed their father, that they may give priestly ministry to me. Their anointing is to authorize them* ᵃ *for priestly ministry down through their generations in perpetuity."*

¹⁶ *So Moses did everything that Yahweh commanded him: he did it precisely.* ᵃ ¹⁷ *Thus it was that in the first month of the second year,* ᵃ *on the first day of the month, the Tabernacle was set up.*

¹⁸ *Moses set up the Tabernacle; he put down its pedestals, then he placed its supports, and he put up its cross-members and he set up its columns.* ¹⁹ *He spread out the*

tent ᵃ *over the Tabernacle, and he placed the cover of the tent upon it at the top, exactly as Yahweh had commanded Moses.*

²⁰*Next, he took the Testimony, and he put it into the Ark, and he placed the carrying-poles onto the Ark, and he put the Ark-Cover onto the top of the Ark.* ²¹*Then he brought the Ark into the Tabernacle, and he placed the Veil of the Screen, and so he screened off the Ark of the Testimony, exactly as Yahweh had commanded Moses.*

²²*He then put* ᵃ *the Table into the Tent of Appointed Meeting, on the northern side of the Tabernacle outside the Veil,* ²³*and he arranged upon it in order the Bread in the Presence of Yahweh, exactly as Yahweh had commanded Moses.*

²⁴*Next, he put the Lampstand into the Tent of Appointed Meeting, in front of the Table on the southern side of the Tabernacle,* ²⁵*and he set in place* ᵃ *the lamps in the Presence of Yahweh, exactly as Yahweh had commanded Moses.*

²⁶*Then he placed the Altar of Gold into the Tent of Appointed Meeting, before the Veil,* ²⁷*and he made Special Formula Incense smoke upon it,* ᵃ *exactly as Yahweh commanded Moses.*

²⁸*He next placed the Screen at the opening of the Tabernacle,* ²⁹*and the Altar of the wholly-burned offerings there at the opening of the Tabernacle of* ᵃ *the Tent of Appointed Meeting, and he offered upon it the wholly-burned offering and the cereal offering, exactly as Yahweh had commanded Moses.*

³⁰*He then placed the Laver between the Tent of Appointed Meeting and the Altar, and he put water into it, for washing.* ³¹*Moses and Aaron and his sons washed their hands and their feet in it:* ³²*whenever they entered the Tent of Appointed Meeting and whenever they came near the Altar, they washed, exactly as Yahweh had commanded Moses.*

³³*Finally, he set up the Courtyard and all four sides of the Tabernacle and the Altar, and he put the Screen at the entrance of the Courtyard. Thus Moses completed the work.* ᵃ

³⁴*Then the cloud covered the Tent of Appointed Meeting, and the Glory of Yahweh filled the Tabernacle,* ³⁵*and Moses was not able to enter the Tent of Appointed Meeting, because the cloud had settled down upon it and the Glory of Yahweh had filled the Tabernacle.* ³⁶*Whenever the cloud was raised up from upon the Tabernacle, the sons of Israel journeyed forth in their various travels;* ᵃ ³⁷*but if the cloud was not raised up, they did not journey forth until the day when it was raised up.* ³⁸*Indeed* ᵃ *the cloud of Yahweh* ᵇ *was upon the Tabernacle in the daytime, and fire was in it in the nighttime for the whole family of Israel to see throughout all their journeyings.*

Notes

2.a. LXX and Cairo Geniza fragment omit "the Tabernacle of."

3.a. SamPent has הארון את הכפרת "the Ark Cover."

4.a. MT has וערכת את ערכו, lit., "and you are to set in order its arrangement"; cf. n. 27:21.a.

4.b. והעלית "and you are to set in place" refers to the elevation of the lamps, setting them up high on the branches of the Lampstand to make the best use of their light; see 25:37.

6.a. SamPent has the definite article.

8.a. סביב "around, surrounding."

10.a. קדש קדשים "utterly holy."

12.a. See n. 29:3.b.

15.a. Lit., "it is to be for them, their anointing."

16.a. כן "so."

17.a. The second year counting from the exodus, a point made specific by SamPent, which adds here לצאתם ממצרים "with reference to their departure from Egypt." LXX has the same addition, also at 40:17.

19.a. LXX has τὰς αὐλαίας "the curtains," the term used in 26:1–6 and its parallels to translate יריעת. The appropriate word for LXX, on the basis of its reading of 26:7, would have been δέρρεις "curtains, screens of hide"; cf. LSJ, 380.

22.a. SamPent has וישם "he then set."

25.a. ויעל "and he set in place"; cf. n. 4.b.

27.a. SamPent adds לפני יהוה "in the Presence of Yahweh" here.

29.a. See n. 2.a.

33.a. SamPent, LXX, Vg have "all the work."

36.a. בכל מסעיהם "in all their journeyings-forth."

38.a. כי "for, because."

38.b. LXX omits "Yahweh."

Form/Structure/Setting

See *Form/Structure/Setting* on 25:1–9 and 35:1–36:7.

This chapter, the conclusion to the composite Exodus by reason of its location, is more intentionally the conclusion to the Priestly sequence of narratives of instruction and narratives of construction connected with the media of worship in Yahweh's Presence. Indeed, it not only summarizes the broad outline of Exod 25–31 and 35–40, it does so by paralleling the narratives of instruction of 25–31 with a narrative of Yahweh's instruction to Moses regarding setting up the Tabernacle and its Courtyard and arranging their furnishings (vv 1–11) and by paralleling the narratives of construction of 35–40 with a narrative of Moses' work in strict obedience to all Yahweh's instructions (vv 16–33).

The instructions of Yahweh concerning the anointing and the vesting of Aaron and his sons (the climactic ordination following these two acts is not mentioned here; cf. Exod 29 and discussion above) are not reported as carried out by Moses here, but in Lev 8, a passage that parallels the instruction narrative of Exod 29 and is regarded by many commentators as the continuation of the Priestly narrative of Exod 35–39, interrupted by the summary material of Exod 40 and the directions for sacrifices and offerings in Lev 1–7. (Cf., e.g., Noth, *Leviticus*, OTL [Philadelphia: Westminster, 1965] 68–69; K. Elliger, *Leviticus*, HAT [Tübingen: J. C. B. Mohr, 1966] 106–7; J. R. Porter, *Leviticus*, CBC [Cambridge: University Press, 1976] 59–60; G. J. Wenham, *Leviticus*, NICOT [Grand Rapids: Eerdmans, 1979] 129–35.)

The conclusion to Exod 40 (vv 34–38) and therefore to the entire book is a careful recapitulation of the primary theme of Exodus, appropriately restated both as a summary and also by way of a preparation for what is to follow, the narrative of the beginning of Israel's corporate worship in Yahweh's Presence and the narrative of Yahweh's guidance of Israel through the wilderness to and then into the land promised to the fathers. While it is necessary to keep in mind that the division of Exodus from Leviticus is, like the division of Leviticus from Numbers, somewhat arbitrary, and that the end of Exodus is not really the end of the larger tetrateuchal narrative, Exod 40:34–38 can nevertheless be seen as an effective summary and conclusion of one part of this larger narrative and an equally effective anticipation and beginning of its next part.

Comment

1–11 The instructions of Yahweh to Moses concerning the setting up at last of the Tabernacle, its Courtyard, and their furnishings amount to a kind of review of the basic information of the narratives of instruction and construction, from which these verses appear to have been drawn. There is no new information here, apart from the specification of the date for setting up the Tabernacle: the first day of the first month (v 2) of the second year (v 17) following the exodus from Egypt. The sequence Moses is to follow involves (1) setting up the Tabernacle, (2) placing its furniture, (3) placing the furniture that stands outside the Tabernacle, (4) setting up the Courtyard around all this, and anointing everything set up and placed, beginning with the Tabernacle and its contents.

12–15 The instruction regarding Aaron and his sons, though it makes no use of the terms "ordain" and "ordination," and though it is reported as carried out beyond the Exodus narrative, in Lev 8, is nevertheless an instruction to ordain, as the mention of the ritual of vesting and the ritual of anointing and the reference to the continuing ministry of Aaron and his sons and a comparison with Exod 29 and Lev 8 clearly show.

16–33 The account of Moses' action upon Yahweh's instructions is, like the account of the making of the sacral vestments (39:1–31) and the summary of the construction of the Tabernacle, its Courtyard, and their furnishings (39:32–43) punctuated with assurances that Yahweh's expectations have been carried out literally and without variation. Indeed, following the assertion of v 17, this assurance is given, almost like a refrain, at the end of the seven successive paragraphs describing the work of Moses in the sequence established in vv 1–11 (cf. vv 19, 21, 23, 25, 27, 29, 32). Once again there is no new information here, apart from the statement of the date on which the Tabernacle and its equipment were set up.

30–32 Following the report of the placement of the Laver, Moses and Aaron and his sons are said to have washed their hands and feet in its water, an action in keeping with the requirements given in 30:19–21, and a necessary preparation for any further ministry in the places of Yahweh's Presence. The order of this work, like the order of Yahweh's instructions, follows a sequence moving outward from the symbolic center of Yahweh's Presence, the Ark in the Holiest Space of the Tabernacle.

34 Immediately following the sonorous statement "Thus Moses completed the work," there is begun the concluding paragraph of Exodus, the language of which is semipoetic (cf. Cassuto, 483–85), almost hymnic. The impression is given of a Yahweh waiting with impatience for the completion of the symbolic place of his Presence and descending upon it the moment it is finally ready. The double reference to the cloud covering the Tent of Appointed Meeting and the Glory of Yahweh filling the Tabernacle is connected with the other cloud and Glory passages in Exodus (cf. 13:21–22; 14:19, 24; 16:10; 24:16–18; 33:9–10, 22; 34:5) and is a particular allusion to the narrative of Yahweh's descent onto Mount Sinai in the sight of Israel in 24:16–18 (see above), also a passage generally assigned to P.

35 There is no real discrepancy in the statement that Moses could not enter the Tent filled and surrounded with Yahweh's Presence, as Hyatt (332), among others, suggests. As in the approach to Sinai following the covering of the cloud and the settling of the Glory (24:15–18), Moses must await Yahweh's invitation before he can draw nearer to the Presence. In the narrative of Exod 24, that invitation is given in v 17; here, that invitation comes farther along in the narrative, perhaps, as Cassuto (484) suggests, in Lev 1:1. Another possibility is that it stands reflected at the end of the narrative of the ordination of Aaron and his sons, following Aaron's first sin-offering and atonement offering, after he had blessed Israel: "and then Moses and Aaron entered the Tent of Appointed Meeting" (Lev 9:23). The reference of 33:9 is of course not to the Tabernacle (see *Form/Structure/Setting* on 33:7–11).

36–38 Finally, and appropriately, Israel's further journeyings are linked to the guiding Presence of Yahweh, not only at hand but also visible to all the people as a cloud by day and as a fire by night. As long as the cloud remained upon the Tabernacle, Israel made no move to any new journey; when the cloud was raised, Israel too made preparations to travel, and in the direction indicated, no doubt (cf. 13:21–22) by the movement of the cloud. Thus Exodus ends as it began, in the multiplication of Israel in Egypt and in the singling-out of Moses, with Yahweh present and in charge of things.

Explanation

With Yahweh's Presence promised, then demonstrated, then given to Israel in theophany at Sinai, the first half of Exodus ends. The second half of the book is preoccupied with response to that Presence, in life, in covenant, in worship, and even in disobedience. The largest part of that second half has to do with the communication to Israel of the reality of that Presence, through a series of set-apart places, set-apart objects and set-apart acts, all of them intimately connected, in one way or another, with Yahweh's Presence.

This final chapter sums up the symbolisms of those places, objects, and acts, then recounts the fulfillment of the ideal of the Exodus theology of the Presence: Yahweh among his people, not in his mighty deeds, or in his rescue, or in his provision, or in his guidance, or in his judgment, or at a distance on a forbidden and foreboding mountain, but there in their midst; the symbol of his nearness visible to all, and all the time, Yahweh protecting and guiding, Yahweh teaching and blessing; Yahweh's Presence settled in Israel's center, Yahweh's Presence filling their Holiest Space, Yahweh's Presence in their living place, wherever it might be, and when; Yahweh's Presence in them.

Index of Authors Cited

Index of Principal Subjects

Index of Biblical Texts

A. Old Testament

B. Apocrypha

C. New Testament

Index of Hebrew Words